W9-APD-777

Visual Basic .NET
BY EXAMPLE

201 West 103rd Street
Indianapolis, Indiana 46290

Gabriel Oancea
and Bob Donald

Visual Basic .NET by Example

Copyright © 2002 by Que

All rights reserved. No part of this book shall be reproduced, stored in a retrieval system, or transmitted by any means, electronic, mechanical, photocopying, recording, or otherwise, without written permission from the publisher. No patent liability is assumed with respect to the use of the information contained herein. Although every precaution has been taken in the preparation of this book, the publisher and authors assume no responsibility for errors or omissions. Nor is any liability assumed for damages resulting from the use of the information contained herein.

International Standard Book Number: 0-7897-2583-5

Library of Congress Catalog Card Number: 2001096459

Printed in the United States of America

First Printing: December 2001

04   03   02   01   4   3   2   1

Trademarks

All terms mentioned in this book that are known to be trademarks or service marks have been appropriately capitalized. Que cannot attest to the accuracy of this information. Use of a term in this book should not be regarded as affecting the validity of any trademark or service mark.

Warning and Disclaimer

Every effort has been made to make this book as complete and as accurate as possible, but no warranty or fitness is implied. The information provided is on an "as is" basis. The authors and the publisher shall have neither liability nor responsibility to any person or entity with respect to any loss or damages arising from the information contained in this book.

Associate Publisher
Dean Miller

Executive Editor
Candy Hall

Acquisitions Editor
Michelle Newcomb

Development Editors
Sarah Robbins
Leah Williams

Technical Editor
Paul W. Richardson

Project Editor
Karen S. Shields

Indexer
D&G Limited, LLC

Proofreader
D&G Limited, LLC

Team Coordinator
Cindy Teeters

Interior Designer
Anne Jones

Cover Designer
Rader Design

Page Layout
D&G Limited, LLC

Contents at a Glance

Table of Contents

About the Authors

Gabriel Oancea has more than 16 years of experience in software development, mostly in object-oriented analysis and design. He has designed and developed medium- and large-scale distributed applications in a number of languages, including C++, Visual Basic, and Java. Recently, he has focused on distributed systems architecture as a chief architect at ONTOS, Inc. He is the author of a number of patents and publications, including *Visual Basic 6 from Scratch*, Que, 1999 (with Bob).

Bob Donald has more than 13 years of experience designing and building standalone applications, client/server applications, and enterprise applications. He is a proponent of the use of UML during the analysis and design phases of software development and has broad experience working with various languages, such as Visual Basic, Visual C++, and Java. Bob has also been a guest speaker at the Connecticut Object Oriented Users Group, Microsoft TechNet, and in the Boston area COM Users Group. At ArsDigita, Bob is currently engaged in the architecture and design of their new collaborative workspace enterprise application.

Dedication

To A. and F.

—Gabriel Oancea

To Patty, Bobby, Alex, and my new son, Ryan, for their patience and support during the writing of this book.

To the heroism, patriotism, determination, and resolve of the American people.

—Bob Donald

Acknowledgments

We would like to thank everyone at Que who helped develop this book and specifically acknowledge Michelle Newcomb for her continued communication and support.

Tell Us What You Think!

As the reader of this book, *you* are our most important critic and commentator. We value your opinion and want to know what we're doing right, what we could do better, what areas you'd like to see us publish in, and any other words of wisdom you're willing to pass our way.

As an associate publisher for Que, I welcome your comments. You can fax, e-mail, or write me directly to let me know what you did or didn't like about this book—as well as what we can do to make our books stronger.

Please note that I cannot help you with technical problems related to the topic of this book, and that due to the high volume of mail I receive, I might not be able to reply to every message.

When you write, please be sure to include this book's title and author as well as your name and phone or fax number. I will carefully review your comments and share them with the author and editors who worked on the book.

Fax: 317-581-5831

E-mail: feedback@quepublishing.com

Mail: Dean Miller
           Associate Publisher
           Que
           201 West 103rd Street
           Indianapolis, IN 46290 USA

Introduction

The *by Example* Series

How does the *by Example* series make you a better programmer? The *by Example* series teaches programming using the best method possible. After a concept is introduced, you'll see one or more examples of that concept in use. The text acts as a mentor by figuratively looking over your shoulder and showing you new ways to use the concepts you just learned. The examples are numerous. While the material is still fresh, you see example after example demonstrating the way you use the material you just learned.

The philosophy of the *by Example* series is simple: The best way to teach computer programming is using multiple examples. Command descriptions, format syntax, and language references are not enough to teach a newcomer a programming language. Only by looking at many examples in which new commands are immediately used and by running sample programs can programming students get more that just a feel for the language.

Who Should Use This Book

Anyone who wants to learn Visual Basic .NET should read this book. The prerequisites include having a basic understanding of Microsoft Windows. As long as you understand some of the simple concepts such as files and directories, the Internet, and applications and programs, you should not have a problem reading this book.

The book covers some of the essential background material necessary for developing Visual Basic .NET applications. This includes an overview of the development environment, the language itself, object-oriented concepts, database concepts, and XML.

This book is for you if you can answer true to one of the following statements:

- I know how to use Microsoft Windows (95, 98, NT, or 2000) and want to learn how to program.

- I am a C++ and/or Java developer and I want to learn how to develop applications for Microsoft .NET.

- I am a Visual Basic 6.0 developer and want to learn the new Visual Basic .NET language.

- I design and build enterprise applications and want to learn a language that can help me.

This Book's Organization

This book is presented in six parts. The first part gives a basic overview of Microsoft .NET and Visual Studio .NET. This sets the context for the reader in developing Visual Basic .NET applications. The reader is then presented with his/her first view of a very simple application. This application is then built and executed to acquaint the user with building an application using Visual Studio .NET.

The second part covers the Visual Basic .NET language basics. This is the first step in understanding the language itself and covers such things as data types, variables, and language statements.

The third part moves into object-oriented concepts. This is necessary due to the language improvements of Visual Basic .NET. Prior versions of Visual Basic do not require any object-oriented knowledge. With this new version, it is a must and this book tries to present the material in order to make you a very good Visual Basic .NET developer.

The fourth part covers user interface development using Visual Basic .NET. This includes developing forms and controls as part of your application.

The fifth part covers data access. Most applications today deal with some form of data. ADO.NET and XML are popular ways of dealing with data. As a result, these technologies are covered to show how these can be used from Visual Basic .NET. This part also includes a basic overview of SQL, which is used in database access provided by ADO.NET.

The sixth part covers developing Web applications using Web Forms. Here we discuss the issues involved in developing Web applications and actually how to do it using Visual Basic .NET.

At the end of the book, there is an appendix that covers UML (Unified Modeling Language) in a quick crash course. The Web site includes migrating Visual Basic 6.0 to Visual Basic .NET applications, XML (eXtensible Markup Language), and a reference of the Visual Basic .NET language.

Conventions Used in This Book

Examples are indentified by the icon shown at left of this sentence.

The source code listing is printed in a monospace font, for example:

EXAMPLE

```
Module Module1
    Sub Main()
        System.Console.Out.WriteLine("An Example")
    End Sub
End Module
```

Frequently, example code contains lines in **bold** text. These lines are in bold to draw the reader's attention to them. The reason for this is because the focus of the example and the corresponding explanation is centered around these lines. As you go through the book and the examples, pay particular attention to reviewing the highlighted lines of code in order to understand and absorb the meaning of each of the examples.

OUTPUT

The output of an example is indentified by the icon shown at left of this sentence.

NOTE

Notes add more information about the material just presented. These notes clarify concepts and procedures.

TIP

Tips provide shortcuts or workarounds to a particular problem.

CAUTION

Cautions provide warnings regarding things to watch out for. These should save you time and trouble.

CHANGES FROM VISUAL BASIC 6.0

These messages indicate the changes in Visual Basic from Visual Basic 6.0 to Visual Basic .NET.

NEW IN VISUAL BASIC .NET

These messages indicate the additional features added to Visual Basic .NET

On the Web Site

Code examples in the book, the answers to the "Checking," "Reviewing," and "Applying" questions at the end of each chapter, and additional references are available at www.quepublishing.com.

What's Next

The book starts with an overview of Microsoft .NET and what it is all about. Then you take a tour of the Visual Studio .NET environment so that you can become familiar with the development environment used throughout the book.

Part I

First Steps in Visual Studio .NET Environment

Overview of the Environment

Creating the First Application

Compiling and Running the Application

Visual Basic .NET Project Types

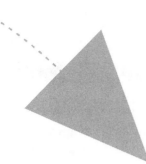

Overview of the Environment

This chapter introduces Visual Basic .NET by presenting an overview of the development environment. The goal here is to allow you to become acquainted with the development environment before actually jumping into learning the Visual Basic language itself.

In this chapter, you will

- Be presented with an overview of Microsoft .NET, Visual Studio .NET, and Visual Basic .NET
- Take a tour of Visual Studio .NET

Introduction

Visual Basic 6 users will see that Visual Basic .NET is not just an upgrade from Visual Basic 6. Instead, it catapults the Visual Basic language into a much broader arena that allows you to create many types of applications previously too difficult (if at all possible) to implement using previous versions of Visual Basic. If this is your first introduction to Visual Basic, welcome aboard and enjoy the ride. Hopefully you will find Visual Basic .NET to be a powerful language that will empower you to build world class applications.

Visual Basic has come a long way since its infancy. Visual Basic (or VB for short) has traditionally been a language that simplifies the development of software applications that run on Microsoft Windows. This includes Windows 3.1, Windows 95, Windows 98, Windows NT, and most recently Windows 2000. The most common types of applications written in Visual Basic have been *standalone applications* that run on a single computer. An example of a simple application is the Calculator program, as shown in Figure 1.1, that comes with Microsoft Windows. Using VB, you were able to develop applications in a very short amount of time. Before VB, one would need to write an application using a more complicated language, such as C or C++, which would require a steeper learning curve and more development time. A new VB developer could write a simple application faster than a moderate C developer. As a result of VB's productivity enhancement benefits, VB became a very popular language.

Figure 1.1: *A simple application.*

Developers then started using VB to write applications that needed to store data in a *database*. This way the application could store data in a structured format and the data would remain on the computer when it was turned off. The next time you turned on the computer and ran the application you would be able to view the data again and add new data. The databases started out by existing on the same computer as the application. Later, the databases were moved to a central location on a network where computers on the same network could talk to the same database. This way a single database could be used by many users, which meant the data could also be shared by those users. These types of applications are called *client-server applications*. The program itself is the client and the database is the server. Figure 1.2 depicts a client-server application where an application running on one computer communicates with a database running on another computer.

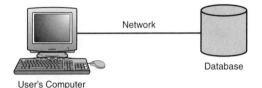

Network

Database

User's Computer

Figure 1.2: *A client-server application.*

As of Visual Basic 6, this client-server paradigm is still being used by many developers. The successor to client-server is called an *n-tiered application* (shown in Figure 1.3) and involves developing an application in layers. Today's typical application uses three distinct layers: the presentation layer, application logic layer, and data services layer. Each layer provides a specific function and is used by a layer above it. Assuming an online e-commerce–type application, the presentation layer of an application displays useful information to the application's user, such as the user's account information and order form. The presentation layer communicates with the application logic layer, which provides the application with specific functionality, such as how much to decrement the user's account based on the products they purchased. The application logic layer communicates with the data services layer for reading and writing persistent data, such as storing the order information in a database. Now, in terms of an n-tiered application, each layer of an application could potentially be running on a separate computer. If all the layers are running on the same computer, the application is considered a standalone application, or single tiered. If the application is running on three separate computers (each layer running on a separate machine), the application is considered a three-tiered application, and so on. Another way of expressing layers and tiers is that layers represent a logical separation of code within an application. A tier represents where the code actually runs.

For the layers to talk to other layers running on different computers they need a way of communicating across a network. Many *Web applications* follow the n-tiered paradigm as part of their architecture. Examples of Web applications are www.cnn.com, www.yahoo.com, and www.amazon.com. The communication mechanism on the Microsoft Windows platform is based on *COM* (Component Object Model) technologies.

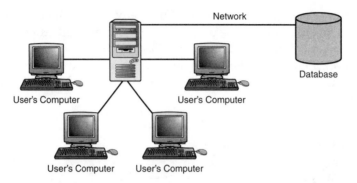

Figure 1.3: *An n-tiered application.*

COM started out with the goal of supporting the development of components that can easily be shared among different applications. These components can be built and installed on computers as basic building blocks that are used by applications. A simple example of a component is a credit card number verifier. By writing code to verify credit card numbers and placing this code in a component, applications then are able to share this component and reduce complexity and maintenance costs along the way.

As the paradigm of building applications changed from applications running on a single computer to client-server and then to n-tiered (or multi-tiered) computing, COM has been trying to keep up. Microsoft has recognized that in order to facilitate the development of n-tiered applications, Web applications, and beyond, it had to redesign some of its architecture and way of building applications. To that end came *Microsoft .NET*, which is a new platform for building distributed Web applications. Visual Basic .NET is the successor to Visual Basic 6.0 that allows you to build applications that support Microsoft .NET.

I am assuming you have heard something about Visual Basic .NET by now (based on the fact that you bought this book), but what exactly is it? What does it really mean? And, most importantly, what does it mean to you?

The Visual Basic language has undergone some major structural changes in order to address some of the deficiencies of the previous Visual Basic versions. With Visual Basic .NET, you are now able to develop standalone applications like before plus you can now create Web applications and Web services. The specifics of these are explained throughout the book. Before getting deeper in Visual Basic .NET, you need to better understand where Visual Basic .NET fits into Microsoft's .NET strategy as this will be important when you start writing .NET applications.

Let's start by defining these three Microsoft terms: *Microsoft .NET*, *Visual Studio .NET*, and *Visual Basic .NET*.

What Is Microsoft .NET?

Microsoft .NET is a new platform for building distributed Web applications.

In Web development today, the focus is on building a Web site that runs an application specific to the business. There is little thought (as a whole) to integrating the Web site with other services provided on the Web. The result is the development of Web-enabled applications that enable users to perform very specific tasks. These applications are not very flexible as they are only intended to fulfill the specific business needs related to the Web site. With Microsoft .NET this no longer needs to be the case.

Microsoft .NET is the platform for the development of a new breed of applications. These applications no longer need to be specific to a single computer or set of computers. You are able to build software services that run in a Web environment. These building block services can then be invoked by Web applications or bundled with other services as part of an even richer application. Using Microsoft .NET, these services and applications can run on any number of computers and the user interface for the applications can be displayed on different types of devices.

Along these lines, Microsoft is developing a set of services that can be used as part of building a Web site. One of the sample services is Microsoft Passport. This service enables you to visit `http://www.passport.com` and obtain your own passport ID using your e-mail address and a password. When you obtain a valid passport ID, it can be used to automatically log you in to any Web site that supports Microsoft Passport. Participating Web sites would invoke a call to the Passport service for verification. The result is that you have a single sign-in capability for the Web.

There are several components to Microsoft .NET. They are *.NET Infrastructure and Tools*, *XML Web Services*, *.NET device software*, and *.NET User Experience*.

The .NET Infrastructure and Tools includes Visual Studio .NET, the .NET Enterprise Servers, the .NET Framework, and Windows .NET. Visual Studio .NET is, of course, the development tool of choice for building .NET applications and services. Visual Studio .NET presently supports 20+ languages. This allows you to develop software in the language in which you are most comfortable. The really interesting (and innovative) part here is that code written in any of the supported languages is first compiled into Intermediary Language (IL). This means that .NET is essentially language neutral. IL then is executed as part of the Common Language Runtime

(CLR), which has automatic support for safe, secure (otherwise referred to as "managed") code and garbage collection.

The .NET Enterprise Servers are designed to be very scalable and suitable for Enterprise applications, which tend to have very strict requirements for stability. The *NET Framework* includes a common library of services that can be leveraged independent of the device the software is running on. This allows you to develop software using the .NET Framework and have it run on a device that supports the .NET Framework. This includes a PC, cellular phone, pager, PDA, and other Internet-ready devices.

The XML Web Services are a set of building block services that can be consumed by applications built on Microsoft .NET technology. Microsoft will provide many services and other vendors will provide even more. At some point there will be a wealth of services to choose from that can be brought together as part of a Web solution, a solution that would be too complex and unwieldy if it were based on the current Microsoft technology. Microsoft .NET greatly simplifies the development and deployment of these services.

The .NET device software enables new kinds of Internet devices to use Web services. This allows the development of new solutions using additional types of devices beyond that of the PC. Microsoft is currently engaging in writing software that supports many types of devices. This includes anything from cellular phones to PDAs.

The .NET User Experience will be much different than today's user staring at a computer screen. The applications built on Microsoft .NET can provide a user experience that transcends computer boundaries by providing different application views on a variety of different devices. For example, you may trade stock on your computer at home, view email from your cellular phone, transfer funds from your Personal Digital Assistant (PDA), and get a meeting reminder on your pager. All of these services can be part of the same overall solution built on .NET.

The complete .NET package means that you can easily create a much richer solution for your users, and deploy that solution in a scalable and reliable environment. It also means you can leverage existing services or provide new services. And, you will start to see a wider variety of devices in conjunction with Web solutions. This allows for the construction of new types of applications not dreamt of before.

The purpose of this chapter is to give you a basic idea of the big picture of .NET. However, the purpose of this book is to teach the reader Visual Basic .NET. If you require more information on other aspects of .NET please refer to www.microsoft.com/net.

What Is Visual Studio .NET?

Visual Studio .NET is "the" development environment for creating software solutions targeted for the Microsoft .NET platform. You use Visual Studio .NET to write your application code, build the solution, debug the code to find your errors, and to help in deploying your application to other computers.

If you are familiar with previous development tools from Microsoft, you might be familiar with Visual Studio. Visual Studio is the development environment for Visual C++ 6.0. Visual Basic 6 had its own separate development environment for building Visual Basic applications. With the advent of Visual Studio .NET, you can build applications using Visual Basic, C# (pronounced see-sharp), and 18 or so other languages.

The advantage with Visual Studio .NET is that you, as a developer, only need to learn one development tool. This will save you time if you ever get to the point of having to develop an application using multiple languages. This may seem unnecessary to you now but this is becoming more common in the software industry. Having a tool like Visual Studio .NET, where you can develop applications in multiple languages, is a huge step forward in the world of software development.

What Is Visual Basic .NET?

Visual Basic .NET is the successor to Visual Basic 6. It is a software language used to build applications targeted for the Microsoft .NET platform. It has undergone some major changes in order for the language to support the Microsoft .NET platform.

Tour of Visual Studio .NET

Now let's take a tour of the development environment so that you can begin to know your way around. The goal, at this point, is to allow you to become familiar with the most common windows in the Visual Studio .NET development environment. Because it would be overwhelming to present all the windows at this point, we shall tour the most common ones now and then cover the rest later in the book as they become relevant.

Let's now start our tour of Visual Studio .NET.

Visual Studio .NET

If you are reading this book next to your computer, you may want to open Visual Studio .NET at this point so that you can get a better feel for it. Click Start, Programs, Microsoft Visual Studio .NET 7.0. When Visual

Studio .NET opens for the first time, you are presented with the default Start Page, which looks similar to the one in Figure 1.4.

Figure 1.4: *Visual Studio .NET Start Page.*

At first sight, Visual Studio .NET looks very much like other software development tools in that it has menus, toolbars, and a variety of windows for handling specific tasks. However, the more I use it the more I appreciate the power of this tool.

TIP

If the Start Page is not immediately visible to you, it can be opened again using the Help menu. Select Help, Show Start Page.

Menus

As with most software applications, Visual Studio .NET has a set of menus and toolbars to help you in your work. Take a minute to scan the menus by clicking on the word File to display the File menu. Then move the mouse left to right to view the submenus. Each of the menus and their functions are explained throughout the book. That way their meaning can be introduced and explained in the context of relevant examples.

Notice some of the menu items are grayed out. This is because those menu items are not currently available. Menu items are available or unavailable based on the current state of your work and based on the type of work you are currently doing. For example, the menu item Close Solution is grayed out because you have not opened a solution yet. Keep this in mind if you run into other menu items that are grayed out. Figure 1.5 shows the File menu.

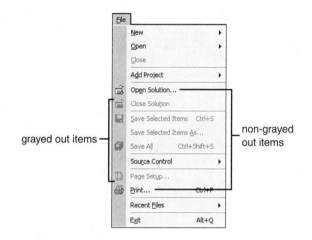

Figure 1.5: The File menu.

Toolbars

Toolbars contain a group of related buttons that each perform a specific task when clicked with the mouse. Figure 1.4 shows the standard toolbar that is visible when you first open Visual Studio .NET. It is displayed immediately below the Visual Studio menus.

You can rearrange the toolbars by clicking and holding the mouse button down on the grab bar at the left of the toolbar. To locate the grab bar, hover your mouse at the left end of the toolbars until the cursor changes to a cross. While holding down the mouse button, you can move the toolbar to a new location. If you drag the toolbar off the toolbar area, the toolbar will stay floating over the application. Whether you want the toolbar fixed at the top of the main window or floating is strictly a user preference.

You also have the capability to specify which toolbars are displayed and which are not. If you right-click the mouse in the toolbar area you will see a list of available toolbars as shown in Figure 1.6. You can get the same list by clicking on the View, Toolbars menu item. The ones with the check marks on them are currently visible. The remaining ones are not visible.

If you want to make one visible, simply click the one on the list you wish to make visible. We recommend that you leave enabled the toolbars that are visible by default (when you opened Visual Studio .NET for the first time), until you get more familiar with the environment. The same idea applies to all the other customizable settings for the environment—stay with the "factory" defaults until you have a better understanding of what the specific settings mean.

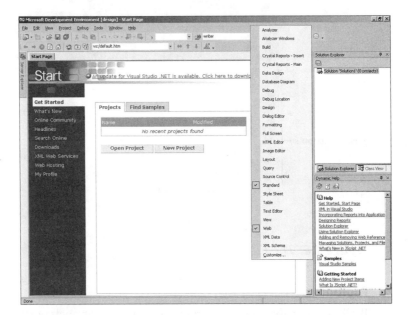

Figure 1.6: *List of available Visual Studio .NET toolbars.*

VS Start Page

The *VS Start Page* is your main starting page when working with Visual Studio .NET. The left side of the VS Start Page window contains a list of sections as shown in Figure 1.4. You can click on each of these sections to display relevant information on the right side of the window pertaining to the selected section.

The *Get Started* section allows you to open recently used projects, open existing projects (any project that you can navigate to using the File Explorer), or create a new project. The recently used projects are shown directly on the window so that you can quickly open the project (or projects) you have been working on. This saves time by not having to keep searching for the project and its location every time you open Visual Studio .NET.

The *What's New* section shows a list of help topics describing new features and changes in Visual Studio .NET. If you are currently a Visual Basic 6 user this may be helpful if you want to jump right in and find out only what's new without having to read the entire documentation first. If you click on an item in the What's New topic the relevant Web page is opened.

The *Online Community* section is quite nice because it shows you a list of public newsgroups related to Visual Studio .NET. You can communicate to other developers like yourself in the event you need answers to specific technical questions or you can just browse the messages as a supplemental learning exercise.

The *Headlines* section shows the latest MSDN (Microsoft Developer Network) news and information. You may want to periodically view this to keep abreast of the information and changes released by Microsoft.

The *Search Online* section allows you to search Microsoft's online MSDN database. This can be very useful when you start to develop your own software. The database contains a wealth of information including articles and code examples. If you come across something that you need more information on you can type a few keywords into the text box and click the Go button. If there is any help available for the keywords you entered the results will show in this window sorted by relevance.

The *Downloads* section provides a central place for obtaining the latest add-ons, service packs, and product upgrades. This also includes sample code and other various Microsoft SDKs.

The *Xml Web Services* section provides a convenient way for finding and registering services that can be used in your applications. Web Services is discussed in more detail later in the book.

The *My Profile* section allows you to customize Visual Studio .NET for your use. You can specify the type of developer you are. The main benefit of this is for the help system. When you use the help system, only information relevant to your profile will show up. For example, if you are a Visual Basic Developer and you click for help on a topic you should not see help information pertaining to Visual FoxPro. This is a major improvement as previous versions of Visual Basic and Visual Studio gave you mounds of help on any given topic. This required you to weed through the results, wasting your time.

At this point, you might want to set your profile to be Visual Basic Developer. This basically tells Visual Studio that you are going to use Visual Basic as your primary development language. This allows Visual Studio to display help in the context of Visual Basic as well as laying out the windows in a fashion that is familiar to most Visual Basic developers.

You also can specify the keyboard scheme. This is similar to the Profile setting but instead of laying out the windows differently the keyboard mapping is different. If you press the F10 key, the resulting action for this key depends entirely on the keyboard scheme you have. You can change the window layout. If you have previously used Visual Studio or Visual Basic 6 you can specify your profile accordingly so that Visual Studio .NET lays out its windows similar to those other tools. For example, if you set your profile to Visual Basic 6.0 the windows are initially laid out as you would see them in Visual Basic 6.0. The goal with this feature is so that you can continue to use a development tool that is familiar to you. If you have not used any previous development tool from Microsoft or if you do not have any strong preference, just leave the Window Layout set to Visual Studio Default, which is what you are going to use through this book.

Solution Explorer

Click View, Solution Explorer or press Ctrl+R to open the *Solution Explorer.* This displays all the different types of elements that are part of the solution. In Figure 1.4, the Solution Explorer is empty because you have not opened a Solution yet. In the next chapter, you will create a new Solution and explorer the types of elements then.

Working with Windows

You will find that after working with Visual Studio .NET for awhile, you may want to display only a specific set of windows. Fortunately, Visual Studio .NET allows you to customize your environment so that you can choose to show only the windows that you use most frequently. In addition to setting the options in My Profile to set the basic layout of the windows, you can further specify which windows to show and hide as well as their position. To show a particular window click on the View menu. This shows a list of windows, as shown in Figure 1.7, that you can display as part of the environment.

The View menu contains a list of the most common windows plus a menu item for Other Windows. Clicking this menu item displays the remaining list of windows available to you. As an example, click View, Other Windows, Output to display the output window. Figure 1.8 shows the output window now visible to you, docked below the *Get Started* window.

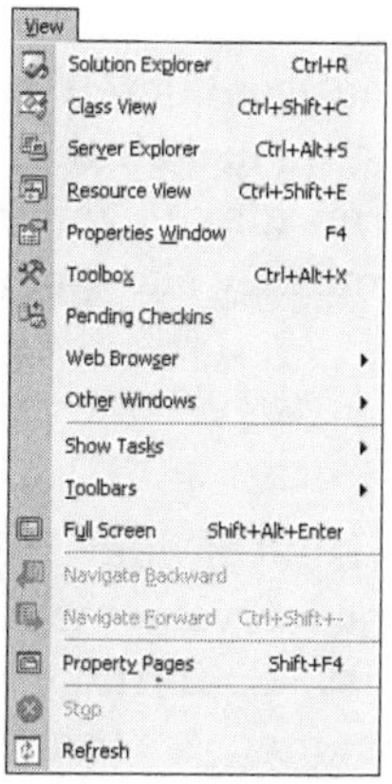

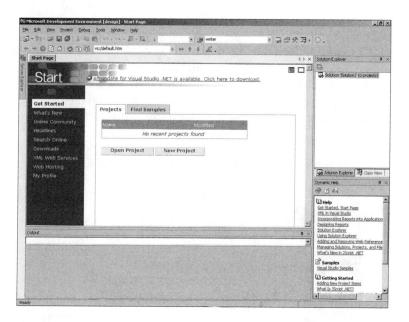

Figure 1.7: *View menu.*

Figure 1.8: *Output window.*

There are two important icons to note in the title bar of the *Output* window. The icon with the "X" should be familiar to you already. It allows you to close that particular window which makes it no longer visible. The other icon that looks like a push pin puts the window in Auto Hide mode. This is a very nice feature that you may find useful the more you use Visual Studio .NET. If a window is in Auto Hide mode, the window tab is displayed on the outer edges of the Visual Studio environment or workspace.

If you move the mouse over the tab and wait a second or so (also know as *hovering*) you will notice the window becomes completely visible in order for you to interact with it. If you then move the mouse off the window, it automatically hides itself again. This way you can maximize the screen real estate as you are developing software and quickly show particular windows when you need them.

Using Help

You will surely come across something in Visual Studio .NET in which you need help or more information. Like any good development tool, Visual Studio .NET comes with online help to assist you in the process of learning the tool and developing your solution. You can access the help information using the Help menu. This menu has four important ways of looking at the help information. They are *Contents*, *Index*, *Search*, and *Dynamic Help*.

Contents

Click Help, Contents to open the Contents window. This shows the table of contents for the help. The information is presented using a table of contents approach. The information is grouped into a hierarchy list of related topics. You can view the high-level topics and drill down to learn more. You click on a topic to display the detailed information in the main window for the topic. Figure 1.9 shows the Contents help window.

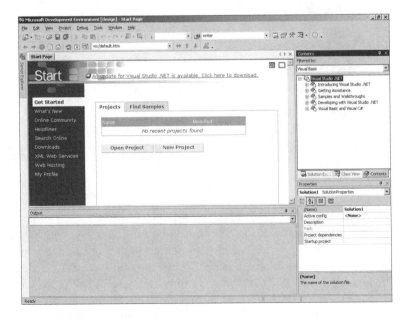

Figure 1.9: *Contents window.*

Index

Click Help, Index to open the Index window. This contains the same information as the Contents window except it displays it in a different way. Instead of showing the table of contents, it displays an alphabetical list of detailed topics. As in the Contents window, you would click on the topic to display the detailed information in the main window. Figure 1.10 shows the Index window.

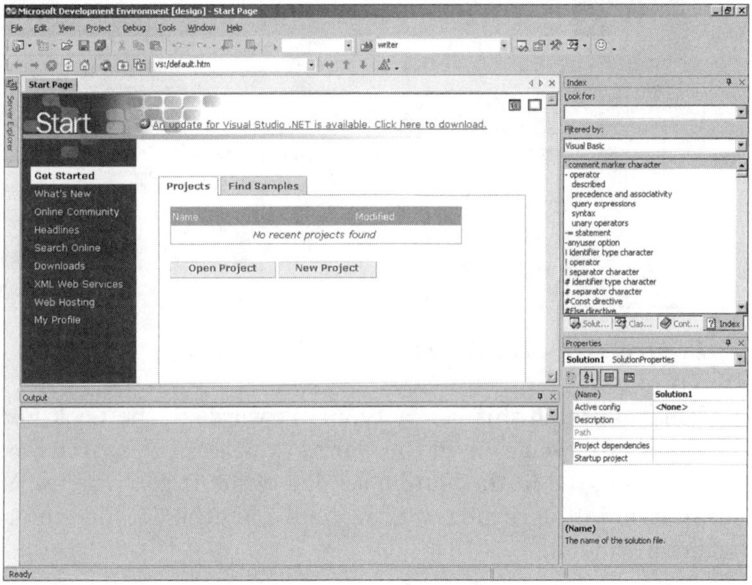

Figure 1.10: Index window.

If you have set the Profile option in My Profile (on the VS Start Page) to indicate the type of developer you are the help system will use this to only display the help index relevant to you. Since this book focuses on Visual Basic .NET you may want to set your profile to Visual Basic Developer. This way you will only be presented with help information that is relevant to Visual Basic.

Search

Click Help, Search to open the Search window. The Search Help window allows you to find help about something using one word or a set of words. Figure 1.11 shows the Search window.

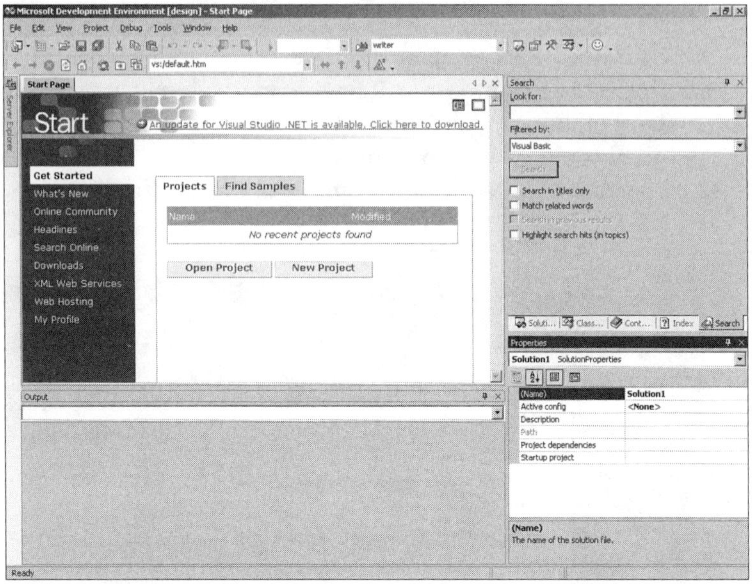

Figure 1.11: Search window.

You can search this list by typing in words in the Look For field. Press Enter after you type in the word(s) you want to search for and the results are displayed in the bottom section of the Index window. You would click on an item in the results window to display the detailed information in the main window.

Dynamic Help

Dynamic Help is new to Visual Studio .NET. If you click on Help, Dynamic Help, this displays the Dynamic Help window. While this help window is visible, any relevant help information is displayed for anything you click. Figure 1.12 shows the Dynamic Help window.

It's that simple but keep in mind that using Dynamic Help can be an intensive operation for your computer. Try it out on your computer and if it helps you then keep using it. Otherwise, do not display the Dynamic Help window.

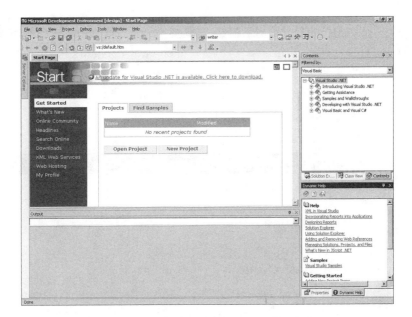

Figure 1.12: *Dynamic Help window.*

What's Next?

We have covered some of the history of the Visual Basic language and presented Microsoft .NET. You also learned about the distinctions between Microsoft .NET, Visual Studio .NET, and Visual Basic .NET. Based on this, you took a tour of the Visual Studio .NET development environment which you will be using throughout the remainder of the book.

In the next chapter you create your first application so that you can introduce Visual Basic .NET for the first time. This is accomplished by creating a new project using a menu item within Visual Studio .NET. All of the necessary files and project information is generated for you. You will go through the generated code to highlight some of the new changes in Visual Basic .NET. For those readers new to Visual Basic, this will also help get you started on the road to learning and being productive with Visual Basic .NET.

NOTE

The answers to the Reviewing It, Checking It, and Applying It are available on the book's Web site.

REVIEW

Reviewing It

This section presents a review of the key concepts in this chapter. These questions are intended to gauge your absorption of the relevant material.

1. What is the Microsoft .NET Framework?

2. What are Microsoft .NET Services?

CHECK

Checking It

Select the correct answer to the following questions.

Multiple Choice

1. Visual Basic .NET is:

    a. A development environment.

    b. An object-oriented software development language.

    c. A simple scripting language.

    d. A financial planning application.

2. Visual Studio .NET is:

    a. A development environment.

    b. An object-oriented software development language.

    c. A simple scripting language.

    d. A financial planning application.

3. Microsoft .NET is:

    a. A new operating system.

    b. A new platform for developing distributed Web applications.

    c. A new Internet Service Provider (ISP).

    d. The new name for the bundled package of all Microsoft products.

4. The VS Start Page allows you to:

    a. View and open the most recently used Visual Studio .NET projects on your computer.

    b. Get help on "What's New" and display common newsgroups that might help in your Visual Basic .NET development.

    c. Set up some default settings for Visual Studio .NET.

    d. All of the above.

5. The Solution Explorer window:

    a. Contains output messages informing you of the success or failure of building your project.

    b. Allows you to directly edit properties of elements in your project.

    c. Contains all the elements contained within your project and allows you to navigate to them.

    d. None of these.

True or False

Select one of the two possible answers and then verify from the book's Web site that you picked the correct one.

1. The Calculator program in Microsoft Windows is an example of a Web application.

    True/False

2. Visual Basic .NET can be used to build standalone applications and Web applications.

    True/False

3. Visual Basic .NET is a minor upgrade from Visual Basic 6.0.

    True/False

4. Changing your profile in Visual Studio .NET affects the Dynamic Help system.

    True/False

APPLY

Applying It

Try to complete the following exercise by yourself.

Independent Exercise

Because this is the first chapter and only an introductory overview is presented, please take this opportunity to read more about Microsoft's .NET strategy and technologies at www.microsoft.com/net.

Creating the First Application

In this chapter you create your first Visual Basic .NET application and learn the source code that is automatically generated by Visual Studio .NET. If you have used prior versions of Visual Basic, the goal of this chapter is to quickly show you the structure of a new application. This is to ease you into the dramatic changes that have occurred in Visual Basic since version 6.0. If you have not used prior versions of Visual Basic, the goal of this chapter is to give you a quick preview of what you will learn reading this book. This chapter does not cover the specific language details so don't worry if some of the language syntax is unclear. You will start learning the Visual Basic .NET language in detail in Part II, "Language Basics."

In this chapter, you will

- Create a new Windows Application project using Visual Studio .NET

- Tour the structure of the new application as generated by Visual Studio .NET

- Learn about more of the features of Visual Studio .NET such as the Code Editor and the Object Browser

Introduction

An *application* is a software program that runs, or executes, on a computer. An application typically has a user interface that allows you, as a user, to interact with it. There are many types of applications in existence such as word processors and e-mail programs. You can buy applications at a store, download them from the Internet, or you can build them yourself (although it is often simpler to buy one rather than build one).

A *project* is a term used to defined the set of files that are the ingredients of an application. An application can be made up of many types of files. The most common type of file used in an application is called the *source* file. A source file contains the steps that are performed when the application runs. These steps, or instructions, are written in a computer language such as Visual Basic .NET. Image files are another type of file that may be part of a project. Images are commonly used as icons or pictures to make the application easier to use by associating pictures with commonly used tasks.

In this chapter, you are going to create a new Windows Application project to demonstrate how you would start building an application. Once the project is created you will continue with your tour of Visual Studio .NET.

A Windows Application is a specific type of application that allows you create menus, toolbars, buttons, and other user interface components that you would normally expect to see in an application that runs on Microsoft Windows. In contrast, another type of application, a Console Application, runs only in a window that displays text output. A console window does not support any of the user interface components previously mentioned. Throughout the book there are examples of different types of applications that illustrate this.

When you create a new project, Visual Studio .NET automatically creates an initial set of files and some code to get you jump-started with your application. As you can probably tell, this is an extremely useful time-saving feature of Visual Studio .NET.

Creating a New Project

You can create a new project in Visual Studio .NET at any time by clicking on the File, New Project menu (or by pressing Ctrl+N). The dialog shown in Figure 2.1 is displayed as the initial step in creating a new project.

Here you would select the type of application you wish to create and specify the name and location of the project. Select Visual Basic Projects as the project type and select Windows Application as the desired template. You can specify any name you want for your project and the location is typically somewhere on your computer or on an accessible network drive.

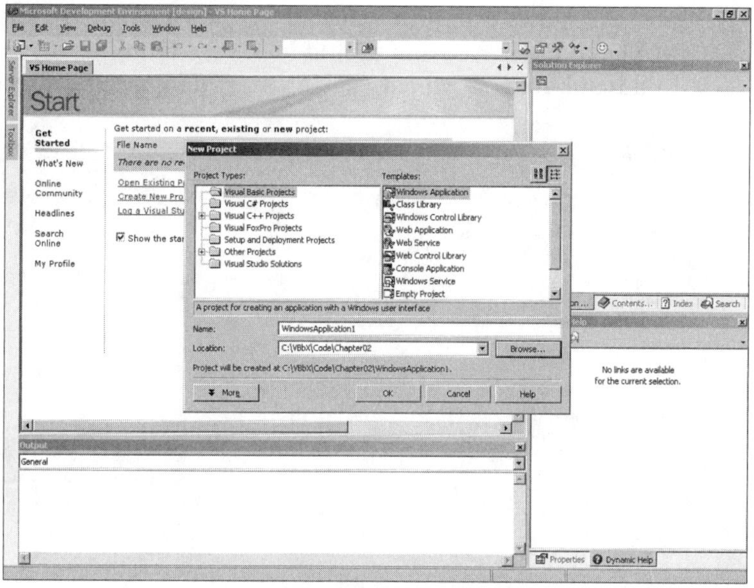

Figure 2.1: *New Project dialog box.*

TIP

You may want to create a folder on your computer for the purpose of placing all of your projects. This way you can manage all of your projects in a central location rather than having to search your hard disk later. Although this concern is somewhat addressed by the VS Start Page because it lists the recent projects, once you start developing new projects on your own this list may become large.

A new project containing a single blank form is generated for you when you click the OK button. The project and its initial files are placed in a subdirectory under the location you specified in the New Project dialog box. The name for the subdirectory is the same name as the project name when you first created the project.

NOTE

The format of the default name for a new project is the project type you selected appended with a number. The very first time you select a project type and empty project location (a directory that does not contain any projects), the appended number is "1." For example, the first time you create a Windows Application in an empty location, the default project name is "WindowsApplication1." The next time I create a Windows Application project in the same location, the default name becomes "WindowsApplication2." And so on.

Figure 2.2 shows the initial view of the newly created project. If you have used Visual Basic 6.0, this should look very familiar to you. You start out with a blank form in which you can start adding UI controls.

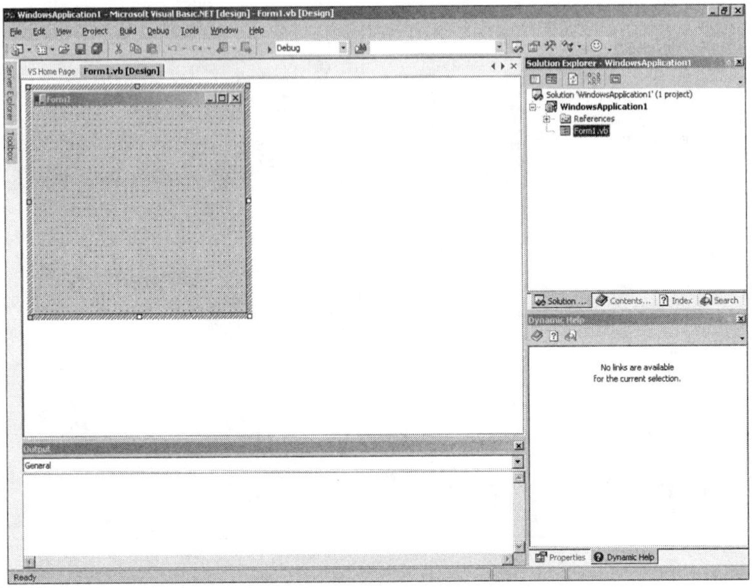

Figure 2.2: *A simple application.*

A Tour of the Generated Project

The Solution Explorer displays all of the different types of elements that are part of the *solution*. A solution is a grouping of one or more projects. If you are just starting to use Visual Studio .NET most of your solutions are probably going to contain just one project. As you become more experienced you may develop many projects as part of one overall solution.

Figure 2.2 shows this solution contains one project. You can create another project and add it to this solution by selecting File, Add Project, New Project. This displays the Add New Project dialog box shown in Figure 2.1. After you select the type of project you want to create, name it, and give it a location, the new project is added to the solution that is currently open. If you select the Close Solution, the current solution is closed and a new solution is created that contains the new project.

Under the project in the Solution Explorer, you can see the References (which is explained later) and the default form created as part of the new project.

Notice that the solution and project have the same name. This is the default behavior when you create a new project that is not part of another solution. If you want to change the name of the solution or project for any reason you can do so by using the Properties Window. Select View, Properties Window or press the F4 key. The Properties window is a dynamic window that displays the properties for the selected element in your project. You can select an element by clicking on it with the mouse. The Properties Window then displays a specific set of properties for that element and a description for that property in the lower part of the window. You can view the elements by using the scrollbar to scroll up and down. Figure 2.3 shows the solution element selected in the Solution Explorer and the properties for the solution displayed in the Properties Window.

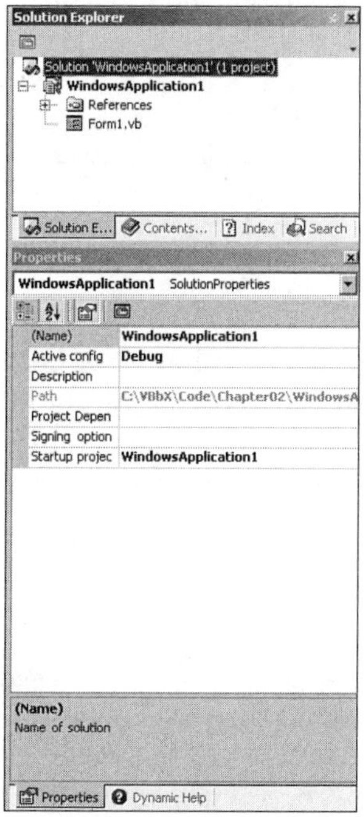

Figure 2.3: *Solution Explorer and Properties Window.*

The name of each property is displayed on the left side of the window and the corresponding value is displayed to the right of each property. Some properties are editable and some are not. If you see a property that appears to be grayed out then this signifies that you cannot change the value and you will be unable to change it. If it is not grayed out, you can change the value by clicking on the value and entering in a new value. For example, you can see the Path property in Figure 2.3 is grayed out because you cannot change the location of the project from the properties window.

Properties can have different types as values. For example, some properties may allow text as a value. A text value can contain a set of characters that you type in using the keyboard. Some properties only allow True or False. Others only allow a predefined list of values. If you click on the value of the property, you can at that point tell what values you can enter for the property. If it is a text property, a blinking cursor appears signifying you can enter text using the keyboard. If the property can only contain True/False or a predefined list of values, you can either type the first character of the value or use the drop-down combo list to select the desired value. For example, if you wanted to change a property value from True to False, you could click on the property and press the F key on the keyboard. Another approach is to click on the value and double-click the mouse. This causes the property to cycle through the possible values. Each double-click of the mouse moves to the next value.

TIP

If you want to quickly change a property value to another value in a predefined list, just double-click the property to cycle through the possible values.

Also notice that the values of the properties change to bold when you edit them. Values that are bold in the Properties window signify that the property has been changed from its default value. This is a quick way to tell what property values have been changed since you first created the element in the project.

TIP

Property values that are displayed in bold mean the value has been changed from its default value. This is a quick way to identify property values are different from their initial default values.

The Properties window could contain many properties based on an element selected. If you click once on the form displayed in Figure 2.2, you will see the form's properties as shown in Figure 2.4. The Properties window has an icon for displaying the properties in a categorical grouping or alphabetically. You have the option of switching between these two displays, allowing you to list the properties in whichever way is most appealing to you. Figure 2.4 shows the properties in alphabetical order and Figure 2.5 shows the properties grouped by category.

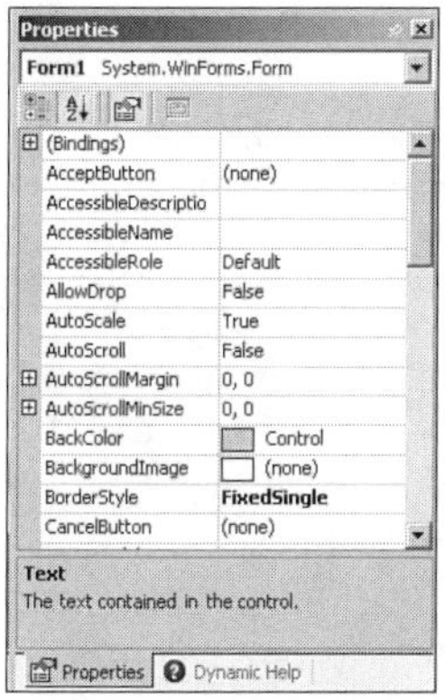

Figure 2.4: *Properties in alphabetical order.*

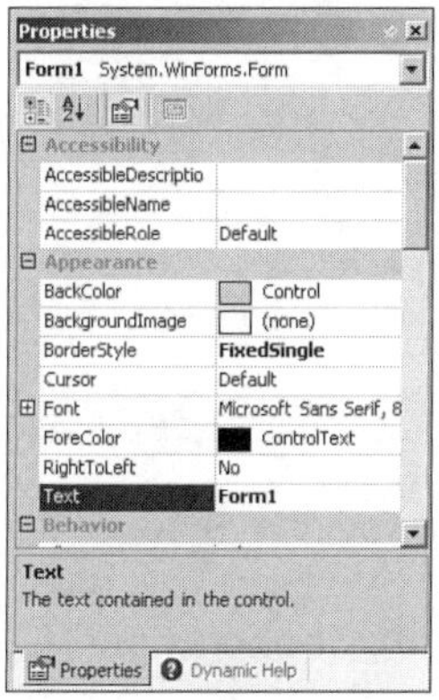

Figure 2.5: *Properties grouped by category.*

As stated earlier, a default form is automatically created for you when you create a new "Windows Application" project (which is what you saw in Figure 2.2). Forms have two parts to them—the Designer and the Code. The Designer shows the visual representation and allows you to visually design the form by placing other visual elements on the form. The Code represents the logic of the form as defined using a software language such as Visual Basic .NET.

If you double-click on the form in Figure 2.2 you will see the source code for that form. This is shown in Figure 2.6. To get back to the visual representation of the form you can double-click the form element in the Solution Explorer window. An even easier way to move between the Code and the Designer is to remember these two keystrokes:

- F7 to display the Code

- Shift+F7 to display the Designer

TIP

Use F7 and Shift+F7 to switch between the Code window and the Designer window.

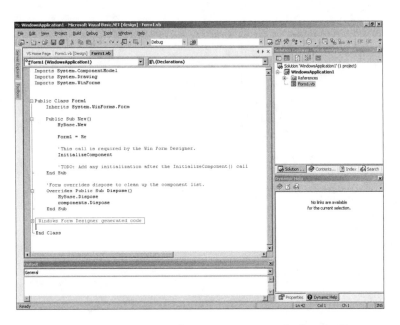

Figure 2.6: *Code window showing source code for the Form.*

If you are new to programming, I would not expect you to understand the code in Figure 2.6 at this point in the book. Also, many Visual Basic 6.0 developers do not have an object-oriented programming background so some of the code is going to look very unfamiliar to those readers as well. The reason it is presented this early is so that you can continue the tour of Visual Studio .NET within the context of a real project and at the same time point out a couple of useful things along the way.

The rest of Part I of this book continues with the tour of Visual Studio .NET. In Part II, the Visual Basic .NET language is presented and explained thoroughly. In Part III object-oriented concepts are covered to ensure you have the appropriate background before reading Part IV, which covers Forms and UI related material. By the time you get to Part IV, you should be in a good position to understand and internalize the generated code.

Let's not worry about the exact purpose of every line in the following code. Instead, focus on some of the structural elements first. Here is the generated code for the form:

```
Public Class Form1
    Inherits System.Windows.Forms.Form

#Region " Windows Form Designer generated code "

    Public Sub New()
        MyBase.New()

        'This call is required by the Windows Form Designer.
        InitializeComponent()

        'Add any initialization after the InitializeComponent() call

    End Sub

    'Form overrides dispose to clean up the component list.
    Protected Overloads Overrides Sub Dispose(ByVal disposing As Boolean)
        If disposing Then
            If Not (components Is Nothing) Then
                components.Dispose()
            End If
        End If
        MyBase.Dispose(disposing)
    End Sub

    'Required by the Windows Form Designer
    Private components As System.ComponentModel.IContainer

    'NOTE: The following procedure is required by the Windows Form Designer
    'It can be modified using the Windows Form Designer.
    'Do not modify it using the code editor.
    <System.Diagnostics.DebuggerStepThrough()> Private Sub InitializeComponent()
        '
        'Form1
        '
        Me.AutoScaleBaseSize = New System.Drawing.Size(5, 13)
        Me.ClientSize = New System.Drawing.Size(292, 273)
        Me.Name = "Form1"
        Me.Text = "Form1"

    End Sub

#End Region

End Class
```

Notice the use of the System.Windows.Forms.Form. This represents a reference to a predefined class that is provided as part of the Microsoft .NET Framework Library. In every program or application that you are going to develop in Visual Basic .NET, you will not want to write everything yourself. You will want to use code that you have previously written or take advantage of code that someone else has written. For example, if you want to draw a line on a form you would not want to write code to draw every pixel that exists in a direct line between two points. You would never get your application finished if you took this approach. The best approach is to leverage as much existing code as possible so that you are not reinventing the wheel (so to speak).

Visual Studio .NET provides a Framework Library of code that you can use in building your software. *Namespaces* are used to avoid naming collisions (such as classes) in code. For example, using namespaces you could name a class "Form" in your own namespace named "MyCode" and refer to the Form class in your code as MyCode.Form. This allows your Form class to coexist with the System.Windows.Forms.Form class provided with the .NET Framework Library since they are in different namespaces. For example:

```
Dim form as MyCode.Form = new MyCode.Form()
```

The `Imports` statement is also provided as part of the Visual Basic .NET language so that you can include a namespace at the top of your source code and just refer to the class name within your code. This way you do not need to continuously write the fully qualified class name including the namespace. Using the `Imports` statement, the previous code snippet could be changed to the following:

```
Imports MyCode
Dim form as Form = new Form()
```

Namespaces are partitioned into *assemblies*. An assembly is simply a prepackaged container of code. Specifically, an assembly is a DLL containing managed code that runs in Microsoft .NET. The meaning of managed code versus unmanaged code is explained later in this book. For now, recognize that namespaces allow you to segment your code to avoid naming collisions with pre-existing classes and types. Assemblies are the deployable units in which your code resides (i.e., a DLL). You will learn more about namespaces and assemblies as well as the Microsoft .NET framework throughout this book.

When a namespace is imported or referred to in code, the assembly which contains the namespace is shown in the Solution Explorer under the "References" element. This way you can easily figure out which assemblies are being referenced by the project. Figure 2.7 shows the references defined in the project you just created. If you are ever in doubt whether a particular assembly is being referenced by your project, you can always check the references in the Solution Explorer to find the answer.

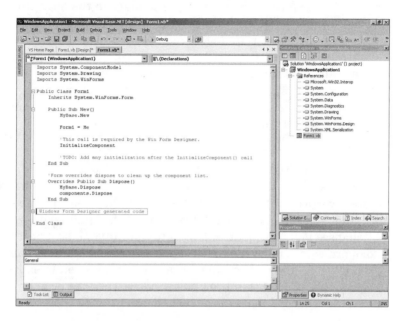

Figure 2.7: *Assembly References for a project.*

NOTE

Although assemblies are new to Visual Basic .NET, they are a different way of implementing what most Visual Basic 6.0 users know of as Project References. In Visual Basic 6.0, you would specify a reference to another project by selecting it from a list of known libraries installed on the computer. Once the reference was established, the code from the referenced library was available to the program. In Visual Basic .NET, after the assembly is imported the program can use the imported code.

Everything between the `Public Class Form1` and `End Class` lines define the Form1 element you see in the Solution Explorer. You can think of this as the beginning and ending points of the Form1's definition in the source code. All of the form's logic must exist between these two lines of code.

NOTE

If you haven't noticed yet, Visual Basic .NET is now a fully object-oriented language. This is a major change that existing Visual Basic 6.0 developers should realize. Don't be alarmed by this as change sometimes causes concern. Part III of this book presents a thorough overview of object-oriented development so that you can better understand and learn the language.

Another interesting point is the code between the #Region and #End Region lines. This region of code is automatically updated by the Designer window. The Designer window allows you to graphically place objects, such as buttons, on the form. When you make changes to the form with the Designer, the Designer adds the necessary code changes to your form in the region between the #Region and #End Region lines. At the beginning phase of learning Visual Basic .NET you should not be changing these lines of code manually as it may cause problems with your program.

NOTE

Novice programmers should NOT edit the code between the #Region and #End Region lines. This code is automatically updated by the Designer.

As shown in Figure 2.6, the Code window also has an addition from previous versions of Visual Basic. In the left margin of the Code window you can see a vertical line going down the page with some squares with plus (+) or minus (–) symbols in them. If you click on a square with a minus, the code collapses and the square changes to contain a plus sign. If you click on a square with a plus, the code reappears and the square changes to contain a minus. Clicking on the squares this way allows you to expand and contract sections of code within the Code window. This can be very helpful if you have lots of code in one window and you want to only see certain sections at a time.

What's Next

You have created your first Visual Basic .NET project and toured more aspects of Visual Studio .NET. You have also skimmed through the structure of the autogenerated code for this project.

In the next chapter, you build the application using this project and run it to see what happens. Generally, when you feel your application is complete and bug-free (no defects) you would want to make your application available to others. This is called deploying your application and you will learn how to do this with Visual Studio .NET.

REVIEW

Reviewing It

This section presents a review of the key concepts in this chapter. The question is intended to gauge your absorption of the relevant material.

1. Describe an application, a project, and a solution and how they relate to one another.

CHECK

Checking It

Select the correct answer to the following questions.

Multiple Choice

1. If you are viewing a form in the Designer window, you can view the form's code using:

   a. F5.

   b. F6.

   c. F7.

   d. Ctrl+C.

2. If you are viewing a form in the Code window, you can view the visual representation in the Designer window using:

   a. Shift+F5.

   b. Shift+F6.

   c. Shift+F7.

   d. Shift+C.

3. Property values that are uneditable are displayed:

   a. With a "lock" icon next to them.

   b. As grayed out.

   c. Just like any other property.

   d. In red.

True or False

Select one of the two possible answers and then verify on our Web site that you picked the correct one.

1. There are several additions to Visual Basic .NET but there are very little changes to the language itself.

   True/False

2. Solutions contain projects.

   True/False

3. The Imports statement is for using assemblies.

   True/False

4. The #Region and #End Region statements are used to delineate comments in your code.

   True/False

5. Bold property values in the Properties window represent properties that have been modified from their original value.

   True/False

6. Property values can only be viewed in alphabetical order.

   True/False

APPLY

Applying It

Try to complete the following exercise by yourself.

Independent Exercise

Create a new "Windows Application" project and make sure the Form's properties are displayed in the Properties window by selecting the form (select the form by clicking on it). Turn off the maximize box by changing the MaximizeBox property to False, change the form's title by editing the Text property, and change the border style to FixedSingle. After you change these properties, notice which form properties are bold and which are not.

Compiling and Running the Application

In this chapter you will learn how to turn your project into a running application. This is more commonly referred to as "building" your project. You will build the sample project created in the previous chapter and then run it to see what it looks like. In the process of doing this, these topics will be covered:

- Building the project
- Explaining Build messages
- Building and Rebuilding
- Running the application

Building the Project

Once you have typed in your source code, using the source code editor in Visual Studio .NET, you probably want to run it to verify that it works. Unfortunately, your computer does not understand how to execute or run your program using the source code directly. Your computer can only run software that is written in a language called *machine code*. Machine code is a format that is directly understood by your computer and is not humanly comprehensible (at least not for most of you).

Most software developers use a language such as Visual Basic to write code and then use a tool such as Visual Studio to convert this code into machine code for the purpose of having the computer understand it. This allows you to develop software in a format that is comprehensible to humans and then convert it to a format that a computer can process.

In order to build your project, you would use the Build Solution menu item on the Build menu in Visual Studio .NET.

Figure 3.1 shows the result of building the project you created in Chapter 2, "Creating the First Application."

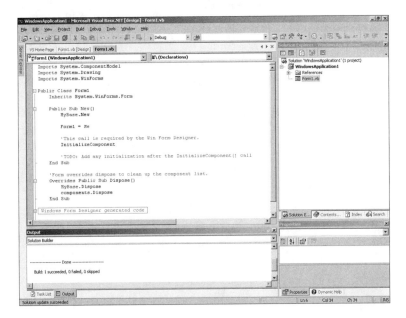

Figure 3.1: *Building the Project.*

When you build a project in Visual Studio .NET, you have the option of building it in *Debug mode* or *Release mode*. In Debug mode, the generated code contains extra information for use by the *debugger*. A debugger is a tool used by software developers to execute software step by step. Using a debugger, you can stop at any point in your software and inspect it to see if it is behaving as you expected. In Release mode, there is no extra information created as part of the generated code. The resulting code is lean and optimized for faster and better performing code.

Most developers build their project in Debug mode until the project is nearly finished. Once the project is fairly stable in its development, you may want to start building it in Release mode to further test it and verify that the project continues to run normally. The build mode (Debug or Release) is set using the Configuration Manager on the Build menu.

Build Messages

At this point, notice the text displayed in the Output Window. As a result of this build, the Output Window contains text informing you that one project was built successfully, zero projects failed building, and zero projects were skipped. Remember that each Solution in Visual Studio .NET can contain multiple projects. Obviously, the goal is to have all of your projects in your solution built successfully.

So, based on this, I can assume the project was built successfully and move on. But, what do I do if my project does not build successfully? To show this, I have typed garbage (random characters) into my source code before trying to build it. Figure 3.2 shows the erroneous text I added and the output of the Build process.

This time I am not presented with the Output Window. Instead, there is a Task List window displaying a list of tasks I must perform before the Build process can complete successfully. Each task generated as a result of a failed build shows an informative description of the task and the file where the error originated. If you double-click on the task, the offending line is highlighted and immediately made visible in the code editor for you to deal with. This is a very nice feature that you will find yourself using quite often as you fix problems in your projects.

If I select View, Other Windows, Output I would see the error message from the build process shown in Figure 3.3. As you can see, this time the output of the build process tells you that zero projects were built successfully and that one project failed to build.

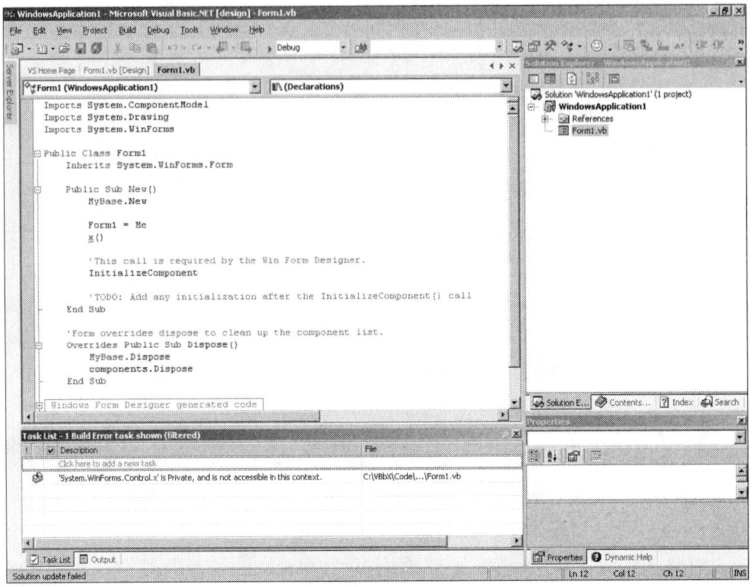

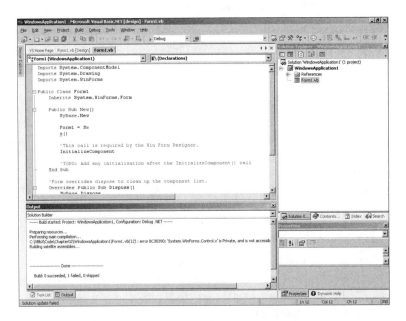

Figure 3.2: *Building a project with errors.*

Figure 3.3: *Output window containing build errors.*

Building and Rebuilding

You may have noticed that there is a Build and a Rebuild menu item. After you build your project for the first time, selecting Build will only build the files that have changed since the last build. This way if you have many files in one project only the files that changed would be built again. This saves time if you have large projects containing hundreds of files and you only make a single change to one file. Only that file would be built when you select the Build menu item from the Build menu.

The Rebuild menu item is available for the situation where you want to rebuild the whole project no matter what. Selecting the Rebuild option does not take into account which files have changed and which have not. They are all rebuilt regardless.

Running the Application

If I remove the erroneous text I just added so that the project is back to the way it was originally I can build the project and run it. If you have built the project in Debug mode you can execute the project in the debugger.

If you are like most developers, you will probably want to start running your newly built projects in the debugger. At some point, your project becomes stable and is free of notable errors. This is when you would start to run it outside the debugger. You can run a project that was built in Debug mode or Release mode outside the debugger.

NOTE

Actually, you can execute code in the debugger regardless of whether the project was built in Debug mode or Release mode. However, the debugger will only be able to perform debugging functions such as setting breakpoints and watching variables if the project was built in Debug mode.

If you intend on using the debugger with your built project, verify the project was built in Debug mode first. If it was not built in Debug mode just set the configuration to Debug in the Configuration Manager and rebuild the solution.

You can execute the project in the debugger by selecting Debug, Start or by pressing the F5 key. If you do not want to run in the debugger you can select Debug, Start Without Debugging or by pressing the Ctrl+F5 keys simultaneously. Figure 3.4 shows the sample application running using the F5 key to start it. This example shows nothing more than a simple blank form. Once again, this example was only intended to provide some context while presenting the Visual Studio .NET development environment.

For those readers familiar with debuggers and stepping through applications, the F9 key is used to toggle a breakpoint on and off on the current line in the Code window. Once a breakpoint is hit and program execution stops on a particular line of code, you can step through the code using the F8 key. At any point, you can press the F5 key to resume execution of the program.

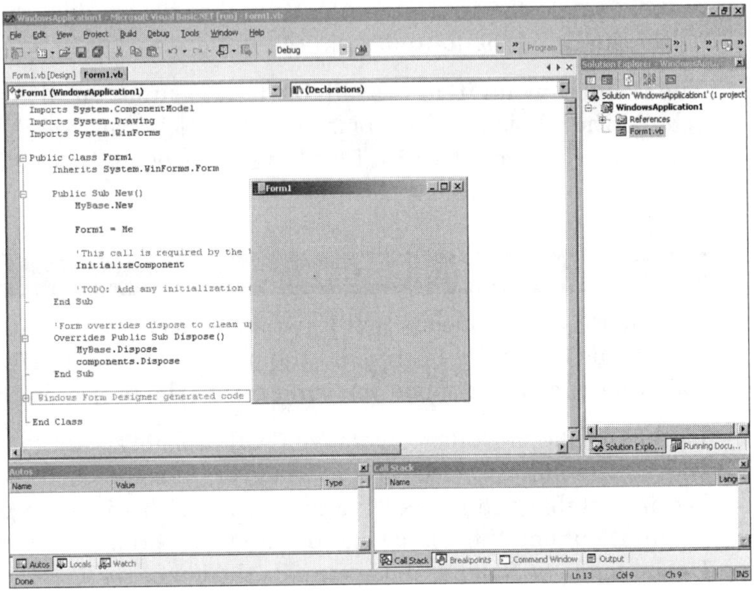

Figure 3.4: *Sample project running.*

NOTE

You can close the application by clicking the close box (the button with the "X") in the titlebar or by pressing Alt-F4.

Once a project is built and free of errors, you will want to deploy it to other computers so that other users can use it. The simplest way to achieve this is to just copy the files to the computer you wish to run it on. It is as simple as that. With Visual Basic .NET, you no longer need to register anything on the computer where the software is going to run. Prior to Visual Basic .NET, you were required to register COM dlls, as an example, using regsvr32.exe prior to using the dlls. If the dll's were not registered they could not be used.

Deploying your software can be more involved if you wish to create an installation program to do the job of installing your software on another computer. This tends to give your program a professional polish to it and helps the user install it in a much more elegant way. There are a number of different types of deployment options available to you (besides copying the files) and these are discussed later in the book.

Under the Covers

I sort of skimmed over the details of what happens under the covers during the build process on purpose so that you could focus more on understanding the process of building rather than low-level details of what's happening. Now that you have gone through the process of building and running the application let's take a look at what's happening so that you can appreciate some of the major improvements of Microsoft .NET.

Existing Visual Basic developers are aware that they can build their projects into *P-Code* or directly into *Native* code. P-Code is an intermediate step between your Visual Basic code and Native code. P-Code is then compiled at runtime by the Visual Basic runtime services into Native code. Native code is the format that is directly understood by the processor on your computer.

With Visual Basic .NET, P-Code is no longer used and you no longer have the capability to generate Native code directly. Instead, Visual Basic .NET source code is compiled into the Intermediary Language (or IL for short). This applies to all of the other available languages in Visual Studio .NET as well. The compilation process checks the code for correct syntax as defined by the specific language.

The IL that gets generated contains *managed code* and *metadata*. Managed code is a term used to express code that is generated by Visual Studio .NET and managed by the Microsoft .NET Framework. The metadata is language neutral type information used to describe the generated code and data types, location of references to other objects, and exception handling tables.

The Common Language Runtime (CLR), which is part of the Microsoft .NET Framework, loads the IL code (and metadata) at runtime and compiles it to Native code using a Just-In-Time (JIT) compiler before the code is executed by the computer's processor. The code is compiled the first time the code is accessed. Subsequent accesses of the same code use the already compiled code created by the JIT.

Managed code is intended to be safer and more reliable since it is being "managed" by the Microsoft .NET Framework, which handles the execution, versioning, security, and deployment issues. Managed code does not require any registration unlike COM dlls generated with Visual Basic 6.0 or Visual

C++ 6.0. The framework provides application isolation so that different versions of the same application can run on the same computer. Also, you can have different versions of the same assembly installed and running on the same computer without breaking existing applications.

NOTE

All source code written in Visual Studio .NET supported languages are compiled into the Intermediate Language (IL for short) during the build process.

This is what enables code written in one language to access data types and code written in another language seamlessly. You can even use code written in different languages within the same project.

The good news is that this all happens under the covers and you really don't need to understand the details. The important point to remember is that all source code is compiled to IL code and the IL code is managed by the Common Language Runtime.

What's Next

You have gone through the process of building the project. This included an explanation of the build messages in the Output Window and tasks in the Task window in the event a build fails. You then executed the application in order to see it working.

In the next chapter, we discuss the types and structures of the various VB projects that you can create. A description of each project type is given along with an example to show what each type of project looks like when it is running. This is intended to give you an idea of the types of applications you can build with Visual Basic .NET.

REVIEW

Reviewing It

This section presents a review of the key concepts in this chapter. These questions are intended to gauge your absorption of the relevant material.

1. Describe what the Intermediate Language (IL) is.

2. Describe the difference between Building and Rebuilding.

CHECK

Checking It

Select the correct answer to the following questions.

Multiple Choice

1. If you want to start debugging your project, you could press which key?

   a. F5.

   b. F6.

   c. F7.

   d. None of the above.

2. If you want to start the application without debugging it you could press which key combination?

   a. Ctrl+F5.

   b. Ctrl+F6.

   c. Ctrl+F7.

   d. None of the above.

3. IL stands for:

   a. Interface Language.

   b. Instructor Lounge.

   c. Inspector Larry.

   d. Intermediate Language.

4. CLR stands for:

   a. Common Language Runtime.

   b. Common Line Return.

   c. Clear Language Reform.

   d. None of the above.

True or False

Select one of the two possible answers and then verify on our Web site that you picked the correct one.

1. All applications developed in Microsoft .NET *must* be registered on the target computer before it can run.

   True/False

2. Managed code is compiled just-in-time by the Common Language Runtime.

   True/False

3. Only Visual Basic .NET source code is ever compiled to IL code.

   True/False

APPLY

Applying It

Try to complete the following exercise by yourself.

Independent Exercise

The purpose of this exercise is to familiarize yourself with building a project and viewing the build messages. Create a new "Windows Application" project and build it. Once it builds, introduce an error into the source code by typing anything in the Code Window and select Build Solution from the Build menu. Remove the text you typed in so that the Code Window is back to what it was and rebuild the project.

Visual Basic .NET Project Types

There are several different types of projects that you can create using Visual Basic .NET. This chapter presents the project types so that you can understand the types of software projects you can create as you read the rest of the book. When you create one of these projects, all of the initial files and source code are generated to give you a head start. Once the project is created, it is up to you to then add the specific code that is unique to your project. Hopefully, the descriptions of these project types give you a better understanding of the true breadth and power that Visual Basic .NET provides you as a developer:

- Windows Application
- Class Library
- Windows Control Library
- ASP .NET Web Application
- ASP .NET Web Service
- Web Control Library
- Console Application
- Windows Service
- Empty Project
- Empty Web Project

Windows Application

The Windows Application project is used to create applications that are installed and run on Microsoft Windows. This is the traditional type of application that has existed on Microsoft Windows for years. These types of projects generally contain a user interface similar to what you are used to seeing in most Microsoft Windows applications. It usually contains common user interface features such as a menu, toolbar, buttons, and so on. Visual Basic 6.0 users should be familiar with this type of project already. When you start developing applications of your own, you will be creating projects of this type for those applications that are not Web-related and are intended to run on the computer where it is installed.

Figure 4.1 shows the Visual Studio.NET workspace after a new Windows Application project is created. All of the necessary code to get your application started is created for you and the project's main form is visible. At this point you can start enhancing the project as you like by adding a menu, toolbar, and buttons to the form. You can even add additional forms. It is up to you to construct your application as simple or as complex as you like. The initial structure of this project includes the default form and references to any assemblies.

The form has a visible component that is editable using the Designer window. This is the window shown in Figure 4.1. You can also edit the form's code directly using the Code window. You can access the Code window for a form using the F7 key. To get back to the Designer window for a form you can press Shift+F7. You will learn about the Designer Window in much more detail in Part IV, "Working with Forms and Controls," when you are dealing with forms and controls.

TIP

You can press F7 to display the form's Code window and Shift+F7 to display the form's Designer window.

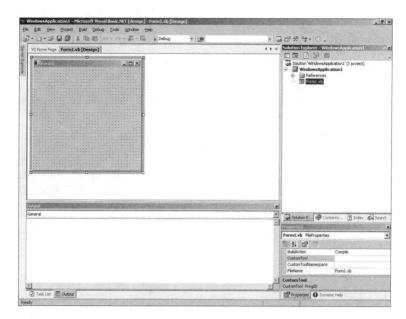

Figure 4.1: *Windows Application project.*

Class Library

A Class Library project is used to create a set of classes that can be used by one or many other projects. The project itself becomes an "assembly" that can be used by other projects once it is built. In Part III, "Working with Objects," you learn about object-oriented concepts and this is where this type of project will be demonstrated. Visual Basic 6.0 users are probably already familiar with this type of project as you can create a Class Library in Visual Basic 6.0 which essentially enables you to build a COM dll.

Figure 4.2 shows the Visual Studio.NET workspace after a new Class Library project is created. All of the source code is generated to give you a head start in building your class library. Notice that the "Class1" is initially visible in the Designer window. Just like with the forms, you can access the code for the class using F7 and back to the Designer window using Shift+F7. The initial structure of this project includes a default Class and any project references as a result of importing assemblies.

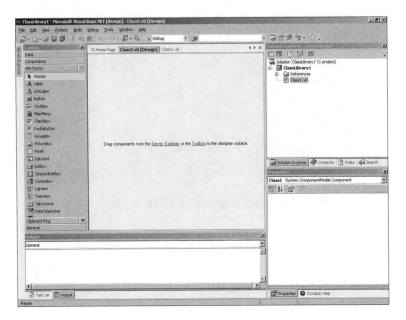

Figure 4.2: *Class Library project.*

For now, think of this type of project as a way to create a library of source code that can be shared and used by many projects without having to duplicate the code in each of those other projects. Each project that wants to refer to code in this project would simply import a reference to this project using the assembly name. The assembly name is defined in the Property Pages for the project. You can display this by right-clicking on a project in the Solution Explorer and then selecting the Properties menu item from the pop-up menu. The project Property Pages window is shown in Figure 4.3.

When you get to the point of wanting to develop your own assemblies, you will create one or more projects of this type for that purpose.

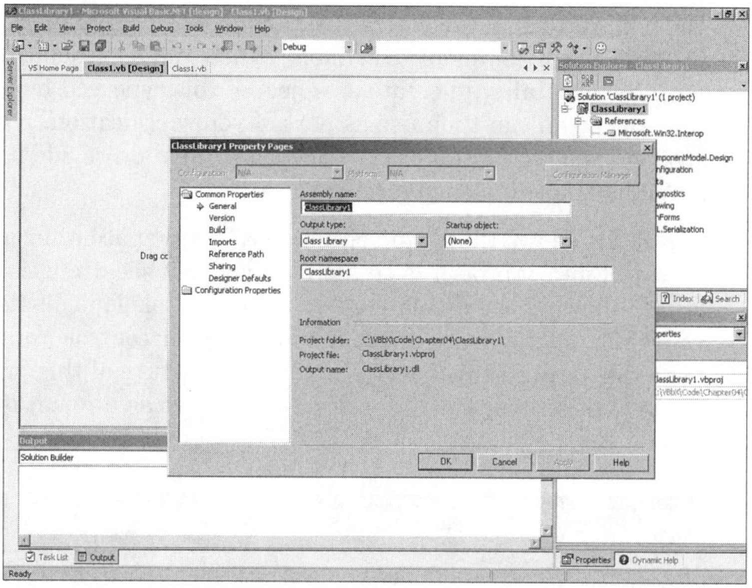

Figure 4.3: *Project Property Pages.*

Windows Control Library

A Windows Control Library project is used to create a customized control that can be used by other projects. A Windows Control is a user interface artifact that usually has a unique look and feel to it. It may also provide the capability of user interaction such that the user could possibly click on it or enter some values.

Windows provides a set of Common Controls that you can immediately use in your development. This includes a Label control for displaying text on a form, a Textbox control for allowing the user to enter data onto a form, and a Button control for providing the capability for the user to click on something visual which then performs a task. Most of you are familiar with these types of controls.

You will inevitably come across a particular situation where you need a control that is not commonly available. When you do reach that point, you have the capability to create a project of this type and build your own control which you can then use as part of your application. If the control is good enough, you could easily package it up and provide it for sale to other developers needing such a control.

Figure 4.4 shows the Visual Studio.NET workspace after a new Windows Control Library project is created. As you can see, the Designer Window is visible showing the display area for the control. This display area is where you would manage and direct the look of your control. You will see how to do this later in this book. The initial structure of this project includes the default control and any project references as a result of importing assemblies.

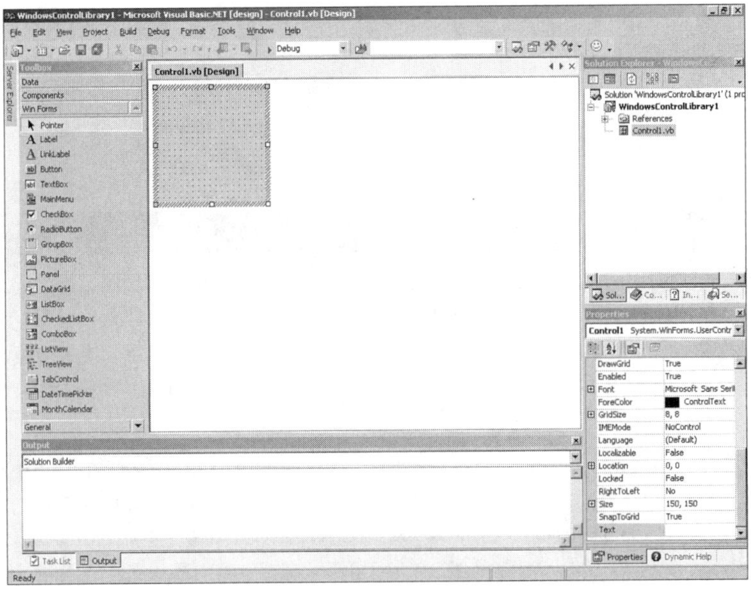

Figure 4.4: Windows Control library project.

ASP .NET Web Application

A Web Application project allows you to develop applications for the Web that are accessed through a Web browser. If you are currently familiar with ASP, think of this project type as ASP development on steroids. This type of project is actually based on ASP.NET using Visual Basic as the development language.

Using a Web Application project you can create *Web Forms*. Web Forms is a major new development as part of Microsoft.NET and ASP.NET in particular. Web Forms allow you to design and develop forms that render themselves according to the target browser or display device on which they run. This frees you from having to know and deal with the specific issues around the type of browser your user may be using, for example.

Figure 4.5 shows the Visual Studio.NET workspace after a new Web Application project is created. As you can see, the Designer Window is visible showing the display area for the Web Form. This is where you would probably add controls and provide any additional graphical output for the form. The initial structure of this project includes several different files. It's better to talk about these files in the context of learning about developing a Web application. Because of this, these files are discussed in Part VI, "Developing for the Web," when we talk about Web Forms and developing for the Web.

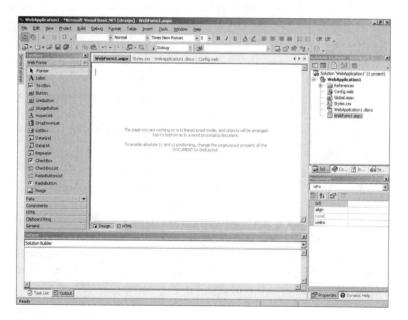

Figure 4.5: *Web Application.*

Although ASP.NET is not covered at any great length in this book, you will be covering Web Forms in Part VI of this book as you take a look at Web development.

ASP.NET Web Service

A Web Service project allows you to develop an entirely new brand of software. From a high-level standpoint, a Web Service is basically a component that can be invoked across the Web. The service itself can be developed by you and would reside on a server somewhere on the Web waiting for consumers of it. Along with Web Services, there is a mechanism for the discovery of Web services enabling users to quickly find out the details and use the service.

For example, wouldn't it be nice if there were an easy way to add simple local weather forecasts to an application you are building for the Web? This could be provided as a Web Service and published so that developers would be able to utilize it. An XML message would be constructed that included the zip code of the user (including other optional data) and dispatched to the Web Service. The Web Service would receive the message, process it, and send back an appropriate response containing the current day's local weather report. The client that initiated the call to the Web Service would then process the response and display the data appropriately.

As a Web Service, this functionality can be included in any web application without having to rewrite the server code to get the relevant data. As more and more interesting building block services are built, applications will become richer and more rewarding since there will be a lot to offer without the traditional expense incurred to make these features available.

It is true that invoking components remotely is not a new concept; however, you now have the capability to develop software that can be called over the Web. And because it uses SOAP (Simple Object Access Protocol, see `http://www.w3.org/TR/SOAP/` for more information) as the protocol it can be accessed from any other computer. This includes computers running UNIX. So, essentially you can now develop a service that is accessible by any other computer. The additional benefit is that Web Services can be invoked without having to download or install any software on the client computer. This further supports the accessibility of future Web Services as they become available.

The types and number of services that will be developed using this technology is unclear at this point. This is going to be left up to developers like you to provide these services to the marketplace. A good place to start, as a developer, is `http://www.gotdotnet.com`. This place provides lot of .NET information as well as interesting code samples.

The initial structure of this project includes several different files similar to the files you may have seen in the Web Application project. These files are discussed in Part VI when we talk about developing for the Web.

Web Control Library

Along the same idea as a Windows Control Library project, the Web Control Library project allows you to develop a control that is intended for use on Web Forms. This type of project enables developers to create customer user interface components that are meant to be used specifically for Web applications or an Internet device.

The initial structure of this project includes the default Web control and any project references as a result of importing assemblies.

Console Application

Microsoft Windows provides a command prompt window that allows you to type in commands using the keyboard to perform everyday tasks such as displaying lists of files, copying files, and deleting files. Figure 4.6 shows the command prompt window. A Console Application project allows you to build a program that can be run within the command prompt window. Console Applications are limited to text output and do not have any associated graphical display. The text output is limited to a command prompt window in which the Console Application runs.

The initial structure of this project includes the default module and any project references as a result of importing assemblies.

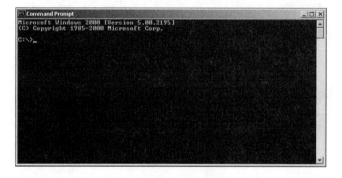

Figure 4.6: *Command Prompt window.*

A Console Application project is used in the next chapter so you can see it first hand then.

Windows Service

A service in Microsoft Windows is a specific type of program that performs a specific job or function in the background. This type of program does not have a user interface that you can interface with. A Windows Service project allows you to develop this type of program using Visual Basic .NET.

The initial structure of this project includes the default service and any project references as a result of importing assemblies.

Your computer currently has a set of services that was installed as part of Microsoft Windows. You can display the list of registered services by clicking on the Services icon in the Administrative Tools in your Control Panel. Figure 4.7 shows the Administrative Tools folder and the Services icon you would need to click on. Figure 4.8 shows the list of registered services on my computer. Once you develop a service and install it, you would see it displayed in the list in Figure 4.8 on your computer.

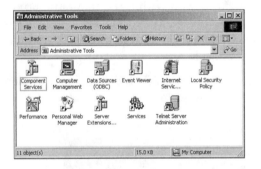

Figure 4.7: *Administrative Tools folder in the Control Panel.*

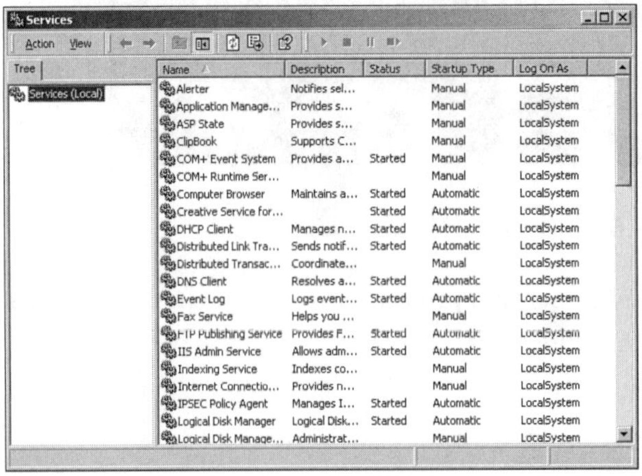

Figure 4.8: *My computer's list of installed services.*

Empty Project

You can also create an Empty Project project. You may want to do this if you are planning on creating a solution that contains many projects. You could first create the empty project, name the solution, and then start adding projects to it.

You could also start with an empty project if you wanted to start out by writing all of the source code yourself. This would not be recommended as you can benefit from choosing one of the other type of projects to get you started faster.

Empty Web Project

This is along the same lines as the Empty Project. The difference here is that this project is going to be Web-related whereas the Empty Project type is not Web-related.

You would create a project of this type if you were starting out by creating a solution in which you are going to then add more than one other project to it. Otherwise, it is just as easy to create one of the other project types such as Web Application, Web Service, or Web Control Library.

What's Next

We have touched on most of the project types that are available to you as you develop software using Visual Basic .NET. Each of the types will start to have more meaning to you as you progress through the book. If you don't quite have a handle on these project types yet, please refer back to this chapter.

In the next chapter you will start learning the Visual Basic .NET language in detail. The chapter starts out with an introduction to programming for those readers just starting out in software development. After that, this book's first programming example is presented so that you can start down the road of learning VB.NET.

REVIEW

Reviewing It

This section presents a review of the key concepts in this chapter. The question is intended to gauge your absorption of the relevant material.

1. Describe the purpose of having different types of projects. Also, describe the Windows Application and Console Application project and their differences.

CHECK

Checking It

Select the correct answer to the following questions.

Multiple Choice

1. Which project would you used to develop a common program that runs in Microsoft Windows?

   a. Windows Control Library.

   b. Windows Application.

   c. Windows Service.

   d. Class Library.

2. If you found yourself needing to develop a new user interface control for your Microsoft Windows application, what type of project would you create to start developing it?

   a. Windows Application.

   b. Console Application.

   c. Windows Control Library.

   d. None of the above.

3. Let's say you came up with an award-winning idea for developing a brand-new service that other developers could invoke over the Internet. What type of project would you create to start developing it?

   a. Web Service.

   b. Windows Service.

   c. Neither a nor b.

   d. My Great Idea Service.

4. If you found yourself needing to develop a new user interface control for your Web application, what type of project would you create to start developing it?

   a. Windows Control Library.

   b. Console Application.

   c. Web Control Library.

   d. None of the above.

True or False

Select one of the two possible answers and then verify in Appendix A that you picked the correct one.

1. A Window Application project is used to create a graphical application that looks and feels like other programs that run on Microsoft Windows.

   True/False

2. A Class Library project is essentially used to create a library of source code that can be used by other projects.

   True/False

3. A Windows Control Library project is used to create custom graphical controls that can be used by other programs.

   True/False

4. A Web Application project is used to develop an application that runs on the World Wide Web.

   True/False

5. A Web Service project is used to develop a service that can be used across the Web by applications that know how to communicate with the service.

   True/False

6. A Web Control Library project is used to create custom graphical controls that can be used in Web Applications.

   True/False

7. A Console Application project is used to develop a program that runs solely within a command prompt window.

   True/False

APPLY

Applying It

Try to complete the following exercise by yourself.

Independent Exercise

The purpose of this exercise is to familiarize yourself with building a Console Application project. Create a new Console Application project and build it. Run the project using the F5 key so that you can familiarize yourself with the output of a Console Application. This type of application is used in the next few chapters so it's a good idea to learn it now.

Part II

Language Basics

Language Description

Fundamental Data Types

Data Conversion and Expressions

Arrays, Enumerations, and Structures

Control Statements

Subroutines and Functions

Introduction to Debugging and Exception Handling

Microsoft .NET Framework—Assemblies and Namespaces

Language Description

In this chapter you will take a tour of the Visual Basic language. We will start with a brief history of programming languages in general and BASIC and Visual Basic in particular. Next you will learn the structure of a Visual Basic project as it integrates into a Visual Studio .NET solution.

You will also write and then dissect and analyze a very simple console application written in Visual Basic .NET. You will use this application to introduce the first and most fundamental concepts of the language: identifiers and literals, comments and whitespace, as well as the general structure of a Visual Basic .NET program.

The material for the chapter is structured into these topics:

- Introduction to programming
- Programming languages
- Structure of a Visual Basic project
- Identifiers, literals, keywords, and whitespace
- Comments

Introduction to Programming

To understand what programming and programming languages are all about, you need to understand first how a computer works. Even if you are familiar with this subject please do not skip the next few paragraphs, which define a few fundamental notions used throughout the rest of the book.

A computer consists of *hardware* and *software*. By *hardware* we understand normally the physical (material) components of the computer, of which the most important are

- The processor or processors, also known as Central Processing Unit(s) or CPU(s).

- The working memory (mostly known as RAM, for Random Access Memory), which is a transient location in which software executes. This memory is in use only while the computer is powered; that is why it is called transient. When the computer is powered off, whatever is in memory will be lost.

- The permanent memory (or permanent storage), which is where software and data are stored while the computer is powered down. Some examples of permanent memory are hard disks, floppy disks, CDs, and so on, together with the devices that link them with the CPU and RAM.

- Other devices and peripherals that are of less interest for you currently include the monitor, keyboard, mouse, miscellaneous video and sound cards, and so on.

By *software* we understand a program that can execute (run) on the hardware. The software program (or program, in short) consists of a set of instructions expressed in a language the CPU can understand (called machine code).

The way this execution (running) of a program occurs is (in a simplified version): the program is loaded from permanent memory into working memory. Then the CPU executes sequentially all instructions in the program. These instructions may require some input data and may produce output data. For example, a word processor program would normally require input from the user (the user must enter some text from the keyboard) and the program may output the document to a printer or save it to a file.

It is important to understand that the whole program execution takes place in working memory, which is manipulated by the CPU according to the instructions provided in the program. The program itself may use additional resources such as disk files, and so on.

You probably are wondering how the program is loaded in working memory and who is managing the miscellaneous resources that the multitude of software programs requires. One special type of software, which is known as the *operating system*, does all this (and much more). The operating system (OS) loads a program in response to a request from the user, for example. It also provides a variety of resources to the programs that run, from simple input/output (IO) to network and database services. Examples of operating systems include the Windows family, Linux, and Solaris.

One of the most important concepts that you need to understand is how the working memory (RAM) is structured because it is in this memory where all software runs. The working memory is a sequence of bits. A *bit* is the fundamental type that computers use to represent data and software, and it can have two possible values: 0 and 1. These bits are organized in bytes—each *byte* consists of 8 bits. Therefore you can represent the working memory as a sequence of bytes. A *memory address* is the number (index) of that byte in the sequence. The term memory address is commonly used as the shorthand *address*, when speaking of software and programming. See Figure 5.1 for a diagram of how working memory is organized.

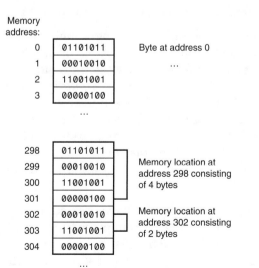

Figure 5.1: *Working memory (RAM) organization in a computer.*

All data and software that a computer uses is represented in memory as bytes—single bytes or bytes grouped together to represent more complex data. For example a UNICODE character requires 2 bytes of memory. A normal Integer value requires 4 bytes of memory. The contiguous memory where a piece of data is stored is known as a *memory location*. We will use this term frequently in the rest of the book.

Programming Languages

You have seen that a program consists fundamentally of a series of steps (instructions) to the CPU on how to manipulate working memory and other resources to produce some useful output, based on some kind of input from the user or other programs.

The programmer provides these instructions to the CPU in a format that it understands. As you already learned, this format is known as machine code (also known as machine language). The first programs written were indeed written in machine code. However, this code is not easy to use or read, and it is even harder to maintain over time (especially if there are changes to the set of instructions the CPU supports). The next step in the evolution of programming languages is the *assembly languages*. These languages require one simple translation to machine code before the CPU can understand it. This translation step is achieved using a program called an *assembler*. However, the assembly languages were not a big step forward; they retained all the complexity and unintuitive features of the machine code.

Further down the evolution line of the programming languages is the first generation of high-level languages. They are named high-level because they require a special (non-trivial) step to transform them into code that the CPU can understand. This step is called *compilation* and is performed by special programs called *compilers*. The compiler will take the *source code* written in the respective language (for example Fortran or C) and translate it into machine code for a given hardware platform and operating system. By *source code* we understand the instructions in the original (high-level) language. We use the term *executable* format for the (compiled) final format that can be executed.

The high-level languages themselves have evolved through a series of steps (sometimes known as *generations*), from procedural languages to structured languages and then to object-oriented languages, such as C++ and Eiffel. The latest generation of languages add a new step into the translation from source code to executable format: an intermediary step called *byte codes* in the case of Java and *intermediate language* (IL) in the case of the Visual Studio .NET. Although the two are not identical in implementation, they share a set of common good ideas, one of which is ease of use and maintenance. In both cases a final (but easy) translation step is required to transform the intermediary code into machine instructions.

BASIC stands for Beginner's All Purpose Symbolic Instruction Code and it is a system developed at Dartmouth College beginning in 1964. It was originally meant to be a very simple language both from a learning and translation perspective. Indeed the first generations of BASIC were quite simplistic, lacking a lot of features that more powerful languages of the day (like Fortran and Algol) had.

Both Microsoft and IBM provided a very successful interpreted version of BASIC for the PC (known as GWBASIC and BASICA). Later on Microsoft, realizing the potential of the new language, provided a compiler for it, known as QBasic (for Quick-Basic) and a very short-lived professional version (PDS Basic). Some competition came from Borland with its version of TurboBasic, which was also quite popular in the late eighties.

The first version of Visual Basic become available at the beginning of the nineties, and evolved through version 3 for Windows 3.x, and then from version 4 and up to today's Visual Basic .NET, for 32-bit versions of Windows. Microsoft currently still supports Visual Basic 6.

Visual Basic was (and is) a very successful language for the same reason as its venerable ancestor BASIC was: it has a simpler syntax and faster learning curve for beginners, while at the same time allowing advanced programmers to achieve complex tasks with ease. That said, one has to understand that, apart from the name and some syntax constructs, there is little resemblance from the original BASIC and the current component-oriented Visual Basic .NET. There are a lot of new features that make this popular language the language of choice for some 4 million programmers across the world. In the rest of the book you will learn some of the most important of these features.

Structure of a Visual Basic Project

You have seen in the previous chapters what are the mechanics of creating a new Visual Basic project. In this section we will discuss this topic in more detail. You will create a simple project that does only one thing: it displays a "Hello World!" message to the console.

NOTE

The *console* is the name for the command prompt (DOS) window, in programmer's parlance. Writing a console application means in effect that all the user interaction takes place using the simple command prompt interface and no graphical user interface (GUI) is involved.

It may seem strange to some readers that you start learning Visual Basic—one of the languages that is specifically designed to ease GUI development—by writing a console application. The reason we believe this is the best approach is that Visual Basic was dramatically changed (for the better) by introducing a series of features that make it a full-blown object-oriented language. These changes include introduction of object-oriented features like inheritance, method overloading, and shared (static) members, to name just a few. We do believe it is easier to understand these concepts exemplified by using simple programming examples, without adding the complexity of GUI forms and controls, until after the basic object-oriented paradigm has been successfully learned. Therefore start simple, and add complexity as you continue learning.

Let's start by creating a new Visual Basic project. From the New Project dialog select Visual Basic projects on the left side and Console Application in the Templates pane on the right side. Change the name of the project to HelloWorld. The dialog should look like the one in Figure 5.2. Click the OK button to create the new project.

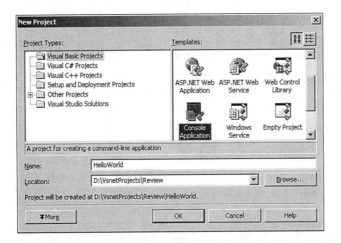

Figure 5.2: *New project dialog for HelloWorld.*

Now the Visual Studio IDE shows the newly opened project, similar to the one shown in Figure 5.3.

As you have seen in the previous chapters, you have a main window that contains the miscellaneous project components that are open. If more than one project component is open, multiple tabs will be present on the top of the main view. Right now you should have only one tab labeled Module1.vb. On the right you see the project window (labeled Solution Explorer) and the Properties window—which were briefly discussed in the previous chapters. We will explore these and other windows in more detail in this chapter.

Figure 5.3: *The Visual Studio IDE with the newly created HelloWorld.*

In the Solution Explorer you can look at all the component parts of your solution and project. When you create a new project, the IDE creates a new solution with the same name as the project. A solution may be comprised of one or more projects. If you click on the solution in the Solution Explorer you will see in the Properties window (below it) the properties of the newly created solution. We will return to this later on in the book. For now, let's continue our exploration.

Click on the project (HelloWorld). The Properties window will now show the properties of the project. Notice that the project file has an extension, .vbproj, which indicates that this is a Visual Basic project. Each project in a solution is developed in a language—Visual Basic, C#, and so on, although projects may interact with one another as you will see. Under the project, you have two entries—one labeled References (which you will ignore for now) and another labeled Module1.vb.

Now click on the Module1.vb in the Solution Explorer window. The Properties window changes again to show the properties of Module1.vb, which is the currently selected object. Module1 is a Visual Basic *module*, which is one of the fundamental components that can be part of a project. Each module consists of source code that, when compiled, will yield executable code (after passing through intermediate language code, first).

The first (Module Module1) and last (End Module) lines of code indicate where the module starts and ends, and are (as you have seen) generated by the wizard. Also generated by the wizard are the two lines in the middle: Sub Main() and End Sub. You can think of these for now as being the entry and exit points of the program. That means your program will start with the statement immediately following Sub Main() and will end the moment it reaches the End Sub. In between these two statements it will execute sequentially all the steps that you will enter. For now this would mean nothing because there is nothing between the Sub Main() starting point and the End Sub ending point. That means that if you ran the program as it is, it would do nothing.

Let's give the computer something interesting to do. Click in the Module1 main view (on the left) and enter the lines shown in bold below, as indicated. You will notice that when you enter the period between different parts of each statement, a drop-down prompt will appear below as you type text. This feature is known as IntelliSense; do not worry about it for now, you will come back to it later.

EXAMPLE

```
Module Module1

    Sub Main()
        Console.Out.WriteLine("Hello World!")
        Console.Out.WriteLine("Press the <Enter> key to end the program")
        Console.In.ReadLine()
    End Sub

End Module
```

Save the program and now let's build (compile) and run (execute) your new application. Select the Debug, Start menu (or simply press F5) to have the IDE compile the code for us and then run it. You should see the output of the program as shown in Figure 5.4.

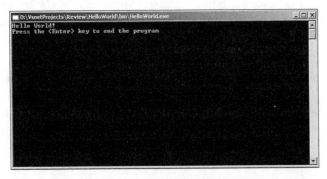

Figure 5.4: *Running the HelloWorld application.*

Notice the "Hello World!" and "Press the <Enter> key to end the program" message displayed in the command prompt window. Press the Enter key to end the program—the focus will return to the Visual Studio IDE.

You have just coded, compiled, and executed your second simple program in Visual Basic. Let's see what the structure of a Visual Basic program is.

You have a Solution (HelloWorld) that contains your Visual Basic project (also HelloWorld). The Visual Basic project is a collection of code and components grouped together to constitute a program. In your case you have only one component—a module, named Module1. This module contains the entry and exit points of the program, and between these, the steps that the CPU must execute. You can think for now of the module as a container for a part of the program.

In this case you have three steps. First you request the text "Hello World!" to be displayed to the console. You achieve this by using the WriteLine() method of an object called Console.Out. Do not worry if you do not understand exactly what the previous sentence means, we will get back to it later on and explain it in detail, in later chapters. For now think of the Console.Out.WriteLine() statement as an instruction to write to the console the text passed to it in parentheses. The second line is very similar to the first line, except the text written to the console is different ("Press the <Enter> key to end the program").

In a similar fashion, the last line before the End Sub exit point reads a line of input from the console until the Enter key is pressed. The reason you have the last two statements is so that you can read the console output—the computer will wait until you press the Enter key. If you delete the last line, the program will run just as fine, except that it would not wait for us to read the "Hello World!" text, it would see that the program has finished and it would close the console window. You can try (as an exercise) to delete the last line and see what happens when you run the program.

Identifiers, Literals, Keywords, and Whitespace

Now that you have seen what a Visual Basic program looks like, you can define some of the fundamental language components.

An *identifier* is what is commonly referred to as a name in programming. It can be the name of a project, module, variable, object, method, and so on. You have seen some identifiers; you will see much more as you go along. An identifier in Visual Basic must conform to some naming rules: it must start with a letter and it must not contain any other symbol than letters, digits and the _ (underscore) character. Valid identifier names are Module1, Main, x, bFound, m_name, and NUMBER_PI. Any identifier that violates these rules is not valid and the IDE and then the compiler will signal you with a syntax error if you try to run the program. Examples of invalid identifiers are m-name, 3stooges, and joe smith.

NOTE

An identifier can also start with an underscore, although it is better to use a letter. The detailed syntax for identifiers (and in general for the Visual Basic .NET language) is presented on our Web site.

You have probably noticed that some of the identifiers in the program you have written are colored in light blue. These are a special class of identifiers known as *keywords*. Keywords are reserved identifiers that the language itself defines and that cannot be used, except in the way defined by the language itself. The compiler detects these keywords and highlights them (in blue, by default), so that you can read the code easier. For example if is a keyword used in a branching statement, as you will see. That means that you cannot name a module if.

Literals are values that are used in code as they are. Examples are numbers like 0, 1, 2.5, or string literals like "Hello World!".

Whitespace is defined as the spaces between different symbols used. It consists of the space, tab, and new line characters.

It is important to remember that Visual Basic is a case insensitive language—that means an identifier can be written in any combination of upper and lowercase letters. For example if, If, iF and IF are all the same identifier. You will notice that the IDE is going to change the capitalization of the keywords to a standard format. This is an option called "code beautification" that can be disabled if you choose to, although we recommended that you keep it on.

Comments

The sample program you wrote is a very simple example of code—there is nothing complicated going on. However, a real-life program is normally more complicated and lives a longer life than a sample program in a book for learning programming. The people developing these programs have realized very early that a mechanism to add notes and comments about what certain pieces of code do is an absolute must—from the human perspective. These comments are required as an additional explanation for what a given piece of code does. They are useful to somebody who uses the code to extend (improve) it or is just reading it trying to understand what different parts of it are doing, or as input for a documentation generation tool.

In programming, these are called comments and all high-level languages have them, although the way they are marked differs. The compiler removes the comments when the code is compiled.

In Visual Basic the comments are delimited by the single quote ('), and end at the end of the line. Let's add the bold line from the code snippet below in your program and run the program again.

EXAMPLE

```
Module Module1

    Sub Main()
        Console.Out.WriteLine("Hello World!")
        Console.Out.WriteLine("Press the <Enter> key to end the program")
        ' The next line prevents the console window to be closed
        Console.In.ReadLine()
    End Sub

End Module
```

As you have noticed already the IDE has colored the line you entered in green. This is the default color used for comments in Visual Studio .NET. It seems that most IDE manufacturers have adhered to this convention in the past few years. One older (and still supported) way of adding comments to code is to use the Rem keyword (from REMark). You could have entered the comments above as

```
Rem The next two lines prevent the console window to be closed prematurely
```

A comment can be also placed at the end of a line of code (normally a shorter comment) as shown below:

```
Console.In.ReadLine() ' waits until the user presses Enter
```

As you have seen by running the program, no changes in behavior occurred because of the added comments—the compiler stripped them away from the compiled code, as you have expected.

What's Next

You have learned of the fundamental language features of Visual Basic .NET and you have also seen a very brief history of the evolution of the programming languages.

In the next chapter you will start the study of the fundamental Visual Basic data types and the operators associated with them. You will also write a few simple examples using the data types that you will learn.

NOTE

The answers to the "Reviewing It," "Checking It," and "Applying It" sections are available on our Web site.

REVIEW

Reviewing It

This section presents a review of the key concepts in this chapter. These questions are intended to gauge your absorption of the relevant material.

1. What do we understand by software? Describe the way a software program executes.

2. What is the role of the operating system?

3. What is a high-level programming language?

4. What is the console?

5. What is a Visual Basic identifier?

6. What is a comment?

CHECK

Checking It

Select the correct answer(s) to the following questions.

Multiple Choice

1. RAM is:

   a. Random Access Memory.

   b. Working memory.

   c. Transient memory.

   d. All of the above.

2. Memory address is:

   a. The physical location of memory bit.

   b. The index of a byte in RAM.

   c. The index of a cluster on a hard disk.

   d. The absolute position of a transistor gate in RAM.

3. A compiler is:

    a. A plug-and-play device that translates source code.

    b. A software program that helps us build user interface projects.

    c. A software program that translates source code into machine code.

    d. A part of the operating system that reads machine code.

4. What is the relationship between a solution and a project in Visual Basic .NET?

    a. A solution can have many projects.

    b. A project can have many solutions.

    c. A solution can have exactly one project.

    d. A project can have exactly one solution.

5. A module is:

    a. A fundamental component that is part of a solution.

    b. A fundamental component that can be part of a project.

    c. A Visual Basic .NET statement.

    d. A set of instructions on how to build a project.

6. Which of the characters shown are *not* allowed in a Visual Basic .NET identifier?

    a. Underscore (_).

    b. Dot (.).

    c. Dash (-).

    d. Colon (:).

7. A comment is used to:

    a. Give additional hints to the compiler or interpreter.

    b. Disable lines of code that are inconvenient.

    c. Give additional explanations about a piece of code.

    d. Tell the user what to do when he reaches the comment line.

True or False

Select one of the two possible answers and then verify on our Web site that you picked the correct one.

1. One bit has 8 bytes.

   True/False

2. A memory location and memory address are the same thing.

   True/False

3. In the sample project shown earlier in this chapter, Sub Main is the entry point for the program.

   True/False

4. The console is the command prompt (DOS) window.

   True/False

5. A Visual Basic .NET identifier can contain an underscore character (_).

   True/False

6. A keyword is used to supply additional information to the compiler.

   True/False

APPLY

Applying It

Try to complete the following exercises by yourself.

Independent Exercise 1

Create a new console project and have it output the text "My first project" to the console, and then wait for the user to press Enter to terminate the project.

Independent Exercise 2

Try the same as in Exercise 1 without the statements that wait for the user. Execute the program and see what happens.

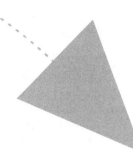

Fundamental Data Types

We will start this chapter by defining data types and then looking at the fundamental data types used by Visual Basic. You will write a few examples to illustrate the concepts that you learn. Specific topics are

- Numeric data types

- Boolean data type

- String and Char data types

- Date data type

- Other data types

As you have seen, a computer program is a series of instructions that tell the computer how to operate on some input data to produce output data. You have also seen that the data (both input and output) is usually represented in the working memory of the computer. This memory is organized in bytes. You could use bytes and memory addresses of these bytes to represent any form of data that you need, and indeed that is the way the low-level languages operate. However, it is not an easy task to deal with data in this raw format: it is easy to make mistakes and hard to track them down, to name just a few issues. Therefore, all high-level languages (Visual Basic included) have a predefined set of *data types* that the programmer can use, to ease data manipulation. Most of these languages also allow the programmer to define new data types, as required.

A *data type* can be thought as a common way to represent the same type of value in the working memory of the computer. We will extend this concept further when you will learn of classes. For example, an Integer value requires a memory location of four bytes in size, whereas a Short value requires only 2 bytes (simply said, Short has a storage size of 2 bytes, or it takes 2 bytes). Some data types use a fixed memory size (as the Integer) while others (like String) take a variable amount of space in memory.

The *fundamental data types* used in Visual Basic are the simple data types that are used as building blocks for the more complex data types. They are defined by the language and cannot be modified. They are the most common data types used in Visual Basic. You will see later in this chapter that the data types (or, in short, "types") can be further classified by additional criteria. You will start by learning the numeric data types, and move next to the Boolean, String, Char, and Date types.

NOTE

All data types used by Visual Basic (as well as other languages in Visual Studio .NET) are actually defined in the .NET Framework—the infrastructure that underlies Visual Studio .NET. We will come back to this topic later on in the book.

Numeric Data Types

The Visual Basic language defines the numeric types as described in Table 6.1.

Table 6.1   Numeric Data Types in Visual Basic .NET

Name	Size	Value Range and Description
Byte	1 byte	0 to 255. An unsigned byte.
Short	2 bytes	–32,768 to 32,767. Integer value.
Integer	4 bytes	–2,147,483,648 to 2,147,483,647. Integer value.
Long	8 bytes	–9,223,372,036,854,775,808 to 9,223,372,036,854,775,807. Integer value.
Decimal	12 bytes	+/–79,228,162,514,264,337,593,543,950,335 with no decimal point; +/–7.9228162514264337593543950335 with 28 places to the right of the decimal; smallest non-zero number is +/–0.0000000000000000000000000001.
Single	4 bytes	3.402823E38 to –1.401298E-45 for negative values; 1.401298E-45 to 3.402823E38 for positive values. Floating point decimal value.
Double	8 bytes	–1.79769313486231E308 to –4.94065645841247E-324 for negative values; 4.94065645841247E-324 to 1.79769313486232E308 for positive values. Floating-point decimal value.

As you see you have a rich set of numeric types, both integral and decimal, covering a wide range of scale and precision. Except for Byte, all the other types are signed—that means they can be used to represent both negative and positive values. Byte can store only positive numbers between 0 and 255 (the numbers that can be stored using 1 byte = 8 bits of memory).

NOTE

Byte is sometimes treated differently from numeric types, namely as a binary data type. For simplicity, we have included it with the numeric types.

From the integral types (types that support integer numbers without decimals), the most commonly used is Integer, which has the convenience of a wide enough value range and at the same time, it takes a reasonable 4 bytes of memory. From the types that support decimal places, Double and Decimal are the most commonly used. One thing to remember is that both Single and Double are using a floating-point storage mechanism that allows for a wider range of numbers, at the price of the precision of the numbers stored. The operations on these types of values may be subject to small rounding errors. This is not the case for the Decimal type; we will revisit this issue later in this chapter.

Variable Declaration and Assignment

Now that you have seen the main numeric types you can start using them. Let's create a new console project (follow the same instructions as for the previous chapter and name the new project DataTypes). In the Sub Main of Module1 add the following lines of code in bold:

```
Module Module1

    Sub Main()
        Dim i As Integer
        i = 6
        Console.Out.WriteLine("The value of i is {0}", i)

        Console.Out.WriteLine("Press the <Enter> key to end the program")
        Console.In.ReadLine()
    End Sub

End Module
```

Save and run the program. You will notice the message saying that the value of i is 6. Press Enter to finish the program and return to the IDE. In this very simple program you have declared a *variable*, you have *assigned* a value to it, and then written its value to the console. Let's analyze each step. The first line after the entry point of the program (Sub Main()) is

```
Dim i As Integer
```

This is a variable declaration. The compiler needs to know what are the types of values that you use in your program. You use a *type declaration*, like the one above to tell the compiler that you intend to use an Integer value named i. A *variable* is a name for a value that you use in your program for making calculations, storing data, and so on. A variable can be thought as a name for a memory location, which memory location is of the type you declared. In your case you tell the compiler to reserve 4 bytes of memory for an Integer value that you intend to use, and that the name associated to this particular memory location is "i".

NOTE

A *variable* is a Visual Basic identifier, and therefore is subject to the naming rules for such an identifier: it must start with a letter and can contain only letters, digits, and the underscore character.

```
i = 6
```

The next line is an *assignment* statement—that is, you tell the compiler what value to store in the memory location that the variable i is associated with (6 in this example). When you declare a variable, the compiler will reserve the memory for it and will initialize it to be 0 (for numeric types). To change this value you must use an assignment statement. After this statement the value of i should be 6. You will verify that the compiler did the right assignment by writing the value to the console using the next statement. It is a variation of the method you have seen before, but you need not worry about it yet. Think of it as simply a way to display a string and a value to the console.

The last lines are familiar: you need to stop the console window from being closed before you can see the output of your sample program.

There is a way to combine the type declaration and the initial assignment of a value to a variable. Replace the lines

```
Dim i As Integer
i = 6
```

with

```
Dim i As Integer = 6
```

This is the exact equivalent of the first two lines and is more compact and readable. If the initial value is 0, you need not place the initialization (= 0) after the type declaration because this is the default value the compiler uses.

If you need more than one variable you can use multiple statements to declare them as

```
Dim i As Integer = 6
Dim noOfApples As Short = 7
```

Or on the same line:

```
Dim i As Integer = 6, noOfApples As Short = 7
```

If the variables are of the same type you can use a declaration like

```
Dim x, y, z As Double
```

This line will declare three variables (x, y, and z) of type Double, and will initialize them all with 0.

Arithmetic Operators on Numeric Values

The arithmetic operators are used to perform simple arithmetic calculations on the values that your program uses. They are the regular arithmetic operators (addition, subtraction, multiplication, and division) with the addition of some special operators: modulo (or remainder of integer division) and exponentiation. The following example can be used to illustrate these operators. Change the code in the example to look like

```
Module Module1

    Sub Main()
        Dim i, j, k As Integer
        i = 11
        j = 3

        k = i + j ' addition
        Console.Out.WriteLine("The value of k is {0}", k) ' 14

        k = i - j ' subtraction
        Console.Out.WriteLine("The value of k is {0}", k) ' 8

        k = i * j ' multiplication
        Console.Out.WriteLine("The value of k is {0}", k) ' 33

        k = i \ j ' integer division
        Console.Out.WriteLine("The value of k is {0}", k) ' 3
```

```
        k = i Mod j ' modulo
        Console.Out.WriteLine("The value of k is {0}", k) ' 2

        Dim d, f As Decimal
        d = 2
        f = d / 17 ' floating point division
        Console.Out.WriteLine("The value of f is {0}", f) ' 0.1176...

        Dim x, y As Double
        x = 2
        y = x / 17 ' floating point division
        Console.Out.WriteLine("The value of y is {0}", y) ' 0.1176...

        y = x ^ 31 ' exponentiation
        Console.Out.WriteLine("The value of y is {0}", y) ' 0.1176...

        Console.Out.WriteLine("Press the <Enter> key to end the program")
        Console.In.ReadLine()
    End Sub

End Module
```

Save and run the program. Your output should match the one in Figure 6.1.

Figure 6.1: *Output of running the DataTypes sample program.*

As you can see you use the variable k to assign to it the results of addition, subtraction, multiplication, and then integer division of the variables i and j. For each operation you output the results to the console (as the value of the variable k). It is important to note the integer division (\) produces an integer result, namely the integer part of the division after eliminating the decimal part. No rounding is done, for example, 11 \ 3 yields 3, not 4 (as 3.6666... rounded would yield).

Another interesting operator for integral data types is modulo or the remainder of integer division, written as mod. The result of 11 modulo 3 will be 2.

Normal division can be used for non-integral data types (either floating point or fixed precision decimal numbers). You can also note the difference in precision between the Decimal and Double data types.

Finally the exponentiation operator (^) is used to compute 2^{31}.

TIP

You have used the Dim declaration statements interspersed within code, closed to the point where they are actually used. This is against traditional (structured) programming style, which recommends that all variables be declared at the top of the procedure where they are used (in this case it would be the Sub Main()). We believe that this approach is more readable, as you do not need to scroll to the top of the procedure to find out what type of variable is f, which is used towards the bottom of the procedure.

Boolean Data Type

The Boolean data type can hold two values, True and False; both True and False are keywords in Visual Basic. For example:

```
Dim b As Boolean = True
```

Boolean variables are used in various ways such as loop statements, as you will see later on in the book. The default value of a Boolean variable is False. That means if you don't initialize a Boolean variable when declaring it, it will be automatically initialized to False.

String and Char Data Types

Individual characters (letters, digits, symbols) can be represented using the Char data type, which takes 2 bytes of memory, and represents a UNICODE character.

NOTE

UNICODE is an international standard that defines how all characters in all known languages are mapped to a value stored in 2 bytes—that is, a number between 0 and 65635. An older standard was (and still is) in used in some older versions of Windows and other operating systems. This standard is known as *ASCII* and uses only one byte to represent a character. The .NET Framework automatically takes care of converting strings and characters to and from ASCII.

To represent strings of characters (normal text) you use the String data type. A String is an array of UNICODE characters that can have between 0 and approximately 2 billion characters. It is, therefore, a variable size data type where size depends upon the number of characters it holds. A String variable can be declared and initialized in the usual fashion:

```
Dim s As String = "Mark Twain"
```

The literal String values are represented as text delimited by the " (double quote) character. The String values support the & operator that can be used to concatenate two String values together. For example:

```
Dim firstName As String = "Mark"
Dim lastName As String = "Twain"
Dim name As String
name = firstName & " " & lastName
' name is now "Mark Twain"
```

This example declares and initializes two String variables (firstName and lastName) and then declares the name variable and assigns to it the result of the concatenation of the firstName and lastName. Note the literal String consisting of one space that is placed in between firstName and lastName. If the space was missing the name variable would hold the result "MarkTwain."

The + can be used instead of the concatenation operator & with the same results. The previous statements can be written also as follows:

```
Dim firstName As String = "Mark"
Dim lastName As String = "Twain"
Dim name As String
name = firstName + " " + lastName
' name is now "Mark Twain"
```

We recommend you use the &, which cannot be confused with the arithmetic + operator. In any case, even if you decide to use the + operator, be consistent in your code; do not mix them in the same project.

Date Data Type

Dates and times are represented in Visual Basic using the Date data type. A Date value takes 8 bytes of memory and can represent dates and times between January 1, 1 CE to December 31, 9999. The precision of the date is up to milliseconds. Following are a few examples of declaring and initializing a date variable:

```
Dim d As Date = #2/2/2001#
Dim dt as Date = #January 1 1900 12:32:45 PM#
```

The literal date values are represented using the # delimiter. They can consist of a date or time expressed in the appropriate format for the country and time zone. Months can be expressed either as numeric values or as literal values (in the appropriate language).

Other Data Types

There are many other predefined data types that can be used in Visual Basic—all of which come from the .NET Framework. We have UInt32, UInt64, and so on. All the data types you have learned, as well as the ones that you will see later, are actually classes or structures defined in the .NET Framework. You will understand better what the meaning of the previous statement is as you learn more about the data types and then classes and objects.

What's Next

In this chapter you have seen what are the fundamental data types that Visual Basic defines. You have also learned how to declare a variable of a given type, how to initialize a variable, and how to assign a value to a variable. You have also learned a few operators on the fundamental data types.

You will continue by studying conversions between data types, as well as other operators and usage of the fundamental data types.

NOTE

The answers to "Reviewing It," "Checking It," and "Applying It" are available on our Web site.

REVIEW

Reviewing It

This section presents a review of the key concepts in this chapter. These questions are intended to gauge your absorption of the relevant material.

1. What is a data type? Why do you need data types?

2. What is a variable?

3. Describe what happens in memory when an assignment statement is executed for a Double value.

4. What is an operator? Give examples.

5. What values can a Boolean variable have?

6. What is the difference between String and Char?

CHECK

Checking It

Select the correct answer to the following questions.

Multiple Choice

1. The size of the memory location required by a fundamental data type is:

    a. Fixed size, depending on the actual type.

    b. Fixed size, always 4 bytes.

    c. Fixed size for some types, variable size for others.

    d. Not applicable. Fundamental data types are always allocated by the compiler.

2. Integral numeric types are:

    a. Integer.

    b. Short, Integer, and Long.

    c. Byte, Short, Integer, and Long.

    d. Byte, Short, Integer, Long, and Char.

3. Which fundamental numeric type can represent a decimal number with the highest possible precision?

    a. Double.

    b. Single.

    c. String.

    d. Decimal.

4. A variable declaration is:

    a. Telling the compiler about a new data type.

    b. A statement used to initialize a variable.

    c. A statement used to tell the compiler about a new variable.

    d. There is no such thing. Variables cannot be declared.

5. Which is the initial value for a variable of type Single?

    a. 0.

    b. 0.0.

c. The initial value specified in the Dim statement. 0.0 if no initial value is specified.

d. The initial value specified in the Dim statement. Infinity, if no initial value is specified.

6. What is the difference between the \ and the / operators?

a. / is used for division and \ is used for fractions.

b. / is used for division and \ is used for string concatenation.

c. / is used for integer division and \ is used for floating point division.

d. / is used for division of decimal types and \ is used for integer division.

7. To concatenate strings "A" and "B" into a new variable s you would write a statement like:

a. s = "A" + "B"

b. s = "A" & "B"

c. s = "A" . "B"

d. Strings cannot be concatenated.

True or False

Select one of the two possible answers and then verify on our Web site that you picked the correct one.

1. A Boolean can have only two values (True and False).

> **NOTE**
>
> The above True and False are the values for the Boolean data type, and as such are different from the answer to the question (true or false).

True/False

2. A variable of String type has a fixed size.

True/False

3. More than one variable can be declared in the same Dim statement.

True/False

4. All variables have a value when first declared, even if not initialized.

True/False

5. A variable of type Date can be used to represent dates in the Cretaceous period (when dinosaurs were still roaming the Earth).

   True/False

6. Assignment and initialization of a variable is the same thing.

   True/False

APPLY

Applying It

Try to complete the following exercises by yourself.

Independent Exercise 1

Create a new console project that outputs area of a circle with a radius of 1.526 units.

Independent Exercise 2

Create a program that computes the modulo of 143 and 13.

7

Data Conversion and Expressions

In this chapter you will learn about data conversions (conversions between different data types), and you will learn a few conversion functions and some new operators. You also will learn about comparison operators and Boolean (logical) operators and expressions.

The chapter contains in the following topics:

- Implicit data conversion
- Explicit data conversion
- In-place arithmetic operators
- Comparison operators
- Boolean operators
- Expressions and operator precedence

You will start by studying conversion between the fundamental data types. By *data conversion* we understand the transformation of one data type into another. In any given program you will use multiple data types, as you have seen even from the simple examples you have studied so far. It will be often required to assign a value of a type to a variable that was declared as being of a different type. As you have seen the assignment can take place only between identical data types, that is, you can assign an Integer value only to an Integer variable, and not to a Date variable. The purpose of the first part of this chapter is to determine how data conversions take place.

In the second part of the chapter you will look at a few new operators and then at the expressions that you could build with them.

This chapter (as well as the rest of the book) assumes you are using the strict type checking added to Visual Basic .NET. This option can be set in the Project Properties dialog box in the category Build by setting the Option Strict On. Alternatively, you can have this statement at the beginning of all your programs:

```
Option Strict On
```

There is no reason not to use the strict option, unless you are porting code from a previous version of Visual Basic, and wish to keep the code as is. This option will enforce a strict type checking and will allow you to catch a lot of programming errors early in the development cycle.

Implicit Data Conversion

When the compiler encounters an assignment statement it will ensure that the data type of the variable being assigned matches the type of the value being assigned to it. If the two are not of the same type it will verify that the two types are compatible, that is, the compiler can implicitly convert the value into the variable data type. This is called an *implicit conversion*. If this is not the case a syntax error will be raised—the program is invalid (cannot be compiled).

For example the following code will compile and run correctly:

```
Dim i As Integer, d As Double
d = i
```

While the next lines of code will not compile:

```
Dim i As Integer, d As Double
i = d
```

You will notice the fact that d is underlined, and if you place the mouse cursor above d and hold it still for a few seconds, a ToolTip will be displayed. The ToolTip text will indicate the cause of the error, as illustrated in Figure 7.1.

From the first example you can infer that the compiler 'knows' to convert an Integer to a Double, but not the other way around. In other (more technical) words: there is an implicit conversion from Integer to Double, but not from Double to Integer.

How would you know what all the existing implicit conversions are? You could look up in the reference online help that comes with Visual Studio .NET, or you could remember the following simple rules:

The only implicit conversions are among numeric data types, with one exception: from Char to String.

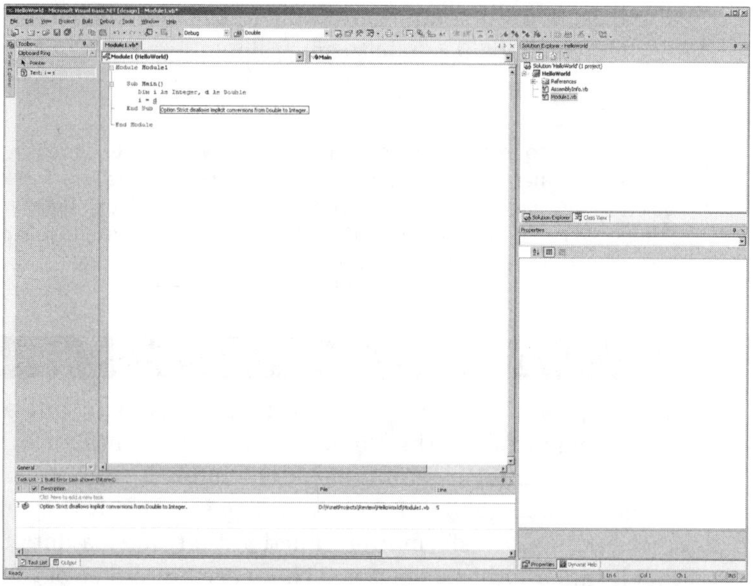

Figure 7.1: *Error message attempting to convert a Double to an Integer.*

The implicit conversions between numeric data types are always from a 'smaller' type to a 'larger' type, i.e. from a type that can have a narrower range of values to one that can hold a wider range. For example Byte can be implicitly converted to any other numeric type, while Double can be implicitly converted to no other numeric type. The logic behind this rule is (as you have probably guessed) quite simple: the variable that gets assigned the new value can always hold it, if the value is between the range of acceptable values for that type or smaller.

NOTE

There may be a precision loss when converting a Long or Decimal value to Single or Double variables, but the number magnitude will be preserved.

The next line shows the implicit conversions for numeric types. Any type in the list can be converted implicitly to any other type in the list that is on its right. For example, Long can be implicitly converted to Decimal, Single, and Double, but not to Integer, Short, or Byte.

Double ← Single ← Decimal ← Long ← Integer ← Short ← Byte

String ← Char

You will see a few examples of implicit conversion shortly, immediately after you learn about explicit conversions.

NOTE

It is possible to extend the range of implicit conversions to converting any type to almost any other type, by setting the `Option Strict` to False. This will in effect disable the type checking of the compiler, and will permit writing unsafe code. The errors introduced can be very subtle and hard to catch. These are the reasons for which we strongly recommend that you set the `Option Strict` to True.

Explicit Data Conversion

What happens if you need to convert a Double to an Integer, and you know that the magnitude of the Double value is within the range of acceptable values for the Integer data type? If the implicit conversions would be the only mechanism available, you would be stuck. But they are not. An *explicit conversion* is a transformation function that takes a data type and transforms it into another data type. There are a number of conversion functions available in the Visual Basic language, some of which are in Table 7.1.

Table 7.1: Conversion Functions in Visual Basic .NET

Name	Converts To	Comments and Parameter Range
CByte	Byte	0 to 255 (same as for Byte data type)
CShort	Short	Same as for Short data type
CInt	Integer	Same as for Integer data type
CLng	Long	Same as for Long data type
CDec	Decimal	Same as for Decimal data type
CSng	Single	Same as for Single data type
CDbl	Double	Same as for Double data type
CBool	Boolean	String ("True"/"False") or numeric (0 will be converted to `False`, anything else will be converted to `True`)
CChar	Char	Cannot be numeric, may be String
CStr	String	Anything that can be converted to a String
CDate	Date	A string that holds a valid date/time representation

The naming rule for these functions is that they begin with "C" (from Conversion) and continue with an abbreviation of the data type to convert to. For example to convert a Double to an Integer one could use code similar to the one in the following example:

```
Dim i As Integer, d As Double
' get the value of d from someplace
i = CInt(d)
```

The CInt is the name of the conversion function (and it is a Visual Basic language identifier). Following CInt is the Double value d that you need to convert to Integer, enclosed in parentheses. This is a standard way to *call* or *invoke* a function in Visual Basic, and it is similar to the mathematical notation for functions learned in high school. The value in parentheses is called a *parameter* (or *argument*) of the function, and must be in the function domain (in this case the domain is not restricted; any value is acceptable as a parameter). In the example, the function CInt has only one parameter, but you will encounter functions with more than one parameter. In this case the parameters will be separated by commas. In a similar way to that of mathematical function, the CInt function (as well as all Visual Basic functions) will process the value passed in as parameter and return a value. In this case the Double passed in is transformed to an Integer and the resulting Integer value is returned from the function. This value is known as the *return value* of the function, and it will always by in the range or *return type* of the function; in our case the return type is the set of values that would fit in the Integer data type. In short, it is said that the function *takes* a Double and *returns* an Integer. The returned value is the value that will be assigned to i.

NOTE

With the analogy you use for functions, it becomes more clear what data types are, namely sets of values, like the Real, Integer, and Rational numbers you learned in school. They can be used as a function's domain or range, or just as a set of all possible values for a given variable. And similar to mathematics you will be able to define your own subsets and operations and functions on these subsets.

An obvious question here is what happens if the value of d is greater than it would fit into an Integer (it is larger that 2,147,483,647 or smaller than –2,147,483,648), or if the value passed in is of a type incompatible with Integer. The compiler has no means of knowing what the value of d is until the program is run, so there is no way of warning you during program compilation. What is going to happen is this: when the program is executed (at *runtime*) the function CInt will check the value passed in and if it is outside the range acceptable for the return value (Integer) it will throw an exception. You will learn more about exceptions later on. For now what you need to understand is that an error message will be displayed, and then the running program will be stopped prematurely.

There are two ways to avoid this premature termination. One would be to ensure that the value passed to the conversion function is within the correct bounds, and if it is not, you should let the user know somehow and correct the problem. The other (which you will learn later on in the book) is to handle the exception so that the program will continue.

Let's use an example to practice what you learned so far in this chapter. Create a project as you have done before, change its name to DataConversion, and enter the following code in the Sub Main:

```
Sub Main()
    System.Console.Out.WriteLine("Please enter a number and then press <Enter>:")

    Dim s As String
    s = Console.In.ReadLine()

    Dim d As Double
    d = CDbl(s)
    Console.Out.WriteLine("The Double value d is {0}", d)

    Dim i As Integer
    i = CInt(d)
    Console.Out.WriteLine("The Integer value i is {0}", i)

    Console.Out.WriteLine("Press the <Enter> key to end the program")
    Console.In.ReadLine()
End Sub
```

Save and run the program, enter (type in) a number when prompted, and press Enter. Make sure you are entering a valid number like 16.67. The output screen should be similar to the one shown in Figure 7.2.

Figure 7.2: Output of running the DataConversion example.

The first noticeable statement you observe is the one using the Console. In.ReadLine() method to get input from the user (you in this case). It is enough (for now) to say that this method returns whatever the user types on the console on one line (until it presses Enter). The input is returned as a String. You will learn more about the input and output methods later on in the book; until then you will use them to output data to the console and to get data inputted by the user back from the console.

The second thing to notice is that you have used another conversion function CDbl to convert the String value the user has entered (s) into a Double variable . It is very similar to the CInt function you saw earlier; it will take a value and attempt to convert it to a Double. You output this value to the console using the known method.

Next you convert the Double d to an Integer i and again output the result to the console.

Now let's see what happens when the user makes a mistake and enters some value that cannot be converted to a number. Run the sample program again, but this time enter a few letters, such as "joe". You will get an error message saying that an unhandled exception (of type System. FormatException) occurred, and giving you the possibility to *break* or *continue*. Break means suspend program execution at the point where the exception occurred so that you can see what was the problem. Continue means (in this case) go ahead and terminate the program. Because you know what the problem is, click on continue. This will direct the IDE to terminate the program.

This example was intended to show what would happen if an attempt to convert a value to another type fails.

As you saw in Table 7.1, there are a number of different operators to convert numbers into other numbers, strings to numbers and dates, and so on. However, Table 7.1 does not list any functions to convert a Char into a number or a number into a Char. These functions exist, and an example using them is presented in the following code. You can incorporate the bold lines into the sample project you just created.

```
Sub Main()
    System.Console.Out.WriteLine("Please enter a number and then press <Enter>:")

    Dim s As String
    s = System.Console.In.ReadLine()

    Dim d As Double
    d = CDbl(s)
    Console.Out.WriteLine("The Double value d is {0}", d)

    Dim i As Integer
    i = CInt(d)
    Console.Out.WriteLine("The Integer value i is {0}", i)

    Dim c As Char
    c = Chr(i)
    Console.Out.WriteLine("The Character value c is {0}", c)
```

```
    i = Asc(c)
    System.Console.Out.WriteLine("The Integer value i is {0}", i)

    Console.Out.WriteLine("Press the <Enter> key to end the program")
    Console.In.ReadLine()
End Sub
```

When you run the project, type **65.4** when prompted to enter a number. The output should look like the one in Figure 7.3.

Figure 7.3: *Output of running the modified DataConversion example.*

The Chr function converts an Integer to a Char, while the Asc function is the reverse, and will convert a Char to an Integer. In your example the Integer value i was 65 (if you typed the indicated number) and was transformed in the Char value 'A' when assigned to the variable c. The value 65 is the UNICODE number (code) for the character 'A'. Each character in the UNICODE set has (as you saw in Chapter 6, "Fundamental Data Types,") a number or code associated with it. The Chr function transforms an Integer representing this code into a Char, while the Asc function transforms a Char into the associated code.

NOTE

Asc and Chr are quite venerable BASIC functions, standing for "to character" and "to ASCII." As we mentioned above, ASCII is a subset of UNICODE characters that was (and still is sometimes) used in older computers and operating systems to represent characters.

In the rest of this chapter you will look at a few different types of operators and functions. In the final part of the chapter you will learn how to combine variables, values, operators, and functions into expressions.

In-place Operators

You have seen what the arithmetic operators are for the basic operations: addition, subtraction, multiplication, division, modulo, and exponentiation. You will learn now a few new operators that are based on these arithmetic operators. They are called *in-place* arithmetic operators.

Consider the following example, which declares a variable i as Integer and initializes it to 6, and then increments its value by 3.

```
Dim i As Integer = 6
i = i + 3
```

It happens that this type of code occurs quite frequently in day-to-day programming. As programmers (and language architects) are practical people, they decided that the expression could be simplified by writing it as:

```
Dim i As Integer = 6
i += 3
```

Note how the i was omitted from the right side of the assignment operator, and the plus sign was moved in front of equal to create the new in-place operator "+=". The two expressions are identical in results, with the exception of the second version being shorter and somewhat more intuitive: you are not assigning a brand new value to i, which happens to be made of the old value of i + 3. But rather you increment i "in-place" by 3. It is up to you to use the form that you like. Most people with background in C/C++/Java will use the second form, while people who use an older dialect of BASIC or Visual Basic are more familiar with the first form.

Similar operators are available for most of the other arithmetic operators (except modulo). The following example illustrates some of these in-place operators. Create a new console project and name it "InPlaceOps," and then add the following lines to it.

```
Sub Main()
   Dim i As Integer = 12
   i -= 3 ' i is now 9
   Console.Out.WriteLine("The Integer value i is {0}", i)
   i *= 3 ' i is now 27
   Console.Out.WriteLine("The Integer value i is {0}", i)
   i \= 9 ' i is now 3
   Console.Out.WriteLine("The Integer value i is {0}", i)

   Dim d As Double = 33.27
   d /= i ' d is now 11.09 (i is still 3)
   Console.Out.WriteLine("The Double value d is {0}", d)
```

```
        d ^= 3 ' d is now 1363.938029
        Console.Out.WriteLine("The Double value d is {0}", d)

        Dim s As String = "i is "
        s &= CStr(i) ' s is now "i is 3"
        Console.Out.WriteLine("The String value s is '{0}'", s)

        Console.Out.WriteLine("Press the <Enter> key to end the program")
        Console.In.ReadLine()
End Sub
```

Save and run the program, and ensure the values displayed are as predicted in the comments. The only other notable operator you used is the in-place String concatenation operator &=. It is used to concatenate the result of the String conversion of the Integer i (using CStr(i)) to the original value of s ("i is "). The result is the displayed string "i is 3" delimited by single quotes.

Comparison Operators

Another class of operators commonly used in programming is the *comparison* operators, also known as relational operators in mathematics. These operators compare two values and return a Boolean value (True or False) depending on the result of the comparison. For example:

```
Dim i As Integer = 3, b As Boolean
b = i < 5
```

The expression i < 5 on the right side of the assignment operator = is a relational expression, and < is the comparison operator known as "less than." It has the same meaning as its mathematical counterpart. The expression will be evaluated to True since i is 3 and therefore, is less than 5. The result of this evaluation (the Boolean value True) will then be assigned to the variable b. The Table 7.2 lists the comparison operators in Visual Basic and their mathematical counterparts (if any are existing).

Table 7.2   Comparison Operators in Visual Basic .NET

Operator	Mathematical	Comments
=	$\equiv$	Equality, a equals b
<>	$\neq$	Inequality, a is not equal to b
<	<	Less than, a is less than b
<=	$\leq$	Less than or equal to, a is less than or equal to b
>	>	Greater than, a is greater than b

Table 7.2   continued

Operator	Mathematical	Comments
>=	$\geq$	Greater than or equal to, a is greater than or equal to b
Like		Special operator for strings, used for pattern matching
Is		Special operator for objects, True if object a is the same as object b

With the exception of the last two special operators (Like and Is, which you will study later on) the rest are common mathematical operators. The symbols used are slightly different, but the meaning is the same.

One thing to note is that the = symbol is used for both assignment and equality. This can cause confusion sometimes because an expression like "i = 3" can mean either "assign 3 to i" or "verify if i is equal to 3," depending on the context in which it is used.

Boolean Operators

The *boolean* or *logical* operators are commonly used to combine Boolean values or expressions into more complex Boolean expressions. For example

```
Dim i As Integer = 3, j As Integer = 5, b As Boolean
b = i < 5 And j >= 6 ' b is False
```

The comparison expressions i < 5 and j >= 6 are combined by the logical operator And. And has the exact meaning as in English: if both comparison expressions (i < 5 and j >= 6) are true, the result is True. If at least one of the expressions is false, the result of the logical And operation is False. This result will be assigned to the Boolean variable b.

Visual Basic also has an Or logical operator, which is the equivalent of the English meaning of the word "or". Here is the same example as before:

```
Dim i As Integer = 3, j As Integer = 5, b As Boolean
b = i < 5 Or j >= 6 ' b is True
```

In this case b will be True if at least one of the expressions i < 5 and j >= 6 is true, or potentially both of them are true. It will be False if both i < 5 and j >= 6 are false.

There is also an exclusive-or operator (Xor) that can be used to determine if one or the other of the expressions is True, but not both at the same time. Reusing the same example:

```
Dim i As Integer = 3, j As Integer = 5, b As Boolean
b = i < 5 Xor j >= 6 ' b is True
```

```
j = 7
b = i < 5 Xor j >= 6 ' b is False
```

The fourth logical operator used is the unary Not operator. It can be applied to a Boolean expression to negate (reverse) the value, that is, if the value is True it will yield False, and the opposite. For example:

```
Dim i As Integer = 3, j As Integer = 5, b As Boolean
b = i < 5 Or j >= 6 ' b is True
b = Not b ' b is False
```

The last statement assigns to b the opposite of what the current value of b is currently. In your case b is True; therefore it will assign False to it.

Expressions and Operator Precedence

The arithmetic, comparison, and Boolean operators, as well as data conversion and other types of functions, can be used to create powerful expressions that can be used in your computations and programs.

An *expression* is a combination of values and operators. The values can be literals or variables, the operators can be any combination of known operators, and a few more that you will learn later on in the book.

The *type of an expression* is the data type of the result of the evaluation of an expression. An expression 2 + 3 is a numeric (Integer) expression. i > 5 is (as you have seen) a logical or boolean expression. An expression that evaluates to a String will be a String expression. By *evaluating* an expression we understand replacing all the variables with their current values, and then performing all the calculations (according to the operators in the expression) in the appropriate order.

An expression can be as simple as i + 3 and as complicated as required by the computations in your program. Similar to mathematical expressions, the operators have different *operator precedence*, which will determine the order in which the expression is evaluated. For example in the following expression:

```
i = 5 + 3 * 2
```

i will be assigned the value of the expression 5 + 3 * 2. The compiler will first multiply 3 with 2, will then add 5 to the result (6) and will assign the total result (11) of this expression to i. Operator precedence indicates to the compiler in what order the operations should take place. In your example multiplication has a higher precedence than the addition, as you have probably expected based on elementary mathematics. Again, as in math, you can use parentheses to change the order of evaluating any given expression. For example, reusing the same code, if you intended that the compiler first add 5 and 3 and then multiply the result by 2 you would write it as:

```
i = (5 + 3) * 2
```

In Table 7.3 you can see the three types of operators and their precedence and operator type, from the highest ones to the top of the table to the lowest precedence to the bottom of the table.

Table 7.3 Operator Precedence in Visual Basic .NET

Operator	Type	Comments
^	Arithmetic	Exponentiation
-	Arithmetic	Negation –i (this is not the same as subtraction)
* and /	Arithmetic	Multiplication and division
\	Arithmetic	Integer division
mod	Arithmetic	Modulus
+ and -	Arithmetic	Addition and subtraction
bitwise	Arithmetic	Bitwise operators (you will study these operators later)
& and +	Special	String concatenation (not to be confused with addition)
=	Comparison	Equality
<>	Comparison	Inequality
<	Comparison	Less than
>	Comparison	Greater than
<=	Comparison	Less than or equal to
>=	Comparison	Greater than or equal to
Like, Is	Comparison	Specialized comparison operators
Not	Boolean	Unary not
And	Boolean	And
Or	Boolean	Or
Xor	Boolean	Exclusive or

As you can see the operators are grouped based on their type. The ones with the higher precedence are the arithmetic and concatenation operators, followed by the comparison operators, and at the end you have the logical operators.

Operators that are of the same precedence (like addition and subtraction, for example) are evaluated in order from left to right.

Expressions are the most common programming construct of any programming language. They are used in all statements that you have seen and in many more that you will learn about in this book.

Although expressions are not complicated, it is important that you understand them properly before proceeding forward.

What's Next

In the next chapter you will learn about some slightly more complicated data types that Visual Basic .NET uses. You will study arrays, enumerations, and structures—the first user-defined data type.

You will learn how to declare single and multi-dimensional arrays, and how to access array elements and use them in expressions. Next you will look at enumerations: why would one use them and how.

The second part of the next chapter will be concerned with structures. You will learn the basic concepts of these user-defined data types: how to declare and use them, as well as some introductory concepts on objects and references.

NOTE

The answers to the "Reviewing It," "Checking It," and "Applying It" sections are available on our Web site.

REVIEW

Reviewing It

This section presents a review of the key concepts in this chapter. These questions are intended to gauge your absorption of the relevant material.

1. What is the difference between implicit and explicit data conversion?

2. Can you convert a String value to a double? If yes, how?

3. What is an in-place operator?

4. What is a comparison operator? Give examples.

5. What is a Boolean operator? Give examples.

6. What is an expression?

CHECK

Checking It

Select the correct answer to the following questions.

Multiple Choice

1. An implicit numeric conversion is performed when:

   a. A numeric value is assigned to another numeric value of a type that is of a larger size.

   b. A numeric value is assigned to another numeric value of a type that is of a smaller size.

   c. Both a and b.

   d. Neither a nor b.

2. `CSng()` is used to convert:

   a. Numeric types to Decimal.

   b. Numeric types to Single.

   c. Numeric types to Double.

   d. Any type to Single.

3. What is the result of the following expression: Asc(Chr(66))?

   a. Character B.

   b. 66.

   c. It is an invalid expression; `Chr()` does not accept an Integer parameter.

   d. It is an invalid expression, `Asc()` does not accept a Char parameter.

4. Is "`0 <= i <= 100`" a valid Visual Basic expression?

   a. Yes.

   b. No. Correct would be "`0 <= i Or i <= 100`".

   c. No. Correct would be "`0 <= i And Not i <= 100`".

   d. No. Correct would be "`0 <= i And i <= 100`".

5. Assuming all variables (i, j, and k) are Integers initialized to 2, what is the outcome of the expression "`i * 4 \ j \ k`"?

   a. 1.

   b. 2.

   c. 4.

   d. 8.

6. Assuming all variables (i and j) are Integers initialized to 2, what is the outcome of the expression "`i ^ 2 >= 0 And j - 2 <= 0`"?

   a. 0.

   b. 4.

    c. True.

    d. You cannot evaluate the expression until it is executed at runtime.

7. What means to short-circuit evaluate a Boolean expression?

    a. Evaluate from left to right in a fast manner.

    b. Bypass type checking when evaluating a Boolean expression.

    c. Evaluate the expression until the first False is encountered.

    d. Evaluate the expression until the result is determined and ignore the rest of the expression.

True or False

Select one of the two possible answers and then verify on our Web site that you picked the correct one.

1. A numeric type can be implicitly converted to Boolean.

    True/False

2. A numeric type can be explicitly converted to Boolean.

    True/False

3. A numeric type can be explicitly converted to Char.

    True/False

4. A numeric type can be explicitly converted to Date.

    True/False

5. Boolean operators have highest precedence.

    True/False

6. Expressions can contain only comparison and Boolean operators.

    True/False

APPLY

Applying It

Try to complete the following exercises by yourself.

Independent Exercise 1

Create a new console project that reads two Double numbers from the user, multiplies the two, and displays the result.

Independent Exercise 2

Create a program that reads two Boolean values from the user, computes the exclusive or of the two values, and displays the result.

Arrays, Enumerations, and Structures

In this chapter you will study a few more advanced and also more useful data types: arrays, enumerations, and structures. These data types are also known as *structured data types*.

The chapter is structured as follows:

- Arrays
- Enumerations
- Structure declaration
- Using the structured data types

You will start by learning about arrays: what an array is, how to declare an array, how to access the elements of an array, how to modify the size of an array, and how to remove all elements from an array.

Next you will look at enumerations. You will learn how to declare and use them, as well as when to use an enumeration versus using regular integral data types.

In the second part of the chapter you will learn about structures and the art of user-defined types. You will learn how to declare a structure, what are structure members, and some issues related to members visibility.

You will also learn the basic steps in using structured data types: arrays, enumerations, and structures, namely assignment behavior for structured data types.

Arrays

You have seen how a variable of a given data type is but a name for a memory location that can store a value of that type. Now what would you do if you would like to have a whole bunch of values of the same type stored as compact as possible and have the same name and some indexing scheme to be able to identify any given value? The answer is quite simple: you would have an array.

For example let's consider that you need to operate on five accounts, namely on the balances of these accounts. You could declare a variable for each account that will hold the balance for that account, as in the following example:

```
Dim balance1 As Decimal
Dim balance2 As Decimal
Dim balance3 As Decimal
Dim balance4 As Decimal
Dim balance5 As Decimal
```

Or you could use an *array* of five account balances—in this case an array of five Decimal values. An array is a type of data that can hold more than one value of a given data type. These values are called *array elements* (or *items*) and they are of the same data type (as specified in the array declaration). You can think of an array as a list of items, each item in the list being an array element. You would declare an array as shown in the following example:

```
Dim balance(4) As Decimal
```

This statement will do something very similar with the previous one, which declared five variables of Decimal type. It will allocate memory for five values of Decimal type. The way to access these values is slightly different, as you will soon see. The number in parentheses following the name of the array variable balance is known as the *array upper bound*, and represents the number of values in the array, plus one. In order to access any value in the array you would use its *index*. The index of an array element is the actual position of that element in the array. The first element in the array is at position (or index) 0. The next one is at position 1, and so on, up to position *array upper bound − 1*, where array size is the size declared in the array declaration. Have a look at the following example:

```
Dim balance(4) As Decimal
balance(0) = 100
balance(4) = 250
```

The first statement declares an array of Decimals having five elements (indexes from 0 to 4). The next statement is assigning the literal value 100 to the first element of the array. The last statement assigns the value 250 to the last element of the array. Note the way an individual element of the array is accessed is by specifying in parentheses the index of the element you mean to access. Therefore balance(0) will represent the first element in the array, while balance(4) will represent the last element in the array. If you were to try to access an element that is not in the array—say element 7, as in balance(6) you would get a runtime exception and the program would be terminated. This type of exception is known as an out-of-bounds array access exception and is not uncommon.

The values at any given index in the array may be used in an expression, the same as any other regular variable. And indeed they are (from the point of view of the compiler) just a regular variable, just the notation is different. For example:

```
Dim balance(4) As Decimal
balance(0) = 100
Dim b As Boolean
b = balance(0) <= 250
```

This code will create an array of five Decimals, will set the value of the first element of the array to be 100, and then will declare a Boolean variable and assign to it the result of evaluating a logical expression. The logical expression compares the value of the array element at position 0 (the one you just set to be 100) to the literal value 250. In a similar fashion you could use array elements in any type of expression.

You have seen that regular variables can be initialized when declared. Could you do the same thing for arrays? The answer is yes and the example that follows illustrates how to do it. Create a new console project and name it ArrayExample. Then enter the code as shown in the Sub Main:

```
Sub Main()
   Dim balance() As Decimal = {100, 200, 300, 400, 250}
   Console.Out.WriteLine("The value of array element 0 is {0}", balance(0))
   Console.Out.WriteLine("The value of array element 1 is {0}", balance(1))
   Console.Out.WriteLine("The value of array element 2 is {0}", balance(2))
   Console.Out.WriteLine("The value of array element 3 is {0}", balance(3))
   Console.Out.WriteLine("The value of array element 4 is {0}", balance(4))

   Dim b As Boolean
   b = balance(0) <= 500
   Console.Out.WriteLine("The value b is {0}", b)
```

```
    Console.Out.WriteLine("Press the <Enter> key to end the program")
    Console.In.ReadLine()
End Sub
```

Please note the first line, which is the declaration and initialization statement for the array. The first difference you see is that there is no array size specified in parentheses (although the parentheses themselves are still present). Next, it is easy to see the initialization code following the = sign. The arrays are initialized using a set of literal values of the appropriate type, delimited by the open and closing curly braces. A comma is required to delimit any individual array element from the next one. Because the compiler knows exactly how many elements are in the initialization values *literal array* (that is, the values between the { and } braces), it does not need a size for the arrays that are initialized as shown. It is actually a syntax error to provide a size, and the IDE and compiler will flag it appropriately.

Next in the sample you output the value of each array element to the console, and then you declare a Boolean and set it to be the result of the expression, as described previously. You then output the value of the variable b to the console. Save and run the project and the results should be similar to those shown in Figure 8.1.

Figure 8.1: *Array example output.*

It is quite seldom that you know up front what is the size of the array that you will need. Quite often this size is determined at runtime. This implies that you need the capability to declare an empty array (or a placeholder) and then initialize it when you know what the size of the array is. This is called *dynamic initialization* of an array. Our example can be modified to illustrate this way of using an array:

```
Sub Main()
    Dim balance() As Decimal
```

```
balance = New Decimal(4) {100, 200, 300, 400, 250}
Console.Out.WriteLine("The value of array element 0 is {0}", balance(0))
Console.Out.WriteLine("The value of array element 1 is {0}", balance(1))
Console.Out.WriteLine("The value of array element 2 is {0}", balance(2))
Console.Out.WriteLine("The value of array element 3 is {0}", balance(3))
Console.Out.WriteLine("The value of array element 4 is {0}", balance(4))

Dim b As Boolean
b = balance(0) <= 500
Console.Out.WriteLine("The value b is {0}", b)

Console.Out.WriteLine("Press the <Enter> key to end the program")
Console.In.ReadLine()
End Sub
```

As you can see the modifications are minor: you have removed the initialization code from the array declaration line, and you have added a new line that assigns a new array of five Decimal values (specified between the { and } braces) to the balance array variable. If you did not know the values for the new array you could use something like:

```
balance = New Decimal(n) {}
```

Where n is the upper bound of the new array (and it can be a variable), while the empty curly braces are needed to indicate it is an array that is being constructed. Note also the use of the keyword New—we will come back to it when you learn about objects and classes.

This simple example is meant to illustrate how to declare and initialize the values in an array, and then how to access these values. An array is quite similar to the mathematical concept of a matrix with one dimension (for the examples you have seen so far). But as you will see next, arrays can have more than one dimension. For example, to represent the values of the balances of the five accounts over the course of three years you would need either three arrays (one per year, each array with five values for the balances in that year) or you could use a matrix with two dimensions. In programmer parlance this construct is called a two-dimensional array. Arrays in Visual Basic can have up to 60 dimensions (dimensions, not elements!), although more than three dimensions is quite unusual.

Declaring a multidimensional array is very similar to declaring a one-dimensional array you have seen. The following example illustrates this:

```
Dim balance(2, 4) As Decimal
```

This declaration declares a two-dimensional array of Decimals. The upper bound of the first dimension is 2; the upper bound of the second dimension is 4. This is similar to a matrix of 3×5 elements, where each matrix element corresponds with an array element (a Decimal value in our example). If you needed the array to have more dimensions, the sizes for the dimensions are separated with commas, exactly as in the previous example. A three-dimensional array declaration would look like:

```
Dim coordinates(9, 9, 9) As Double
```

This declares an array with three dimensions, the upper bound of each dimension being 9 (a total of 1,000 Double elements). As you can see the size of the array increases very fast for multidimensional arrays, so one has to be careful on when and how one of these arrays is used.

To access an array element from a multidimensional array you need to specify an index for each of the dimensions of the array. In the case of your two-dimensional array you could use code like this:

```
Dim balance(2, 4) As Decimal
balance(0, 2) = 300
```

This example sets the value for the element identified by the indices (0, 2) to be 300. In the case of a two-dimensional array you can picture this in terms of rows and columns: the third element on the first row. The indices are in row-column order, which means that the first dimension (and index) represents the row(s), and the second dimension represents the column(s). This type of representation becomes less intuitive when dealing with arrays with three or more dimensions, but these are rare cases.

Can you initialize a multidimensional array in the same fashion in which you initialized the one-dimensional array you used in your example? The answer is yes, and let's see how. Modify the sample project you used previously so that the code looks like this:

```
Sub Main()
    Dim balance(,) As Decimal = {{100, 200, 300, 400, 250}, _
                                 {100, 200, 300, 400, 250}, _
                                 {100, 200, 300, 400, 250}}
    Console.Out.WriteLine("The array element 0,0 is {0}", balance(0, 0))
    Console.Out.WriteLine("The array element 0,1 is {0}", balance(0, 1))
    Console.Out.WriteLine("The array element 0,2 is {0}", balance(0, 2))
    Console.Out.WriteLine("The array element 0,3 is {0}", balance(0, 3))
    Console.Out.WriteLine("The array element 0,4 is {0}", balance(0, 4))

    Dim b As Boolean
    b = balance(0, 0) <= 500
    Console.Out.WriteLine("The value b is {0}", b)

    Console.Out.WriteLine("Press the <Enter> key to end the program")
    Console.In.ReadLine()
End Sub
```

Do not omit the _ (underscore) characters at the end of the lines after the commas. This is the *line-continuation* character in Visual Basic. If you need to write a line that is longer than will fit in the editor window (or if you simply want to make the code look better), you can continue that line on the next line by adding the underscore character at the end of the line. Each statement in Visual Basic ends at the end of the line unless you have the underscore symbol as the last symbol on the line, in which case the compiler will interpret the following line as a continuation of the current line.

In this case you are declaring an array with two dimensions and then initializing it to the set of values specified after the = symbol, between curly braces. The values are entered as the array would contain other arrays, and each of these arrays in turn contains the values. Note the fact that the two dimension sizes are empty "(,)", for the same reason as in the case of the one-dimensional array: the compiler can determine the sizes of each dimension. The number of dimensions is indicated by the number of commas between the parentheses (0 = one-dimensional array, 1 = two-dimensional array, and so on). It now becomes clear why you split the initialization line into three lines: the values are positioned in the same way as the corresponding elements would be represented in the array after it is initialized.

The rest of the program is very much the same, except that the individual elements of the array are now accessed using two indices instead of one (the row and column).

In a similar fashion to the one-dimensional arrays, you can use a notation to declare an array of a known number of dimensions but unknown sizes, and then use the New keyword to construct an array and assign it to the declared variable. For example:

```
Dim balance(,) As Decimal
balance = New Decimal(2, 4) {}
```

This example creates a new two-dimensional array of 3×5 Decimals.

Most of the examples that you use are going to be one-dimensional arrays, although the use of two-dimensional arrays is quite common also.

Enumerations

Let's assume you have been given the task of writing a subsystem for a game of cards (like bridge, for example). Your task is to determine if a given card from the deck was used already. That means you need some means to represent the deck of cards and remember for each card if it was used or not. A deck of cards consists of 52 cards divided into 4 suits (clubs, diamonds, hearts, and spades). Each suit consists of the cards from 2 to 10, the Jack, Queen, King, and Ace of the suit.

To store the fact that a card was used you can use an array of 52 Boolean values. Or even better (more intuitive) you could use a two-dimensional array of 4 rows (one per suit) and 13 columns (one for each card in the suit). Deciding that you use the latter version, you are faced with another issue. What would the correlation be between the indices and the suits and cards? That is, to find out if the Queen of Hearts was used, at what row and column do you need to retrieve the element in the array? You could arbitrarily establish that you use 0 for clubs, 1 for diamonds, 2 for hearts, and 3 for spades, and 0 for the Two, 1 for the Three, ..., 12 for the Ace in each suit. That means you could find out if the Queen of Hearts was used by getting the value of the array element at position (2, 10). However this is not really intuitive and it is error prone: assume that somebody else looks at your program and tries to figure out what card you are referring to. There is nothing that tells him that the element at (2, 10) is really the Queen of Hearts.

But Visual Basic allows you to use a better approach to this problem using enumerations. An *enumeration* is a set of values that are given a name, and can be used as a data type. For example you could define an enumeration for the card suits:

```
Enum CardSuit
    clubs
    diamonds
    hearts
    spades
End Enum
```

You can see that the enumeration declaration is delimited by the keyword Enum followed by the enumeration name, and End Enum, which marks the end of the declaration. This declaration declares a new data type that consists of only four possible values. You can use this data type to declare new variables and build expressions, like any of the fundamental data types. For example you could write code like this:

```
Dim cs As CardSuit = CardSuit.hearts
cs = CardSuit.clubs
```

You declare and initialize the cs variable to be of type CardSuit, which you have defined as an enumeration with the four possible values. You can assign new values (from the enumeration) to the new variable, or output the value of the variable to the console (as you will see soon).

Create a new console project and name it EnumExample. Enter the code that follows.

NOTE

The Enum declarations are outside the Sub Main body. This is because they are type declarations—they define new types.

```
Module Module1

    Enum CardSuit
        clubs = 0
        diamonds = 1
        hearts = 2
        spades = 3
    End Enum

    Enum CardRank
        two = 0
        three = 1
        four = 2
        five = 3
        six = 4
        seven = 5
        eight = 6
        nine = 7
        ten = 8
        jack = 9
        queen = 10
        king = 11
        ace = 12
    End Enum

    Sub Main()
        Dim deck(4, 13) As Boolean

        Dim cs As CardSuit = CardSuit.hearts
        Console.Out.WriteLine("The value cs is {0}", cs)

        Dim cr As CardRank = CardRank.queen
        Console.Out.WriteLine("The value cr is {0}", cr)

        Dim bUsed As Boolean
        bUsed = deck(cs, cr)
        Console.Out.WriteLine("The value bUsed is {0}", bUsed)

        bUsed = deck(CardSuit.spades, CardRank.ace)
        Console.Out.WriteLine("The value bUsed is {0}", bUsed)
```

```
      Console.Out.WriteLine("Press the <Enter> key to end the program")
      Console.In.ReadLine()
   End Sub

End Module
```

When you declare the type for the cs and cr variables, the newly defined types (CardSuit and CardRank) are in the IntelliSense list of available types. The same applies for when you assign a value to one of the two variables: a list of possible values is displayed. That makes it easier to use than using the Integer values.

The Enum elements are in effect Integers, and, as you can see from the previous code listing, you can explicitly assign values to each element of en enumeration. If you do not assign any value, the elements will have the value equal to their position in the enumeration (starting with 0). You can have negative values and multiple elements with the same value, if required.

If you execute this program you will notice that the output values for both cs and cr are the element names hearts and queen, respectively. But you can use these enumerated values as regular Integers. This is illustrated by the two assignments to the bUsed variable. The first one uses the cs and cr variables to access the array element for the Queen of hearts. The second assignment uses the explicit enumerated values to get the array element for the Ace of Spades.

In summary you can say that enumerations are useful in defining new data types that are subsets of the Integer data type. Each element in the subset has a name—which is a valid Visual Basic identifier. Elements can be used in the same way as any literal value. So instead of using the Integer literal 2 you use CardSuit.hearts.

Structure Declaration

A structure is a complex data type that consists of one or more *members* (also known as fields). Let's look at an example so that you understand better. Assume that you are dealing with a graphics application that requires you to access (get and set) the color of a point (known as *pixel*) anywhere on the display, as well as other graphic operations that require the pixel coordinates. You can represent the address of any point on the screen as a pair of x and y coordinates. That means that any time you need to operate on a given point you need to specify both the x and the y coordinate. It would be useful to be able to treat each pixel as a unit, rather than dealing with independent x-y numbers. That is where the structures come into consideration. You can declare a structure that consists of the x and y coordinates for any pixel.

Create a new console project and name it StructExample. Enter the following code in Module1. Note that the Structure declaration is outside the body of Sub Main, as expected, because it is a type declaration.

```
Module Module1

    Structure PixelCoord
        Public x As Single
        Public y As Single
    End Structure

    Sub Main()
        Dim p As PixelCoord

        p.x = 200
        p.y = 100
        Console.Out.WriteLine("The value p.x is {0}", p.x)
        Console.Out.WriteLine("The value p.y is {0}", p.y)

        Console.Out.WriteLine("Press the <Enter> key to end the program")
        Console.In.ReadLine()
    End Sub

End Module
```

From this code you can see that the structure declaration is delimited by the keyword Structure, followed by the structure name, and the End Structure keyword, which marks the end of the declaration. Inside the structure declaration you have the *structure member* declarations. Each member of a structure is a variable of a specified type. You use syntax similar to the Dim statement you have used in declaring variables so far, except for the fact that the keyword Public is used to declare the members of the structure.

NOTE

The Public keyword indicates that the member is *visible* (accessible) outside the structure. You will understand more when you will learn of visibility later on in the book.

You are declaring a new data type that consists of two Single values, the first one named x and the second one named y. When the compiler will allocate memory for a variable of this type it will allocate a memory location that is equal with the combined sizes of its members (two Single values in this case).

This structure allows you to declare variables that better represent one pixel. You can access structure members using the *dot-notation*. That is you use the period (known as "dot" in programmer dialect) after a variable of structure type, to access any of its members. You have probably noticed that, when you type the dot after the name of the variable p, a list of members appears that includes the x and y members you declared, and some other names that are not present in your structure declaration. This is quite all right; you can think of these as some members that all structures have. You will understand better what these members are when you are going to study objects and classes. You will ignore them for now.

In the Sub Main you declare a variable of the PixelCoord type, you set the values of the two structure members and then you output these values to the console. You could use any of these values in an expression, as you would any variable of Single type. The difference is that the name of the variable is composed of the name of the structure variable + the name of the member, accessed using the dot-notation, p.x.

As mentioned earlier, the data types of the structure members can be any valid data type. That of course includes all the fundamental data types (like Integer, String, and so on), but it also includes arrays, enumerations and other structures. Let's look at a more complex example. Modify the code you have entered to look like the code listed below:

```
Module Module1

    Enum PixelColor
        red
        green
        blue
    End Enum

    Structure PixelCoord
        Public x As Single
        Public y As Single
        Public flags() As Byte
        Public color As PixelColor
    End Structure

    Structure Rectangle
        Public topLeft As PixelCoord
        Public topRight As PixelCoord
        Public bottomLeft As PixelCoord
        Public bottomRight As PixelCoord
        Public fillColor As PixelColor
    End Structure
```

```
Sub Main()
    Dim r As Rectangle

    r.topLeft.x = 100
    r.topLeft.y = 100
    r.topLeft.color = PixelColor.green

    r.topRight.x = 300
    r.topRight.y = 100
    r.topRight.color = PixelColor.green

    r.bottomLeft.x = 100
    r.bottomLeft.y = 300
    r.bottomLeft.color = PixelColor.green

    r.bottomRight.x = 300
    r.bottomRight.y = 300
    r.bottomRight.color = PixelColor.green

    Console.Out.WriteLine("The value r.topLeft.x is {0}", r.topLeft.x)
    Console.Out.WriteLine("The value r.topLeft.y is {0}", r.topLeft.y)

    Console.Out.WriteLine("Press the <Enter> key to end the program")
    Console.In.ReadLine()
End Sub

End Module
```

You have added a PixelColor enumeration with three elements (red, green, and blue). You will use this enumeration to indicate the color of a given pixel. You have changed the PixelCoord structure to include an array of flags as Byte values, and a color member declared as an enumerated value of type PixelColor.

You have also added a new structure named Rectangle that contains four members of PixelCoord type (one of each of the four corners of the rectangle) and one member of the enumerated PixelColor type, which indicates the color used to fill the rectangle.

In the Sub Main you declare a variable of type Rectangle and then you assign values to its members. Because some of its members are structures too, you use the dot-notation recursively to access the members of its members that are structures. For example to access the x and y coordinates of the top-left corner of the rectangle you use r.topLeft.x and r.topLeft.y. In this example r is the variable of Rectangle type, topLeft is a member of the Rectangle structure, and it is of type PixelCoord. The x and y are members of the PixelCoord structure and are of Single type.

There are many other issues related to declaring structures in addition to what you have learned in this chapter. You will learn them as you get a deeper understanding of the Visual Basic language and of some basic object-oriented concepts.

Using the Structured Data Types

Arrays, enumerations, and structures can be grouped together under the label *structured types*. They are custom and/or complex data types, based on the fundamental data types.

Variables of these types can be declared and used in the same way as any fundamental type variable can be used. There are some differences that need to be understood before you proceed with your learning. One of the most important is the way the assignment works between different variables of the same type.

In the case of fundamental data types, the assignment is said to occur *by value (ByVal)*. That means that when you assign an Integer variable i to another Integer variable j, the compiler will copy the contents of the memory location that the variable i refers to into the memory location to which j refers to.

Alternatively, the compiler could have the variable j refer to the same memory location as the variable i. This behavior is known as assignment *by reference (ByRef)* because the only thing that is assigned is the reference to a new memory location, no values are copied as in the *by value* case. The implication of this type of behavior is that, after an assignment by reference, modifying the value of the i variable will modify also the j variable (because they both refer to the same location in memory).

It is very important to understand these two fundamental behaviors because all data types in Visual Basic (and in the .NET Framework for that matter) use one or the other. Figure 8.2 summarizes the two behaviors and the preceding comments.

All the data types you have seen so far, with the exception of arrays, are using ByVal behavior. The arrays use ByRef behavior. The following example will illustrate this for some of the fundamental types, arrays, and structures. Create a new console project and name it AssignExample, and then enter the following code:

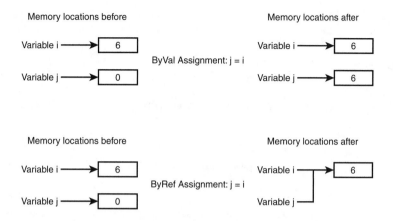

Figure 8.2: *ByVal versus ByRef assignment behavior.*

```
Module Module1

    Structure Card
        Public name As String
        Public pcid As Integer
    End Structure

    Sub Main()
        Dim i As Integer = 7, j As Integer = 3
        System.Console.Out.WriteLine("BEFORE i is {0} and j is {1}", i, j)
        i = j
        j = 2
        System.Console.Out.WriteLine("AFTER i is {0} and j is {1}", i, j)

        Dim c1 As Card, c2 As Card
        c1.name = "Video card"
        c1.pcid = 0
        c2.name = "Audio card"
        c2.pcid = 6
        Console.Out.WriteLine("BEFORE c1.name is {0} and c1.pcid is {1}", _
                        c1.name, c1.pcid)
        Console.Out.WriteLine("BEFORE c2.name is {0} and c2.pcid is {1}", _
                        c2.name, c2.pcid)

        c1 = c2
        c2.name = "Joe"
        c2.pcid = 123
        Console.Out.WriteLine("AFTER c1.name is {0} and c1.pcid is {1}", _
                        c1.name, c1.pcid)
```

```
        Console.Out.WriteLine("AFTER c2.name is {0} and c2.pcid is {1}", _
                        c2.name, c2.pcid)

        Dim a1() As Integer = {1, 2, 3, 4, 5}
        Dim a2() As Integer = {6, 7, 8, 9, 0}

        Console.Out.WriteLine("BEFORE a1(3) is {0} and a2(3) is {1}", _
                        a1(3), a2(3))
        a1 = a2
        a1(3) = -1
        Console.Out.WriteLine("AFTER a1(3) is {0} and a2(3) is {1}", _
                        a1(3), a2(3))

        Console.Out.WriteLine("Press the <Enter> key to end the program")
        Console.In.ReadLine()
    End Sub

End Module
```

First you declare a two-member structure that you will use in the example. Your example consists of three parts: the assignment of two Integer variables, two Card structure variables, and two arrays.

In the case of the Integer variables you declare and initialize them, and then output their values to the console before the assignment. You then assign j to i and then change the value of j. If the assignment would be by reference, you would see the value of i change as well. You verify that this is not the case by outputting the values of i and j to the console, and indeed the i and j hold different values.

You apply the same procedure for two variables, c1 and c2, of Card structure type. You declare and initialize the variables, then their values BEFORE the assignment are outputed to the console. Then you assign c2 to c1, and change the values for both members of c2. If the assignment would be by reference, that would change the values of c1 as well. You output the value of both variables and verify that indeed this is not the case.

The final portion of your test will verify that the array assignment takes place by reference. Create two arrays (a1 and a2) of Integer values, and initialize them with different values. Verify that the element 3 of both arrays contains different values BEFORE the assignment. Then assign a2 to a1, and then change the value of the element 3 of the a1 array to −1. When you output the values to the console for the element three in both arrays, you will find out that both values are −1. You have never assigned −1 to the a2(3), therefore the only way it can have this value is if both a1 and a2 arrays are actually referring to the same array now. That means the assignment operator is behaving by reference for arrays.

What's Next

In this chapter you studied how to declare and use some advanced data types. You learned what arrays, enumerations, and structures are and a few examples of how to use them. You have also seen what by value and by reference behavior is for assignment.

In the next chapter you will study some of the control statements of Visual Basic, namely branching and loop statements.

You will study the `If` and `Select Case` statements, and then the `Do While`, `While`, and `For` loops.

NOTE

The answers to the "Reviewing It," "Checking It," and "Applying It" are available on our Web site.

REVIEW

Reviewing It

This section presents a review of the key concepts in this chapter. These questions are intended to gauge your absorption of the relevant material.

1. What is an array?
2. Enumerate all methods by which you can set the values of array elements.
3. What is an enumeration?
4. What is a structure?
5. What is the purpose of the dot-notation?
6. What is the difference between by-value and by-reference assignment?

CHECK

Checking It

Select the correct answer to the following questions.

Multiple Choice

1. By array dimension you understand:
    a. The number of elements the array holds.
    b. The measure of the array in one direction (coordinate).
    c. The structure of the memory location for the array.
    d. The size of the array as a whole.

2. An array element can be accessed by:

    a. Its name.

    b. Its index in the array.

    c. Dot-notation using the array name followed by its index.

    d. Specifying its position using an index for each dimension of the array.

3. How many elements hold an array declared as `Dim a(2, 3, 4) As Integer`?

    a. 45.

    b. 60.

    c. 345.

    d. As many as required; it will grow to accommodate new elements.

4. Can enumeration elements be used as array indices?

    a. Yes.

    b. No. Only integers can be used as array indices.

    c. Yes, but a conversion function must be used.

    d. No. Array indices must be literals.

5. Can a structure member (field) be an array?

    a. Yes.

    b. No.

    c. Yes, but only one-dimensional arrays.

    d. Yes, but only uninitialized (dynamic) arrays.

6. Can array elements be structures?

    a. Yes.

    b. No.

    c. Yes, but only structures without array fields.

    d. No, arrays must be of fundamental types only.

7. If you have an array A and an array B, and you assign B to A, and then change the value of one element of A (for example A(0)), what happens to the corresponding element B(0)?

   a. It remains unchanged, it is a different array.

   b. The value of A(0) is copied in B(0) too.

   c. A(0) and B(0) refer to the same element, therefore they have the same (changed) value.

   d. A(0) and B(0) refer to the same element, but when assigned a new value A(0) will be copied to a different memory location.

8. Array index values start at:

   a. 0.

   b. 1.

   c. You define it when you declare the array.

   d. 0 for fixed arrays, 1 for dynamic arrays.

True or False

Select one of the two possible answers and then verify on our Web site that you picked the correct one.

1. The size of an array is the sum of the sizes of each dimension.

   True/False

2. The elements of an array are all of the same type.

   True/False

3. An array must be initialized upon declaration.

   True/False

4. An enumeration is the same as an array, but it has names for its elements.

   True/False

5. Structures can contain other structures as members.

   True/False

6. Structures are assigned by value (values of individual members are copied into the assignment target).

   True/False

APPLY

Applying It

Try to complete the following exercises by yourself.

Independent Exercise 1

Create a new console project that declares a one-dimensional array of Strings of size 3. Have the user enter values for the elements of the array and then concatenate the elements and display the result.

Independent Exercise 2

Create a program that declares a structure for the personal information about an individual: last name, first name, date of birth, and gender. Then get the user to fill in information about itself and output this information to the console.

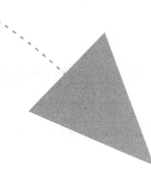

Control Statements

In this chapter you will learn the fundamental control statements used by the Visual Basic language. These are statements that control the flow of the programs, and they can be classified in two categories: branching statements and loop statements. You will study the fundamental Visual Basic branching and loop statements in this chapter, structured as follows:

- The `If` statement
- The `Select Case` statement
- The `For` loop
- The `Do` loop
- The `While` loop

The programs you used as examples up to this point were linear programs; that is, they started in one point (after the `Sub Main`) and continue in a *linear* fashion by executing all statements between the starting point and the end point (the `End Sub` statement). Real-life programs are seldom that simple. Most frequently you must execute some block of statements only if some condition is met. Or you may need to execute one statement multiple times. That is, you must be able to control the execution flow of the program—hence the name *control statements*.

There are two types of control statements: branching statements and loop statements. The *branching statements* are used to selectively execute a group of statements only when a condition is met. Branching statements are the `If` and `Select Case` statements. The *loop statements* are used to execute a group of statements multiple times. The loop statements that you will learn in this chapter are the `For` loop, `Do` loop, and `While` loop.

The If Statement

The If statements is one of the most common Visual Basic statements. It allows you to execute one or more statements only when a specific condition is met. This condition is a Boolean expression that will evaluate to True or False. Let's look at an example:

```
Sub Main()
   Console.Out.WriteLine("Enter a value for i and press <ENTER>: ")
   Dim i As Integer
   i = CInt(Console.In.ReadLine())

   Console.Out.WriteLine("Enter a value for j and press <ENTER>: ")
   Dim j As Integer
   j = CInt(Console.In.ReadLine())

   If i < j Then
      Console.Out.WriteLine("i is less than j")
   End If

   Console.Out.WriteLine("Press the <Enter> key to end the program")
   Console.In.ReadLine()
End Sub
```

These example declare two Integer variables i and j and gets some values for them from the user. Then if i is less than j it will output to the console the string "i is less than j". For this you used an If statement. The If statement consists of the keyword If followed by the Boolean expression and the keyword Then. On the next line you have the statement that you want to execute conditionally. You can have more than one statement here. The If statement must always end with the End If keywords.

What happens at runtime is probably quite clear by now: first the Boolean expression "i < j" is evaluated. If this expression is true (that is, if i holds a value that is less than the one j is holding), the statements between the Then and End If statement are executed. If the expression is false (that is, i is less than or equal to j) the statements are not executed. That means control will be transferred to the first statement following the End If statement.

To run the example, create a new console project and call it IfExample, and then enter the code as shown previously, and run it. If you enter a value for i that is less than the value for j (such as 3 and 5) the output will look like Figure 9.1.

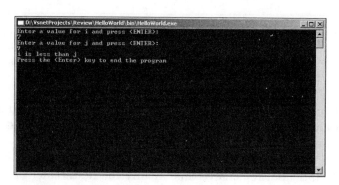

Figure 9.1: If example output 1.

If i is greater than or equal to j then the output will look like the one in Figure 9.2.

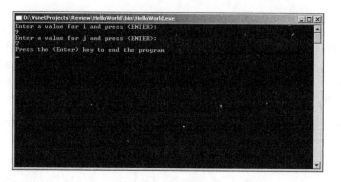

Figure 9.2: If example output 2.

The conditional expression used in an If statement is a Boolean expression, and can be as complex as required. We recommend keeping it simple and clear to improve the readability of your programs.

There is another (less common) form of the If statement that is sometimes used, called a *single-line If statement* because it is written on a single line. For distinction, the form we have used is called a block-If statement. You could rewrite the If statement as:

```
If i < j Then Console.Out.WriteLine("i is less than j")
```

This line of code does the same thing as the If you have seen previously. The differences are that the statement that is executed when the expression is true is on the same line as the If...Then statement, and the End If is missing.

NOTE

This form of If is useful in some instances when there is only one statement following the Then and it is short. If there is an Else part (described later in this chapter) or more than one statement, then the block-If statement form should be used.

There are cases when you would like to execute some statements when a condition is true, and some other statements when the condition is false. To continue this example, you would like to display the text "j is less than or equal to i" if your expression (i < j) is false. You can use another form for the If statement to achieve this. Modify the If statement in the previous example to look like the code in bold:

```
If i < j Then
    Console.Out.WriteLine("i is less than j")
Else
    Console.Out.WriteLine("j is less than or equal to i")
End If
```

You use the keyword Else to delimit the statements that will be executed if the condition is true and the ones that are executed when the condition is false. If the expression i < j is true then the statements between Then and Else are executed; otherwise the statements between Else and End If are executed. This form of the If statement is also quite common.

There is a corresponding form of the single-line If statement that uses the Else keyword as well:

```
If bDebug Then Stop Else End
```

In this example if the value of the bDebug variable is True then the statement Stop is executed; otherwise, the statement End is executed.

WARNING

We believe this form is less readable than the block-If statement, and should not be used. It is included here for completeness.

Any statement can be placed in the block of statements inside a block-If statement, including other If statements. If you had an If statement inside another If statement, you would call the interior If statement *nested*. This term is often used to indicate a construct or statement within other constructs or statements. You will encounter it later in the chapter when you learn about loop statements.

What would happen with your example if you wanted to distinguish between the case when i is equal to j and the other two cases? You would need somehow to have the program branch in three cases: i is less than j, i is equal to j, and finally i is greater than j. You can achieve this by using another form of the If statement, presented in the following example. Modify the code of the If to look like this:

```
If i < j Then
    System.Console.Out.WriteLine("i is less than j")
ElseIf i = j Then
    System.Console.Out.WriteLine("i equals j")
Else
    System.Console.Out.WriteLine("j is less than i")
End If
```

The new lines (in bold) illustrate a way to branch in three cases. First the expression i < j is evaluated, and if it is True, the statement between Then and ElseIf is executed. If i < j is False, the expression of the following ElseIf is evaluated. If it is True the statements following the Then and the following Else or ElseIf are executed. Finally if none of the expressions evaluated are True the Else statements are executed. The If statement is equivalent to a group of nested If statements as in the following example:

```
If i < j Then
    System.Console.Out.WriteLine("i is less than j")
Else
    If i = j Then
        System.Console.Out.WriteLine("i equals j")
    Else
        System.Console.Out.WriteLine("j is less than i")
    End If
End If
```

The former example is clearer, in this case. The ElseIf form becomes more readable if there are multiple conditions to test. A few important things to remember are that you can have more than one ElseIf part and that the Else part is not mandatory.

Considering what you have learned about the If statement so far you could use the following expression to describe the general syntax of an If statement:

```
If <expression-1> Then
    <statements-1>
[ElseIf <expression-2> Then
    <statements-2>]
...
[ElseIf <expression-n> Then
    <statements-n>]
[Else
    <else-statements>]
End If
```

The detailed syntax for the If and all other statements in the book is shown on our Web site.

The keywords are in bold. <expression-1>, <expression-2>, and so on are placeholders for the actual Boolean expressions that would be used. <statements-1>, <statements-2>, ..., <else-statements> are placeholders for the actual statement(s) that will be placed in the respective position in the statement. The use of braces [ ] denotes an optional part of the statement, that is, it can be omitted and the statement would still be correct. The use of ... (ellipsis) denotes the fact that the part of the statement preceding it can be repeated. In our example here we mean that the ElseIf optional part can be repeated more than once. You can have 0 or more ElseIf parts of the statement. We will use the same conventions to formally illustrate the syntax of the other statements you will encounter in this book.

The Select Case Statement

The Select Case statement is used as a convenient replacement for an If statement with a large number of ElseIf branches. Let's write a simple example to illustrate the use of a Select Case. Your task is to develop a funny oracle that will guess the gender of the user, based on its first name. Create a new console project and name it SelectCaseExample, and then enter the code as shown in the following example.

```
Sub Main()
    Console.Out.WriteLine("I am the Oracle and I will guess your gender")
    Console.Out.WriteLine("Enter your first name and press <ENTER>: ")
    Dim s As String
    s = Console.In.ReadLine()

    Select Case s
        Case "Bob"
            Console.Out.WriteLine("Hi Bob!")
        Case "Gabriel"
            Console.Out.WriteLine("You again?!")
        Case "Jim"
            Console.Out.WriteLine("You are a male!")
        Case "John"
            Console.Out.WriteLine("You are a male!")
        Case "Tom"
            Console.Out.WriteLine("You are a male!")
        Case "Rob"
            Console.Out.WriteLine("You are a male!")
        Case "Joanne"
            Console.Out.WriteLine("You are a female!")
```

```
      Case "Sarah"
         Console.Out.WriteLine("You are a female!")
      Case "Betty"
         Console.Out.WriteLine("You are a female!")
      Case "Jane"
         Console.Out.WriteLine("You are a female!")
      Case Else
         Console.Out.WriteLine("I do not know. Are you an alien?")
   End Select

   Console.Out.WriteLine("Press the <Enter> key to end the program")
   Console.In.ReadLine()
End Sub
```

The logic is quite simple: if you can recognize the name as male or female (or one of the two authors) you print a message to the console and then exit. If the name is not recognized, you print a default message and exit. The implementation of this logic gets the input from the user into the String variable s and then uses a `Select Case` statement to branch to the appropriate statement to execute. Each branch is made of the keyword `Case` and the expression that follows it, plus the statements that follow it until the next `Case` branch or the end of the statement (`End Select`) is encountered. The way the `Select Case` works is the `Select Case` expression is evaluated first (in this case the expression is the String variable s). Next, each `Case` expression is evaluated to see if it matches the value of the `Select Case` expression. For example, if the user types in "John" the statements following the `Case "John"` branch would be executed. If no match is found and there is a `Case Else` branch present, the statements in the `Case Else` are executed. In either case, the execution is then transferred to the statement following the end of the statement (`End Select`).

If you run this example you will get an output similar to the one in Figure 9.3.

Figure 9.3: `Select Case` *sample output.*

You have probably noticed that you have multiple branches that to the same thing for different values of the Case expression. For example for all the male names that you know will write the same message ("You are a male!") to the console. The same for all the female names. It would be good if you could somehow compress these branches into one. The Select Case statement allows you to do this. You can specify multiple values following the same Case statement, delimited by commas. Change the preceding example code to the following:

```
Sub Main()
    System.Console.Out.WriteLine("I am the Oracle and I will guess your gender")
    System.Console.Out.WriteLine("Enter your first name, then press <ENTER>: ")
    Dim s As String
    s = System.Console.In.ReadLine()

    Select Case s
        Case "Bob"
            Console.Out.WriteLine("Hi Bob!")
        Case "Gabriel"
            Console.Out.WriteLine("You again?!")
        Case "Jim", "John", "Tom", "Rob"
            Console.Out.WriteLine("You are a male!")
        Case "Joanne", "Sarah", "Betty", "Jane"
            Console.Out.WriteLine("You are a female!")
        Case Else
            Console.Out.WriteLine("I do not know. Are you an alien?")
    End Select

    Console.Out.WriteLine("Press the <Enter> key to end the program")
    Console.In.ReadLine()
End Sub
```

As you can see this is much easier and compact code. The comma is equivalent to the logical Or statement: if the value of the s string (Select Case expression) matches any of the values delimited by commas then the statements following this Case will be executed.

The type of the Select Case expression must be either a numeric value or a string value. The values of the Case expressions must match the type of the Select Case expression. There are other valid expressions for the Case expressions, especially when dealing with numeric types. For example, when using an Integer i:

```
Select Case i
    Case 1, 3, 5
        Console.Out.WriteLine("1, 3 or 5")
    Case 7 To 11, Is >= 15
```

```
        Console.Out.WriteLine("Between 7 and 11, or >= 15")
    Case Else
        Console.Out.WriteLine("Other number")
End Select
```

You can specify an interval using the keyword To, or use a comparison operator (like >=) and the keyword Is. The interval and comparison operators could be used also for Strings, although is not that frequent.

You could express the syntax of the Select Case statement formally as follows:

```
Select Case <select-expression>
    Case <case-expression-1>
        <statements-1>

    ...

    [Case Else
        <else-statements>]
End Select
```

The <select-expression> is a placeholder for a numeric or String expression. You have one or more Case branches, each with its expression and set of statements that will be executed if the expression matches the select-expression. Optionally you have a Case Else branch (also known as a *default branch*) that will be used if none of the case-expressions match the select-expression.

WARNING

You are not allowed to place any statements between the Select Case line and the first Case branch.

You are probably wondering whether you could implement the same example using an If statement with a lot of ElseIf branches, something like this:

```
If s.Equals("Bob") Then
    Console.Out.WriteLine("Hi Bob!")
ElseIf s.Equals("Gabriel") Then
    Console.Out.WriteLine("You again?!")
ElseIf s.Equals("Jim") Or s.Equals("John") Then
    Console.Out.WriteLine("You are a male!")
...
Else
    Console.Out.WriteLine("I do not know what you are. Are you an alien?")
End If
```

The answer is yes, you could. It is entirely up to you which version of branching you use; both the If and Select Case statements offer similar functionality.

The For Loop

You have seen how to selectively execute statements based on some conditions. Another frequently used feature in programming is to repeat a group of statements for different values of one or more variables. For example, to sum all the values in an array of numbers into one variable, you could use code like this:

```
Dim vals As Integer() = {1, 2, 3}
Dim total As Integer
total = vals(0) + vals(1) + vals(2)
```

If you know the size of the array (the number of elements in the array) that is a very easy task. What happens if you do not know the size of the array when you write the program, but rather this information will be supplied to you when you are at runtime? In this case this method would not work anymore. You need a new type of statement that would allow you to execute something like: *for each element i of the array vals, get its value and add it to the variable total.* This statement exists and it is called a For loop. Let's create a new console project and name it ForLoopExample. Enter the code as follows in the Sub Main.

```
Sub Main()
   Dim vals() As Integer = {1, 2, 3, 4, 5, 6, 7, 8, 9, 10}

   Console.Out.WriteLine("Enter the start index and press <Enter>:")
   Dim index As Integer
   index = CInt(Console.In.ReadLine())

   If index < 0 Or 9 < index Then
      Console.Out.WriteLine("Invalid index, must be between 0 and 9")
      Console.Out.WriteLine("Press the <Enter> key to end the program")
      Console.In.ReadLine()
      End
   End If

   Dim i As Integer, total As Integer
   For i = index To 9
      total += vals(i)
   Next
   Console.Out.WriteLine("The total value is {0}", total)

   Console.Out.WriteLine("Press the <Enter> key to end the program")
   Console.In.ReadLine()
End Sub
```

This program will calculate the sum of the elements of the Integer array vals from an index given by the user to the last item in the array. To do this you first get an integer value for the index variable from the user. Then you check that the value of the index is within the bounds of the array, between 0 and 9 inclusive. If this is not the case you display a message informing the user of the problem, and terminate the program using the End statement.

NOTE

The End statement can be used as an extreme resort to terminate a Visual Basic application. It should be used only in cases when the program cannot continue, and a normal termination is not possible. You will learn more about End later on in the book.

If the value of the index is valid, you then declare two integer variables. One is used as a *counter* (you will see soon what this means). The other one (total) is used to store the sum of all elements of the array that are between index and the last element of the array (9).

Then you have the actual For loop, delimited by the keywords For and Next. The statements inside the loop (between the For and the Next) are known as the *loop body*. The variable i is known as the *loop counter*. The expressions following the = and the To keyword are known as the *range* of the counter, or *start* and *end values*, respectively, of the counter. The body of the loop will be executed a number of times (determined by the value's start and end). One such execution is called an *iteration*. The value of the counter will be incremented for each iteration of the loop. In effect the statements in the body of the loop will be executed (end – start + 1) times with the counter starting at start at the first iteration and ending at end value.

In our example, assuming you entered the value 3 for the index variable, the loop body will be executed $9 - 3 + 1 = 7$ times. The counter i will start as 3 and end up as 9. The body of the loop consists of the statement that adds to the current value of the variable total the value of the element of the vals array at position i. That means you will add to total all elements of the vals array from 3 to 9. And this is exactly what you wanted to do.

If you would like to see how the value of the total variable evolves in time, you could add an output statement in the loop to display the current value of the i and the total variables. Modify the For loop to look like this example:

```
For i = index To 9
    total += vals(i)
    Console.Out.WriteLine("The total value is {0} at i = {1}", total, i)
Next
Console.Out.WriteLine("The final total value is {0}", total)
```

If you run the program and enter 3 a start index you should get an output like the one in Figure 9.4.

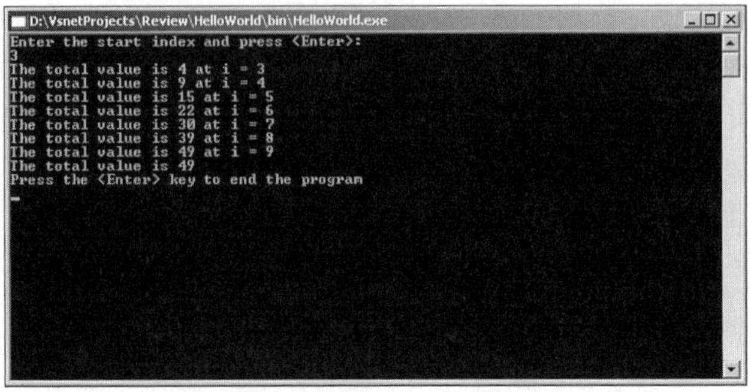

Figure 9.4: For loop sample output.

If the index variable in the example is 9, the loop body would be executed only once. If the index is greater than 9, the loop body would not be executed at all.

The formal syntax for the For loop is

```
For <counter> = <start> To <end> [Step <step>]
   <body-statements>
Next [<counter>]
```

You have seen what most of these keywords and expressions are. The optional Step and the expression <step> following are used to control the value by which the counter is incremented at every iteration, as you will see later in this chapter. The other element that you have not seen so far is the optional <counter> following the Next keyword.

Qualified Next

The qualified Next is a feature that allows you to identify easily which Next belongs to which For, especially in nested loops like the one in the following example.

```
Dim i As Integer, j As Integer
For i = 0 To n - 1
   For j = 0 To m - 1
      ' statements
   Next j
Next i
```

The compiler does not require that you use the Next j and Next i, but if you do, you must match it with the appropriate For. For example the following code is also correct:

```
Dim i As Integer, j As Integer
For i = 0 To n - 1
   For j = 0 To m - 1
      ' statements
   Next
Next
```

But the code is not correct, and will not compile:

```
Dim i As Integer, j As Integer
For i = 0 To n - 1
   For j = 0 To m - 1
      ' statements
   Next i
Next j
```

The use of the qualified Next makes your code more readable, but it is also more difficult to change. For example, if you need to change the counter variable name, you will need to change it in one more place. Therefore, it is a question of personal preference which form you use; each one has its small advantages and disadvantages.

Using the Step

If you would like the counter to be incremented by two at each iteration of a For loop, you would use Step 2. The following example illustrates a simple program that computes the sum of all odd numbers between 1 and 31:

```
Dim i As Integer, t As Integer
For i = 1 To 31 Step 2
   t += i
Next
Console.Out.WriteLine("The final value of t is {0}", t)
```

The counter variable i will start as 1 and will be incremented at every iteration by 2, that is, 3, 5, and so on up to 31.

This feature can be useful to walk through a string or array in reverse order (from end to start). The next code example will reverse a string the user enters and output it to the console:

```
Sub Main()
   Console.Out.WriteLine("Enter the string to revert and press <Enter>:")
   Dim s As String = Console.In.ReadLine()
   Dim i As Integer, n As Integer
   n = s.Length()
```

```
    Dim z As String
    For i = n - 1 To 0 Step -1
        z &= s.Substring(i, 1)
    Next
    Console.Out.WriteLine("The reverted string is {0}", z)

    Console.Out.WriteLine("Press the <Enter> key to end the program")
    Console.In.ReadLine()
End Sub
```

Note how the Step -1 is used in conjunction with the reversion of the values for start and end (the smaller value is to the right of the To keyword) to have the loop reversed. (Start with the higher value and decrement at each step by one, until the lesser value is reached.) This allows you to "walk" the s String variable in reverse order, from end to start, and add each character at the current counter position i to the output String z.

Exit For

There are rare cases when you need to exit a For loop before the whole number of iterations were performed—such as when an error condition occurs that prohibits the rest of the iterations from being completed. In a case like this you can use a loop exit statement:

```
For i = 0 To n - 1
    ' normal loop body
    If <some error condition> Then Exit For
Next
```

The bold statement illustrates the use of the Exit For statement to leave a For loop before its natural completion. We do not recommend the usage of this technique in the following pattern: search for something using a For loop, and when found exit the loop and continue. A Do loop would be much better for implementing this algorithm, as you will see next.

The For loops are very useful in a lot of programming tasks, from array manipulation and graphics rendering to database and string handling. But the For loops are not covering the whole domain of loop programming.

The Do Loop

There are certain cases in which you need to execute the body of the loop while a specific expression is True (or False). This means executing a loop an unknown number of times. You would not be able to use a counter and a range of values, as in a For loop. You can use a Do loop to solve this type of problem.

In the following example you would like to allow the user to perform a simple mathematical computation as many times as he or she wishes. To run the example, create a new console project and enter the code as shown.

```
Sub Main()
    Dim sContinue As String = "yes"

    Do While sContinue.Equals("yes")
        Console.Out.WriteLine("Enter the value for i and press <Enter>:")
        Dim i As Integer
        i = CInt(System.Console.In.ReadLine())
        Console.Out.WriteLine("Enter the value for j and press <Enter>:")
        Dim j As Integer
        j = CInt(Console.In.ReadLine())
        Console.Out.WriteLine("The complex math computation yields {0}", i + j)
        Console.Out.WriteLine("")
        Console.Out.WriteLine("Enter 'yes' to continue, anything else to end,")
        Console.Out.WriteLine("then press <Enter>")
        sContinue = Console.In.ReadLine()
        sContinue = sContinue.ToLower()
        sContinue = sContinue.Trim()
    Loop
End Sub
```

You use the String variable sContinue to determine whether the user wants to execute the body of the Do loop one more time. In the actual body of the loop, you get two Integer values from the user, add them, and display the result. Next you ask the user if he or she wants to continue, and store the String answer into the sContinue variable declared outside the loop. You convert the string to lowercase (in case the user typed "YES," for example) and then you call the Trim() method of the string object (which will remove the beginning and trailing whitespace characters, such as spaces and tabs, from the string). When the execution point reaches the Loop keyword (which marks the loop end) the expression following the Do keyword is evaluated. In this case the loop will be executed While the expression sContinue.Equals("yes") is True, while the user enters "yes" at the console. Equals can be thought of as a comparison operator for strings. You will learn more about it when we learn about classes and objects.

If you run the program and enter some numeric values for i and j, and enter "yes" when asked to continue, you will get an output like the one shown in Figure 9.5.

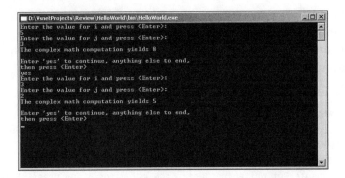

Figure 9.5: *Do loop sample output.*

As you can see from this example the Do loop is different from the For loop. There is no counter variable, no range for the counter, and no Step. The body of the loop will be executed as long as the conditional expression of the loop is evaluated to True. Therefore, a loop like the one in the next bad example will never exit, and it is called an *infinite loop*.

```
Do While True
    ' any statements
Loop
```

Writing a loop like this makes little sense because it is unlikely that you want to execute this loop for the rest of the eternity. You may encounter cases where this approach is used in conjunction with the Exit Do statement (which, similar to the Exit For, allows you to unconditionally leave the loop). The next example illustrates this pattern:

```
Do While True
    ' any statements
    If <condition> Then Exit Do
Loop
```

This can be written better as:

```
Do While Not <condition>
    ' any statements
Loop
```

Or as an alternative form of the Do loop (you will look at this form shortly):

```
Do
    ' any statements
Loop Until <condition>
```

Any of the two alternatives is better because it is clearer what is the condition for which the loop is executed as part of the loop statement, instead of being hidden inside the loop body.

The Do loop can also be written using a slightly different form:

```
Sub Main()
   Dim sContinue As String

   Do
      Console.Out.WriteLine("Enter the value for i and press <Enter>:")
      Dim i As Integer
      i = CInt(Console.In.ReadLine())
      Console.Out.WriteLine("Enter the value for j and press <Enter>:")
      Dim j As Integer
      j = CInt(Console.In.ReadLine())
      Console.Out.WriteLine("The complex math computation yields {0}", i + j)
      Console.Out.WriteLine("")
      Console.Out.WriteLine("Enter 'yes' to continue, anything else to end,")
      Console.Out.WriteLine("then press <Enter>")
      sContinue = Console.In.ReadLine()
      sContinue = sContinue.ToLower()
      sContinue = sContinue.Trim()
   Loop Until Not sContinue.Equals("yes")
End Sub
```

This example is the exact equivalent of the first Do loop example, and will execute with identical results. The difference is that the conditional expression is placed at the bottom, after the Loop keyword. The implication of this placement is that the loop will be executed at least once before the expression will be evaluated. In the first form it is possible that the loop will be executed 0 times because the expression will be evaluated *before* the loop is executed for the first time. If the expression returns false, the loop body will not be executed at all.

You can formally describe the two types of Do loop statements as shown here:

```
Do {While | Until} <conditional-expression>
   <statements>
Loop
```

And:

```
Do
   <statements>
Loop {While | Until} <conditional-expression>
```

The vertical bar between the keywords While and Until, delimited by braces {}, denotes that only one of the two keywords must be present. You will use this notation technique for other statements too.

Now that you know what both `For` and `Do` loops are you can easily show that a `For` loop can always be re-written as a `Do` loop. For example, the `For` loop here (from one of our previous examples):

```
Dim i As Integer, t As Integer
For i = 1 To 31 Step 2
    t += i
Next
Console.Out.WriteLine("The final value of t is {0}", t)
```

can be rewritten as a `Do` loop:

```
Dim i As Integer = 1, t As Integer
Do While i <= 31
    t += i
    i += 1
Loop
Console.Out.WriteLine("The final value of t is {0}", t)
```

The two loops are doing exactly the same thing, but in slightly different ways. In the `Do` loop you need to initialize and increment the counter variable, and the `While` condition becomes that the counter is less than or equal to the end value of the `For` loop. The moral is that if you rely on a counter and have a range of values the counter navigates, use a `For` loop; for all your other needs use a `Do` loop.

The `While` Loop

The `While` loop is a less used variation of the `Do` loop, and was maintained in the language mostly for historical reasons (in our opinion). It is totally superseded in functionality by the `Do` loop. We will present it for completeness, but recommend that you do not use it.

The formal syntax is

```
While <conditional-expression>
    <statements>
End While
```

The last example could be re-written using a `While` loop as shown:

```
Dim i As Integer = 1, t As Integer
While i <= 31
    t += i
    i += 1
End While
Console.Out.WriteLine("The final value of t is {0}", t)
```

As you can see it is virtually identical to the `Do` loop, except for the lack of the `Do` keyword and the use of `End While` as loop terminator.

Another important thing to remember is that the While loops cannot be exited using an Exit Do statement. There is no equivalent Exit While. This means an infinite While loop cannot be exited, short of interrupting the program in some fashion. You will learn about this later on in the book.

What's Next

In this chapter you have learned the fundamental control statements in Visual Basic. These statements allow you to control the execution flow or your program, and make decisions on what parts of the program are executed in what conditions and/or how many times. You have seen that the control statements can be classified further in branching statements (like the If and Select Case statements) and loop statements (like For, Do and While).

In the next chapter you will learn how to structure your program into smaller pieces, known as subroutines, procedures, and functions. You will also learn why this is important and see a few examples of writing and using procedures and functions and passing parameters.

NOTE

The answers to Reviewing It, Checking It, and Applying It are available on our Web site.

REVIEW

Reviewing It

This section presents a review of the key concepts in this chapter. These questions are intended to gauge your absorption of the relevant material.

1. What are the differences and similarities between branching and loop statements?

2. What is the syntax of the If statement?

3. What is a For loop?

4. What is a Do loop?

5. What are the differences between the For and Do loops?

CHECK

Checking It

Select the correct answer to the following questions.

Multiple Choice

1. The *type* of the expression of an If statement is:

   a. Numeric.

   b. Logical.

   c. True or False.

   d. Depends upon the programmer.

2. Given an If statement without an Else part, what happens if the If expression is False?

   a. The statements inside the If are not executed.

   b. The statements inside the If are executed.

   c. An exception is thrown and the program ends.

   d. Both b and c.

3. The type of the expression of a Select statement must be:

   a. Numeric.

   b. String.

   c. Anything.

   d. Numeric or String.

4. When does a For loop end (according to what you've learned so far)?

   a. After a number of iterations equal to the difference between the upper bound and the lower bound.

   b. When the counter value is $\geq$ the upper bound (for incrementing loops) or is $\leq$ lower bound (for decrementing loops).

   c. When an Exit For statement is encountered.

   d. When the Next statement is encountered.

5. Can you modify the value of the counter variable inside a For loop? For example, assuming i is the counter variable can you execute the statement i += 1 inside the loop?

   a. Yes.

   b. No.

   c. Yes, but it will affect the loop (number of iterations).

   d. Yes, but it has no effect on the loop (it will be reset when Next is encountered).

6. A Do loop will be executed at least once if:

   a. The Do While ... Loop format is used.

   b. The Do Until ... Loop format is used.

   c. The Do ... Loop While format is used.

   d. The Do ... Loop Until format is used.

7. The loop counter in a Do loop is incremented:

   a. Automatically.

   b. Manually.

   c. In the Do expression.

   d. There is no loop counter in a Do loop.

8. How many times would the following loop be executed?
   `For i = 10 To 0 Step -3`

   a. 3.

   b. 4.

   c. 9.

   d. 10.

True or False

1. An If statement can have exactly one of each: If, ElseIf, and Else parts.

   True/False

2. Else is for If as Case Else is for Select Case.

   True/False

3. The Select Case is by far more efficient (in terms of performance) than an If statement with many ElseIf branches.

   True/False

4. A For loop can be executed 0 times.

   True/False

5. A Do loop can be executed 0 times regardless of the Do format used.

   True/False

6. It is better to use an Exit Do and Exit For to exit a loop than to specify a clear loop termination condition.

   True/False

APPLY

Applying It

Try to complete the following exercises by yourself.

Independent Exercise 1

Write a program to calculate the factorial of all numbers supplied by the user. (The factorial of an integer n is the product of all numbers between 1 and n: 1*2*3*...*n). The program should work as follows:

1. Ask the user to enter a number n between 1 and 20, or 0 to exit the program.

2. Validate n, if 0 exit program, if invalid display error message and go back to step 1.

3. Calculate the factorial of n.

4. Display n.

5. Go back to Step 1.

Note that factorials grow *very* fast, so limit the number to 20 or less to avoid arithmetic overflow errors. You will need a Long or larger type to hold the factorial value.

Independent Exercise 2

Create a program that counts the number of spaces in a string entered by the user. Note: you can use a property of the String type called Chars(index) to get the character in a string at a given position.

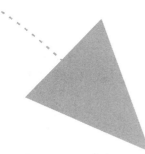

Subroutines and Functions

In this chapter you will learn about ways to structure your programs in a better way. You will study Visual Basic subroutines and functions, which are known generically as procedures. The chapter will be divided in the following categories:

- Introduction to structured programming
- Subroutines
- Functions
- Scope and lifetime

All the programs you have written so far used the same pattern: you have a module (`Module1`) created by default, and this module has a `Sub Main`, in which your code resides. When the `End Sub` is reached, the program ends. As you probably imagined, these were just simple examples to illustrate the introductory concepts of the language. A real-world program would contain much more code than the few lines in these examples. That code could not fit in the `Sub Main` that you used so far, and even if it did, it would be hard to read, understand, and modify. That was the reason that programmers and language architects have introduced the concept of splitting programs into smaller units called procedures. Each procedure works like a small standalone program, accepting input and producing output. As you will see in the rest of this chapter, this input and output can have different sources.

Each language has its own name or names for procedures. In Visual Basic there are two types of procedures, called *subroutines* and *functions*. They are almost identical except for the name and the fact that functions return a value (like a mathematical function does, for example *sin(x)*), while subroutines do not return any value. We will explain shortly what this means through the use of a few examples.

In the last part of this chapter, you will learn a few things about passing parameters to subroutines and functions, as well as rules regarding the scope of subroutines and functions within modules, and scope and lifetime of variables within subroutines and functions. You will also learn about constants and variables declared at module-level.

Introduction to Structured Programming

As you have seen in the previous chapters, a software program consists of a sequence of statements that the computer executes. There is a start point (the first statement that will be executed) and an end point (the last statement of the program). In the Visual Basic examples you have seen so far, the start point is the Sub Main statement and the end point is the End Sub statement. The statements between the start and end points are executed sequentially. The currently executing statement is known as the *current statement* or the *execution point*. You have seen that there are statements that allow you to control which statements are executed (the branching statements, like If and Select Case) and statements that allow you to repeat some statements a number of times (the loop statements, like For and Do). These statements are, in effect, controlling the execution flow of the program by determining which statement gets to be executed next based on some specific criteria that you supply.

There are cases when a program must be split into smaller units, called *procedures*, which execute a specific task. The reasons to split a program are that a program could become too large to understand and, most importantly, there may be parts of a program that do the same (or a very similar) task, over and over. If you have a procedure that is able to execute a specific task, you could call this procedure every time that task needs to be executed. The alternative would be to write the code for that task in every place in your main program where this task needs to be executed. Let's take an example to illustrate better what we have described so far.

```
Module Module1
    Sub Main()
        Dim vals() As Integer = {1, 2, 3, 4, 5, 6, 7, 8, 9, 10}

        Console.Out.WriteLine("Enter the start index and press <Enter>:")
        Dim index As Integer
        index = CInt(Console.In.ReadLine())

        If index < 0 Or 9 <= index Then
            Console.Out.WriteLine("Invalid index, must be between 0 and 9")
            Console.Out.WriteLine("Press the <Enter> key to end the program")
            Console.In.ReadLine()
```

```
        End
    End If

Dim i As Integer, total As Integer
For i = index To 9
    total += vals(i)
    Console.Out.WriteLine("The total value is {0} at i = {1}", total, i)
Next
Console.Out.WriteLine("The final total value is {0}", total)

Console.Out.WriteLine("Press the <Enter> key to end the program")
Console.In.ReadLine()
End Sub

End Module
```

This is the example used to illustrate a For loop. The lines in bold in the previous example are identical; they perform the same task (prevent the console window from closing—wait for the user to press Enter). You have to type the same identical code twice. And if you would like to change this piece of code, you have to change it in every location that you typed it in the first place. That is not only a waste of time, but it is also error-prone.

NOTE

It is actually one of the major causes of errors in any real system. The technique of duplicating portions of code in different places in the program (with eventually slight modifications) is known as the *copy-paste* technique. The most common error related to the copy-paste technique is to modify the code in a few places and forget to change it in other places.

There is a better way to deal with this issue: define a procedure that executes the task that you need to repeat, and call this procedure from the main program any time the task needs to be executed. Consider the following improved example.

```
Module Module1

Sub Main()
    Dim vals() As Integer = {1, 2, 3, 4, 5, 6, 7, 8, 9, 10}

    Console.Out.WriteLine("Enter the start index and press <Enter>:")
    Dim index As Integer
    index = CInt(Console.In.ReadLine())

    If index < 0 Or 9 <= index Then
        Console.Out.WriteLine("Invalid index, must be between 0 and 9")
        WaitForEnter()
```

```
        End
    End If

    Dim i As Integer, total As Integer
    For i = index To 9
        total += vals(i)
        Console.Out.WriteLine("The total value is {0} at i = {1}", total, i)
    Next
    Console.Out.WriteLine("The final total value is {0}", total)
    WaitForEnter()
End Sub

Sub WaitForEnter()
    Console.Out.WriteLine("Press the <Enter> key to end the program")
    Console.In.ReadLine()
End Sub

End Module
```

In this example we have moved the repetitive code into a new procedure (named WaitForEnter), and then in the main program we replaced the code with a call to this procedure. Let's do an in-depth analysis of this.

The first step was to create a new procedure named WaitForEnter. This procedure is known in Visual Basic as a *subroutine*, or a *sub*. Sometimes the term procedure is used to mean a sub, although it is incorrect. A procedure can also be a function.

A sub is nothing more than a small program in itself. You can give it any name you choose (as long as you remember that it is a language identifier, and stick to the rules for identifiers). It is quite common to give it a meaningful name related to what it does, so that you can remember easily what task the subroutine is solving. The subroutine is very similar to the Sub Main, except for the different name. It uses the keyword Sub followed by its name and a set of parentheses () to mark its start point, and the keywords End Sub to mark its end.

The *body* of the subroutine is the code between the Sub declaration and the End Sub. This code will be executed when this subroutine is called, in the same manner as the code in the Sub Main: starting with the first statement following the Sub declaration line, and continuing up to the end point, which is the End Sub. You can write any code you want in the body of the subroutine, following the same rules as you did for the Sub Main. In particular you can declare variables, use control statements, and so on.

The next step was to *call* or *invoke* the subroutine from the points in Sub Main where the replaced code was. This is done by simply placing the name of the subroutine, followed by parentheses, where the replaced code was. This will tell the compiler that when it reaches this line of code, it should invoke the subroutine. That is, the execution point will move to the first executable statement inside the called subroutine, in this case the Console.Out.WriteLine statement.

NOTE

An *executable statement* is a statement that does something at runtime. A comment is not an executable statement.

The compiler will then execute the rest of the subroutine and output the "Press the <Enter> key to end the program" string to the console, and then wait for the user to press Enter. As soon as the code in the subroutine has finished executing, the execution point will return to the next statement in the main program, which follows the call to the subroutine. This will be either the End statement or the End Sub statement, depending from where the subroutine was called in the first place.

This subroutine is part of the module Module1, as the Sub Main is. To better organize the procedures in a program, Visual Basic groups them in modules. A *module* is a collection of procedures as well as type declarations (as you have seen for enumerations and structures) and some other things that you will see later on. A Visual Basic project can have many modules, and each module can contain many procedures.

The code in a procedure also can call other procedures, either the ones you defined, or system-defined procedures. And indeed, if you look at the code in your Sub WaitForEnter you will notice that you call two system defined subroutines: Console.Out.WriteLine() and Console.In.ReadLine(). These are special forms of procedures defined by the programmers from Microsoft who built the .NET Framework. In effect, an executing (running) program is a stack of procedures that call one another to resolve different tasks. The first one in the stack is the one called the Sub Main, which can call other procedures to do some work, and these others can in turn call others, and so on.

This is in brief what structured programming is about. We will have much more to say about it in the next sections of this chapter.

Subroutines

As you have seen, a subroutine is a language construct that allows you to split a large task into smaller pieces. In the previous example, you implemented a subroutine that does the same thing every time it is called: outputs the same string to the console, and then waits until the user presses Enter. This case is rarely useful. There are many cases when you would like the subroutine to do the same operation, but on different data. In this example, we would like to output a different string when the user has entered an incorrect value and the program will terminate abnormally, and a success message when the task of summing the array elements is successful. This is achievable through the use of subroutines with arguments, as illustrated in the next example.

```
Module Module1

    Sub Main()
        Dim vals() As Integer = {1, 2, 3, 4, 5, 6, 7, 8, 9, 10}

        Console.Out.WriteLine("Enter the start index and press <Enter>:")
        Dim index As Integer
        index = CInt(Console.In.ReadLine())

        If index < 0 Or 9 <= index Then
            WaitForEnter("Invalid index, must be between 0 and 9")
            End
        End If

        Dim i As Integer, total As Integer
        For i = index To 9
            total += vals(i)
            Console.Out.WriteLine("The total value is {0} at i = {1}", _
                                  total, i)
        Next
        WaitForEnter("The final total value is " & CStr(total))
    End Sub

    Sub WaitForEnter(ByVal message As String)
        Console.Out.WriteLine(message)
        Console.Out.WriteLine("Press the <Enter> key to end the program")
        Console.In.ReadLine()
    End Sub

End Module
```

You have modified the `Sub WaitForEnter` to accept an *argument.* An argument is a variable that is declared on the subroutine declaration line, and which will have its value allocated by the caller of this subroutine. In your case the argument is named `message` and it is of type `String` (like any other variable it must have a type). The keyword `ByVal` in front of the variable name indicates how is the value passed—we will return to this shortly. The *caller* of the subroutine is said to be the subroutine that invoked this one (`Sub Main` here).

Inside the subroutine you can use the argument (sometimes called *formal argument*) as you would use any normal variable. In your case you will output it to the console, using the `Console.Out.WriteLine()`.

The definition of your subroutine now includes one argument of type String. This definition is called the *signature* of the subroutine, and tells the potential callers *how* this subroutine should be called. Because you have an argument of type String, the caller must provide a value for this argument whenever it makes the subroutine call. You have modified the calls to the subroutine `WaitForEnter` to provide the String value required. In one case you supply the String `"Invalid index, must be between 0 and 9"`, to let the user know what went wrong. In the other case you use a String expression resulted by concatenating the literal String `"The final total value is "` with the value of the `total` variable converted to String. At runtime the compiler will take the value and, when starting the subroutine `WaitForEnter`, will pass it as the value of the argument `message`. The values passed to a subroutine are known as *parameter values*, or in short *parameters*.

NOTE

The terms *argument* and *parameter* are often interchangeably used in programming literature to mean the same thing, argument in some cases, parameter in others. We are trying to keep it consistent in this book. In real life be prepared to make the distinction based on the context.

Next you will look at subroutines with more than one argument and at how parameters are passed to subroutines.

Multiple Arguments and `ByVal` versus `ByRef`

You have seen how to define a subroutine with one argument. In many cases you will find that you need to pass two or more values to a subroutine.

The *argument list* of a subroutine is defined as the sequence of arguments between the ((open parenthesis) and) (close parenthesis) that follow the name of a subroutine. You can have more than one argument in the list of arguments by simply separating the arguments with commas. This is very similar to the syntax used in the Dim statement. For example, if you need to define a subroutine that requires three arguments you would write something like

```
Sub MyProcedure(ByVal count As Integer, ByVal name As String, ByVal dob As Date)
…
End Sub
```

The three arguments defined would require the subroutine call to look something like this:

```
MyProcedure(6, "Joe", #02/02/2002#)
```

We have used the keyword ByVal (standing for *By Value*) so far to indicate to the compiler a certain way of handling the values passed to the subroutine. The alternative is known as ByRef (standing for *By Reference*). As the name suggests in the first case, ByVal, the compiler will pass the value of the variable. That is, it will make a copy of the variable, and pass the copy to the subroutine. The subroutine may change the value, but when the subroutine exits the original value of the variable will be unchanged. Consider the following example:

```
Module Module1

  Sub Main()
    Console.Out.WriteLine("Enter a value for i and press <Enter>:")
    Dim i As Integer
    i = CInt(Console.In.ReadLine())

    Console.Out.WriteLine("Enter a value for j and press <Enter>:")
    Dim j As Integer
    j = CInt(Console.In.ReadLine())

    Console.Out.WriteLine("In Main before calling Add. j is {0}", j)
    Add(i, j)
    Console.Out.WriteLine("In Main after calling  Add. j is {0}", j)
    WaitForEnter("The final value of j is " & CStr(j))
  End Sub

  Sub Add(ByVal i As Integer, ByVal j As Integer)
    Console.Out.WriteLine("In Add before addition. j is {0}", j)
    j += i
    Console.Out.WriteLine("In Add after addition. j is {0}", j)
  End Sub
```

```
Sub WaitForEnter(ByVal message As String)
    Console.Out.WriteLine(message)
    Console.Out.WriteLine("Press the <Enter> key to end the program")
    Console.In.ReadLine()
End Sub
```

```
End Module
```

You are declaring two integers i and j, which you initialize with the values entered by the user. You also have defined the subroutine Add, which takes two arguments, both by value. The subroutine will add the value of the first argument to the second argument. You also have a set of "trace calls" (output values of some expression to the console) to view the value of j at different points in the program. If you execute the program, and enter the values 1 and 2 for i and j, respectively, the output of the program will look like the one in Figure 10.1.

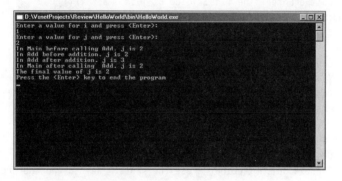

Figure 10.1: Sample output for ByVal.

You will notice that the value of j is changed to 3 in the Add subroutine, after the addition of i took place. However, when you return in Main, the value of j is back to 2! The reason for this apparently strange behavior is that the variable j in the Main and the argument j in Add are different entities; they refer to two different values in memory (they are at different memory locations). Changing one will not affect the other. The compiler made a copy of the value of the variable j from Main and assigned the value to the argument j when the Add subroutine was called. But, when the subroutine Add ended, the changed value of the argument j in Add was not stored back into the variable j. Actually, as you will see shortly, the compiler never does this.

If you intended to have the Add subroutine behave such that the value of the argument j reflects, upon return, the sum of itself and i, you need to rewrite your code using the ByRef keyword in front of j. Make this one change and run the example again.

```
Module Module1

    Sub Main()
        Console.Out.WriteLine("Enter a value for i and press <Enter>:")
        Dim i As Integer
        i = CInt(Console.In.ReadLine())

        Console.Out.WriteLine("Enter a value for j and press <Enter>:")
        Dim j As Integer
        j = CInt(Console.In.ReadLine())

        Console.Out.WriteLine("In Main before calling Add. j is {0}", j)
        Add(i, j)
        Console.Out.WriteLine("In Main after calling  Add. j is {0}", j)
        WaitForEnter("The final value of j is " & CStr(j))
    End Sub

    Sub Add(ByVal i As Integer, ByRef j As Integer)
        Console.Out.WriteLine("In Add before addition. j is {0}", j)
        j += i
        Console.Out.WriteLine("In Add after addition. j is {0}", j)
    End Sub

    Sub WaitForEnter(ByVal message As String)
        Console.Out.WriteLine(message)
        Console.Out.WriteLine("Press the <Enter> key to end the program")
        Console.In.ReadLine()
    End Sub

End Module
```

Now the output of the program (shown in Figure 10.2) shows the variable j with a value of 3, after the call to Add.

The reason is that the compiler now handles j differently. It will not make a copy of variable j value and assign it to the argument j of the subroutine Add. Rather it will have both the variable and the argument *refer to the same memory location* (hence the ByRef keyword). Modifying the argument j of the subroutine, you actually are changing also the value of the variable j in the Main. It is very important to understand this behavior correctly because it can have nasty side effects. This difference is similar to the difference you have seen for variable assignment by value and by reference.

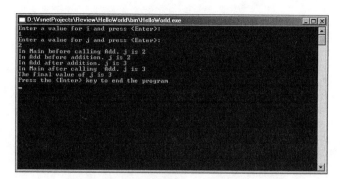

Figure 10.2: *Sample output for* `ByRef`.

We recommend that you use the `ByVal` method of passing values as much as possible; use `ByRef` only when the subroutine does actually modify the value.

NOTE

We have used in the previous example the same identifier (`j`) for both the variable in `Main` and the argument in the `Add` subroutine. This was done for the purpose of illustrating `ByRef` versus `ByVal` behavior. Normally we recommend that you use more meaningful names for arguments.

Next you will look at a special form of procedures called functions.

Functions

You have seen examples of Visual Basic built-in functions when you learned about conversion between different data types. We have used these functions in some of the examples you have seen since then. A function is a subroutine that returns a value. The syntax is slightly different but the functionality is identical. The difference is that it returns a value. Let's modify your last example to transform the `Add` subroutine into a function.

```
Module Module1

    Sub Main()
        Console.Out.WriteLine("Enter a value for i and press <Enter>:")
        Dim i As Integer
        i = CInt(Console.In.ReadLine())

        Console.Out.WriteLine("Enter a value for j and press <Enter>:")
        Dim j As Integer
        j = CInt(Console.In.ReadLine())
```

```
    Dim sum As Integer
    sum = Add(i, j)
    WaitForEnter("The value of i + j is " & CStr(sum))
End Sub

Function Add(ByVal i As Integer, ByVal j As Integer) As Integer
    ' Add i to j and return the result
    Return j + i
End Function

Sub WaitForEnter(ByVal message As String)
    Console.Out.WriteLine(message)
    Console.Out.WriteLine("Press the <Enter> key to end the program")
    Console.In.ReadLine()
End Sub
```

End Module

The first thing you have to do is change the keywords from Sub and End Sub to Function and End Function. The argument list is identical in syntax as the one used for subroutines. However, after the closing parenthesis of the argument list you notice the type declaration As Integer. This is the data type of the return value of the function, also known as the *function return type*, or in short *return type*. The return is one of the regular data types, and it is used by the compiler to ensure the function is used properly. For example in an expression it will ensure that the proper conversions are executed, or in an assignment that the variable is of the appropriate type.

The body of the function is similar to the body of a subroutine, with one exception: it must return a value of the type indicated in the declaration line (the first line). In our example this must be an Integer value. This is achieved using the Return statement. The value of the expression following the Return keyword is what the function will return. In your case, this is going to be the result of adding i to j. The Return statement does not have to be the last statement in a function, as you will see shortly.

The way a function is used is identical to the way the system or built-in functions are used: in an expression, or as part of an assignment (the way you used it). You assigned the return value of the function to the variable sum and then you output this variable to the console, to ensure the result is what you expected.

As a twist on this example let's assume that you are required to make the function return a positive value or 0, if the sum of i and j is negative. The modified example is shown here.

```
Module Module1

    Sub Main()
        Console.Out.WriteLine("Enter a value for i and press <Enter>:")
        Dim i As Integer
        i = CInt(Console.In.ReadLine())

        Console.Out.WriteLine("Enter a value for j and press <Enter>:")
        Dim j As Integer
        j = CInt(Console.In.ReadLine())

        Dim sum As Integer
        sum = Add(i, j)
        WaitForEnter("The value of i + j is " & CStr(sum))
    End Sub

    Function Add(ByVal i As Integer, ByVal j As Integer) As Integer
        Dim sum As Integer
        sum = i + j

        ' if sum is negative return 0
        If sum < 0 Then
            Return 0
        End If

        ' Otherwise return the sum
        Return sum
    End Function

    Sub WaitForEnter(ByVal message As String)
        Console.Out.WriteLine(message)
        Console.Out.WriteLine("Press the <Enter> key to end the program")
        Console.In.ReadLine()
    End Sub

End Module
```

You have modified the body of the Add function to illustrate a few important points. The first is that you can have variable declarations in a function (and in subroutines). You are declaring the sum variable to be of type Integer. This variable is not related in any way with the variable with the same name in Main. This is a very important fact that you need to remember: variables declared in a function or subroutine are *local* to that function or subroutine. You will learn more on this subject in the remainder of this chapter.

Next you test to see if the sum variable is negative, and if it is you use the Return statement to exit the function and return 0. This is meant to illustrate that when a Return statement is encountered, the function body is exited, and the value after the Return becomes the function return value.

Older versions of Visual Basic are using a different syntax for returning a value from a function. Namely the return value is assigned to the pseudo-variable that is the function name itself, as in the following example:

```
Function Add(ByVal i As Integer, ByVal j As Integer) As Integer
    Dim sum As Integer
    sum = i + j

    ' if sum is negative return 0
    If sum < 0 Then
        Add = 0
        Exit Function
    End If

    ' Otherwise return the sum
    Add = sum
End Function
```

We find this notation harder to read, and less intuitive, and therefore we do not recommend it. Another reason not to use it is that there is a possibility that Microsoft will render this syntax obsolete at some point in the future.

The Return statement can be used also in subroutines, to exit before reaching the end of the subroutine. In this case there is no return value specified. An example follows:

```
Sub WriteMessage(ByVal messages() As String, ByVal index As Integer)
    If index < 0 Or messages.Length() <= index Then Return
    Console.Out.WriteLine(messages(index))
End Sub
```

This example shows a subroutine that will output a message from an array of string messages, at a specified index. If the index value passed in is invalid (that is, less than 0 or greater than or equal to the length of the array), the code simply returns without doing anything. This is achieved by calling Return in conjunction with a single-line If statement.

The example also illustrates how to declare an argument of an array type, and how to use it (like any other array variable) inside the body of the subroutine.

Scope and Lifetime

The *scope* of a variable is the part or parts of the program in which a variable can be accessed by code. It is also known as the *visibility* of the variable. When we say that a variable *is visible* in a specific procedure, for example, we say that the code in that procedure can access the variable. We can also say the *scope* of the variable is that procedure—and mean the same thing. We are going to use both terms in the rest of this book.

Normally the scope of any variable declared with Dim inside a subroutine or function is from the line following its declaration, up to the end of the subroutine or function. These variables are known as *local* variables. However, the scope is not extended to the code before the declaration (Dim) line. For example:

```
Sub Main()
    ' code before the declaration cannot use i
    Dim i As Integer = 0
    i = 5
    …
    ' any code after the declaration can access i
End Sub
```

If you had a line of code before the Dim statement that would refer to i, it would be a syntax error. Visual Studio and the compiler are happy to point this out to you. Most of the time an Unknown variable *<yourVariableNameHere>* error would occur. Also the variable i cannot be accessed by code that is outside the Sub Main where it is declared.

This is one more reason to keep the variable declarations close to the point where they are used. In this way, they cannot be inadvertently modified, therefore reducing the risk of errors.

You cannot have two variables with the same name declared in the same scope. The reason is quite simple: the compiler would not know which one to use.

A variable can be declared also within a smaller scope than the whole subroutine. For example if it is declared in a block statement like an If, For, Do, or similar, the scope is limited to the block statement. For example, next we show code declaring and using an Integer j inside a For loop.

```
Sub Main()
    Dim i As Integer
    For i = 0 To 9
```

```
      Dim j As Integer
      j = j + i
   Next
   ' j cannot be accessed here
End Sub
```

If the code outside the loop tries to access the variable, a syntax error is fired, and the program will not compile.

The *lifetime* of a variable is the period of time between the moment it is declared and initialized and the moment the variable is discarded. It is in effect the period of time the variable has a memory location allocated to it. For most local variables, the lifetime is the period between their declaration and the end of the procedure. In this example, the variable i has a lifetime that spans from the moment it is declared up to the end of the Main subroutine. The lifetime of i is the time while the Sub Main executes.

In the previous example, the scope of the variable j is the For loop in which it is declared. However, the lifetime of j is (same as in the case of i) the duration of the Main subroutine. You can test that this is the case if you display the value of j at each iteration of the loop, you will find out that is every time incremented by i. Which means that the value of j is preserved between loop iterations; it is not reinitialized with 0.

If you would like j to be 0 every time a loop iteration is starting) you need to write the code differently:

```
Sub Main()
   Dim i As Integer
   For i = 0 To 9
      Dim j As Integer = 0
      j = j + i
   Next
   ' j cannot be accessed here
End Sub
```

This modification (adding = 0 to the declaration of j) will ensure the value of j is set to 0 for each iteration of the loop.

In short, if a variable is declared inside a block statement that is inside a subroutine or function, the compiler will allocate memory for it when the subroutine or function is entered (and not every time the loop is executed, as it may appear). That memory will not be initialized until the block statement where the variable is declared is entered. If an explicit initialization is provided, this will be executed every time the block statement (loop) is executed. Do not worry if this seems complicated. Your code will be all right if you declare variables at the subroutine level and not inside loops.

Module Level Variables and Constants

So far you have seen variables declared inside subroutines and functions. However, there are cases when a variable must be accessed by more than one subroutine or function in a given module. This is especially the case with constant values. A *constant value* (abbreviated as *constant*) is a special type of variable that is declared and initialized, but which cannot be modified after this declaration. Constants are useful to represent values that do not change during the execution of the program. For example, a program that would deal with trigonometric calculations will use the value π a lot. Instead of using the numeric approximate value 3.141592 in every expression that use π, a smart programmer would define a constant value for it, and use that value in the whole program. The declaration must be placed at module level:

```
Module Module1
    Public Const PI As Double = 3.141592
    Sub Main()
        ' any code can use PI
    End Sub
End Module
```

A constant declared like this is visible to the whole project (and in some cases to other projects as well, as you will see). The lifetime of module level constants and variables is the whole duration of the program execution.

The names and types of variables and constants declared at module level also appear in the class view of the module. In the Solution Explorer, open the tab labeled Class View and expand the tree until you see the contents of the module.

The `Dim` statement was replaced by the keyword `Const` and the qualifier `Public`, which is also a reserved keyword. `Const` means the value of the variable is constant and cannot be changed. `Public` means that the visibility of the constant is set to be the whole project. It is okay to have a few widely used constants declared as public constants, although you should try to limit this number. The qualifier `Public` allows you to define constants and variables that are visible to code in the whole program, regardless of what module or class the code is in.

NOTE

Although it is okay to have public constants, it is highly recommended that you do not use public variables. There are many reasons for this; one of the most important is that it makes it very hard to write modular code (because a public variable can be modified anywhere in the program).

If a constant is only accessed by procedures from this module, it is better to declare it as `Private`, as in the next example:

```
Module Module1
    Private Const PI As Double = 3.141592
    Private outputBuffer As String
    Sub Main()
        ' only code in this module can use PI
        ' code in this module can use and
        ' modify outputBuffer
    End Sub
End Module
```

The qualifier `Private` allows you to define constants and variables that are visible in any subroutine or function in this module. Private constants are very useful, but there is little use for private variables in modules. They can be easily replaced by other means, as you will see when you learn about classes and objects. There are some cases in which you may want to use one. The syntax of the declaration is the same as for the `Dim` statement, with the exception that it is done outside any subroutine or function. A module-level variable (as they are called) can be accessed and modified in any subroutine and function in the module, and this can cause issues when writing multi-threaded code. You will learn more about this issue when you study classes and objects in Part III, "Working with Objects."

What happens if you have a subroutine that declares a variable with the same name as a module-level variable? For example, if you have code like this:

```
Module Module1
    Private Const PI As Double = 3.141592
    Sub Main()
        Console.Out.WriteLine(PI)
        Dim PI As String = "Joe"
        Console.Out.WriteLine(PI)
    End Sub
End Module
```

What is the output of this program going to be? The first output statement will see the constant `Double` variable `PI`, and will output its value (`3.141592`). The second output statement is placed after the declaration of a local variable with the same name, but of different type. Its output will be the value of this local variable. This means that the local variable PI takes precedence over (or *shadows*) the module-level constant PI. This example illustrates variable shadowing, but not good coding practice. We strongly discourage using the same name for module-level and local variables and constants. In addition we suggest that you use meaningful names for module-level variables. The rule of thumb is that the wider the scope of the variable, the more descriptive the name should be. For a local variable used as a loop counter for a two-line loop i is sufficient—you can see the whole scope of the variable on one screen. For a module-level a meaningful name in combined case (like outputBuffer, overdrawProtectionEnabled, and so on) should be used. It is also common practice to start the names of module (and class) variables with the prefix "m_", which can avoid naming conflicts. We will expand on this issue in the chapters on classes and class fields.

One more point: the Const keyword can be used to declare constant values local to a subroutine or function. In this case the qualifiers Public and Private cannot be used. For example:

```
Module Module1
    Sub Main()
        Const PI As Double = 3.141592
        ' only code in this sub can use PI
    End Sub
End Module
```

Argument Visibility and Lifetime

The same rules that apply to variables and constants apply to the arguments to subroutines and functions. An argument is visible in the procedure in which it is declared, and its lifetime is the same as the lifetime of the procedure. The compiler will allocate the memory for it when the procedure starts and will de-allocate the memory when the procedure finishes execution. This applies to arguments that are passed by value.

In the case of the arguments that are passed by reference, the actual value will exist as long as the caller of the procedure has a variable that refers to it, potentially long after the procedure has finished execution.

It is important to remember that there is a relationship between the type of the argument (by value or by reference) and the effect of the ByVal and ByRef argument modifier. If the argument data type is of by-value type, either ByVal or ByRef can be used and they will have the expected behavior. However, in the case of data types that are by-reference, the ByVal modifier has no influence whatsoever. They will always be treated by value. Consider the following example:

```
Module Module1
    Structure Test
        Public x As Double
    End Structure
```

```
Sub Main()
   Dim o As Test
   o.x = 4
   TestS(o)
   Console.Out.WriteLine(o.x)

   Dim a() As Integer = {1, 2, 3}
   TestA(a)
   Console.Out.WriteLine(a(2))
End Sub

Sub TestS(ByRef o As Test)
   o.x = 6
End Sub

Sub TestA(ByVal a() As Integer)
   a(2) = 7
End Sub

End Module
```

Structures use by-value semantics; therefore the ByVal versus ByRef modifier for the argument of the TestS subroutine makes a difference. The o.x will remain 6 after the function returns because the parameter modifier is ByRef. If the parameter modifier is ByVal then o.x would remain 4 after the function returns.

In the case of the TestA subroutine the modifier ByVal makes no difference whatsoever. Regardless of whether it is ByVal or ByRef, the array element is always changed in the original array, as declared in Main. The reason for this is that the arrays use by-reference semantics.

Optional Arguments

There are cases when a subroutine or function can be called in some instances with a value and sometimes without that value. For example, assume you would like to write a function to copy part of a given array of integers into a new array and return this new array. The function will have as arguments the original (source) array, the position in this array where to start copying elements, and the end position. However, you would like to be able to not specify the end position, and then it should default to the end of the array. Here is the finished example:

```
Module Module1

   Sub Main()
      Dim a() As Integer = {1, 2, 3, 4, 5, 6, 7, 8, 9, 10}
```

```
        Dim c() As Integer = CopyArray(a, 4)
        Dim d() As Integer = CopyArray(a, 4, 9)
        ' c and d are now identical clones of elements 4-9 of a
    End Sub


    ' This function will make a copy of the elements from
    ' the array of Integers a() passed in, starting at
    ' startAt position, up to endAt position
    ' If endAt is not specified, will copy to the end of the array
    Function CopyArray(ByRef a() As Integer, _
                    ByVal startAt As Integer, _
                    Optional ByVal endAt As Integer = -1) As Integer()
        If endAt < 0 Then
            endAt = a.Length() - 1
        End If


        ' Determine the size of the new array
        Dim n As Integer
        n = endAt - startAt + 1
        If n <= 0 Then
            Return Nothing
        End If


        ' Create the new array
        Dim cpy() As Integer = New Integer(n) {}


        ' Copy elements from a to the cloned array cpy()
        Dim i As Integer
        For i = 0 To n - 1
            cpy(i) = a(startAt + i)
        Next


        Return cpy
    End Function


End Module
```

The first thing to notice is that we have split the function declaration on multiple lines (using the underscore _) and arranged it nicely.

The next thing to notice is that we have a function that will return an array; the syntax used is similar to the one used to declare arrays. No size or dimensions are required for the array, and should not be used. (It is a syntax error to use size or dimensions).

The third argument of the function is preceded by the specifier Optional, which indicates that the value may be specified or not when the function is called. You need to provide a default value for the argument—this is the value that the argument will have if no other value is specified. We have chosen –1; this is also an invalid value, therefore it is easy to determine in the function body if a value was supplied for the argument or not.

The logic of the function is simple. First determine if the optional argument endAt has a valid value. If not, set its value to be the last element of the array (which is the length of the array minus 1). Then you determine the number of elements to copy in the new array (its size), and allocate it using the syntax that you have seen in the previous chapters.

Finally you use a For loop to copy each element from position startAt + i of the source array a into the cloned array cpy at position i. You then return the cpy array as the return value of the function.

In Main you create a source array a, and initialize its elements. Then you call the CopyArray function twice, once specifying the optional argument, once not specifying it, to illustrate that your code works.

We leave it as an exercise for you to add trace statements to ensure the results are correct.

There are a few rules involving optional arguments:

- If you have only one optional argument, it must be the last argument in the list.

- If you have more than one optional argument, all the arguments after the first optional argument must also be optional. Optional arguments are always grouped at the end of the argument list.

- A default value must be specified for all optional arguments.

- There are some restrictions on what the optional argument types can be (for example, structures cannot be used as optional arguments). You will learn a few more in the next few chapters.

The optional arguments can be useful if used within reason. It makes little sense to have more than one, at most two optional arguments. If you do, maybe you want to consider creating two or more specialized subroutines or functions, since the usage is so varied. As a rule you are trying to avoid using them—it makes code harder to read and understand, and it may cause problems with maintenance.

Visibility of Procedures and Functions

The Public and Private modifiers also can be applied to subroutines and functions, with similar effects as for the module-level variables and constants. A public procedure is visible outside the module—that means that anyone who can see the module can call that procedure. In contrast the private subroutines and functions can only be called from the module in which they were declared. By default subroutines and functions in modules are Public. The following example illustrates this.

```
Module Module1

   Sub Main()
      ' code
   End Sub

   Public Sub PublicSub()
      ' can be called from other modules
   End Sub

   Private Sub PrivateSub()
      ' cant be called from other modules
   End Sub

End Module
```

If you had a second module in this project, and a subroutine in that module, you could call the PublicSub() but not the PrivateSub(). If the PublicSub() would be declared without the keyword Public you still could call it from the other module.

You will learn more about subroutine and function visibility when you learn about classes and objects.

What's Next

This chapter covered a lot of ground in the fundamental principles of structured programming. You will continue your study with exception handling in Visual Basic .NET and learn how this affects your programming style.

You will also learn the fundamental concepts of debugging using the Visual Studio .NET.

NOTE

The answers to "Reviewing It," "Checking It," and "Applying It" are available on our Web site.

REVIEW

Reviewing It

This section presents a review of the key concepts in this chapter. These questions are intended to gauge your absorption of the relevant material.

1. Why do you need to structure your programs?

2. What are the differences between a subroutine and a function?

3. What is the signature of a subroutine or function?

4. What is the difference between an argument and a parameter?

5. What is the scope of a variable? What is the variable lifetime?

6. What is the meaning of visibility in programming?

7. Discuss the difference between by-value and by-reference passing of arguments to subroutines and functions, by analogy with the by-value and by-reference assignment.

CHECK

Checking It

Select the correct answer to the following questions.

Multiple Choice

1. Invoking a sub-program (subroutine or function) means:

   a. Terminating the current program and starting the invoked sub-program.

   b. Telling the compiler to take that code and embed it into the current subroutine.

   c. Executing the sub-program in parallel with the current program.

   d. Executing the sub-program invoked, and then, when this returns, continuing with the current code.

2. The parameter values of a subroutine (or function) are used to:

   a. Transmit required values into the subroutine.

   b. Return values from the subroutine.

   c. Both transmit and return values.

   d. Neither; they are used by the compiler only to make sure the right subroutine is called.

3. What can you say about the return value of a function?

    a. Cannot be an array.

    b. Cannot be a structure.

    c. Must be a fundamental data type.

    d. Can be any data type.

4. If private function F of module Module1 has an argument named arg, its scope (visibility) is:

    a. The body of F.

    b. The body of Module1.

    c. Neither; being a private function no one can access its arguments.

    d. Both a and b.

5. What is the lifetime of a regular variable declared inside a For loop?

    a. The loop.

    b. The subroutine containing the loop.

    c. The whole project.

    d. Being a local variable of the loop has no lifetime.

6. If an array is passed to a function using ByVal, and one of the array elements is modified inside the function, which of the statement(s) is true?

    a. The local copy of the array is modified; the original array from the caller is not affected.

    b. Both copies are modified and kept in synch by the compiler.

    c. The ByVal is ignored for by-reference types, therefore there is only one instance of the array (and it is modified).

    d. No modifications are made to the array until the function returns.

7. An optional argument is:

    a. An argument that can be omitted when the function is called.

    b. An argument that has optional semantics, either by-value or by-reference.

c. A hint for the compiler to optimize the passing of this argument.

d. All of the above.

True or False

Select one of the two possible answers and then verify on our Web site that you picked the correct one.

1. A `Dim` statement like `Dim i As Integer` is an executable statement.

   True/False

2. A `Dim` statement like `Dim i As Integer = 0` is an executable statement.

   True/False

3. A subroutine or function can invoke itself.

   True/False

4. A subroutine (function) can invoke another subroutine that in turn can invoke itself.

   True/False

5. The value of a constant can be changed in the subroutine where it is declared.

   True/False

6. A private subroutine in a module can be invoked by any subroutine in the same module, but by no subroutine outside that module.

   True/False

APPLY

Applying It

Try to complete the following exercises by yourself.

Independent Exercise 1

Change exercise 1 from Chapter 9, "Control Statements," to calculate the factorial using a function that calls itself—a recursive function. Hint: Define a function called `Factorial` with one argument n, and have it compute the factorial of the argument by calling itself. You will need to specify a condition to end the recursion.

Independent Exercise 2

Create and test a function that "pads" a String s with spaces up to a specified length n. If the length of the string passed in exceeds n, trim it to be at most n characters. The function should have an optional parameter that indicates whether the padding (spaces added) should be done to the left or to the right of the original string. You will need the method Substring(i, n) of the String type (which returns a sub-string of n characters, starting at position i) and the global function Space(n), which creates and returns a string of n spaces.

Introduction to Debugging and Exception Handling

In this chapter you will learn the basic concepts of debugging an application and of handling exceptions. The chapter will be divided into the following categories:

- Preparing to debug a program
- Stepping through code
- Structured exception handling
- Unstructured exception handling

You will start by understanding the basic concepts of debugging a program (what is debugging and why do you need it), and then you will learn the fundamentals: how to step through code, set breakpoints, look at the value of variables, and more.

Next you will learn what errors and exceptions are and what are the mechanisms the .NET Framework provides to describe and deal with exceptions. You will look at examples of how to deal with exceptions in a structured manner.

In the last part of this chapter you will look briefly at the older (unstructured) method for exception handling.

Preparing to Debug a Program

A "bug" in programmer dialect is a code defect that can cause anomalous behavior. Bugs are normally caused by errors in the code; for example, you type + when you actually meant to type *. This would result in addition instead of multiplication and a totally different result from what you had expected. Other bugs are cause by mistakes in the program logic (the algorithm that underlies your program). An *algorithm* is a series of steps that are required to execute a task. These steps are (in your case) statements that a computer can execute.

NOTE

In a more general sense the word *algorithm* can be used to describe any series of steps that accomplishes a task, such as the steps required to withdraw money from an automatic banking machine (enter card, enter code, specify amount, get money and receipt, get card back).

A bug, therefore, is an error in the algorithm. The process to eliminate these bugs is called debugging. You may think that careful planning and analysis of the algorithm before coding (a process that is called analysis and design) can eliminate all the bugs. Although it is certain that a good analysis and design phase will reduce (sometimes drastically) the number of bugs in a program, it is also proven that for any real-life program no amount of analysis and design can eliminate all the bugs, as anyone working in the software industry will tell you. That is the reason that you need to learn to debug programs.

It turns out that the debugging process can be helped a lot by a good debugging tool. Microsoft's Visual Studio .NET is such a tool—it is very good in helping you eliminate the bugs from your code, as you will see shortly.

Historically, debugging was performed by executing the program in a test environment and comparing the actual output of the program with the expected output, for as many sets of input variables as possible. For example, if you had a program to compute the exponential of a decimal number, you would try as many combinations of numbers and exponents as possible, with care to ensure the limits of the domains were tested—0, 1, and very large numbers. The issue with this approach is that the expected output was quite often computed by hand, and if it failed, it was hard to say what caused the failure.

To help this process, the programmers started using trace statements. Trace statements are simply outputting the values of some of the important variables at some crucial points in the execution of the program, so that the programmer can then look at them and determine the cause of a bug. This is very similar to what you did in your sample programs so far using the `Console.Out.WriteLine`. This technique is, of course, much better than analyzing the final output of the program. It would allow you to narrow down the statements that were causing a problem, which is the first step in solving it.

Stepping through Code

The modern debuggers (normally integrated with the IDE) are much better than this. As you will see shortly, they will allow you to *step through* your program (execute one statement at a time) and look at the values of variables. Also the debugger will allow you to set *breakpoints*, which are statements in your programs that you mark and tell the debugger to suspend program execution when it gets there, so that you can have a look at what is happening. Let's try an example. Create a new console project and enter the code as shown:

```
Module Module1

    Sub Main()
        Dim a() As Integer = {1, 6, 6, 9}

        Dim s As String = "The array has "
        s += CStr(Count6es(a))
        s += " elements that have a value of 6"

        Console.Out.WriteLine(s)
    End Sub


    ' This function will count all sixes in ints(), and return it
    Private Function Count6es(ByRef ints() As Integer) As Integer
        Dim count6 As Integer = 0 ' sixes counted so far
        Dim n As Integer = ints.Length() ' array size
        Dim i As Integer ' loop counter
        For i = 0 To n - 1
            If ints(i) = 6 Then count6 += 1
        Next
        Return count6
    End Function


End Module
```

In the following, assume that you are using the default key mappings as they ship with Visual Studio .NET.

NOTE

If you changed the key mappings please make the adjustments in the following code too; that is, if you changed the mapping for the "step-over" command from F10 to another key, please make the mental adjustment when we mention F10 in the book. The key mappings can be viewed and/or changed in a number of places (Tools,Options dialog; debug menu and tool bar; profile settings on the start page; etc.)

You will debug this program and step through all the statements in the program. To do this place a breakpoint on the first executable statement of the program. Click on the margin of the code window, to the right of the first `Dim` statement in Main. A red dot should be displayed, and the statement now has a red background, as illustrated in Figure 11.1.

Figure 11.1: *Setting a breakpoint.*

This will tell the debugger to suspend program execution (to break) when it encounters this line. You can have as many breakpoints as required in your code.

To activate the debugger you can use the Debug, then Start menu, or press the shortcut key F5, or click on the run icon in the toolbar (see Figure 11.1). Press F5, and the IDE will start the program, and it will stop at the breakpoint you set, as shown in Figure 11.2. The line is now displayed on a yellow background, which indicates that this is the current statement (the statement that is going to be executed next).

The current statement background color will depend upon your system settings. It shows as light gray in Figure 11.2.

Figure 11.2: *Stop at the breakpoint.*

Press F10 to execute this line. The current statement now becomes the next executable line, as shown in Figure 11.3.

Please note in Figure 11.3 how the IDE layout is now changed. In the two lower windows you can see the *local* variables and the *call stack*.

Figure 11.3: *Stepping through code.*

The window labeled *locals* is used to display the names, values, and types for the local variables. In the previous example you see the array a and string s. In the value column the array length is indicated, while for s an empty string (" ") shows. Finally the Type column indicates what is the type of each variable. It is Integer() (array) for a and String for s. If you press F10 one more time you will notice that the value for s has changed to "The array has ", and it is colored in red (which means it was changed by the statement that you just executed).

The current statement consists of a call to the Count6es function, which passes in the array a() and converts the returned integer value to a string, and concatenates it to the current value of s. If you press F10 (which stands for *step over*) all this would happen, but you will not be stepping into the Count6es function. You need to step into the function, and for this you use the F11 key. This will bring you into the function, as shown in Figure 11.4.

Figure 11.4: *Stepping into the function.*

If you press the wrong key at any time, you can let the program finish (press F5) and then redo the steps again.

You can step over the first two Dim statements (use F10), and you will notice that the Dim statement for i is skipped over. The reason is that a Dim statement without initialization is not an executable statement. It is just a declaration.

You can step into the loop, and you will see how the current statement is moving four times through the loop, with the value of i (shown in the locals window) changing at every iteration. In the same locals window you can see all the local variables, and the function argument ints(). You can look at the values of the individual array elements by clicking the + sign to the left of the variable name. You will also notice a variable that you did not declare: Count6es. This is actually the name of the function and functions as a pseudo-variable, for the code that uses the older form of assigning to the function name the return value, rather than using Return.

What is also interesting is that on the Call Stack window (bottom right) you can see what is known as the *call stack*. This is the sequence of procedures that are on the stack of execution at this point. Note that there are multiple tabs in both bottom windows that offer different views in the debugging process. Please select the Call Stack (if not already selected). The IDE will remember the settings of your debugging session and will restore them next time your debug a program. See Figure 11.5 for reference.

Figure 11.5: *Debugging the function.*

The top-most line in the call stack window is the currently executing procedure (or function). In your case it is the Count6es function, and it is shown with the parameter values with which it was invoked. Next down is the caller of this function, in your case the sub Main, and the position in main from where it was called. The language in which these procedures are written is also shown (in your case Basic). The last entry is a system entry point, which calls out Main.

The call stack can be useful if you have an error in a function that is called from many places in your program, and it fails only in some instances. You would place a breakpoint in the function at the line that fails, and when it fails you would look at the call stack to determine from where it is called and what values were passed as parameters.

You also can set break points while the program is running. To toggle a breakpoint on and off just click on the margin near the statement that you would like to break on.

Other useful debugger commands are:

- *Step out of a procedure/function (Shift+F11).* This command will execute the rest of the code in the current procedure/function without stopping and then it will stop as soon as it returns to the caller.

- *Run to cursor (Ctrl+F10).* This command allows you to execute all statements between the current statement and the statement the cursor (blinking caret, not mouse) is on. It is equivalent to setting a breakpoint on the line the cursor is on and then executing the program, and when it reaches the current line, toggling the breakpoint off.

- *Continue execution (F5).* This allows the program to continue executing until the next breakpoint or the end of the program is encountered.

There are other commands available under the Debug menu, some of which are useful. We will explain them as we use them in examples throughout the book.

One other useful feature is the capability to view the values or variables and expressions. You have seen how to do that in the Locals window. But there are other ways to do it, too. When you return in the Main procedure with the execution point, select Debug, Quick Watch. A dialog window like the one in Figure 11.6 will be shown, and you can enter any valid expression that you would like to evaluate. Enter **s.Length()** and click on the Recalculate button. The length of the string s will be displayed.

If you would like to monitor this expression as the code executes you can add it to the Watch window, by clicking on the Add Watch button. This is illustrated in Figure 11.7. You can have many expressions that you can monitor at one time. You can add and remove expressions in the watch window. The same conventions as for the Locals window apply: if the statement executed changes the value of the expression, the value is displayed in red.

Figure 11.6: *Quick watch of an expression.*

Figure 11.7: *The watch window.*

In this example you can step through the program until you reach the End Sub statement. At this point you can switch to the console window (using Alt+Tab) and look at what the output is. Or, you can look at the value of the string s to see what it is.

NOTE

If you keep the mouse cursor still over any variable name in the currently executing procedure for a few seconds, the IDE will display the current value for that variable. That is the same value as the one displayed in the locals, but sometimes it is more convenient to do it this way.

This is a summary of the main functions and commands of the debugger. You will learn a few more advanced techniques later on in the book.

Structured Exception Handling (SEH)

The errors in a software program can be classified as *syntax errors*, *runtime errors,* and *logical errors*.

The *syntax errors* are caught by the compiler and signaled by the IDE. You are by now familiar with the underlining of an undeclared variable name or invalid expression with the blue line. If you keep the mouse cursor hovering over the respective expression, the actual error message will be shown. The errors are also shown in the output window (at the bottom of the Visual Studio .NET IDE) when you try to compile a program with syntax errors.

The *runtime errors* (most commonly known as *exceptions*) are problems that arise when the program is executed. For example, let's assume that you have a statement like:

```
result = x / y
```

This is a valid statement. If you try to execute this statement with a value of zero for the y variable, the result will be undefined. In other words, you have attempted to execute an invalid operation. The result of this action is that your program will be interrupted, and *an exception will be thrown*. An *exception* in this context is an object of a special data type; we will describe it in more detail later. *Thrown* means that the compiler will check your code to see whether it is prepared to deal with the exception. If it is not prepared, it will display an error message, and your program will be terminated. If you are running the program in the debugger, you will get the option to debug your code, with the current statement being the one that caused the exception.

NOTE

The term *exception* is used with two meanings in the text: one meaning the runtime error that occurs, the other an object (variable) of a special type. These two are related: The exception object is generated as a result of the runtime error and contains information about the runtime error for which it was generated.

If your code is prepared to handle the exception, the appropriate handler is called. You will look at what the exact meaning of this statement is in the next example. To be prepared to deal with an exception you need to use a special language construct, named a `Try-Catch` statement.

```
Module Module1
    Sub Main()
        Dim i As Integer = 5
        Dim j As Integer = 0 ' Explicit
        Dim result As Integer

        Try
            result = i \ j
        Catch e As DivideByZeroException
            MsgBox("We caught a divide by 0 exception")
        End Try
    End Sub
End Module
```

The `Try-Catch` statement is delimited by the keywords `Try` and `End Try`. The two keywords are strictly delimiters; they are non-executable statements. Inside the statement you have two blocks. The first one (known as the `Try` block) consists of the statement or statements that you believe may cause exceptions to be thrown. The next block is known as the `Catch` block, or the exception *handler*. The exception handler *body* is the code between the line with the `Catch` keyword and the `End Try`. It is possible to have more than one handler, as you will see shortly.

The way a `Try-Catch` statement works is as follows: if an exception occurs while executing the code in the `Try` block, the program execution is interrupted, and the control is passed to the appropriate `Catch` handler. In your case this handler has just one line of code, which is displaying a message using the `MsgBox()` function.

NOTE

The `MsgBox()` function is used to display a message dialog box and then waits for the user to take some action. You will see more options of this function later in the book.

There may be multiple statements in the `Try` block, including loops, control statements, and so on.

The `Catch` handler you used will not handle any type of exception, just a specific type. The `Catch` keyword is followed by the code `e As DivideByZeroException`. This type declaration indicates what type of exception this `Catch` block handles. In this case it will handle only exceptions of type `DivideByZeroException` (which is a system-defined exception type). You will see that the only types that can be handled (*caught*) are a special subset of types, derived from a system type named Exception. You will learn more about the exception types when you learn of classes and objects. For now, it is important to remember that not any type can be handled as exceptions, for example String, Integer, and all other type you have learned cannot be caught.

As mentioned previously, you can have multiple Catch blocks, each one catching different exceptions. There is also a special form of the Catch statement that will catch any exception. Let's modify the code in your example to look like this:

```
Module Module1
    Sub Main()
        Dim i As Integer = 5
        Dim result As Integer

        Try
            result = Integer.MaxValue * i
        Catch e As DivideByZeroException
            MsgBox("We caught a divide by 0 exception")
        Catch e As Exception
            MsgBox("We caught a generic exception")
            Console.Out.WriteLine(e.StackTrace)
            Throw
        End Try
    End Sub
End Module
```

This changes the example so that now it will handle a DivideByZeroException, as well as any other type of exception. The Catch e As Exception is a generic catchall. When an exception is thrown, the runtime will check the Catch clauses in the order they are in code. If it finds a Catch block for the type of exception being thrown, it will execute it; otherwise it will continue the search with the next Catch. In your example, the following statement will cause what is known as an overflow exception—an attempt to assign to a type a value that is larger than it can store:

```
result = Integer.MaxValue * i
```

In your case you attempt to assign to an Integer the maximum value that can be stored in an Integer (Integer.MaxValue) multiplied with i (5). The result is not going to fit in an Integer, and an exception will be thrown. The runtime will first check to see whether the first Catch block can handle the exception (it can't). Then it will move to the next Catch block, and this one can handle all exceptions; therefore, it will be executed.

NOTE

Instead of using `Catch e As Exception`, you can use just `Catch` (without any type declaration following). It has the same effect, with the difference being that you do not have any information on what the exception was (since the variable e is not present). We recommend the first form.

Because the catchall block catches all exceptions, it should always be the last `Catch` in the `Try-Catch` statement (if is used).

Inside an exception handler (`Catch` block) you may have multiple statements that deal with the exception. For example, you may set the value of the `result` variable to 0. In your last example you also printed the *call stack* to the console. The call stack in this case indicates where in code the exception occurred, and it can be useful for debugging. All exceptions have this property (as well as other useful properties that you will learn later in this book).

A special statement that can occur only in a `Catch` block is called a `Throw` statement. The `Throw` statement without any arguments is used to re-throw the same exception, so that another handler deals with it. A usage scenario would be if the `Catch` block is used to log a debugging message, but it does not deal with the exception. The exception is then re-thrown for some other handler to deal with. In your case there is no other handler; therefore, the program is terminated.

In the next example you look at how exceptions are propagated on the call stack. That is, if an exception occurs in a function that you call from another function, how is the exception handled?

```
Module Module1
    Sub Main()
      Dim result As Integer

      Try
         result = MultiplyInts(Integer.MaxValue, 5)
      Catch e As DivideByZeroException
         MsgBox("We caught a divide by 0 exception")
      Catch e As Exception
         MsgBox("We caught a generic exception")
         System.Console.Out.WriteLine(e.StackTrace)
      End Try
    End Sub

    Function MultiplyInts(ByVal i As Integer, ByVal j As Integer) As Integer
      Dim result As Integer
      result = i * j
```

```
      Return result
    End Function
End Module
```

The function `MultiplyInts` is used to illustrate how exceptions are propagated on the call stack. If passed invalid (too large) values, the statement `result = i * j` will throw an exception. The function does not have a `Try-Catch` statement that will deal with the error. The runtime will look at the procedure that called this function and check whether it does have a `Try-Catch` statement that will handle this type of exception. If it does, the appropriate `Catch` block in the calling procedure will be called. This is the case with our example.

Fundamentally the rule is this: The runtime will look on the call stack for the first suitable handler (a `Catch` that can handle the type of exception being thrown). It will start with the top of the stack (the currently executing procedure) and move down the stack to the caller, until it can find a suitable handler. If none can be found the program is terminated (or in Debug mode a dialog box will inform you of an unhandled exception).

You have learned the basis of structured exception handling. We will come back to exception handling later on, after you learn about classes and objects.

Unstructured Exception Handling

This section will explain the older technique of dealing with exceptions, used in previous versions of Visual Basic. We strongly recommend that you use the structured exception handling (`Try` statements) as you just learned. This section is included for those who need to understand or migrate projects from previous versions of Visual Basic.

In Visual Basic there is a unique global object named `Err`. You can think of this as being a public variable of a special structure type. This object represents the last exception that has occurred anywhere in the program. It has a number of properties (fields), among which the most important are the `Number` and `Description` of the exception. We will explain what these are soon.

When an exception occurs, the runtime will set the properties for this object. Then it will look for an active *error handler*. An error handler is a statement that tells the runtime what to do if an error occurs in a portion of code. Note that this is different from an *exception handler* (the `Catch` block). The most commonly used one is `On Error GoTo <label>` as illustrated here:

```
Module Module1
   Sub Main()
       Dim i, j As Integer

       On Error Goto Main_Failed
       i = i \ j
       Exit Sub

Main_Failed:
       If err.Number = 11 Then
          j = 1
          Resume
       ElseIf err.Number = 10 Then
          Resume Next
       Else
          MsgBox(Err.Description)
       End If
   End Sub
End Module
```

The main components of an error handler are shown in the previous code. The On Error GoTo statement tells the runtime that for any error that occurs between itself and the end of the current procedure, it should transfer control to the label mentioned after the keyword GoTo. In this case this label is Main_Failed. A *label* is similar to a line number, it is a way to identify a place in a subprogram where other statements may jump to. In this case it identifies the sequence of statements that will be executed if an error occurs.

The code that deals with the errors is looking at the Number property of the Err object and based on what the error was, it will take appropriate action. The possible actions are to try again the statement that failed, ignore the statement that failed, and continue with the next statement after it, or do something else. We illustrate each one of these cases in your example. If the error number is 11 (which corresponds to the DivideByZeroException), you will change the value of j to 1 and re-execute the same statement. If the error number is 10, you will ignore the offending statement and continue with the statement that follows after it. And, finally if it is something else, you will display the error description and exit the program.

There are two more statements (variations of the On Error GoTo) that are used in error handling. The first is On Error Resume Next, and it tells the runtime to ignore any error it encounters and continue with the next statement. This can be a very dangerous statement because it will ignore all errors and exceptions, including serious system-level exceptions, and can lead to program crashes that are very difficult to debug.

The On Error GoTo 0 statement is used to disable error handling. It also clears the Err object, resetting all its properties to blank (empty) values. It is used to disable a previous On Error.

Although the preceding mechanism may appear to offer slightly more functionality than the structured handling of exceptions, programming practice proved the Try-Catch blocks to be easier to use and more solid. We strongly recommend that you use the Try-Catch blocks whenever possible.

What's Next

In this chapter you learned how to debug a program, how to step through code, and how to look at the values of variables and expressions as the program is executed line-by-line.

You also have learned the basis of what exceptions are and how to deal with them in a structured fashion. You also have seen the older version of unstructured exception handling.

In the next chapters you will learn how a Visual Basic project is organized hierarchically. You will learn about assemblies, namespaces, and modules. You will also look at the most commonly used assemblies and namespaces in the .NET Framework, and their contents.

NOTE

The answers to the "Reviewing It," "Checking It," and "Applying It" are available on our Web site.

REVIEW

Reviewing It

This section presents a review of the key concepts in this chapter. These questions are intended to gauge your absorption of the relevant material.

1. What is a bug, and why do you need a debugger?

2. What is a breakpoint?

3. What is meant by exception?

4. What is structured exception handling?

5. What is an exception handler?

CHECK

Checking It

Select the correct answer to the following questions.

Multiple Choice

1. To step through code means:

    a. To execute the program line by line.

    b. To execute the program statement by statement.

    c. To browse the code looking for problems.

    d. All the above.

2. In the locals window you can see:

    a. Names of the local variables.

    b. Names and values of the local variables.

    c. Names, values, and data types of the local variables.

    d. Names, values, data types, and status (modified or not) of the local variables.

3. The call stack is:

    a. The stack of all variables in the procedure.

    b. The stack of all variables used in the procedure.

    c. The sequence of procedures and functions that were called to get to this point into the execution.

    d. Both a and b.

4. Exceptions are:

    a. Runtime errors.

    b. Objects of a special data type used in SEH.

    c. Both a and b.

    d. Allowed deviations from a syntactic rule of the language.

5. If an exception is thrown and not caught, the result is:

    a. The IDE will stop the program and point you to where the exception happened.

    b. The program will be terminated and execution halted (if outside IDE).

    c. Since no handler is available, the runtime will ignore it and continue.

    d. a or b depending whether the IDE is available.

6. If an exception occurs in a function with no SEH, but its caller has a `Try-Catch` block, what is the outcome?

    a. The program is terminated (or stopped if in the IDE).

    b. The exception is caught by the handler in the caller.

    c. The exception is caught by the handler in the caller, but only if the caller has the appropriate handler type and the function was called from within the `Try` block.

    d. A trace message is outputted to the console, and the program ends.

True or False

Select one of the two possible answers and then verify on our Web site that you picked the correct one.

1. Proper analysis and design normally can eliminate a large number of bugs.

True/False

2. A trace statement is used to output the value(s) of variables to help debugging.

True/False

3. The step-over command of the debugger is used to skip one statement and execute the next one.

True/False

4. If the try block of a `Try` statement finishes without exceptions, the Catch blocks are executed in order.

True/False

5. There is a `Catch` handler version that can catch any exceptions.

True/False

APPLY

Applying It

Try to complete the following exercises by yourself.

Independent Exercise 1

Debug all the examples listed in this chapter, using step-through and looking at all variables and the call stack.

Independent Exercise 2

Create a program that gets two integer values (i and j) from the user and then executes the following operation "result = 256 * i \ j". Make sure that regardless of the values the user enters no exception is unhandled and DivideByZeroException and OverflowException are handled specifically.

Microsoft .NET Framework— Assemblies and Namespaces

This chapter is dedicated to the structure of a Visual Basic application. You will learn of assemblies and namespaces. The chapter will be divided in the following categories:

- Software development life cycle

- Assemblies

- Namespaces

- Useful namespaces

To help you better understand the structure of an application, we also give a succinct overview of the development life cycle for a software product. Then you will look at an example of an assembly and its properties in detail. Next you will look at what a namespace is and some examples. You will also build a more complex example that consists of two projects, one project (client) using the other project's procedures and functions (server). This will illustrate the use of the Namespace and Imports statement.

In the final part of the chapter you will look at some of the commonly used namespaces that come with the .NET Framework and Visual Studio .NET.

Software Development Life Cycle

A software product is the final goal of software development, and it is an application that a user can interact with to resolve a specific problem (or set of problems). As a very simple example you have the venerable Notepad application, which can be used to read or write simple text from or to computer files. A complicated example would be a distributed application with a Web front-end and mobile clients, with Web and application servers, using several heterogeneous databases and legacy systems (mainframes) as a back-end.

An application's user(s) do not have to be human(s); the term *user* can also include non-human users such as other applications. This is quite common actually, because most applications use the services offered by other existing applications. This is done mostly to save work and not reinvent the wheel. For example, Notepad uses the graphical and text services (functions) offered by some system-level libraries to draw its window and manipulate the text, fonts, and so on. The whole idea behind software development is reusing the existing services and combining them to solve a problem and create new functionality.

The software development is the process of creating one of these applications. It normally goes through a series of steps (phases):

- *Analysis*—This is the process of gathering the requirements about the application (defining what the input and output should be).

- *Design*—Drawing the blueprints for the application, (determining structure and how different parts are interacting with one another). Normally a modeling tool is used. Most modern tools are based on the Unified Modeling Language (UML).

- *Development*—Build all components that make up the application and link them together. This is the part upon which you are concentrating.

- *Testing*—Make sure the application performs as required in as many cases as possible. Unfortunately the importance of this step is very often overlooked.

- *Deployment*—Provide the means to install and configure the application on the user's computer. This step is also quite often ignored.

These steps are presented as logical steps, rather than physical ones. Each step can be very extensive and detailed, even split in many sub-steps and iterations, or it can be as simple as a sketch on a piece of paper, all depending on the software project type, size, and numerous other factors. We will concentrate on development—the actual implementation of the design, but you will use some elements of design, especially in the next few chapters.

Assemblies

Now that you have seen the overall picture of software development, you can better understand the structure of a Visual Studio .NET application. In all .NET languages the application is represented by an *assembly*. An assembly is a collection of all software of which the application consists. It is called the *unit of deployment* for a .NET application. That means that you need an assembly to install an application. This assembly is normally an executable file (.exe) or a dynamic link library file (.dll). Each assembly contains an *assembly manifest*, which is similar to a table of contents for the assembly. It contains information about the assembly (name, version, and so on), a list of files that are in this assembly, and a list of *external references*. This assembly manifest is automatically created for you when you build the assembly, based on the code you developed. Let us look at a very simple example. You create a new console project called AssemblyExample and have a Sub Main that outputs one line of text to the console. The example is shown in Figure 12.1.

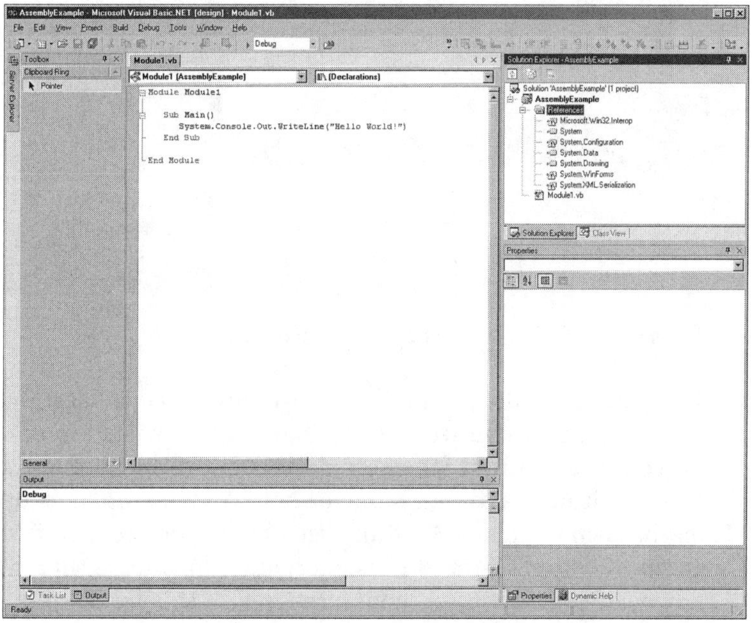

Figure 12.1: *Assembly example project.*

In the Solution Explorer window pane, on the right, you can see the assembly structure. You have one project named AssemblyExample, and it has some references and one file, Module1.vb. The project is the assembly, in this case.

The references indicate what other assemblies you use. All projects in Visual Studio .NET must have a reference to the System assembly. Depending on the project type, some other assemblies may be required. If you click on one of the references (for example, System) it will update the properties pane (below the Solution Explorer) to show the properties of this assembly. You should see something similar to Figure 12.2.

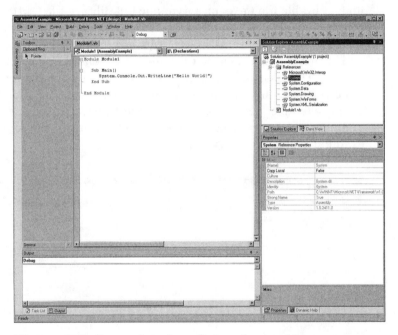

Figure 12.2: *Properties of a referenced assembly.*

There are a number of properties that are used to identify the assembly (such as name, identity, version, build, and revision numbers) and some miscellaneous others (the actual filename of the assembly, its type, and whether it uses a strong name or not.) A *strong name* is used as a security mechanism to ensure that an assembly cannot be modified by anybody except its developer and uses encryption to enforce that. This is an advanced topic that will not be covered in this book.

Because your project is an assembly too, you can set some of its properties. If you right-click on the project name and select Properties from the pop-up menu, you will see a dialog box similar to the one in Figure 12.3.

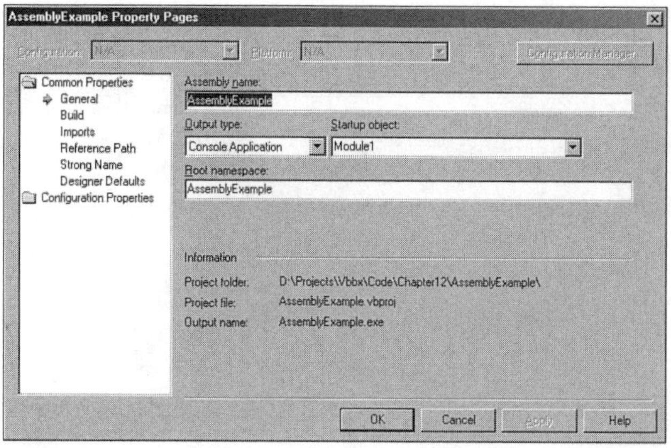

Figure 12.3: Assembly common properties—General.

On the left of the dialog there is a list of property categories, grouped under two folders (Common and Configuration properties) from which you can select. The Common categories refer to all configurations of this assembly, while the Configuration properties are particular for one configuration. That is why when selecting a category under the Common folder, the configuration and platform drop-down lists at the top are grayed out (not available).

A *configuration* is a way to build an assembly. The most common use for configurations is to build debug and release configurations. The *debug configuration* is used by the developer during the development and testing phases of development. It contains information and statements that allow the developer to quickly and easily identify bugs. This is achieved at the price of a performance decrease, which is sometimes quite severe. That is why, when the testing is finished and the final version of the product is built, a *release configuration* is built, which has all the debug information and statements stripped out, but has a better performance. You can manage the configurations for any project using the Configuration Manager button on the top right of the dialog. We will return to the Configuration Manager later in the book.

The currently selected category is indicated by the small arrow to its left. The properties that you are now interested in are the general and build categories, shown in Figures 12.3 and 12.4, respectively.

In the General category you can modify the assembly name, its type (that is, the project type—we selected console), the startup object, and the root namespace. We will return to the root namespace later. The startup object is the module that contains the Sub Main that you want executed when the application is run. As you will see shortly, you can change this setting.

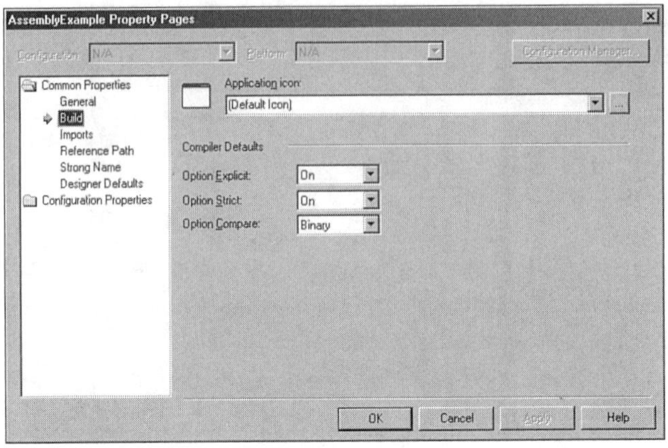

Figure 12.4: *Assembly common properties—Build.*

The Build category is used to select an icon for the application and to set some basic options for the compiler. Your project is a console application; therefore, you have no icons. The three options determine how the compiler behaves in certain cases. You encountered the Option Strict when you learned about data conversion (this option enforces type checking). The Option Explicit is used to enforce variable declarations. We strongly suggest that you leave both of them on. The third option is used for character and string comparison. If set to binary, the characters are compared based on the value of their code (UNICODE). Otherwise, if set to text, a language-specific set of rules is applied, which correctly deals with accented and special characters in each language. If the latter option is selected, it will slow down somewhat character and string comparison.

The rest of the categories under the Common categories folder are more advanced topics. We will come back to some of them later in the book.

In the configuration-specific folder, you have three categories—debugging, optimizations, and build—shown in Figures 12.5, 12.6, and 12.7. Depending on what configuration and platform you select, you will have different values for the settings in each category. The drop-down lists also indicate the *active configuration*. The active configuration is the configuration that is currently built when you build the project (by selecting the Build menu, toolbar button, or the shortcut key F7). You also can see the properties in a category that are common to all configurations by selecting the All Configurations item in the drop-down list.

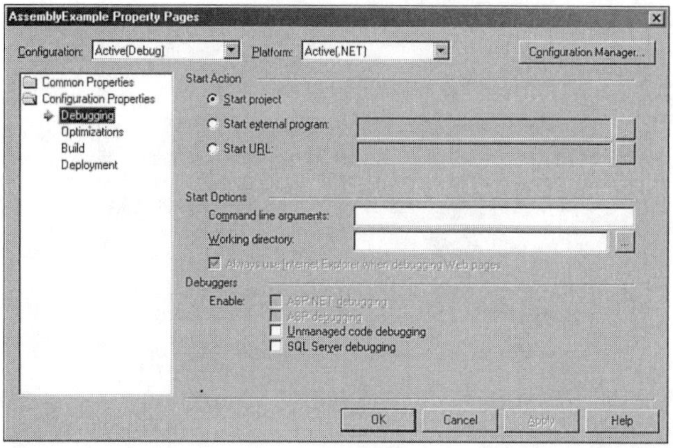

Figure 12.5: *Assembly configuration-specific properties—Debugging.*

In the debugging category you can select some options for building the debugging information into the assembly. These properties normally do not apply to the release configuration. The Start Action property tells the compiler what to do when a debugging session starts, and default is to run the project. You will see later on in the book what command-line arguments and the working directory are used for. The last three properties are used with ASP (Active Server Pages) projects or with non-Visual Basic projects.

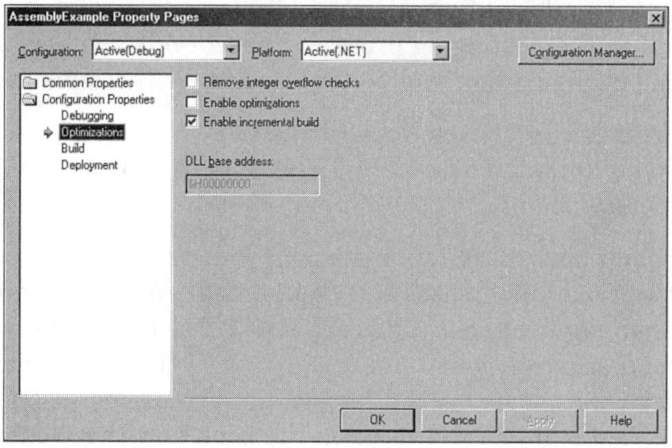

Figure 12.6: *Assembly configuration-specific properties—Optimizations.*

The properties in the optimizations category are used to tell the compiler whether to use some advanced optimization techniques. These are beyond the scope of this book for beginners.

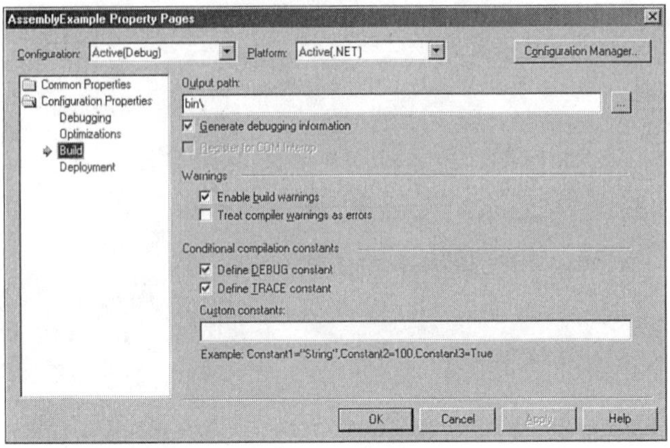

Figure 12.7: *Assembly configuration-specific properties—Build.*

In the Build category you have a few properties that you will use to customize the debug and release configurations. The output path is the place where the build assembly will be stored for each configuration. By default, both configurations end up in the *bin* subfolder of the project folder. That means that building the debug and then the release configurations will result in the latter overwriting the former. If you want to keep both, you will need to change this property. The checkbox labeled Generate Debugging Information will, if checked, instruct the compiler to include all the necessary information when building the assembly so that the debugger can use it in the debugging process. This checkbox is normally checked for the debug configuration and is not checked for the release configuration.

The Warnings checkboxes instruct the IDE what to do if a warning shows up while building the assembly. These should be normally left at their default values.

In the conditional compilation section, you instruct the compiler whether to define two constants (DEBUG and TRACE), and any other compilation constants that you need, per configuration. These constants are different from the normal program constants declared with the Const keyword and should be thought of as some special form of pre-processing instructions for the compiler. You will learn later on in the book how these constants are used and what they are used for.

Namespaces

A software project consists normally of a number of pieces of code (declarations, procedures and functions, classes, and so on), known generically as *components* of an assembly. For large projects the number of these components can be quite large. To ease the use of these components by further grouping them into smaller categories, a new construct was introduced. It is known as a *namespace*. A *namespace* is a group of components that are somehow related. These components can be type declarations, constants, procedures, functions, classes, and so on.

Namespaces also resolve naming ambiguity issues with which programmers in older languages were confronted. Let us assume your program uses an external function called WriteError to log an error to a file. Let's further assume that this function comes from a software library called A. You will add to your application a reference to A, and the function WriteError becomes available to your application. At some point you decide to extend the functionality of your program, and you need to add another reference to another software library B (for example to gain access to some mathematical routines). It just so happens that the developer of B decided to define its own function WriteError. At this point your program will not build properly because the compiler will not know which function WriteError you refer to when calling it: the one in A or the one in B.

The namespaces resolve this problem by allowing you to call either function, if they are grouped in a namespace. The next example will illustrate the concept of namespaces and their usage. You will construct two console projects, NamespaceExample and NamespaceExampleClient. The latter is using the services of the former. Follow these steps to create the two projects:

1. First create a new console project and call it NamespaceExample. Change the default name of Module1 to ModMain in the code. Then change the name of the file from Module1.vb to Main.vb in the properties window. Figure 12.8 illustrates this step completed.

   We will explain shortly why the names of the module and file were changed.

2. Now change the code in Main.vb to look like this:

```
Namespace NSEx1

    Public Module ModMain

        Sub Main()
            ' test the two methods
            Println("A test")
            NSEx2.Println("A test")
        End Sub

        ' Write the message to the console
        Public Sub Println(ByVal message As String)
```

```
                   Console.Out.WriteLine(message)
              End Sub

       End Module

End Namespace

Namespace NSEx2

    Public Module ModAux

        ' Write the message to the console, adding the current date and time
        Public Sub Println(ByVal message As String)
           Dim dt As Date = Now
           Console.Out.WriteLine(CStr(dt) + " : " + message)
        End Sub

    End Module

End Namespace
```

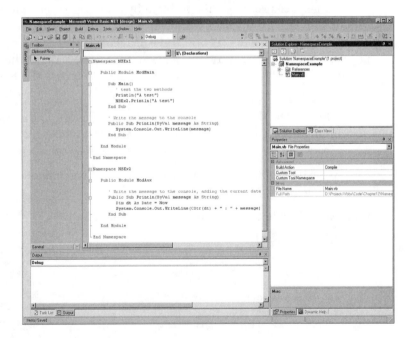

Figure 12.8: *Namespace example—step 1.*

3. Before running the example you need to make one more change, then we will examine what you did in detail. Open the properties for the project (right-click on the project name in the Solution Explorer window and select Properties). Select the General category under the common properties folder. Change the Root namespace property from NamespaceExample to `NamespaceExampleLib`. Now, from the Startup drop-down list select the first entry (which should read NamespaceExampleLib.NSEx1.ModMain). Figure 12.9 illustrates the dialog with the changes made.

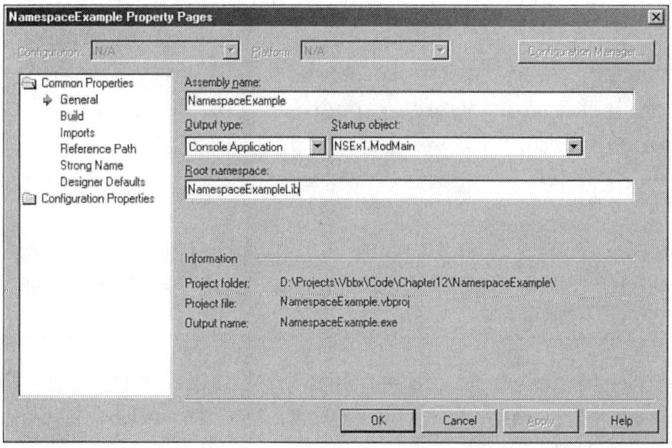

Figure 12.9: *Namespace example—step 2.*

Each assembly consists of a root namespace that contains all the components in the assembly. By default this namespace has the same name as the assembly and the project. You may change this to an empty string, effectively removing the root namespace, but this is not recommended. The root namespace may contain other namespaces (and these in turn may contain other namespaces, as required). No declaration is required for the root namespace; just change the property in the dialog as shown. In this example the root namespace contains two other namespaces. You need to declare these two namespaces using the `Namespace` keyword followed by the name of the namespace (`NSEx1` in this case). This name is a Visual Basic identifier and must conform to the language-naming rules. Each namespace can contain modules or, as you will see later, classes. The namespace ends with the `End Namespace` keywords; everything between the `Namespace` and `End Namespace` statements is part of that namespace.

The second namespace is named `NSEx2` (standing for NameSpace Example 2) and it contains one module named `ModAux`.

In the ModMain module you have your Sub Main. This is the one you choose in the Properties dialog when you selected the startup object. Each of the two modules (ModMain and ModAux) has a procedure named Println, which takes a string argument and outputs this string to the console. The second version of the function prefixes the message with the current date and time.

In the Sub Main you used the Println sub in the NSEx1 namespace as usual (just call it by name), but you needed to prefix the call to the second version of the Println sub by the name of its namespace (NSEx2). This is because, within a namespace, all components declared in that namespace are available. You could access the first Println method by prefixing it with NSEx1, but you do not need to; it is redundant. However, in order to access a component declared in another namespace, you need to prefix it with the name of its namespace.

NOTE

If namespaces are *nested* (a namespace that contains another namespace, and so on) you need to fully qualify the component, that is, use notation like Namespace1. Namespace2.Component.

Another very important aspect of namespaces is the fact that they allow only certain components to be exported and used by external code. This is achieved by declaring as Public only the components that need to be visible from the outside of this namespace. Only Public components of a namespace can be used outside the namespace itself. It is very good practice to declare all utilities and components that need not be exposed to the outside world as Private. This gives you the opportunity to change these private components as you like (for example, to improve performance or fix bugs), without worrying that you may break somebody else's code. In effect it shields the clients of your namespaces from the internal implementation of the exposed functionality. This is a fundamental object-oriented (OO) concept called *encapsulation*, and you will learn a lot more about it in the next few chapters.

Next you will expand your example to use the two namespaces in a new project. Follow these steps to reproduce the example.

1. Create a new project for this solution: right-click on the solution in the solution explorer and select Add/New Project menu item. The regular project dialog will open; select Console Project and rename the project NamespaceExampleClient.

2. Now right-click on the References node under the new project and select Add Reference. A dialog labeled Add Reference will be shown.

There are three tabs on this dialog. The first one shows references from the .NET Framework; the second displays COM components; and the third displays projects from this solution. This is the one you are interested in. You can see NamespaceExample assembly listed as the only entry. Select it by clicking on the Select button and then click OK to add it to your project's references. You will see it now listed under the references for the NamespaceExampleClient project.

3. You can now use the Println procedures you defined in the last project as if they were part of this project. Enter the code as shown:

```
Module Module1

    Sub Main()
        Dim s As String

        Do
            Console.Out.WriteLine("Enter some text and press ENTER")
            Console.Out.WriteLine("(leave empty and press ENTER to end)")
            s = Console.In.ReadLine()

            NamespaceExampleLib.NSEx1.Println(s)
            NamespaceExampleLib.NSEx2.Println(s)
        Loop Until s.Length = 0
    End Sub

End Module
```

4. You loop as long as the user inputs any text and output that text using both versions of the Println procedures you have developed in the other project. Before you can run it you need to set this project as the startup project for this solution. Right-click on the NamespaceExampleClient and select the menu item Set as Startup Project. The startup project is displayed in bold in the Solution Explorer. Now you can run the example, enter some text, and watch in amazement how the Println procedures output it to the screen. Press Enter without any text to end the program.

You probably have noticed in this example how you need to specify the full name of the two procedures using the root namespace and then the namespace and the procedure name. There is a better way to do this. You could use the Imports statement. Modify the code to look like this:

```
Imports NamespaceExampleLib

Module Module1
```

```
Sub Main()
    Dim s As String

    Do
        Console.Out.WriteLine("Enter some text and press ENTER")
        Console.Out.WriteLine("(leave empty and press ENTER to end)")
        s = Console.In.ReadLine()

        NSEx1.Println(s)
        NSEx2.Println(s)
    Loop Until s.Length = 0
End Sub

End Module
```

The Imports statement makes all public components in the specified namespace public in the current namespace (by importing them). Hence, you do not need to prefix the nested namespaces NSEx1 and NSEx2 with the root namespace qualification.

If this is true then, you may ask, why not import the actual NSEx1 and NSEx2 themselves? You could write code like such:

```
Imports NamespaceExampleLib.NSEx1
Imports NamespaceExampleLib.NSEx2

Module Module1

    Sub Main()
        Dim s As String

        Do
            Console.Out.WriteLine("Enter some text and press ENTER")
            Console.Out.WriteLine("(leave empty and press ENTER to end)")
            s = Console.In.ReadLine()

            Println(s)
            Println(s)
        Loop Until s.Length = 0
    End Sub

End Module
```

This code will not work; the compiler will rightly complain that both Println procedure calls are ambiguous. If two namespaces contain conflicting component declarations, the solution is to import just one of them (namely the one that contains the conflicting components that you would use most). You would use those without a qualified name and use the other components with a qualified name. The next example illustrates how to do this:

```
Imports NamespaceExampleLib
Imports NamespaceExampleLib.NSEx2

Module Module1

   Sub Main()
      Dim s As String

      Do
         Console.Out.WriteLine("Enter some text and press ENTER")
         Console.Out.WriteLine("(leave empty and press ENTER to end)")
         s = Console.In.ReadLine()

         NSEx1.Println(s)
         Println(s)
      Loop Until s.Length = 0
   End Sub

End Module
```

Assuming that you use the second version of the `Println` procedure more often, you import its namespace (`NSEx2`) and use it without a qualified name. If you want to use the `NSEx1` version of the `Println` you need to qualify the call using the namespace.

You have probably observed that the IntelliSense drop-down prompts for the namespaces that you created to be the same as the system namespaces.

Another important feature is that, when debugging, you can step from one project into the other project's code. Try to set a breakpoint on the first call to `Println` and step into it; you can see the call stack showing the two projects.

Useful Namespaces

The *System* namespace (within the assembly with the same name) is the fundamental namespace that all Visual Studio .NET projects import by default. It contains the fundamental data type definitions, as well as utility classes and the fundamental class `Exception` and some of the commonly used exceptions. It also contains other specialized namespaces, some of which are discussed next. The most important ones for you in this book are highlighted in bold.

The `System.Collections` namespace contains the definitions for the most commonly used collection classes, such as arrays, lists, hash-tables, indexed lists, queues, stacks, and so on.

The **System.Data** namespace deals with data manipulation when interacting with external data storage, normally with databases. It is the place for the ADO.NET classes, and it has some namespaces of its own.

System.Diagnostics is useful for debugging, testing, and performance-monitoring tools. It has classes that deal with debugging, tracing exception logging, and others.

System.DirectoryServices provides easy access to Active Directory services.

System.Drawing is mainly used to access the graphics functions of Windows. It has classes used to draw lines, fonts, and images, as well as help with printing and 2D drawing.

The **System.IO** classes are used to develop applications that read from and write to streams. A stream can be a file, a network connection, an array of bytes, the console, and so on.

System.Messaging and **System.Net** provide components that enable programs to communicate with other programs on different machines using messages and network protocols.

The namespace **System.Runtime** contains components designed for run-time support. It contains other specialized namespaces for remoting, serialization, compiler, and interoperability services.

The **System.Security** namespace is designed to provide security and cryptography services to Visual Studio .NET applications.

System.Text is designed for parsing, encoding, and decoding of text streams, and together with the **System.Xml** namespace is used to handle XML documents.

System.Threading and **System.Timers** offer access to operating system-level functions regarding thread handling and timer components.

The **System.Web** is used to offer a variety of components that will be needed to develop and deploy Web-enabled applications.

And finally the **System.WinForms** namespace is the basis for the user interface developed in Visual Basic .NET and one that you will study in great detail.

Another namespace that is very useful in Visual Basic .NET is the Microsoft.VisualBasic namespace. This namespace contains a large number of useful enumerations that most programmers familiar with older versions of Visual Basic will recognize. It also contains some useful structures and global functions. You will encounter these in most sample projects from now on.

What's Next

You have seen in this part what the fundamental Visual Basic .NET language constructs are. You have also learned the basis of programming for Visual Studio .NET in Visual Basic using structured programming constructs. You know the fundamental and complex data types, basic statements, procedures and functions, and the structure of an application. You also have basic knowledge of debugging a program and handling exceptions. If you are uncertain about any of these concepts, this is a good time to review the concepts introduced in Part II and make sure that you have a firm grasp on them.

Moving forward you will start to learn object-oriented concepts and implementations using the Visual Basic .NET environment. We will use what you have learned so far and expand on some of the concepts. You will see that there is no magic involved in OO, and developing code in OO fashion is easier and more natural than what you have seen in Part II.

NOTE

The answers to the "Reviewing It," "Checking It," and "Applying It" are available in Appendix A, "Answers," at the end of the book.

REVIEW

Reviewing It

This section presents a review of the key concepts in this chapter. These questions are intended to gauge your absorption of the relevant material.

1. Define and describe the software development life cycle.

2. What is an assembly? Enumerate its major properties.

3. What is a build configuration used for?

4. What is a namespace?

5. What does the Import statement do?

Checking It

Select the correct answer to the following questions.

CHECK

Multiple Choice

1. The relationship between assembly, solution, and namespace is:

   a. Assemblies have solutions, solutions have namespaces.

   b. Namespaces have solutions, solutions have assemblies.

   c. Solutions have assemblies, assemblies have namespaces.

   d. Assemblies have namespaces, namespace has solutions.

2. The root namespace of an assembly is:

   a. A formal name for the assembly.

   b. The namespace that contains the assembly.

   c. An advanced property used only in special circumstances that you have not learned about.

   d. The main namespace of that assembly, which contains all other assembly components and namespaces.

3. Namespaces are useful when:

   a. You would like to better structure a large project.

   b. You would like to prevent name ambiguity with other projects.

   c. You would like to hide implementation details for the project.

   d. All of the above.

4. If a function F is declared as Private in a namespace N that resides in module M, who can call the function?

   a. Anyone.

   b. Anyone in module M.

   c. Anyone in namespace N.

   d. Anyone in namespace N or who imports namespace N.

5. If a function F is declared as Public in a namespace N that resides in module M, who can call the function?

   a. Anyone.

   b. Anyone in module M.

   c. Anyone in namespace N.

   d. Anyone in this project or who imports namespace N.

6. If a function F is declared as Public in Module M, which is contained in namespace N2, which is contained in namespace N1, how can you call the function from another assembly? (Select all that apply.)

   a. Import N1 and then access as N2.F.

   b. Import N1 and then access F by name.

   c. Import N2 and then access F by name.

   d. Import N1.N2 and then access F by name.

True or False

Select one of the two possible answers and then verify on our Web site that you picked the correct one.

1. The design phase comes before the development phase.

   True/False

2. The only supported configurations for an assembly are debug and release.

   True/False

3. Generating debugging information when building an assembly slows down the performance of your project at runtime.

   True/False

4. A namespace must not contain other namespaces.

   True/False

5. If two namespaces imported in a project contain a function with the same name and signature, you cannot compile the project.

   True/False

APPLY

Applying It

Try to complete the following exercise by yourself.

Independent Exercise

Modify the example you used for namespaces to export an enumeration and a function that transforms a string to the enumerated value. For example, use CardSuit enumeration containing the four suits (spades, hearts, diamonds, and clubs), and create a function that will accept a String parameter (like heart) and return the enumerated value that corresponds.

Part III

Working with Objects

Objects and Classes—Introduction to Object-Oriented Programming

Properties

Methods

Static Class Members

Inheritance

Interfaces

Collections

Advanced OO Topics

13

Objects and Classes—Introduction to Object-Oriented Programming

This chapter presents the fundamental concepts that constitute the basis of object-oriented programming (OOP). The chapter is broken down into the following topics:

- Introduction to objects and classes
- Defining a class in Visual Basic .NET
- Class fields
- Class constructors

You will start by looking at what objects and classes are, from a general (non-programmer) perspective. You will then learn a few formal definitions for the concepts of class and object, as applied to programming. You will then continue with a few examples of simple classes. You will create the class definition, and declare and use objects. The final section of this chapter talks about constructors.

Note for the readers familiar with previous versions of Visual Basic: the concepts and implementation related to the object-oriented part of Visual Basic .NET are completely different from the ones in Visual Basic 6 and earlier. We recommend reading carefully the chapters in Part III, "Working with Objects," and trying the examples so that the concepts presented get crystallized.

Introduction to Objects and Classes

You have seen in Part II, "Language Basics," how programming languages evolved from assembler to object-oriented languages. We have not explained then what exactly *is* an object-oriented programming language. You will learn this in this chapter and in Part III.

We all know what an object is in day-to-day life: a rock found on the beach, the oak tree in front of the house, or Bucefalus—the horse of Alexander the Great. All these are examples of objects, each one of them having its own characteristics, quite different from those of other objects. We can speak of an object to someone who has never seen it and still convey an idea of what that object looks like. For example, I have never seen Alexander's horse (nor have you, probably), but reading the description made by one of his historians, you will have an idea on what Bucefalus looked like. The image of Bucefalus will form in your mind, based on what you know about horses from your own experiences *plus* the description made by the historian, which details what special characteristics Bucefalus had. That is, you use your *general* knowledge of horses and the *particular* information about this specific horse (that which distinguishes him from other horses) to construct your representation of Bucefalus.

This general/particular combination is a very powerful mechanism of transmitting information. It is considered to be one of the fundamental mechanisms that underlie the language (symbolic representation) used by humans. A similar mechanism (but far more simplistic) is used by the object-oriented (OO) programming languages.

The *general* information about a specific set of objects is known as a *class*. In your example you know there is a type of objects named horses, which have four legs, a head, a tail, are used for riding, and so on. If you collect all the information common to all horses and group this information under the abstract name of *horse*, you have an idea what a class is. Horse is then the generic name for any member of the set of all particular horses.

> **NOTE**
>
> The Greek philosopher Plato was the first to formulate this idea about 2,500 years ago, when developing his concept of *forms*. He claimed that these forms (his name for classes) physically exist in a parallel/abstract world.

The *particular* information that differentiates one horse from other horses is used to build the mental image of a horse (or in the general case of any object) in our minds. For example: the generic class horse has a color, which is a characteristic of the class. That is, you know that any horse has a color. You cannot predict what the color for a specific horse would be without more information about the horse. This information would be the actual color of the horse, which is in effect the value of the color characteristic of the class.

The same general/particular mechanism is used by OO programming languages to define *classes* and *objects*. A *class* is a user-defined data type that describes a set of objects that share some characteristics. An *object* is a member of this set. It is said that an object is an *instance* of the class to which it belongs. An object cannot belong to more than one class; an object cannot be a horse and a rock at the same time. You will see later when you will learn about inheritance, that this statement must be understood in a certain way.

NOTE

For example you can have a more general class called Mammal, that would include all mammals, and therefore all horses. In mathematical terms it is a superset of the Horse class. Therefore, in this sense a Horse is also a Mammal. The catch is that the Mammal and Horse classes are related in a special way, while the Horse and Rock class are not related (presumably).

A class is a way of grouping objects that share a number of characteristics: attributes (like name, color, height, weight, etc.) and behavior (such as ability to perform jumps, to run, to swim, etc.). All objects in the class *horse* will have an attribute named *height*, for example. That means that all objects in that class have a height—the *value* of the attribute height will be different for each instance of the class (i.e., for each particular horse). This is a very important concept that you need to understand: All instances of a class (objects) have all the attributes defined by the class. Each individual object has its own value(s) for these attributes.

Formally a *class* is a set of objects that share a common data structure and behavior. An *object* is a data structure (also known as *state*) and the behavior associated with it.

You will notice in the rest of this chapter that there are similarities between structures and classes in Visual Basic .NET. We will discuss these similarities, as well as differences between classes and structures, in the next two chapters, after you learn about methods and behavior.

Defining a Class in Visual Basic .NET

A class is a user-defined data type. Its declaration is similar to the declaration of structures. You can declare it as part of a module; however, due to the fact that classes tend to be much larger (have more lines of code) than structures, they are usually declared in separate files (using the same .vb extension).

Create a new console project and give it the suggestive name ClassExample1. From the Project menu select Add Class and change the filename from Class1.vb to Horse.vb. Enter the lines of code shown in bold in the following example:

```
Public Class Horse
    Public m_name As String
    Public m_color As String
    Public m_height As Single
End Class
```

This is a class definition. Apparently there are no major differences between a class and a structure (except the keyword Class, which replaces Structure). A class can have fields, which have the same semantics as the fields in structures. In this example you have three public fields m_name, m_color, and m_height.

NOTE

The prefix m_ is a notation convention used for class fields and stands for data member (another name for field in C++ classes; C++ was one of the first object-oriented languages). We will use this convention throughout the book. It is helpful in that it allows you to distinguish between fields and properties.

All instances of this class will have these three fields; each instance may have different values for the fields. This is similar to the real life, where all horses have a name, height, and color, but each horse has its own values for these attributes. The idea behind the object-oriented paradigm is to try and emulate real life in a natural, intuitive way.

You can now use the class you defined. You can declare variables of this class type, which are known as *object variables*. These variables are referring to *objects* (or *instances*) of type Horse. You can use a variable declared in this way to access the members of the class (fields, in the example). You can set the values of these fields, and in general use the variables as you would use any structure variable, with one important difference: Objects have by-reference assignment semantics. That means that assigning a variable of type Horse to another one will not make a copy of the object, but rather have the latter refer to the same object as the first one.

Enter the following code in Sub Main, in Module1. The code illustrates an example of using the Horse class.

```
Module Module1
    Sub Main()
        Dim h As Horse = New Horse()
        h.m_name = "Bucefalus"
        h.m_color = "black"
```

```
        h.m_height = 2

        Dim g As Horse
        g = h
        g.m_height = 1.8
        Console.Out.WriteLine("Height of h is now {0}", h.m_height)
    End Sub
End Module
```

First you declare a new variable of type Horse and initialize it. You could say in other words that you create a Horse instance, or create a Horse object. This is done using the New keyword, which you have seen briefly before. New is used to create a new object of the specified type. It is followed by a class name and the parentheses. The New operator instructs the compiler to allocate the memory required for one object of the specified class.

VB6 COMPATIBILITY

The Set keyword used in previous versions of Visual Basic when dealing with objects is not supported in Visual Basic .NET. The IDE will automatically remove it if you use it.

NOTE

You could write the declaration for the h variable as:

```
    Dim h As New Horse()
```

This is the older form of a new object declaration, which is equivalent with the new form used previously. This form may be familiar to programmers using older versions of Visual basic.

The variable h is said to *refer to* the object. You use it to access the fields of the Horse object; namely you set the values for these fields. You will encounter often the use of the variable name as a substitute for the object. For example you could say "you set the properties of the object h." This is just a shortcut for saying that you set the values for the object the variable h refers to. Although the shortcut is quite commonly used, it is important to understand the subtle difference between the variable and the object. The variable has as a value a reference to the object; whereas the object is the physical memory location where the data for this instance of the class is maintained.

In the second part of our simple example you declare another variable (g) of type Horse. You then assign to it the h variable. The effect of this assignment is that g will refer to the same object as h. To illustrate this, our example changes the value of the m_height field of g. You then output the value of the m_height field of h, and you will see that it has changed. That means that the two variables h and g refer to the same object. This confirms the fact that the assignment (g = h) is done by reference and not by value.

When a variable of an object type is declared but not initialized (as you did when declaring g), it gets initialized to a special default value named Nothing. Nothing is a keyword that indicates that the object variable does not refer to any valid object. In our example g would have the value Nothing before you assign h to it in the next statement. You can verify this by using the debugger to step through the program and watch the value of g, just before the assignment. If you attempt to use an object variable that is Nothing to access the underlying object, it will cause an exception (NullReferenceException) to be thrown stating that the object reference is invalid.

NOTE

Those coming from other languages such as C, C++, or Java, will notice that Nothing is very similar to the NULL value for a pointer, or the Java null value for a reference. All mean the same thing: The variable does not point/refer to a valid object.

You can also explicitly set the value of an object variable to be Nothing when you no longer need the variable. This is normally not required; the compiler will do that for you when the variable goes out of scope (in your example g will be set to Nothing at the end of Sub Main). However, we illustrate this technique in the next example because there are cases when you may need to use it.

```
Module Module1
    Sub Main()
        Dim h As Horse = New Horse()
        h.m_name = "Bucefalus"
        h.m_color = "black"
        h.m_height = 2

        Dim g As Horse
        g = h
        g.m_height = 1.8
        g = Nothing ' Any reference to g after this line will cause an exception
        Console.Out.WriteLine("Height of h is now {0}", h.m_height)
    End Sub
End Module
```

To check whether an object is valid (if it is not Nothing), you can use the Is operator, as illustrated in the next example:

```
Dim h As Horse
' later on in the code
```

```
If h Is Nothing Then
   ' the object is nothing, take action
Else
   ' we have a valid object, use it
End If
```

NOTE

You can use the negation of the expression h Is Nothing as Not h Is Nothing. A common mistake is to write it as h Is Not Nothing, which is syntactically incorrect.

In this section you have learned how to create and declare a simple class in Visual Basic. You have also learned how to declare variables of object type, initialize them, and use them to access the fields of the object.

Class Fields

The fields of a class constitute its data, what the compiler will allocate in memory when an object of this class is instantiated. The fields are fundamental to the class: Defining the correct fields is crucial. This is normally done as part of the design stage of the software development life cycle (SDLC).

Class fields can have access modifiers similar to the ones you encountered for the structure fields:

- Public means that the field is accessible by anyone in this project and in other projects that use the class. Anyone can get the value of the field and set it back (if it is not a constant field).

- Private means that the field is not visible to anyone but the object itself. You will see in the next chapter why this is useful.

- Protected is a special modifier used in inheritance hierarchies. You will learn more about it there; we just mention it here for completeness.

- Friend is used to define fields that can be accessed by anyone in the current assembly, but they will not be visible to those outside the assembly. In effect it means public for the purpose of the current assembly and private for the rest of the world.

If you would like the external users of the class Horse to be prevented to access the m_height field, you can make it Friend. That will allow you to continue accessing it from the code in this assembly (as you did previously), but it will be invisible to the users who use the assembly and import the class Horse.

```
Public Class Horse
    Public m_name As String
    Public m_color As String
    Friend m_height As Single
End Class
```

If you change the height to Private, no one (except the code in the class Horse itself) can access it. This will cause your previous example to fail to compile.

We mentioned that the classes are normally defined in the design stage of the SDLC. You will need to graphically represent classes and fields, make diagrams with classes, and in general visually represent classes and their members. You will present the fundamental notions required to understand the notation you use—which is the almost universally accepted symbolic notation known as the Unified Modeling Language or UML. You can find a summary of UML at the end of the book in Appendix A, "UML Crash Course."

Classes are represented as rectangles with two or three compartments. The class name is always in the upper compartment; the attributes of the class are always in the second compartment. The third compartment is used for methods; we will go into details about methods in Chapter 15, "Methods." Figure 13.1 illustrates an example of your class Horse.

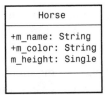

Figure 13.1: *Class Horse representation in UML.*

The attributes in UML correspond (roughly) to your fields. The convention to indicate the type of an attribute is to use notation like

```
attributeName : TypeName
```

That means that the attribute name attributeName is of type TypeName. We will be using this notation for examples throughout the book. In addition to this, the following symbols are used to denote the visibility of an attribute:

- + is used to indicate Public visibility

- # is used to indicate Protected visibility

- - is used to indicate Private visibility

The Friend visibility is indicated by not using any of these notations. The next example shows the attributeName attribute with Public visibility:

```
+attributeName : TypeName
```

The type of the fields in a class can be any valid type. They can be fundamental data types, as in the previous example. They can be structures, enumerations, or arrays. They can be objects of another class, or even of the same class. The next example illustrates some of these types:

```
Public Class Foo
    Private m_dob As Date        ' date
    Protected m_list() As Horse  ' list of Horse objects
    Friend m_suit As CardSuit = CardSuit.diamonds
    Public m_aFoo As Foo
End Class
```

CardSuit is assumed to be an enumeration, similar to the one you used earlier in the book. It is important to note that an array of objects must be populated in a different way than one of structures. For example in this case you will need code to create the array (which is itself an object, as you will see later) and then to create each object and assign it to the array elements. By default the array elements are Nothing when first created. For example, to initialize your list of Horse object, you need to follow these steps:

```
m_list = new Horse(2) {} ' create the array
m_list(0) = New Horse() ' create the first horse object
m_list(1) = New Horse() ' create the second horse object
```

The fields of a class can be initialized to a default value, as shown for m_suit in the previous example and the m_height in the next example:

```
Public Class Horse
    Public m_name As String
    Public m_color As String
    Friend m_height As Single = 1.5
End Class
```

Every time a new object is created, all fields will be initialized to the default values specified in the class definition. If no default value exists, the value will be set to the default value for the type. That is 0 for numeric values, empty string for strings, False for Boolean, Nothing for objects.

In your original example, when you will construct a Horse instance, the m_name and m_color will be initialized to empty strings (" "), but the m_height will be initialized to 1.5, which is the value you specified.

You can test this, using a modified version of the preceding example.

```
Module Module1
    Sub Main()
```

```
        Dim h As Horse = New Horse()
        Console.Out.WriteLine("Height of h is {0}", h.m_height)
    End Sub
End Module
```

You create a new horse and, without doing anything else, you output the value of its height to the console, which will show 1.5.

Class Constructors

In code, you can frequently encounter a case where an object must be created and immediately after its properties must be set to a set of values. For example, if you continue with the Horse class:

```
Module Module1
    Sub Main()
        Dim h As Horse = New Horse()
        h.m_name = "Lightning"
        h.m_color = "Brown"
        h.m_height = 1.9

        Console.Out.WriteLine("Name is {0}", h.m_name)
        Console.Out.WriteLine("Color is {0}", h.m_color)
        Console.Out.WriteLine("Height is {0}", h.m_height)
    End Sub
End Module
```

The example is pretty common: Create an object and set the values for its fields. This task can become tedious, especially for classes with a large number of fields. That is one of the reasons why *class constructors* (or *constructors*, in short) were introduced in the object-oriented languages. A *constructor* is a special Sub procedure, named New, which allows a new object to be initialized in a certain way. The next example shows the class Horse with a constructor.

```
Public Class Horse
    Public m_name As String
    Public m_color As String
    Friend m_height As Single = 1.5 ' in meters

    Public Sub New(ByVal name As String, _
                   ByVal color As String, _
                   ByVal height As Single)
        m_name = name
        m_color = color
        m_height = height
    End Sub
End Class
```

The constructor is a normal Sub procedure, except that it has a special keyword name (New), and it must be declared as part of a class. Class procedures and functions are usually known as class methods (or *methods* in short). Therefore, a constructor is a special type of method. You can declare it with any arguments you think are appropriate for the class. The constructor will be called when you construct a new object passing in parameters that match its argument list, the way it is illustrated in the next example:

```
Module Module1
    Sub Main()
        Dim h As Horse = New Horse("Lightning", "Brown", 1.9)

        Console.Out.WriteLine("Name is {0}", h.m_name)
        Console.Out.WriteLine("Color is {0}", h.m_color)
        Console.Out.WriteLine("Height is {0}", h.m_height)
    End Sub
End Module
```

Notice that the parentheses after the class name (Horse) following the keyword New in the initialization of h now include the parameters that you wish to pass to the constructor. This statement will call the constructor you defined in the previous class. You could re-write the code in a different way, but the end result will be identical:

```
Dim h As Horse
h = New Horse("Lightning", "Brown", 1.9)
```

The only difference is that the variable h will be Nothing to start with, and then a new object will be created and a reference to it will be assigned to h.

The constructor procedure will be executed in both cases, setting the values for all the fields of the class. A constructor is a regular Sub procedure, and it may contain any other statements that can be part of a procedure: branching statements, loop statements, and so on. For example, let's assume that you would like to make sure that the value for the height is within reasonable limits for a horse (at least 1 meter and at most 2.5 meters high). You can modify the class as shown here:

```
Public Class Horse
    Public m_name As String
    Public m_color As String
    Friend m_height As Single = 1.5 ' in meters

    Public Sub New(ByVal name As String, _
                   ByVal color As String, _
                   ByVal height As Single)
        m_name = name
```

```
        m_color = color
        If 1 <= height And height <= 2.5 Then
            m_height = height
        End If
    End Sub
End Class
```

If the conditions are met (height between 1 and 2.5), the m_height field will be set to the height parameter; otherwise it will keep the default value of 1.5, as specified in the field declaration.

The fields are initialized before the constructor is executed. In your case the m_height will have a value of 1.5 before the constructor is executed. So if an invalid height is passed to the constructor, the m_height will remain 1.5.

In UML you represent the methods of a class (known in UML as *operations*) in the third compartment of the class rectangle as shown in Figure 13.2. Because the constructors are just a special type of method, you will place them there, too, as shown.

```
          Horse

+m_name: String
+m_color: String
m_height: Single

+New()
```

Figure 13.2: *Class Horse representation in UML (version with constructor).*

What would happen with your example if you would like to construct a Horse object sometimes with the three arguments shown previously, and sometimes only with two of them? You have two options:

- You could use a constructor with optional arguments.
- You could have more than one constructor.

Both examples will be illustrated; let's start with the first.

```
Public Class Horse
    Public m_name As String
    Public m_color As String
    Friend m_height As Single = 1.5 ' in meters

    Public Sub New(ByVal name As String, _
                Optional ByVal color As String = "", _
                Optional ByVal height As Single = 0)
```

```
        m_name = name
        m_color = color
        If 1 <= height And height <= 2.5 Then
            m_height = height
        End If
    End Sub
End Class
```

In this case you declare the last two arguments as optional. You could call the constructor now with any of the following:

```
Dim h As Horse = New Horse("Lightning")
Dim h As Horse = New Horse("Lightning", "Brown")
Dim h As Horse = New Horse("Lightning", , 1.9)
Dim h As Horse = New Horse("Lightning", "Brown", 1.9)
```

The second solution to your problem involves the use of *overloaded* methods. *Overloaded* methods are methods that have the same name but have a different signature. You recall that the signature of a procedure or function involves the number, type, and order of its arguments. When one of these overloaded methods is called, the compiler will figure out which one of them to call, based on the signature (number, order, and type of the parameters passed).

NOTE

The overloaded methods should be semantically close related—that is, do similar things. For example you could have two overloaded methods named Print, of which the first one prints a document to the printer, and the second one calculates the probability that tomorrow it will rain. This is legal, but nevertheless misleading at best. The language does not enforce semantics (it can't); it is you who must preserve this similarity, or change the names of the methods to reflect the reality, if they are not similar!

Overloading is extensively used both in mathematics and in programming (computer science in general). For example the operator + is overloaded to mean addition of integers, reals, and complex numbers as well as things that are not numbers at all (vectors, matrices, and others).

If you have two constructors with the same name you *must* specify Overloads for both of them, otherwise the program will not compile. We illustrate with an example:

```
Public Class Horse
    Public m_name As String
    Public m_color As String
    Friend m_height As Single = 1.5 ' in meters

    Public Sub New(ByVal name As String, _
                   ByVal color As String, _
                   ByVal height As Single)
```

```
        m_name = name
        m_color = color
        If 1 <= height And height <= 2.5 Then
            m_height = height
        End If
    End Sub

    Public Sub New(ByVal name As String, ByVal color As String)
        m_name = name
        m_color = color
    End Sub
End Class
```

The second constructor takes only the name and color as arguments. You can construct a new `Horse` object with any of the following two:

```
Dim h As Horse = New Horse("Lightning", "Brown")
Dim h As Horse = New Horse("Lightning", "Brown", 1.9)
```

Both solutions have their own advantages, and it is up to you to figure out which one to use. As a general guideline, if a method has more than two optional parameters, it is better probably to write a few overloaded versions of the method.

NOTE

Special care should be taken when the two approaches are mixed: You can end up with overloaded methods with optional parameters that could (if some parameters were missing) be interpreted as another overload of the same method. This could be a major source of debugging pain. Therefore, if any ambiguities are possible, the compiler will refuse to build your project.

If you attempt to create a `Horse` object using the first form of the constructor that you used (also known as the *empty* or *default* constructor), you will discover that the compiler complains that there is no such constructor defined.

```
Dim h As Horse = New Horse()
```

And it is right; there is no constructor (in either solution) that takes 0 parameters. So how come you could construct a `Horse` object in your first iteration of the example without having a proper constructor? The explanation is that Visual Basic .NET provides a public empty constructor for any class that does not have *any* constructor. The moment you declare one or more constructors, you lose this default constructor. You can either add it as an overloaded method or make all arguments optional. In either case you can now construct objects using the empty constructor. This is useful in particular when you declare and initialize arrays made of the instances of the class.

Constructors have access modifiers similar to the fields; they can be Public, Private, Protected, or Friend. The same UML visibility notations apply to methods (and constructors) as for attributes (+ for Public, # for Protected, - for Private, and no symbol for Friend). The meaning is the same as for the fields—public is visible for anyone and so on. A Private constructor, for instance, may be called only by the other methods of the class. You can call a constructor from another constructor by using the keyword MyClass. The following example expands the class Horse to include a default constructor and a private constructor that is called from the other two public ones.

```
Public Class Horse
    Public m_name As String
    Public m_color As String
    Friend m_height As Single = 1.5 ' in meters

    Public Sub New()
        MyClass.New("", "", 0)
    End Sub

    Public Sub New(ByVal name As String, ByVal color As String)
        MyClass.New(name, color, 0)
    End Sub

    Private Sub New(ByVal name As String, _
                    ByVal color As String, _
                    ByVal height As Single)
        m_name = name
        m_color = color
        If 1 <= height And height <= 2.5 Then
            m_height = height
        End If
    End Sub
End Class
```

Notice how the two public constructors access the private constructor using MyClass.New. The keyword MyClass represents this object (for those coming from C++ or Java it is the equivalent of the this keyword). MyClass can be used inside any class method to access any other method of the object. You could use MyClass.m_height to access the field m_height, but it would be redundant. MyClass is normally required only in some special cases, when qualification is needed for the field or method. In the previous example, New is a keyword, and it must be accessed in this way. The appropriate overloaded New method is called (based on the signature, as explained previously). You also would be required to use it if you did not use the m_ prefix for the fields, and you would have an argument with the same name. Consider the following example:

```
Public Class Horse
    Public name As String

    Public Sub New(ByVal name As String)
        MyClass.name = name
    End Sub
End Class
```

You have both a class field named name and a method argument named name. To distinguish between the two, you must use the MyClass keyword to prefix the class field. This technique is a bit risky, especially if the method is larger than a few lines of code, as one might inadvertently use one when he meant to use the other. This can yield to subtle and hard to discover bugs. That is one reason why we recommend using the m_ prefix for class fields (data members).

As you can see in the examples presented in this chapter, you can access the class fields from within the constructor. That is, you can set the value of m_name, for example, from the constructor method. What this implies is that the constructor method has knowledge of these fields, by the fact that it is part of the class. As you will see in more detail in Chapter 15, this is one of the major features of the object-oriented paradigm: to couple the data with the methods that operate on it under one entity called a class.

What's Next

You have learned in this chapter the basic elements of object-oriented programming: how to access and use classes, objects, and class fields. You learned about constructors and how to overload them. You also learned how to represent a class with attributes.

In the next chapter you will learn about the class properties. You have seen that classes have fields, but you will learn of a better way to express (get and set) the properties of an object. You will learn the syntax and semantics related to class properties using (as always) a number of examples.

NOTE

The answers to the "Reviewing It," "Checking It," and "Applying It," are available on our Web site.

REVIEW

Reviewing It

This section presents a review of the key concepts in this chapter. These questions are intended to gauge your absorption of the relevant material.

1. What is a class, and what is an object? Explain the difference.

2. What is a class field?

3. What is a constructor?

4. What is a method?

5. What does it mean to overload a constructor?

6. What is a default constructor?

CHECK

Checking It

Select the correct answer to the following questions.

Multiple Choice

1. The relationship between class and object is similar to the relationship between:

    a. Mammal and horse.

    b. Mammal and rock.

    c. Horse and Bucefalus.

    d. Rock and Bucefalus.

2. If you have a friend class field, it can be accessed from:

    a. Anyone in this assembly and outside it.

    b. Anyone in this assembly.

    c. Anyone in the same namespace.

    d. Anyone in the same class.

3. When a new object is constructed using an empty constructor:

    a. Fields get initialized before the constructor is executed.

    b. Fields get initialized after the constructor is executed.

    c. Fields do not get initialized; the constructor must do that.

    d. Fields do get initialized only if the constructor fails.

4. A private constructor can be called from:

   a. Anyone in this assembly and outside it.

   b. Anyone in this assembly.

   c. Anyone in the same namespace.

   d. Anyone in the same class.

5. A variable of type object has as default value (value that it gets if not explicitly initialized):

   a. An empty object.

   b. Nothing.

   c. NULL.

   d. 0.

6. An overloaded constructor is used to:

   a. Hide the default implementation, when not required.

   b. Provide alternative ways to build the project.

   c. Allow the clients access to the class internals.

   d. Allow different ways to construct a new object.

True or False

Select one of the two possible answers and then verify on our Web site that you picked the correct one.

1. Classes are user-defined (custom) data types.

   True/False

2. Objects and variables are the same thing.

   True/False

3. A class can have fields of the same type as itself (a class A can have a field m_a declared of type A).

   True/False

4. The default value of an object variable is Nothing.

   True/False

5. A class constructor is a method used to create a new object and initialize it in a certain way.

   True/False

6. The MyClass keyword can be accessed only inside the class.

   True/False

7. An overloaded method cannot have optional parameters.

   True/False

APPLY

Applying It

Try to complete the following exercises by yourself.

Independent Exercise 1

Draw the UML class diagram for the class Foo presented in code earlier in this chapter.

Independent Exercise 2

Write a class that corresponds to the following UML diagram (see Figure 13.3).

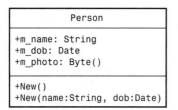

Figure 13.3: Class Person in UML.

14

Properties

This chapter continues to build on the previous chapter's object-oriented concepts. You will learn about class properties, including the following topics:

- What are properties
- The `Property` statement
- Using properties
- Parameterized properties
- Fields and properties

First you will look at what class properties are, why you need them, and a comparison between properties and fields. Next you will look at details on how to implement properties in a class declaration. You will also look at property access modifiers and their relation to visibility of a property. You will continue with a few examples of read-only, read-write, and write-only properties. You will look at parameterized properties, or how to implement properties to access data represented as arrays. You will conclude the chapter with a short discussion and examples on how to combine efficiently the properties and fields of a class, as well as a few guidelines and conventions used commonly.

What Are Properties?

One of the examples from the previous chapter was the class Horse, which had three fields: name, color, and height. We are showing only one constructor, in order to keep the example simple.

```
Public Class Horse
    Public m_name As String
    Public m_color As String
    Public m_height As Single = 1.5

    Public Sub New(ByVal name As String, _
                   ByVal color As String, _
                   ByVal height As Single)
        m_name = name
        m_color = color
        If 1 <= height And height <= 2.5 Then
            m_height = height
        End If
    End Sub
End Class
```

In the constructor you are forcing the height to be a valid height for a horse (between 1 and 2.5 meters). That will ensure that your horse is a valid object. Well, actually, not quite so. The user can set the m_height field (which is a Single variable) to any value within the Single domain. That is, it can be negative, 0, and so on. For example:

```
Dim h As Horse = New Horse("Bucefalus", "black", 2)
h.m_height = -250.34
```

If the user would set the height of the horse to a negative value, it would make your horse an invalid object. It is also said about an invalid object that it has an *inconsistent state*, meaning that there are mismatches or incorrect values among the class fields (data members).

At this point you need to make a short digression to explain the distinction between class *attributes* (which we mentioned briefly before when speaking of UML) and class fields. Class *attributes* are the characteristics of a class from a logical point of view. For example, you can say that name, color, and height are attributes of class Horse. Fields are the physical way you implement these attributes in your code. In this case you have three public fields that correspond to the three attributes: m_name implements the name attribute, m_color implements the color attribute, and m_height implements the height attribute. By *implements* here we understand that it is the physical representation of the logical attribute.

The problem is that, if you use a public field (m_height) to represent the height attribute of the class, the users of the class may inadvertently change the value of height to an invalid value. There is no way to prevent this, if you use fields to represent class attributes. You may limit access to the field by making it Friend, and in this case only the code in the current assembly can damage the class. But then no one outside the package can find out what the height of the horse is! This is a severe limitation in functionality. To overcome this type of problem, the notion of class *properties* was introduced.

From a conceptual point of view, fields and properties are very similar: They both are used to implement the value of an attribute of the class. The way this feat is achieved is different. You have seen that fields are just variables that hold data. *Properties* are a special form of procedure that allows you to customize the way a value for a class attribute is get or set by the users of the class. It normally uses a private or protected field to hold the data. Next we will illustrate the implementation of properties in Visual Basic .NET.

The Property Statement

A solution to the problem is given in the following example.

```
Public Class Horse
    Public m_name As String
    Public m_color As String
    Private m_height As Single = 1.5

    Public Property height() As Single
        Get
            Return m_height
        End Get
        Set
            If 1 <= Value And Value <= 2.5 Then
                m_height = Value
            End If
        End Set
    End Property

    Public Sub New(ByVal name As String, _
                   ByVal color As String, _
                   ByVal height As Single)
        m_name = name
        m_color = color
        MyClass.height = height
    End Sub
End Class
```

The first thing to observe is that the `m_height` field is now private; it can be accessed from the members of the class, but it will be invisible to anyone outside the class.

Then you have added the `Property` statement, which is somewhat similar to that of a `Function` statement. It has a type, which indicates the property type. In this case the type is `Single`. The `Property` statement is composed of two parts (blocks of statements): a `Get` block and a `Set` block. At least one of the two blocks must be present. You will see shortly when one of them can be omitted.

VB6 COMPATIBILITY

Users of previous versions of Visual Basic are familiar with Property Get and Property Set statements. These two statements have been combined into one Property statement with two blocks Get and Set as explained next. The Property Get and Property Set are no longer supported in Visual Basic .NET.

The `Get` block is the one that is executed when the user accesses the property. This is also known as a read block. The block is delimited by the `Get` and `End Get` statements. This block can contain any regular statements and should end with returning the value of the property. The return value must match the property type. In this case you return the value of the private field `m_height`.

The `Set` block is used to set the value for the property. This would happen when the user intends to change this value. It is expected that the value set will be stored someplace (for example in a private field, like we do) and when read later, will be returned. Like the `Get` block, the `Set` block is delimited by the keywords `Set` and `End Set`. Inside the block you can have regular statements. Normally you have code that verifies that the value set by the user is valid. It is important to understand that this value is of the same type as the property type (`Single`) and it is represented by the keyword `Value`. This keyword is not declared anywhere, and it must be accessed only inside the `Set` block. In the example you verify that the `Value` is within the correct range for a horse height, and if it is you modify the private field to the new value.

NOTE

If the value is not correct you do nothing. That is not what you would do in a real-life program; it is done so in the example to avoid complications. You would normally raise an exception, telling the user that the property value the user set was incorrect.

Normally a property uses a field to store and retrieve the value of the property. The field is usually declared as private or protected. The use of properties satisfies one of the fundamental OO principles known as *encapsulation*. The *encapsulation* principle states that the way a specific attribute of a class is implemented should not be exposed outside the class. That means that the class fields should be declared as private, and properties should be used to access them. The most important reason for doing so is illustrated in the next paragraph.

If you implement an attribute as a public field of a type and later on decide to change the field type to some other type to improve the class in a way, this change would break the user code that has used that field. For example, in a class Account you decide to implement the balance attribute using a Double field m_balance. You develop the class and publish it so that others (or even you) can use it to develop an application. After one year you discover that there can be rounding errors using a Double, and decide that you must change the type of m_balance to Decimal. If you do this, you will need to go through all the code that uses your class and change it so that it uses Decimal variables when using the m_balance. That can be a lot of work and can be also dangerous. The easy solution would have been to have Double private field and a public Double property. If you need to change the field, change it, but keep the property, and add a conversion routine to it so that it converts from Decimal to Double.

The properties in Visual Basic .NET can have the access modifiers as functions and procedures (Public, Protected, Friend, or Private). Usually properties are not declared as Private. Private properties would be accessible only from the class, but that means you can use directly the field that underlies the property.

The last thing to notice in the class is that you used the property also in the constructor to ensure that the height is properly initialized. You needed to use MyClass here because you have already an argument called height. Also observe that you can access any member of a class from inside the class itself by using the MyClass keyword.

Using Properties

Properties can be used exactly as the fields are used. For example, if you use the class you defined previously, you could write code as shown:

```
Module Module1
    Sub Main()
        Dim h As Horse = New Horse("Bucefalus", "black", 2)
        h.height = 1.9
```

```
        Console.Out.WriteLine("The height is {0}", h.height)
    End Sub
End Module
```

You construct a new Horse object and then you set its height to 1.9, and you output the value of the height property to the console. The second line in Sub Main (h.height = 1.9) will call the property procedure and execute its Set block. The Value implicit variable will be set to 1.9. That means it would pass verification using the If statement and will set the m_height field value to be 1.9.

Next you read the value (execute the get) of the height property (h.height) and output it to the console. This will execute the property procedure again, this time the Get block. This will simply return the value of the field m_height, which you set previously to 1.9.

You can (and should) use the debugger to step through these few lines of code; step into the property procedure to see how it works.

Properties are also useful if you have a property that is read-only or (seldom) write-only. Often you would like to prevent users from directly changing a property. If you have a class Person that models a person with a name and a date of birth, you may choose to initialize the person's name and date of birth upon creating a new object and disallow the users to change them later. This can be achieved using a read-only property. This is a property that the users can read (get) but not set:

```
Public Class Person
    Private m_name As String
    Private m_dob As Date

    Public ReadOnly Property name() As String
        Get
            Return m_name
        End Get
    End Property

    Public ReadOnly Property dob() As Date
        Get
            Return m_dob
        End Get
    End Property

    Public Sub New(ByVal name As String, ByVal dob As Date)
        m_name = name
        m_dob = dob
    End Sub
End Class
```

Both properties of this class are using the ReadOnly modifier to indicate that there is only a Get block defined—that this property cannot be set (assigned to). An example of usage is shown here:

```
Module Module1
    Sub Main()
        Dim p As Person = New person("John G.", #7/4/1960#)
        Console.Out.WriteLine("The name is {0} and dob is {1}", p.name, p.dob)
    End Sub
End Module
```

If the user would write code like p.name = "Ragnar D.", it would not compile (the IDE would flag it as a syntax error). This is a very useful mechanism, employed in encapsulating (protecting) the data for the instances of a class.

You can use a write-only property by using the WriteOnly modifier for the property and implementing only a Set block. This will force the property to only accept assignments to it, but disallow reading from it, the opposite of a ReadOnly property. Write-only properties are used seldom and normally for volatile data (for example in implementing output streams, like an out console). For example:

```
Public Class OutTextStream
    Public WriteOnly Property outText() As String
        Set
            Console.Out.WriteLine(Value)
        End Set
    End Property
End Class
```

You create a class that allows you to output text to the console by setting a property named outText. This time there is no field to store the data, so it makes no sense to have a Get (what would you return?). This can be used as shown:

```
Module Module1
    Sub Main()
        Dim o As OutTextStream = New OutTextStream()
        o.outText = "This goes to the console!"
    End Sub
End Module
```

This is an example only for illustrating the write-only properties, it would make little sense to use a class for something that can be done with the system stream classes.

Another useful type of property is the calculated property. These are normally properties that do not have an underlying field to store that data, but rather the property value is calculated from other fields. For this reason calculated properties are often read-only properties. For example if you were to implement a property called age for your Person class, you would not need another field for age. You have one for the date of birth, so you can easily calculate the age of the person using the Date functions. We illustrate the modified person class in the next example.

```
Public Class Person
    Private m_name As String
    Private m_dob As Date

    Public ReadOnly Property age() As Integer ' in years
        Get
            Return Now.year - m_dob.year
        End Get
    End Property


    ' rest of the code omitted
End Class
```

You have added the read-only age property, which is going to return the age of the person in years. In the implementation of the Get block, you use the built-in object Now to get the current date and time, and then the year property of the Date type to access the year of Now and of the m_dob variable. The difference between the two is the age, and you return it. You can now use it as illustrated:

```
Module Module1
    Sub Main()
        Dim p As Person = New person("John G.", #7/4/1960#)
        Console.Out.WriteLine("The name is {0} and dob is {1}", p.name, p.dob)
        Console.Out.WriteLine("The age is {0}", p.age)
    End Sub
End Module
```

Because it is a read-only property, you cannot set it; you can only read it.

Parameterized Properties

You know you can have array fields in structures and classes. You also can have attribute of type array, or more generally parameterized attributes. How can you implement these attributes using properties? Let's look at an example. Assume that your Person class can have a number of accounts with a financial institution. You plan to store the balances of these accounts in the Person class. You can further assume (for simplification) that the maximum number of accounts is five. You decide to implement this attribute using an array field of five Decimal values. If you were to use the public array field, you could write the class as follows:

```
Public Class Person
    Private m_name As String
    Private m_dob As Date
    Public m_balances() As Decimal

    ' properties code omitted

    Public Sub New(ByVal name As String, ByVal dob As Date)
        m_name = name
        m_dob = dob
        m_balances = New Decimal(5) {}
    End Sub
End Class
```

We have omitted the properties because they are not changed. We illustrate how to set up an array field and how to allocate it in the constructor (the bold code). To access it you could write code like the following example:

```
Module Module1
    Sub Main()
        Dim p As Person = New person("John G.", #7/4/1960#)
        ' we assume we get these values from some place
        p.m_balances(0) = 2100
        p.m_balances(1) = 10000

        Console.Out.WriteLine("Balance of account 0 is {0}", p.m_balances(0))
        Console.Out.WriteLine("Balance of account 1 is {0}", p.m_balances(1))
    End Sub
End Module
```

There is nothing new here: You access each element of the array field as though it would be a normal array, except that it is a member of the object p. Therefore, you prefix it with the object variable, similar to any regular field access. However, this poses a problem. You break the encapsulation principle by allowing users direct access to the implementation of the class! You should use a property to expose the balances, not a public field. Let's modify the code to make the class obey the encapsulation principle. Make the m_balances array private, create a new property called balances, and use a *parameterized property* this time because it is an array that you wish to expose to your users.

```
Public Class Person
    Private m_name As String
    Private m_dob As Date
    Private m_balances() As Decimal
```

```
    ' other properties code omitted

    Public Property balances(ByVal index As Integer) As Decimal
        Get
            Return m_balances(index)
        End Get
        Set
            m_balances(index) = Value
        End Set
    End Property

    Public Sub New(ByVal name As String, ByVal dob As Date)
        m_name = name
        m_dob = dob
        m_balances = New Decimal(5) {}
    End Sub
End Class
```

The property statement is very similar to the ones you have seen previously, except that now the property procedure has an argument, the index argument (some call it a parameter, hence the name *parameterized* properties). This argument is used to identify which item of the array you wish to get or set, and as such can be accessed by both the Get and Set blocks. You simply return the value of the requested balance in the Get block and set its value to the implicit Value in the Set block. If the value of the index argument is out of bounds (less than 0 or greater than 4) an out of bounds exception will be thrown by the .NET Framework runtime.

Now you can access the new property the same way you would access a regular field, as illustrated by the next example.

```
Module Module1
    Sub Main()
        Dim p As Person = New person("John G.", #7/4/1960#)
        ' we assume we get these values from some place
        p.balances(0) = 2100
        p.balances(1) = 10000

        Console.Out.WriteLine("Balance of account 0 is {0}", p.balances(0))
        Console.Out.WriteLine("Balance of account 1 is {0}", p.balances(1))
    End Sub
End Module
```

However the programmers using your classes do not have access to the underlying array field, and therefore, they cannot make mistakes like deleting the whole array, or resizing it. In the previous version (with the public m_balances field) a user could write code like

```
Module Module1
   Sub Main()
      Dim p As Person = New person("John G.", #7/4/1960#)

      p.m_balances = New Decimal(2) {} ' legal but bad!
   End Sub
End Module
```

This code would break the class code that relies on the fact that the size of the array is 5! In the better version of the class (using the parameterized property) the only actions they can perform are set and get the values of the elements in the array. You can make the property read-only if you wish to restrict write access, the same way you did it for a regular (non-parameterized) property.

It is a good idea to combine a parameterized property with another property that can indicate to the users the valid bounds (indices) for the property, such as a *count calculated* property. In our example this would simply return the number of elements in the array. For example the noOfBalances property shown here:

```
Public Class Person
   Private m_name As String
   Private m_dob As Date
   Private m_balances() As Decimal

   ' rest of code omitted
   Public ReadOnly Property noOfBalances() As Integer
      Get
         Return m_balances.Length
      End Get
   End Property
   ' rest of code omitted
End Class
```

You can have properties that have multiple indices (for example to access a multi-dimensional array). Also the types of the indices are not restricted to Integer or numeric types. You can have a property indexed by a String, such as a phone list indexed by the person name.

A somewhat advanced feature is that you can have overloaded parameterized properties—properties with the same name but different parameters. You can have another balances property that uses a String as an index (for example to identify the balance by some sort of ID string). For example:

```
Public Class Person
   Private m_name As String
   Private m_dob As Date
```

```
    Private m_balances() As Decimal

  ' unchanged code omitted
  Public Property balances(ByVal index As Integer) As Decimal
     Get
        Return m_balances(index)
     End Get
     Set
        m_balances(index) = Value
     End Set
  End Property

  Public Property balances(ByVal index As String) As Decimal
     Get
        Return m_balances(CInt(index))
     End Get
     Set
        m_balances(CInt(index)) = Value
     End Set
  End Property
  ' unchanged code omitted
End Class
```

The use of the `Overloads` keyword is not required in this case. This is somewhat inconsistent with the methods, which require it. This fact proves that all languages, even the best, have their own set of inconsistencies.

To use the new property you could write code such as

```
p.balances("0") = 2100
```

Note the use of the string `"0"` as a parameter to the property. This allows for more powerful constructs than the arrays because you can define the type of the indices. We will look into this more when you learn about collection classes.

Fields and Properties

You have seen what a property is and why you need properties. A normal class should have all its attributes implemented using a combination of private fields and public (or friend) properties. In some cases it may be useful to give access to the class fields to classes in the same assembly as itself. In this case you can use friend fields and public properties. That would ensure that no one outside the assembly has access to the class internals.

Using public fields is the only big no-no. It would break the encapsulation principle, which is one of the most important OO principles.

In UML notation, the class attributes normally represent both the property and the field. The attribute specification will indicate whether a combination of property and field, or just a field, or just a property, should be used to implement the attribute. Each UML element (such as classes and attributes) has a specification attached to it that describes some of its properties. For an attribute this specification includes how to implement it, what is its access modifier (public, private), if it is parameterized, and so on.

As a general naming guideline, you use the attribute name as the property name, starting with a lowercase letter and then using mixed case. For the field you use the same name as the attribute, but with a prefix of m_ as illustrated by all your examples.

It is a good idea to use a plural form for the name of a parameterized property (such as "balances" not "balance," or "items" not "item"). It is more suggestive for the user, and because there is no indication in the drop-down IntelliSense box that a property is or is not parameterized, it can help with usability of your classes.

What's Next

In this chapter you studied another member of a class: properties. You have seen what they are and how to implement and use regular and parameterized properties. You learned how to code read-only, write-only, and calculated properties. You also learned about the important OO principle of encapsulation.

Next you will study the class methods. You will learn what methods are and how to declare and use them. You will learn more about overloading methods in general (not only class constructors). You will also learn about method parameters and in general how to use methods to implement class behavior.

NOTE

The answers to "Reviewing It," "Checking It," and "Applying It" are available on our Web site.

REVIEW

Reviewing It

This section presents a review of the key concepts in this chapter. These questions are intended to gauge your absorption of the relevant material.

1. What is a class attribute?

2. What is a property?

3. What is the difference between a property and a field?

4. What is a read-only property?

5. Enounce the principle of encapsulation.

6. What is a parameterized property?

Checking It

Select the correct answer to the following questions.

CHECK

Multiple Choice

1. Which of the following statements is true?

   a. An attribute is implemented using a property.

   b. An attribute is implemented using a field.

   c. An attribute is implemented using a property and a field.

   d. An attribute is implemented using a property, field, or both.

2. A friend property can be accessed from:

   a. Anyone in the same assembly and outside it.

   b. Anyone in the same assembly.

   c. Anyone in the same namespace.

   d. Anyone in the same class.

3. A read-only property has:

   a. A Set block only.

   b. A Get block only.

   c. A Get block and sometimes a Set block.

   d. Both a Get and a Set block.

4. A calculated property is normally used to:

   a. Calculate the return value of a property.

   b. Implement a read-only attribute through a property.

   c. Implement an attribute that can be calculated based on other attributes.

   d. Implement a computing-intensive property.

5. A parameterized property is used to:

   a. Access array fields.

   b. Implement indexed attributes.

   c. Enforce encapsulation.

   d. All of the above.

True or False

Select one of the two possible answers and then verify on our Web site that you picked the correct one.

1. Attributes are the abstract representation of a class characteristic; whereas properties and fields are concrete implementation of these attributes.

   True/False

2. Read-only properties can be parameterized properties at the same time.

   True/False

3. Read-write properties have optional `Get` and `Set` blocks.

   True/False

4. The `Value` keyword can be used both in the `Get` and the `Set` properties.

   True/False

5. The `MyClass` keyword can be used in a parameterized property.

   True/False

6. The use of a field is optional when implementing a property.

   True/False

APPLY

Applying It

Try to complete the following exercises by yourself.

Independent Exercise 1

Implement the class illustrated in the following diagram, noting the specifications for each attribute.

Person
+name: String +dob: Date +age: Integer +balances: Decimal()
+New() +New(name:String, dob:Date)

Figure 14.1: *Class Person in UML.*

Independent Exercise 2

Implement the class illustrated in the following diagram, noting the specifications for each attribute.

Account
+id: String +balance: Decimal +type: Integer
+New() +New(id:String, iType:Integer)

Figure 14.2: *Class Account in UML.*

15

Methods

In Chapter 13, "Objects and Classes—Introduction to Object-Oriented Programming," you saw briefly what a class method is. In this chapter you are going to learn more about class methods. The chapter is structured in the following topics:

- Class methods defined
- Method overloading
- Using methods

We will start by formally defining the syntax of a method and give some examples to illustrate different types of methods. Next you will look in more detail at method overloading—what it is and how and when can you use it. This will include some examples, hints, and good practices of method overloading. We will conclude the chapter with a few examples that illustrate the concepts you learned and how to use them efficiently, as well as how to represent methods in UML.

Class Methods Defined

In the first chapter of Part III we defined a class as being a set of objects that share common attributes and behavior. Objects that are part of this set are known as instances of the class. You have so far learned that the attributes of a class are implemented as fields and properties. You know now that fields hold the data for an object (the object state) and properties provide controlled access to this state.

In this chapter you will look at the behavior, which is the second dimension of classes. *Behavior* means describing what an instance of the class (an object) can do. For example a horse can trot, jump, eat, and so on. All horses can perform these actions. The set of all the actions that the objects of a class can perform is called behavior. In programming, behavior is represented by the methods of the class.

A *method* is a function or subroutine defined inside the class body, which performs some action when invoked. For example, a method named Jump on the class Horse could calculate how high the horse can jump based on its height (for simplification) and return the value to the caller. Let us look at this example.

```
Public Class Horse
    Private m_name As String
    Private m_color As String
    Private m_height As Single

    Public ReadOnly Property name() As String
        Get
            Return m_name
        End Get
    End Property

    Public ReadOnly Property color() As String
        Get
            Return m_color
        End Get
    End Property

    Public Property height() As Single
        Get
            Return m_height
        End Get
        Set
            If 1 <= Value And Value <= 2.5 Then
                m_height = Value
            End If
```

```
        End Set
    End Property

    Public Sub New(ByVal name As String, _
                   ByVal color As String, _
                   Optional ByVal height As Single = 1.5)
        m_name = name
        m_color = color
        MyClass.height = height
    End Sub

    ' We assume that a horse can jump 75% of its height
    Public Function Jump() As Single
        Return CSng(0.75 * m_height)
    End Function
End Class
```

You are using a slightly modified version of your Horse class. You have all fields as private members now, and you also have public properties for all the attributes. The name and color must be provided when constructing a Horse object because the name and color properties are declared as read-only. The height is optional and can be modified later.

The new function Jump is a method of the class that returns the height the horse jumps. In this very simple example, this is always 75 percent of its height. This value is calculated, converted to a Single, and returned.

NOTE

You have learned before that a constructor is also a method, albeit a special type of method, used only to construct a new object.

To use the new method you defined write a short example:

```
Module Module1
    Sub Main()
        Dim h As Horse = New Horse("Bucefalus", "black", 2)
        Console.Out.WriteLine("The horse jumps {0} meters high!", h.Jump())
    End Sub
End Module
```

The normal methods of a class (not constructors or properties) can be called using the familiar dot-notation and providing the parentheses after the method name. If the method would have an argument defined, you would place the parameter values in parentheses. If you had more than one value, you need to separate them by commas.

Class methods have access modifiers, similar to the fields and properties. These can be Public, Private, Protected, or Friend. The meanings of the modifiers are the same as for the properties and fields. Public methods can be called by anyone; private methods can be called only by other methods or properties of the same class.

As you see from the previous example, methods have access to the other class members. For example your Jump method uses the m_height field to perform its task. Some methods may alter some of the object attributes, either through the use of properties (such as in the constructor, where you use the height property) or through the use of the class fields.

If you were to create two Horse objects, each with its own height, and then call Jump on each, the return values would be different because in each case the method will return 75 percent of the height of the object you are invoking it on. For example:

```
Module Module1
    Sub Main()
        Dim h As Horse = New Horse("Bucefalus", "black", 2)
        Dim g As Horse = New Horse("Lightning", "brown", 1.75)
        Console.Out.WriteLine("The horse (0) jumps {1} meters!", _
                         h.name, h.Jump()) ' 1.75
        Console.Out.WriteLine("The horse (0) jumps {1} meters!", _
                         g.name, g.Jump()) ' 1.3125
    End Sub
End Module
```

It is important to understand that the class methods use the data of the object on which they are invoked. This is one of the powerful paradigms of object-oriented programming: The data (fields, properties) and the methods that operate on it are represented as a unit—the class. If you were to use structured programming, you would define a structure and a number of functions that operate on that structure, but which are in no way associated with it. They could be in different modules or even in different programs. This leads to a very fragile architecture because changes to the structure can affect parts of the program that you do not know about. When using classes, the data and methods are all in the same place. This allows for better encapsulation (no need to expose implementation details) and a more robust architecture (all changes go in one place only).

In summary you can say that a method is a subroutine or function defined in the class body that you can call on an object (using the dot-notation) to ask the object to perform a specific task.

Method Overloading

There are cases when a class needs to achieve the same task starting with different input values—that is, with different arguments. You have seen examples of this behavior when you learned about constructors. The same rules apply to regular method overloading. The overloading of regular methods is less common than the constructor overloading, which is used in almost every class. A class that models a calculator could have a method called Add that can be overloaded to take different types of numeric values (Short, Integer, Long, and so on).

```
Public Class Calculator
    Public Overloads Function Add(ByVal x As Short, ByVal y As Short) As Long
        Return x + y
    End Function
    Public Overloads Function Add(ByVal x As Integer, ByVal y As Integer) As Long
        Return x + y
    End Function
    Public Overloads Function Add(ByVal x As Long, ByVal y As Long) As Long
        Return x + y
    End Function
End Class
```

The Overloads keyword modifier is used to indicate that the method is overloaded. You can now use the class to calculate the sum of two integers, longs, and so on. For example you could use the Calculator class as follows:

```
Module Module1
    Sub Main()
        Dim result As Long
        Dim calc As New Calculator()

        Dim s1 As Short = 3, s2 As Short = 5
        result = calc.Add(s1, s2)

        Dim i1 As Integer = 3, i2 As Integer = 5
        result = calc.Add(i1, i2)

        Dim j1 As Long = 3, j2 As Long = 5
        result = calc.Add(j1, j2)
    End Sub
End Module
```

The use of the Overloads keyword is required for all methods that have the same name. Also, overloaded methods must differ in their argument list: They must have different number or different types of arguments, or have them in a different order.

CHANGES FROM VISUAL BASIC 6.0

Method overloading was not supported in Visual Basic 6.0 and previous versions.

Overloaded methods should be used to perform tasks that are very similar but can have different input parameters. You should not use overloaded methods to perform tasks that are semantically different, that is, tasks that do not perform the same action.

You will learn more about overloading methods when you learn about inheritance and interfaces in the next chapters.

Using Methods

Class methods can be used as you would use any function or subroutine, except that you need a valid object on which to invoke the method. Use the dot-notation to invoke the method and place the parameters (if any) in parentheses after the method name. If the method is a function, you can assign the result value to a variable of the appropriate type or use the function in an expression.

You have probably noticed that the properties and methods are relatively similar from the implementation point of view. For example you could easily rewrite the Horse class presented previously to replace all properties with functions and subroutines, as shown in the example:

```
Public Class Horse
    Private m_name As String
    Private m_color As String
    Private m_height As Single

    Public Function name() As String
        Return m_name
    End Function

    Public Function color() As String
        Return m_color
    End Function

    Public Function getHeight() As Single
        Return m_height
    End Function
```

```
Public Sub setHeight(ByVal v As Single)
    If 1 <= v And v <= 2.5 Then
        m_height = v
    End If
End Sub

Public Sub New(ByVal name As String, _
               ByVal color As String, _
               Optional ByVal height As Single = 1.5)
    m_name = name
    m_color = color
    setHeight(height)
End Sub

' We assume that a horse can jump 75% of its height
Public Function Jump() As Single
    Return CSng(0.75 * m_height)
End Function
End Class
```

You have replaced the name and color properties with functions with the same name. The property height you replaced with a getHeight function to get the value and a setHeight subroutine to set the value. The class functionality is unchanged. You can use it in the same way you did the original version:

```
Module Module1
    Sub Main()
        Dim h As Horse = New Horse("Bucefalus", "black", 2)
        h.setHeight(1.9)
        Console.Out.WriteLine("The height is {0}!", h.getHeight())
    End Sub
End Module
```

You need to replace the use of the height property with the getHeight and setHeight methods.

Although this example is working, it is not the recommended way of implementing properties. The languages that do not have a separate statement for properties use this technique (and call the methods used for accessing the fields *accessors*). However, Visual Basic .NET supports properties, therefore it is better to use them. The code is easier to read and understand if there is a clear distinction between a property (which is meant to access the value of a field) and a method (which is an action that the object can perform). You could fall into the other extreme and create properties that do things other than setting or getting the value of an attribute.

As a general set of guidelines you should use properties strictly to get or set the value of an attribute (either a field or a calculated property) and eventually to validate the input value provided for the property. You should use methods whenever the object performs other tasks (calculations affecting multiple fields, interaction with other objects and the environment, and so on). Adhering to these two simple guidelines will make your code readable and easier to understand for others and for yourself.

Methods can invoke other methods or properties on the same object. You have seen an example of this invocation in the constructor. This can be done by either directly calling the method (without the dot-notation) or using the MyClass keyword and the dot-notation to call the method.

You will now look at a more complicated example, which consists of two classes that interact with each other. You will analyze each step you took to implement this example. You have to implement a class named Person, which models a person entity in a banking application, having a number of accounts. Some of the methods you need for this person will be to deposit a sum into an account, to withdraw an amount, and to transfer money from one account to the other. The Account is also a class, but a very simple one, having only a balance and an account identifier. The Account class is shown next.

```
Public Class Account
    Private m_id As String
    Private m_balance As Decimal

    Public ReadOnly Property id() As String
        Get
            Return m_id
        End Get
    End Property

    Public Property balance() As Decimal
        Get
            Return m_balance
        End Get
        Set
            m_balance = Value
        End Set
    End Property

    Public Sub New(ByVal id As String, ByVal balance As Decimal)
        m_id = id
        m_balance = balance
    End Sub
End Class
```

The Account class has two private fields to store the account ID and balance, two properties that allow you to get the account ID, and get and set the balance. You also have a constructor that takes an account ID and a starting balance. The account ID cannot be changed after the Account object is created, but the balance can. Let's have a look at the Person class. We will split the class definition in a few parts, so that we can better discuss the methods. First implement the fields, a get property for the name, and the constructor:

```
Public Class Person
    Private m_name As String
    Private m_accounts() As Account

    Public ReadOnly Property name() As String
        Get
            Return m_name
        End Get
    End Property

    Public Sub New(ByVal name As String)
        m_name = name
        m_accounts = New Account(2) {}
        ' here we should initialize the accounts from a data source
        m_accounts(0) = New Account("Checking", 2100) ' we just pick a number
        m_accounts(1) = New Account("Savings", 11000) ' we just pick a number
    End Sub
End Class
```

You have a field and a property for the Person name, both String. The name once set in the constructor will not change. You also have an array of Account objects named m_accounts. These accounts will hold the banking information for this person. In the constructor you set the m_name field and then you create a new array that can hold two Account objects. This is separate from creating the actual objects in the array, which is a separate step. Then you create the two Account objects and assign them to the corresponding array element. You create an account with the ID "Checking" and a balance of 2100 and assign it to the first element of the array (m_accounts(0)). Next you create the second Account object that will hold the "Savings" information. In real life you would read this information from a database, but the code to do this is beyond the level you are at currently, so you just fake it.

You now need to add a property for the users of the class person to access their account balances. You could simply expose the Account objects in the m_accounts array as a property. But this will allow the users to change their balances, and this is not something you want to do. Therefore, you add a calculated parameterized property called `balance`, which will return the balance of a specified account. The first version of this property is illustrated next:

```
Public ReadOnly Property balance(ByVal accountId As String) As Decimal
    Get
        Dim i As Integer
        For i = 0 To m_accounts.Length - 1
            If m_accounts(i).id.Equals(accountId) Then
                return m_accounts(i).balance
            End If
        Next
    End Get
End Property
```

Loop through the accounts in the `m_accounts` array until you find the one that has an ID that matches the `accountId` argument that was passed in (the account for which the user wants the balance). When you find it, return the balance and exit the property procedure.

You are going to use this type of code (which finds an account in the array based in its ID) also in the deposit, withdraw, and transfer methods. So you decide to make a private function that will do this finding for you, instead of repeating the same `for` loop over and over. This is another fundamental object-oriented principle, known as the principle of reusing. You will write a method that can be reused whenever that task is needed, rather than having a piece of code repeated all over. It is a commonsense way to code, if you think about it. So rewrite the code:

```
Public ReadOnly Property balance(ByVal accountId As String) As Decimal
    Get
        Dim a As Account = GetAccountById(accountId)
        Return a.balance
    End Get
End Property

' utility function: find the account specified by the accountId
Private Function GetAccountById(ByVal accountId As String) As Account
    Dim i As Integer
    For i = 0 To m_accounts.Length - 1
        If m_accounts(i).id.Equals(accountId) Then
            Return m_accounts(i)
        End If
    Next
End Function
```

The utility function `GetAccountById` will return an account from the array of accounts of this object (`m_accounts`), which matches the `accountId` parameter passed in to the function. If no account is found that matches, Nothing will be returned, and the code calling this function will most likely crash (indicating that the account was not found). You should add exception handling to this class, but for simplicity reasons we will leave it out.

You also have changed the property balance to take advantage of the new function. Namely it is trying to find the account and then it returns its balance. This is simpler than before and easier to understand.

You are now ready to implement the Deposit, Withdraw, and Transfer methods. Deposit and withdraw should increment or decrement the balance of the account (specified by accountId) by the amount specified in the amount argument. The Transfer method will Withdraw from the accountIdFrom account and Deposit it into the accountIdTo account. You can now look at the final version of the Person class, with the three methods shown in bold.

```
Public Class Person
    Private m_name As String
    Private m_accounts() As Account

    Public ReadOnly Property name() As String
        Get
            Return m_name
        End Get
    End Property

    Public ReadOnly Property balance(ByVal accountId As String) As Decimal
        Get
            Dim a As Account = GetAccountById(accountId)
            Return a.balance
        End Get
    End Property

    Public Sub Deposit(ByVal accountId As String, ByVal amount As Decimal)
        Dim a As Account = GetAccountById(accountId)
        a.balance += amount
    End Sub

    Public Sub Withdraw(ByVal accountId As String, ByVal amount As Decimal)
        Dim a As Account = GetAccountById(accountId)
        a.balance -= amount
    End Sub

    Public Sub Transfer(ByVal accountIdFrom As String, _
                        ByVal accountIdTo As String, _
                        ByVal amount As Decimal)
```

```
        Withdraw(accountIdFrom, amount)
        Deposit(accountIdTo, amount)
    End Sub

    Public Sub New(ByVal name As String)
        m_name = name
        m_accounts = New Account(2) {}
        ' here we should initialize the accounts from a data source
        ' i.e. read the value of the balances, etc.
        m_accounts(0) = New Account("Checking", 2100) ' we just pick a number
        m_accounts(1) = New Account("Savings", 11000) ' we just pick a number
    End Sub


    ' utility function: find the account specified by the accountId
    Private Function GetAccountById(ByVal accountId As String) As Account
        Dim i As Integer
        For i = 0 To m_accounts.Length - 1
            If m_accounts(i).id.Equals(accountId) Then
                Return m_accounts(i)
            End If
        Next
    End Function
End Class
```

Both `Deposit` and `Withdraw` are using identical mechanisms: find the account requested and then increment/decrement the account by the amount specified. The `Transfer` method is even simpler, as it calls first `Withdraw` and then `Deposit` to execute the transfer.

You can now use the classes you developed. The next example illustrates a possible scenario.

```
Module Module1

    Sub Main()
        Dim p As Person = New Person("Dagny T.")

        Console.Out.WriteLine("Checking balance is {0}", p.balance("Checking"))
        Console.Out.WriteLine("Savings  balance is {0}", p.balance("Savings"))

        p.Deposit("Savings", 1200)
        p.Transfer("Savings", "Checking", 450)

        Console.Out.WriteLine("Checking balance is {0}", p.balance("Checking"))
        Console.Out.WriteLine("Savings  balance is {0}", p.balance("Savings"))
    End Sub


End Module
```

You have seen an example that is more involved and which illustrates most of what you learned so far in the realm of objects and classes. It would be a good idea to implement this example yourself and step through it to see how the properties and methods work. Look at the local variables in every method and property and try to understand what happens under the hood (when are objects created, and so on).

You have learned how to represent properties and fields in design using UML. Methods are also represented in design, using the third (and lowermost) compartment of the class container. The same notation is used to denote the visibility of the methods, as for the regular attributes (+ for `Public`, # for `Protected`, - for `Private`, or nothing for `Friend`). Figure 15.1 illustrates the `Person` and `Account` classes you have implemented previously.

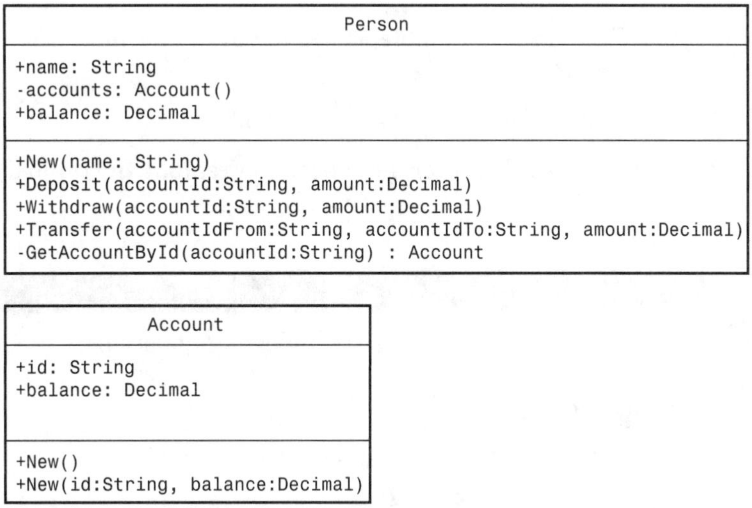

```
                              Person
─────────────────────────────────────────────────────────────
+name: String
-accounts: Account()
+balance: Decimal
─────────────────────────────────────────────────────────────
+New(name: String)
+Deposit(accountId:String, amount:Decimal)
+Withdraw(accountId:String, amount:Decimal)
+Transfer(accountIdFrom:String, accountIdTo:String, amount:Decimal)
-GetAccountById(accountId:String) : Account
```

```
            Account
─────────────────────────────────
+id: String
+balance: Decimal
─────────────────────────────────
+New()
+New(id:String, balance:Decimal)
```

Figure 15.1: *UML diagram of the Person and Account classes*

The two classes are shown with all their methods and attributes. Notice the way the return type of a method (if present) is displayed in UML.

What's Next

In this chapter you looked at class methods in detail. You now know how to overload methods and how to use methods to implement the class behavior. You also know what the differences are between methods and properties and when to use one or the other.

In the next chapter you will study special types of properties and methods, known as shared or static. You will see when shared methods and properties are useful, and you will, of course, do this by using a number of examples.

NOTE

The answers to "Reviewing It," "Checking It," and "Applying It" are available on our Web site.

REVIEW

Reviewing It

This section presents a review of the key concepts in this chapter. These questions are intended to gauge your absorption of the relevant material.

1. What is a method?

2. What are the possible access modifiers for methods (that you learned so far)?

3. What means to overload a method?

4. What are the differences between regular (module) subroutines and functions and class methods?

CHECK

Checking It

Select the correct answer to the following questions.

Multiple Choice

1. A class method is a way to model:

   a. Class attributes.

   b. Object state.

   c. Object state and behavior.

   d. Class behavior.

2. A public method can be invoked from:

   a. Anyone in this assembly or outside it.

   b. Anyone in this assembly.

   c. Anyone in the same namespace.

   d. Anyone in the same class.

3. The `Overloads` keyword is used to:

   a. Indicate that a method is going to be overloaded later.

   b. Indicate that the method is overloaded by another method.

   c. Indicate that the method overloads another method.

   d. Both b and c because they mean the same thing.

4. Overloaded methods must differ by:

   a. Name.

   b. Number of arguments.

   c. Number and/or type of the arguments.

   d. Number and/or type and/or order of the arguments.

5. If `Elevator` is a class, which would be valid candidate for a method?

   a. Elevator license number.

   b. Move to specified floor.

   c. Emergency brake.

   d. Interior decoration.

6. If the price of a Product class is computed based on some fields (such as list price, discounts, tax rate), is the price a property or a method?

   a. Property because it is an attribute of the class.

   b. Method because it is calculated.

   c. Calculated property because it does not model an action of the class.

   d. Parameterized property because it requires other data to be calculated.

True or False

Select one of the two possible answers and then verify on our Web site that you picked the correct one.

1. A class method is a function or subroutine that can be invoked on any object of the class, given that the caller has visibility (access).

   True/False

2. An overloaded method can differ from another method by return type only.

   True/False

3. Overloaded methods must not have optional parameters.

   True/False

4. Two overloads of a method can differ by the ByVal/ByRef argument modifiers.

   True/False

5. To invoke a class method from the body of another method or property of the same class, you must use the MyClass keyword.

   True/False

Applying It

Try to complete the following exercises by yourself.

Independent Exercise 1

Extend the methods Withdraw and Transfer of the Person/Account example presented previously to include verification of overdraft (to make sure that there is enough money before making a withdrawal—that the balance after withdrawal is always ≥ 0).

Independent Exercise 2

Modify the balance property of the Person class to deal with the case when an invalid account ID is provided in a better fashion (i.e., detect the error and warn the user).

Shared Class Members

You have learned about class members such as fields, properties, and methods. In this chapter you will study a special type of class members named *shared* members. The chapter is structured as follows:

- Shared members definition

- Shared methods

- Hints and tips regarding shared members

The shared member is a new concept in Visual Basic .NET; it did not exist in the previous versions of the language. For those familiar with other object-oriented languages, it is similar to the concepts of *static* members.

You will start with some definitions and an easy example that illustrates a shared field and property. Next you will look at some more complex examples to illustrate the usage of shared methods, in combination with properties and fields.

The chapter concludes with a general discussion on shared members, namely on when and how to use them. You will also learn some hints and guidelines for coding.

Shared Members Definition

To better understand shared members, we will start with an example. Let's assume that you have to code a class that models a product sold in a shop and that the shop is geographically situated in a state or country that has a sales tax. Your product class will have to calculate the price charged for the product, based on the list price of the product, the sales tax, any discounts entered by the sales clerk, and the quantity purchased. You could design and then implement a class like the one shown here:

```
Public Class Product
    Private m_name As String ' product name
    Private m_listPrice As Decimal ' the list price
    Private m_taxRate As Double

    Public ReadOnly Property name() As String
        Get
            Return m_name
        End Get
    End Property

    Public ReadOnly Property listPrice() As Decimal
        Get
            Return m_listPrice
        End Get
    End Property

    Public ReadOnly Property taxRate() As Double
        Get
            Return m_taxRate
        End Get
    End Property

    Public Sub New(ByVal name As String, _
                ByVal listPrice As Decimal, _
                ByVal taxRate As Double)
        m_name = name
        m_listPrice = listPrice
        m_taxRate = taxRate
    End Sub

    Public Function GetPrice(ByVal discount As Double) As Decimal
        Dim price As Double
        price = m_listPrice + m_listPrice * m_taxRate - m_listPrice * discount
        Return CDec(price)
    End Function
End Class
```

One can use this class as in the next example:

```
Module Module1
    Sub Main()
        Dim p As Product = New Product("Coconuts", 2, 0.08)
        Console.Out.WriteLine("The price is {0}", p.GetPrice(0))
    End Sub
End Module
```

This is a perfectly valid class that would perform the task for which it was designed. However, if you think about the way it is going to be used, you will find a problem with this implementation. The tax rate is the same for all products in the shop (assuming a flat tax rate). This means that in each object you store the same value for the field m_taxRate. This is a waste of memory because each instance of the class allocates the eight bytes (for Double) required to hold the tax rate. Moreover, the users of the class must specify the same value for the tax rate every time, when they construct an instance of the class. You could place the tax rate into a global variable in the program, but this raises encapsulation issues. Because only this class (Product) uses the value, it should not be made public so that anyone could get at it. It would be much better if you could somehow have a variable or field that would be common for all objects of this class.

This is exactly what *shared* fields are: variables that are declared at class level and shared among all instances of the class. In other object-oriented languages these variables are called *static*, and you will find them defined as static in parts of the .NET Framework documentation. They are also known as *class variables* (or methods), in the sense that they are declared and can be used at class level, as compared to the regular fields, which are considered to be at the object or instance level. We will call them *shared* fields, properties, and methods. They are declared using the special modifier Shared, which can be used only inside classes.

Let's rewrite the example to take advantage of the shared members:

```
Public Class Product
    Private m_name As String ' product name
    Private m_listPrice As Decimal ' the list price

    Private Shared s_taxRate As Double

    Public ReadOnly Property name() As String
        Get
            Return m_name
        End Get
    End Property
```

```
      Public ReadOnly Property listPrice() As Decimal
         Get
             Return m_listPrice
         End Get
      End Property

      Public Shared Property taxRate() As Double
         Get
             Return s_taxRate
         End Get
         Set
             s_taxRate = Value
         End Set
      End Property

      Public Sub New(ByVal name As String, ByVal listPrice As Decimal)
         m_name = name
         m_listPrice = listPrice
      End Sub

      Public Function GetPrice(ByVal discount As Double) As Decimal
         Dim price As Double
         price = m_listPrice + m_listPrice * s_taxRate - m_listPrice * discount
         Return CDec(price)
      End Function
End Class
```

The first change that you notice is that the field m_taxRate is now Shared and was renamed to s_taxRate (the s_ is our convention, used to mark shared fields to distinguish them from regular m_ member fields). The fact that s_taxRate is Shared means that any object of the class Product can now access the value of s_taxRate, and if anyone is changing it, the changes will be reflected immediately to all objects that use it. This is a very good reason to keep it private, so that only objects of this class have direct access to it.

Another change you did is to have a shared property, which will allow controlled access to the value of the shared field. Normally for shared fields you implement shared properties. A shared property is not different from a normal property, with the exception of the keyword Shared. It can be Readonly, Writeonly, or both read and write (as in the example, where it has both a get and a set). One difference between the shared and regular properties is that a shared property cannot access fields or properties that are not shared themselves. The reason for this is that the shared properties are not invoked on any particular instance of the class. No instances means no fields; therefore, the compiler will prevent you from accessing any non-shared member (field, property, or method) from a shared property or method. The opposite is not valid: any instance of the class can access any shared field, property, and method, because these are defined at class level. Another difference between shared properties and regular properties is the way the user accesses them, as illustrated in the next example.

```
Module Module1
    Sub Main()
        Product.taxRate = 0.08
        Dim p As Product = New Product("Coconuts", 2)
        Console.Out.WriteLine("The price is {0}", p.GetPrice(0))
    End Sub
End Module
```

The user uses the dot-notation on the class name itself (`Product.taxRate = 0.08`) to access the shared members. The reason for this is that the shared members are not "part" of any particular object from the set, but rather they apply to the whole set of objects (the class). The statement in bold sets the value s_taxRate to be 0.08, which can subsequently be accessed by any instance of the class.

The rest of the code is virtually unchanged, except that you removed the argument `taxRate` from the constructor and now use the s_taxRate field instead of the `m_taxRate` in the `GetPrice` function.

Notice that the class is now easier to use and understand from a coding perspective: You have only one variable that holds the tax rate for all the objects of the class. You initialize it only once during the lifetime of the program, and then it stays at that value.

The *lifetime* of the static fields is the duration of the program. The value of the variable may change in this time. If it is an object then, it may be allocated with New at some point, or the field may be Nothing.

Shared Methods

Shared methods are similar to shared fields and properties in the fact that they are not actions performed on an object, but rather actions performed on the class level that do not require the existence of an object.

If you continue with the example, you may want to add a function that will calculate the price for an unknown product. As it happens in any shop, you might find a product without a label, or with a deteriorated label. In this case the cashier will assign it a list price and will ask for the final price. But because there is no product object that matches the description, you need to provide a mechanism to calculate the price that is not based on an existing product. The solution is to create a shared function that takes the list price assigned by the cashier (instead of, say, the product code or ID) and calculates the final price.

You can add this function (shown in the next example) to the class Product you developed previously.

```
Shared Function GetPriceUnknown(ByVal price As Decimal) As Decimal
    Return CDec(price + price * s_taxRate)
End Function
```

The method is declared with the modifier Shared, as you did before for methods and properties. It does calculate the final price based on the assigned price (passed in as an argument) and the shared field s_taxRate. It is important to notice that you do not access any instance members (fields starting with m_, or properties). This is not allowed in a shared method, and attempting to do so will cause the IDE and compiler to signal a syntax error (Cannot access non-shared class members from shared method).

You can also have overloaded shared methods. You can use the exact syntax you used for regular methods, except that you must add the Shared keyword to indicate that the methods are also shared.

To continue the example let us assume you also need a version of the function GetPriceUnknown in which the price and a discount is given. You would end up with two overloaded methods as shown in the next example.

NOTE

You could have used one shared method with an optional parameter discount (and in this case it would be a better choice probably). However, the purpose is to show how to implement shared overloaded methods.

```
Overloads Shared Function GetPriceUnknown(ByVal price As Decimal) As Decimal
    Return CDec(price + price * s_taxRate)
End Function

Overloads Shared Function GetPriceUnknown(ByVal price As Decimal, _
                                          ByVal discount As Double) As Decimal
    Return CDec(price + price * s_taxRate - price * discount)
End Function
```

Overloaded shared methods are useful in some cases, although the same warnings apply for these, as for regular overloaded methods.

In UML you use the prefix notation $ to denote a shared attribute (field/property) or method.

Hints and Tips Regarding Shared Members

To determine whether a field, property, or method would be better modeled as shared than as an instance member, you can look at a few criteria. We present a few of the most common ones later in this chapter.

If you have a class method or property that does not use or refer to any instance members, it is a good candidate for becoming a shared method or property.

If a field value is the same value in all objects, then it is almost certain that it would be better to be a shared field.

Sometimes, you will find out that a class, especially if imported from an older version of Visual Basic, would have a lot of methods and properties that are really shared, but they were not declared as such because the language did not support it then.

Shared members are a very good addition to the Visual Basic language, and we recommend that you use them whenever appropriate because they save memory and will make the logic behind the class easier to understand.

What's Next

In this easy chapter you looked at shared members (fields, properties, and methods). You learned that shared members are class-level members that do not operate or exist at the instance level, as was the case with the regular members that you have studied before. We call these latter members instance members, to distinguish them from the class-level or shared members.

In the next chapter you will start what probably could be considered the most important topic of object-oriented programming: inheritance. You will learn the basis of inheritance—what it is, how it is implemented, and what are its consequences in the whole way you program, as well as in the details of how you implement classes.

> **NOTE**
>
> The answers to "Reviewing It," "Checking It," and "Applying It" are available on our Web site.

REVIEW

Reviewing It

This section presents a review of the key concepts in this chapter. These questions are intended to gauge your absorption of the relevant material.

1. What is a shared class member?

2. What is the lifetime of a shared field?

3. What is the scope of a shared private field? What is the scope of public and friend shared fields?

CHECK

Checking It

Select the correct answer to the following questions.

Multiple Choice

1. A shared property or method can access a regular (non-shared) field if:

   a. The field is public.

   b. The field is protected.

   c. The field is friend.

   d. It cannot access the field.

2. A regular property or method can access a shared field if:

   a. It is not private.

   b. It is friend.

   c. It can access any shared field.

   d. It can access no shared field.

3. Can a shared method be recursive (can it call itself)?

   a. Yes.

   b. No.

   c. Yes, if it is public.

   d. Yes, if it is overloaded.

4. Can a shared field have an initializer? (Hint: If you don't know, try writing a quick example.)

   a. Yes.

   b. No.

    c. Not unless it is an object field.

    d. Yes, but not for arrays.

5. What access modifiers are allowed for shared members?

    a. Must be public.

    b. Public, private, and friend.

    c. All that are available for regular members.

    d. No access modifiers are allowed for shared members.

6. To access a shared property you need:

    a. An instance of the class to invoke the method on.

    b. An object variable.

    c. Both a and b.

    d. Nothing; use class name and the dot-notation.

True or False

Select one of the two possible answers and then verify on our Web site that you picked the correct one.

1. A shared or class-level method means a method that is invoked on the class and not on a particular instance of the class.

True/False

2. Shared properties and method cannot be overloaded.

True/False

3. Shared fields must use the s_ prefix.

True/False

4. Shared properties can be `Readonly`, `Writeonly`, and normal (read-write), the same as regular properties.

True/False

5. You would use a shared method when the action performed by the method does not involve any of the regular (non-shared) fields, properties, or other methods of the class it is on.

True/False

6. Using shared methods allows for better encapsulation and readability of code.

True/False

Applying It

Try to complete the following exercise by yourself.

APPLY

Independent Exercise

Create a class that models a pizza ordering system. You must have a class for the pizza order. The class must specify the name of the caller (the person who ordered the pizza), the size of the pizza (small or large), and the ingredients (pepperoni, sausage, cheese, and so on). Each ingredient has a fixed price based on the size of the pizza ($1.00 for small and $2.00 for large). The base price for a pizza with no ingredients (sauce and cheese only) is $6.00 for a small and $10.00 for a large.

Your class must have methods to change the size, add ingredients, and calculate the final price for the pizza.

Make a UML model of the class and then implement the class and write a unit test program to ensure that it works.

Inheritance

In this chapter you will learn about one of the most important features of object-oriented design and programming, inheritance. The chapters is structured as follows:

- What is inheritance?
- Simple inheritance
- Implications of inheritance
- Multi-level inheritance
- Polymorphism
- Abstract classes
- Inheritance in the .NET Framework

First you will look at what inheritance is and how to use inheritance to model the real world. You will look at a few theoretical examples to understand the semantic meaning of inheritance. Next we will give an example of simple inheritance. You will learn what the syntax is for inheriting from a class and then some of the implications of inheritance on different members of a class. You will also look at how inheritance influences other aspects of OO programming, such as visibility and life span of members.

You will then learn about polymorphism: what it is and how to implement it in Visual Basic .NET. You will see a few examples of method and property overriding. The next topic, abstract classes, deals with a special feature of object-oriented languages: classes that do not have instances. We will explain their use and look at some examples.

At the end of the chapter you will look at the inheritance hierarchy of the .NET Framework in the light of the concepts you just learned.

What Is Inheritance?

Let's assume you need to model and program a Human Resources (HR) system, which deals with the employees of the company and customer contacts, among other entities. The approach based on what you know today (and what you would do in a previous version of Visual Basic) would be to design two classes: one for employees and one for customer contacts. They would look like the UML diagram in Figure 17.1 and be implemented as shown in the code that follows.

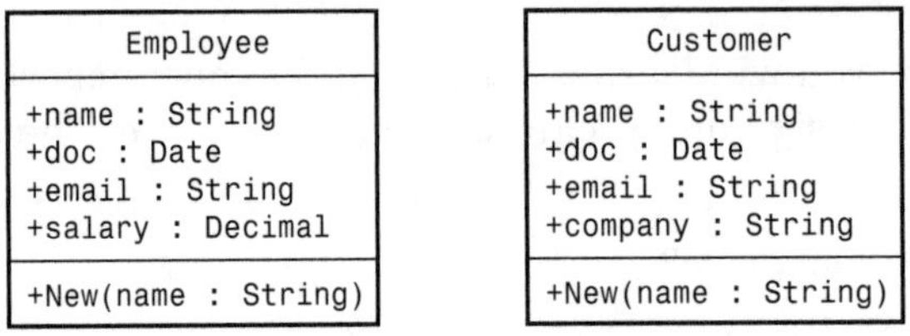

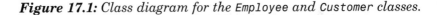

Employee
+name : String
+doc : Date
+email : String
+salary : Decimal
+New(name : String)

Customer
+name : String
+doc : Date
+email : String
+company : String
+New(name : String)

Figure 17.1: *Class diagram for the* `Employee` *and* `Customer` *classes.*

The implementation for the `Employee` class would be:

```
Public Class Employee
    Private m_name As String
    Private m_dob As Date
    Private m_email As String
    Private m_salary As Decimal

    Public Property name() As String
        Get
            Return m_name
        End Get
        Set
            m_name = value
        End Set
    End Property

    Public Property dob() As Date
        Get
            Return m_dob
        End Get
        Set
            m_dob = value
        End Set
    End Property
```

```
    Public Property email() As String
        Get
            Return m_email
        End Get
        Set
            m_email = value
        End Set
    End Property

    Public Property salary() As Decimal
        Get
            Return m_salary
        End Get
        Set
            m_salary = value
        End Set
    End Property
End Class
```

And the Customer (short for customer contact) class would look like:

```
Public Class Customer
    Private m_name As String
    Private m_dob As Date
    Private m_email As String
    Private m_company As String

    Public Property name() As String
        Get
            Return m_name
        End Get
        Set
            m_name = value
        End Set
    End Property

    Public Property dob() As Date
        Get
            Return m_dob
        End Get
        Set
            m_dob = value
        End Set
    End Property

    Public Property email() As String
        Get
            Return m_email
```

```
        End Get
        Set
            m_email = value
        End Set
    End Property

    Public Property company() As String
        Get
            Return m_company
        End Get
        Set
            m_company = value
        End Set
    End Property
End Class
```

There is nothing fancy in the two classes, just private fields and public properties to get and set their values. We have omitted constructors and methods for simplicity.

You have probably noticed that a large part of the code repeats itself, the fields and properties for name, dob (date of birth), and email. If you stop and think about it, this is quite normal because both a customer contact and an employee are humans; therefore, they would have a lot in common (all have names, dates of birth, and so on). Although apparently there is nothing wrong with implementing the two classes this way, you will learn that there are good reasons to use another mechanism to do it. But first let's look at some of the issues. Let's call the code that is identical in both classes *common code* for simplicity.

The first and most important issue is that this common code is repeated in each class. That means that someone would have to type in the same code for each class that uses it. In our example this would be any class that models a human being who has a name, date of birth, and email address. This process has the disadvantage of being error-prone (through typing or copy/paste errors). But the more important consequence is that of code maintenance: whenever a change to this common code is made (for example to split the name property in first and last names) the change will have to be done in every single class that uses the common code.

The second issue is that you have no means of treating an employee and a customer contact in the same manner. If you have a procedure that deals with an employee's name, date of birth, and email (say for sending a birthday greeting email), and want to apply a similar procedure to a customer contact, you need to write another procedure. The example is illustrated here.

```
Public Sub SendCongratulationE(ByVal employees() As Employee)
   Dim i As Integer, e As Employee
   For i = 0 To employees.Length - 1
     e = employees(i)
     If e.dob = now Then ' his birthday!
        ' send the person an email with "Happy Birthday " + name
        ' at his email address
     End If
   Next
End Sub

Public Sub SendCongratulationC(ByVal customers() As Customer)
   Dim i As Integer, c As Customer
   For i = 0 To customers.Length - 1
     c = customers(i)
     If c.dob = now Then ' his birthday!
        ' send the person an email with "Happy Birthday " + name
        ' at his email address
     End If
   Next
End Sub
```

You cannot reuse the first procedure for Customer objects because they are of a different type than the Employee objects. Therefore, you need a second procedure. The more classes that share common code, the more procedures you would need. As a consequence the program would become more complex and hard to maintain.

Inheritance resolves both these issues:

- It allows common code to exist in one place only and not be replicated in all classes that share it. This also solves the maintenance problem because, being stored in one place, the code can be changed in that one place. The changes will be reflected in all classes that use it.

- It allows classes that share a subset of properties and methods to be treated in the same way. We will explain how shortly.

So what is inheritance? *Inheritance* is defined as the process of extending the functionality of a class by adding new properties and methods and creating in this way a new class. The new class (known as the *derived*, or *specialized class*) has all the methods and properties of the original class (known as the *base class*), plus a set of properties and methods that are its own. The new class is said to *inherit* from the base class, or that it is *derived* from the based class, or that it *specializes* the base class. All these terms are equivalent and can be used interchangeably. You will understand better these terms by following the text and examples in the rest of this chapter.

From a more philosophical point of view, you can think of inheritance as the process of going from general to particular. If you had a class Car, which represents the general concept of a car (an object that can be used to transport individuals or objects over some distance) you could specialize it in a few subcategories: town cars, SUVs, trucks, flying cars. All of these are sharing all properties of a car, and have some more of their own. A truck has a larger engine and can carry massive objects; a flying car can fly, has a set of parachutes, and redundant rotative engines; and so on. But all of them are also cars, not trains, ships, or planes.

The reverse process of going from particular to general (known as generalization, or abstraction) is looking at a set of classes and determining that they have common properties and behaviors. These common properties and behaviors are then used to construct a new class—which is the generalization (abstraction) of the particular classes involved in the first place. You would look at some species of animals (like humans, rats, baboons, parrots, and so on) and determine that they share some common properties. You would place those properties in a new class: Animal. You can go further and determine that the human, rat, and baboon share a property that the parrots do not have (namely, giving birth to live offspring, and feeding them with milk after birth). You would classify them as mammals, and the parrot as a bird.

Both these techniques end up with a classification hierarchy in which you have the more general classes being subclassed in more specialized classes. You will look at some examples next.

Simple Inheritance

How does inheritance solve the issues you had with your Employee and Customer classes? Well, you can apply the generalization process and move from particular to general. In your example you noticed that three of the properties are common to both classes. That means that you could have a base class named Person, for example, in which you place the common properties. Then you inherit from this class both your Employee and Customer classes. In this way you solve both issues (code reuse and common behavior). Let's see how this is done. First you write the base class:

```
Public Class Person
    Private m_name As String
    Private m_dob As Date
    Private m_email As String

    Public Property name() As String
        Get
```

```
            Return m_name
        End Get
        Set
            m_name = value
        End Set
    End Property

    Public Property dob() As Date
        Get
            Return m_dob
        End Get
        Set
            m_dob = value
        End Set
    End Property

    Public Property email() As String
        Get
            Return m_email
        End Get
        Set
            m_email = value
        End Set
    End Property
End Class
```

This is a regular class, with just the three properties and fields that are common to both `Employee` and `Customer` classes. Now you rewrite the `Employee` class:

```
Public Class Employee
    Inherits Person

    Private m_salary As Decimal

    Public Property salary() As Decimal
        Get
            Return m_salary
        End Get
        Set
            m_salary = value
        End Set
    End Property
End Class
```

And the Customer class:

```
Public Class Customer
    Inherits Person

    Private m_company As String

    Public Property company() As String
        Get
            Return m_company
        End Get
        Set
            m_company = value
        End Set
    End Property
End Class
```

You have removed the common fields and properties from both classes and replaced them with the Inherits statement. This statement tells you (and the compiler) that the class *is a* Person. That means it inherits from the class specified after the Inherits statement (Person, in this example) all its fields, properties, and methods. Indeed, if you write a short test program to verify that this is true, you can see all properties of Person show up in the drop-down list of members of a variable of type Employee or Customer (when you use the "." —dot). The example code is shown here:

```
Sub Main()
    Dim e As New Employee()
    e.name = "Hank R."
    e.dob = #1/1/1928#
    e.email = "hank@rearden.com"
    e.salary = 45000

    Dim c As New Customer()
    c.name = "Dagny T."
    c.dob = #1/1/1930#
    c.email = "dagny@taggart.com"
    c.company = "Taggart Intl."
End Sub
```

You can use the name, date of birth, and email properties as they would be declared by the Employee or Customer class themselves. As far as the client is concerned, the inherited properties (as well as inherited methods) appear to be part of the derived class.

Now you can address the second issue, namely you can now write a procedure that will deal with both the Employee and Customer classes through their common properties. You can convert your email sending procedure from the previous example to the following:

```
Public Sub SendCongratulation(ByVal persons() As Person)
    Dim i As Integer, p As Person
    For i = 0 To persons.Length - 1
        p = persons(i)
        If p.dob = now Then ' his birthday!
            ' send the person an email with "Happy Birthday " + name
            ' at his email address
        End If
    Next
End Sub
```

The first difference (to the two procedures shown previously) is that you now use an array of Person objects and not of Employee or Customer. This will allow you to pass in either employees or customers, or a mixture. Indeed, because both the Employee and Customer are also Person, you can use them as such.

You could modify your test code to declare an array of two persons, populate it with one employee and one customer, and call the procedure to send them an email.

```
Sub Main()
    Dim persons() As Person = New Person(2) {}
    Dim e As New Employee()
    e.name = "Hank R."
    e.dob = #1/1/1928#
    e.email = "hank@rearden.com"
    e.salary = 45000
    persons(0) = e
    Dim c As New Customer()
    c.name = "Dagny T."
    c.dob = #2/2/1930#
    c.email = "dagny@taggart.com"
    c.company = "Taggart Intl."
    persons(1) = c
    SendCongratulation(persons)
End Sub
```

As you can see from the code, you can assign an object of a derived class (Employee or Customer) to a variable declared to be of the base class (Person). You could also pass a variable of a derived class to a procedure or property that expects a variable of the base type.

You could have code like this:

```
Sub Main()
    Dim e As New Employee()
    e.name = "Hank R."
    e.dob = #1/1/1928#
    e.email = "hank@rearden.com"
    e.salary = 45000
    MySub(e)
End Sub

Public Sub MySub(ByVal p As Person)
    Console.Out.WriteLine("Name is " + p.name)
    Console.Out.WriteLine("DOB is " + CStr(p.dob))
    Console.Out.WriteLine("Email is " + p.email)
End Sub
```

You construct a new Employee and pass it to a procedure that expects a Person. Because the Employee inherits from Person, or in other words is derived from Person, you usually say that *is a* Person. The inheritance is known as a relationship of type *is-a* between two classes. The meaning is the exact English meaning—that an instance of the derived class is also an instance of the base class.

One important fact to remember is that one class can be derived from one class only (it can have at most one base class). That is, you cannot have two or more Inherits statements in a class. This is known as *single inheritance* model, as opposed to languages that support a *multiple inheritance* model (like C++). Multiple inheritance means that the class can inherit from two or more classes.

NOTE

There is an on-going argument in the OO community of whether multiple inheritance is a theoretically sound concept or not. Regardless of this argument, the practical experience has shown that programs and libraries making use of multiple inheritance tend to be more complex and, as a result, harder to maintain and more error-prone. Therefore, more recent languages like Java and most of the .NET languages do not support multiple inheritance. Interfaces are used to achieve the same results, as you will see in the next chapter.

In UML you represent inheritance by a line uniting the two classes (base and derived) that has a triangle at the base class end, which points to the base class. An example is shown in Figure 17.2.

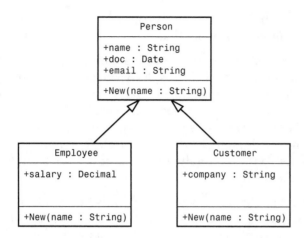

Figure 17.2: *Class diagram for the* Person, Employee, *and* Customer *classes.*

Implications of Inheritance

You have seen what inheritance is. Now you will look at the implications of inheritance in some key areas you have learned so far, namely visibility of members, constructors, overloading of methods, and shared members.

Visibility

You have seen that members of a class can have one of the three standard access modifiers (Public, Private, and Friend). We also mentioned that you can have members declared as Protected. You will now learn what protected members are and how to use them.

First we need to mention that the public, private, and friend modifiers are exactly the same in the case of both base and derived classes. A Public member is accessible to anyone in the assembly and outside it. A Private member is accessible only inside the class it is declared in, but *not* in any classes derived from that class! Friend members are visible to anyone inside the assembly of which the class is part. These modifiers do not cover some special cases, and because of this some new modifiers had to be added.

A private field declared in a base class cannot be accessed in any of the properties or methods of a derived class. In our example, the m_name field declared in Person could not be accessed in a method in Employee. The Employee class could access the property name, which is declared as Public. In general you can use public properties to offer access to private members. Unfortunately, this will make the properties accessible to anyone. Alternatively, you could make the properties Friend, so that they can be accessed only from this assembly. But in this case you cannot use it from classes in a different assembly that wish to inherit from your class.

There are often cases when some members must be accessed by the class they are declared in and all classes derived from it, but not by anyone else. These types of members should be declared as Protected. It makes sense to declare a member (normally a field or property) as Protected only if it is intended to be used by classes derived from the class in which they are declared. If no one is going to inherit from the class (if it is a friend class, not visible outside the assembly) then Protected members function the same as private members.

If a class member should be accessible by anyone in this assembly and only to derived classes outside this assembly, then the Protected and Friend modifiers can be combined. Protected Friend fields, properties, and methods are accessible by anyone in the assembly the class is declared in and only to derived classes from other assemblies, which extend the class in question.

In the examples you should declare the m_name, m_dob, and m_email as protected, as shown, to be visible in both the Employee and Customer classes.

```
Public Class Person
    Protected m_name As String
    Protected m_dob As Date
    Protected m_email As String
    ' the rest of the class is omitted (unchanged)
End Class
```

As a general rule, fields in a class intended as a base class should be declared as Protected, and properties and methods as Public or Friend.

Constructors and the MyBase Keyword

To understand what the implications are of inheritance on constructors you first need to understand the way derived class objects are constructed. The .NET runtime first allocates memory for one object of the appropriate type (for an Employee object). It will then initialize all the members of the object, according to their declarations, but starting with the base class members. In the example this will initialize the m_name, m_dob, and m_email first, then the derived class members, m_salary. Then it will call the appropriate constructor on the derived class and execute the code in this constructor. This constructor may in turn call the base class constructor. If it does call it, it must use the keyword MyBase, which is used to indicate the base instance, in this case a "virtual" instance of the class Person:

```
Public Class Person
    Protected m_name As String
```

```
Protected m_dob As Date
Protected m_email As String
' the rest of the class is omitted (unchanged)
Public Sub New(Optional ByVal name As String = "", _
               Optional ByVal dob As Date = #1/1/1900#, _
               Optional ByVal email As String = "")
   m_name = name
   m_dob = dob
   m_email = email
End Sub
End Class
```

You added a constructor with three optional parameters to the Person class. This is a regular constructor, which will set the three fields to the given parameter values.

```
Public Class Employee
   Inherits Person

   Private m_salary As Decimal

   Public Property salary() As Decimal
      Get
         Return m_salary
      End Get
      Set
         m_salary = value
      End Set
   End Property

   Public Sub New(Optional ByVal name As String = "", _
                  Optional ByVal dob As Date = #1/1/1900#, _
                  Optional ByVal email As String = "", _
                  Optional ByVal salary As Decimal = 0)
      MyBase.New(name, dob, email)
      m_salary = salary
   End Sub
End Class
```

You also added a constructor to the Employee class, which first calls the constructor in MyBase (the Person class) and then sets the m_salary (which is a derived class field).

MyBase can strictly be used within a derived class to access its base class members. MyBase is not really an object; it can be better described as a syntactic placeholder for the base class. You do not have to use it if the base class member can be accessed directly. However, this is not the case in the example (Sub New also exists in Person); that is why you need it.

NOTE

The MyBase is the counterpart of the MyClass keyword, which you learned before, and their usage has many things in common. Neither is a real object, both are used to access members that may be otherwise inaccessible, neither can be used for the Is operator, and so on.

Now you can construct a new employee and trace with the debugger to see the order of the operations executed in the following example:

```
Sub Main()
    Dim e As Employee
    e = New Employee("Joe", #1/3/1986#, "Joe@thecomp.com", 45000)
End Sub
```

Method Overloading

The methods and properties of base classes can be overloaded in the same way as for a single non-inherited class. The only interesting case arises when a derived class overloads a method that was originally declared in a base class. In this case the base class does not have to declare the method with the Overloads keyword. If you were to develop the class B and someone else were to inherit from it class D and overload the MyMethod, it would do it as shown in the following example.

```
Public Class B
    Public Sub MyMethod()
        ' do something
    End Sub
    ' rest of class omitted
End Class
Public Class D
    Inherits B
    Public Overloads Sub MyMethod(ByVal anArg As String)
        ' do something
    End Sub
    ' rest of class omitted
End Class
```

That is, only the derived class must declare the method with the Overloads keyword. There is currently no way to prevent someone from deriving from your class to overload one of your visible methods (Public, Protected, or Friend).

Shared Members

Shared members are declared and used the same way as non-inherited classes. All visible (non-private) shared members declared in a base class are accessible to the derived classes. Next is a valid example:

```
Public Class B
   Public Shared Sub MyMethod()
      ' do something
   End Sub
   ' rest of class omitted
End Class
Public Class D
   Inherits B
   Public Overloads Shared Sub MyMethod(ByVal anArg As String)
      MyBase.MyMethod()
      ' do something
   End Sub
   ' rest of class omitted
End Class
```

The inherited shared methods can be overloaded in the same way as non-shared methods. You can use the MyBase keyword to access a shared method declared on the base class.

If a shared member is declared in a derived class, it is not accessible to the base class, although it is a class-level member. The next example is incorrect, and it would not compile:

```
Public Class B
   Public Shared Sub MyMethod()
      MyOtherMethod() ' wrong!
   End Sub
   ' rest of class omitted
End Class
Public Class D
   Inherits B
   Public Shared Sub MyOtherMethod()
      ' do something
   End Sub
   ' rest of class omitted
End Class
```

The same applies to all members, not only shared members. A member declared in a derived class is not accessible in the base class.

Multi-level Inheritance

Inheritance can have multiple levels. That is, a base class can have derived classes, each of which can have derived classes, and so on. These classes constitute what is known as an *inheritance hierarchy* (or *inheritance tree*). All the rules that apply for single-level inheritance also apply for multiple level inheritance. You can extend your example with the Person, Employee, and Customer to add two more classes to the hierarchy: SalesEmployee and Manager. These are both derived from the Employee class. The sales employees have a base salary (represented by the base class Employee m_salary) and a monthly bonus, calculated based on a percentage of the salary. The managers have a salary (like all employees) and a managerial bonus (which is a fixed amount every month). We have changed the m_salary in Employee to be Protected and added two new classes as shown.

```
Public Class SalesEmployee
    Inherits Employee

    Protected m_bonusRate As Decimal

    Public Property bonusRate() As Decimal
        Get
            Return m_bonusRate
        End Get
        Set
            m_bonusRate = value
        End Set
    End Property

    Public Sub New(Optional ByVal name As String = "", _
                   Optional ByVal dob As Date = #1/1/1900#, _
                   Optional ByVal email As String = "", _
                   Optional ByVal salary As Decimal = 0, _
                   Optional ByVal bonusRate As Decimal = 0)
        MyBase.New(name, dob, email, salary)
        m_bonusRate = bonusRate
    End Sub
End Class

Public Class Manager
    Inherits Employee

    Protected m_bonus As Decimal

    Public Property bonus() As Decimal
        Get
            Return m_bonus
        End Get
        Set
            m_bonus = value
        End Set
    End Property
```

```
Public Sub New(Optional ByVal name As String = "", _
               Optional ByVal dob As Date = #1/1/1900#, _
               Optional ByVal email As String = "", _
               Optional ByVal salary As Decimal = 0, _
               Optional ByVal bonus As Decimal = 0)
    MyBase.New(name, dob, email, salary)
    m_bonus = bonus
  End Sub
End Class
```

You can use these classes in a similar fashion with the `Employee` class. You can write code such as

```
Sub Main()
  Dim se As SalesEmployee
  se = New SalesEmployee("Joe", #1/3/1986#, "Joe@hiscomp.com", 45000,
CDec(0.15))
End Sub
```

One thing that is notable about the classes that are derived from other derived classes is the usage of the `MyBase` keyword. When used in the `SalesEmployee` class, for instance, it does not reflect only the members of the base class of `SalesEmployee` (`Employee`), but rather all the members of `Employee`, and any members which `Employee` inherits from its parent (`Person`), and so on. These members will be visible when you type MyBase followed by a period and get the drop down list of members.

Polymorphism

Polymorphism comes from the Greek roots *polu* (many) and *morphe* (form), and it means (in computer science) an entity that can have multiple forms or different behavior. In the specific case of inheritance it means that derived classes may have different behavior for the same method.

Let's assume that you need to add a method that calculates the monthly salary of an employee. The normal place you would add this would be the `Employee` class, where you have the `m_salary` field, from which you calculate the income. You could write a function `GetMontlyPay()` as shown:

```
Public Class Employee
  Inherits Person
  Protected m_salary As Decimal
  ' the rest of the class is omitted (unchanged)
  Public Function GetMonthlyPay() As Decimal
    Return m_salary / 12
  End Function
End Class
```

This would work fine for regular employees. But, it would not work well for managers and sales employees, who both have a bonus or a bonus rate added to their base salary. You could write another method that calculates the salary of a sales employee on the SalesEmployee class, and yet another one on the Manager class. But this is not the best solution because you do not have a generic method that you can call on any Employee to find its monthly pay.

To have this functionality you need a method that is implemented on the Employee class (as you have seen previously) but whose functionality you can overwrite in any of the derived classes. This is exactly what *polymorphism* is: the capability to define generic methods in a base class that could be altered in derived classes—implicitly conferring on the derived class a different behavior. Because you can have many derived classes from one base class, each may have its own behavior, and hence the *polymorphism* (many forms of behavior in this case, for the same method).

To implement *overridable methods* (which is what they are usually known as) you first add the Overridable modifier on the method in the base class:

```
Public Class Employee
   Inherits Person
   Protected m_salary As Decimal
   ' the rest of the class is omitted (unchanged)
   Public Overridable Function GetMonthlyPay() As Decimal
      Return m_salary / 12
   End Function
End Class
```

Then you override the method in both the SalesEmployee and Manager classes, as shown:

```
Public Class SalesEmployee
   Inherits Employee
   Protected m_bonusRate As Decimal
   ' the rest of the class is omitted (unchanged)
   Public Overrides Function GetMonthlyPay() As Decimal
      Return (m_salary / 12) * (1 + m_bonusRate)
   End Function
End Class

Public Class Manager
   Inherits Employee
   Protected m_bonus As Decimal
   ' the rest of the class is omitted (unchanged)
```

```
Public Overrides Function GetMontlyPay() As Decimal
   Return MyBase.GetMonthlyPay() + m_bonus
End Function
End Class
```

As you can see from this example, you use the Overrides keyword for the methods in the derived classes to specify that they overwrite the behavior of a method declared in the base class. You can access from an overridden method in a derived class the base class method implementation by using the MyBase keyword (as illustrated in the Manager class).

The reason that overriding (polymorphism) is such a popular technique in object-oriented programming is the fact that the compiler knows what type of object it is dealing with, even if the object is used through a reference to its base class. You could have a variable of type Employee that refers to a SalesEmployee object. When you call GetMontlyPay() the runtime knows that the object is a SalesEmployee and not an Employee, as the variable types seems to indicate, and calls the right version of the method. This is illustrated in the next example, and we recommend that you use the debugger to step through the code and see which method is actually called.

```
Sub Main()
   Dim e As Employee, d As Deciaml
   e = New SalesEmployee("Joe", #1/3/1986#, "Joe@hiscomp.com", 48000, CDec(0.15))
   d = e.GetMonthlyPay() ' calls SalesEmployee.GetMonthlyPay()
End Sub
```

This can be extremely useful because you can deal with objects in a uniform and generic fashion without knowing exactly what type they are. You can define an Overridable method on the base class and then use base class variables to deal with any derived class objects. You can call the method, and each object will execute the appropriate method as defined by its class override of that particular method.

If a class does not provide an override of an overridable method, the runtime will use the base class version of the method. If in this case you would add another class called TelecomutingEmployee that uses the same way to calculate the monthly pay as the regular Employee, it does not need to provide an override for the GetMonthlyPay() method. When the method will be invoked on an instance of the class, the base class method will be executed.

It is important that you understand that there is a fundamental difference between the concept of *overloaded* methods and properties and the concept of *polymorphism* (*overridable* methods and properties). *Overloading* means having more than one method with the same name, but *a different list of arguments* (number, order or type), in the same class or in a combination of base and derived classes. *Overriding* a method means having a method with the same name and *the same arguments* in a derived class, a method that will be called automatically when an object of the derived type is the target of the invocation. When an overloaded method is called, it is determined by the caller which variation of the method is desired (by specifying the appropriate parameters). When calling an overridden method, the runtime decodes what implementation of the method to call (base class or derived class) depending on the object type.

NOTE

If a method or property is declared with a specific visibility modifier in a base class, this modifier *must* be preserved in the derived classes. A method declared as Public Overridable in the base class cannot be overridden as Private Overrides. It must remain Public.

It is very important to understand correctly how polymorphism works and when to use it, as it is one of the most useful techniques in object-oriented programming when coupled with inheritance and use of interfaces, as you will see in the next chapter. As you advance in your study of the language, and you gain more experience in writing code, you will see that it becomes a natural concept easy to understand and use.

Abstract Classes

There are some cases in which the base class of an inheritance hierarchy needs to declare an overridable method, but the class itself is unable to provide any implementation for the method. In this case what you need is a way to force the derived classes to override the method in discussion. For an example, let's consider a banking application that has an Account base class, of which you derived two classes: CheckingAccount and SavingsAccount. We illustrate these three classes as follows.

```
Public Class Account
    Protected m_balance As Decimal

    Public Property balance() As Decimal
       Get
          Return m_balance
       End Get
       Set
          m_balance = value
       End Set
    End Property
```

```
    Public Sub New(Optional ByVal startBalance As Decimal = 0)
        m_balance = startBalance
    End Sub
End Class
```

The base class `Account` is quite simple; it has only one field and property called balance, which is the balance of the account. You also include a constructor, for convenience.

```
Public Class CheckingAccount
    Inherits Account

    Public Sub New(Optional ByVal startBalance As Decimal = 0)
        MyBase.New(startBalance)
    End Sub

    Public Sub CloseMonth()
        If m_balance < 0 Then
            ' If the balance is negative, apply a charge of 25 dollars
            m_balance -= 25
        ElseIf m_balance < 2500 Then
            ' If the balance is less than 2,500, apply monthly charge
            m_balance -= 4
        End If
        ' otherwise no action is taken (no interest)
    End Sub
End Class
```

The `CheckingAccount` class inherits from `Account`, and it has a method that adjusts the end of the month balance according to the policy for this type of account: if the balance is negative (overdraft) the bank will charge an amount; if the balance is less that 2,500 it will charge the monthly fee. Otherwise, if the balance exceeds 2,500 the charge is waived.

```
Public Class SavingsAccount
    Inherits Account

    ' shared interest, default to 0.5% monthly
    Protected Shared s_interest As Decimal = CDec(0.005)

    Public Shared Property interest() As Decimal
        Get
            Return s_interest
        End Get
        Set
            s_interest = value
        End Set
    End Property
```

```
    Public Sub New(Optional ByVal startBalance As Decimal = 0)
        MyBase.New(startBalance)
    End Sub

    Public Sub CloseMonth()
        If m_balance < 0 Then
            ' If the balance is negative, apply a charge of 25 dollars
            m_balance -= 25
        Else
            ' apply an interest of whatever the interest
            ' stored in the s_interest value
            m_balance *= 1 + s_interest
        End If
    End Sub
End Class
```

The savings account class has a shared field and property for the monthly interest that the savings account will earn (if the balance is positive). The shared interest has a (generous) default value of 0.5% monthly. It also has a procedure for the end of the month calculation, which is different from the one in the CheckingAccount class.

You could use these classes as illustrated in the following example:

```
Module Module1
    Sub Main()
        Dim ca As CheckingAccount = New CheckingAccount(1200)
        ca.CloseMonth()
        Console.Out.WriteLine("The checking balance is {0}", ca.balance)
        ' output is 1194
        Dim sa As SavingsAccount = New SavingsAccount(7600)
        sa.CloseMonth()
        Console.Out.WriteLine("The savings balance is {0}", sa.balance)
        ' output is 7638
    End Sub
End Module
```

The problem with these classes is that you have a method on both derived classes that is semantically identical (it performs the end of the month calculation for the account). It is not declared as overridable in the base class because there is nothing the base class can provide as an implementation for that particular method that is common to both the savings and checking derived classes. This is a typical pattern encountered frequently in OO design and programming. The implication is that the Account class is what is known as an *abstract class*. You can declare the CloseMonth() method in the Account class and use the keyword MustOverride to indicate that classes that are derived from this class *must* provide an implementation for this method, and that this class does *not* provide one. If you do this, the implication is that the Account class cannot be instantiated (no objects of type account can be created with the New keyword). The reason for this is simple: If the method CloseMonth() is called on an object of type Account, the runtime will look for the implementation of the method, but it will find none! To prevent this and indicate to the compiler that you declare this Account class as abstract, use the class modifier MustInherit so that no one will be able to create objects of this class, but rather only of its derived classes. Let's look at the modified example:

```
Public MustInherit Class Account
    Protected m_balance As Decimal


    ' the rest of the class is omitted (unchanged)


    Public MustOverride Sub CloseMonth()


End Class
```

The methods declared as MustOverride must not have a body, and no End Sub or End Function should be entered. Also a class that contains one or more methods of this type (known as *abstract* method) must be declared as MustInherit. A class can be declared as *abstract* (MustInherit) even if it does not have any abstract methods, just to prevent clients from creating instances of this type.

```
Public Class CheckingAccount
    Inherits Account


    ' the rest of the class is omitted (unchanged)


    Public Overrides Sub CloseMonth()
        If m_balance < 0 Then
            ' If the balance is negative, apply a charge of 25 dollars
            m_balance -= 25
        ElseIf m_balance < 2500 Then
            ' If the balance is less than 2500, apply monthly charge
            m_balance -= 4
        End If
        ' otherwisse no action is taken (no interest)
    End Sub
End Class

Public Class SavingsAccount
    Inherits Account


    ' the rest of the class is omitted (unchanged)
```

```
    Public Overrides Sub CloseMonth()
        If m_balance < 0 Then
            ' If the balance is negative, apply a charge of 25 dollars
            m_balance -= 25
        Else
            ' apply an interest of whatever the interest
            ' stored in the s_interest value
            m_balance *= 1 + s_interest
        End If
    End Sub
End Class
```

The derived classes both now must use the Overrides keyword to indicate that the method is overriding a base class method (although in this case there is no real overriding, rather it is implementing). Now you can actually have variables declared as type Account and call the CloseMonth() method on it, as shown here:

```
Module Module1
    Sub Main()
        Dim a As Account = New CheckingAccount(1200)
        a.CloseMonth()
        Console.Out.WriteLine("The checking balance is {0}", a.balance)

        a = New SavingsAccount(7600)
        a.CloseMonth()
        Console.Out.WriteLine("The savings balance is {0}", a.balance)
    End Sub
End Module
```

That means you can now treat any account generically, although there is no such thing as an Account (you can have only derived class instances, such as CheckingAccount and SavingsAccount). It also implies that if you add a new class to the hierarchy (say, InvestmentAccount) you must provide an implementation for all methods declared as MustOverride in the base class.

In general you are allowed to have an inheritance hierarchy with multiple levels of abstract classes, but this is unusual. In case this cannot be avoided, the derived classes must implement all methods declared as MustOverride from all abstract classes in its inheritance ancestors, or become themselves abstract (by using the MustInherit modifier).

Abstract classes are represented in UML the same way as regular classes, except that the name of the class is italicized, as shown in Figure 17.3.

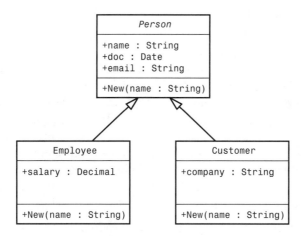

Figure 17.3: *Class diagram (version 2) for the* Person, Employee, *and* Customer *classes.*

This concludes your introduction to inheritance, and at this point you are supposed to understand the basic terms and concepts used in inheritance. You will see more examples in the rest of the book, as all classes in .NET Framework are actually inherited from some class.

Inheritance in the .NET Framework

As you saw from the moment you wrote your first example of a class, when you used the period to access a variable's members, the IntelliSense drop-down list will contain some "mysterious" members that you never declared. These members are Equals, GetHashCode, GetType, and ToString. Now you know enough to understand that these members must come from some base class. But how, because your classes did not used Inherits at that point?

The mystery is solved quite simply. All classes in the .NET Framework (and in general in all .NET languages) inherit (directly or indirectly) from a base class called Object. This inheritance is implicit; you do not need to declare it, the compiler assumes that if your class does not have an Inherits statement, it inherits from Object. If it does inherit from another class, that class in turn will inherit from Object (directly or indirectly). In short, Object is the base class of all classes.

The Object class declares a few methods, and the public ones are your mysterious members, which we illustrate here with some examples.

Equals is used to compare two instances for equality:

```
Dim d As Decimal = 5
Dim e As Decimal = 5
```

```
If d.Equals(e) Then ' True
   MsgBox "d and e hold the same value"
End If
```

You can override this method and provide your own comparison. The default implementation compares the object passed in as a parameter to the current object and, if they are the same object (reference comparison), it returns true. You could override it to provide a comparison between the values of different fields and return true if they are identical. Some classes in the .NET Framework override this method so that the comparison is between values, not references. This includes most fundamental data types (such as `Integer`, `Decimal`, `String`, and so on). You have seen in one of our previous examples the Equals method used on a String.

The `GetHashCode` method provides a hash code used for hash tables. In case you are not familiar with hash tables, they are indexed collections of objects, and the key, known as a hash key, is generated by this method. You will learn of them in the next chapter.

`GetType` is a method that returns an instance of a class named `Type`. This is a special class whose instances describe other classes. It is usually known as a metadata class.

The `ToString` method returns the state of the object in a String format. It can be used for debugging purposes (output to a console for example). The fundamental data types override this method to return their value converted to a string.

These are the fundamental methods of the Object class that are available to all objects in the .NET Framework. If you look in the help file, you can find inheritance hierarchies for most assemblies in .NET Framework. The fundamental one is the `System` hierarchy, which is quite large. You will review some of the more important classes next. For details on any class, you can look that class up in the reference section of the MSDN .NET Framework (in the Index for example).

`Exception` is a base class for all exceptions thrown in the .NET Framework. It has members to access the error message, the source, and stack trace of the exception. You can extend it for creating your exceptions.

`Math` is a class that contains a shared method corresponding to major mathematical functionality (such as the absolute of a number, trigonometric functions, powers, square root, and so on).

`Random` is a class used to generate random numbers and initialize the algorithms that generate these (pseudo) random numbers.

ValueType is a very important class, from which most of the fundamental data types are derived. Boolean, all numeric types (and other numeric data types not mentioned yet), enumerations, structures, Date, and many others are derived from ValueType. The ValueType derived classes are the ones that have a by-value assignment semantic. String, for example, is not ValueType derived, but Decimal is. The ValueType class does not have any additional methods or properties. It is used mainly to indicate that the classes derived from it should use by-value assignment and copy semantics.

The Console class that you used in basically every example in this book so far, is also derived from Object and is part of the System assembly. The two members that you used, Out and In, are used to get data from a console user, or to output data to the console, as you already know.

There are many other important classes and many other assemblies (as you have seen before). You will encounter and explore many of them in the rest of the book, although some of the more advanced or esoteric ones will be left out.

What's Next

You have learned what inheritance is and how to use it to better your programs by using the fundamental OO paradigms. You also learned about the related concept of polymorphism and how to best make use of it. These are fundamental OO concepts, and we recommend that you review them carefully until you understand them. The exercises and questions that follow will help crystallize these concepts.

Next we will talk about interfaces: What is an interface, why do we need them, and how to use one. You will learn about the tight coupling between interfaces and class inheritance in implementing polymorphic behavior.

NOTE
The answers to "Reviewing It," "Checking It," and "Applying It" are available on our Web site.

REVIEW

Reviewing It

This section presents a review of the key concepts in this chapter. These questions are intended to gauge your absorption of the relevant material.

1. What do you understand by inheritance?

2. What is a base class?

3. What is a derived class?

4. Define and exemplify polymorphism.

5. What is an abstract method?

6. What is an abstract class?

7. Name the base class for the following groups of classes:

   • cheetah, hamster, dolphin, human

   • oak tree, fir tree, grass, mushroom

   • square, rectangle, circle, triangle

CHECK

Checking It

Select the correct answer(s) to the following questions.

Multiple Choice

1. What are the reasons the use of inheritance is a good programming practice (select all that apply)?

   a. Code reuse.

   b. Permits the use of polymorphism.

   c. Promotes encapsulation.

   d. It is a more structured approach.

2. What is the correct term for a class that inherits from another class (select all that apply)?

   a. Abstract class.

   b. Specialized class.

   c. Generalized class.

   d. Derived class.

3. Polymorphism is implemented using:

   a. Method overloading.

   b. Method overriding.

   c. Both.

   d. None.

4. Can a method that overrides a base class method call the base method?

   a. No, this is illegal.

   b. Yes it can, nothing special must be done.

   c. Yes, but it must use the `MyBase` keyword to prefix it.

   d. Yes, but it must use the `MyClass` keyword to prefix it.

5. An abstract method is:

   a. Any method in an abstract class.

   b. Any method that cannot be overridden in the derived classes.

   c. Any method that must be overridden in the derived classes.

   d. Any method that must be overridden in the base class.

6. An abstract class is:

   a. A class that has at least one abstract method.

   b. A class that has at least one method marked as `MustOverride`.

   c. A class declared as `MustInherit`.

   d. A class that has no fields.

True or False

Select one of the two possible answers and then verify on our Web site that you picked the correct one.

1. Inheritance is one of the cornerstones of OO programming.

   True/False

2. If you have a class called Kid and an instance of the class (a child named Joe) you can say that Joe inherits from Kid.

   True/False

3. If you have an abstract class called `FoodItem` with an overridable method called `CalculateCalories()` and a class `Pie`, which inherits from `FoodItem`, the class `Pie` must implement `CalculateCalories()`.

   True/False

4. A `Protected Overridable` method in a base class can be overridden and its visibility changed to `Public`.

   True/False

5. Abstract classes must have at least one abstract method.

   True/False

6. A class containing an abstract method must be abstract.

   True/False

APPLY

Applying It

Try to complete the following exercise by yourself.

Independent Exercise

Make the Person class (which you used in the first part of this chapter) an abstract class and add an abstract property called title. Implement the property in each class, adding fields and changing constructors as required.

Interfaces

In this chapter you will learn about a new and very important object-oriented concept: interfaces. We will discuss the following topics:

- What is an interface?
- Using interfaces
- Interface inheritance
- Interfaces in the .NET Framework

You will begin by learning what interfaces are and what are the differences between implementing an interface and inheriting from another class. You will continue with a few examples of how to use interfaces, including some of the most common .NET Framework interfaces.

We will then discuss interface inheritance, interfaces that inherit from other interfaces. You will also look at examples and discuss when it is better to use interfaces and when it is not.

In the final part of the chapter we will present a few of the most commonly used interfaces in the .NET Framework, together with some examples illustrating their use.

What Is an Interface?

To understand what an interface is let's start with an analogy. Any of the tools in a Swiss army knife is analogous to an interface. A Swiss army knife has a set of tools, such as a blade, can opener, screwdriver, and so on. But it is still a Swiss army knife; it is neither a blade, nor a can opener. It *can* perform the same actions as a can opener or a screwdriver, without being one. From the point of view of someone who needs a can opener, a Swiss army knife acts like a can opener. From the point of view of someone who needs a screwdriver, the same Swiss army knife is a screwdriver. In programming you would say that the can opener, blade, and so on are interfaces that define certain capabilities, and the Swiss army knife is a class that implements these interfaces.

Therefore, an *interface* is a definition for certain behavior. This behavior is *implemented* by any class that wishes to appear as that interface to someone who needs it. The next example illustrates the .NET Framework interface IComparable.

```
Public Interface IComparable
    Function CompareTo(ByVal o As Object) As Integer
End Interface
```

This interface is designed to be implemented by any class that wishes to offer the functionality defined by the interface, in this case the capability to compare two objects.

NOTE

The IComparable interface is normally implemented by classes that need to use a better comparison than the default Equals method in the Object base class, which only checks whether the two references are referring to the same object.

There is an unwritten convention (mostly in the Microsoft Windows programming world) that all interface names begin with the uppercase letter I, followed by the name of the interface. We find this convention useful, as it indicates at a glance whether a data type is class or an interface.

The interfaces are similar to classes: They can have member properties and methods (but not fields). All the properties and methods of an interface are abstract; they have no body, just the declaration. The class implementing the interface will supply the body. Also no modifiers for the properties and methods are allowed. That means that no Public, Protected, Private, Friend, Shared, Overrides, MustOverride, and NotOverridable are permitted inside an interface. All methods and properties are public and must be overridden. The interface itself maybe declared with the modifiers Public, Friend, or Private, which control its visibility in the assembly and outside of it.

After an interface is defined, it can be implemented by any class that chooses to. Implementing an interface is like a contract: The class implementing the interfaces "promises" that it will provide an implementation (body) for all methods and properties of the interface. There is no such thing as a "partial implementation," implementing only some methods from the interface.

In UML you represent an interface as illustrated in Figure 18.1. Note that the name of the interface is in italics, and the stereotype "<<interface>>" is added above or below the name to indicate clearly that is not an abstract class. The *stereotype* is just a way to classify entities in a UML model, and it has the regular English meaning of the word.

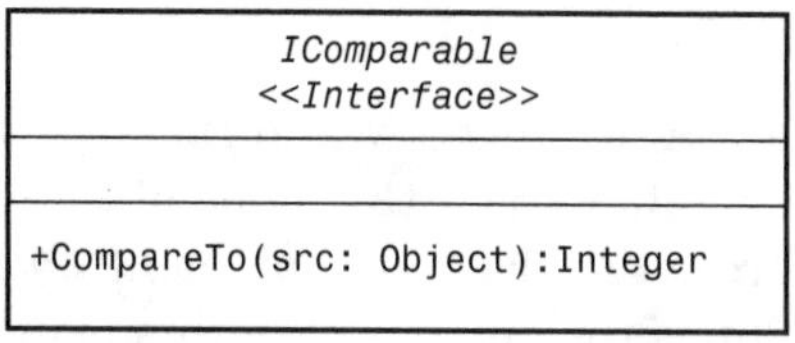

```
IComparable
<<Interface>>


+CompareTo(src: Object):Integer
```

Figure 18.1: *Interface* IComparable *in UML.*

Using Interfaces

We will show an example of a class implementing the IComparable interface next. Let's assume that you have the class Test, which has a field named m_testNo. You intend to use this class in a sorted collection, which requires the class to implement the IComparable so that it can be sorted by the m_testNo field.

NOTE

We will discuss collections later in the book. The only fact that matters now is that some of them require classes that implement the IComparable interface, which we use as an example.

The next example illustrates this class, implementing the interface IComparable.

```
Public Class Test
   Implements IComparable

   Protected m_testNo As Integer

   Public Property testNo() As Integer
      Get
```

```
        Return m_testNo
    End Get
    Set
        m_testNo = value
    End Set
End Property

Function CompareTo(ByVal o As Object) As Integer _
        Implements IComparable.CompareTo
    Dim t As Test = CType(o, Test)
    If m_testNo = t.m_testNo Then Return 0
    If m_testNo < t.m_testNo Then Return -1
    Return 1
End Function
End Class
```

To implement the interface you first need to add the Implements statement at the beginning of the class, followed by the name of the interface you want to implement. This forces the class to implement all methods and properties declared in the interface. In your case this is just one method, CompareTo.

You implement the CompareTo function using the syntax shown previously. You use a regular function syntax, except that you specify that this function implements a function of the interface (Implements IComparable.CompareTo). If you omit this specification, the compiler will consider the function as a regular method of the Test class and not an implementation of the CompareTo from IComparable method.

One thing to notice is that inside the method you use the generic (and very important) CType conversion function, which will convert an expression of any type to any other type. CType takes two parameters: the object that you want to convert, followed by the class name to which you want it converted. If the conversion is legal, the function returns a valid reference to the requested type; otherwise an exception is thrown.

In this case you convert a generic Object to a Test instance. Because Object is the base class for all data types in the .NET Framework, it can be used as a generic placeholder. In this instance it is used to confer generality to the CompareTo method. If the reference passed in is not actually an instance of the Test class (this class) then an exception is going to be thrown. Otherwise, the method compares the m_testNo values of both objects and returns: −1 if this value is less than the parameter's, 0 if they are equal, and 1 if this value is greater than the parameter's. This is what a class implementing IComparable is supposed to do.

In UML you can represent the fact that a class implements an interface using the symbols in Figure 18.2. Note that the methods (CompareTo here) are not repeated in the class. It is assumed that the class will implement all methods in the interface.

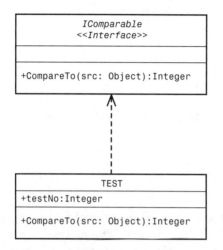

Figure 18.2: Implementing IComparable shown in UML.

One class can implement multiple interfaces—similar to the original analogy with the Swiss army knife: It can have a blade, a can opener, and so on. In a similar way, classes can implement multiple interfaces. If you would like your class Test to implement also the ICloneable interface (which is a useful interface of the System assembly) you would proceed as shown in the following code. The interface ICloneable looks like:

```
Public Interface ICloneable
    Function Clone() As Object
End Interface
```

And it is used (through its only method, Clone) to denote that the object can make copies of itself. The modified class Test is shown next.

```
Public Class Test
    Implements IComparable,ICloneable

    Protected m_testNo As Integer

    Public Property testNo() As Integer
        Get
            Return m_testNo
        End Get
        Set
```

```
        m_testNo = value
    End Set
End Property

Function CompareTo(ByVal o As Object) As Integer _
        Implements IComparable.CompareTo
    Dim t As Test = CType(o, Test)
    If m_testNo = t.m_testNo Then Return 0
    If m_testNo < t.m_testNo Then Return -1
    Return 1
End Function

Function Clone() As Object Implements ICloneable.Clone
    Dim t As Test = New Test()
    t.m_testNo = m_testNo
    Return t
End Function
End Class
```

As you can see we added one more interface to the `Implements` statement and then implemented the `Clone` method. The method implementation creates a new object of type test, copies the value of the field m_testNo into the new object, and returns it. In UML this could be represented as shown in Figure 18.3.

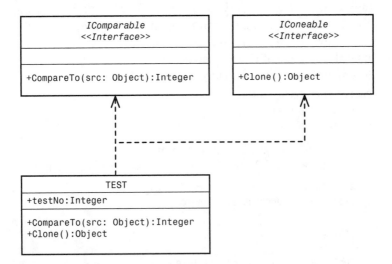

Figure 18.3: *Class Test implementing* `IComparable` *and* `ICloneable`*.*

You can now use any instance of the `Test` class anywhere where an `ICloneable` or `IComparable` variable is required. You could have a procedure that compares two IComparable objects and outputs a message if they are equal or not, as shown here.

```
Sub CheckEquality(ByVal o1 As IComparable, ByVal o2 As IComparable)
    If o1.CompareTo(o2) = 0 Then
        Console.Out.WriteLine("o1 is equal to o2")
    Else
        Console.Out.WriteLine("o1 is NOT equal to o2")
    End If
End Sub
```

You can call this procedure with two of your objects, as well as any other class that implements IComparable (as String, for instance).

```
Sub Main()
    Dim t1 As New Test()
    t1.testNo = 5
    Dim t2 As New Test()
    t2.testNo = 5
    CheckEquality(t1, t2)

    Dim s1 As String = "Joe"
    Dim s2 As String = "Joe"
    CheckEquality(s1, s2)
End Sub
```

In both cases the method will show the message "o1 is equal to o2", regardless of what the actual objects are.

Interfaces and Inheritance

There is one important point that we need to clarify next, the difference between inheritance and implementing an interface. You have probably noticed that there are similarities between an interface and an abstract class (especially if you rule that the class has only abstract public methods and properties). So, how is implementing an interface different from inheriting from an abstract class? The answer is that although there are similarities between the two, the main differences are summarized in the next paragraph.

- A class can inherit from one class only, but it can implement any number of interfaces.

- An interface is different from a base class: An interface defines behavior only, whereas a base class can hold state (have fields), define, and implement behavior.

- A base class defines what a derived class *is* (a Swiss army knife); whereas an implemented interface defines how the object behaves in certain circumstances (when opening a can, for instance).

- An object is not said to *be* an `ICloneable`, but it is said to *be* a `ValueType`, for instance (if you take the `Decimal` class as an example). It is instead said to be cloneable—that is, it can *behave* as described by the interface, but *is* an instance of the base class.

The value of using interfaces is that you can write generic classes and procedures that deal with any type of object, with the condition that it implements an interface you define. In this way you leave the door open for other assemblies to use the functionality of your classes and procedures, while still remaining free to design their classes as they wish, with the condition that they implement your interfaces.

The alternative would be to use abstract classes and ask your clients to inherit any class that would be used in one of your procedures from your abstract class. This is a more error-prone scenario: It is not really feasible in a single-inheritance language (you must have multiple inheritance). But even if you assume that you have multiple inheritance, the link between a class and its base class is much tighter than between a class and an implemented interface. This is mostly because interfaces do not have state (fields) and also do not implement behavior. Practical experience has shown that, although the two scenarios look similar from a theoretical point of view, the single-inheritance + interfaces works much better in the real world.

Interface Inheritance

Interfaces can inherit from other interfaces, in a similar way in which classes may inherit from other classes. The syntax and semantic of interface inheritance is very similar to that of class inheritance. If interface D *inherits* from interface B, it is said that D *extends* B, or D is a *specialization* of B. D is the *derived interface*; B is the *base interface*. If a class implements the derived interface D, then it must implement all methods of both D and B.

NOTE

Interfaces do not inherit from the `Object` base class. They actually do not inherit from anything, unless another interface is specifically mentioned.

There is one major difference from class inheritance: Interface inheritance can be multiple. That is, one interface can inherit from more than one base interface. You could create your own interface and inherit from both `IComparable` and `ICloneable`.

```
Public Interface ITest
    Inherits IComparable, ICloneable
    ReadOnly Property textValue() As String
End Interface
```

Any class that implements `ITest` must implement all the methods and properties in `ITest` and its base interfaces: `CompareTo` from `IComparable`, `Clone` from `ICloneable`, and the property `textValue` from `ITest`. You could modify the Test class to implement the new interface:

```
Public Class Test
    Implements ITest

    Protected m_testNo As Integer

    Public Property testNo() As Integer
        Get
            Return m_testNo
        End Get
        Set
            m_testNo = value
        End Set
    End Property

    ReadOnly Property textValue() As String Implements ITest.textValue
        Get
            Return CStr(m_testNo)
        End Get
    End Property

    Function CompareTo(ByVal o As Object) As Integer Implements ITest.CompareTo
        Dim t As Test = CType(o, Test)
        If m_testNo = t.m_testNo Then Return 0
        If m_testNo < t.m_testNo Then Return -1
        Return 1
    End Function

    Function Clone() As Object Implements ITest.Clone
        Dim t As Test = New Test()
        t.m_testNo = m_testNo
        Return t
    End Function
End Class
```

Interface inheritance is used mostly to group together some methods and properties. It does carry less meaning (compared to class inheritance, which is always meaningful).

You would represent this in UML as shown in the diagram in Figure 18.4.

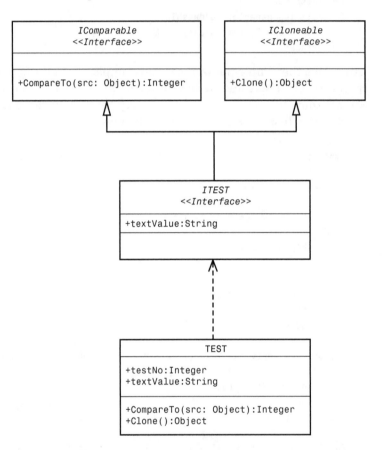

Figure 18.4: *Class Test implementing* `ITest`, *derived from* `IComparable` *and* `ICloneable`.

Interface inheritance is not as frequently used as class inheritance.

Interfaces in the .NET Framework

We will present an overview of some of the most common interfaces in the .NET Framework. We will also specify where in the book they are described in more detail.

You have already seen the `ICloneable` and `IComparable`, which are the most-used general purpose interfaces in .NET Framework. Another useful interface is `IConvertible`, which defines methods to convert a value (normally derived from `ValueType`) into any of the fundamental data types (as well as some .NET Framework–specific data types). It has methods like `ToString`, `ToDouble`, `ToDecimal`, and so on. If you would like your class to implement this interface, you must implement all these methods.

The `System.Collections` namespace has a few very useful interfaces such as `IEnumerable` (exposes an enumerator for a collection of objects), `ICollection` (a generic collection of objects), and `IList` (a list collection). You will learn more about the collections and the interfaces in the collections namespace in the next chapter.

In the `System.ComponentModel` namespace you have two important interfaces for people developing visual controls (components): `IComponent` and `IContainer`. These are used in conjunction with the `Component` and `Container` classes to implement custom component libraries.

The `System.Data` namespace (and some of its nested namespaces, like ADO and SQL) contain a large number of interfaces and classes that deal with data storage and retrieval, as well as with the metadata associated with them. You will learn more about these in Part V.

The `System.Web` and `System.WindowsForms` also have a number of important interfaces that describe behavior related to the HTTP protocol and UI Web controls, as well as standard UI controls, forms, menus, and other UI components. You will learn more about these in Parts IV and VI of this book, respectively.

What's Next

In this chapter you learned what interfaces are and the first steps in how to use them. You have seen the differences between implementing polymorphism using inheritance, or using interfaces. You will use this knowledge in the rest of the book, so it is important that you have a sound understanding of this chapter.

The next chapter will deal with a specific type of classes and interfaces located in the `System.Collections` namespace. These are objects that contain other objects, either as arrays, lists, queues, stacks, or other forms. In general these classes are known as collection classes in all languages, and they are very useful. You will learn the specific .NET Framework collection classes as used from the Visual Basic .NET language.

NOTE

The answers to "Reviewing It," "Checking It," and "Applying It" are available on our Web site.

REVIEW

Reviewing It

This section presents a review of the key concepts in this chapter. These questions are intended to gauge your absorption of the relevant material.

1. What is an interface?

2. What does it mean when we say that a class implements an interface?

3. What is the difference between an interface and an abstract class?

4. How is polymorphic behavior implemented using interfaces?

5. Describe interface inheritance in four sentences.

CHECK

Checking It

Select the correct answer to the following questions.

Multiple Choice

1. What field modifiers are allowed in interfaces?

   a. `Public` and `Private`.

   b. `Public`, `Protected`, and `Private`.

   c. None, all fields are public by default.

   d. None, interfaces do not have fields.

2. What modifiers can have properties and methods in an interface (mark all that apply)?

   a. Access modifiers (`Public`, `Protected`, `Friend`, and `Private`).

   b. `Shared`.

   c. `Overridable`, `NotOverriddable`, `MustOverride`.

   d. `Overloads`.

3. If a class chooses to implement only some of the methods of an interface, you call it:

   a. A partial implementation. The clients can use only the implemented methods.

   b. Not possible, the class must implement all methods.

   c. The class is abstract, and its derived classes must implement the remainder of the methods.

   d. It is legal only as a partial solution, while the program is in development.

4. The ICloneable interface is used to:

   a. Create a copy of the object (byte-by-byte).

   b. Create a clone of the object (a copy of all its fields).

   c. Allow the class to define its own cloning mechanism.

   d. All of the above.

5. The IComparable interface is used to:

   a. Compare any two objects.

   b. Compare any two classes.

   c. Compare two instances of a class.

   d. Allow the class to define its own compare method.

True or False

Select one of the two possible answers and then verify on our Web site that you picked the correct one.

1. Interfaces have constructors.

   True/False

2. Interfaces are not derived from Object.

   True/False

3. Interfaces cannot be Friend, Private, or Public.

   True/False

4. Interfaces can inherit from more than one other interface.

   True/False

5. A class cannot implement more than one interface.

   True/False

6. Interfaces cannot have fields or methods that have an implementation (body).

   True/False

Applying It

Try to complete the following exercise by yourself.

APPLY

Independent Exercise

Provide implementation for the interfaces and classes in the next UML diagram. Do not implement the Draw method, just provide the correct signature.

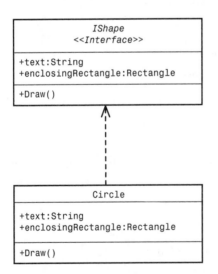

Figure 18.5: Exercise class diagram.

Collections

In this chapter you learn about collection classes: what they are, different types of collections, and how to use them. The chapter contains the following topics:

- Collections basics
- ArrayList
- Hashtable
- SortedList
- Queue and stack
- Making your own collections
- Tips on using collections

You start by looking at what collections are and some of the most used interfaces in the `System.Collections` namespace. You will learn what are the members of the `ICollection`, `IList`, `IEnumerable`, and `IEnumerator` interfaces. Then you will look at examples of the most useful classes in the namespace: `ArrayList`, `HashTable` (and its non–case-sensitive counterpart `CaseInsensitiveHashTable`), `SortedList` (and its case-insensitive counterpart `CaseInsensitiveSortedList`), `Queue`, and `Stack`. Finally you learn how to create custom collections for your classes, using the `NameObjectCollectionBase` and its members.

The collection classes have changed a lot from the previous versions of Visual Basic. If you plan to use collections in your programs, you should carefully read this chapter. The collection classes and interfaces are explained without assuming any prior knowledge (other than elementary mathematics).

Collections Basics

As the name suggests, *collections* are classes that contain a variable number of other objects. They normally have methods to add and remove objects to and from the collection, to search for objects, to navigate the collection (that is, iterate through the objects in the collection), and so on.

Collection Features

The collection classes can be characterized by many different criteria, including:

- Dynamic—Whether they can increase the number of objects they hold dynamically

- Indexed—Whether the collection is indexed

- Sorted—Whether the collection is sorted

- Access—How they allow access to the objects in the collection

The preceding characteristics are briefly discussed next from a general point of view. Then, they will be illustrated using actual collection examples during the rest of the chapter.

- **Dynamic.** All collections in the System.Collections namespace are dynamic, meaning that they can increase their capacity as required, when new objects are added to the collection.

- **Indexed.** Another important criterion is whether the collection is indexed, meaning that the order in which the elements are added in the collection is maintained, and each element can be accessed by its *index*. This is similar to a regular array. For example, the ArrayList, BitArray, and SortedList classes are indexed.

- **Sorted.** Another criterion is whether the collection is *sorted*, meaning that the objects in the collection are placed in order, based on the values of a certain other object, known as a key. This is similar to a dictionary: when a new word and its description is added, the new word is not added at the end of the dictionary, but rather in a position that is determined alphabetically. The SortedList is an example of a sorted collection class. A hybrid between indexed and sorted collections is the HashTable class, which uses a key to find an object, but objects are not stored in a sorted way.

- **Access.** Depending upon the way a collection item (element) can be retrieved after it is added to a collection, you have collections that allow access based on an index, based on a key associated with the object, or based on the position of the object in the collection. Examples of the latter types of collection are Queue (which uses a first-in, first-out algorithm, abbreviated as FIFO), and Stack (which uses a last-in, first-out algorithm, known as LIFO).

Collection Interfaces

The basic collection interfaces are IEnumerable and its related cousin IEnumerator. They are used to retrieve an enumerator for a collection, and respectively enumerate (navigate) a collection. The enumerator maintains a position in the collection, and when requested returns the current object or moves to the next object in the collection. In the following string, the IEnumerable interface has only one member, the method GetEnumerator(), which returns an IEnumerator object:

```
Public Interface IEnumerable
    Function GetEnumerator() As IEnumerator
End Interface
```

The IEnumerator interface has three members:

```
Public Interface IEnumerator
    ReadOnly Property Current As Object
    Function MoveNext() As Boolean
    Sub Reset()
End Interface
```

These members are

- The property Current, which returns the current object in the collection.

- The MoveNext method is used to move the position of the enumerator to the next item in the collection. It returns true if successful, false if there are no more items in the collection.

- Reset is used to reset the position of the iterator to the first element of the collection.

The core interface used by the collection classes is ICollection, which is implemented by virtually all collection classes, except the special cases of Queue and Stack. ICollection inherits from the IEnumerable, and hence classes implementing ICollection must also implement the IEnumerable. The most important members of the ICollection interface are presented here:

```
Public Interface ICollection
    ReadOnly Property Count As Integer
    Sub CopyTo(ByVal array As System.Array, ByVal index As Integer)
```

```
    ReadOnly Property IsSynchronized As Boolean
    ReadOnly Property SyncRoot As Object
End Interface
```

The interface members are

- Property Count is used to get the number of items in the collection.

- Method CopyTo is used to copy the collection items to an array (provided as an argument) starting at a specified position in this array.

- The two advanced properties IsSynchronized and SyncRoot are used to set and get the synchronization object and status of the collection (that is, whether the collection is thread-safe).

Another important interface used by most collections is IList. IList defines add, insert, and remove operations, as well as indexed find methods, which the collection class implements. We summarize the members of IList as follows:

```
Public Interface IList
    ReadOnly Property IsReadOnly As Boolean
    ReadOnly Property IsFixedSize As Boolean
    Property Item(ByVal index As Integer) As Object
    Function Add(ByVal value As Object) As Integer
    Sub Clear()
    Function Contains(ByVal value As Object) As Boolean
    Function IndexOf(ByVal value As Object) As Integer
    Sub Insert(ByVal index As Integer, ByVal value As Object)
    Sub RemoveAt(ByVal index As Integer)
    Sub Remove(ByVal value As Object)
End Interface
```

The most important members are explained as follows:

- Property Item is used to get an object from a collection at a specified index.

- Method Add is used to add an object to the collection (as the last item).

- Method Insert is used to insert an object into the collection at a specified position.

- Methods Remove and RemoveAt allow objects to be removed from a collection based on either the object or its index, respectively.

- Method Contains is used to find out whether an object is contained in a collection.

- Method IndexOf is used to get the index (position) of an object in this collection.

- Method Clear is used to remove all items from the collection.

The IDictionary is another important interface, normally implemented by classes that store collections of key-value pairs. It defines add and remove operations, as well as methods to retrieve all keys and all values in the collection. IDictionary inherits from ICollection.

```
Public Interface IDictionary
    ReadOnly Property IsReadOnly As Boolean
    ReadOnly Property IsFixedSize As Boolean
    Property Item(ByVal key As Object) As Object
    Function Add(ByVal value As Object) As Integer
    ReadOnly Property Keys As ICollection
    ReadOnly Property Values As ICollection
    Sub Add(ByVal key As Object, ByVal value As Object)
    Sub Clear()
    Function Contains(ByVal key As Object) As Boolean
    Function GetEnumerator() As IDictionaryEnumerator
    Sub Remove(ByVal key As Object)
End Interface
```

The most important members are explained as follows:

- The Item property is used to get an object from a collection based on its associated key (passed in as an argument).

- The properties Keys and Values are used to get a collection (as ICollection) of all keys and values in this dictionary.

- The Add method is used to add a key-value pair into the collection. Keys must be non-null and unique.

- The Remove method allows objects to be removed from the collection, based on the key the object is associated with.

- The Contains method is used to find out whether a key exists in this collection (and, implicitly, if its associated object exists).

- The GetEnumerator method is used to get a specialized enumerator, of type IDictionaryEnumerator, shown next.

- The Clear method is used to remove all items from the collection.

The IDictionaryEnumerator is extending (inheriting from) IEnumerator and is used by classes that implement IDictionary to enumerate their items. In addition to its base interface members, it has three members.

```
Public Interface IDictionaryEnumerator
   ReadOnly Property Entry As DictionaryEntry
   ReadOnly Property Key As Object
   ReadOnly Property Value As Object
End Interface
```

These members are explained as follows:

- The `Entry` property is used to retrieve both the key and value at the current position in the dictionary. It is a simple structure with two members: the key and the value.

- The `Key` property is used to retrieve the key at the current position.

- The `Value` property is used to retrieve the object at the current position.

You will better understand these methods when you use some examples (like `ArrayList`) to illustrate the classes that implement these interfaces.

ArrayList

The `ArrayList` is a collection class that models a dynamic array, whose size increases as required when new objects are added to the array. The items in the array are Object instances, which means that you can use instances of this class to hold any type of variable.

The `ArrayList` implements the `IList`, `ICollection`, and `ICloneable` interfaces. Let's look first at a simple example of how to use it:

```
Sub Main()
   Dim a As ArrayList = New ArrayList()

   a.Add("Joe")
   a.Add("Jane")
   a.Add("Jim")

   Dim i As Integer
   For i = 0 To a.Count - 1
      Console.Out.WriteLine(a.Item(i))
   Next
End Sub
```

First you create the `ArrayList` a using the regular object variable declaration and initialization. Then you use the `Add` method (from `IList`) to add three literal strings to the array. Next you iterate through the array from item 0 to item a.Count - 1, and you output the value of the object at the respective position (accessed through the `Item` property) to the console.

You could achieve the same result using the IEnumerator interface, as illustrated here:

```
Sub Main()
    Dim a As ArrayList = New ArrayList()

    a.Add("Joe")
    a.Add("Jane")
    a.Add("Jim")

    Dim e As IEnumerator
    e = a.GetEnumerator

    Dim s As String
    Do While e.MoveNext()
        s = CType(e.Current, String)
        Console.Out.WriteLine(s)
    Loop
    e.Reset()
End Sub
```

You get the enumerator for this collection, and then you use it to navigate through all its items. The enumerator is initially not positioned on the first item in the collection (as one may expect), but rather on a somewhat abstract position *before* the first item in the collection. Therefore, you need to initialize it by calling MoveNext() as the first action, otherwise you get an exception stating that the enumerator is not correctly positioned.

We have used strings in both preceding examples, but you can use any object you like, instances of your classes included. Since in Visual Basic .NET all objects are derived from the Object base class, you can store any object in an array (and in general in all untyped collections). You can have arrays of integers, decimals, dates, etc. This is different from the previous versions of Visual Basic (that allowed only the use of objects in collections), in the sense that now everything is an object and can therefore be stored in a collection.

The next example shows a few more of the properties and methods of the ArrayList class:

```
Sub Main()
    Dim a As ArrayList = New ArrayList()

    a.Add("Joe")
    a.Add("Jane")
    a.Add("Jim")
```

```
    Dim sObject As String = "theObject"
    a.Insert(2, sObject)

    If a.Contains(sObject) Then
        Console.Out.WriteLine("a contains sObject")
        Dim index As Integer
        index = a.IndexOf(sObject)
        Console.Out.WriteLine("the index of sObject in a is {0}", index)
    End If

    If a.IsReadOnly Then
        Console.Out.WriteLine("a is read-only")
    Else
        Console.Out.WriteLine("a is not read-only")
    End If

    a.RemoveAt(2) ' remove the sObject
    If a.Contains(sObject) Then
        Console.Out.WriteLine("a STILL contains sObject")
    Else
        Console.Out.WriteLine("a does not contains sObject")
    End If
    a.Clear() ' remove all items from the array
End Sub
```

You Insert a string into the array at index 2, and then you verify with Contains that the array indeed contains the string, and you ensure that its index is 2, using the IndexOf method. Make sure the array is not read-only and then remove the string object you inserted at index 2. Then make sure that the array no longer Contains the string. Use Clear in the end to remove all items in the array.

As you can see from the previous examples, the ArrayList class is a versatile replacement for the regular arrays: You can insert and add objects dynamically, find objects, and much more. The overhead (additional memory) involved when using this class, compared to a regular array, is minimal, and it is balanced by its vastly extended functionality.

In summary: If you plan to use an array to store dynamic data use the ArrayList class. If you are using an array for static data (which does not change in time), and you do not need the added functionality of the ArrayList, use a regular array.

However, the search for an item in an ArrayList is performed sequentially, and this means it is slow. When performance of the search counts, you may want to consider another collection type, such as Hashtable or SortedList.

Hashtable

The Hashtable class implements the IDictionary and ICollection interfaces, as well as ICloneable, ISerializable, and IDeserializationEventListener (which are not collection-specific, so you will ignore here).

A *hash table* is a collection of key-value pairs implemented using a hash table algorithm. The keys must override the GetHashCode and Equals methods of the Object class. Key objects must be also *immutable* (that is, their attributes or state cannot be changed). The most commonly used keys are String objects, which match all these criteria. The values can be any objects.

NOTE

A hash table can be thought of as an array of buckets holding key-value pairs; each bucket is indexed by a value that is derived from the key, using a special function known as a *hash function*. The actual theory behind hash tables is beyond the scope of this book; you may want to consult a book on algorithms, if you need more details. Normally you can use this class without any additional understanding of the internals of hash tables.

Next we show a simple example using String values as keys and one of our objects as a values. Create the class Person, as shown here:

```
Public Class Person
    Private m_name As String
    Private m_dob As Date

    Public Property name() As String
        Get
            Return m_name
        End Get
        Set
            m_name = value
        End Set
    End Property

    Public Property dob() As Date
        Get
            Return m_dob
        End Get
        Set
            m_dob = value
        End Set
    End Property
```

```
     Public Sub New(Optional ByVal name As String = "", _
                    Optional ByVal dob As Date = #1/1/1900#)
        m_name = name
        m_dob = dob
     End Sub

     Public Function getAge() As Integer
        Dim ts As TimeSpan = Now.Subtract(m_dob)
        Return ts.Days \ 365 ' approximate, ignore leap years
     End Function
End Class
```

And store it in a hash table, as shown:

```
Sub Main()
   Dim ht As Hashtable = New Hashtable()

   Dim p1 As Person = New Person("Joe", #1/1/1961#)
   ht.Add(p1.name, p1)

   Dim p2 As Person = New Person("Jane", #2/2/1962#)
   ht.Add(p2.name, p2)

   Dim p3 As Person = New Person("Jim", #3/3/1963#)
   ht.Add(p3.name, p3)

   Dim p As Person
   If ht.Contains("Jim") Then
      p = CType(ht.Item("Jim"), Person)
      Console.Out.WriteLine("The age of {0} is {1}", p.name, p.getAge())
   End If
End Sub
```

You can use the Add method (from IDictionary) to add items to the hash table; you use Contains and Item to check for existence and retrieve items from the hash table. The Add method takes two parameters: the *key* and the *object* to be added to the collection. In this example, the key is the person name, and the object is the person.

The Hashtable class has a number of other features and can be highly customized, to achieve better performance. You can use a custom hash code generator, set the load factor (see next paragraph), initial capacity, and many other properties using one of the 11 overloaded constructors.

The big advantage of the Hashtable is that the search is very fast, based on its load factor. The *load factor* is the ratio between the size of the array of buckets and the maximum load of each bucket. The higher the value of this factor, the faster the search, but at a price: The memory consumption is also increased a lot. In short: Hash tables are big but fast.

One disadvantage of the Hashtable class is that values stored in the hash table cannot be accessed by index, which may present a problem in some instances. This issue is solved by the SortedList class.

If you need a balance between the ArrayList's slow performance and compactness and the great performance but high memory usage of a Hashtable, you should look at the SortedList class.

SortedList

A *sorted list* is a collection that holds a set of key-value pairs. The keys and values are stored in two sorted arrays. This allows the list to function both as an array (indexed access to values) as well as a *sorted list* (search based on the keys).

A sorted list may not contain duplicate keys. A hash table can have duplicate keys.

The SortedList implements the IDictionary and ICollection interfaces. It has similar methods to the Hashtable, and the same requirements for the keys: They must implement IComparable, or a custom comparator implementing IComparer must be added. The capacity of the list increases as required to accommodate new items added.

The same example used in the preceding section can be modified to use a SortedList instead of the Hashtable as follows:

```
Sub Main()
    Dim sl As SortedList = New SortedList()

    Dim p1 As Person = New Person("Joe", #1/1/1961#)
    sl.Add(p1.name, p1)

    Dim p2 As Person = New Person("Jane", #2/2/1962#)
    sl.Add(p2.name, p2)

    Dim p3 As Person = New Person("Jim", #3/3/1963#)
    sl.Add(p3.name, p3)
```

```
    Dim p As Person
    If sl.Contains("Jim") Then
        p = CType(sl.Item("Jim"), Person)
        Console.Out.WriteLine("The age of {0} is {1}", p.name, p.getAge())
    End If
End Sub
```

Sorted lists offer a balanced solution between a hash table and an array, offering both good performance and reasonable memory usage. The next example shows a list with a custom key and a comparator class. First we need to define the two structures to use as keys (Name) and value (Person).

```
Structure Name
    Public firstName As String
    Public lastName As String
    Public ReadOnly Property completeName() As String
        Get
            Return firstName + " " + lastName
        End Get
    End Property
    Public Sub New(ByVal fName As String, ByVal lName As String)
        firstName = fName
        lastName = lName
    End Sub
End Structure


Structure Person
    Public fullName As Name
    Public age As Integer
    Public Sub New(ByVal fName As String, _
                   ByVal lName As String, _
                   ByVal theAge As Integer)
        fullName.firstName = fName
        fullName.lastName = lName
        age = theAge
    End Sub
End Structure
```

Both structures have a constructor, and Name also has a property used to display the complete name of the person. The person's name is an instance of the Name structure. Next, implement a comparator class, which is used to compare two instances of the Name structure:

```
Class NameComparer
    Implements IComparer

    Public Function XCompare(ByVal x As Object, ByVal y As Object) As Integer _
    Implements IComparer.Compare
```

```
        Dim n1 As Name = CType(x, Name)
        Dim n2 As Name = CType(y, Name)
        If n1.lastName.Equals(n2.lastName) Then
            Return n1.firstName.CompareTo(n2.firstName)
        End If
        Return n1.lastName.CompareTo(n2.lastName)
    End Function
End Class
```

The function XCompare is named this way because Compare is a reserved word in Visual Basic .NET; therefore, you need to use a different name than the one the interface specifies. The implementation code first casts (using CType) the objects to Name objects and then compares the last names, and if these are equal, compares the first names. If the last names are different, the code uses the String CompareTo method to determine the value.

The Sub Main shown next is an example of using the custom comparator class.

```
Sub Main()
    Dim comp As NameComparer = New NameComparer()
    Dim sl As SortedList = New SortedList(comp)

    Dim p1 As Person = New Person("Joe", "Smith", 23)
    sl.Add(p1.fullName, p1)

    Dim p2 As Person = New Person("Sarah", "Jones", 18)
    sl.Add(p2.fullName, p2)

    Dim p3 As Person = New Person("Jim", "Smith", 20)
    sl.Add(p3.fullName, p3)

    Dim p As Person
    Dim n As Name = New Name("Sarah", "Jones")
    If sl.Contains(n) Then
        p = CType(sl.Item(n), Person)
        Console.Out.WriteLine("The age of {0} is {1}", _
                            p.fullName.completeName, p.age)
    End If

    Dim q As Person
    Console.Out.WriteLine("USING THE GetByIndex")
    Dim i As Integer
    For i = 0 To sl.Count - 1
```

```
        q = CType(sl.GetByIndex(i), Person)
        Console.Out.WriteLine("At index {0} we have {1}", _
                              i, q.fullName.completeName)
    Next

    Console.Out.WriteLine("USING THE Enumerator and the DictionaryEntry")
    i = 0
    Dim e As IEnumerator, de As DictionaryEntry
    e = sl.GetEnumerator()
    Do While e.MoveNext()
        de = CType(e.Current, DictionaryEntry)
        q = CType(de.Value, Person)
        Console.Out.WriteLine("At sort position {0} we have {1}", _
                              i, q.fullName.completeName)
        i += 1
    Loop
End Sub
```

The `SortedList` object is now constructed using a comparator. It calls this object every time it needs to compare two keys (`Name` objects) to sort them—for example, when `Add` is called.

Now to do a search you construct a Name object, set its fields, and then pass it to the `Contains` or `Item` methods. The `GetByIndex` can be used to retrieve an object at its index in the array. The enumerator interface for a `SortedList` actually returns an `IDictionaryEnumerator`, and the `Current` property returns an instance of the `DictionaryEntry` structure. This latter contains a key-value pair (as properties `Key` and `Value`, respectively). You use it to get the value (`Person`) and display it using the `Console.Out` object.

A SortedList may be used either with or without a custom comparator. If you use as a key a class that implements IComparable (which most system types like Integer, String, etc., do), then there is no need to implement a custom comparator. A custom comparator must be used when using key classes that do not implement the IComparable interface. It is usually easier and more convenient to implement IComparable than to create a specialized comparator class.

The `SortedList` can be used instead of `ArrayList` and `Hashtable` when both accessing by index and sorting are important.

Queue and Stack

Queues and stacks are two special types of collections that use a different access mechanism than the ones we have already discussed, where any item in the collection is accessible at any time, one way or the other.

Queues are used to model a first-in, first-out (FIFO) type of scenario, like a one-way pipe or stream. *Stacks* are used for, well, stacks of objects, where the next object is added "above" the previous one, and needs to be removed before the ones underneath it. This scenario is a last-in, first-out scenario, used for example to model something like a mail in-box, where the next piece of paper thrown in sits above all the ones that were there before it.

Our example uses a queue object and two stack objects to simulate a mail sorting procedure: Mail gets thrown into a queue, and then the queue is processed, and mail sorted in two stacks—one for urgent messages and one for normal messages. You use the MailMessage structure as a data to fill in the queue and stacks:

```
Structure MailMessage
   Public isUrgent As Boolean
   Public messageBody As String
   Public Sub New(ByVal u As Boolean, ByVal m As String)
      isUrgent = u
      messageBody = m
   End Sub
End Structure
```

The structure has a constructor, for convenience, so you can create objects easier. The next example, using the structure, illustrates the basic methods of the Queue (Enqueue and Dequeue) and of the Stack (Push and Pop). Enqueue and Push are used to add an item to the Queue and Stack, respectively, while Dequeue and Pop are used to remove the first/last item in the Queue/Stack:

```
Sub Main()
   Dim q As Queue = New Queue()
   Dim m As MailMessage

   ' 1. Populate the queue
   m = New MailMessage(True, "message 1")
   q.Enqueue(m)
   m = New MailMessage(False, "message 2")
   q.Enqueue(m)
   m = New MailMessage(False, "message 3")
   q.Enqueue(m)
   m = New MailMessage(True, "message 4")
   q.Enqueue(m)
   m = New MailMessage(False, "message 5")
   q.Enqueue(m)
```

```
' ... later
' 2. Read from the queue and place items in the stacks
Dim sUrgent As Stack = New Stack()
Dim sNormal As Stack = New Stack()

Do While q.Count > 0
    m = CType(q.Dequeue(), MailMessage)
    If m.isUrgent Then
        sUrgent.Push(m)
    Else
        sNormal.Push(m)
    End If
Loop

' ... later
' 3. Lets look at the contents of the stacks
Do While sUrgent.Count > 0
    m = CType(sUrgent.Pop(), MailMessage)
    Console.Out.WriteLine("Urgent message : " + m.messageBody)
Loop

Do While sNormal.Count > 0
    m = CType(sNormal.Pop(), MailMessage)
    Console.Out.WriteLine("Normal proiority message : " + m.messageBody)
Loop
End Sub
```

The output of the program shows the stacks emptied in the reverse order (with urgent messages first). If you step through the code with the debugger, you will be able to see the contents of the queue and stacks as the program runs.

NamedObjectCollectionBase—Making Your Own Collections

All the collections you have seen so far can be used as they are—that is, out of the box. This is a good thing, but it has its price: None of these collections are strongly typed, meaning that the methods of the collection use Object base class references in all methods. This means that you can easily make a mistake and pass in the wrong type of object, and the compiler would not be able to tell you that you made a mistake. This is sometimes an acceptable risk, especially if the code that deals with a collection is contained. However, there are cases when you need to expose collections of some of your objects to the outside world. Exposing an ArrayList of Person objects, say, would allow a client of your class to call the Add method with an object of another class. At this point your class has a runtime problem (because the compiler will not detect it).

In these types of cases, the best approach is to develop custom collection classes. You have two choices: Use one of the standard collections internally (as a private field) and expose to the outside world only the safe methods. Alternatively, you could inherit the `NameObjectCollectionBase` class, which is designed to function as a base for a custom collection.

There are other classes that can be used as bases for custom collections, such as CollectionBase, ReadOnlyCollectionBase, and DictionaryBase. We choose the `NameObjectCollectionBase` as the most representative of them. The process is very similar for any of the other base classes.

Let's look at an example using the first method—that is, aggregate a standard collection and expose only the methods you choose. You use the class shown next as an example of a value class (however, it can be any other custom class):

```
Public Class CollValue
    Public m_key As String
    Public m_value As String
    Public Sub New(Optional ByVal key As String = "", _
                   Optional ByVal value As String = "")
        m_key = key
        m_value = value
    End Sub
End Class
```

The custom collection class would look like this:

```
Public Class CustCollAgg
    Implements ICollection

    Private m_coll As ArrayList = New ArrayList()

    Public ReadOnly Property count() As Integer _
    Implements ICollection.Count
        Get
            Return m_coll.Count
        End Get
    End Property


    Public ReadOnly Property isSynchronized() As Boolean _
    Implements ICollection.IsSynchronized
        Get
            Return m_coll.IsSynchronized
        End Get
```

```
        End Property
        Public ReadOnly Property syncRoot() As Object _
        Implements ICollection.SyncRoot
            Get
                Return m_coll.SyncRoot
            End Get
        End Property

        Public Function GetEnumerator() As Collections.IEnumerator _
        Implements System.Collections.ICollection.GetEnumerator
            Return m_coll.GetEnumerator()
        End Function
        Public Sub CopyTo(ByVal array As System.Array, ByVal index As Integer) _
        Implements System.Collections.ICollection.CopyTo
            m_coll.CopyTo(array, index)
        End Sub

        Public Sub Add(ByVal v As CollValue)
            m_coll.Add(v)
        End Sub

        Public Sub Insert(ByVal index As Integer, ByVal v As CollValue)
            m_coll.Insert(index, v)
        End Sub

        Public Sub Remove(ByVal v As CollValue)
            m_coll.Remove(v)
        End Sub

        Public Sub RemoveAt(ByVal index As Integer)
            m_coll.RemoveAt(index)
        End Sub

        Public Function IndexOf(ByVal v As CollValue) As Integer
            Return m_coll.IndexOf(v)
        End Function

        Public Sub Clear()
            m_coll.Clear()
        End Sub
End Class
```

You implement the ICollection interface to provide a standard interface to your clients who may use the ICollection. You delegate all methods to the private field m_coll, which holds an array of CollValue objects.

You then expose a set of methods to add and remove objects to the collection. But these methods use CollValue as an argument type instead of Object. This prevents a client of this class from adding a String to the collection in error.

The second approach to customized collections is shown in the next example:

```
Public Class CustCollInh
    Inherits Specialized.NameObjectCollectionBase

    Public Overloads Property item(ByVal key As String) As CollValue
        Get
            Return CType(BaseGet(key), CollValue)
        End Get
        Set
            BaseSet(value.m_key, value)
        End Set
    End Property

    Public Overloads ReadOnly Property item(ByVal index As Integer) As CollValue
        Get
            Return CType(BaseGet(index), CollValue)
        End Get
    End Property

    Public Sub Add(ByVal v As CollValue)
        BaseAdd(v.m_key, v)
    End Sub

    Public Sub Remove(ByVal v As CollValue)
        BaseRemove(v.m_key)
    End Sub

    Public Sub RemoveAt(ByVal index As String)
        BaseRemove(index)
    End Sub

    Public Sub Clear()
        BaseClear()
    End Sub
End Class
```

You inherit from the NameObjectCollectionBase and add your own methods for the properties and methods the base class does not support: item (access the value by index or key), Add, Remove, RemoveAt, and Clear. Use the base-protected methods to implement the calls: BaseGet (to retrieve an item by key or index), BaseSet (to set a value at an index or key), BaseRemove (overloaded to remove an object identified by index or key), and BaseClear (to remove all values and keys from the collection).

The base class (NameObjectCollectionBase) uses an array and a hash table to implement the base for the collection. You can provide constructors that take a custom comparator, hash key generator, and an initial capacity of the collection, if you like. You can also add more functionality, but all is in terms of a collection of *your* objects—that is, CollValue objects.

The second approach involves less code and also offers more functionality. It is easier to use and generally recommended over the first approach (implementing ICollection).

Tips and Hints on Using Collections

Depending on the nature of the problem you are trying to solve, different approaches can be considered as optimal, with collections as well as with other software problems. We try to address a few typical scenarios in the following list:

- *Small/medium collection, does not change much (no items added or removed) after it is created, no searches.* Use a regular Visual Basic .NET array. If you need to expose it to client objects, use ArrayList and get the clients a read-only copy.

- *Small/medium collection, does change (many items added or removed) after it is created, no searches.* Use an ArrayList or a custom collection derived from it, if the additions are always at the end. If you expect many inserts and removes, use a Hashtable.

- *Small/medium collection, does not change much (no items added or removed) after it is created, lots of searches.* Use a Hashtable or a SortedList or a custom collection derived from NameObjectCollectionBase.

- *Large collection (thousands of items).* Try to avoid it if possible, as it is slow and it is not scalable. Use a database or data store and retrieve data as required. If you can't avoid it, use arrays or ArrayList, which are compact but slower in the search operation. Use a SortedList if you must. Hashtable can cause serious memory loads, especially if the load factors are large.

Use custom collections whenever possible to avoid runtime exceptions. Always think of some usage scenarios (best case/worst case/average usage) for the collection before deciding which one to pick.

The next table summarizes the main characteristics of different collection types discussed. Queue and Stack are not included, because they are intended for special cases and are not comparable with normal collections.

Table 19.1: Collection Comparison Table

Collection Type	Memory Usage	Add, Remove Speed	Search Speed	Types of Access
Normal array	Very compact	N/A directly	Slow	Indexed
ArrayList	Compact	Slow	Slow	Indexed
HashTable	Large	Fast	Very fast	Key (sorted)
SortedList	Medium	Fast	Fast	Index + key (sorted)
Specialized collection	Large	Fast	Very fast	Key (sorted)

What's Next

In the next chapter we will discuss some advanced OO concepts, as well as looking at a few common patterns in software engineering as they apply to Visual Basic .NET. We will give examples for these patterns, and explain how they would fit into your applications.

NOTE

The answers to "Reviewing It," "Checking It," and "Applying It" are available on our Web site.

REVIEW

Reviewing It

This section presents a review of the key concepts in this chapter. These questions are intended to gauge your absorption of the relevant material.

1. What is a collection class?

2. What are the characteristics of an ArrayList?

3. What are the characteristics of a Hashtable?

4. What are the characteristics of a SortedList?

5. How do you implement a custom collection?

CHECK

Checking It

Select the correct answer to the following questions.

Multiple Choice

1. An indexed collection is a collection that:

    a. Implements the `IList` interface.

    b. Implements the `IDictionary` interface.

    c. Has items that can be retrieved by their index.

    d. Uses key-value pairs as collection items.

2. A sorted collection is

    a. A collection of values sorted using a specified key.

    b. A collection of key-value pairs.

    c. A collection that implements `IEnumerable`.

    d. A collection that implements `IList`.

3. Are the `Queue` and `Stack`:

    a. Indexed.

    b. Sortable.

    c. Neither.

    d. Both.

4. What would you use to implement a collection for all the bank accounts of a person:

    a. `Hashtable`.

    b. `SortedList`.

    c. `ArrayList`.

    d. `Stack`.

5. What would you use to implement a collection of Product (custom) objects that can be searched by product ID or index?

    a. `ArrayList`.

    b. `Hashtable`.

c. SortedList.

d. Custom collection derived from NameObjectCollectionBase.

True or False

Select one of the two possible answers and then verify on our Web site that you picked the correct one.

1. The IList interface is implemented by indexed collections.

   True/False

2. The IDictionary interface is implemented by sorted collections.

   True/False

3. All collection classes implement ICollection.

   True/False

4. The Hashtable is faster on searches than SortedList

   True/False

5. The ArrayList is using less memory than a SortedList

   True/False

APPLY

Applying It

Try to complete the following exercises by yourself.

Independent Exercise 1

Write an example that measures the performance of the Add methods for an ArrayList, HashTable, and SortedList.

Hint: Use a large number of objects (10000, for instance) so that you can measure the time consistently. Also see the note that follows on how to measure the length of an operation.

Independent Exercise 2

Modify the preceding example to measure the performance of a search operation for the three classes. For the ArrayList use a loop. Alternatively, you could use the advanced BinarySearch method.

NOTE

To measure the time it takes to execute an operation, you can use code like the code shown next.

```
Dim startTime As Date = Now    ' Get the start time
' Execute the operation that is to be timed
Dim elapsedTime As TimeSpan = Now.Subtract(startTime)
Dim elapsedMillsecs As Integer = elapsedTime.Milliseconds
' or
Dim elapsedTicks As Integer = elapsedTime.Ticks
```

The Milliseconds measure the elapsed time in milliseconds, the Ticks in clock ticks (1 tick = 100 nanoseconds). The tick is the smallest unit of time in .NET.

Advanced OO Concepts

In this chapter you will explore a few advanced concepts of Object Oriented methodologies. You will learn the elementary concepts about the following methodologies:

- Relations

- Object persistence

- Development methodologies

You will start by learning about relations, as they apply to classes and interfaces. You will learn how to identify, declare, and implement class and object relationships.

Next, we will talk briefly about object persistence. We will introduce the basic fundamental concepts of persistence without going into details. Part V, "Manipulating Data with ADO+ and XML," is dedicated to this subject. The scope of the brief introduction done in this chapter is to give you an idea on the fundamental concepts of object persistence.

In the final portion of this chapter (and also in Part III, "Working with Objects") you will study in brief a few methods for developing object-oriented systems. You will learn about three methodologies for developing a software system: top-down, bottom-up, and mixed.

Relations

Most of the classes used as examples in the book so far were very simple. To keep things as clear as possible we have removed any unnecessary features (unnecessary from the point of view of the example we were presenting). This included in most cases any relations between classes.

Relations can be looked at from two different points of view. From a practical, hands-on view a *relation* is a connection between a number of objects or classes. For example a purchase order *has* items. The word *has* indicates the relationship between the two entities: the purchase order and the items ordered. Each item in the order *refers to* a product (that is, what the item is). The *refers to* is also a relation between the order item class and a product class.

In practical terms you could have a class named `PurchaseOrder` and a class named `OrderItem`. The class `PurchaseOrder` would contain a collection of `OrderItem` objects. Each `OrderItem` object would have a reference to a `Product` object (representing the catalog products).

From a mathematical point of view, *relations* can be viewed as relations between sets. A *class* represents a set of objects. It can have a relationship to another set of objects (another class). Each object in one set can have relations to one or more objects in the other set. These relations can be categorized from a few points of view: cardinality, navigability, containment, visibility, and so on:

- *Cardinality* is the number of objects that participate in the relation. It is normally expressed as the number of objects on each side of the relation, for example one-to-one, or one-to-many. If the `PurchaseOrder` has one or more `OrderItems`, you say the cardinality of the relation is one-to-many.

- *Navigability* is a property of a relation that indicates whether the relation can be traversed in either direction. If the `PurchaseOrder` has a collection of `OrderItems`, you say that the relation is navigable from the `PurchaseOrder` to the `OrderItem` (that is, you have a property that allows you to access the `OrderItems` from the `PurchaseOrder`). If the `OrderItem` does have a reference to the `PurchaseOrder` that owns it, you say that the relation is also navigable from the `OrderItem` to the `PurchaseOrder` (that is, you can get the `PurchaseOrder` when given an `OrderItem` object).

- *Containment* indicates whether one end of the relation owns the other end, or if it is simply associated with it. In the case of the `PurchaseOrder` you can say the `OrderItems` are owned (*aggregated*) into the order. The relation between `OrderItem` and `Product` can be described as an *association* because the `OrderItem` does not own the product. An easy mental test to determine whether a relationship is an association or an aggregation is to determine what happens to the other end of the relation when this end is deleted. If you delete a `PurchaseOrder`, all its `OrderItems` are deleted; therefore, it is aggregated. If you delete an `OrderItem`, the catalog `Product` it refers to is unaffected; therefore, it is an association.

- *Visibility* is the same as for an attribute: It indicates what parts of this class, component, or application can access the properties that represent the relation. It can be one of the familiar: `Public`, `Protected`, `Private`, or `Friend`.

Returning to the purchase order example, you can say that the data members described previously (the collection of `OrderItems` and the reference to the `Product`) are known as the *implementation* of the relation. This is very similar to the concept of class attribute, which is implemented as a class data member (field) and a property. In a similar fashion, a relation can be implemented as a data member and a property (or a few properties, in some cases), in each class that is part of the relation.

In UML, a relation is represented as a line between two classes, having a *role* at each end. For example, the line connecting the `PurchaseOrder` and `OrderItem` classes in Figure 20.1 represents a relationship between these classes. The role consists of the role name (for example, `items` and `order` in the same relation in Figure 20.1), a multiplicity (1 and 1..*), and the end-of-line adornments (plain, arrow, diamond, and others). A UML role represents the properties of one end of the relation, toward the other end. The role has a name, multiplicity, navigability, and visibility, as illustrated in Figure 20.1. These concepts are explained next.

Multiplicity is one side of the cardinality of the relation and is usually indicated as a number (1, as in the role `product`) or a range such as `1..*` (as in the role `items`) indicating that this end can have any number of objects between 1 and infinity. If the multiplicity of a role is missing, it is usually assumed to be 1. In some cases it is considered to be undefined.

Navigability is usually indicated by the presence or absence of an arrow at the end of the relation line. If no arrows are present the relation is navigable both ways, as is the case with the relationship between `PurchaseOrder` and `OrderItem`. If an arrow is present, the relation is navigable only in one direction, as is the case with the relation between `OrderItem` and `Product`, which is navigable only between the `OrderItem` to the `Product`, but not the other way.

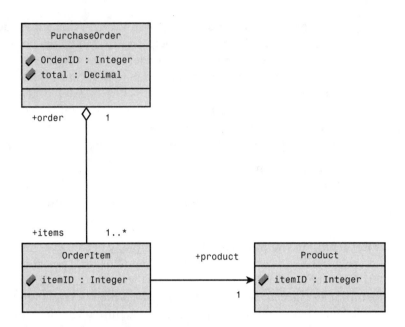

Figure 20.1: *UML relations.*

The **containment** of a relation is indicated by the presence of a diamond ending (either hollow or filled) at one end of the line that symbolizes the relation. The diamond is situated at the line end towards the class that is the owner (also known as *container*) in the relation. In the example shown in Figure 20.1, it is towards the PurchaseOrder class, which owns the OrderItems.

NOTE

If the diamond is hollow it is said that the object at the other end of the relationship is contained *by reference*. If it is filled it is said that the object is contained *by value*. In our example the PurchaseOrder class contains a list of OrderItems by reference. This type of relationship is known as a *has-a* type of relationship. Containment by reference is also known as *aggregation*, while containment by value is known as *composition*. Composition means that the contained object is an integral part of its container (it cannot exists outside its container, and it cannot be moved to a different container). *Aggregation* means the object is contained, but it can be moved to a different container. Aggregation and composition are advanced OO concepts.

The **visibility** is indicated by the + signs that precede the role names in all relations shown. The same convention applies as in the case of attributes: + is used to denote public, # to denote protected, - to denote private, and no symbol to denote friend visibility.

A relation is implemented usually as two attributes, one in each class, in the case when the relation is navigable in both directions. This is the case with the relation between the PurchaseOrder and OrderItem classes, as shown here.

```
Public Class PurchaseOrder
    Protected m_orderID As Integer
    Protected m_items As ArrayList

    Public Property orderID() As Integer
        Get
            Return m_orderID
        End Get
        Set
            m_orderID = value
        End Set
    End Property

    Public ReadOnly Property items() As ArrayList
        Get
            Return m_items
        End Get
    End Property

    Public Sub New(Optional ByVal id As Integer = 0)
        m_orderID = id
        m_items = New ArrayList()
    End Sub
End Class

Public Class OrderItem
    Protected m_itemID As Integer
    Protected m_order As PurchaseOrder
    Protected m_product As Product

    Public Property itemID() As Integer
        Get
            Return m_itemID
        End Get
        Set
            m_itemID = value
        End Set
    End Property

    Public Property order() As PurchaseOrder
        Get
            Return m_order
```

```
        End Get
        Set
            m_order = value
        End Set
    End Property

    Public Property productRef() As Product
        Get
            Return m_product
        End Get
        Set
            m_product = value
        End Set
    End Property

    Public Sub New(Optional ByVal id As Integer = 0)
        m_itemID = id
    End Sub
End Class

Public Class Product
    Protected m_productID As Integer

    Public Property productID() As Integer
        Get
            Return m_productID
        End Get
        Set
            m_productID = value
        End Set
    End Property

    Public Sub New(Optional ByVal id As Integer = 0)
        m_productID = id
    End Sub
End Class
```

The example illustrates one way to implement the class diagram illustrated in Figure 20.1. In this example the PurchaseOrder class implements its relation to OrderItem as a data member—ArrayList of OrderItem objects and its corresponding property. The OrderItem implements both the relation to its owner (PurchaseOrder) and its related catalog Product as single object reference attributes (m_order and m_product, respectively, and the corresponding properties).

There can be many variations of this implementation. You could force the objects of type OrderItem to be created only from a PurchaseOrder container by making the constructor of the class `OrderItem` `Friend` and adding a method named `addOrderItem` on the `PurchaseOrder` class. This method would create a new `OrderItem`, set its order to be itself, add it to the array, and return a reference to it to the caller. In this case you can change the property `order` to a read-only property (so that no one can change the owner, once it is set).

You could also not expose the `PurchaseOrder` relation to `OrderItem` as a property returning an `ArrayList`, but rather as a parameterized read-only property, plus a few methods to add and remove `OrderItem` objects from the array.

These are just examples of the many ways a relation could be implemented. It is your decision, based on the concrete circumstances in each case, how to best implement relations.

One thing that is worth nothing is that because all data types in the .NET Framework are classes, one could look at all attributes as being in fact relations. In the previous example, the class `PurchaseOrder` has an `Integer` attribute named `orderID`, which could be viewed as the implementation of a relationship between the classes `PurchaseOrder` and `Integer`. While this is correct from a theoretical standpoint, there are very few developers that would choose to represent this as a relation (as shown in Figure 20.2) and not as an attribute (as in Figure 20.1).

Figure 20.2: *Relation versus attribute.*

In the same spirit, you could represent the relations shown previously as attributes. For example, you could show the class `OrderItem` as having an attribute of type `Product`, rather than a relation to the product class.

Common sense dictates that if a relation is one of containment, navigable one way, and it is between one of your classes and a fundamental data type (such as `String`, `Integer`, and so on) you should use an attribute, not a relation. In this light, the example in Figure 20.2 would be better represented as an attribute (as it was originally in Figure 20.1).

If the relation is navigable both ways, or it involves non-fundamental data type classes, it is probably better represented as a relation than a pair of related attributes.

Object Persistence

In the examples from the book we have shown a multitude of classes from different aspects of business and programming. Examples included accounts, orders, addresses, and persons, to name just a few. Most examples involved creating new objects and manipulating their data. In all the cases shown, you have assumed that the data for these objects (that is, the objects' state) is either entered by the user or created by you at runtime.

This is normally not the case. Most software systems store large parts of the data they operate upon in such a way that it is accessible also after the program has finished execution. For example, the account balance for all your bank or investment accounts is stored safely in some database of your bank, along with all the information required to identify it as being yours. The database is known in a more generic term as *persistent storage*, meaning that the information stored is stored in a persistent manner—that is, the information is retained even after the computer is turned off. This is unlike the information that exists while a program is running, which disappears if the program exits or if the power goes down.

When you make a withdrawal or deposit, the information is retrieved from persistent storage, updated (based on the operation you performed), and then saved back in the persistent storage, overwriting the old data that was there. If the power goes down, or the network fails, or any other disaster strikes while you are you are making the withdrawal, the persistent storage will be unaffected, keeping the last known valid state of your account.

NOTE

The preceding bank example is a simplified version of the actual persistent storage mechanism, especially in large-scale systems. It is used only to illustrate the concept of persistent storage.

In short, most software systems use some sort of persistent storage to deposit the information they deem persistent. The most common persistent storage devices used are relational databases (SQL Server, Oracle, and so on) and regular disk files (XML documents, configuration files, and so on).

The persistent classes are marked as such in UML (by default classes are *transient*, that is, non-persistent). A persistent class would define a mechanism by which the state of any of its objects is stored and retrieved from a specific persistent storage device. A persistent object would be used to retrieve data from the persistent storage, and after the data is modified according to the program's algorithm, would be used again to store it back into the persistent storage.

It is common practice that the tasks of retrieving and saving data from/into persistent storage be separated from the actual business rules that modify the data. This is illustrated in distributed systems in the separation of classes in two distinct categories:

- *Business classes*—transient objects, which hold transient or no state and implement business algorithms

- *Data classes*—persistent objects, which implement methods to retrieve and store their state, and very little else

For example, you could have a business class `WireTransfer`, which has the appropriate methods to execute a wire transfer from one account of one customer to another account of the same or other customer, but in a different financial institution. This business class would use a few data classes like `Customer` and `Account` to perform its functions. It would first retrieve the `Customer` and `Account` information on this end of the transaction, then make the appropriate verifications that the transfer is a valid one, and then send a message to its peer at the other end that the transfer is ready. Upon receiving notification that the other end is ready, and all is well, the transfer would be executed. The `Account` would be debited or credited for the proper amount; the necessary fees would be applied; and then the Account state would be saved back into the database.

It is also worth mentioning that the object persistence is not a simple problem as it may appear (except in very simple systems). Among the issues that complicate it is the frequently encountered requirement that the data be shared between multiple users (and therefore protected from simultaneous updates—something known as *concurrency control*). Normally persistence involves transactions (we will cover this in Part V). Another issue is the discrepancies between the Object-Oriented paradigm (widely used today for software development) and the persistent storage paradigms (normally relational databases or some sort of hierarchical file system). These discrepancies are evident mostly when dealing with inheritance and complex relationships, concepts not well supported in a relational database or file system.

You will learn more about databases and storing objects in a persistent fashion using ADO.NET and XML.NET, in Part V.

Development Methodologies

You have learned a lot about object-oriented concepts; you now know what classes and objects are, as well as more advanced concepts of inheritance, polymorphism, and interfaces, in Chapters 13 through 19.

The next step in developing a system (after you learn about the theory and the tools) is to actually start working on a real example, or even better a subsystem of a real application.

NOTE

Right now you could not really do this because we haven't yet discussed a user interface (presented in the next chapters) or how to persist data (shown in Part V).

Assuming you have all the theoretical knowledge required, where would you start? Would you start developing a UML model, detailing each class, attribute, and method? Would you start by coding the classes first and then reverse-engineer them into a UML model?

These questions are normally asked at the beginning of each new software project. They have little to do with the actual language structure and the theory behind it, at least on the surface. But what use would a book that teaches programming have if it would not dedicate at least a small amount of time to the practical aspect of things? This is the reason we will present in the closing of this chapter a summary of the principal development methodologies used today.

The development methodologies can be categorized as top-down, bottom-up, and mixed. Following are summary overviews of each of these categories:

- *Top-down methodologies* generally start with identifying the high level abstractions and business entities, as well as the relations among them, based on use cases or other analytical methods. Then they start drilling down in a process called refining of the design and identifying the concrete packages and classes, and then the class attributes and methods. This process can be done in a few iterations, each one more detailed and fixing any issues that the previous iteration had. Finally a good and solid design is developed, and the final code can then be written based on it. This type of approach is normally very useful on large or very large systems, especially when resources and time are of less importance than quality and reliability. One of the best known methodologies to use this approach is the *Rational Unified Process* (in short RUP). It was developed at Rational Corporation by the same people who have originally developed the UML.

- *Bottom-up methodologies* involve starting to code with minimal design. The concept behind it is that the modern IDE tools (such as Visual Studio .NET) are powerful and integrated enough that no detail design is needed to develop a sound system. It is based on the basic idea that once you develop a number of working classes you can easily identify the abstractions, build the base classes and interfaces, and add polymorphism. This approach is well suited for small- to medium-size projects, especially when time and resources are scarce. The best example of such a methodology is known as Extreme Programming (XP).

- The *mixed approach* is (as the name suggests) a hybrid of the two methodologies. There are many in-house versions of methodologies devised especially for a specific project, or for a specific class of projects. The fundamental idea is to balance between the time spent analyzing the problem and the time spent developing the solution.

The process is usually as follows:

1. **Develop a prototype of what the final system will look and feel like.** This is usually a quick task, often using public fields and hardcoding difficult to implement or expensive features (threat synchronization, persistence, and so on).

2. **Design the final system based on lessons from the prototype.** Detail on this varies, but usually includes class.

3. **Implement the design.** It's best here to reuse what makes sense from the prototype code.

It normally involves developing a prototype (or proof of concept) of what the final system will look and feel like. This is done in a quick fashion (using public fields and hardcoding some hard-to-implement or expensive features such as thread synchronization, persistence, and so on. After the prototype is up and running, a design of the final system is done, based on the lessons learned from the prototype. The detail of this design can vary a lot from project to project, but in most cases includes at least all classes and attributes, as well as the crucial methods and state diagrams. The final step in the mixed methodologies is to implement the design, reusing what it makes sense from the prototype code.

The best methodology to use depends on a lot of factors, from available resources and time to quality requirements and organization culture and development history. It is a good thing to understand what the benefits and drawbacks of each category are, even if you will have little say in which methodology is selected for any given project.

What's Next

In Part III of the book you learned all the fundamental concepts of object-oriented development. You started with the simple concepts of class and object, their attributes (fields and properties), and their operations (methods), both object and class level (non-shared and shared). You then learned the fundamental concepts of object-oriented development: inheritance, interfaces, and polymorphism. You learned about the basic principles of OO: encapsulation and abstraction, and how to use them. You also learned some of the advanced concepts: collections and relations, and an intro to object persistence principles.

A lot of the material covered in this part will constitute the fundamental building blocks for the rest of the book. Many concepts that may seem unclear now will become clear when you use them throughout the rest of the book and even clearer when you start developing your own applications.

The next part of the book will deal with the visual (and way more spectacular) part of Visual Basic .NET: developing a user interface using the new .NET Framework.

NOTE

The answers to the Reviewing It, Checking It, and Applying It sections are available on our Web site.

Reviewing It

REVIEW

This section presents a review of the key concepts in this chapter. These questions are intended to gauge your absorption of the relevant material.

1. What is a relation?

2. What do we mean by the cardinality of a relation?

3. What is navigability?

4. What is a role in UML?

5. What is the difference between transient and persistent classes?

6. What are the categories of development methodologies in software engineering?

CHECK

Checking It

Select the correct answer to the following questions. There may be more than one answer to some questions.

Multiple Choice

1. Select all valid multiplicities.

    a. 0..1

    b. 1..1

    c. −2..*

    d. 2..*

2. What are valid containments for a relation?

    a. Association.

    b. Substitution.

    c. Aggregation.

    d. Distribution.

3. What does a many-to-many cardinality of a relation between classes A and B mean?

    a. Many objects of type A contain many objects of type B.

    b. Each object of type A contains many objects of type B.

    c. Each object of type B contains many objects of type A.

    d. Both b and c.

4. If relation A→B is navigable from A to B that means:

    a. A has an attribute of type B.

    b. B has an attribute of type A.

    c. Both a and b are true.

    d. Neither a and b are true.

True or False

Select one of the two possible answers and then verify on our Web site that you picked the correct one.

1. Aggregation is represented graphically by an arrow.

    True/False

2. The role name is usually the attribute name used to implement the relation.

   True/False

3. Persistent classes and business classes usually serve different purposes.

   True/False

4. Relations to fundamental data types are usually represented as attributes.

   True/False

5. If an object contains a collection of other objects it is said that the former aggregates the latter.

   True/False

6. The RUP process is known as a bottom-up category of development methodology.

   True/False

APPLY

Applying It

Try to complete the following exercises by yourself.

Independent Exercise 1

Develop the UML class diagram for classes in Figure 20.1 using only attributes, no relations, so that they have the same functionality.

Independent Exercise 2

Write the code that implements the classes in the diagram shown in Figure 20.3 as a prototype (that is, use public fields).

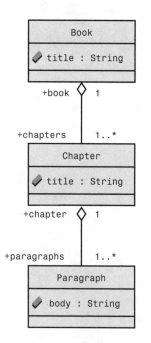

Figure 20.3: *Book, chapter, and paragraph class diagram.*

Part IV

Working with Forms and Controls

Programming the User Interface—Fundamental Concepts

Forms

Controls

Menus

Program Flow Control in the User Interface

Graphics Programming

Printing

Developing a Help System for the User Interface

Programming the User Interface—Fundamental Concepts

An important part of any good application is the user interface or UI. After all, this is what the user of your application sees and works with. To the user, the visual aspects of the application represent the entire application. They do not necessarily have interest in understanding the underpinnings of the application nor should they need to care. Users are happy if they can accomplish their task using the graphical interface that the application presents. This also means users are unhappy if they do not understand how the application works or meets their needs. So don't just think in terms of building a flashy user interface; make sure what you are building addresses the needs of the user.

The goal in this chapter is to introduce you to some fundamental user interface development topics. These topics cover the components and concepts used in the development of the user interface and sets the foundation for the user interface code examples in the chapters that follow.

The following user interface topics are covered in this chapter:

- Proper partitioning of your application code
- Single document interface versus multiple document interface
- Forms
- Controls
- Menus
- Events
- Multilanguage support
- Supporting the keyboard and mouse
- Fonts and colors

Introduction

Your goal should always be happy users. To accomplish this you must be clear on the requirements of the application and, most importantly, your application user interface should support these requirements in a very simple and friendly way. Before sitting down and writing code, you should always have a plan. This means you should know who the users of your application are and what they wish to accomplish.

If you do not take the initial steps to figure out this information, you will not be in a position for success. You will end up developing an application that most likely will not address the needs of the user. This can be frustrating for both you and the users. To avoid this you simply need to take the appropriate steps to identify your audience and actually talk to a few of them to agree on the purpose and deliverables of the application you are going to build. Even if the audience is yourself, you should develop a design and plan of what you are going to build before writing any source code.

This chapter does not cover User Interface Design specifically. Instead, this chapter covers more of the programming and development aspects related to the coding of a user interface. After you have read through this book, you may want to read a book on designing an effective user interface if you are (or will be) a user interface developer. Unfortunately, designing a good user interface is beyond the scope of this book.

The topics presented in this chapter lay a foundation for the next several chapters. It is important for you to understand this material before moving on to the code examples shown later. The purpose is to give you some context in how to develop a user interface before throwing some arbitrary code at you without giving you some background information.

Once you have read through Part IV, "Working with Forms and Controls," you should be in a position to start developing your own user interface using VB .NET.

Proper Partitioning of Your Application Code

By this point in the book you have already learned about the Visual Studio .NET development environment, the Visual Basic .NET language basics, and object-oriented concepts. Now you are moving on to learn about developing the user interface for an application.

One of the most common overlooked aspects of software development is the proper partitioning of your code. When most programmers start out in the software industry, their approach has been to sit down and start coding.

This approach assumes the application is going to magically appear from energetic creative people. Although this approach can foster very interesting outcomes, more often than not, this path produces code that is not very well thought out or maintainable.

There exist many philosophies and processes in the software development industry to address this. Deciding which process to adopt can be a daunting task by itself. The best advice I can give you is to use common sense and choose a process that is not extremely fine grained and rigid. The process should have a repeatable pattern. For example, use a process such as gather requirements, produce design, implement code, test and verify code, gather more requirements, and so on. And most importantly, follow it.

During the design phase, you should take a high-level view of your application and place pieces of your planned functionality into one of three common layers—User Interface, Application Logic, and Data Services. Figure 21.1 shows these three layers.

User Interface | Application Logic | Data Services

Figure 21.1: Logical partitions of application code.

The first layer of an application is commonly referred to as the User Interface layer or Presentation layer. This layer consists of everything the user sees and interacts with to use your application. The following several chapters are devoted to programming this layer.

The second layer of an application is commonly referred to as the Application Logic (or Business Logic) layer. This layer consists of code that performs logic (contains algorithms) that form the basis of the application intelligence. A simple example that you are probably familiar with is an ATM. When you go to the bank to take some money out of your checking account, you put your ATM card into a machine. This machine then starts asking you questions on a screen. First you must tell the machine what your personal identification number is. Next, you select a task such as "withdrawal" and then specify the amount. Everything you see on the screen is the user interface (that is, you, as a human, are interfacing with the computer). There is also code, as part of the ATM application, that verifies who you are and that you entered a valid personal identification number. If everything is okay at this point, money is withdrawn from your account by the amount you specified, and money comes out of the machine. The logic for verifying that you are the valid owner of the ATM card and for deducting the proper money from your account exists in the Application Logic of the ATM application.

The third layer of an application is the Data Services layer. Most applications use a database such as Oracle or SQL Server to store data. However, some don't use a database at all. They may store their data in a mainframe or by sending a message to a service exposed on the Web. The term "Data Services" is used to encompass all types of mechanisms that persist data in some form.

So now that you know what the common layers of an application are, why should you care? And, why bring this up when you are just trying to learn about programming a user interface? The reason is that if you take the time to partition your code this way, then you will be able to better maintain your application once it is complete. You would be able to put an entirely different kind of user interface on top of the application logic layer, for instance, without having to modify the application logic or data services layers. Each layer is distinct and can be enhanced without breaking the other layers—as long as you spend time during the design phase. The user interface code should be lightweight and deal only with user interface issues.

The other reason I mentioned this layering approach is to give you an understanding of why some of the sample user interface code is built the way it is. I could have chosen to put all of the sample code in Part IV right into the user interface classes. This would have been easier for me; however, this is not the approach you should be learning. Instead, some of the examples include additional classes that perform the application logic portion. I strongly encourage you to take a similar approach in code that you develop yourself. This may become clearer to you once you get to the code examples.

NOTE

This layering approach is similar to the Model-View-Controller design pattern. The Model represents the actual data representation only. The View is the display and is responsible for presenting a display of the data existing in the Model. When the View needs to change the data, it does so through the Controller. The Controller deals with the logic for manipulating the data.

NOTE

You should be designing your application into logical layers regardless of whether you are developing a standalone application for a single user or an *n*-tiered Web application.

This is also a reminder that application layers and tiers were formerly introduced in Chapter 1, "Overview of the Environment," and expanded in this chapter.

Single Document Interface versus Multiple Document Interface

Your Windows application can have one of two main styles—a single document interface (SDI) or a multi-document interface (MDI). An SDI application has one main window as part of the application. An MDI application has a main window that can contain multiple child windows. Figure 21.2 shows an SDI application next to an MDI application to illustrate the visual differences.

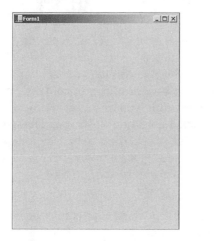
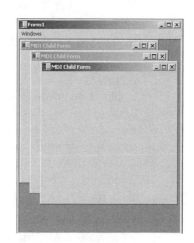

Figure 21.2: Single document interface versus muti-document interface.

An SDI application is generally used if you need only one main window to present the application's view to the user. This is the simplest kind of user interface to build and is quite common. Notepad, which comes with Microsoft Windows, is an example of an SDI application.

An MDI application is used when an application needs to display several windows to the user at the same time. These windows could be several different kinds of windows or several windows of the same type. The driving factor with an MDI application is that the application needs to display many different windows to the user in a straightforward manner. The child windows in an MDI application can be moved around within the main window but not outside the main window. The child windows can also be minimized within the main window. This type of application is more difficult to develop and requires more up-front thought about the types of windows the application needs to support. Microsoft Word is an example of an MDI application.

I referred to the term "windows" in introducing SDI and MDI applications. Actually, the main window and child windows are really instances of the Form class in the System.Windows.Forms namespace. In VB .NET, you will be using the Form class in the development of your applications as part of your graphical user interface. The Form class is part of the System. Windows.Forms namespace and is essential in developing a Windows application.

Forms can be modal or modeless. A *modal* form blocks any input to the rest of the application while it is displayed on the screen. You can move a modal form anywhere on the screen, but you cannot interact with the rest of the application while the form is up and running. In contrast, a modeless form can be displayed on the screen while you are interacting with the rest of the application. A modeless form does not block you. The use of modal and modeless depends entirely on your specific needs. Use a modal form when you want to get input from a user before allowing the user to continue. Use a modeless form when you want users to see the form at the same time that they need to interact with the rest of the application.

Dialogs are a special type of a Form class that can be used to gather input from a user. After the user has entered the required information, he or she would click on a button (typically the OK button) to accept the data and close the window. If you plan on building your own dialogs as part of an application you would use the Project—Add Windows Form menu item to create your new dialog class. Your dialog classes will inherit from the Form class in System.Windows.Forms.

The following example shows how to create a new form and display it on the screen:

```
Dim form As New Form()
form.Show()
```

Figure 21.3 shows the visual form displayed as a result of the previous example code.

Figure 21.3: *A form.*

The first line of code instantiates (or creates) a new Form object. The second line calls the Show method, which displays the form on the screen. The Show method displays the form as a modeless form. The ShowDialog method can be used to display the form as a modal form. This sample code is just illustrating how to create a new form and display it. It is not really interesting because there is nothing on the form. In the next chapter we will discuss forms in more detail and show you how to make more interesting forms.

Controls

Controls are special-purpose artifacts used in graphical user interfaces. There is a set of common controls provided as part of the Microsoft .NET Framework that you can use to build your applications. This includes (but is not limited to) the following set of standard controls that Windows developers are familiar with: Label, TextBox, Button, RadioButton, and CheckBox. These controls, and more, are covered in detail in Chapter 23, "Controls." Figure 21.4 shows some example controls on a form.

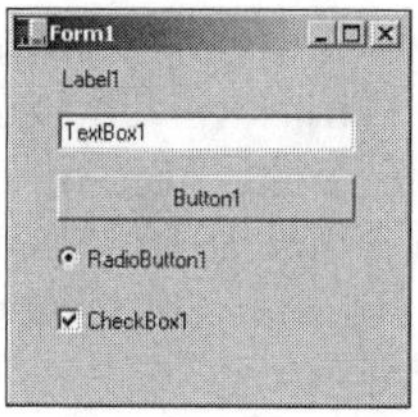

Figure 21.4: *Some common controls.*

If you find yourself needing a control to do a job that cannot be easily accomplished by using one of the existing controls that are displayed in the Visual Studio .NET toolbox, you can initiate a search for a control that is commercially available. Although this may incur a cost to you, it may be worth it if it saves you time from having to build it yourself. This is the traditional buy versus build dilemma.

You always have the option of building new controls yourself to meet your specific needs. This may be a result of needing to build a control for an application you are building or you may choose to build a library of controls and sell them commercially to other developers. You may even choose to build them and make them publicly available for free to anyone who wants to use them. Whatever the circumstances, you do have the ability to create your own custom controls, and this is covered in Chapter 23.

Menus

What would a Windows application be without menus? Menus provide a convenient way for the user to initiate defined tasks in your application. Menus usually appear across the top portion of your application window starting from the left. Related tasks can be grouped together on a menu so that the user can learn and understand your application faster and at the same time give the user quick access to the functionality provided by your application.

Visual Studio .NET has an extensive set of menus that you use in the development of your software projects. Visual Basic .NET also gives you the ability to create and define menus for your own applications. In Chapter 24, "Menus," you will see how to define your own menus and write code that is executed when the user selects the menu items you define. Figure 21.5 shows an example. The menu is referred to as the Windows menu because the name of the menu on the menu bar is Windows. The single menu item in the Windows menu is named New Child Form. This menu item is used to create a new child form in the application window. In Chapter 24, you will see how to define your own menus and write code that gets executed in response to the user selecting the menu items.

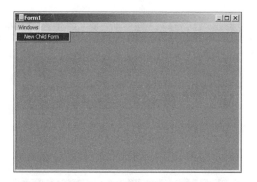

Figure 21.5: *Example menu.*

Events

When you first learn any programming language you are taught how to program using a procedural approach. This is on purpose to focus your attention on the language itself without having to explain some of the more complex concepts in programming. In fact, this is the approach we took early on in this book to get you started learning Visual Basic .NET.

In contrast, developing a user interface requires an event-driven programming model. Instead of having a predefined start point and end point with a set of code in the middle, event-driven programming requires that you develop snippets (or small sections) of code that get executed when an event happens in your application. When an event occurs, it is said that the event "fires." Any code that is defined to respond to the specific event would then be executed.

The most common event would be a click of a button. You can write code that is executed when a user clicks a button. Figure 21.6 shows an event being fired as a result of a user clicking a button.

Using this approach, you should design and develop your user interface using specialized forms and controls along with code snippets that are executed when certain events occur. You have control over which events you care to write code for and which events you do not necessarily care about. We will get into more detail regarding events in the next several chapters as events are an extremely important part of developing a user interface.

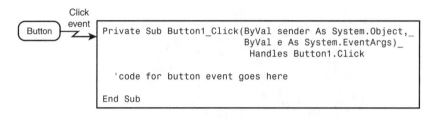

Click
event
Button
Private Sub Button1_Click(ByVal sender As System.Object,_
ByVal e As System.EventArgs)_
Handles Button1.Click
'code for button event goes here
End Sub

Figure 21.6: *Events.*

Multilanguage Support

If you ever plan on building a software application for users who understand different languages, you need to plan on building multilanguage and localization support into your application. Suppose you need to build an application that contains a form for entering personal information such as your name and address. You would presumably create a form similar to the one shown in Figure 21.7.

Enter Name and Address
First Name:
Last Name:
Address:
City:
State:
Zip:
Ok
Cancel

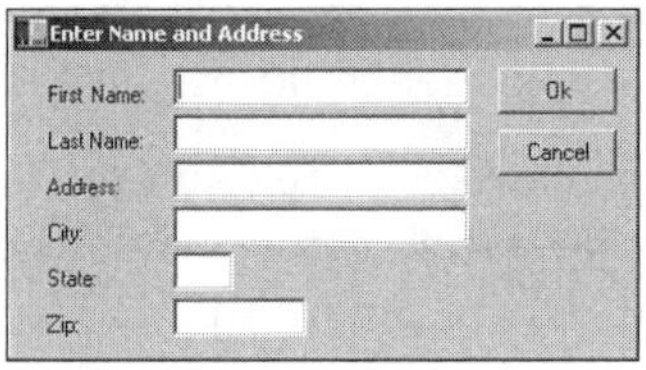

Figure 21.7: *Dialog for entering name and address.*

Ideally, you would want to be able to display the same form using different languages depending on the country in which you are selling your software. Using other software development tools in the past, you would have to store all of the phrases you used in your application in a resource file and reference them using a unique ID. Then, when your application was installed, the user would pick the preferred language during the installation process, and the appropriate resource file would be installed on the user's computer. Your program would then use the installed resource file, and the correct localized words would be displayed in the user interface.

Although this approach has worked in the past, the amount of effort involved in programming an application this way (let alone testing it) precluded many developers from actually implementing multilanguage support in their applications.

Luckily for you, Visual Basic .NET has this support built in and it is very easy to use. After you have developed your user interface, you need to revisit each form in your project and turn on the Localizable property as shown in Figure 21.8. This signifies that the selected form supports multiple languages.

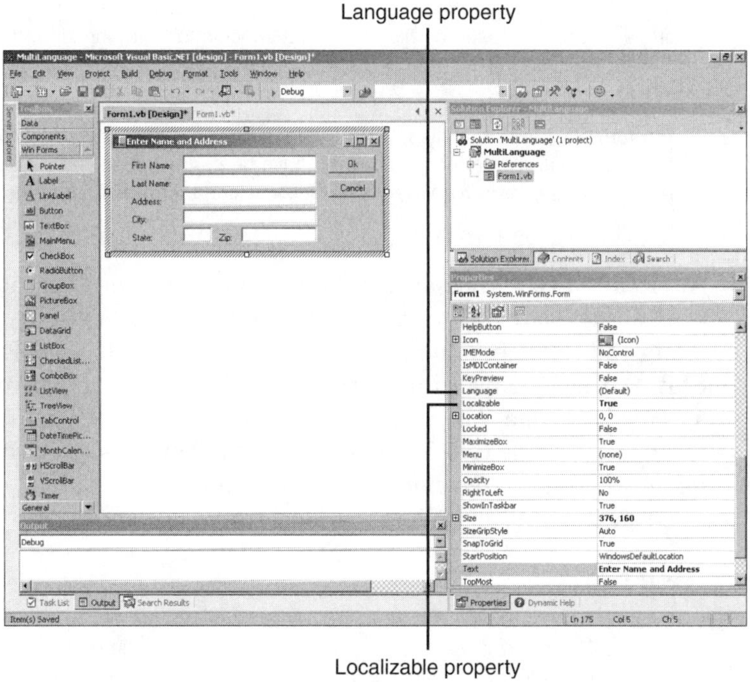

Language property

Localizable property

Figure 21.8: *Localizable property on a form.*

If you choose to turn on the Localizable property (by setting the property to True), you would want to lay out your form with the Language property set to Default. This allows you to define how the form looks in the default case. When you are comfortable with the basic look of the form, you would select the specific language (using the Language property on the form) for the purpose of modifying the form for that language. After you change the language on a form, you can change the strings on all of the controls to contain text specific to the language you choose. Also, you can resize the form and add controls as part of a specific language setting. This way you can completely customize the look of a form depending on the specific language setting as part of the operating system. This is very useful in the cases where the size of the text on a control is language-dependent. This requires the layout of the controls on the form to be different for different languages.

NOTE

Setting the `Localizable` property to `True` on your form initiates the creation of a resource file in your project behind the scenes. The resource file is based on your form name and has a file extension of .resx. If your form name is Form1, the resource file created is Form1.resx. This resource file is used to store the strings associated with the default language. When you choose a specific language in the form's `Language` property, another resource file is created specific to that language. If you choose English (United States) a resource file named Form1.en-US.resx is generated for the form named Form1.

The format of the .resx files is XML. This allows you to use the XML Designer to view and edit these files directly once they have been generated and included in the project. The XML Designer is displayed by double-clicking the .resx files in the Solution Explorer window.

After you have turned on `Localization` and set the `Language` property for your forms, your application's user interface is adjusted by the Language setting on the user's computer. If the language setting is English (United States), then the user interface is based on the design of your forms for this specific language. The great part in all of this is that you do not need to write any specific code to get this benefit. This has traditionally required a lot of work on the developer's part in the past to obtain this type of localization functionality in an application.

NOTE

A simple way of testing the results of localization of your application is to set the specific locale directly in your code. This is much simpler than updating the settings on your computer. To set the locale in your code you need to set the `CurrentUICulture` for the current thread. The following code sets the current locale to be French (Cananda):

```
Thread.CurrentThread.CurrentUICulture = New CultureInfo("fr-CA")
```

The following namespaces need to be imported as well:

```
Imports System.Threading.Thread
Imports System.Globalization
```

Figure 21.9 started with the form shown in Figure 21.7 and localizes it for Romanian. Notice that the strings appear in the appropriate language. Also, the TextBoxes needed to be moved over to the right slightly since the Romanian text is longer than the English versions. Once again, you can change the layout as well as the strings for each language that your form supports. The form will display based on the language setting on the computer on which it runs.

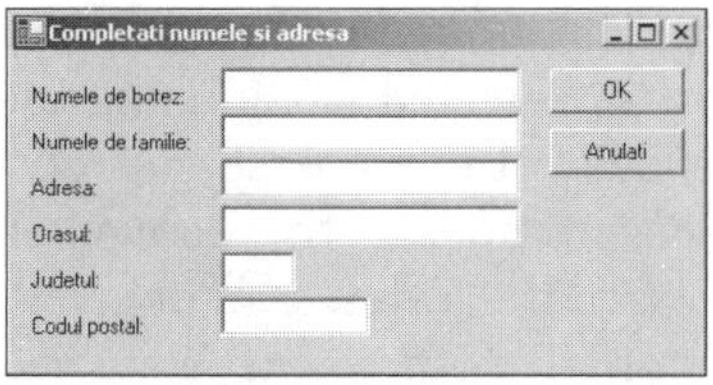

Figure 21.9: *Localized form to support Romanian.*

Supporting the Keyboard and Mouse

The keyboard and the mouse are the primary inputs for your application. Because this is what the user is going to use to work with your application, you should spend some time during your development to make sure your application works well with the keyboard and not just the mouse. Most developers using Visual Studio .NET are very accustomed to using the mouse and lose sight of the application support for the keyboard.

Tab Order

One of the most common problems in this area is not setting the *Tab order* on a form. The Tab order is the order in which the controls on your form are visited when the user presses the Tab key. When a form is first displayed, the selected control is the one that is the first in the Tab order. When the Tab key is pressed, the control that is second in the Tab order is then selected. Each successive press of the Tab key moves the selection through all of the controls in the Tab order list. When the last control is selected and the Tab key is pressed, the selection reverts back to the first control in the Tab order list. Shift+Tab can also be used at any time to move through the Tab order list in reverse order.

To set the Tab order on a form, you need to modify the properties of each control on the form. Using the form shown in Figure 21.7 to illustrate this, you would need to go through each control's property list setting the TabStop and TabIndex properties. The TabStop property is a Boolean property meaning it can contain only a True or False value. If the TabStop property is set to True then this control is visited at some point during the process of pressing Tab many times on the form. Exactly when the control becomes the selected control is based on the TabIndex property value. TabIndex is a numeric property. The value for this property is the position in the list of controls that becomes selected when using the Tab key. A TabIndex value of 1 means this control is the first control selected when the form is displayed. If the TabIndex value is 2, this control is the second control selected when the user presses the Tab key. When you are developing your forms, you would go through all of the controls on each form and set the TabStop and TabIndex properties so that the selection process of the controls is a natural progression on the form.

Using the form shown in Figure 21.7, a natural progression for the Tab Order would be the First Name text box, the Last Name text box, the Address text box, the City text box, the State text box, the Zip Code text box, the OK button, and lastly the Cancel button. For your forms, you would obviously use your best judgement but make sure your Tab order does not jump in all different directions on the form as this will confuse the user. A good approach to take when dealing with Tab order on a form is to start at the top left and end at the bottom right.

Accelerator Keys

Accelerator keys, also called mnemonics, are represented by the underlined characters you see as part of menus and menu items. They represent a keyboard shortcut key that can be used by the user to invoke the menu immediately as opposed to having to click on it with the mouse.

You can define accelerator keys on menus and command buttons by placing the ampersand character (&) somewhere in the text of the menu or command button. The character in the text that follows the ampersand becomes the accelerator key. To use the accelerator key, you need to press the Alt key plus the accelerator key at the same time. Figure 21.10 shows an example menu and menu item with accelerator keys defined. The menu accelerator key is Alt+F and is defined by setting the menu text property to &File. The menu item accelerator key is Alt+O and is defined by setting the menu item text property to &Open. It is very easy to discern the accelerator keys because the F and the O are underlined respectively.

To open the File menu, you would press Alt+F. While the menu is visible, you can select and invoke the menu item by pressing Alt+O.

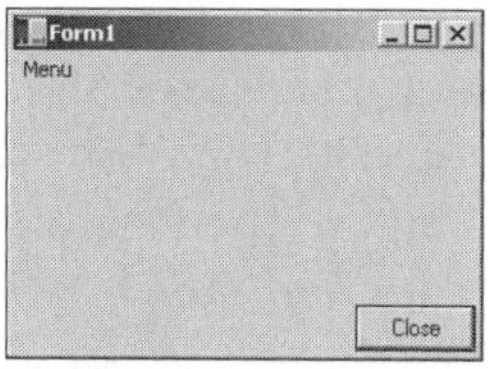

Figure 21.10: *Accelerator keys.*

Also in Figure 21.10, a command button with the text Close is displayed on the form. The button has an accelerator key of Alt+C defined for it. Again, this was created by specifying &Close in the button's Text property.

Drag and Drop

"Drag and Drop" is a phrase used to describe the process of selecting something with the mouse and then dragging it into a different area of the same window or another completely different window. This can be a very useful feature that allows users to work with your application in a very natural way. Moving things around visually is much easier to understand than, for example, having to select some things in a window and then press a button to move the selection.

Fonts and Colors

Fonts allow you to display text in a variety of different shapes and sizes within your application. This gives it a more unique and flashy look that can be appealing to users. Or, you can be like most developers and accept the default font setting to be displayed in your application user interface. However, please try to be creative with your applications as the world already has enough boring stale user interfaces. You should want users to enjoy using the software you build. Good use of fonts and colors can go a long way toward this end.

While you are attempting to be creative, keep in mind that consistent standards are extremely important across the application or set of applications you are developing. As a Microsoft Windows developer, you should be aware of the guidelines presented by Microsoft so that your applications conform to a consistent look and feel. The *Microsoft Windows User Experience* book is a good place to gain this knowledge. For more information regarding this book check out this link: http://www.microsoft.com/MSPress/books/2466.asp.

You can change the font in a form by setting its font property. A form's font is used by all of the controls placed on the form unless the control specifically overrides the form's font. If you set a form's font size to be 20 and then you place a control on the form, the control assumes the font size of 20. If you change the form's font size to 10, the form and all of the controls on the form assume the font size of 10. However, if you change the font size of a control to a different size, say 30, then the control has just overridden the font size of the form. Changing the form's font size at this point has no affect on that specific control's font size.

Figure 21.11 shows two labels on a form. The top label has a font size of 30 and the bottom has a font size of 10. The form's font size is 10. In this example, the label at the top of the form has its font changed to override the form's font. At this point, I could change the form's font size, and only the bottom label would change its font size according to the form's font size.

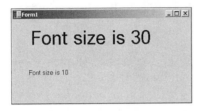

Figure 21.11: Font sizes on forms.

The font size was used as an example to show how the form's font properties are related to the font properties of the controls on the form. Fonts have additional properties that you can change to customize the look to suit your needs. Figure 21.12 shows some sample font settings.

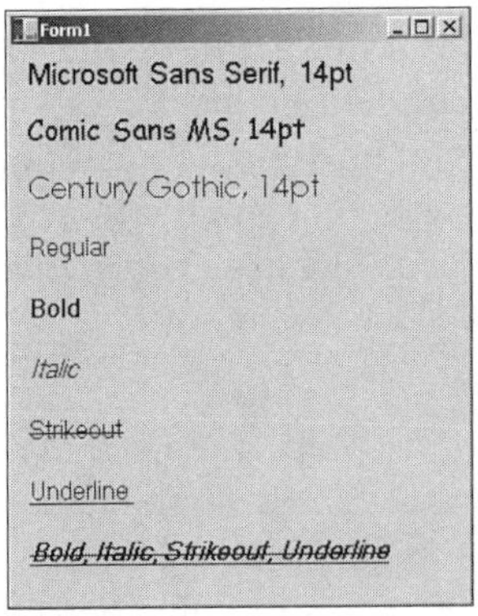

Figure 21.12: Example fonts.

The top three labels on the form in Figure 21.12 show examples of different fonts. You should have several fonts available on your computer to use in your development, and these three are just examples. The next five labels illustrate the use of regular, bold, italic, strikethrough, and underlined text. You can also combine these as you choose. The last and bottom label shows the combination of bold, italic, strikethrough, and underlined to illustrate how this looks.

As you have probably guessed by now, you can also change the font settings through code rather than having to use the Properties window. This involves using the System.Drawing namespace, which we will get into more in Chapter 26, "Graphics Programming." For now, to change the font of a control programmatically you would write code similar to the following:

```
Dim label As Label = New System.Windows.Forms.Label()

label.Text = "Bold"
label.Font = New Font("Microsoft Sans Serif", 12!, System.Drawing.FontStyle.Bold)
```

The first line defines and creates a new `Label` control. The next line sets the displayed text of the label. The last line updates the label's font. This is done by creating a new System.Drawing.Font object and setting this to the label's `Font` property. The constructor of the `Font` object takes three parameters in this example. The first parameter is the name of the font to use for the label. The second parameter is the point size of the font. And lastly, the third parameter is the font style. This example shows the use of a predefined constant representing the bold style.

What's Next

In this chapter we introduced you to some introductory user interface concepts. These concepts are just the first step in developing a user interface in Microsoft .NET. In the following chapters, you will get into more detail about how to develop a user interface.

In the next chapter, Windows Forms is covered in extensive detail. Windows Forms is the next generation class library for building user interfaces for Windows applications. This class library can be used by any language that is supported by Microsoft .NET. You no longer need to make language choices that depend on the richness of the available user interface libraries.

NOTE

The answers to "Reviewing It," "Checking It," and "Applying It" are available on our Web site.

REVIEW ## Reviewing It

This section presents a review of the key concepts in this chapter. These questions are intended to gauge your absorption of the relevant material.

1. What are the three common layers of an application?

2. What is the difference between MDI and SDI?

3. What are Controls?

4. What are Menus?

5. What is Localization?

Checking It

Select the correct answer to the following questions.

CHECK **Multiple Choice**

1. What are the two possible modes that forms can be in?

    a. Public and private.

    b. Modal and shared.

    c. Modal and modeless.

    d. None of the above.

2. What are Accelerator keys?

    a. Keyboard shortcuts for menus and controls.

    b. Keys that type faster than others.

    c. Keys that specify the Tab order.

    d. All of the above.

3. In Microsoft .NET, forms are:

    a. Windows.

    b. Used to display data and gather user input.

    c. Either modal or modeless.

    d. All of the above.

4. Accelerator keys are defined using:

    a. Brackets.

    b. Parentheses.

    c. Ampersand.

    d. Quotes.

5. Events are:

    a. Special times to install Microsoft .NET.

    b. Special times when forms, controls, or other classes need to communicate something to other code that may be listening.

    c. Not part of the Microsoft .NET.

    d. None of the above.

True or False

Select one of the two possible answers and then verify on our Web site that you picked the correct one.

1. The font and color of a dialog are specified by the system colors only.

   True/False

2. An SDI application has only one main form.

   True/False

3. Forms can have menus to provide the user access to functionality provided by the form.

   True/False

4. Drag and drop is not handled in Microsoft .NET.

   True/False

5. Accelerator keys allow you to define a shortcut to menu items.

   True/False

6. Controls on a form can be tabbed through successively in the order defined by the developer.

   True/False

APPLY

Applying It

Try to complete the following exercises by yourself.

Independent Exercise 1

Check out the online resources for user interface design at `http://msdn.microsoft.com/library/default.asp?url=/nhp/Default.asp?contentid=28000443`. Familiarize yourself with the standards so that you can develop professional-quality applications in Microsoft Windows. In addition, you may want to purchase *Microsoft Windows User Experience* if you are a serious UI developer.

Independent Exercise 2

Create a new Windows Application project and localize a form. To do this, first add a Label control to the form by dragging it from the Toolbox and drop it onto the form.

Forms

In this chapter, you explore Forms in detail as they are an essential part of creating a Windows application.

The following form topics are covered in this chapter:

- Size and position
- Color and background
- Border styles
- Forms Designer
- Docking and anchoring
- Events
- Scrolling
- Message boxes
- Dialog boxes
- Single document interface and multiple document interface

Introduction

Prior to the development of the Microsoft .NET Framework, if you wanted to develop Windows Applications in C++ you would use MFC, ATL, or down and dirty Win32 to develop your user interface. This was not something that was entertaining for most developers. Yes, some developers grew accustomed to writing lots of code to gain the full power of implementing a powerful UI, but most became frustrated with the complexity of trying to build even the simplest user interfaces.

Visual Basic 6 was an alternative for developing a modest user interface using forms, especially because one could develop the user interface in VB and write COM components in either VB or C++ (for those serious developers). Even in Visual Basic 6 though, it was sometimes necessary to make calls into Win32 to perform specific tasks not readily available in VB.

In Microsoft .NET, it appears the simplicity of Visual Basic forms and the power of Win32 has produced what is now called Windows Forms. Windows Forms refers to the System.Windows.Forms namespace in the Microsoft .NET Framework, which contains a set of classes necessary to build a user interface in Microsoft .NET. This includes the Form class and common control classes such as Button, Label, TextBox, and ListBox to name a few. Although this book covers Visual Basic .NET, we must point out once again that Visual Studio .NET allows you to develop in basically any language use choose. This means that you can use Windows Forms in other languages such as C# (pronounced "C sharp"). This solves the problem of having to learn how to develop user interfaces in different languages. You can now develop using Windows Forms without worrying about the language you are using for development.

You will explore the Form class in detail as part of this chapter and move on to controls in the next chapter. To explain some Forms concepts, there are examples in this chapter that use some of the controls defined in the System.Windows.Forms namespace but this is only a preview of those controls.

In Visual Studio .NET, creating forms in Windows applications is very much the same as it was in Visual Basic 6.0. For example, there is a Form Designer that allows you to resize the form and add controls to the form. A form also consists of a code file that contains the logic for the form. The big difference between Visual Basic 6.0 and Visual Basic .NET (in regards to forms) is that much more of the guts of the form are exposed to you as a developer. Visual Studio .NET simplifies this by hiding the complexity and automatically updating a form's code based on the visual designing you do. The Form Designer is covered over the course of the next several chapters.

However, in order to help you understand the details of the
System.Windows.Forms.Form class, the examples start simple and progressively explain more and more capabilities of forms.

For your first example you'll create a new Empty project and then add a
new Windows Form to the project. If you do this on your own, you may
notice a few additional lines of code that are automatically generated for
you as part of the Form class. To simplify the example please refer to the following code for the Form class:

```
Imports System.Windows.Forms

Public Class Form1
    Inherits System.Windows.Forms.Form

End Class
```

The first line imports the System.Windows.Forms namespace for use within
the class file for the form. Next, a new class is defined with the name of
Form1 and it inherits from the System.Windows.Forms.Form class. All forms
that you develop are going to inherit from the System.Windows.Forms.Form
class (or a subclass of System.Windows.Forms.Form class). The last line ends
the declaration of the class. There is nothing really exciting going on here
except that a new Form1 class is defined as part of the project.

A shared main method is added to the Form1 class to provide a starting
point for the application as shown in the following code example.

```
Imports System.Windows.Forms

Public Class Form1
    Inherits System.Windows.Forms.Form

    Shared Sub Main()
        Dim form As Form1
        form = New Form1()
        Application.Run(form)
    End Sub

End Class
```

In the Main subroutine, a new variable of type Form1 is declared and then
it is assigned a new instance of the Form1 class. The last line in the Main
subroutine uses the shared (or static) method Run in the Application class
to display the form. Actually, the Application.Run method starts the message pump for the form. If you are familiar with Win32 or MFC this should
sound familiar to you. If not, basically applications written for Microsoft
Windows must have a message processing loop for the purpose of dealing

with Windows messages and events within the application. As events are sent to the form, the message processing loop continuously looks for messages on a queue and processes them as they appear on the queue. The Application.Run accomplishes this automatically for you.

NOTE

The Application object has shared properties for the current application. This includes StartupPath, which signifies the location where the application is started from, and ExecuteablePath, which signifies where an application's executable file is stored. This should sound familiar to any VB6 developer who has used App.Path to get the application path.

You also need to specify the startup object in your project settings. This allows you to set the exact starting point of your application. Because this project only contains the Form1 class your options are limited, but if you had a large project with lots of Form classes and Modules you would have a variety of places to define the starting point of your application.

You can set the startup object by right-clicking on the project in the Project Explorer window and selecting the Properties menu. This displays a dialog box for editing the project's properties. In the General section of the Common Properties, you can select the startup object by choosing an item in the list box. Figure 22.1 shows this dialog and where to choose the startup object.

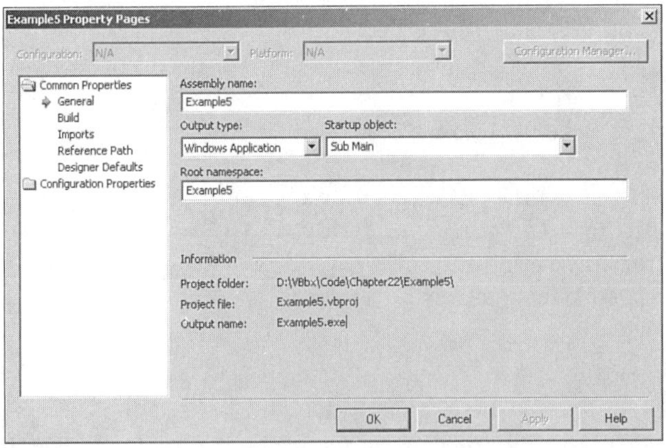

Figure 22.1: Setting the startup object.

Size and Position

A form has two distinct sizes that you need to be aware of. The first size is the overall size of the entire form as displayed on the screen. The second size is the internal area of the form where other components can be drawn. The internal area is referred to as the client area of the form and is obviously smaller in size than the form's overall size. The value for the height and width of a form can have different meanings depending on the PageUnit property of the System.Drawing.Graphics object associated with the display of the form. The PageUnit property's data type is System.Drawing.GraphicsUnit and can have these possible values: Display, Document, Inch, Millimeter, Pixel, Point, and World. PageUnit is discussed in more depth in Chapter 26, "Graphics Programming."

For the remainder of this chapter, the size of the form uses the default PageUnit which is Pixel. A pixel standards for "picture element" and is the smallest unit of display on a computer screen. The number of pixels that can be displayed on the screen is defined in the Display Properties panel in Microsoft Windows. Figure 22.2 shows the Display Properties panel, which can be accessed by right-clicking the Desktop, selecting Properties from the menu, and then clicking on the Settings tab.

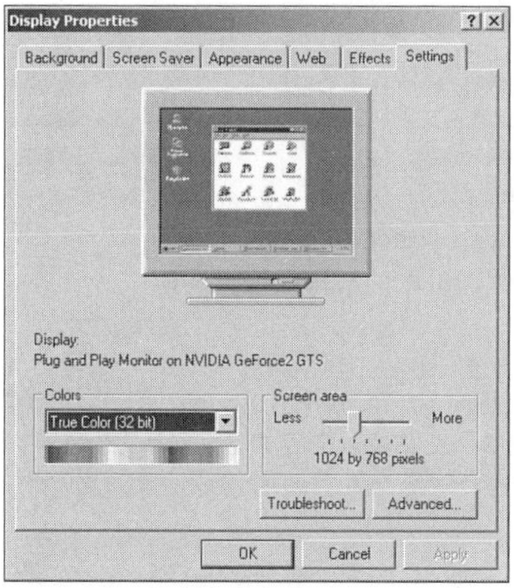

Figure 22.2: *Setting the screen area.*

You should also keep this in mind when you are developing Windows applications. If you define the sizes of your forms using the standard pixel setting, the forms may or may not show up on your users' computers. For example, if your display is set to 1152x864 and you set the size of a form to the entire screen on your computer, this form will not display correctly on a screen that is set to 800x600. The form will be too big for that screen.

To alleviate some of this concern, you should set your computer's display settings to 800x600 resolution. 800x600 is generally the smallest acceptable display setting on a computer. Therefore, if you develop a user interface on a computer that has its display resolution set to 800x600, your forms and applications should show up just fine on your users' computers.

To set the overall size of a form you would set the form's Size property. To set the client size of a form you would call its ClientSize property. The following code sets the size of the form, displays both the size and client size, sets the client size, and displays both the size and client size again.

```
Imports System.Windows.Forms

Public Class Form1
    Inherits System.Windows.Forms.Form

    Sub DisplaySizes()
        System.Console.Out.WriteLine("Form Size: {0}, {1}", _
                                     Size.Width, _
                                     Size.Height)
        System.Console.Out.WriteLine("Form Client Size: {0}, {1}", _
                                     ClientSize.Width, _
                                     ClientSize.Height)
    End Sub

    Shared Sub Main()
        Dim form As Form1
        form = New Form1()

        'sets size of entire form window
        form.Size = New System.Drawing.Size(300, 300)
        form.DisplaySizes()

        'sets size of client area of form
        form.ClientSize = New System.Drawing.Size(300, 300)
        form.DisplaySizes()

        Application.Run(form)
    End Sub

End Class
```

The output of running the code is:

```
Form Size: 300, 300
Form Client Size: 292, 273
Form Size: 308, 327
Form Client Size: 300, 300
```

The output tells you that when you set the size of the form the client size is also changed. The results are based on running on my computer with the display settings set to 1024x768 pixels. Notice that the client size is slightly smaller. Running on my computer, the difference in width appears to be 8 units (pixels) and the difference in the height is 27 units (pixels). This means that the height of the form is 27 units larger than the form's client area height, and the width of the form is 8 units larger than the form's client area width. This extra size difference is taken up by the title area of the form and the form's border area, both of which are not considered part of the client area of the form.

Also note that the minimum size of a form is 112 units by 27 units. So, if you try to set the size of the form to a width and height of zero, the form's size will be width of 112 units and a height of 27 units.

Again, these numbers are totally dependant on the display settings of the computer on which the application is running. The main point in going over these numbers is to illustrate that the client area is smaller than the form's overall size.

The `System.Drawing.Size` class is provided as part of the System.Drawing namespace and is used throughout the set of user interface classes as a standard way of representing size information. The `Size` class has `Width` and `Height` properties for the purposes of setting or getting the width and height values within a `Size` object.

To retrieve a form's size and client size, you would access the form's `Size` and `ClientSize` properties depending on your needs (whether you are interested in the entire size of the form or only the client area of the form). In the previous example, the first line in the `DisplaySizes` method gets the value for the form's `Size` property and then reads the value for the `Width` property of the `Size` object using the code `Size.Width`. The code gets the form's Size property again and reads the Height property from the Size object using the code `Size.Height` and both the width and height values are displayed in the output window. The second line in the `DisplaySizes` method does the same thing except it gets the form's client size information using the code `ClientSize.Width` and `ClientSize.Height`.

The `Form` class also has `Height` and `Width` properties for setting the size of the form. The `Height` property is a shorthand way of getting or setting the form's height. The `Width` property is a shorthand way of getting or setting the form's width. The following two code fragments have the same effect:

```
Dim form As Form1
form = New Form1()
form.Size = New System.Drawing.Size(250, 250)
```

```
Dim form As Form1
form = New Form1()
form.Width = 250
form.Height = 250
```

A form can be displayed on the computer screen in three possible states: normal, maximized, and minimized. A form displayed in a normal state is visible on the screen but does not take up the entire display area. You would still be able to see other forms or windows when a form is displayed in a normal state. If a form is displayed in a maximized state, then it takes up the entire screen. You would not be able to see any other forms or windows at the same time the maximized form is being displayed. And lastly, a minimized form is not visible on the screen except for the form's entry on the task bar (or as an iconized window in an MDI parent as you'll see later).

You can set a form's display state if you wish to have the form be displayed in any one of these ways. The Form class has a property named WindowState. The data type for this property is System.Windows.Forms.FormWindowState, which only allows for three possible values. Table 22.1 describes the values for the window state.

Table 22.1: Possible Window States for Forms

FormWindowState	Description
Normal	Form is visible but does not cover entire screen so that other forms or windows are partially visible as well.
Maximized	Form is visible and covers entire screen.
Minimized	Form is not visible except for entry in task bar or iconized in MDI parent window.

The following code fragment shows how to create a new form object and display it in a maximized state so that it takes up the entire screen.

```
Imports System.Windows.Forms

Public Class Form1
    Inherits System.Windows.Forms.Form

    Shared Sub Main()
        Dim form As Form1
        form = New Form1()
        form.WindowState = FormWindowState.Maximized
        Application.Run(form)
    End Sub

End Class
```

The default window state of a Form is set to Normal. Once again this means the Form is visible but does not cover the entire screen. Forms that are displayed in a Normal state also have a screen position that can be set. The System.Windows.Forms.Form class has a StartPosition property for specifying the position of a Form when it is displayed. The data type for the StartPosition property is System.Windows.Forms.FormStartPosition. Table 22.2 lists the possible values of the StartPosition property and the corresponding descriptions.

Table 22.2: StartPosition Values

StartPosition	Description
CenterScreen	The form is automatically centered on the screen.
CenterParent	The form is automatically centered in its parent (or screen if it does not have a parent).
Manual	The exact position is defined in your code or specified in the properties window for the form.
WindowsDefaultBounds	Microsoft Windows chooses an appropriate location and size for the form. This overrides any sizing you may have done to the form.
WindowsDefaultLocation	Microsoft Windows chooses an appropriate location for the form. The size of the form is not affected.

If I wanted to set the exact position on the screen for a form I would need to set the form's FormWindowState to Normal and also set the form's StartPosition to Manual. Next, I would need to set the exact position. So how is this done? The position of a form is set using the form's Top and Left properties. The Top property specifies the number of units the form is from the top of the screen (or top of the client area of a parent window). The Left property specifies the number of units from the left of the screen (or left of the client area of a parent window). To illustrate, the following code creates a new form and positions the window 200 units from the top of the screen and 200 units from the left of the screen:

```
Imports System.Windows.Forms

Public Class Form1
    Inherits System.Windows.Forms.Form

    Shared Sub main()
        Dim form As Form1
        form = New Form1()

        ' sets size of entire form window
        form.Size = New System.Drawing.Size(200, 200)
```

```
        ' set window state to normal (default)
        form.WindowState = FormWindowState.Normal

        ' set start position to be manually defined
        form.StartPosition = FormStartPosition.Manual

        ' set exact position
        form.Left = 200
        form.Top = 200

        ' display form
        Application.Run(form)
    End Sub

End Class
```

Figure 22.3 shows the form displayed 200 units from the top of the screen and 200 units from the left of the screen.

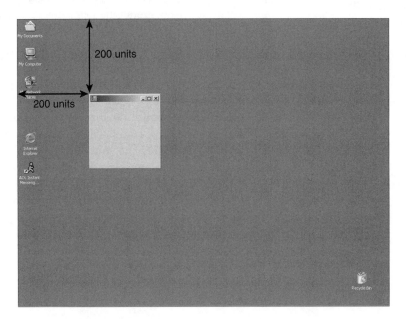

Figure 22.3: *Setting position of a form.*

If I wanted to center a form, I could always calculate the position of the form based on the form's size and the size of the screen. But why bother! Just use the CenterScreen (or CenterParent) start position value. Here's an example:

```
Imports System.Windows.Forms

Public Class Form1
    Inherits System.Windows.Forms.Form

    Shared Sub main()
        Dim form As Form1
        form = New Form1()

        ' sets size of entire form window
        form.Size = New System.Drawing.Size(200, 200)

        ' set window state to normal (default)
        form.WindowState = FormWindowState.Normal

        ' set start position to be center on the screen
        form.StartPosition = FormStartPosition.CenterScreen

        ' display form
        Application.Run(form)
    End Sub

End Class
```

Color and Background

Forms automatically take on the color scheme that is defined in Microsoft Windows. Therefore, most of the time you do not need to specify colors for your forms. You do have the option, however, of changing the colors for a form if you desire. You could either change the colors in the Properties window for the form that you want to change, or you can write code to change it as well.

There are two color settings that you should be concerned with if you choose to deal with colors on a form. The first color is the back color and is represented by the BackColor property on the form. The back color is the background color of the form. The second color is the foreground color and is represented by the ForeColor property on the form. The foreground color is the color by which any text or characters would be displayed in. For example, newspapers are primarily printed with a black foreground color and a white background color (black text on white paper).

The data type for both of the color properties on the form is System. Drawing.Color. A Color object can be created using a combination of three numbers that make up an RGB color. The first number represents the intensity of the color red; the second number represents the intensity of the color green; and the third represents the intensity of the color blue. By combining these three intensities any color can be generated.

The following code sets the background color of the form to be black:

```
Imports System.Windows.Forms

Public Class Form1
    Inherits System.Windows.Forms.Form

    Shared Sub main()
        Dim form As Form1
        form = New Form1()

        ' set color to black
        form.BackColor = System.Drawing.Color.FromArgb(0, 0, 0)

        ' display form
        Application.Run(form)
    End Sub

End Class
```

This works okay because I know that a zero intensity for red, green, an blue results in black. But, what if I want to use the colors orange or purple? Do I really have to figure out the intensities for each color I want to use? The answer is no. You can use instead a predefined list of color names. The following code illustrates this for setting the background of the form to orange and the forecolor to blue:

```
Imports System.Windows.Forms

Public Class Form1
    Inherits System.Windows.Forms.Form

    Shared Sub main()
        Dim form As Form1
        form = New Form1()

        ' set background and foreground colors
        form.BackColor = System.Drawing.Color.Orange
        form.ForeColor = System.Drawing.Color.Blue

        ' display form
        Application.Run(form)
    End Sub

End Class
```

In addition to setting the colors on a form, you may want to display an image on the background of a form to give it a little more sizzle. You can set the background image of a form using an image file. When the form is displayed, the image file is loaded and painted onto the form before any of the form's controls. Here is an example of setting up a background image for a form using an image file:

```
Imports System.Windows.Forms

Public Class Form1
    Inherits System.Windows.Forms.Form

    Shared Sub main()
        Dim imagePath As String
        Dim form As Form1
        form = New Form1()

        ' specify an image file
        imagePath = Application.StartupPath() + "\.net.gif"

        ' set the background image for a form
        form.BackgroundImage = System.Drawing.Image.FromFile(imagePath)

        ' display form
        Application.Run(form)
    End Sub

End Class
```

Figure 22.4 shows the result of the previous code example that sets the background image on a form.

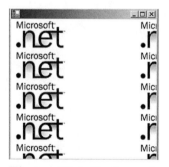

Figure 22.4: Setting a background image on a form.

Border Styles

Forms can have different border styles as defined by the FormBorderStyle property. Figures 25.5 through 25.10 show the possible border styles for a form.

Figure 22.5: Fixed3D border style.

Figure 22.6: FixedDialog border style.

Figure 22.7: FixedSingle border style.

Figure 22.8: FixedToolWindow border style.

Figure 22.9: *Sizable border style.*

Figure 22.10: *SizableToolWindow border style.*

The Fixed3D border style defines a form that is not resizable and shows a 3D effect around the borders of the form. The form also has a title bar and minimize, maximize, and close icons on the right of the title bar.

The FixedDialog border style defines a form that is not resizable and has a normal form display instead of the 3D effect. The form also has a title bar and minimize, maximize, and close icons on the right of the title bar.

The FixedSingle border style appearance looks identical to the FixedDialog border style except that the FixedDialog border style does not have an icon at the top left corner of the form. This way the form conforms to the look of a dialog.

The FixedToolWindow border style gives the appearance of a toolbox window similar to the ToolBox in Visual Studio .NET. A form with this style is not resizable and does not have a title bar or the window icons on the right of the title bar.

The Sizable border style displays a form identical to the FixedDialog border style. The difference is that the Sizeable border style allows the user to resize the form.

The SizableToolWindow is identical to the FixedToolWindow except that the user can resize the form.

Forms Designer

The Forms Designer allows you to graphically design your forms in Visual Studio .NET. When you click on forms in the Solution Explorer window, the default view of the form is the Forms Designer. This is shown in Figure 22.11.

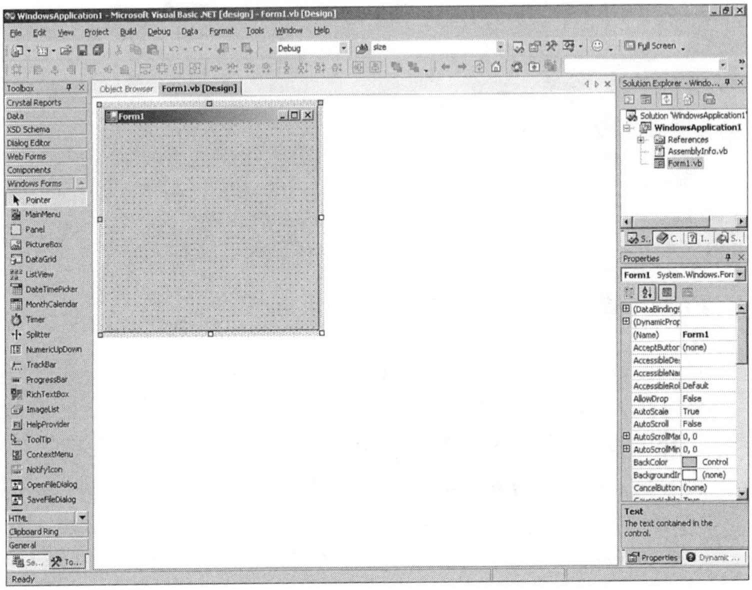

Figure 22.11: *Forms Designer.*

The Forms Designer allows you to see what the form actually looks like while you are designing it. This allows you to set the size and position of controls on the form while you are designing it as opposed to doing this in your code and seeing the form's look when your application runs. It is obviously easier to see the form as you are designing it.

Using the Forms Designer, it is also much easier to adjust the form size by dragging the control points until the form reaches its desired size. This is much easier than calculating the size of the form each time modifications are made to it. This saves a huge amount of time during development.

Forms also have a corresponding Code Window. This is where the logic for the form resides. You can bring up a form's Code Window by right-clicking the form in the Forms Designer window and choosing the View Code option. Or, you can right-click the form in the Solutions Explorer window and choose View Code to bring up the Code Window for the form.

The Toolbox window is helpful while you are designing forms as you can drop controls from the toolbox directly onto a form. This allows you to easily pick the controls you want on your form. Once the controls are on your form you can position them and resize them as you choose. You can move the controls by clicking and dragging them with the mouse. And, you can resize a control by clicking it to select it and then moving the mouse over any of the edges (or corners) of the control until the mouse cursor changes to one of several arrow cursors. At this point, you can click the mouse and drag the edge (or corner) until the control is the desired size.

You can also position controls by clicking on the controls to select them and using the Format menu to perform formatting functions such as sizing, aligning, and spacing controls. Controls can also be cut, copied, and pasted around the form. This allows you to quickly create a form by rapidly adding controls and positioning them as you see fit.

NOTE

This note is for existing VB6 users who are familiar with control arrays. Control arrays are NOT supported in Visual Basic .NET.

By default, there is a grid that is displayed on the form for helping you to align your controls. When you move or size your controls, the position or size snaps to the edges of the grid displayed on the form. You can set the grid options in the Options page accessible from the main menu in Visual Studio .NET (see Figure 22.12).

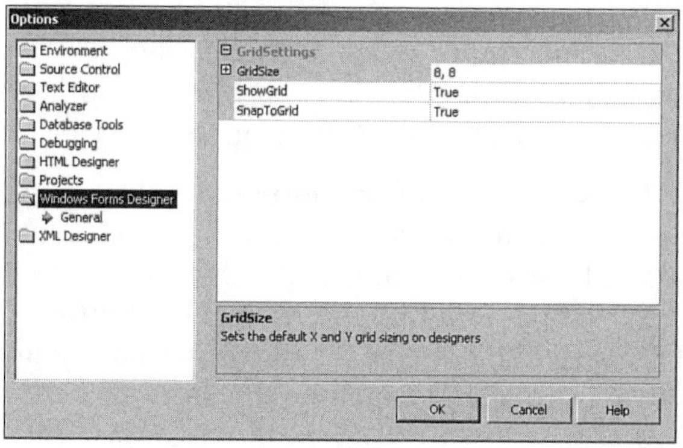

Figure 22.12: *Grid options.*

This allows you to set the size of the grid, whether to have the grid visible, and whether controls should snap to the grid or not. If the grid snapping is turned off, the controls can be positioned any place on the form and will not have its position adjusted to the grid.

NOTE

When you add controls to a form, the Forms Designer creates a region in your source code and labels the region "Windows Form Designer generated code." This region is solely maintained by the Forms Designer, and you should not directly edit this code.

Docking and Anchoring

If you have used prior versions of Visual Basic or even Visual C++, you are probably familiar with having to write code to correctly position controls after the user has resized one of the forms you developed. You now have additional options available to you (provided by the .NET Framework and Windows Forms) so that you can automatically position controls without having to write any code.

The first option is called *Docking*. Docking allows you to automatically position a control at the edge of its parent. You can dock a control to the top, bottom, left, or right edge of its parent so that the control's placement is always aligned with the edge that it is docked to.

The second option is called *Anchoring*. Anchoring allows you to place controls relative to its parent and the distance from the edge of the parent remains constant. You can pick the edges of the parent to which you wish to anchor the control.

The `System.Windows.Forms.RichControl` class provides the docking and anchoring support for controls in the .NET Framework. This means that any class that subclasses `System.Windows.Forms.RichControl` also automatically has the support for handling docking and anchoring. The ListBox control, Button control, and the StatusBar controls inherit from the `System.Windows.Forms.RichControl` class can, therefore, be used to illustrate this support.

Figure 22.13 shows a basic resizable form that allows a user to select a fruit from a list and then click on the OK button to accept the selection and close the form. If the user resized the form by clicking and dragging the lower-right corner of the form, the position of the buttons would need to be changed and the size of the list box updated so that the presentation of the form still looks appealing and usable to the user.

Figure 22.14 shows an example of the same form that has been resized so that more of the contents of the list box is visible. More importantly, the buttons have moved appropriately as a result of the form resizing.

Figure 22.13: *Resizable form for selecting fruit.*

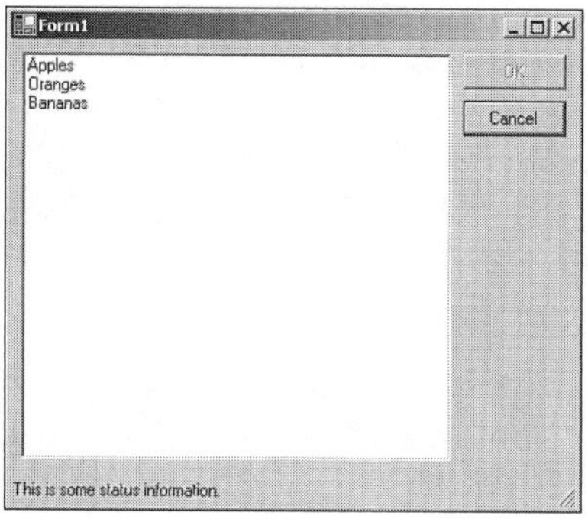

Figure 22.14: *The same form, resized.*

The StatusBar at the bottom of the form is positioned with the bottom edge of the StatusBar touching the bottom edge of the form. When the form is resized, the StatusBar remains touching the bottom edge of the form. This is because the StatusBar is docked to the bottom of the form. The System.Windows.Forms.RichControl class provides the Dock property for specifying which sides of the control are docked to its parent. Table 22.3 lists the possible values for the Dock property of a RichControl object.

Table 22.3: Values for the **Dock** *Property of a* **RichControl** *Object*

Dock Property	Description
DockStyle.Bottom	The control is docked to its parent's bottom edge.
DockStyle.Fill	The control fills the entire client area of its parent.
DockStyle.Left	The control is docked to its parent's left edge.
DockStyle.None	The control is not docked to its parent.
DockStyle.Right	The control is docked to its parent's right edge.
DockStyle.Top	The control is docked to its parent's top edge.

Rather than having to write code that correctly positions the buttons a certain number of units from the right side of the form and resizing the list box relative to the form, anchoring is used to automatically update the position of the controls on the form. The System.Windows.Forms.RichControl class provides an Anchor property for this purpose. Table 22.4 lists the possible values for the Anchor property of a RichControl object.

Table 22.4: Values for the **Anchor** *property of a* **RichControl** *Object*

Anchor **Property**	**Description**
AnchorStyle.All	The control is anchored to all of the edges of its parent.
AnchorStyle.Bottom	The control is anchored to the bottom edge of its parent.
AnchorStyle.BottomLeft	The control is anchored to the bottom and left edges of its parent.
AnchorStyle.BottomLeftRight	The control is anchored to the bottom, left, and right edges of its parent.
AnchorStyle.BottomRight	The control is anchored to the bottom and right edges of its parent.
AnchorStyle.Left	The control is anchored to the left edge of its parent.
AnchorStyle.LeftRight	The control is anchored to the left and right edges of its parent.
AnchorStyle.None	The control is not anchored at all.
AnchorStyle.Right	The control is anchored to the right edge of its parent.
AnchorStyle.Top	The control is anchored to the top edge of its parent.
AnchorStyle.TopBottom	The control is anchored to the top and bottom edges of its parent.
AnchorStyle.TopBottomLeft	The control is anchored to the top, bottom, and left edges of its parent.
AnchorStyle.TopBottomRight	The control is anchored to the top, bottom, and right edges of its parent.
AnchorStyle.TopLeft	The control is anchored to the top and left edges of its parent.
AnchorStyle.TopLeftRight	The control is anchored to the top, left, and right edges of its parent.
AnchorStyle.TopRight	The control is anchored to the top and right edges of its parent.

You can specify exactly which sides of a control are to be anchored to its parent (the form). If a control's right side is anchored to the parent, the control will always remain the same distance from the right side of the edge of the parent.

In Figure 22.14, the buttons are anchored to the top and right side of the form. The list box is anchored to the left, right, top, and bottom of the form. This way the list box is resized relative to the form's size, and it always maintains a consistent margin on all sides relative to the form.

You can set the anchor property for a control using the Properties window in Visual Studio .NET, or you can set the property directly in your code.

The following code fragment shows how you would set the anchor properties on the list box and buttons shown in Figure 22.14.

```
lbFruit.Anchor = AnchorStyles.All
btnOK.Anchor = AnchorStyles.TopRight
btnCancel.Anchor = AnchorStyles.TopRight
```

Events

Events are an important part of the Windows Forms programming model. They are used to communicate particular actions or "events" that occur during an application lifecycle. The most common example of an event is a button click. When a user clicks a button on a form an event is fired. Events can be caught (or listened to), and as a result you can specify code that is run only when a particular event occurs. The procedures that receive events are called event handlers.

The next set of examples illustrate the Event mechanism in .NET and how you can use it to develop an event-driven user interface in Windows Forms. In Windows Forms, forms and controls have a set of predefined events that can be fired and caught in your code. In the next chapter, we will discuss how you would create your own events.

There are two ways you can handle events in .NET:

- Using the `WithEvents` keyword and the `Handles` keyword
- Using `AddHandler`

Using the common button click example as shown in Figure 22.15 and Figure 22.16, let's walk through an example.

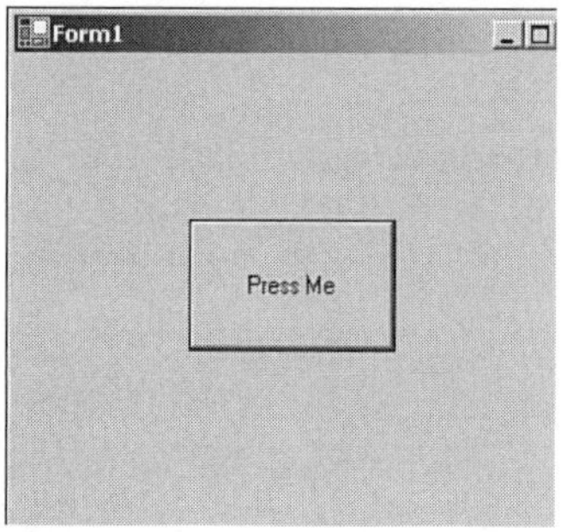

Figure 22.15: Form with a button.  *Figure 22.16: Result of clicking button.*

Create a new Windows Application project and add a button to the form. The name of the button is defaulted to Button1. Set the text of the button to Press Me. Now, double-click the button. Visual Studio .NET automatically creates an event handler to handle the Click event for the button. Also, the Code Window appears with the cursor in the newly created event handler so that you can immediately start writing code that responds to the button's Click event. Here is the code that handles the event and displays a message.

```
Private Sub Button1_Click(ByVal sender As System.Object,
                          ByVal e As System.EventArgs) _
                          Handles Button1.Click
    MsgBox("Button Pressed!", MsgBoxStyle.OKOnly, "")
End Sub
```

The nice part about using Visual Studio .NET this way is that you don't need to concern yourself with the details. You can just add buttons to forms and double-click them to handle their events.

However, let's take a look at the complete picture using the following concise code example.

```
Imports System.Windows.Forms

Public Class Form1
    Inherits System.Windows.Forms.Form

    Private WithEvents m_button As System.Windows.Forms.Button

    Private Sub New()

        StartPosition = FormStartPosition.CenterScreen

        m_button = New System.Windows.Forms.Button()

        m_button.Location = New System.Drawing.Point(88, 80)
        m_button.Size = New System.Drawing.Size(104, 64)
        m_button.Text = "Press Me"

        Controls.Add(m_button)

    End Sub
```

```
Protected Sub MyButtonClick(ByVal sender As Object, _
                            ByVal e As System.EventArgs) _
                            Handles m_button.Click
    Dim msgBox As MessageBox
    msgBox.Show("Button Pressed!")
End Sub

Shared Sub main()
    Application.Run(New Form1())
End Sub
```

```
End Class
```

The button must be defined using the `WithEvents` keyword in order for the buttons events to be handled. When you use the `WithEvents` keyword, this tells the Visual Basic compiler that your code is interested in events generated by the object stated after the WithEvents keyword.

The Handles keyword is used at the end of the method definition to stipulate that the method's purpose is to handle the `Click` event for the m_button data member.

The `Handles` keyword is followed by `<control name>.<event name>`. This tells the Visual Basic compiler that this method handles the specified event for the specified control. In this case, this means the `MyButtonClick` method handles the `Click` event generated by the `m_button` control. When the button is clicked, the event is dispatched to the `MyButtonClick` method.

This example shows how to respond to an event generated by a control. However, the method that responds to the event responds only to a single event generated by a single control. The next example shows how you can catch events generated by multiple controls.

```
Imports System.Windows.Forms

Public Class Form1
    Inherits System.Windows.Forms.Form

    Private m_button1 As System.Windows.Forms.Button
    Private m_button2 As System.Windows.Forms.Button

    Private Sub New()

        m_button1 = New System.Windows.Forms.Button()
        m_button2 = New System.Windows.Forms.Button()
```

```
        m_button1.Location = New System.Drawing.Point(104, 64)
        m_button1.Size = New System.Drawing.Size(79, 30)
        m_button1.Text = "Press Me!"

        m_button2.Location = New System.Drawing.Point(104, 114)
        m_button2.Size = New System.Drawing.Size(79, 30)
        m_button2.Text = "And Me!"

        Controls.Add(m_button1)
        Controls.Add(m_button2)

        AddHandler m_button1.Click, AddressOf Me.ButtonClicked
        AddHandler m_button2.Click, AddressOf Me.ButtonClicked

    End Sub

    Protected Sub ButtonClicked(ByVal sender As Object,
                                ByVal e As System.EventArgs)
        Dim msgBox As MessageBox
        msgBox.Show("Button Pressed!")
    End Sub

    Shared Sub main()
        Application.Run(New Form1())
    End Sub

End Class
```

In this example, the first parameter to AddHandler takes a `<control name>`. `<event name>`, and the second argument is a reference to the method that is to receive the event when it is fired. You can call RemoveHandler to unregister event handling if you needed to.

Delegates

The second argument to the AddHandler function is made possible through the use of delegates. Delegates are an integral part of the Microsoft .NET event architecture. They allow you to obtain the address (or reference point) of any procedure or method and then call the procedure or method through the delegate. The following code gives an example of this:

```
Module Module1

    Delegate Sub MessageProcedure(ByVal msg As String)

    Sub Main()
        Dim msg As MessageProcedure
```

```
        msg = AddressOf ShowMyMessage
        msg.Invoke("Hello")

    End Sub


    Public Sub ShowMyMessage(ByVal msg As String)
        MsgBox(msg, MsgBoxStyle.OKOnly, "")
    End Sub

End Module
```

A delegate is declared near the start of the program. It is essentially a pre-defined declaration of a procedure. Inside the main procedure, the new variable msg is created and has a data type of MessageProcedure (a delegate). After the variable is created, it is assigned the address of the ShowMyMessage procedure. The AddressOf call creates an actual Delegate object that references the ShowMyMessage procedure. The next line calls the Invoke method of the Delegate object referenced by the msg variable. This internally calls the ShowMyMessage procedure through the delegate. If you are familiar with function pointers in C or C++, this should be familiar to you. If not, just recognize that you can call procedures using delegates instead of actually calling the procedure directly.

Event Delegates and Arguments

You may have been wondering if the format of the methods in the event examples have to be in a particular format. Take the ButtonClicked method for example:

```
Protected Sub ButtonClicked(ByVal sender As Object, ByVal e As System.EventArgs)
```

Does this method need to have these two parameters defined or can you add parameters? The answer is the method must follow the definition of the event. Every event is defined by these two things:

- A delegate class
- An event arguments class

The event delegate dictates the definition of an event handler (the procedure that receives the event). For example, the Click event for a button has the following delegate defined to handle the event:

```
Public Sub Click(ByVal sender As Object, ByVal e As System.EventArgs)
```

Because of this, every event handler that you write to handle the Click event generated by a button must follow this declaration. The compiler checks the syntax of your event handlers against the delegates that are defined for the events.

The argument class defined as part of an event must ultimately inherit from System.EventArgs. When defining your own events, you can create a subclass of the EventArgs class if there is additional information you needed to send along with your events. As you can see in the Click event for the Button class, the standard System.EventArgs is used.

Scrolling

System.Windows.Forms.Form is a subclass of System.Windows.Forms. ContainerControl, which is a subclass of System.Windows.Forms. ScrollableControl. The System.Windows.Forms.ScrollableControl class gives forms the capability to be scrollable. Even though forms have a defined size, you can add controls (such as labels and buttons) outside the size of the form. When the form is displayed, anything outside the size of the form is not visible. It is essentially outside the display area of the form. If the AutoScroll property on the form is set to True, then scrollbars are automatically displayed on the form if the form detects that there are controls on the form and outside the display area. This allows the user to scroll the form vertically and horizontally to bring the rest of the form into view.

Here is a code example that illustrates the scrolling capability of forms:

```
Imports System.Windows.Forms

Public Class Form1
    Inherits System.Windows.Forms.Form

    Shared Sub main()
        Dim form As Form1
        Dim label As System.Windows.Forms.Label

        ' create a new form and a label
        form = New Form1()
        label = New Label()

        ' turn on the auto scrolling feature of the form
        form.AutoScroll = True

        ' set the text display for the label and its position
        label.Text = "My Label"
        label.Left = 300
        label.Top = 300

        ' add the label to the form
        label.Parent = form
```

```
' set the size of the form so that the label is hidden
' and see the scrollbars turned on
form.Size = New System.Drawing.Size(200, 200)

    Application.Run(form)
End Sub
```

```
End Class
```

The first two lines in the main method of the form create a form variable and a label variable. The next line creates a new Form object and assigns it to the form variable. Then, a new Label object is created and assigned to the label variable. The form's AutoScroll property is set to True, which allows the scrollbars to show up automatically if needed. The next three lines set the text and position of the label. The label is then added to the form by setting the label's parent property to the form variable. The form's size is then set to 200 by 200 pixels. Notice the result of this code sets the label's position outside the size of the form. The last line runs the form and displays it on the screen. Figure 22.17 shows the initial display based on this code.

Figure 22.17: *Display of scrollable form.*

If you use the vertical scrollbar on the right of the form to scroll down and the horizontal scrollbar on the bottom to scroll to the right, you will soon see the label come into view as shown in Figure 22.18. The result of all this is that you can create forms that are virtually larger than the display area on the screen. Using scrollbars you allow the user of your application to scroll through the form.

Figure 22.18: *Display of scrollable form with label visible.*

NOTE

It is not good practice to create forms that are larger than the display area. This is because it makes it harder for the user to find the desired information. Users may miss some relevant information on the form because they may not even notice it was there.

There are, however, some cases where it can be useful to use scrolling, such as displaying the results of a report. Displaying the results of a report usually involves allowing the form to be vertically scrollable only. Vertically scrollable windows are understandable by most users because most users are accustomed to using browsers such as Internet Explorer and Netscape.

The bottom line here is to use your best judgement and always make the most important information immediately visible to the user.

Message Boxes

Occasionally, you as a developer may want to show a textual message to the user of your application. You may even want to ask a question at a strategic point in your code. Message boxes are the standard way of presenting messages to users, and they allow you to ask questions of the user and get their responses. The `System.Windows.Forms.MessageBox` class is provided as part of the .NET Framework for the exact purpose of informing the user and eliciting user responses.

To show a message to the user, you can call the shared `Show` method of the `System.Windows.Forms.MessageBox` class. The following code displays a basic message to the user and Figure 22.19 shows the output of this code:

```
MessageBox.Show("This is a message.")
```

Figure 22.19: *A simple message.*

As you can see, the message is displayed for the user to see along with a default OK button. The message stays on the screen until the user clicks the OK button. The previous example shows how to call the `Show` method on the `MessageBox` class; however there are actually several `Show` methods to choose from when developing your application. Let's discuss the following four first:

```
Public Shared Function Show(ByVal text As String) _
                    As System.Windows.Forms.DialogResult

Public Shared Function Show(ByVal text As String, _
```

```
                          ByVal caption As String) _
                          As System.Windows.Forms.DialogResult
Public Shared Function Show(ByVal text As String, _
                          ByVal caption As String, _
                          ByVal buttons As MessageBoxButtons) _
                          As System.Windows.Forms.DialogResult
Public Shared Function Show(ByVal text As String, _
                          ByVal caption As String, _
                          ByVal buttons As MessageBoxButtons, _
                          ByVal icon As MessageBoxIcon) _
                          As System.Windows.Forms.DialogResult
```

NOTE

There are actually several versions of the Show method you can use. For more information, you can use the Object Browser to see a complete list of methods on the MessageBox class.

Also, you can use the IntelliSense feature of Visual Studio .NET to browse the versions of the Show method using the up- and down-arrow keys to scroll through the options while the IntelliSense is displayed. Pressing the Tab key selects the current option displayed.

The first Show method takes a single argument, which is the text of the message. The method also returns a value of type System.Windows. Forms.DialogResult. System.Windows.Forms.DialogResult is a structure defined in the System.Windows.Forms namespace and it contains public properties that represent the buttons that can be clicked on a MessageBox. The return value from the Show method signifies which button was clicked by the user. In the previous example we did not care which button was clicked because the example only showed a simple message. Therefore, you did not create avariable to hold the return value from the Show method. It is just ignored. If you were interested in which button the user clicked, the following code stores the return value of the Show method and can be used to test which button was clicked:

```
Dim result As DialogResult

result = MessageBox.Show("This is a message.")

If result = System.Windows.Forms.DialogResult.OK Then
    ' do something
End If
```

Here is a list of the DialogResult values that can be used to test which button was clicked on the MessageBox form:

The only button available on the form at this point is the OK button.

- `DialogResult.Abort`
- `DialogResult.Cancel`
- `DialogResult.Ignore`
- `DialogResult.No`
- `DialogResult.None`
- `DialogResult.OK`
- `DialogResult.Retry`
- `DialogResult.Yes`

Each of these result values will become obvious as you continue with more advanced uses of `MessageBox`. The next `Show` method takes two arguments, the message text and a caption for the form. The following code displays a message box with a message and the caption My Application, and Figure 22.20 shows how the message appears to the application user:

```
MessageBox.Show("This is a message.", "My application")
```

Figure 22.20: *A simple message with a caption.*

The next `Show` method is where it starts to get interesting and more useful. This version of the `Show` method takes three arguments: the text message, the caption, and an Integer value representing the style of the `MessageBox`. The `MessageBox` style is comprised by combining a value from one of three groups of values.

To illustrate this, three tables are shown describing the values in each group. After each table is sample code showing the usage of the values in the table and the corresponding outputs.

Table 22.5 shows the values that can be used to specify which buttons are displayed on the `MessageBox`. Table 22.6 shows the values that can be used to pick the icon to be displayed on the `MessageBox`. And, Table 22.7 shows the values that can be used to set the default button on the `MessageBox`. A value from each of these tables can be combined together to create the overall style for a `MessageBox`.

Table 22.5: **MessageBox** *Style Value for Buttons*

Value	Description
MessageBoxButtons.OK	Displays only an OK button.
MessageBoxButtons.OKCancel	Displays an OK button and a Cancel button.
MessageBoxButtons.AbortRetryIgnore	Displays the Abort, Retry, and Ignore buttons.
MessageBoxButtons.YesNoCancel	Displays the Yes, No, and Cancel buttons.
MessageBoxButtons.YesNo	Displays a Yes button and a No button.
MessageBoxButtons.RetryCancel	Displays a Retry button and a Cancel button.

Based on the values shown in Table 22.5, the following code examples use these values to define the set of buttons to be shown on the MessageBox. After each example, you can see what the resulting MessageBox looks like (see Figures 22.21 through 22.26).

```
MessageBox.Show("Completed Successfully!", "My application", _
            MessageBoxButtons.OK)
```

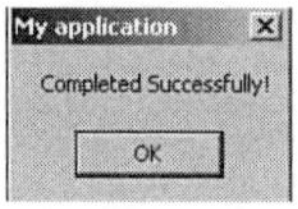

Figure 22.21: *MessageBox with an OK button.*

```
MessageBox.Show("Begin printing report.", "My application", _
            MessageBoxButtons.OKCancel)
```

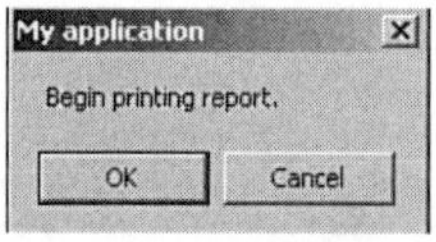

Figure 22.22: *MessageBox with OK and Cancel buttons.*

```
MessageBox.Show("Encountered problem, what do you want me to do?", _
            "My application", _
            MessageBoxButtons.AbortRetryIgnore)
```

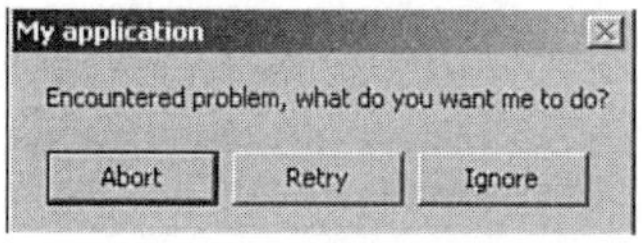

Figure 22.23: *MessageBox with Abort, Retry, and Ignore buttons.*

```
MessageBox.Show("Save before exiting?", _
            "My application", _
            MessageBoxButtons.YesNoCancel)
```

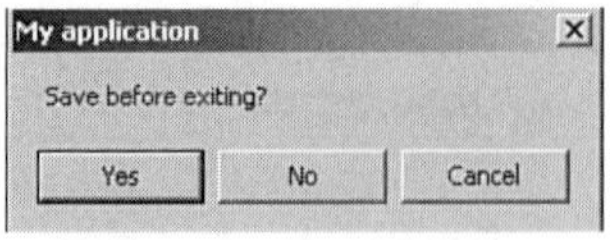

Figure 22.24: *MessageBox with Yes, No, and Cancel buttons.*

```
MessageBox.Show("Do you like Visual Basic.NET?", _
                "My application", _
                MessageBoxButtons.YesNo)
```

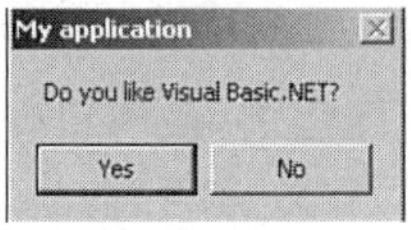

Figure 22.25: *MessageBox with Yes and No buttons.*

```
MessageBox.Show("Problem printing report.", _
                "My application", _
                MessageBoxButtons.RetryCancel)
```

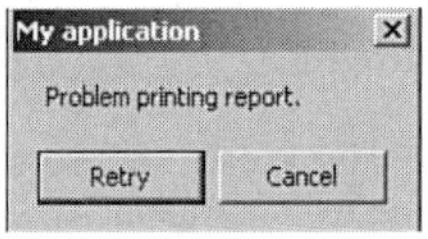

Figure 22.26: *MessageBox with Retry and Cancel buttons.*

Table 22.6: **MessageBox** *Style Value for Icons*

Value	Description
MessageBoxIcon.Asterisk	Same as MessageBoxIcon.Information.
MessageBoxIcon.Error	Display this icon if your program is informing the user of an error.
MessageBoxIcon.Exclamation	Display this icon if you are telling the user something very important.
MessageBoxIcon.Hand	Same as MessageBoxIcon.Stop.
MessageBoxIcon.Information	Display this icon if you are displaying a message for informational purposes only.
MessageBoxIcon.Question	Display this icon if you are asking the user a question.
MessageBoxIcon.Stop	Display this icon in your MessageBox if your program is about to stop performing a task because of some condition.
MessageBoxIcon.Warning	Display this icon if you are displaying a message to warn the user.

Based on the values shown in the previous table, following is a set of code examples using these values to define the icon to be used on the MessageBox. After each example, you can see what the resulting MessageBox looks like (see Figures 22.27 through 22.34).

```
MessageBox.Show("Visual Basic.NET is my kinda language.", _
               "My application", _
               MessageBoxButtons.OK, _
               MessageBoxIcon.Asterisk)
```

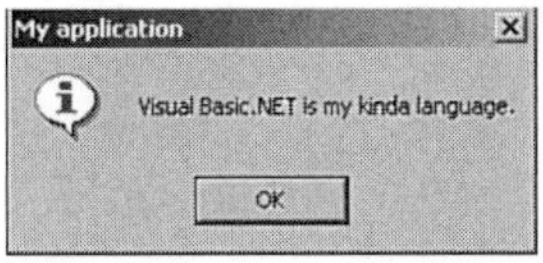

Figure 22.27: MessageBox with Asterisk icon.

```
MessageBox.Show("Oops, there is an error.", _
               "My application", _
               MessageBoxButtons.OK, _
               MessageBoxIcon.Error)
```

Figure 22.28: MessageBox with Error icon.

```
MessageBox.Show("Stop, don't do that.", _
               "My application", _
               MessageBoxButtons.OK, _
               MessageBoxIcon.Exclamation)
```

My application
Stop, don't do that.
OK

Figure 22.29: MessageBox with Exclamation icon.

```
MessageBox.Show("Wait, I have something important to say...", _
               "My application", _
               MessageBoxButtons.OK, _
               MessageBoxIcon.Hand)
```

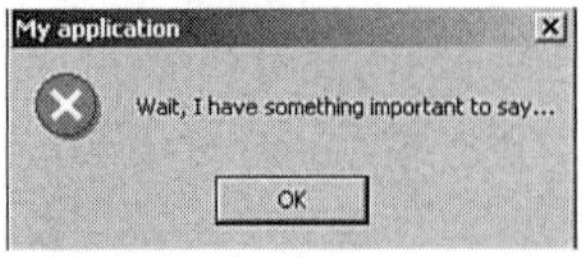

Figure 22.30: MessageBox with Hand icon.

```
MessageBox.Show("Here is some information for you.", _
                "My application", _
                MessageBoxButtons.OK, _
                MessageBoxIcon.Information)
```

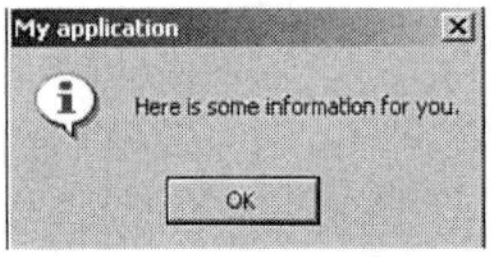

Figure 22.31: MessageBox with Information icon.

```
MessageBox.Show("Do you want the blue pill or the red pill?", _
                "My application", _
                MessageBoxButtons.OK, _
                MessageBoxIcon.Question)
```

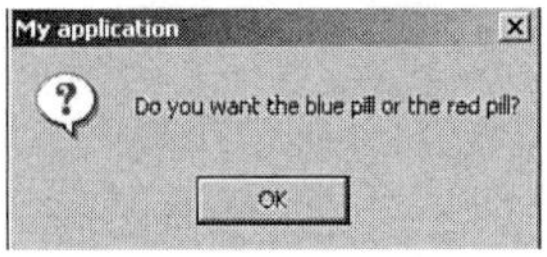

Figure 22.32: MessageBox with Question icon.

```
MessageBox.Show("Stop, don't do that.", _
                "My application", _
                MessageBoxButtons.OK, _
                MessageBoxIcon.Stop)
```

Figure 22.33: MessageBox with Stop icon.

```
MessageBox.Show("I must warn you...", _
                "My application", _
                MessageBoxButtons.OK, _
                MessageBoxIcon.Warning)
```

Figure 22.34: *MessageBox with Warning icon.*

The values in Table 22.7 can be used to set the default button on the MessageBox form. Each value represents the position from left to right as they appear on the form. To set the leftmost button on the form to be the default button, you would use the MessageBoxDefaultButton.Button1, the second button to be the default using MessageBoxDefaultButton.Button2, and lastly the third button using the MessageBoxDefaultButton.Button3.

Table 22.7: **MessageBox** *Style Value for Default Buttons*

Value	Description
MessageBoxDefaultButton.Button1	The first button on the MessageBox form is the default button.
MessageBoxDefaultButton.Button2	The second button on the MessageBox form is the default button.
MessageBoxDefaultButton.Button3	The third button on the MessageBox form is the default button.

The default button is the one that gets selected when the user presses the Enter key when the message box is displayed. This can be useful if you are asking a question and you expect the user to answer a particular way most of the time. If you ask a question with a yes or no answer and you expect the user to answer yes most of the time, in this case you would set the Yes button to be the default button so that the user could immediately press the Enter key and move on. This results in minimal effort on the user's part to answer the question.

Here are three examples using the same MessageBox. The only difference is the default button. The first example sets the Abort button to be the default. The second example sets the Retry button to be the default. And, the third example sets the Ignore button to be the default.

```
MessageBox.Show("Encountered problem, what do you want me to do?", _
                "My application", _
                MessageBoxButtons.AbortRetryIgnore, _
                MessageBoxIcon.Question, _
                MessageBoxDefaultButton.Button1)

MessageBox.Show("Encountered problem, what do you want me to do?", _
                "My application", _
                MessageBoxButtons.AbortRetryIgnore, _
```

```
                MessageBoxIcon.Question, _
                MessageBoxDefaultButton.Button2)

MessageBox.Show("Encountered problem, what do you want me to do?", _
                "My application", _
                MessageBoxButtons.AbortRetryIgnore, _
                MessageBoxIcon.Question, _
                MessageBoxDefaultButton.Button3)
```

Now that you've gone through the MessageBox extensively let's review the DialogResult once more. The return value for the Show method (regardless of which one you end up using) is a value of type DialogResult. The possible values for DialogResult are listed earlier in the chapter. If I wanted to write code to figure out which of the three buttons (Abort, Retry, or Cancel) the user clicked, I could write the following code:

```
Dim result As DialogResult
result = MessageBox.Show("Encountered problem, what do you want me to do?", _
                "My application", _
                MessageBoxButtons.AbortRetryIgnore, _
                MessageBoxIcon.Question)

Select Case result
    Case DialogResult.Abort : MessageBox.Show("Abort Pressed!")
    Case DialogResult.Retry : MessageBox.Show("Retry Pressed!")
    Case DialogResult.Ignore : MessageBox.Show("Ignore Pressed!")
End Select
```

The previous code displays a message box with three buttons, and the result is returned into the result variable. The code then checks the value of the result variable using the Select Case statement and displays a message signifying which button was clicked. Instead of displaying the message you would probably write code that responded to the appropriate button click. If the user clicked the Ignore button, for example, you would ignore the problem encountered in the code and continue on normally.

Dialog Boxes

Dialog boxes are forms that are displayed on top of other application windows. Each dialog typically has a defined purpose in the application to present additional information or gather specific input from the user. When displaying a dialog to the user, you have two modes that a dialog can be displayed in—*modal* and *modeless*.

Modal dialogs, when displayed, block input to the rest of the application. This forces the user to fill out the information correctly on the dialog before moving on. To display a modal dialog, you can call the ShowDialog method on the `System.Windows.Forms.Form` class. This example shows a form in a modal state:

```
Dim form As New Form()
form.ShowDialog()
```

Modeless dialogs, when displayed, do not block input to the rest of the application and can be displayed for an extended period of time and allow accessibility to the rest of the application. To display a modeless dialog box, you can call the `Show` method on the `System.Windows.Forms.Form` class. This example shows a form in a modeless state:

```
Dim form As New Form()
form.Show()
```

Single Document Interface and Multiple Document Interface

In the previous chapter we briefly touched upon the meaning of SDI and MDI. At the beginning of this chapter, the first code examples showed an SDI application where the application consisted of just one form. Again, this is the simplest type of application to build and because we have already shown you examples of an SDI application there is no reason to do so again.

In the previous chapter you saw what an MDI application looked like, but how do you build one? The answer lies with the `IsMDIContainer` and the `MDIParent` properties of the `System.Windows.Forms.Form` class. To build an MDI application you must start with the application's main form. This main form must have the `IsMDIContainer` property set to `True`, which signifies it is the container of all MDI child forms. Then for each child form you must set the `MDIParent` property to an instance of the main form.

To show how this works in actual code, the following code defines a `ChildForm` class that doesn't really do anything. It just defines a form class that can be used as the MDI child forms. The purpose here is to only show the necessary code involved in creating an MDI application.

```
Imports System.Drawing
Imports System.Windows.Forms

Public Class ChildForm
    Inherits System.Windows.Forms.Form

End Class
```

The next set of code defines the MainForm class, which is used for the main form of the MDI application. As you can see, the main method of the MainForm class creates a new instance of the MainForm class and starts running the application by calling Application.Run(). In the New procedure of the MainForm, the object sets its Text property to "MDI Container" so that you can distinguish this window when the application runs. The object also sets itself to be the MDI container by setting its IsMDIContainer property to True. Next, it sets its size to an arbitrary width and height.

A new instance of the ChildForm class is then created for the purposes of adding a single MDI child window to the application's main form. The Text property of the ChildForm object is set to "MDI Child" so that you can distinguish this form when it is visible on the screen. The ChildForm object's MDIParent property is set to Me which, in this case, is the application's main form. Setting the MDIParent essentially adds the ChildForm object as an MDI Child form to the MainForm object. The visible state of the child form is set, and then a call to the Show method is made to make the child form visible.

```
Imports System.Windows.Forms

Public Class MainForm
    Inherits System.Windows.Forms.Form

    Public Sub New()
        MyBase.New()
        Dim child As ChildForm

        Me.Text = "MDI Container"
        Me.IsMDIContainer = True
        Me.Size = New System.Drawing.Size(400, 400)

        child = New ChildForm()
        child.Text = "MDI Child"
        child.MDIParent = Me
        child.WindowState = FormWindowState.Normal
        child.Show()
    End Sub

    Shared Sub main()
        Application.Run(New MainForm())
    End Sub

End Class
```

The result of running this code is the picture shown in Figure 22.35.

Figure 22.35: Sample MDI application.

What's Next

This chapter covered a lot of material. You learned how to set the size and position of a form, how to set the color and background of a form, border styles, and automatic layout using docking and anchoring. We also covered events and scrolling. Lastly, we discussed message boxes, dialog boxes, and more about SDI and MDI. This chapter covered a lot of ground, but as you can see, Windows Forms has lots to cover.

In the next chapter, you will learn about controls. This includes examples using the most common controls that come with the Microsoft .NET Framework. Also, you will learn how to create your own controls. Because controls are used extensively on forms, we will also be covering more information regarding forms. Specifically, we will cover more aspects of the Forms Designer and some of the layout features such as aligning and sizing of controls.

NOTE

The answers to "Reviewing It," "Checking It," and "Applying It" are available on our Web site.

Reviewing It

REVIEW

This section presents a review of the key concepts in this chapter. These questions are intended to gauge your absorption of the relevant material.

1. How would you lay out controls on a form so that they were automatically positioned even when the form is resized?

2. How would you respond to a Button Click event to display a message?

3. When you need to ask a user a question, would you develop your own form or would you use an existing standard form? If so, which one?

4. How would you define a resizable form versus a fixed size form?

5. If I wanted to position a form in the center of the screen would I need to calculate the form's position? If so, why? If not, why not?

CHECK

Checking It

Select the correct answer to the following questions.

Multiple Choice

1. What is the grid used for in the Forms Designer?

   a. To show spacing on the form.

   b. To automatically align controls along a vertical line or horizontal line.

   c. To help judge sizes of controls.

   d. All of the above.

2. What are delegates used for?

   a. As another way to display a message to a user.

   b. To pass an address of a method to some other code where the method can be invoked indirectly.

   c. To represent variables of different types.

   d. None of the above.

3. MessageBoxes can be used to:

   a. Ask a user a Yes/No question.

   b. Ask a user an OK/Cancel question.

   c. Display a message and have users click an OK button when they are ready.

   d. All of the above.

4. Automatic layout of controls is handled by:

   a. Docking and anchoring.

   b. Delegates and events.

   c. Border style.

   d. None of the above.

5. Modal dialogs are displayed using what method?

   a. Show.

   b. ShowDialog.

   c. Display.

   d. DisplayDialog.

True or False

Select one of the two possible answers and then verify on our Web site that you picked the correct one.

1. A form's size and client size have the same meaning.

   True/False

2. A form's default GraphicUnit is Inch.

   True/False

3. Forms do not support inheritance.

   True/False

4. A form's background color can be set.

   True/False

5. An event generated by multiple buttons can be processed by the same event handler.

   True/False

6. Anchoring allows controls to be uniformly spaced to the edge of the parent form even if the form is resized.

   True/False

7. Docking allows controls to be uniformly spaced to edge of parent form even if the form is resized.

   True/False

APPLY

Applying It

Try to complete the following exercise by yourself.

Independent Exercise

Create a Windows Application project. Add a button to a form in the lower right portion of the form. Using the Properties window, anchor the button to the bottom and right sides of the form. Then, write the necessary code to display a message when the user clicks the button.

23

Controls

Controls are a necessary party of user interface development, especially if you are developing Windows applications. In this chapter we explain what a control is, how controls are used, a common set of controls provided by the .NET Framework, and how you would go about creating your own controls.

The focus is on controls used by Windows applications. Specifically, the controls provided in the System.Windows.Forms namespace.

These topics are covered in this chapter:

- Control class
- Working with controls
- Examples using some common controls in .NET
- Creating your own controls

Introduction

This chapter presents controls that are provided by the Microsoft.NET Framework class library. *Controls* are custom user interface artifacts that display information, gather data from the user, or both. They provide the capability of interacting with a user of your application.

For example, you may come across a situation in which you want a user to enter in his name or other information. To accomplish this, you could use a TextBox control (as you will see in the section "Working with Controls"). You may also want to display a list of options and allow the user to select one. In this case you would probably use the RadioButton control or the ComboBox control.

Most, if not all, Visual Basic .NET programs leverage (or will leverage) the user interface classes provided by the Framework. However, this chapter does not cover the entire range of classes provided in the Framework because of the sheer volume of material to cover. The goal is to give you a great starting point into using the user interface classes provided with the Framework as part of your Visual Basic .NET development.

We present the common controls in this chapter, how they work, and potentially why you may want to use them. In addition, we cover how to create your own control in the event you want to develop a custom control for a particular need.

By the end of this chapter, you should know enough about controls (such as how to place them on a form, view the control's properties and methods, and respond to the control's events) that you should have a good head start in figuring out how to use any control. As you become more experienced, you should use the Object Browser in Visual Studio .NET to discover the entire set of classes in the .NET Framework from which your programs can benefit. Also, if you plan on doing intensive UI development, you may want to purchase a reference book that focuses specifically on the control classes and interfaces provided with the .NET Framework.

The controls defined in the .NET Framework utilize inheritance so that a common set of functionality can be defined, which specific controls can leverage through subclassing. A perfect example of this is the System.Windows.Forms.Control class. This class is the base class for all controls used in Windows applications. Every control extends or subclasses the Control class and provides its specific behavior and appearance.

Because the major topic of this chapter is controls, the next several sections focus only on the Control class. This includes the Control class's properties, events, and methods. After that, specific examples are provided that show the different types of controls and their usage.

But first, here is a simple example showing a `Label` control used to display a string on a form. Create a new Windows application project and replace the automatically generated form code with the code shown here:

```
Imports System.Windows.Forms

Public Class Form1
    Inherits System.Windows.Forms.Form

    Private Sub New()

        Dim myLabel As Label = New Label()

        myLabel.Location = New System.Drawing.Point(100, 70)
        myLabel.Size = New System.Drawing.Size(100, 30)
        myLabel.Text = "Visual Basic.NET"

        Me.Controls.Add(myLabel)

    End Sub

End Class
```

The reason this example replaces the auto-generated code is so that you can focus on a very concise programming example. This way, you will have a better understanding of the code involved in displaying a control on a form. In your own development, you will probably use the Toolbox and Form Designer to add controls to a form. However, this process is updating the form's code behind the scenes. Therefore, it is useful to understand how the code works, especially as you become a more experienced developer in Microsoft.NET technologies.

In the constructor of the `Form1` class, a new `Label` control is created. The `Label` control's `Location`, `Size`, and `Text` properties are set. Then the control is added to the `Form1`'s `Controls` property. The *Controls property* is a collection of controls that are owned by the form. When the form is displayed, it also displays all of the controls defined in the `Controls` property.

Figure 23.1 shows what this form looks like when it is displayed.

This example is quite simple but illustrates a couple of simple concepts. It shows how controls can be created and added to a form when the program runs. You don't need to just use the Form Designer to lay out a form. You can also programmatically lay out your controls as well. It also shows how setting the control's properties affects its layout. In this example, the label's position on the form and the label's size are set by the form. In addition, the text that is displayed by the label is also set.

Figure 23.1: Example `Label` control.

There is nothing wrong with programmatically creating your forms and, in fact, once you become an advanced Visual Basic .NET programmer you may find yourself doing this in some cases. However, as you start out learning Visual Basic .NET there is an easier and preferred way of adding controls to your forms. This preferred way involves using the Toolbox and the Forms Designer.

You can select controls from the Toolbox window, drag them onto a form, and then resize or position the controls visually. This allows you to graphically see how the controls look as you are designing the form. Because you can adjust the sizes and positions accordingly, without having to build the project and run it, you are able to increase your productivity and reduce the development time to create a form.

Now let's get into more detail regarding the Control class itself.

Control Class

Once again, the `Control` *class* is the base class for all controls, including forms, in the .NET Framework. This class provides the basic support for a control's visual appearance including the background and foreground color, for specifying the control's size, dragging and dropping onto a control, mouse events such as clicking and double-clicking, and keyboard events.

The base support provided by the `Control` class is accomplished through the use of properties, events, and methods. There are several `Control` class properties that are used to describe the control and its behavior. These properties are presented in the next section. Events are also defined for the `Control` class. The events are generated by the control based on specific actions. The most common event for a control is the `Click` event. This occurs when the user clicks the mouse while hovering over the control. This allows you to respond to the event, giving the appearance that the control is performing an action. All the control events are presented so that you can understand the breadth of support relating to the events (both generated and handled) for controls. Also, the Control class contains lots of methods for interacting with a control and for overriding the control's behavior (as you'll see later in this chapter).

A *Form* is a specific type of a control; you may notice some familiarity between what you learned in the last chapter about forms and what you are about to read in regard to controls. Also, as you learn more about controls in this chapter, you are also learning more about forms.

Controls can also contain other controls, allowing you to create more complex controls. A perfect example of this is any form that you develop. A form can contain lots of other controls to address a specific user interface need. By creating a form that contains other child controls, the form can be treated as a single complex control and used as needed. When you design your own applications, you should consider designing your forms so that they can be used by several applications and not make them too specific or overly complicated. If you take the necessary design steps before developing your controls or forms, you will find yourself building a library of controls that you can use again and again. This usually results in a huge time savings (and potential cost savings).

Tables 22.1 through 22.3 list a set of properties and events defined for the Control class. The tables are presented here so that you can quickly get an idea of the types of properties you can define for a control and what they mean. Also, you can get an idea of some of the events generated and consumed by controls. After you read through these tables, we will start to present examples of working with controls so that you can see how these properties and events are used to perform common actions with controls such as tabbing, validating, and drag and drop.

These tables are not the complete set of properties and events because they are too large to present and cover in this book. The intent here is to present the most common properties and events. After you complete this chapter, you may want to use the Object Browser or Help in Visual Studio .NET to read more about the Control class and its additional capabilities.

Table 23.1: **Control** *Class Public Shared Properties*

Property	Description
DefaultBackColor	Gets the default background color for the control.
DefaultFont	Gets the default font for the control.
DefaultForeColor	Gets the default foreground color for the control.
ModifierKeys	Gets the current state of the SHIFT, CTRL, and ALT keys (whether or not they are pressed).

Table 23.1: continued

Property	Description
MouseButtons	Gets the current state of the mouse buttons. This allows you to tell which mouse buttons are currently pressed and which are not.
MousePosition	Gets the current position of the mouse on the screen.

Table 23.2: **Control** *Class Public Properties (Partial List)*

Property	Description
AllowDrop	This property signifies whether the control supports dragging and dropping data onto the control.
Anchor	Defines the edges of the container (or parent control) that this control maintains a uniform distance to.
BackColor	Defines the background color for the control.
BackgroundImage	Defines an image displayed in the control's background.
Bottom	The position of the bottom edge of the control and the top of the parent controls' client area.
Bounds	The bounding rectangle of the control.
CanFocus	Signifies whether a control can receive input focus. If it can, this means the control can receive mouse and keyboard events. The control must also have the Visible and Enabled properties set to True to receive focus.
CanSelect	Signifies whether a control can be selected.
CausesValidation	Describes whether the control causes validation to occur. When this control gets the focus and this property is set to True, all other controls on the form that require validation are validated.
ClientRectangle	This is the rectangular display area within the control where drawing can occur and where child controls can be displayed. The upper-left corner of the client area is (0,0).
ClientSize	This is the size of the display area within the control where drawing can occur and where child controls can be displayed. This size represents the width and a height of the client area.
CompanyName	Gets the company name of the creator of the control.
ContainsFocus	Tells whether the control currently has input focus.
ContextMenu	Defines the context menu (pop-up menu) for the control.
Controls	A control collection that represents child controls displayed within this control.

Table 23.2: continued

Property	Description
Cursor	Defines the cursor that is displayed when the mouse moves over this control.
DataBindings	Defines bindings of this control's properties to properties of another object. By doing data binding, you can have the control automatically have its properties updated by another object.
DisplayRectangle	The rectangular display area of the control. Normally, this is the same as the client area. However, subclasses of a control may change the client area as desired. The display area remains the entire display surface of the paint process.
Disposing	Tells whether this control is currently in the process of being disposed.
Dock	Defines the edges of the container (or parent control) that this control maintains a uniform distance to.
Enabled	Defines whether this control is enabled.
Focused	Defines whether this control currently has the input focus.
Font	Defines the current font for the control.
ForeColor	Defines the current foreground color for the control.
HasChildren	A value indicating whether the control has child controls.
Height	Represents the height of the control.
Left	Defines the position of the left side of the control (x-coordinate) in relation to its parent control.
Location	Defines the location of the upper-left corner of the control in relation to its parent's upper-left corner of control.
Name	Defines the name of the control.
Parent	Defines the control's parent control.
ProductName	Gets the name of the application containing this control.
ProductVersion	Gets the version of the application containing this control.
Region	Defines the graphics shape of a window. By default, a window (a form for example) is rectangular and does not have an associated Region. Regions are used to create non-rectangular windows.
Right	Defines the position of the right side of the control (x-coordinate) in relation to its parent control.
RightToLeft	Defines the alignment for child controls of the control. Default value is `False`.
Size	Defines the height and width of the control.

Table 23.2: continued

Property	Description
TabIndex	Defines the Tab order for the control.
TabStop	Defines whether input focus for the control can be caused by using the Tab key.
Tag	Defines an object that contains data for the control.
Text	Defines text for this control.
Top	Defines the position of the top side of the control (y-coordinate) in relation to its parent control.
TopLevelControl	Defines the top-level control that contains the control.
Visible	Defines whether the control is visible.
Width	Defines the width of the control.

Table 23.3: **Control** *Class Events (Partial List)*

Event	Description
Click	Event occurs when the control is clicked.
DoubleClick	Event occurs when the control is double-clicked.
DragDrop	Event occurs when the drag and drop process is completed.
DragEnter	Event occurs when an object is dragged into the control's boundary.
DragLeave	Event occurs when an object is dragged into and then out of the control's boundary.
DragOver	Event occurs when an object is dragged over the control.
Enter	Event occurs when the control is entered.
GiveFeedback	Event occurs during a drag operation.
GotFocus	Event occurs when the control receives input focus.
Invalidated	Event occurs when a control's display is updated.
KeyDown	Event occurs when a key is pressed down while the control has input focus.
KeyPress	Event occurs when the key is pressed while the control has input focus.
KeyUp	Event occurs when the key is released after it was pressed down and while the control has input focus.
Leave	Event occurs when the control is left but before it has lost focus.
LostFocus	Event occurs when the control has lost focus.
MouseDown	Event occurs when the mouse button is clicked while the mouse cursor is over the control.
MouseEnter	Event occurs when the mouse cursor enters the boundaries of the control.
MouseHover	Event occurs while the mouse cursor is hovering over the control.

Table 23.3: continued

Event	Description
MouseLeave	Event occurs when the mouse cursor is leaving the control.
MouseMove	Event occurs while the mouse is moving over the control.
MouseUp	Event occurs when the mouse button is released while the mouse cursor is over the control.
MouseWheel	Event occurs when the mouse wheel is moved and the control has input focus.
Paint	Event occurs when the control is redrawn.
Resize	Event occurs when the control is resized.
SizeChanged	Event occurs when the Size property of the control is changed.
Validated	Event occurs when the control's validation is complete.
Validating	Event occurs when the control is in the process of validating.

The Control class methods are not listed here because of the large number of methods. The common methods are better presented through examples in this chapter. As you become more experienced with Visual Basic .NET and user interface development in regards to Windows applications, you will find yourself using the Object Browser and Help to learn more about the properties, events, and methods not covered here. You may also decide to purchase a reference book devoted to the Microsoft.NET Framework in which the Framework classes should be completely explained in detail.

Working with Controls

Now that you have read about the common properties and events of the Control class, let's go through some examples so that you can learn more about working with controls in Visual Basic .NET. The examples in this section are focusing on the properties, events, and methods of the Control class; therefore, the examples are relevant for any control that you want to use.

The previous chapter presented information about sizing, color, docking, and anchoring (in regards to a form). Each of these topics is actually related to the Control class itself. Each of these topics is usually thought of when dealing with forms, which is why the material was presented in the previous chapter. We did not want to present the Control class at that point because we just wanted to focus on a form. Also, the Form class and Control class is too much material to present in one chapter. Now that you understand that a form is also a control, it should be clearer that some of the information presented in the previous chapter is relevant to controls. Specifically, the information about sizing, color, docking, and anchoring all apply to controls. Please refer back to the previous chapter if you want to see examples of these again.

When working with controls in general, there are some common tasks that you may want to do in your programming. As such, here is a list of tasks that this section covers pertaining to controls:

- Adding controls to a form

- Tabbing

- Focus and validation

- Drag and drop

- Keyboard shortcuts

A single Visual Basic .NET Windows application project is going to be used to demonstrate each of these tasks. Figure 23.2 shows Visual Studio .NET after a new Windows application project is created. As you can see the Forms Designer is displayed so that you can immediately start to define the form. Using this project, let's go through the tasks.

Adding Controls to a Form

Controls can be added to a form in two different ways. First, you can add a control by writing code to programmatically add the control to the form. This approach is used in the example at the beginning of the chapter. The second approach (and probably the most common) is to use the Toolbox and Forms Designer in Visual Studio .NET. This approach involves clicking a control in the toolbox, holding the mouse button down, dragging it onto the form, and then releasing the mouse button. Once the control is on the form, you can click the control to select it. Once selected, you can move it or resize it as you desire.

TIP

Double-clicking a control on the Toolbox puts a control on the form. The location is either the top left or the same as the last control added.

Figure 23.3 shows two TextBox controls added to the form in the project. The TextBox control is used for this example; however, any control can be added this way.

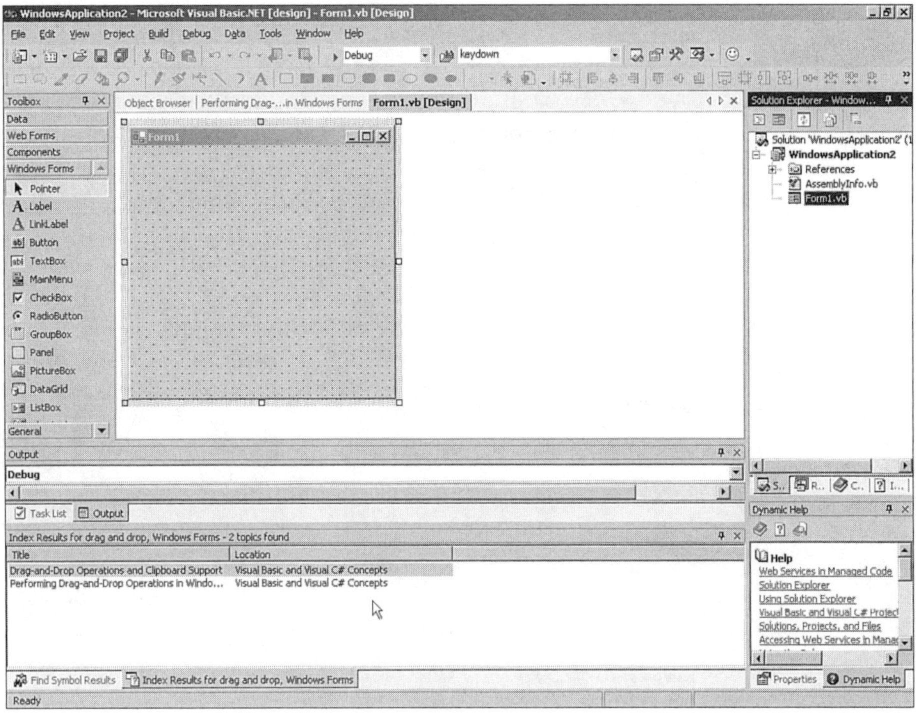

Figure 23.2: *New Windows application project.*

TIP

If there is a control that exists on your computer but it is not visible in the Toolbox, you can right-click the Toolbox to display its context menu. You can then select "Customize Toolbox" to display a dialog box showing the controls installed on your computer. The controls that are checked in the list automatically appear in the Toolbox.

Select the controls you want to appear in the Toolbox by clicking on the control name until a check mark appears; then click the OK button to accept the changes. The controls you selected should now be available on the Toolbox.

The Form Designer automatically updates your code by setting the control's properties appropriately. It also automatically creates a name for the control when it is dropped onto the form.

After controls are added to the form, you can resize them or position them as you like. You can do this manually by clicking them and using the mouse to position or resize them. You can also use the menu items in the Format menu to help you get the look you like. The Format menu provides support for aligning controls together, making controls the same height and/or width, spacing between controls, ordering controls, and locking controls.

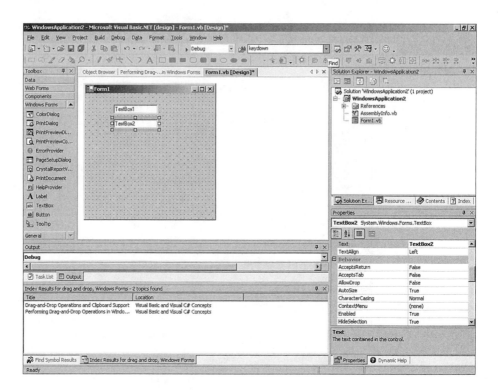

Figure 23.3: *Controls added to form.*

Each of these format options requires multiple controls on the form to be selected. This is accomplished by clicking on each control while holding down the CTRL key at the same time. Alternatively, you can click in an empty spot on the form (not in a control), and, keeping the mouse button pressed, draw a selection rectangle encompassing the controls you want to select. Only the controls fully included in the rectangle will be selected. Once you select the desired controls, you can use the options in the format menu to aid you in laying out the controls on the form.

Controls can be aligned together along any of their sides or middles. Selected controls can automatically be resized to the same size. This includes the height, width, or both. Sometimes when you add many controls to a form the spacing can be off a bit. Rather than manually updating the spacing between all of the controls, you can select multiple controls and automatically adjust the spacing between the controls to be uniform. Controls can also be centered on the form vertically, horizontally, or both. And, controls can be locked. Once locked, you cannot move or resize them until you unlock them. This is useful once you have a form that looks the way you want it. By locking the controls, you prevent yourself from inadvertently changing the size or position of the controls.

Controls can also have their anchoring and docking capabilities set using the Properties window in Visual Studio .NET. You would click on the control in the Form Designer and then set the properties for the control in the Properties window. The specific anchoring and docking capabilities are presented in the previous chapter on forms.

Tabbing

Tabbing support allows the user to use the Tab key to cycle through the controls on a form rather than having to use the mouse to change focus to the next control. To support tabbing, you of course would want to control the order in which the controls are selected when you tab through a form. Also, you want to choose whether a control can be tabbed to or not.

Tabbing is supported through the `TabIndex` and `TabStop` properties on a control. If you set the `TabStop` property to `True`, the control is in the list of controls that can be tabbed to using the Tab key. The `TabIndex` property contains a number. The number is the position in the list used during the tabbing process. For example, if a control has its `TabIndex` property set to `0`, the control will have input focus when the form is first displayed. When the user presses the Tab key, focus moves to the control that has its `TabIndex` set to 1, and so on.

The `TabStop` property defaults to `True`, meaning it will be in the tabbing order. Also, when you drop a control onto a form from the Toolbox, the `TabIndex` is automatically set to the last index in the list.

The following example shows the code generated by Visual Studio .NET after the project was created and two `TextBox` controls were added to the form:

```
Public Class Form1
    Inherits System.Windows.Forms.Form

#Region " Windows Form Designer generated code "

    Public Sub New()
        MyBase.New()

        'This call is required by the Windows Form Designer.
        InitializeComponent()

        'Add any initialization after the InitializeComponent() call
```

```vb
End Sub

'Form overrides dispose to clean up the component list.
Protected Overloads Overrides Sub Dispose(ByVal disposing As Boolean)
    If disposing Then
        If Not (components Is Nothing) Then
            components.Dispose()
        End If
    End If
    MyBase.Dispose(disposing)
End Sub
Friend WithEvents TextBox1 As System.Windows.Forms.TextBox
Friend WithEvents TextBox2 As System.Windows.Forms.TextBox

'Required by the Windows Form Designer
Private components As System.ComponentModel.Container

'NOTE: The following procedure is required by the Windows Form Designer
'It can be modified using the Windows Form Designer.
'Do not modify it using the code editor.
<System.Diagnostics.DebuggerStepThrough()> Private Sub InitializeComponent()
    Me.TextBox1 = New System.Windows.Forms.TextBox()
    Me.TextBox2 = New System.Windows.Forms.TextBox()
    Me.SuspendLayout()
    '
    'TextBox1
    '
    Me.TextBox1.Location = New System.Drawing.Point(64, 24)
    Me.TextBox1.Name = "TextBox1"
    Me.TextBox1.TabIndex = 0
    Me.TextBox1.Text = "TextBox1"
    '
    'TextBox2
    '
    Me.TextBox2.Location = New System.Drawing.Point(64, 56)
    Me.TextBox2.Name = "TextBox2"
    Me.TextBox2.TabIndex = 1
    Me.TextBox2.Text = "TextBox2"
    '
    'Form1
    '
    Me.AutoScaleBaseSize = New System.Drawing.Size(5, 13)
    Me.ClientSize = New System.Drawing.Size(292, 273)
    Me.Controls.AddRange(New Control() {Me.TextBox2, Me.TextBox1})
    Me.Name = "Form1"
    Me.Text = "Form1"
```

```
        Me.ResumeLayout(False)

    End Sub

#End Region

End Class
```

The IntializeComponent method was automatically generated when you created the project. This method is required and utilized by the Windows Form Designer. As a result, you should not be changing the code directly in this method as unpredictable results may occur. You should rely on using the Form Designer to make the changes for you.

The Form1 class contains two TextBox data members. These data members were automatically created when the TextBox controls were added to the form. Each time a control is added, a data member is defined, and the data member is initialized in the form's InitializeComponent method. After the data members are initialized, a call to the SuspendLayout method on the form object is made. This turns off the automatic layout logic associated with the form. This is useful if you are going to add several controls to a form. Rather than having the form perform its layout logic after each control is added, you can turn off the automatic layout, add several controls, and then perform the automatic layout process once.

Next, each data member's properties are set. The Location property is set based on where the control was dropped onto the form. It is also updated appropriately when you adjust the location by moving the control in the Form Designer. A default name is created for a control when it is added by dropping onto the Form Designer. The Name property is set to a value based on the type of control and the total number of controls for the type that already exists on the form. For example, the first time the TextBox control was added to the form a default name of "TextBox1" was generated. The second time a TextBox control was added to the form a default name of "TextBox2" was generated. The TabIndex is also automatically set based on the number of controls currently in the Tab order. A new control is automatically put at the end of the Tab order. The Text property is set to the same value as the Name property.

Each of these properties is set by default when you drop the control on the form. You can modify these values using the Properties window in Visual Studio .NET.

After all of the controls' properties are set, the controls are added to the form. This is accomplished by adding the controls to the form's Controls collection. The AddRange method on the Controls property supports adding multiple controls to the Controls property at once. Also, the Controls property is part of the Control class. Hence, you can add child controls to a control the exact same way. It just so happens that the parent control in this example is a form.

And lastly, the ResumeLayout method is called, telling the form (actually the control) to perform its layout processing.

Figure 23.4 shows the running form based on the just described code example. The form shows two text boxes. When the user presses the Tab key, focus shifts from the first text box to the second text box. Pressing the Tab key again moves the focus to the next control in the Tab order. When the Tab order reaches the highest number and the user presses the Tab key again, the focus moves back to the first control in the Tab order.

NOTE

The Tab key cycles through the controls based on the Tab order defined on a form. Pressing Shift+Tab performs just like the Tab key except in reverse order.

Figure 23.4: *Example Tab order.*

Focus and Validation

The previous example showing tabbing is rather straightforward. What if you wanted to validate the first TextBox to make sure it has a value before moving to the next TextBox? What if you wanted to validate any control for that matter? To do validation in this way, you need to deal with the Control events. In regards to input focus and validation for controls, the following events are generated in this order:

1. Enter

2. GotFocus

3. Leave

4. Validating

5. Validated

6. LostFocus

So how does this work? When a control is about to get the focus, it receives an Enter event followed by a GotFocus event. After these events occur, the control has the input focus. In the case of a text box, the user can enter text into the text box by typing at the keyboard because the text box has the input focus.

When the user changes focus to another control by pressing the Tab key or using the mouse, a Leave event is sent to the current control informing it that the focus is about to leave. Next, a Validating event is sent to the control. The purpose of this event is to allow some level of validation to occur on the control before moving on to the next control. It is possible to handle this event and not allow the input focus to move to the next control. This would mean the user must enter valid text into the TextBox control before moving on. What is meant by *valid text* depends on the application being built. This is where you, as the developer, make this decision. Assuming the control passes the validation step, a Validated event is sent to the control. This signifies to the control that it is valid before moving on. Lastly, the LostFocus event is sent to the control, telling it that it no longer has the focus.

TIP

The Enter and Leave events should be used in regards to controls. The exception to this rule is forms. Form objects suppress the Enter and Leave events and instead use the Activated and Deactivate events respectively.

You should not use the GotFocus and LostFocus events because they are lower-level events. Stick with using the Enter and Leave (or Activated and Deactivate) events.

As long as you understand these events and their sequence, you can write interesting code for special purposes. The most common feature you would develop in regards to these events is validation.

The two TextBoxes in the previous example can be validated by defining event handlers to handle the Validating event for each control. The following two event handlers test whether the controls have an empty Text property, and if they do a message is displayed to the user, and the control is invalidated. This prevents the focus from moving off the control to another control.

```
Private Sub TextBox1_Validating(ByVal sender As Object, _
                    ByVal e As System.ComponentModel.CancelEventArgs) _
```

```
                              Handles TextBox1.Validating
    If Me.TextBox1.Text = "" Then
        MsgBox("Field must not be empty.", MsgBoxStyle.OKOnly, "")
        e.Cancel = True
    End If
End Sub

Private Sub TextBox2_Validating(ByVal sender As Object, _
                        ByVal e As System.ComponentModel.CancelEventArgs) _
                        Handles TextBox2.Validating
    If Me.TextBox2.Text = "" Then
        MsgBox("Field must not be empty.", MsgBoxStyle.OKOnly, "")
        e.Cancel = True
    End If
End Sub
```

In each event handler, a check is made of the control's Text property. If the Text property is empty, the Cancel property on the EventArgs parameter is set to True—meaning cancel the attempt at changing the focus.

Drag and Drop

Drag and Drop is the capability to select something using the mouse and then drag it onto another control and drop the dragged item. The result of a drag and drop operation is that the item dropped is copied or moved from the source location to the target location. Whether it is copied as opposed to being moved depends on the code that is written. You can choose to do either depending on the situation.

Starting the drag and drop process involves calling the DoDragDrop method on the source control that contains the data being dragged. The DoDragDrop method can be called through any means that makes sense in your application. A common way to start a drag and drop process is by responding to the MouseDown event on a control. To show how to do Drag and Drop, the following code is added to the previous example to allow dragging text from the first text box to the second text box.

The first step is to write an event handler for the event in which you want to start the drag and drop process. The following code defines an event handler for the MouseDown event for the TextBox1 control.

The simplest way to do this is to select the TextBox1 control in the ListBox at the top left of the Code window. Then the ListBox at the top right of the Code window displays all of the relevant events for the control. Selecting the MouseDown event places an empty event procedure directly in the code. At this point, you can fill in your additional code in the event procedure.

```
Private Sub TextBox1_MouseDown(ByVal sender As Object, _
```

```
                    ByVal e As System.Windows.Forms.MouseEventArgs) _
                    Handles TextBox1.MouseDown
        TextBox1.DoDragDrop(TextBox1.Text, DragDropEffects.Copy)
End Sub
```

The event handler has a single line of code in its body. This code calls the DoDragDrop method on the TextBox1 control. The object on which you call the DoDragDrop method is the source of the Drag and Drop operation.

Th DoDragDrop method takes two parameters. The first parameter is the content of the data being dragged. In this case it is a string, but the drag and drop operation supports several different formats. The second parameter defines the effect of the drag and drop operation. The DragDropEffects enumeration values are shown in Table 23.4. In this example, the data from the TextBox1 control is copied to the TextBox2 control.

Table 23.4: **DragDropEffects** *Enumeration*

Value	Description
Copy	The data is copied from the source control.
Move	The data is moved from the source control to the target control.
Link	A link to the source data is dropped onto the target control.
Scroll	Data is scrolled in the drop target.
None	The target control does not accept the data being dropped.
All	The data is dropped and scrolled into the target control and removed from the source control.

At this point, the data from the first control is provided to the drag and drop operation, but how is the data dropped onto the second control? The first thing you need to do is set the AllowDrop property on the TextBox2 control to True. This allows the drag and drop operation to detect that the control can be a target of a drag and drop operation.

Next, you need to handle two additional events on the target control. These events are DragEnter and DragDrop. You can do this by using the ListBoxes at the top of the Code window again. This time select the TextBox2 control in the top left ListBox. Then select the DragEnter and DragDrop events in the top right ListBox at the top of the Code window.

The DragEnter event is generated when data is currently being dragged and the mouse cursor enters a control. The control receives a DragEnter event, in which case the control needs to respond regarding whether it can support the data format of the data being dragged. This is done by checking the format of the data and setting the appropriate DragDropEffect. The data format is checked using the GetDataPresent method on the Data property of the DragEventArgs parameter passed to the DragEnter event handler.

If the control supports the data format of the drag and drop operation, the drop effect is set to an appropriate value. In this example, the effect is set to Copy. If the format is not supported the effect is set to None to avoid any potential errors.

```
Private Sub TextBox2_DragEnter(ByVal sender As Object, _
                        ByVal e As System.Windows.Forms.DragEventArgs) _
                        Handles TextBox2.DragEnter
    If e.Data.GetDataPresent(DataFormats.Text) Then
        e.Effect = DragDropEffects.Copy
    Else
        e.Effect = DragDropEffects.None
    End If

End Sub


Private Sub TextBox2_DragDrop(ByVal sender As Object, _
                        ByVal e As System.Windows.Forms.DragEventArgs) _
                        Handles TextBox2.DragDrop
    TextBox2.Text = e.Data.GetData(DataFormats.Text).ToString()
End Sub
```

The list of possible formats is defined in Table 23.5.

Table 23.5: DataFormats Members

Value	Description
Bitmap	Windows bitmap format.
CommaSeparatedValue	Specifies the comma-separated value format (CSV).
Dib	Windows Device Independent Bitmap format.
Dif	Windows Data Interchange format.
EnhancedMetafile	Windows Enhanced Metafile format.
FileDrop	Windows file drop format.
Html	Hypertext Markup Language format (HTML).
Locale	Windows culture format.
MetafilePict	Windows metafile format.
OemText	Windows original equipment manufacturer text format.
Palette	Windows palette format.
PenData	Windows pen data format.
Riff	Resource Interchange File Format (RIFF) audio format.
Rtf	Rich Text Format.
Serializeable	Specifies the format of any serializable object.
StringFormat	Windows Forms String class format.
SymbolicLink	Windows symbolic link format.

Table 23.5: continued

Value	Description
Text	Standard ANSI text format.
Tiff	Tagged Image File format.
UnicodeText	Unicode text format.
WaveAudio	Wave audio format.

When you run the code example, you can select the text in the first text box, press the mouse button down, hold the mouse button down, drag the text onto the second text box, and release the mouse button. This capability can be duplicated for other controls by simply following the steps just described. Also, you provide interesting drag and drop capabilities by utilizing the different drag and drop data formats.

Keyboard Shortcuts

Controls can also have keyboard shortcuts that provide a quick way of setting the input focus to a particular control. To define a keyboard shortcut, you simply need to place an ampersand character (&) somewhere in the value of the Text property for the control. The character after the ampersand becomes the keyboard shortcut.

To show how this works, create a new Windows Application project and add two buttons to the form. The buttons default to the names Button1 and Button2. For each button, double-click the button to generate an event procedure that handles the Click event. In each event procedure, display a message to the user. Now, in order to set the shortcut keys, edit the Text properties of each button using the Properties window. Set the Text property of Button1 to "&One" and the Text property of Button2 to "&Two."

Here is the resulting code:

```
Public Class Form1
    Inherits System.Windows.Forms.Form

#Region " Windows Form Designer generated code "

    Public Sub New()
        MyBase.New()

        'This call is required by the Windows Form Designer.
        InitializeComponent()

        'Add any initialization after the InitializeComponent() call

    End Sub
```

```
'Form overrides dispose to clean up the component list.
Protected Overloads Overrides Sub Dispose(ByVal disposing As Boolean)
    If disposing Then
        If Not (components Is Nothing) Then
            components.Dispose()
        End If
    End If
    MyBase.Dispose(disposing)
End Sub
Friend WithEvents Button1 As System.Windows.Forms.Button
Friend WithEvents Button2 As System.Windows.Forms.Button

'Required by the Windows Form Designer
Private components As System.ComponentModel.Container

'NOTE: The following procedure is required by the Windows Form Designer
'It can be modified using the Windows Form Designer.
'Do not modify it using the code editor.
<System.Diagnostics.DebuggerStepThrough()> Private Sub InitializeComponent()
    Me.Button1 = New System.Windows.Forms.Button()
    Me.Button2 = New System.Windows.Forms.Button()
    Me.SuspendLayout()
    '
    'Button1
    '
    Me.Button1.Location = New System.Drawing.Point(24, 16)
    Me.Button1.Name = "Button1"
    Me.Button1.Size = New System.Drawing.Size(72, 48)
    Me.Button1.TabIndex = 0
    Me.Button1.Text = "&One"
    '
    'Button2
    '
    Me.Button2.Location = New System.Drawing.Point(112, 16)
    Me.Button2.Name = "Button2"
    Me.Button2.Size = New System.Drawing.Size(72, 48)
    Me.Button2.TabIndex = 1
    Me.Button2.Text = "&Two"
    '
    'Form1
    '
    Me.AutoScaleBaseSize = New System.Drawing.Size(5, 13)
    Me.ClientSize = New System.Drawing.Size(216, 77)
    Me.Controls.AddRange(New System.Windows.Forms.Control() {Me.Button2,
Me.Button1})
    Me.Name = "Form1"
    Me.Text = "Form1"
```

```
        Me.ResumeLayout(False)

    End Sub

#End Region

    Private Sub Button1_Click(ByVal sender As System.Object, _
                        ByVal e As System.EventArgs) Handles Button1.Click
        MsgBox("Button One clicked!", MsgBoxStyle.OKOnly, "")
    End Sub

    Private Sub Button2_Click(ByVal sender As System.Object, _
                        ByVal e As System.EventArgs) Handles Button2.Click
        MsgBox("Button Two clicked!", MsgBoxStyle.OKOnly, "")
    End Sub

End Class
```

When you press ALT+O, a `Click` event is generated for Button One. When you press ALT+T, a `Click` event is generated for Button Two.

If you actually want to use an ampersand character as part of the display of a control but don't want it to be a shortcut key, you must use two ampersands in a row. For example, the text "M&&M" produces the text display "M&M" without defining a shortcut key for the M.

Examples Using Common Controls in .NET

Over the next several pages examples are provided to show usage of specific controls that you can use in the development of your Windows applications using Visual Basic .NET.

Labels

Labels are controls used mostly to display static text on a form. Labels are typically used in conjunction with `TextBox` controls to describe the type of data contained in the text boxes. The `Label` class inherits from the `Control` class.

A new kind of label is also introduced as part of the `System.Windows.Forms` namespace. This kind of label is called a `LinkLabel` and allows you to display text on a form just like a normal label. However, you can also define fragments of the text to be Web links such that if you click on the fragment a Web browser opens to the Web page defined for the link.

The following code shows an example of a Label and a LinkLabel:

```
Public Class Form1
    Inherits System.Windows.Forms.Form

#Region " Windows Form Designer generated code "

    Public Sub New()
        MyBase.New()

        'This call is required by the Windows Form Designer.
        InitializeComponent()

        LinkLabel1.Links.Add(17, 3, "www.mlb.com")
        LinkLabel1.Links.Add(28, 7, "www.redsox.com")

    End Sub

    'Form overrides dispose to clean up the component list.
    Protected Overloads Overrides Sub Dispose(ByVal disposing As Boolean)
        If disposing Then
            If Not (components Is Nothing) Then
                components.Dispose()
            End If
        End If
        MyBase.Dispose(disposing)
    End Sub
    Friend WithEvents Label1 As System.Windows.Forms.Label
    Friend WithEvents LinkLabel1 As System.Windows.Forms.LinkLabel

    'Required by the Windows Form Designer
    Private components As System.ComponentModel.Container

    'NOTE: The following procedure is required by the Windows Form Designer
    'It can be modified using the Windows Form Designer.
    'Do not modify it using the code editor.
    <System.Diagnostics.DebuggerStepThrough()> Private Sub InitializeComponent()
        Me.LinkLabel1 = New System.Windows.Forms.LinkLabel()
        Me.Label1 = New System.Windows.Forms.Label()
        Me.SuspendLayout()
        '
        'LinkLabel1
        '
        Mc.LinkLabel1.Font = New System.Drawing.Font("Microsoft Sans Serif", _
                                14.0!, _
                                System.Drawing.FontStyle.Regular, _
                                System.Drawing.GraphicsUnit.Point, _
```

```
                                    CType(0, Byte))
        Me.LinkLabel1.Location = New System.Drawing.Point(16, 64)
        Me.LinkLabel1.Name = "LinkLabel1"
        Me.LinkLabel1.Size = New System.Drawing.Size(344, 72)
        Me.LinkLabel1.TabIndex = 1
        Me.LinkLabel1.TabStop = True
        Me.LinkLabel1.Text = "The best team in MLB is the Red Sox!"
        '
        'Label1
        '
        Me.Label1.Font = New System.Drawing.Font("Microsoft Sans Serif", _
                        12.0!, _
                        System.Drawing.FontStyle.Regular, _
                        System.Drawing.GraphicsUnit.Point, _
                        CType(0, Byte))
        Me.Label1.Location = New System.Drawing.Point(16, 16)
        Me.Label1.Name = "Label1"
        Me.Label1.Size = New System.Drawing.Size(184, 24)
        Me.Label1.TabIndex = 0
        Me.Label1.Text = "Just another label:"
        '
        'Form1
        '
        Me.AutoScaleBaseSize = New System.Drawing.Size(5, 13)
        Me.ClientSize = New System.Drawing.Size(368, 141)
        Me.Controls.AddRange(New Control() {Me.LinkLabel1, Me.Label1})
        Me.Name = "Form1"
        Me.Text = "Form1"
        Me.ResumeLayout(False)

    End Sub

#End Region

    Private Sub LinkLabel1_LinkClicked(ByVal sender As System.Object, _
                            ByVal e As LinkLabelLinkClickedEventArgs) _
                            Handles LinkLabel1.LinkClicked
        LinkLabel1.Links(LinkLabel1.Links.IndexOf(e.Link)).Visited = True
        System.Diagnostics.Process.Start(e.Link.LinkData.ToString())
    End Sub

End Class
```

Both the `Label` and `LinkLabel` were dropped onto the form using the Toolbox and the Form Designer. The `LinkLabel` is similar to the `Label`. The additional capability is shown in the constructor of the form. After the labels have been created by calling the `InitializeComponent` method, The `Links` property on the `LinkLabel` is updated to represent the actual Web links in the text of the `LinkLabel`. The `Add` method is called on the `LinkLabel.Link` object to set up the Web links. This method takes three parameters. The first parameter is that starting position in the `Text` property's string value where the link starts. The next parameter is the length of the string for the link. The third parameter is the link itself.

In this example, links are set up for the string fragments "MLB" and "Red Sox" in the `LinkLabel`'s `Text` property. This is accomplished by the lines in bold. The first number defines the position in the text string to start the link. The second number defines how many characters the link extends.

When the user clicks on the MLB link, her browser is directed to `www.mlb.com`. When the user clicks on the Red Sox link, her browser is directed to `www.redsox.com`. Figure 23.5 shows the labels on the form.

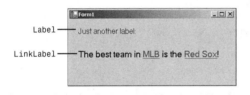

Figure 23.5: `Label` and `LinkLabel`.

Also notice in the example code that the support for opening the browser is not done automatically. You need to create an event handler for the `LinkClicked` event. In this handler, the `Visited` property of the `LinkArea` object is set to `True`. A `True` value for the `Visited` property causes the color of the link to change on the form after the link is clicked. This allows the user to visually see what links they have already visited and is identical to the way links work within a Web browser. The last line in the event handler opens the link in an external Web browser. This is a very handy way of incorporating external Web pages into your Windows application.

TextBoxes

There are two text box controls provided with the .NET Framework. They are `TextBox` and `RichTextBox`. Each of these controls inherits from the `TextBoxBase` class, which in turn inherits from the `Control` class. The `TextBoxBase` class provides a common set of features for both types of text boxes. This includes methods for support text manipulation such as cut, copy, paste, and undo. This also includes multiline text control support and a common set of events.

The TextBox class is used to display and gather single-line or multiline text data. Multiline support is enabled by setting the Multiline property on the TextBox object to True. The RichTextBox is used to display and edit text using the Rich Text Format. This format supports basic formatting capabilities such as bold and italic as well as other formatting features such as bulleted lists.

The following example code, as part of a Windows Application project, demonstrates a TextBox control and a RichTextBox control:

```
Public Class Form1
    Inherits System.Windows.Forms.Form

#Region " Windows Form Designer generated code "

    Public Sub New()
        MyBase.New()

        'This call is required by the Windows Form Designer.
        InitializeComponent()

        Me.RichTextBox1.LoadFile("grocerylist.rtf")

    End Sub

    'Form overrides dispose to clean up the component list.
    Protected Overloads Overrides Sub Dispose(ByVal disposing As Boolean)
        If disposing Then
            If Not (components Is Nothing) Then
                components.Dispose()
            End If
        End If
        MyBase.Dispose(disposing)
    End Sub
    Friend WithEvents TextBox1 As System.Windows.Forms.TextBox
    Friend WithEvents RichTextBox1 As System.Windows.Forms.RichTextBox

    'Required by the Windows Form Designer
    Private components As System.ComponentModel.Container

    'NOTE: The following procedure is required by the Windows Form Designer
    'It can be modified using the Windows Form Designer.
    'Do not modify it using the code editor.
    <System.Diagnostics.DebuggerStepThrough()> Private Sub InitializeComponent()
        Me.TextBox1 = New System.Windows.Forms.TextBox()
        Me.RichTextBox1 = New System.Windows.Forms.RichTextBox()
        Me.SuspendLayout()
        '
```

```
'TextBox1
'
Me.TextBox1.Location = New System.Drawing.Point(8, 16)
Me.TextBox1.Name = "TextBox1"
Me.TextBox1.Size = New System.Drawing.Size(272, 20)
Me.TextBox1.TabIndex = 0
Me.TextBox1.Text = "TextBox1"
'
'RichTextBox1
'
Me.RichTextBox1.Location = New System.Drawing.Point(8, 56)
Me.RichTextBox1.Name = "RichTextBox1"
Me.RichTextBox1.Size = New System.Drawing.Size(272, 208)
Me.RichTextBox1.TabIndex = 1
Me.RichTextBox1.Text = "RichTextBox1"
'
'Form1
'
Me.AutoScaleBaseSize = New System.Drawing.Size(5, 13)
Me.ClientSize = New System.Drawing.Size(288, 273)
Me.Controls.AddRange(New Control() {Me.RichTextBox1, Me.TextBox1})
Me.Name = "Form1"
Me.Text = "Form1"
Me.ResumeLayout(False)

End Sub

#End Region

End Class
```

The output of this example is shown in Figure 23.6. Here you can see the example TextBox and RichTextBox on a form.

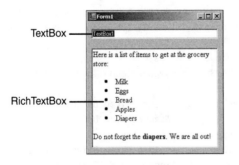

Figure 23.6: *TextBox and RichTextBox.*

Buttons

There are three types of button controls provided by the .NET Framework. These are `Button`, `CheckBox`, and `RadioButton`. Each of these button controls inherits from the `ButtonBase` class. The `ButtonBase` class inherits from the `Control` class and provides a common set of features for the three types of buttons. The `ButtonBase` class mostly provides support for displaying an image associated with the button.

The `ButtonBase` provides an `Image` property for setting a button's image. The `ButtonBase` class also has `ImageList` and `ImageIndex` properties for an alternative way of setting a button's image. `ImageList` objects are used to contain a list of images that may be used by several controls in an application. To use the `ImageList`, the `ImageList` property must be set to an `ImageList` object in your application, and the `ImageIndex` property must be set to the image index in the list. If the `ImageList` property on a button is set then the `Image` property is set to `null`. If an `Image` property is set on a button then the `ImageList` property is set to `null`, and the `ImageIndex` property is reset to `-1`.

The `Button` control provides basic button functionality. This allows you to display a button on a page containing text and/or an image. The user is able to click on the button, and a `Click` event can be handled as desired.

The `CheckBox` control has an on/off state associated with it. It can also be displayed containing text and/or an image. When the user clicks on a `CheckBox` control, the control displays a check mark if the button's state is on; otherwise, the control is displayed without a check mark. This type of control is useful for displaying options that the user can select independent of one another.

The `RadioButton` performs in a similar fashion as the `CheckBox`. The difference is that a solid circle is displayed instead of a check mark. And, `RadioButtons` are typically used within a group of `RadioButtons`. Only one `RadioButton` in the group is allowed to be on at a given time. This type of control is useful for allowing a user to select only one option from a group of options.

The following code, as part of a Windows application project, gives an example using one `Button` control, three `CheckBox` controls, and two `RadioButton` controls.

```
Public Class Form1
    Inherits System.Windows.Forms.Form

#Region " Windows Form Designer generated code "
```

```
Public Sub New()
    MyBase.New()

    'This call is required by the Windows Form Designer.
    InitializeComponent()

    'Add any initialization after the InitializeComponent() call

End Sub

'Form overrides dispose to clean up the component list.
Protected Overloads Overrides Sub Dispose(ByVal disposing As Boolean)
    If disposing Then
        If Not (components Is Nothing) Then
            components.Dispose()
        End If
    End If
    MyBase.Dispose(disposing)
End Sub
Friend WithEvents CheckBox1 As System.Windows.Forms.CheckBox
Friend WithEvents CheckBox2 As System.Windows.Forms.CheckBox
Friend WithEvents CheckBox3 As System.Windows.Forms.CheckBox
Friend WithEvents RadioButton1 As System.Windows.Forms.RadioButton
Friend WithEvents RadioButton2 As System.Windows.Forms.RadioButton
Friend WithEvents Button1 As System.Windows.Forms.Button

'Required by the Windows Form Designer
Private components As System.ComponentModel.Container

'NOTE: The following procedure is required by the Windows Form Designer
'It can be modified using the Windows Form Designer.
'Do not modify it using the code editor.
<System.Diagnostics.DebuggerStepThrough()> Private Sub InitializeComponent()
    Me.CheckBox1 = New System.Windows.Forms.CheckBox()
    Me.CheckBox2 = New System.Windows.Forms.CheckBox()
    Me.CheckBox3 = New System.Windows.Forms.CheckBox()
    Me.RadioButton1 = New System.Windows.Forms.RadioButton()
    Me.RadioButton2 = New System.Windows.Forms.RadioButton()
    Me.Button1 = New System.Windows.Forms.Button()
    Me.SuspendLayout()
    '
    'CheckBox1
    '
    Me.CheckBox1.Location = New System.Drawing.Point(16, 16)
    Me.CheckBox1.Name = "CheckBox1"
    Me.CheckBox1.TabIndex = 0
```

```
Me.CheckBox1.Text = "Magazine"
'
'CheckBox2
'
Me.CheckBox2.Location = New System.Drawing.Point(16, 48)
Me.CheckBox2.Name = "CheckBox2"
Me.CheckBox2.TabIndex = 1
Me.CheckBox2.Text = "Book"
'
'CheckBox3
'
Me.CheckBox3.Location = New System.Drawing.Point(16, 80)
Me.CheckBox3.Name = "CheckBox3"
Me.CheckBox3.TabIndex = 2
Me.CheckBox3.Text = "Newsletter"
'
'RadioButton1
'
Me.RadioButton1.Location = New System.Drawing.Point(16, 144)
Me.RadioButton1.Name = "RadioButton1"
Me.RadioButton1.TabIndex = 3
Me.RadioButton1.Text = "Morning"
'
'RadioButton2
'
Me.RadioButton2.Location = New System.Drawing.Point(16, 176)
Me.RadioButton2.Name = "RadioButton2"
Me.RadioButton2.TabIndex = 4
Me.RadioButton2.Text = "Evening"
'
'Button1
'
Me.Button1.Location = New System.Drawing.Point(144, 16)
Me.Button1.Name = "Button1"
Me.Button1.TabIndex = 5
Me.Button1.Text = "Ok"
'
'Form1
'
Me.AutoScaleBaseSize = New System.Drawing.Size(5, 13)
Me.ClientSize = New System.Drawing.Size(224, 221)
Me.Controls.AddRange(New System.Windows.Forms.Control() {Me.Button1, _
                                              Me.RadioButton2, _
                                              Me.RadioButton1, _
                                              Me.CheckBox3, _
                                              Me.CheckBox2, _
                                              Me.CheckBox1})
```

```
          Me.Name = "Form1"
          Me.Text = "Form1"
          Me.ResumeLayout(False)

      End Sub

#End Region

    Private Sub Button1_Click(ByVal sender As System.Object, _
                            ByVal e As System.EventArgs) Handles Button1.Click
        Me.Close()
      End Sub
End Class
```

In this previous example, each of the Button controls is used to close the form. This is done by defining an event handler for the Button's Click event. In the event handler, the Close method is invoked on the form object, thus closing the form.

The CheckBox controls are used to display three values (Magazine, Book, and Newsletter), which the user can choose to select. After the user selects the desired options, the CheckBox controls can be interrogated to see which options were selected. The selected CheckBox controls will have their Checked property set to True.

The RadioButton controls are used to display two possible values (Morning or Evening). The user can choose either option. If the user chooses an option the other option is automatically unselected. The resulting RadioButton control that is selected has its Checked property set to True.

Figure 23.7 shows a running example that uses a Button, CheckBoxes, and RadioButtons on a form.

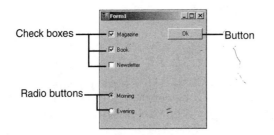

***Figure 23.7:** Button, CheckBoxes, and RadioButtons.*

NOTE

RadioButton controls are automatically sensitive to other RadioButton controls that have the same parent control. If you want to have two sets of RadioButton controls on the same form that represent two different sets of options, you must first place a GroupBox control on the form and then place the set of RadioButtons within the GroupBox. Repeat this process for each set of RadioButtons on the form.

GroupBox

The GroupBox control's main purpose is to group a set of controls on a form within a bounding area. The purpose of this is two fold. First, by grouping a set of controls on a form you are able to simplify your user interface by visually grouping like controls, making it easier for your users to understand. If you do not use GroupBoxes, in the extreme case you may find that your forms contain lots of controls spread out over the form, making the form difficult to read and understand. The second purpose of GroupBox controls is so that controls such as RadioButtons can function together as a group without concern for the rest of the RadioButtons on the form.

Here is a quick example of a GroupBox used within a Windows application project:

```
Public Class Form1
    Inherits System.Windows.Forms.Form

#Region " Windows Form Designer generated code "

    Public Sub New()
        MyBase.New()

        'This call is required by the Windows Form Designer.
        InitializeComponent()

        'Add any initialization after the InitializeComponent() call

    End Sub

    'Form overrides dispose to clean up the component list.
    Protected Overloads Overrides Sub Dispose(ByVal disposing As Boolean)
        If disposing Then
            If Not (components Is Nothing) Then
                components.Dispose()
            End If
        End If
        MyBase.Dispose(disposing)
    End Sub
```

```vbnet
Friend WithEvents Button1 As System.Windows.Forms.Button
Friend WithEvents GroupBox1 As System.Windows.Forms.GroupBox
Friend WithEvents RadioButton1 As System.Windows.Forms.RadioButton
Friend WithEvents RadioButton2 As System.Windows.Forms.RadioButton

'Required by the Windows Form Designer
Private components As System.ComponentModel.Container

'NOTE: The following procedure is required by the Windows Form Designer
'It can be modified using the Windows Form Designer.
'Do not modify it using the code editor.
<System.Diagnostics.DebuggerStepThrough()> Private Sub InitializeComponent()
    Me.Button1 = New System.Windows.Forms.Button()
    Me.GroupBox1 = New System.Windows.Forms.GroupBox()
    Me.RadioButton1 = New System.Windows.Forms.RadioButton()
    Me.RadioButton2 = New System.Windows.Forms.RadioButton()
    Me.GroupBox1.SuspendLayout()
    Me.SuspendLayout()
    '
    'Button1
    '
    Me.Button1.Location = New System.Drawing.Point(144, 16)
    Me.Button1.Name = "Button1"
    Me.Button1.TabIndex = 5
    Me.Button1.Text = "Ok"
    '
    'GroupBox1
    '
    Me.GroupBox1.Controls.AddRange(New System.Windows.Forms.Control() _
                                {Me.RadioButton1, Me.RadioButton2})
    Me.GroupBox1.Location = New System.Drawing.Point(8, 16)
    Me.GroupBox1.Name = "GroupBox1"
    Me.GroupBox1.Size = New System.Drawing.Size(128, 104)
    Me.GroupBox1.TabIndex = 6
    Me.GroupBox1.TabStop = False
    Me.GroupBox1.Text = "Time of Day"
    '
    'RadioButton1
    '
    Me.RadioButton1.Location = New System.Drawing.Point(16, 24)
    Me.RadioButton1.Name = "RadioButton1"
    Me.RadioButton1.TabIndex = 3
    Me.RadioButton1.Text = "Morning"
    '
    'RadioButton2
    '
```

```
        Me.RadioButton2.Location = New System.Drawing.Point(16, 48)
        Me.RadioButton2.Name = "RadioButton2"
        Me.RadioButton2.TabIndex = 4
        Me.RadioButton2.Text = "Evening"
        '
        'Form1
        '
        Me.AutoScaleBaseSize = New System.Drawing.Size(5, 13)
        Me.ClientSize = New System.Drawing.Size(224, 133)
        Me.Controls.AddRange(New Control() {Me.Button1, Me.GroupBox1})
        Me.Name = "Form1"
        Me.Text = "Form1"
        Me.GroupBox1.ResumeLayout(False)
        Me.ResumeLayout(False)

    End Sub

#End Region

    Private Sub Button1_Click(ByVal sender As System.Object, _
                    ByVal e As System.EventArgs) Handles Button1.Click
        Me.Close()
    End Sub
End Class
```

Figure 23.8 shows the GroupBox as it appears on the form.

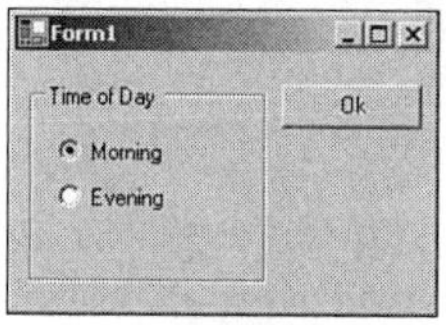

Figure 23.8: *A* GroupBox.

ComboBox and ListBox

The ComboBox class and the ListBox class both inherit from the ListControl class. The ListControl class inherits from the Control class and provides the basic support for containing the list of items or alternatively a reference to a data source for data binding. The ComboBox class and the ListBox class both contain the property Items. The Items property is used to store the items in the list of values for the respective controls.

The ComboBox class is useful for presenting a list of possible values from which the user can choose, plus allowing them to enter in a value by typing into the ComboBox control. This, of course, depends on the value of the DropDownStyle property. The DropDownStyle property is based on the ComboBoxSytle enumeration. This enumeration is listed in Table 23.6.

Table 23.6: **ComboBoxStyle** *Enumeration*

Value	Description
DropDown	The control allows editing to the text portion of the control. The list is displayed by clicking on the drop-down arrow on the control.
DropDownList	Same as DropDown except the text portion of the control is not editable.
Simple	The text portion is editable, and the list portion is always visible.

List boxes are useful for presenting a longer list of possible values from which to choose. This list of values could potentially be a dynamic list of options possibly retrieved from a database as well. ListBoxes support single selection, multiple selection, or no selection depending on the value of the SelectionMode property. This property is based on the SelectionMode enumeration, which is defined in Table 23.7.

Table 23.7: **SelectionMode** *Enumeration*

Value	Description
MultiExtended	Multiple selection is supported using the Shift, Ctrl, and arrow keys.
MultiSimple	Multiple selection is supported.
None	No items can be selected.
One	Only one item can be selected.

The ListBox class is further extended by the CheckedListBox class. This class adds the capability to show the selected items in the list using check marks instead of highlighting the selection.

This Windows application project example uses a ComboBox, ListBox, and a CheckedListBox:

```
Public Class Form1
    Inherits System.Windows.Forms.Form

#Region " Windows Form Designer generated code "

    Public Sub New()
        MyBase.New()

        'This call is required by the Windows Form Designer.
        InitializeComponent()
```

```
        'Add any initialization after the InitializeComponent() call
        PopulateComboBox()
        PopulateListBox()
        PopulateCheckedListBox()

End Sub


'Form overrides dispose to clean up the component list.
Protected Overloads Overrides Sub Dispose(ByVal disposing As Boolean)
    If disposing Then
        If Not (components Is Nothing) Then
            components.Dispose()
        End If
    End If
    MyBase.Dispose(disposing)
End Sub
Friend WithEvents ComboBox1 As System.Windows.Forms.ComboBox
Friend WithEvents ListBox1 As System.Windows.Forms.ListBox
Friend WithEvents CheckedListBox1 As System.Windows.Forms.CheckedListBox
Friend WithEvents Button1 As System.Windows.Forms.Button


'Required by the Windows Form Designer
Private components As System.ComponentModel.Container

'NOTE: The following procedure is required by the Windows Form Designer
'It can be modified using the Windows Form Designer.
'Do not modify it using the code editor.
<System.Diagnostics.DebuggerStepThrough()> Private Sub InitializeComponent()
    Me.ComboBox1 = New System.Windows.Forms.ComboBox()
    Me.ListBox1 = New System.Windows.Forms.ListBox()
    Me.CheckedListBox1 = New System.Windows.Forms.CheckedListBox()
    Me.Button1 = New System.Windows.Forms.Button()
    Me.SuspendLayout()
    '
    'ComboBox1
    '
    Me.ComboBox1.DropDownWidth = 120
    Me.ComboBox1.Location = New System.Drawing.Point(16, 16)
    Me.ComboBox1.Name = "ComboBox1"
    Me.ComboBox1.Size = New System.Drawing.Size(120, 21)
    Me.ComboBox1.TabIndex = 0
    Me.ComboBox1.Text = "ComboBox1"
    '
    'ListBox1
    '
    Me.ListBox1.Location = New System.Drawing.Point(16, 56)
    Me.ListBox1.Name = "ListBox1"
```

```
            Me.ListBox1.Size = New System.Drawing.Size(120, 95)
            Me.ListBox1.TabIndex = 1
            '
            'CheckedListBox1
            '
            Me.CheckedListBox1.Location = New System.Drawing.Point(144, 56)
            Me.CheckedListBox1.Name = "CheckedListBox1"
            Me.CheckedListBox1.Size = New System.Drawing.Size(120, 94)
            Me.CheckedListBox1.TabIndex = 2
            '
            'Button1
            '
            Me.Button1.Location = New System.Drawing.Point(184, 8)
            Me.Button1.Name = "Button1"
            Me.Button1.TabIndex = 3
            Me.Button1.Text = "OK"
            '
            'Form1
            '
            Me.AutoScaleBaseSize = New System.Drawing.Size(5, 13)
            Me.ClientSize = New System.Drawing.Size(280, 165)
            Me.Controls.AddRange(New Control() {Me.Button1, _
                                        Me.CheckedListBox1, _
                                        Me.ListBox1, _
                                        Me.ComboBox1})
            Me.Name = "Form1"
            Me.Text = "Form1"
            Me.ResumeLayout(False)


        End Sub

    #End Region

        Public Sub PopulateComboBox()
            ComboBox1.Items.Add("Red")
            ComboBox1.Items.Add("Green")
            ComboBox1.Items.Add("Blue")
            ComboBox1.SelectedIndex = 0
        End Sub

        Public Sub PopulateListBox()
            ListBox1.Items.Add("Ford")
            ListBox1.Items.Add("Toyota")
            ListBox1.Items.Add("Chevy")
            ComboBox1.SelectedIndex = 0
        End Sub
```

```
    Public Sub PopulateCheckedListBox()
        CheckedListBox1.Items.Add("Four wheel drive")
        CheckedListBox1.Items.Add("Automatic transmission")
        CheckedListBox1.Items.Add("Power windows")
        CheckedListBox1.SelectedIndex = 0
    End Sub

    Private Sub Button1_Click(ByVal sender As System.Object, _
                        ByVal e As System.EventArgs) Handles Button1.Click
        System.Console.Out.WriteLine("ComboBox selection is " + ComboBox1.Text)
        System.Console.Out.WriteLine("ListBox selection is " + _
                        ListBox1.SelectedItem.ToString)
        System.Console.Out.WriteLine("CheckedListBox selection is " + _
                        CheckedListBox1.SelectedItem.ToString)
        Me.Close()
    End Sub
End Class
```

The output of this example is shown in Figure 23.9.

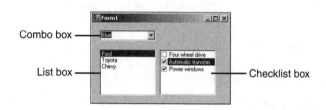

Figure 23.9: *ComboBox, ListBox, and CheckedListBox.*

There are three populate methods in the previous example that show how to populate the Items property of each of the controls. Once each of the controls is populated, you can see the result in Figure 23.9. After the user makes a selection in each of the controls and clicks the OK button, the selected values from each of the controls can be retrieved. In the event handler for the OK button, the values for each of the controls is outputted to the system console. This example code outputs a single selection for each of the controls. If you want to deal with multiple selections you would use the SelectedItems property instead of the SelectedItem property. The SeletedItems property is a collection of only the items selected in the ListBox. The SelectedItems property also has a Count property so that you can call SelectedItems.Count to get the number of selected items in the ListBox. You can also use the SelectedItems.Item method to get each selected item.

ToolBar and StatusBar

The `ToolBar` control supports adding multiple buttons that contain text, an image, or both. The buttons on the `ToolBar` represent the common commands in an application. Because the buttons exist on the toolbar, they can be accessed very quickly which can add an increased level of usability to any application.

Toolbars are constructed by instantiating a `ToolBar` control and adding `ToolBarButtons` to it. The `ToolBarButtons` can have text, an image, or both defined for it. Obviously, a `ToolBarButton` with both text and an image adds the most meaning to what the button actually does. So, it is encouraged that you add both text and images to your toolbars.

The images for each `ToolBarButton` is defined using an `ImageList` object. The `ImageList` object holds a list of images. The list can be dynamically added to as the program runs. The `ToolBar` object sets a reference to the `ImageList` object using the `ToolBar`'s `ImageList` property. Next, the `ToolBarButtons` reference an image by setting the `ImageIndex` property on the `ToolBarButton` to the index of the appropriate image in the `ImageList` object (referenced by the toolbar to which the `ToolBarButton` is added).

Status bars are used to display textual messages at the bottom of a form. These are easily created by instantiating a `StatusBar` object and adding it to the form's Controls collection.

The following example shows how to define and use a `ToolBar` and a `StatusBar`. This example was not automatically created through Visual Studio to show you the most relevant code. Create a new Windows Application project and replace the automatically generated code with the following:

```
Imports System.Windows.Forms

Public Class Form1
    Inherits System.Windows.Forms.Form

    Private Sub New()

        Dim button As ToolBarButton

        m_toolBar = New ToolBar()
        m_statusBar = New StatusBar()

        m_toolBar.ImageList = New ImageList()
        m_toolBar.ImageList.Images.Add(New Icon("go.ico"))
        m_toolBar.ImageList.Images.Add(New Icon("stop.ico"))
```

```
        button = New ToolBarButton()
        button.Text = "Go"
        button.ImageIndex = 0
        m_toolBar.Buttons.Add(button)

        button = New ToolBarButton()
        button.Text = "Stop"
        button.ImageIndex = 1
        m_toolBar.Buttons.Add(button)

        Me.Controls.Add(m_toolBar)
        Me.Controls.Add(m_statusBar)

        AddHandler m_toolBar.ButtonClick, AddressOf Me.ToolBarButtonClick

        m_statusBar.Text = "Ready."

    End Sub

    Private m_toolBar As ToolBar
    Private m_statusBar As StatusBar

    Protected Sub ToolBarButtonClick(ByVal sender As Object, _
                                     ByVal e As ToolBarButtonClickEventArgs)
        Select Case e.Button.Text
            Case "Go" : MsgBox("Go selected.", MsgBoxStyle.OKOnly, "")
            Case "Stop" : MsgBox("Stop selected.", MsgBoxStyle.OKOnly, "")
        End Select
    End Sub

End Class
```

This code requires you have the go.ico and stop.ico files in your project's bin folder in order for the program to run. Feel free to substitute icons if you want to try it out on your computer.

Figure 23.10 shows a toolbar and status bar based on the code in the previous example.

Also notice that to use the ToolBar, an event handler is defined for the ToolBar's ButtonClick event. The second argument to the event handler contains a reference to the button that was actually pressed.

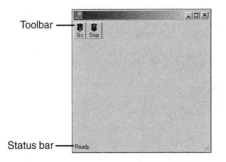

Figure 23.10: *ToolBar and StatusBar.*

TabControl

The TabControl allows you to create a control with several tabs. Each tab can contain specific controls. TabControls are commonly used for option pages in an application. Each tab usually represents a particular group of options. By creating and using multiple tabs, each group of options or settings can be placed on a single tab. This allows some level of organization of the options a user can view and modify within an application. The following example shows how to create a tabbed control with three separate pages. The pages are empty; however, you can add whatever controls you deem necessary for each page. The purpose of the example is strictly to show how to create a tabbed control with multiple pages.

Create a new Windows application project and replace the automatically generated code for the form with the following:

```
Imports System.Windows.Forms

Public Class Form1
    Inherits System.Windows.Forms.Form

    Private Sub New()

        m_tabControl = New TabControl()
        m_tabControl.TabPages.Add(ConstructPageOne())
        m_tabControl.TabPages.Add(ConstructPageTwo())
        m_tabControl.TabPages.Add(ConstructPageThree())
        m_tabControl.Dock = DockStyle.Fill

        Me.Controls.Add(m_tabControl)

    End Sub
```

```
Private m_tabControl As TabControl

Protected Function ConstructPageOne() As TabPage
    Dim page As TabPage = New TabPage()
    page.Text = "Page One"
    ' add code to create controls specific
    ' to the first page
    Return page
End Function

Protected Function ConstructPageTwo() As TabPage
    Dim page As TabPage = New TabPage()
    page.Text = "Page Two"
    ' add code to create controls specific
    ' to the second page
    Return page
End Function

Protected Function ConstructPageThree() As TabPage
    Dim page As TabPage = New TabPage()
    page.Text = "Page Three"
    ' add code to create controls specific
    ' to the third page
    Return page
End Function
```

End Class

As you can see, a page is created using the ConstructPageOne, ConstructPageTwo, and ConstructPageThree methods. The resulting pages are added to the TabControl's TabPages property. The TabControl automatically displays the TabPages that it knows about through the TabPages property. Figure 23.11 shows the resulting TabControl created by this example.

Figure 23.11: TabControl with three TabPages.

TreeView

The TreeView control is a very common user interface control used by many applications. It represents a hierarchical tree of data. Most users tend to understand the tree concept fairly well, which makes it suitable to use in an application to represent hierarchical data. The concept is very simple. The tree contains a root node. Starting from the root node, any node can contain many child nodes (hence the term "tree"). It gives the appearance of a tree branching out from a single root node.

A node in the TreeView is represented by a TreeNode object. Tree node objects contain a Text property that represents the visible text of the item in the tree. TreeNodes can also contain an image index into the tree's ImageList object. A TreeNode has an image index (ImageIndex) that represents the image of the node displayed in the tree. It also has another image index (SelectedImageIndex) that represents the image of the node that represents how the node should appear in the tree when it is selected.

The TreeView control also has several events defined for it that can be handled. For example, events are generated before and after a node is expanded or collapsed, before and after a node is selected, and before and after a node is edited. You can respond to these events depending on how complicated your TreeView control is in your application.

The following example shows how to create a TreeView and respond to the selection of the nodes in the tree:

```
Imports System.Windows.Forms

Public Class Form1
    Inherits System.Windows.Forms.Form

    Private Sub New()
        m_treeView = ConstructTreeView()
        m_treeView.Dock = DockStyle.Fill
        Me.Controls.Add(m_treeView)
    End Sub

    Private WithEvents m_treeView As TreeView

    Shared Sub main()
        Application.Run(New Form1())
    End Sub

    Private Function ConstructTreeView() As TreeView
        Dim tree As TreeView = New TreeView()
        Dim book As TreeNode
```

```
Dim part As TreeNode
Dim chapter As TreeNode

tree.ImageList = New ImageList()
tree.ImageList.Images.Add(New Icon("book.ico"))
tree.ImageList.Images.Add(New Icon("part.ico"))
tree.ImageList.Images.Add(New Icon("chapter.ico"))

book = New TreeNode()
book.Text = "Book"
book.ImageIndex = 0
book.SelectedImageIndex = 0
tree.Nodes.Add(book)

part = New TreeNode()
part.Text = "Part I"
part.ImageIndex = 1
part.SelectedImageIndex = 1
book.Nodes.Add(part)

chapter = New TreeNode()
chapter.Text = "Chapter 1"
chapter.ImageIndex = 2
chapter.SelectedImageIndex = 2
part.Nodes.Add(chapter)

chapter = New TreeNode()
chapter.Text = "Chapter 2"
chapter.ImageIndex = 2
chapter.SelectedImageIndex = 2
part.Nodes.Add(chapter)

chapter = New TreeNode()
chapter.Text = "Chapter 3"
chapter.ImageIndex = 2
chapter.SelectedImageIndex = 2
part.Nodes.Add(chapter)

part = New TreeNode()
part.Text = "Part II"
part.ImageIndex = 1
part.SelectedImageIndex = 1
book.Nodes.Add(part)

chapter = New TreeNode()
chapter.Text = "Chapter 4"
```

```
        chapter.ImageIndex = 2
        chapter.SelectedImageIndex = 2
        part.Nodes.Add(chapter)

        chapter = New TreeNode()
        chapter.Text = "Chapter 5"
        chapter.ImageIndex = 2
        chapter.SelectedImageIndex = 2
        part.Nodes.Add(chapter)

        chapter = New TreeNode()
        chapter.Text = "Chapter 6"
        chapter.ImageIndex = 2
        chapter.SelectedImageIndex = 2
        part.Nodes.Add(chapter)

        part = New TreeNode()
        part.Text = "Part III"
        part.ImageIndex = 1
        part.SelectedImageIndex = 1
        book.Nodes.Add(part)

        chapter = New TreeNode()
        chapter.Text = "Chapter 7"
        chapter.ImageIndex = 2
        chapter.SelectedImageIndex = 2
        part.Nodes.Add(chapter)

        chapter = New TreeNode()
        chapter.Text = "Chapter 8"
        chapter.ImageIndex = 2
        chapter.SelectedImageIndex = 2
        part.Nodes.Add(chapter)

        chapter = New TreeNode()
        chapter.Text = "Chapter 9"
        chapter.ImageIndex = 2
        chapter.SelectedImageIndex = 2
        part.Nodes.Add(chapter)

        tree.ExpandAll()

        Return tree
    End Function
```

```
        Private Sub NodeSelected(ByVal sender As System.Object, _
                         ByVal e As TreeViewEventArgs) _
                         Handles m_treeView.AfterSelect
           MsgBox(m_treeView.SelectedNode.Text + " is selected!", _
                 MsgBoxStyle.OKOnly, _
                 "")
        End Sub
```

```
End Class
```

This code requires the book.ico, chapter.ico, and part.ico to exist in the project's bin folder in order to run. Feel free to substitute icons if you want to try it out on your computer.

The ConstructTreeNode method creates an example tree. The first thing it does is it creates an ImageList object and adds three icons that are going to be used by the nodes in the tree. Next, it creates the root node in the tree. Following that, the rest of the tree nodes are created. All of the nodes have the appropriate images set. The last line in the ConstructTreeNode method before returning expands the entire tree.

There is also a NodeSelected event handler that responds to the AfterSelect event on the TreeView object. After every node is selected, the event handler is called, and a message box is displayed showing the text of the node that was selected. In a real application, this event handler would perform some action based on the node just selected. Figure 23.12 shows the TreeView control after the form is displayed.

Figure 23.12: TreeView control.

There are lots more controls provided with the .NET Framework—too numerous to mention here. You should try working with the remaining controls in the ToolBox so that you can learn to leverage them in your applications. Our intention here was to present some of the most common controls you are probably going to use in building your own Windows applications.

Creating Your Own Controls

The goal in creating your own custom control is to combine the necessary graphics and/or control elements to create a unique user interface element that performs a specific purpose. It is totally up to you how you want your control to look and function. To walk you through creating a custom control, we are going to create a control whose purpose is to edit a person's address. We could choose to just add a bunch of TextBoxes to a form in an application; however, the benefit of creating a control is that it can be used again and again in many different projects.

To create a custom control, you first need to create a new project. However, the type of project you need to create is a "Windows Control Library" project. You need to choose File, New, Project or press Ctrl+N to open the New Project dialog box. In the Name text box, enter the name of your project. The project name used in the example that is about to be presented is *CtlAddressLib*.

After you create this type of project, your Visual Studio .NET environment looks something like that in Figure 23.13.

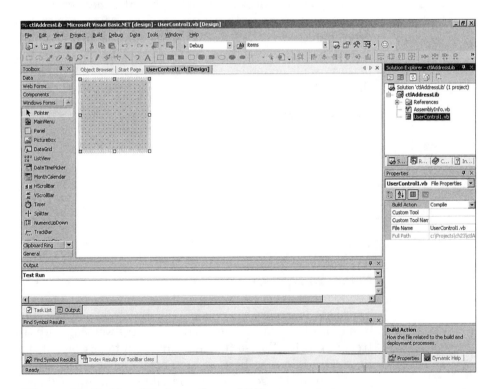

Figure 23.13: *New Windows Control Library project.*

You are presented with the same Designer you have seen already; however the Designer is not showing a form. It shows an area that looks like the interior of a form. It is actually just a Graphics display area which your control can draw onto. A control has a display area just like a form without the title bar and border.

Next, you should change the name of the user control class, which defaults to UserControl1, to a more meaningful name. You can change the name of a control by selecting the control then changing the Name property in the Properties window. In our example, the name is changed to CtlAddress by changing the name in the source code. Right-click the control in the Designer window and then choose the View Code menu item. The control class name should be near the top of the source file.

Now you should add any necessary controls to your control's display. Figure 23.14 shows the address control in the Designer Window after a GroupBox, several Labels, and several TextBoxes have been added.

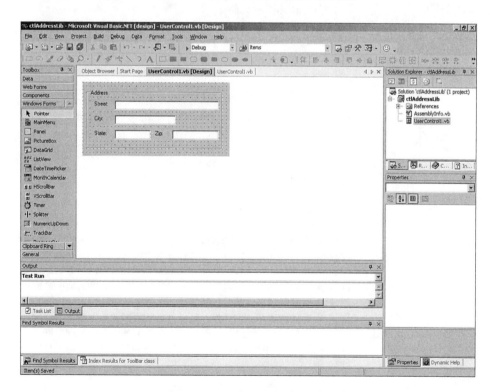

Figure 23.14: Address Control Designer window.

When the controls are in place, add several properties to the control so that code using the control can set and get property values. This allows the control to expose a City property, for example. When the City property is set on the control, the TextBox that contains the City text is populated. When the City property is retrieved from the control, the text value in the city TextBox is returned.

Here is the entire code for the address control:

```
Public Class CtlAddress
    Inherits System.Windows.Forms.UserControl

#Region " Windows Form Designer generated code "

    Public Sub New()
        MyBase.New()

        'This call is required by the Windows Form Designer.
        InitializeComponent()

        'Add any initialization after the InitializeComponent() call

    End Sub

    'UserControl1 overrides dispose to clean up the component list.
    Protected Overloads Overrides Sub Dispose(ByVal disposing As Boolean)
        If disposing Then
            If Not (components Is Nothing) Then
                components.Dispose()
            End If
        End If
        MyBase.Dispose(disposing)
    End Sub
    Friend WithEvents GroupBox1 As System.Windows.Forms.GroupBox
    Friend WithEvents Label1 As System.Windows.Forms.Label
    Friend WithEvents Label2 As System.Windows.Forms.Label
    Friend WithEvents Label3 As System.Windows.Forms.Label
    Friend WithEvents Label4 As System.Windows.Forms.Label
    Friend WithEvents m_street As System.Windows.Forms.TextBox
    Friend WithEvents m_city As System.Windows.Forms.TextBox
    Friend WithEvents m_state As System.Windows.Forms.TextBox
    Friend WithEvents m_zip As System.Windows.Forms.TextBox

    'Required by the Windows Form Designer
    Private components As System.ComponentModel.Container
```

```
'NOTE: The following procedure is required by the Windows Form Designer
'It can be modified using the Windows Form Designer.
'Do not modify it using the code editor.
<System.Diagnostics.DebuggerStepThrough()> Private Sub InitializeComponent()
    Me.GroupBox1 = New System.Windows.Forms.GroupBox()
    Me.Label1 = New System.Windows.Forms.Label()
    Me.Label2 = New System.Windows.Forms.Label()
    Me.Label3 = New System.Windows.Forms.Label()
    Me.Label4 = New System.Windows.Forms.Label()
    Me.m_street = New System.Windows.Forms.TextBox()
    Me.m_city = New System.Windows.Forms.TextBox()
    Me.m_state = New System.Windows.Forms.TextBox()
    Me.m_zip = New System.Windows.Forms.TextBox()
    Me.GroupBox1.SuspendLayout()
    Me.SuspendLayout()
    '
    'GroupBox1
    '
    Me.GroupBox1.Controls.AddRange(New System.Windows.Forms.Control() {Me.m_zip, _
                                                  Me.m_state, _
                                                  Me.m_city, _
                                                  Me.m_street, _
                                                  Me.Label4, _
                                                  Me.Label3, _
                                                  Me.Label2, _
                                                  Me.Label1})

    Me.GroupBox1.Location = New System.Drawing.Point(8, 16)
    Me.GroupBox1.Name = "GroupBox1"
    Me.GroupBox1.Size = New System.Drawing.Size(304, 128)
    Me.GroupBox1.TabIndex = 0
    Me.GroupBox1.TabStop = False
    Me.GroupBox1.Text = "Address"
    '
    'Label1
    '
    Me.Label1.Location = New System.Drawing.Point(16, 24)
    Me.Label1.Name = "Label1"
    Me.Label1.Size = New System.Drawing.Size(72, 20)
    Me.Label1.TabIndex = 0
    Me.Label1.Text = "Street:"
    '
    'Label2
    '
    Me.Label2.Location = New System.Drawing.Point(16, 56)
    Me.Label2.Name = "Label2"
```

```
        Me.Label2.Size = New System.Drawing.Size(56, 20)
        Me.Label2.TabIndex = 1
        Me.Label2.Text = "City:"
        '
        'Label3
        '
        Me.Label3.Location = New System.Drawing.Point(16, 88)
        Me.Label3.Name = "Label3"
        Me.Label3.Size = New System.Drawing.Size(72, 20)
        Me.Label3.TabIndex = 2
        Me.Label3.Text = "State:"
        '
        'Label4
        '
        Me.Label4.Location = New System.Drawing.Point(152, 88)
        Me.Label4.Name = "Label4"
        Me.Label4.Size = New System.Drawing.Size(80, 20)
        Me.Label4.TabIndex = 3
        Me.Label4.Text = "Zip:"
        '
        'm_street
        '
        Me.m_street.Location = New System.Drawing.Point(64, 24)
        Me.m_street.Name = "m_street"
        Me.m_street.Size = New System.Drawing.Size(232, 20)
        Me.m_street.TabIndex = 4
        Me.m_street.Text = ""
        '
        'm_city
        '
        Me.m_city.Location = New System.Drawing.Point(64, 56)
        Me.m_city.Name = "m_city"
        Me.m_city.Size = New System.Drawing.Size(136, 20)
        Me.m_city.TabIndex = 5
        Me.m_city.Text = ""
        '
        'm_state
        '
        Me.m_state.Location = New System.Drawing.Point(64, 88)
        Me.m_state.Name = "m_state"
        Me.m_state.Size = New System.Drawing.Size(80, 20)
        Me.m_state.TabIndex = 6
        Me.m_state.Text = ""
        '
```

```
'm_zip
'

Me.m_zip.Location = New System.Drawing.Point(192, 88)
Me.m_zip.Name = "m_zip"
Me.m_zip.Size = New System.Drawing.Size(104, 20)
Me.m_zip.TabIndex = 7
Me.m_zip.Text = ""
'

'UserControl1
'

Me.Controls.AddRange(New System.Windows.Forms.Control() {Me.GroupBox1})
Me.Name = "UserControl1"
Me.Size = New System.Drawing.Size(328, 160)
Me.GroupBox1.ResumeLayout(False)
Me.ResumeLayout(False)


End Sub


#End Region


    Public Property Street() As String
        Get
            Return m_street.Text
        End Get
        Set(ByVal Value As String)
            m_street.Text = Value
        End Set
    End Property


    Public Property City() As String
        Get
            Return m_city.Text
        End Get
        Set(ByVal Value As String)
            m_city.Text = Value
        End Set
    End Property


    Public Property State() As String
        Get
            Return m_state.Text
        End Get
        Set(ByVal Value As String)
            m_state.Text = Value
```

```
        End Set
    End Property

    Public Property Zip() As String
        Get
            Return m_zip.Text
        End Get
        Set(ByVal Value As String)
            m_zip.Text = Value
        End Set
    End Property

End Class
```

The name of the control is `CtlAddress`. In the `InitializeComponent` method, all the necessary child controls of this address control are created and added to the display. Also, properties have been defined in the address control so that code using this control can set and get the address control data simply by using the properties.

At this point, how do you run and test the control to verify it is working properly? First build the control project to eliminate compile errors. Then, you create a Windows Application Project and add it to the current solution by choosing "File, Add Project, New Project." Once the new project is added to the current solution you need to set a reference to the address control project so that the new project can use it. In the Solution Explorer you would right-click the References node in the newly added project and then choose the "Add Reference" menu item.

At this point, the Add Reference dialog box appears, as shown in Figure 23.15. You click the Project tab, highlight the desired project by clicking on it, and then click the Select button. Press the OK button to accept the reference.

The new Windows application project now has a reference to the `address` control. The `CtlAddress` control is now available in the ToolBox for use in adding it to a form. After you drag it from the ToolBox onto a form, you can set the properties appropriately and run the application. When the form appears, you can see and test your control. Make sure the application project is set up to be the startup project. You can tell which project is the startup project by finding the project in the Solution Explorer that is displayed in a bold font. This indicates the startup project.

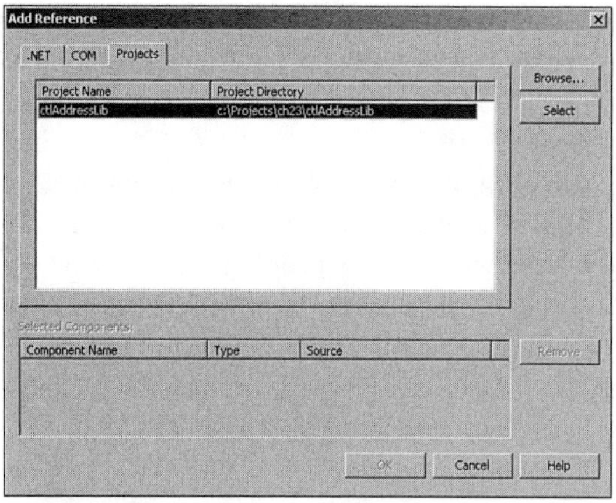

Figure 23.15: Add Reference dialog.

Mouse Events

Another common user interface programming need is the capability to intercept and respond to mouse events. This is very common when creating your own custom controls. When a user moves the cursor to a control and clicks it with the mouse there are actually six different mouse events that are generated and can be handled. The exact mouse events and the order in which they occur is as follows:

1. MouseEnter

2. MouseMove

3. MouseHover

4. MouseDown

5. MouseUp

6. MouseLeave

In the common case, you may not have a need to respond to more than one of these events. However, if you plan on developing your own custom control you may want the control to respond to each of these events to provide a unique capability. For example, a splitter bar that is commonly used between two windows handles most of these events. When the cursor enters the splitter bar control (MouseEnter) the cursor changes to a different icon signifying the splitter can be moved. When you press the mouse down (MouseDown), a visible line is created showing where the splitter bar will end up as you move the mouse (MouseMove). When you release the mouse button (MouseUp), the splitter bar moves to the new location and the windows between the splitter bar are resized. When the mouse moves away from the splitter bar (MouseLeave) the cursor is changed back to its previous state.

Key Events

Similar to mouse events, key events are also frequently handled to provide support for special key commands when a control has focus. The way in which a control knows what key is pressed when it has input focus is through the handling of key events. When a key is pressed there are three events that are generated. The following list shows the events in the exact order they occur:

1. KeyDown

2. KeyPress

3. KeyUp

When dealing with custom controls, instead of using event handlers the preferred way to handle events is by overriding certain methods. Overridable methods that handle events start with the prefix "On". For example, if a custom control wants to handle the Click event the custom control can override the OnClick method. There are several overrideable methods for dealing with control events. If you need to deal with mouse events or key events, keep in mind the sequence of events just described so that you can provide the correct functionality by responding to the appropriate event.

What's Next

In this chapter you learned all about controls; how to work with them, how to use them with specific controls, and also how to create custom controls to meet your needs. We encourage you to try out additional controls provided with the .NET Framework so that you can be acquainted with the entire set of controls you can use. This chapter provided information in regards to using any control so you should have a great head start.

In the next chapter, we cover menus in Visual Basic .NET. You will learn how to create menus and respond to menu clicks. You will also learn how to create context (or pop-up) menus. Menus are an extremely important aspect of any Windows application; therefore, the material is very important to your learning about developing a user interface in .NET.

NOTE

The answers to "Reviewing It," "Checking It," and "Applying It" are available on our Web site.

REVIEW

Reviewing It

This section presents a review of the key concepts in this chapter. These questions are intended to gauge your absorption of the relevant material.

1. What are controls?

2. What is the difference between a Label and TextBox?

3. What is a custom control?

4. What is the difference between a CheckBox control and a RadioButton control?

5. What control would you used to display hierarchical data?

6. What classes are necessary to use in order to display a form with tabbed panes?

CHECK

Checking It

Select the correct answer to the following questions.

Multiple Choice

1. In order for a control to support tabbing, what property(s) must be set on the control?

    a. TabOrder.

    b. TabIndex.

    c. TabOrder and TabIndex.

    d. None, controls do not support tabbing.

2. RadioButtons:

    a. Support exclusive options.

    b. Look like knobs.

    c. Work like regular buttons.

    d. All of the above.

3. Which control allows grouping of child controls?

    a. RadioButton.

    b. CheckBox.

    c. `GroupBox`.

    d. `ListBox`.

4. Buttons can display an image:

    a. By setting the `Image` property.

    b. By setting the `ImageList` and `ImageIndex` properties.

    c. Both a and b.

    d. None of the above.

5. What is the first event sent to a control prior to getting input focus?

    a. `GetFocus`.

    b. `Enter`.

    c. `PreFocus`.

    d. None of the above.

6. What is the last event sent to a control prior to losing input focus?

    a. `LostFocus`.

    b. `EndFocus`.

    c. `Leaving`.

    d. None of the above.

True or False

Select one of the two possible answers and then verify on our Web site that you picked the correct one.

1. Controls support tabbing (move from one control to the next using the Tab key).

   True/False

2. Controls support drag and drop.

   True/False

3. You must use the Designer Window to add controls to a form.

   True/False

4. TextBoxes support line wrapping.

   True/False

5. Labels, in .NET, support links. This allows you to display a link on a form so that a user can click it to display a Web page based on the link.

   True/False

6. LinkLabels, in .NET, support links. This allows you to display a link on a form so that a user can click it to display a Web page based on the link.

   True/False

7. MouseEnter is the first event sent to a control when the mouse cursor enters the area of the control.

   True/False

8. MouseExit is the last event sent to a control when the mouse cursor exits the area of the control.

   True/False

APPLY

Applying It

Try to complete the following exercises by yourself.

Independent Exercise 1

Write an example using the MonthCalendar control and respond to the click event so that when the user clicks on your birthday a message is displayed.

Independent Exercise 2

Write an example using the ProgressBar control.

24

Menus

This chapter explains how to use menus to enable the users of your software to perform certain tasks. These tasks are exposed by you, as a developer, through menus so that a user can quickly and consistently interact with your software application.

In the Microsoft .NET Framework, there are three classes that are essential to providing menus in your software. These are MainMenu, MenuItem, and ContextMenu. This chapter explains these classes through examples so that you will understand how they are used.

The following Menu topics are covered in this chapter:

- Menus and menu items
- Menu item event handlers
- Menu separators and breaks
- Enabling and disabling menu items
- Mnemonics and shortcuts
- Checked menu items
- Radio button menu items
- Nested menus
- Dynamic menus
- Context menus
- Owner drawn menu items

Introduction

If you have used any standard application on Microsoft Windows you should already have a good understanding of what a menu is. If not, Figure 24.1 shows a very simple example menu containing three menu options.

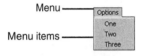

Figure 24.1: Sample menu.

When you start designing how you are going to build your Windows application, you need to spend some quality time thinking about a good menu structure (assuming your application is going to have a menu).

Here are a couple of recommendations for how to go about designing a menu structure for any application. If you are building a Single Document Interface application (one main window), try listing all the features that your application is going to provide. Then, group similar features together and think of a name for each group. Each group would then become its own menu. Each of the features become menu items within the respective menu.

To illustrate this, most applications have features such as "create a new file," "save a file," and "open an existing file." Each of these features can be grouped together because they all share the same common theme (a file). The resulting menu for these features is shown in Figure 24.2.

Figure 24.2: File menu.

If you are building a Multiple Document Interface application, the idea remains the same but the task is a little more complex. You still want to list all of the features your application is going to provide, but you should separate the features by the types of windows in your application. Then, for each type of window create a group of menus the same way as described for Single Document Interface applications. When a window in an MDI application becomes active (by clicking on it), the group of menus for that window is displayed.

Each type of window is presumably going to provide a specific user interface to present information to the user. As such, the different types of windows in your application may also share some of the same features. So instead of having each window display a unique set of menus as the window becomes active, another approach is to create a single menu structure and enable or disable menu items appropriately depending on the window that becomes active.

These recommendations are just guidelines to get you started in building your own menus. The goal of this chapter is to show you how to create menus, so let's get started.

Menus and Menu Items

There are three main classes that you will use to create menus in Microsoft .NET. These classes are `MainMenu`, `MenuItem`, and `ContextMenu`. These classes are part of the `System.Windows.Forms` assembly of the Microsoft .NET Framework.

Let's walk through an example of adding a menu to a form using the Form Designer window. This is the most common way to add a menu to a form, as this is the easiest way to do this. You start by dragging a `MainMenu` control from the toolbox onto the form. Once you drop it on the form, a menu appears, and a `MainMenu1` control appears at the bottom of the Form Designer window. This is shown in Figure 24.3.

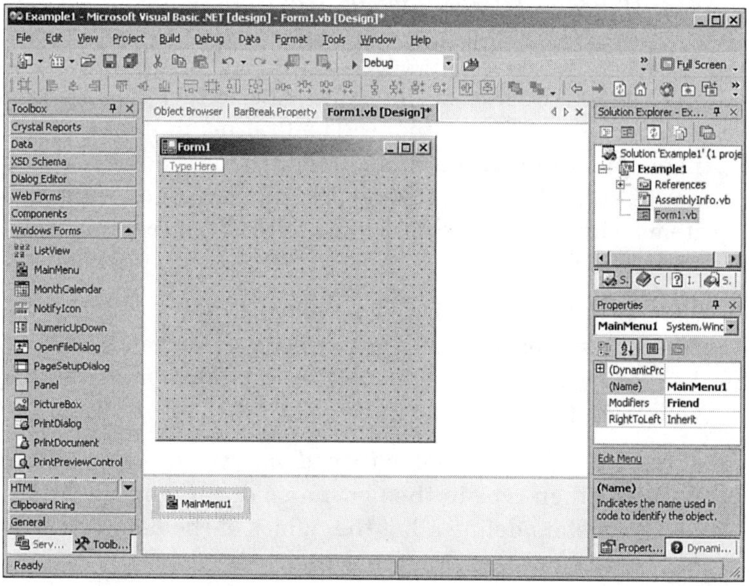

Figure 24.3: Adding a menu to a form.

To define the menu structure, you simply type in the visible text for each menu item directly in the menu where it says "Type Here." After you type in the text for a menu item, new menu items appear to the right and below containing "Type Here" so that you can define more menu items. This is shown in Figure 24.4 after the first menu item is defined.

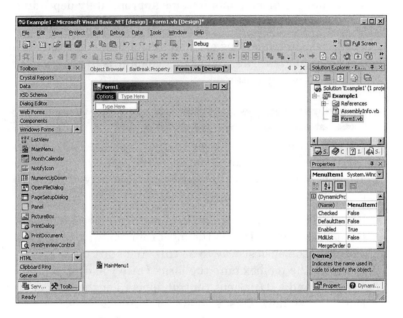

Figure 24.4: *Defining a menu item.*

Each menu item that is created as you create the menu has an automatically generated name. The name is MenuItem, plus a unique number that is incremented for the menu. The first menu item created then has the name MenuItem1, the second MenuItem2, and so on. This may or may not be suitable for you. Some programmers may want to name the menu items with more suitable names so that the resulting code is easier to understand.

The Form Designer window accommodates this by allowing you to also edit the names of each menu item directly in the menu. You can turn on the Edit Names mode by right-clicking the menu and selecting Edit Names. Once you do this, the menu appears as shown in Figure 24.5.

If the Edit Names mode is turned on, you can click the name of a menu item and then type in the new name directly on the form. This is an easy way to custom define all of the names of the menu items visually without having to do this within the actual code.

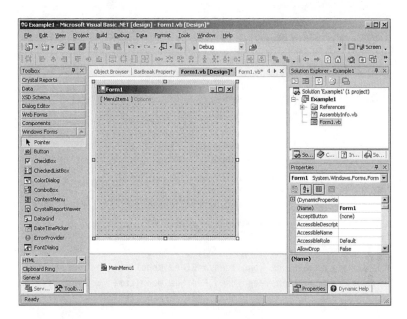

Figure 24.5: *Turning on Edit Names mode.*

So, how do you write code that gets executed as a result of a menu item being clicked? Easy. Just double-click the menu item you want to respond to. This brings up the code window and places the cursor in an event handler for the menu item you just clicked. All you have to do is type in your custom code as you see fit. When the program runs, the appropriate code is executed as each menu item is selected by the user.

Everything mentioned so far has shown how to define menus using the Form Designer. Although this is the most common approach to defining menus, this example does not really demonstrate the power you have in creating menus for your own application. In order to shed some light on this, the remainder of the chapter shows examples where the menus are created in simple code examples. This allows you to actually see what is happening behind the scenes when you are using the Form Designer to define a menu.

Create a Windows application project and replace the automatically generated form code with the following example code:

EXAMPLE

```
Imports System.Windows.Forms

Public Class Form1
    Inherits System.Windows.Forms.Form

    Private m_menu As MainMenu
```

```
Private Sub New()
    MyBase.New()
    CreateMenus()
End Sub

Protected Sub CreateMenus()
    Dim mnuOptions As MenuItem

    ' create main menu
    m_menu = New MainMenu()

    ' create options menu item
    mnuOptions = New MenuItem("Options")
    m_menu.MenuItems.Add(mnuOptions)

    ' add menu items to options menu
    mnuOptions.MenuItems.Add(New MenuItem("One"))
    mnuOptions.MenuItems.Add(New MenuItem("Two"))
    mnuOptions.MenuItems.Add(New MenuItem("Three"))

    ' set the forms main menu
    Me.Menu = m_menu

End Sub


End Class
```

This example was used to produce the sample menu shown in Figure 24.1. The MyBase keyword is used to access methods defined in the base class of the current form. Also, the keyword Me is used to refer to the current object or form in this case.

To construct the menu, an instance of MainMenu is created within the CreateMenus method of the form. The MainMenu object is the root container of all the menu items for the menu. Next, a new MenuItem object is created with the name Options and added to the MainMenu object's collection of menu items.

Three new MenuItem objects are created and added to the Options menu item's collection of menu items. This means that the three new menu items are children, or submenu items, of the Options menu item. When the Options menu is clicked, the submenu will appear.

Lastly, the form's menu property is set to the menu you just constructed. When the form is displayed, the menu is displayed because the form automatically displays the menu referenced by its menu property.

Let's clarify one point. When the form is displayed and the menu is visible, most people would commonly refer to the menu as the Options menu. Although this terminology is useful, distinguish this from what is actually happening in the code. All of the visible elements of a menu are actually instances of `MenuItem`. In our case, the Options menu is actually a menu item with three child menu items. The Options menu item is added to a `MainMenu` object. The `MainMenu` object has no visible component to it.

The `MenuItem` class has several constructors that can be used depending on your needs. In the previous code example, each of the menu items created had a single text value passed as part of the `MenuItem` constructor. The text value represented the text property of the respective menu item and is the label you see on the menu.

The code shows how a menu is constructed, but the menu does not do anything. Ideally, you want to build menus where you can write the code that gets executed when the user clicks any one of the menu items you define. In Microsoft .NET, this is accomplished through the use of event handlers.

Menu Items and Event Handlers

Menu items use `EventHandler` delegates for associating the code that is executed in response to events raised by menu items (just like buttons). One of several constructors provided by the `MenuItem` class allows you to pass in an `EventHandler` delegate that is used to handle the `Click` event generated by the `MenuItem`. A `Click` event can be generated on a menu item by pressing the Enter key on the keyboard, pressing the shortcut key associated with the menu item, or clicking the menu item using the mouse.

NOTE

MenuItems that contain MenuItems do not generate a Click event. Only MenuItems that do not contain child MenuItems can generate Click events.

In the following example, the `Options` menu item will never generate a `Click` event because it contains child `MenuItems`. Let's take a look at the following code to see how this works. Create a Windows application project and replace the generated form code with the following:

```
Imports System.Windows.Forms

Public Class Form1
    Inherits System.Windows.Forms.Form

    Private m_menu As MainMenu
```

```vb
Private Sub New()
    MyBase.New()
    CreateMenus()
End Sub

Protected Sub CreateMenus()
    Dim mnuOptions As MenuItem
    Dim mnuItem As MenuItem

    ' create main menu
    m_menu = New MainMenu()

    ' create options menu
    mnuOptions = New MenuItem("Options")
    m_menu.MenuItems.Add(mnuOptions)

    ' add menu items to options menu
    mnuItem = New MenuItem("One", _
                        New System.EventHandler(AddressOf OptionOneClick))
    mnuOptions.MenuItems.Add(mnuItem)

    mnuItem = New MenuItem("Two", _
                        New System.EventHandler(AddressOf OptionTwoClick))
    mnuOptions.MenuItems.Add(mnuItem)

    mnuItem = New MenuItem("Three", _
                        New System.EventHandler(AddressOf
OptionThreeClick))
    mnuOptions.MenuItems.Add(mnuItem)

    ' set the forms main menu
    Me.Menu = m_menu

End Sub

Protected Sub OptionOneClick(ByVal sender As Object, _
                            ByVal e As System.EventArgs)
    Dim msgBox As MessageBox
    msgBox.Show("Option One Clicked!")
End Sub

Protected Sub OptionTwoClick(ByVal sender As Object, _
                            ByVal e As System.EventArgs)
    Dim msgBox As MessageBox
    msgBox.Show("Option Two Clicked!")
End Sub
```

```
Protected Sub OptionThreeClick(ByVal sender As Object, _
                               ByVal e As System.EventArgs)
    Dim msgBox As MessageBox
    msgBox.Show("Option Three Clicked!")
End Sub
```

```
End Class
```

Figure 24.6 shows the menu based on the previous example and Figure 24.7 shows the result of clicking the first menu item.

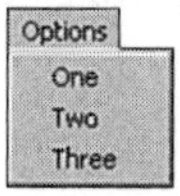

Figure 24.6: Options menu.

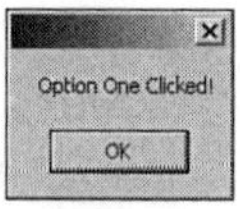

Figure 24.7: MessageBox *displayed as a result of clicking* MenuItem One.

As you can see, handling the Click event is set up by passing an EventHandler delegate to the MenuItem when the MenuItem is created. The EventHandler delegate, in this example, references a method in the Form1 class.

The MenuItem containing the text "One" is given an EventHandler that refers to the OptionOneClick method. Similarly, the MenuItem containing the text "Two" is given an EventHandler that refers to the OptionTwoClick method and so on for MenuItem "Three."

When the first MenuItem (the one containing the text "One") is clicked, a MessageBox is displayed informing the user that option one was clicked. The message box in Figure 24.7 is shown as an example, and you can add whatever code you deem necessary to respond to your MenuItems.

The System.EventHandler is defined in Microsoft .NET as:

```
Public Delegate Sub EventHandler( ByVal sender As Object, ByVal e As EventArgs )
```

If you want to write a method or procedure to handle an event, this definition of the EventHandler delegate forces the method or procedure to have this signature (that is, the method or procedure must take two arguments as defined by the EventHandler delegate). If you do not declare the signature of the event handler correctly, the code will not compile.

In the previous example, it may not be apparent what these arguments are used for. And, in fact, the arguments are not even used in the previous example. However, you may come across a situation where you need to have several MenuItems all using the same method in their event handlers. This allows you to have several MenuItems calling the same method when the user clicks them. This is where the parameters are useful and necessary.

The next example shows how to set up several MenuItems to use the same method when those MenuItems are clicked. Create a new Windows application project and replace the automatically generated form code with the following code:

```
Imports System.Windows.Forms

Public Class Form1
    Inherits System.Windows.Forms.Form

    Private m_menu As MainMenu
    Private m_mnuHearts As MenuItem
    Private m_mnuClubs As MenuItem
    Private m_mnuSpades As MenuItem
    Private m_mnuDiamonds As MenuItem

    Private Sub New()
        MyBase.New()
        CreateMenus()
    End Sub

    Protected Sub CreateMenus()
        Dim mnuSuits As MenuItem
        Dim mnuItem As MenuItem

        ' create main menu
        m_menu = New MainMenu()

        ' create suits menu
        mnuSuits = New MenuItem("Suits")
        m_menu.MenuItems.Add(mnuSuits)

        ' add menu items to options menu
        m_mnuHearts = New MenuItem("Hearts", _
                        New System.EventHandler(AddressOf SuitClick))
        mnuSuits.MenuItems.Add(m_mnuHearts)
```

```
                m_mnuClubs = New MenuItem("Clubs", _
                                New System.EventHandler(AddressOf SuitClick))
                mnuSuits.MenuItems.Add(m_mnuClubs)

                m_mnuSpades = New MenuItem("Spades", _
                                New System.EventHandler(AddressOf SuitClick))
                mnuSuits.MenuItems.Add(m_mnuSpades)

                m_mnuDiamonds = New MenuItem("Diamonds", _
                                New System.EventHandler(AddressOf SuitClick))
                mnuSuits.MenuItems.Add(m_mnuDiamonds)

                ' set the forms main menu
                Me.Menu = m_menu

        End Sub

        Protected Sub SuitClick(ByVal sender As Object, ByVal e As System.EventArgs)
                Dim msgBox As MessageBox
                If sender Is m_mnuHearts Then
                        msgBox.Show("Hearts clicked!")
                ElseIf sender Is m_mnuClubs Then
                        msgBox.Show("Clubs clicked!")
                ElseIf sender Is m_mnuSpades Then
                        msgBox.Show("Spades clicked!")
                ElseIf sender Is m_mnuDiamonds Then
                        msgBox.Show("Diamonds clicked!")
                End If
        End Sub

End Class
```

Figure 24.8 shows the menu created in the previous example. If you click on the first item in the menu, a message is displayed to the user, as shown in Figure 24.9.

Figure 24.8: *Suits menu.*

Figure 24.9: MessageBox *displayed as a result of clicking the Hearts menu item.*

Notice that each EventHandler created for the MenuItems is a delegate to the same method. This means that clicking on any of Hearts, Clubs, Spades, or Diamonds menu items results in executing the SuitClick method.

So, how do you know which MenuItem initiated the event? The answer lies in the parameter values passed to the SuitClick method. The first parameter is the sender or initiator of the event. To find out which MenuItem sent the event, you only need to compare the value of the *sender* parameter to the values of the known menu items. The second parameter is used to pass additional data along with the event. In our example, there is no additional event data; therefore, this parameter is not used.

The key to finding out which menu item generated the event is that when you construct the menu you need to store a reference to the MenuItems somewhere accessible. In this case, the simplest place to put the references is within the Form class itself. After the menu is constructed, the fields in the form that refer to the MenuItems can be used for comparison in the SuitClick method.

But what if you don't want to store references to the MenuItems? Is there another way? The answer is yes. Instead of keeping references to the MenuItems for use in the comparison, you could just test the text of the MenuItem that generated the event. For this to be reliable however, you must store the text used for the MenuItems in a centralized location so that you can use the same variable for specifying the MenuItem text and for use during the test.

Create a new Windows application project and replace the automatically generated code with the following:

```
Imports System.Windows.Forms

Public Class Form1
    Inherits System.Windows.Forms.Form

    Private m_menu As MainMenu
    Private Shared m_hearts As String = "Hearts"
    Private Shared m_clubs As String = "Clubs"
    Private Shared m_spades As String = "Spades"
    Private Shared m_diamonds As String = "Diamonds"
```

```
Private Sub New()
    MyBase.New()
    CreateMenus()
End Sub

Protected Sub CreateMenus()
    Dim mnuSuits As MenuItem
    Dim mnuItem As MenuItem

    ' create main menu
    m_menu = New MainMenu()

    ' create suits menu
    mnuSuits = New MenuItem("Suits")
    m_menu.MenuItems.Add(mnuSuits)

    ' add menu items to options menu
    mnuItem = New MenuItem(m_hearts, _
                New System.EventHandler(AddressOf SuitClick))
    mnuSuits.MenuItems.Add(mnuItem)

    mnuItem = New MenuItem(m_clubs, _
                New System.EventHandler(AddressOf SuitClick))
    mnuSuits.MenuItems.Add(mnuItem)

    mnuItem = New MenuItem(m_spades, _
                New System.EventHandler(AddressOf SuitClick))
    mnuSuits.MenuItems.Add(mnuItem)

    mnuItem = New MenuItem(m_diamonds, _
                New System.EventHandler(AddressOf SuitClick))
    mnuSuits.MenuItems.Add(mnuItem)

    ' set the forms main menu
    Me.Menu = m_menu

End Sub

Protected Sub SuitClick(ByVal sender As Object, ByVal e As System.EventArgs)
    Dim msgBox As MessageBox
    Dim menuItem As MenuItem = sender

    If menuItem.Text = m_hearts Then
        msgBox.Show("Hearts clicked!")
    ElseIf menuItem.Text = m_clubs Then
        msgBox.Show("Clubs clicked!")
```

```
        ElseIf menuItem.Text = m_spades Then
            msgBox.Show("Spades clicked!")
        ElseIf menuItem.Text = m_diamonds Then
            msgBox.Show("Diamonds clicked!")
        End If
    End Sub
```

```
End Class
```

In this example, the text used for the menu items is stored as part of the Form1 class. It is declared as Shared so that all instances of the Form1 class can use the same string values. This saves memory instead of having the strings duplicated for each object instance of Form1. Then in the event handler (SuitClick), the text of the MenuItem object can be compared against the known string values about which the event handler cares.

Before the comparison can be done however, the object passed to the event handler needs to be cast into a MenuItem. Because this event handler is only used for MenuItems this is a safe operation, and you don't need to worry about the sender object not being a MenuItem.

We will discuss more about MenuItem events at the end of this chapter as we show how to extend MenuItems to do fancier things such as displaying icons as part of the menu item.

Menu Separators and Breaks

As you design the menus in your applications, you may come across a need to group menu items within a menu. For example, after you have defined all of your menus, a menu may contain several menu items. Some of those menu items you may want to group together. So far, our examples just listed the MenuItems within a menu so it is not clear yet how to do this.

Figures 24.10 through 24.12 show examples of the available ways you can separate your menu items.

Figure 24.10: *Sample usage of menu separators.*

Figure 24.11: *Sample usage of menu breaks.*

Figure 24.12: *Sample usage of menu breaks with bars.*

Regarding a menu separator, the basic idea is to create a `MenuItem` that "is" the separator and have it display a horizontal line instead of text. Also, the separator should not be selectable in the menu.

Menu breaks and menu breaks with bars are implemented by setting properties on the `MenuItem` objects. You do not need to create additional `MenuItems` to get this behavior as you do with separators. Notice that in Figure 24.11, the menu items are displayed horizontally instead of vertically. This is what is meant by a *Break*. Also, a *BarBreak* displays the menu items horizontally with the addition of a vertical bar between the menu items; hence called a *BarBreak*.

The following code example shows how to create the menus displayed in Figures 24.10, 24.11, and 24.12. Create a new Windows application project and replace the automatically generated form code with the following:

```
Imports System.Windows.Forms

Public Class Form1
    Inherits System.Windows.Forms.Form

    Private m_menu As MainMenu

    Private Sub New()
        MyBase.New()
        CreateMenus()
    End Sub

    Protected Sub CreateMenus()
        Dim mnuMenu, mnuItem As MenuItem

        m_menu = New MainMenu()

        ' Example showing separator
        mnuMenu = New MenuItem("Separator")
        m_menu.MenuItems.Add(mnuMenu)
```

```vbnet
        mnuItem = New MenuItem("One")
        mnuMenu.MenuItems.Add(mnuItem)

        mnuItem = New MenuItem("Two")
        mnuMenu.MenuItems.Add(mnuItem)

        mnuItem = New MenuItem("-")
        mnuMenu.MenuItems.Add(mnuItem)

        mnuItem = New MenuItem("Three")
        mnuMenu.MenuItems.Add(mnuItem)

        ' Example showing break
        mnuMenu = New MenuItem("Break")
        m_menu.MenuItems.Add(mnuMenu)

        mnuItem = New MenuItem("One")
        mnuMenu.MenuItems.Add(mnuItem)

        mnuItem = New MenuItem("Two")
        mnuItem.Break = True
        mnuMenu.MenuItems.Add(mnuItem)

        mnuItem = New MenuItem("Three")
        mnuItem.Break = True
        mnuMenu.MenuItems.Add(mnuItem)

        ' Example showing barbreak
        mnuMenu = New MenuItem("BarBreak")
        m_menu.MenuItems.Add(mnuMenu)

        mnuItem = New MenuItem("One")
        mnuMenu.MenuItems.Add(mnuItem)

        mnuItem = New MenuItem("Two")
        mnuItem.BarBreak = True
        mnuMenu.MenuItems.Add(mnuItem)

        mnuItem = New MenuItem("Three")
        mnuItem.BarBreak = True
        mnuMenu.MenuItems.Add(mnuItem)

        ' set form's menu
        Me.Menu = m_menu

    End Sub

End Class
```

In the example, a separator in the Separator menu is accomplished by creating another `MenuItem` object and setting its text property to the hyphen or dash character (`-`). The `MenuItem` object detects this and produces the necessary behavior for the menu separator.

In the Break menu, the menu items are displayed horizontally by setting the `Break` property. By default, all `MenuItems` are displayed vertically one after another. Any `MenuItem` that has the `Break` property set to `True` will be displayed next to the previous `MenuItem`. The menu items Two and Three have their `Break` properties set to `True`, which forces Two to be displayed to the right of One and Three to be displayed to the right of Two.

In the BarBreak menu, instead of setting the `Break` property you would set the `BarBreak` property to `True`. This allows the menu items to be displayed to the right of the previous menu item including a separator. In this menu, the Two and Three menu items are displayed as they are in the Break, and they have a visible separator between them.

Enabling, Disabling, and Visibility

So far, all of the menu items you have seen in the previous examples have been enabled (meaning they can be clicked) and visible (meaning you can see them). Often, menu items have a context in which they can be used. For example, a File-Save menu item in an application would not be appropriate if the application does not currently have a file opened.

To accommodate the situations where you need to provide menu items that have contextual meaning, `MenuItems` can be disabled or invisible. Disabling a `MenuItem` object is done by setting the `Enabled` property to `False`. This causes the `MenuItem` to have a grayed-out appearance and cannot be clicked in the application.

Menu items can also be invisible, if you choose, by setting the `Visible` property to `False`. The following example shows how to disable menu items and to make menu items invisible. Create a new Windows application project and replace the automatically generated form code with the following:

```
Imports System.Windows.Forms

Public Class Form1
    Inherits System.Windows.Forms.Form

    Private m_menu As MainMenu

    Private Sub New()
        MyBase.New()
```

```
        CreateMenus()
    End Sub

    Protected Sub CreateMenus()
        Dim mnuMenu, mnuItem As MenuItem

        m_menu = New MainMenu()

        mnuMenu = New MenuItem("Menu")
        m_menu.MenuItems.Add(mnuMenu)

        ' create normal menu item that is enabled
        mnuItem = New MenuItem("Enabled")
        mnuItem.Enabled = True
        mnuMenu.MenuItems.Add(mnuItem)

        ' create disabled menu item (grayed out)
        mnuItem = New MenuItem("Disabled")
        mnuItem.Enabled = False
        mnuMenu.MenuItems.Add(mnuItem)

        ' create invisible menu item
        mnuItem = New MenuItem("Invisible")
        mnuItem.Visible = False
        mnuMenu.MenuItems.Add(mnuItem)

        ' set form's menu
        Me.Menu = m_menu

    End Sub

End Class
```

You can see the output of this example in Figure 24.13.

Figure 24.13: *Example of enabled, disabled, and invisible menu items.*

The enabled menu item looks like any other normal menu item shown previously in this chapter. The disabled menu item is shown grayed out. This allows a user of an application to know that the menu item exists but is not available (until something is done in the application to enable it). The invisible menu item is obviously not viewable. Invisible menu items are mostly used when a single menu is created for an application and some menu items within the menu are used in the context of specific windows. One technique to use is to make these menu items visible only when those specific windows are active, thus requiring the menu items to be visible. When those specific windows are not active, the menu items are made invisible.

NOTE

If you have a MenuItem that may or may not be used depending on the context of your application, enabling/disabling menu items is the preferred way instead of making the menu items visible/invisible. This is because if you use the enabling/disabling approach your users can see all of the menu items your application provides, and they can see which are currently available. If the menu items are sometimes invisible, it is much more difficult (and possibly even impossible) to tell (from the user's perspective) the entire set of options that the menus provide. This can lead to frustration on the user's behalf.

Mnemonics and Shortcuts

Mnemonics are used in conjunction with menus to provide better keyboard support with your application. If a user tends to use the keyboard as opposed to the mouse for navigating the user interface, mnemonics allow the user to quickly select a menu item on a menu using the mnemonic key associated with the desired menu item.

The first mnemonic key is pressed together with the Alt key to show a sub menu from the main menu. Then, the subsequent mnemonic keys can be pressed with or without using the Alt key to select a menu item on the sub menu.

You define what the single key is for a menu item by defining the mnemonic character for the menu item. This is done by using the ampersand (&) character within the text of the menu item. The character following the ampersand becomes the mnemonic character and can be pressed when the menu is active. Pressing the mnemonic key results in the Click event firing for the given menu item. The mnemonic character is displayed in the menu item with an underscore. This is how the mnemonic key is expressed to the user so that they would know which key to press to automatically select a menu item.

If you defined a mnemonic for a menu item using the ampersand, the Mnemonic property for the MenuItem object contains the mnemonic character. For example, if you defined the text of a MenuItem text property to be &File, the Mnemonic property has the character F. If no mnemonic is defined for a MenuItem, the Mnemonic property is the character 0.

> **NOTE**
>
> If by chance you wanted to display an ampersand as part of a menu item text and not have it cause a mnemonic key to be defined, you need to specify two ampersands in a row (&&). This causes a single ampersand to be displayed and does not create a mnemonic for the menu item.

Shortcuts are similar to mnemonics except the shortcut keys are not based on the text of the menu item. It could be a function key such as F5. Shortcuts are displayed to the right of the text in a menu item. Also, shortcuts generate a Click event for a menu item regardless of whether the menu is active. The menu does not have to be displayed before pressing the shortcut key. With mnemonics, the menu that contains the desired menu item must be visible before pressing the mnemonic key for the menu item.

The following code example illustrates both mnemonics and shortcuts:

```
Imports System.Windows.Forms

Public Class Form1
    Inherits System.Windows.Forms.Form

    Private m_menu As MainMenu

    Private Sub New()
        MyBase.New()
        CreateMenus()
    End Sub

    Protected Sub CreateMenus()
        Dim mnuMenu, mnuItem As MenuItem

        m_menu = New MainMenu()

        mnuMenu = New MenuItem("Fruit")
        m_menu.MenuItems.Add(mnuMenu)

        mnuItem = New MenuItem("&Apple", _
                    New EventHandler(AddressOf ApplePicked))
        mnuItem.Shortcut = Shortcut.F4
        mnuMenu.MenuItems.Add(mnuItem)

        mnuItem = New MenuItem("&Orange", _
                    New EventHandler(AddressOf OrangePicked))
        mnuItem.Shortcut = Shortcut.F5
        mnuMenu.MenuItems.Add(mnuItem)
```

```
            mnuItem = New MenuItem("&Banana", _
                        New EventHandler(AddressOf BananaPicked))
            mnuItem.Shortcut = Shortcut.F6
            mnuItem.ShowShortcut = False
            mnuMenu.MenuItems.Add(mnuItem)

            ' set form's menu
            Me.Menu = m_menu

        End Sub

        Protected Sub ApplePicked(ByVal sender As Object, _
                            ByVal e As System.EventArgs)
            Dim msgBox As MessageBox
            msgBox.Show("Apple Picked!")
        End Sub

        Protected Sub OrangePicked(ByVal sender As Object, _
                            ByVal e As System.EventArgs)
            Dim msgBox As MessageBox
            msgBox.Show("Orange Picked!")
        End Sub

        Protected Sub BananaPicked(ByVal sender As Object, _
                            ByVal e As System.EventArgs)
            Dim msgBox As MessageBox
            msgBox.Show("Banana Picked!")
        End Sub

End Class
```

You can see the output of this example in Figure 24.14.

Figure 24.14: *Example of mnemonics and shortcuts.*

In the previous example, take a look at the MenuItem defined for Apple. The ampersand character in the MenuItem text defines a mnemonic using the "A" character, because the "A" immediately follows the ampersand. This allows a user to press the A key on the keyboard to activate the menu item when the Fruit menu is displayed on the screen.

Following this logic, the Orange menu item defines a mnemonic using the O key, and the Banana menu item defines a mnemonic using the B key.

Next, notice that a shortcut key is created for the Apple menu item. The shortcut key used is the F4 key. This is accomplished by setting the Shortcut property on the MenuItem object. Also notice that the Orange menu item has the shortcut key F5 defined, and the Banana menu item has the shortcut key F6 defined. This enables the F4 key to always invoke the Click event handler for the Apple menu item regardless of whether the menu is visible on the screen first. The F5 key invokes the Orange menu item event handler. And lastly, the F6 key invokes the Banana menu item event handler.

The MenuItem class also has a ShowShortcut property that can be used. Setting this property to True displays the shortcut key to the right of the MenuItem text in the menu. Setting this property to False turns off the display of the shortcut key but still allows the shortcut key to be used to invoke the event handler. As a rule, if you define a shortcut for a MenuItem, then you should always set the ShowShortcut to True.

Checked Menu Items

Sometimes you may want to inform the user that a feature represented by a particular menu item is already enabled in your application. This may include telling the user that the auto-save feature is already enabled in your application or that the spell checking feature is turned on. The menu items shown so far do not indicate whether the feature is currently on or off in the application.

Checked menu items solve this problem by displaying a check mark to the left of the menu item if the feature represented by the menu item is turned on. The good news is that you have a user interface construct that allows you to do this. The bad news is that you have to manage it yourself. To turn on the check mark, you need to set the Checked property of the MenuItem to True. To turn it off, set it to False. It is up to you to set this property appropriately in your application to correctly reflect this.

This example shows how to create checked menu items and how to manage the check marks. Create a new Windows application project and replace the automatically generated form code with the following::

```
Imports System.Windows.Forms

Public Class Form1
    Inherits System.Windows.Forms.Form

    Private m_menu As MainMenu

    Private m_mnuBob As MenuItem
    Private m_mnuGabriel As MenuItem

    Private Sub New()
        MyBase.New()
        CreateMenus()
    End Sub

    Private Sub CreateMenus()
        Dim mnuAuthors, mnuItem As MenuItem

        m_menu = New MainMenu()

        ' create boolean menu
        mnuAuthors = New MenuItem("Authors")

        ' create True menu item
        m_mnuBob = New MenuItem("Bob", _
                    New System.EventHandler(AddressOf AuthorClick))
        m_mnuBob.Checked = True
        mnuAuthors.MenuItems.Add(m_mnuBob)

        ' create True menu item
        m_mnuGabriel = New MenuItem("Gabriel", _
                    New System.EventHandler(AddressOf AuthorClick))
        m_mnuGabriel.Checked = True

        mnuAuthors.MenuItems.Add(m_mnuGabriel)

        m_menu.MenuItems.Add(mnuAuthors)

        ' set form's menu
        Me.Menu = m_menu

    End Sub

    Protected Sub AuthorClick(ByVal sender As Object, _
                        ByVal e As System.EventArgs)
        If sender Is m_mnuBob Then
            m_mnuBob.Checked = Not m_mnuBob.Checked
        ElseIf sender Is m_mnuGabriel Then
```

```
            m_mnuGabriel.Checked = Not m_mnuGabriel.Checked
        End If
    End Sub

End Class
```

You can see the output of this example in Figure 24.15.

Figure 24.15: *Menu with checked items.*

In Figure 24.15, each of the two MenuItems have their Checked properties set to True. This instructs the MenuItem to draw a check mark on the left side of the menu item when it is displayed. Again, to turn it off just set the Checked property to False.

The AuthorClick event handler manages to turn the check mark off if the check mark is currently on and vice versa. This applies to both of the menu items.

As you can see, the example is not very elaborate primarily because turning on and off the check mark is quite simple. In your application, the logic for setting the Checked property would probably be more complex.

Radio Buttons on Menus

Just like the checked menu items, you can create a set of menu items that display a solid circle to the left of the menu item's text if the menu item is turned on. Turning on the checked menu item involves setting the Checked property just like checked menu items.

However, there are two basic differences. First, you also need to set the RadioCheck property of the menu item so that it displays the solid circle instead of the check mark. Second, radio menu items are intended to be exclusively turned on between one another. For example, if you have three menu items that all have the RadioCheck property set to True, only one of those menu items is supposed to be turned on at a time.

Just as it is with checked menu items, you need to manage the interaction between the menu items yourself. So, if one menu item is turned on, you have to turn the others off in the set of radio menu items.

The following example shows how to define the radio menu items, turning them on and off, and managing the interaction between them. Create a new

Windows application project and replace the automatically generated code for the form with the following:

```
Imports System.Windows.Forms

Public Class Form1
    Inherits System.Windows.Forms.Form

    Private m_menu As MainMenu

    Private m_mnuYes As MenuItem
    Private m_mnuNo As MenuItem
    Private m_mnuMaybe As MenuItem

    Private Sub New()
        MyBase.New()
        CreateMenus()
    End Sub

    Private Sub CreateMenus()
        Dim mnuMultiple, mnuItem As MenuItem

        m_menu = New MainMenu()

        ' create Multiple menu
        mnuMultiple = New MenuItem("Multiple")

        ' create Yes menu item
        m_mnuYes = New MenuItem("Yes", _
                    New System.EventHandler(AddressOf Me.MultipleClick))
        m_mnuYes.RadioCheck = True
        m_mnuYes.Checked = True
        mnuMultiple.MenuItems.Add(m_mnuYes)

        ' create No menu item
        m_mnuNo = New MenuItem("No", _
                    New System.EventHandler(AddressOf Me.MultipleClick))
        m_mnuNo.RadioCheck = True
        mnuMultiple.MenuItems.Add(m_mnuNo)

        ' create Maybe menu item
        m_mnuMaybe = New MenuItem("Maybe", _
                    New System.EventHandler(AddressOf Me.MultipleClick))
        m_mnuMaybe.RadioCheck = True
        mnuMultiple.MenuItems.Add(m_mnuMaybe)
```

```
            m_menu.MenuItems.Add(mnuMultiple)

            ' set form's menu
            Me.Menu = m_menu

        End Sub

        Protected Sub MultipleClick(ByVal sender As Object, _
                                    ByVal e As System.EventArgs)
            Dim msgBox As MessageBox
            If sender Is m_mnuYes Then
                m_mnuYes.Checked = True
                m_mnuNo.Checked = False
                m_mnuMaybe.Checked = False
                msgBox.Show("Yes pressed!")
            ElseIf sender Is m_mnuNo Then
                m_mnuYes.Checked = False
                m_mnuNo.Checked = True
                m_mnuMaybe.Checked = False
                msgBox.Show("No pressed!")
            ElseIf sender Is m_mnuMaybe Then
                m_mnuYes.Checked = False
                m_mnuNo.Checked = False
                m_mnuMaybe.Checked = True
                msgBox.Show("Maybe pressed!")
            End If
        End Sub

End Class
```

The output of this example can be seen in Figure 24.16.

Figure 24.16: *Radio menu items.*

Notice that each of the Yes, No, and Maybe menu items are defined to be radio menu items. This is done by setting their respective RadioCheck property to True. Also in this example, only the Yes menu item is turned on by setting the Checked property to True. This is how you would set the default menu item that is checked when you construct the menu.

The setup is complete at this point; now comes the management behind the scenes. In the event handler for the menu items, a check is made to see which menu item was clicked. Depending on which one was clicked, that menu item's Checked property is set to True, and the other menu items' Checked property is set to False.

Nested Menus

Menus can, of course, be nested. A menu can have a submenu and items. The submenu can also have a submenu, items, and so on. Nested menus are quite simple to create in VB .NET using the Framework classes. Each MenuItem object can contain a list of child MenuItem objects. This list is represented by the MenuItems property on the MenuItem class. MenuItems is a collection of MenuItem objects.

If the MenuItems property contains zero MenuItems this means the MenuItem does not have a submenu and is considered to be a leaf menu. If you think of a tree as an analogy, a tree has branches and each branch extends outward to form more branches. Each branch ends with a leaf. A leaf MenuItem is considered the last MenuItem extending from the main menu. Once again, leaf MenuItems are the only MenuItems that generate a Click event.

To create nested menus, all you have to do is create MenuItem objects and add them to another MenuItem's MenuItems property. The following example shows nested menus for displaying a deck of cards by suit. This would allow a user to select a particular card in the deck by using the defined menus. Create a new Windows application project and replace the automatically generated form code with the following:

```
Imports System.Windows.Forms

Public Class Form1
    Inherits System.Windows.Forms.Form

    Private m_menu As MainMenu

    Private Sub New()
        MyBase.New()
        CreateMenus()
    End Sub

    Private Sub CreateMenus()
        Dim mnuMenu, mnuSubMenu, mnuItem As MenuItem

        m_menu = New MainMenu()

        mnuMenu = New MenuItem("Cards")
        m_menu.MenuItems.Add(mnuMenu)
```

```
mnuSubMenu = New MenuItem("Hearts")
mnuSubMenu.MenuItems.Add(New MenuItem("2"))
mnuSubMenu.MenuItems.Add(New MenuItem("3"))
mnuSubMenu.MenuItems.Add(New MenuItem("4"))
mnuSubMenu.MenuItems.Add(New MenuItem("5"))
mnuSubMenu.MenuItems.Add(New MenuItem("6"))
mnuSubMenu.MenuItems.Add(New MenuItem("7"))
mnuSubMenu.MenuItems.Add(New MenuItem("8"))
mnuSubMenu.MenuItems.Add(New MenuItem("9"))
mnuSubMenu.MenuItems.Add(New MenuItem("10"))
mnuSubMenu.MenuItems.Add(New MenuItem("J"))
mnuSubMenu.MenuItems.Add(New MenuItem("Q"))
mnuSubMenu.MenuItems.Add(New MenuItem("K"))
mnuSubMenu.MenuItems.Add(New MenuItem("A"))
mnuMenu.MenuItems.Add(mnuSubMenu)

mnuSubMenu = New MenuItem("Clubs")
mnuSubMenu.MenuItems.Add(New MenuItem("2"))
mnuSubMenu.MenuItems.Add(New MenuItem("3"))
mnuSubMenu.MenuItems.Add(New MenuItem("4"))
mnuSubMenu.MenuItems.Add(New MenuItem("5"))
mnuSubMenu.MenuItems.Add(New MenuItem("6"))
mnuSubMenu.MenuItems.Add(New MenuItem("7"))
mnuSubMenu.MenuItems.Add(New MenuItem("8"))
mnuSubMenu.MenuItems.Add(New MenuItem("9"))
mnuSubMenu.MenuItems.Add(New MenuItem("10"))
mnuSubMenu.MenuItems.Add(New MenuItem("J"))
mnuSubMenu.MenuItems.Add(New MenuItem("Q"))
mnuSubMenu.MenuItems.Add(New MenuItem("K"))
mnuSubMenu.MenuItems.Add(New MenuItem("A"))
mnuMenu.MenuItems.Add(mnuSubMenu)

mnuSubMenu = New MenuItem("Spades")
mnuSubMenu.MenuItems.Add(New MenuItem("2"))
mnuSubMenu.MenuItems.Add(New MenuItem("3"))
mnuSubMenu.MenuItems.Add(New MenuItem("4"))
mnuSubMenu.MenuItems.Add(New MenuItem("5"))
mnuSubMenu.MenuItems.Add(New MenuItem("6"))
mnuSubMenu.MenuItems.Add(New MenuItem("7"))
mnuSubMenu.MenuItems.Add(New MenuItem("8"))
mnuSubMenu.MenuItems.Add(New MenuItem("9"))
mnuSubMenu.MenuItems.Add(New MenuItem("10"))
mnuSubMenu.MenuItems.Add(New MenuItem("J"))
mnuSubMenu.MenuItems.Add(New MenuItem("Q"))
mnuSubMenu.MenuItems.Add(New MenuItem("K"))
mnuSubMenu.MenuItems.Add(New MenuItem("A"))
mnuMenu.MenuItems.Add(mnuSubMenu)
```

```
mnuSubMenu = New MenuItem("Diamonds")
mnuSubMenu.MenuItems.Add(New MenuItem("2"))
mnuSubMenu.MenuItems.Add(New MenuItem("3"))
mnuSubMenu.MenuItems.Add(New MenuItem("4"))
mnuSubMenu.MenuItems.Add(New MenuItem("5"))
mnuSubMenu.MenuItems.Add(New MenuItem("6"))
mnuSubMenu.MenuItems.Add(New MenuItem("7"))
mnuSubMenu.MenuItems.Add(New MenuItem("8"))
mnuSubMenu.MenuItems.Add(New MenuItem("9"))
mnuSubMenu.MenuItems.Add(New MenuItem("10"))
mnuSubMenu.MenuItems.Add(New MenuItem("J"))
mnuSubMenu.MenuItems.Add(New MenuItem("Q"))
mnuSubMenu.MenuItems.Add(New MenuItem("K"))
mnuSubMenu.MenuItems.Add(New MenuItem("A"))
mnuMenu.MenuItems.Add(mnuSubMenu)

' set form's menu
Me.Menu = m_menu

    End Sub

End Class
```

The output from this example can be seen in Figure 24.17.

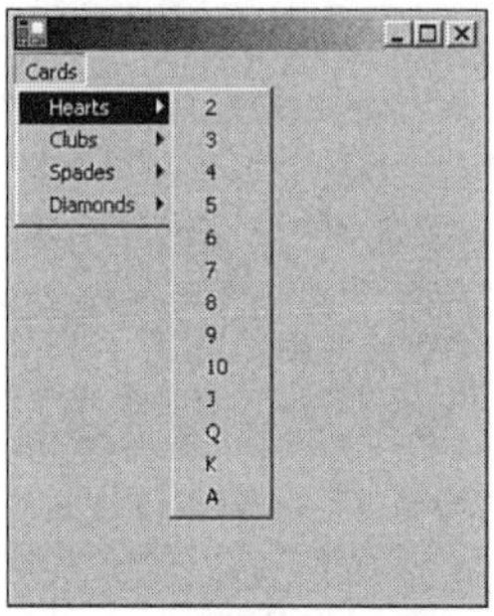

Figure 24.17: *Nested menus.*

Dynamic Menus

All of the menu examples shown so far assume that you know the exact menu structure at the time you develop your application. Sometimes this menu is not known until after the application is built. A list of possible menu items may be defined in a configuration file or come from a database (the support for this is up to you to develop).

In any event, MenuItems allow you to define sub MenuItems while the application is running. This is accomplished through the use of events. When you move the cursor over a MenuItem, a Select event is dispatched to the MenuItem. This event can be intercepted to perform a number of different tasks such as constructing a submenu dynamically.

Using the nested menu example based on a deck of cards again, we are going to show you how to dynamically generate the submenus. The final program looks identical to that previous example from the user's point of view. The result should look identical to Figure 24.17. The difference with this example is that because the menus are constructed dynamically you could write additional code to get the menu items from a configuration file if you choose to.

To handle the Select event, you may decide to write a new class that inherits from MenuItem. Then you can override the OnSelect method, which is invoked when a Select event is sent to it. In the OnSelect method, you can dynamically create the submenu. Here is an example that defines a class that inherits from MenuItem. In the OnSelect method, the class creates a submenu based on the set of cards within a suit.

Create a new Windows application project and add the following class to the project:

```
Public Class CardMenu
    Inherits System.Windows.Forms.MenuItem

    Private m_loaded As Boolean

    Public Sub New(ByVal text As String)
        MyBase.New(text)
        ' add a dummy menu item to indicate menu
        ' contains a submenu before user selects it
        ' (forces display of right arrow on menu)
        MenuItems.Add(New MenuItem("Dummy"))
        m_loaded = False
    End Sub

    Protected Overrides Sub OnSelect(ByVal e As System.EventArgs)

        ' if the submenu has already been loaded exit the
        ' method. If it has not already been loaded then continue
        ' on and load the submenu.
        If m_loaded = True Then
            Exit Sub
        End If

        ' remove "Dummy" menu item
        MenuItems.Clear()
```

```
' add submenu here (this could be redone to read from configuration file)
MenuItems.Add(New MenuItem("2"))
MenuItems.Add(New MenuItem("3"))
MenuItems.Add(New MenuItem("4"))
MenuItems.Add(New MenuItem("5"))
MenuItems.Add(New MenuItem("6"))
MenuItems.Add(New MenuItem("7"))
MenuItems.Add(New MenuItem("8"))
MenuItems.Add(New MenuItem("9"))
MenuItems.Add(New MenuItem("10"))
MenuItems.Add(New MenuItem("J"))
MenuItems.Add(New MenuItem("Q"))
MenuItems.Add(New MenuItem("K"))
MenuItems.Add(New MenuItem("A"))
m_loaded = True

    End Sub


End Class
```

In the constructor of the CardMenu class, a "dummy" MenuItem object is created and added to its MenuItems property. The reason for this is so that the menu decoration (right arrow) is displayed for showing a submenu existing before the user moves the mouse over the menu. If the "dummy" MenuItem were not added, the CardMenu object would be displayed as a normal MenuItem that has no submenu. Then when the user moves the cursor over it, a right arrow would appear and then the submenu. This could be confusing to the user. If a MenuItem contains submenus, regardless of whether the menu is static or dynamic, the submenu decoration, or glyph, should immediately appear for informational purposes to the user.

The CardMenu class also has a private field (m_loaded) for indicating to itself whether the submenu has been loaded.

This next example uses the CardMenu class to show how it works in an application and that the display is identical to the example shown for nested menus. In the same project that contains the CardMenu class, replace the automatically generated code in the form with the following:

```
Imports System.Windows.Forms


Public Class Form1
    Inherits System.Windows.Forms.Form

    Private m_menu As MainMenu
```

```
        Private Sub New()
            MyBase.New()
            CreateMenus()
        End Sub

        Private Sub CreateMenus()
            Dim mnuMenu, mnuItem As MenuItem
            Dim mnuSubMenu As CardMenu

            m_menu = New MainMenu()

            mnuMenu = New MenuItem("Cards")
            m_menu.MenuItems.Add(mnuMenu)

            mnuSubMenu = New CardMenu("Hearts")
            mnuMenu.MenuItems.Add(mnuSubMenu)

            mnuSubMenu = New CardMenu("Clubs")
            mnuMenu.MenuItems.Add(mnuSubMenu)

            mnuSubMenu = New CardMenu("Spades")
            mnuMenu.MenuItems.Add(mnuSubMenu)

            mnuSubMenu = New CardMenu("Diamonds")
            mnuMenu.MenuItems.Add(mnuSubMenu)

            ' set form's menu
            Me.Menu = m_menu

        End Sub

End Class
```

The result of this example is identical to the output shown in Figure 24.17.

Context Menus

In some applications, you can right-click on certain user interface artifacts and a menu pops up. This is commonly referred to as a *pop-up menu* or *context menu*. This ability is also provided to you in Microsoft .NET as part of Windows Forms.

All of the examples shown in this chapter have so far used a MainMenu object as the root container of all the MenuItems. As already demonstrated, the MainMenu object supports displaying menus across a menu bar in your form.

To implement context menus, you would instead use an instance of
ContextMenu instead of MainMenu. Everything explained so far in relation to
MainMenu also applies to ContextMenu. The only difference is that a context
menu can appear at different locations on your screen.

The following example demonstrates using a ContextMenu. Create a new
Windows application project and replace the automatically generated form
code with the following:

```
Imports System.Windows.Forms

Public Class Form1
    Inherits System.Windows.Forms.Form

    Private Sub New()
        MyBase.New()
        CreateContextMenu()
    End Sub

    Private Sub CreateContextMenu()
        Dim ctxMenu As New ContextMenu()
        ctxMenu.MenuItems.Add(New MenuItem("Option 1"))
        ctxMenu.MenuItems.Add(New MenuItem("Option 2"))
        ctxMenu.MenuItems.Add(New MenuItem("Option 3"))
        Me.ContextMenu = ctxMenu
    End Sub

    Protected Overrides Sub OnMouseDown(ByVal e As MouseEventArgs)
        Me.ContextMenu.Show(Me, New Point(e.X, e.Y))
    End Sub

End Class
```

The output of this example can be seen in Figure 24.18.

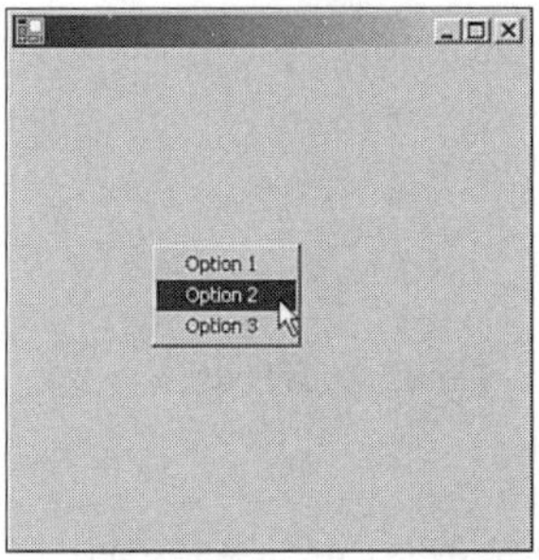

Figure 24.18: Context menu.

In the `CreateContextMenu` method, a new `ContextMenu` object is created and `MenuItem` objects added to it. At the end of this method, the form's `ContextMenu` property is set to the `ContextMenu` object just created. This sets the form's context menu.

The only remaining thing left to do is to display the menu when something is clicked. To demonstrate this, we overrode the form's `OnMouseDown` method to respond to a `Mouse Click` event on the form. In this method, the `ContextMenu` is displayed at the position the mouse was clicked. Once the user selects something on the menu or clicks outside the menu, the menu automatically hides itself again.

Owner Drawn Menu Items

At some point, you may need the capability to create a menu item that has a custom look. For example, most Windows applications today contain menus that have cute little icons on the menu items. The default behavior of the `MenuItem` class does not have support for this. However, you can write code to do this yourself. This concept is called *owner drawing*.

Instead of having the `MenuItem` do all of the drawing, you can subclass `MenuItem` with your own class and override two methods for providing your own drawing routines. Here is example code that creates a subclass of `MenuItem` for the purposes of adding icons to menus. Create a new Windows application project and add this class to the project:

```
Imports System
Imports System.ComponentModel
Imports System.Drawing
Imports System.Drawing.Drawing2D
Imports System.Drawing.Text
Imports System.Windows.Forms

Public Class IconMenuItem
    Inherits System.Windows.Forms.MenuItem

    Private m_icon As Icon
    Private m_font As Font

    Public Sub New()
        MyBase.New("", Nothing, Windows.Forms.Shortcut.None)
    End Sub

    Public Sub New(ByVal text As String, ByVal icon As Icon)
        MyClass.New(text, icon, Nothing, Nothing, Windows.Forms.Shortcut.None)
    End Sub
```

```
Public Sub New(ByVal text As String, ByVal icon As Icon, _
            ByVal onClick As EventHandler, ByVal shortcut As Shortcut)
    MyClass.New(text, icon, Nothing, onClick, shortcut)
End Sub

Public Sub New(ByVal text As String, _
            ByVal icon As Icon, _
            ByVal font As Font, _
            ByVal onClick As EventHandler, _
            ByVal shortcut As Shortcut)
    MyBase.New(text, onClick, shortcut)
    Me.OwnerDraw = True
    If Not font Is Nothing Then
        m_font = font.Clone()
    Else
        m_font = New Font("MS Sans Serif", 8)
    End If
    m_icon = icon
End Sub

Public Overloads Sub Dispose()
    m_font.Dispose()
    m_icon.Dispose()
    MyBase.Dispose()
End Sub

Public Property Icon() As Icon
    Get
        Return m_icon
    End Get
    Set(ByVal Value As Icon)
        m_icon = Value
    End Set
End Property

Public Property Font() As Font
    Get
        Return m_font
    End Get
    Set(ByVal Value As Font)
        m_font = Value
    End Set
End Property

Private Function GetDisplayText() As String
```

```vbnet
    ' There are two parts to the display text
    ' 1 - the value of the Text property
    ' 2 - the value of the shortcut Text
    ' These two parts are combined into one string
    ' in order to get the actual text that is going to be
    ' displayed on the menu item.

    Dim displayText As String = Me.Text

    If Me.ShowShortcut And Me.Shortcut <> shortCut.None Then
        Dim shortCut As Keys
        Dim shortCutText As String
        Dim converter As TypeConverter
        shortCut = CType(Me.Shortcut, Keys)
        ' convert the shortcut key to a visual string representation
        converter = TypeDescriptor.GetConverter(GetType(Keys))
        shortCutText = converter.ConvertToString(shortCut)
        displayText = displayText & ChrW(Keys.Tab) & shortCutText
    End If

    Return displayText

End Function

Protected Overrides Sub OnDrawItem(ByVal e As DrawItemEventArgs)
    MyBase.OnDrawItem

    ' draw the icon if we have one
    If Not m_icon Is Nothing Then
        e.Graphics.DrawIcon(m_icon, e.Bounds.Left + 2, e.Bounds.Top + 2)
    End If

    ' get the rectangle of the area we can draw in
    ' and update the area to not include the icon
    Dim rect As Rectangle = e.Bounds
    rect.X += 24

    ' define a brush to use. If the menu item is not selected
    ' then use the control brush; otherwise use the highlight brush
    Dim brush As Brush
    If CBool(e.State And DrawItemState.Selected) Then
        brush = SystemBrushes.Highlight.Clone()
    Else
        brush = SystemBrushes.Control.Clone()
    End If
```

```
            ' fill the area using the brush
            e.Graphics.FillRectangle(brush, rect)

            ' now draw the text
            Dim formatter As StringFormat = New StringFormat()
            formatter.HotkeyPrefix = HotkeyPrefix.Show
            formatter.SetTabStops(50, New Single() {0})
            e.Graphics.DrawString(GetDisplayText(), _
                            m_font, _
                            New SolidBrush(e.ForeColor), _
                            e.Bounds.Left + 25, _
                            e.Bounds.Top + 2, _
                            formatter)
        formatter.Dispose()
        brush.Dispose()

    End Sub

    Protected Overrides Sub OnMeasureItem(ByVal e As MeasureItemEventArgs)
        Dim formatter As StringFormat

        MyBase.OnMeasureItem

        ' tell the formatter to display hot keys
        ' and set the tab stops far enough out
        formatter = New StringFormat()
        formatter.HotkeyPrefix = formatter.HotkeyPrefix.Show
        formatter.SetTabStops(50, New Single() {0})

        e.ItemHeight = 22
        e.ItemWidth = CInt(e.Graphics.MeasureString(GetDisplayText(), _
                                        m_font, _
                                        10000, _
                                        formatter).Width) + 15

    If Me.MenuItems.Count > 0 Then
        e.ItemWidth += 15
    End If

    formatter.Dispose()
    End Sub

End Class
```

For you to provide your own drawing routines, you need to be aware of a couple of things. First, you should create a class that inherits from System.Windows.Forms.MenuItem. Next, you must make sure that you set the

OwnerDraw property to True. This informs the MenuItem that the default painting behavior is going to be provided by a subclass.

Lastly, you need to provide two methods in your subclass—OnMeasureItem and OnDrawItem. When the menu item is displayed, these two methods are called in succession so that you can do your special drawing. OnMeasureItem is called first so that you can figure out how big the menu item should be. You then set the size by setting the appropriate members of the MeasureItemEventArgs parameter. After that, the OnDrawItem method is called where you actually do your drawing. In the sample code shown previously, the custom drawing routines have to take into account the size of the icon, the size of the menu item text, the size of the text for the shortcut key, and the size of the glyph indicating a submenu.

Here is sample code that uses the class defined in the previous example to demonstrate the icons in the menu. In the same project, replace the automatically generated code with the following:

```
Imports System.Windows.Forms

Public Class Form1
    Inherits System.Windows.Forms.Form

    Private m_menu As MainMenu

    Private Sub New()
        MyBase.New()
        CreateMenus()
    End Sub

    Private Sub CreateMenus()
        Dim mnuMenu, mnuItem As MenuItem
        Dim mnuSubMenu As IconMenuItem
        Dim heartsIcon As Icon = New Icon("Hearts.ico")
        Dim clubsIcon As Icon = New Icon("Clubs.ico")
        Dim spadesIcon As Icon = New Icon("Spades.ico")
        Dim diamondsIcon As Icon = New Icon("Diamonds.ico")

        m_menu = New MainMenu()

        mnuMenu = New MenuItem("Cards")
        m_menu.MenuItems.Add(mnuMenu)

        mnuSubMenu = New IconMenuItem("Hearts", _
                                      heartsIcon, _
                                      Nothing, _
                                      Shortcut.CtrlF5)
```

```
mnuSubMenu.MenuItems.Add(New IconMenuItem("2", heartsIcon))
mnuSubMenu.MenuItems.Add(New IconMenuItem("3", heartsIcon))
mnuSubMenu.MenuItems.Add(New IconMenuItem("4", heartsIcon))
mnuSubMenu.MenuItems.Add(New IconMenuItem("5", heartsIcon))
mnuSubMenu.MenuItems.Add(New IconMenuItem("6", heartsIcon))
mnuSubMenu.MenuItems.Add(New IconMenuItem("7", heartsIcon))
mnuSubMenu.MenuItems.Add(New IconMenuItem("8", heartsIcon))
mnuSubMenu.MenuItems.Add(New IconMenuItem("9", heartsIcon))
mnuSubMenu.MenuItems.Add(New IconMenuItem("10", heartsIcon))
mnuSubMenu.MenuItems.Add(New IconMenuItem("J", heartsIcon))
mnuSubMenu.MenuItems.Add(New IconMenuItem("Q", heartsIcon))
mnuSubMenu.MenuItems.Add(New IconMenuItem("K", heartsIcon))
mnuSubMenu.MenuItems.Add(New IconMenuItem("A", heartsIcon))
mnuMenu.MenuItems.Add(mnuSubMenu)

mnuSubMenu = New IconMenuItem("Clubs", _
                              clubsIcon, _
                              Nothing, _
                              Shortcut.CtrlF6)

mnuSubMenu.MenuItems.Add(New IconMenuItem("2", clubsIcon))
mnuSubMenu.MenuItems.Add(New IconMenuItem("3", clubsIcon))
mnuSubMenu.MenuItems.Add(New IconMenuItem("4", clubsIcon))
mnuSubMenu.MenuItems.Add(New IconMenuItem("5", clubsIcon))
mnuSubMenu.MenuItems.Add(New IconMenuItem("6", clubsIcon))
mnuSubMenu.MenuItems.Add(New IconMenuItem("7", clubsIcon))
mnuSubMenu.MenuItems.Add(New IconMenuItem("8", clubsIcon))
mnuSubMenu.MenuItems.Add(New IconMenuItem("9", clubsIcon))
mnuSubMenu.MenuItems.Add(New IconMenuItem("10", clubsIcon))
mnuSubMenu.MenuItems.Add(New IconMenuItem("J", clubsIcon))
mnuSubMenu.MenuItems.Add(New IconMenuItem("Q", clubsIcon))
mnuSubMenu.MenuItems.Add(New IconMenuItem("K", clubsIcon))
mnuSubMenu.MenuItems.Add(New IconMenuItem("A", clubsIcon))
mnuMenu.MenuItems.Add(mnuSubMenu)

mnuSubMenu = New IconMenuItem("Spades", _
                              spadesIcon, _
                              Nothing, _
                              Shortcut.CtrlF7)

mnuSubMenu.MenuItems.Add(New IconMenuItem("2", spadesIcon))
mnuSubMenu.MenuItems.Add(New IconMenuItem("3", spadesIcon))
mnuSubMenu.MenuItems.Add(New IconMenuItem("4", spadesIcon))
mnuSubMenu.MenuItems.Add(New IconMenuItem("5", spadesIcon))
mnuSubMenu.MenuItems.Add(New IconMenuItem("6", spadesIcon))
mnuSubMenu.MenuItems.Add(New IconMenuItem("7", spadesIcon))
```

```
        mnuSubMenu.MenuItems.Add(New IconMenuItem("8", spadesIcon))
        mnuSubMenu.MenuItems.Add(New IconMenuItem("9", spadesIcon))
        mnuSubMenu.MenuItems.Add(New IconMenuItem("10", spadesIcon))
        mnuSubMenu.MenuItems.Add(New IconMenuItem("J", spadesIcon))
        mnuSubMenu.MenuItems.Add(New IconMenuItem("Q", spadesIcon))
        mnuSubMenu.MenuItems.Add(New IconMenuItem("K", spadesIcon))
        mnuSubMenu.MenuItems.Add(New IconMenuItem("A", spadesIcon))
        mnuMenu.MenuItems.Add(mnuSubMenu)

        mnuSubMenu = New IconMenuItem("Diamonds", _
                                      diamondsIcon, _
                                      Nothing, _
                                      Shortcut.CtrlF8)

        mnuSubMenu.MenuItems.Add(New IconMenuItem("2", diamondsIcon))
        mnuSubMenu.MenuItems.Add(New IconMenuItem("3", diamondsIcon))
        mnuSubMenu.MenuItems.Add(New IconMenuItem("4", diamondsIcon))
        mnuSubMenu.MenuItems.Add(New IconMenuItem("5", diamondsIcon))
        mnuSubMenu.MenuItems.Add(New IconMenuItem("6", diamondsIcon))
        mnuSubMenu.MenuItems.Add(New IconMenuItem("7", diamondsIcon))
        mnuSubMenu.MenuItems.Add(New IconMenuItem("8", diamondsIcon))
        mnuSubMenu.MenuItems.Add(New IconMenuItem("9", diamondsIcon))
        mnuSubMenu.MenuItems.Add(New IconMenuItem("10", diamondsIcon))
        mnuSubMenu.MenuItems.Add(New IconMenuItem("J", diamondsIcon))
        mnuSubMenu.MenuItems.Add(New IconMenuItem("Q", diamondsIcon))
        mnuSubMenu.MenuItems.Add(New IconMenuItem("K", diamondsIcon))
        mnuSubMenu.MenuItems.Add(New IconMenuItem("A", diamondsIcon))
        mnuMenu.MenuItems.Add(mnuSubMenu)

        ' set form's menu
        Me.Menu = m_menu

    End Sub

End Class
```

This example code requires the `hearts.ico`, `clubs.ico`, `spades.ico`, and `diamonds.ico` files to be located in the project's bin folder in order to run. If you want to run this yourself, you can use any existing icon files you have and just update the code to use those files instead.

You can see the output of this example in Figure 24.16.

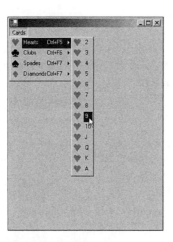

Figure 24.16: *Menu with icons.*

SDI, MDI, and Menus

At the beginning of this chapter, we discussed some issues regarding menus and SDI applications and MDI applications. Now that you have read through this chapter, let's revisit this a little bit. First if you are planning on developing an SDI application, the menu support is quite straightforward. Just create a menu and set the main form's menu property to this menu.

If you are planning on creating an MDI application, you will mostly likely use the default MDI menu behavior. The MDI container form has its own menu (which is the main menu for the application). Each MDI child form that is created has its menu appended to the main menu automatically. As you open each child form you can see the additional menu items added to the main menu. And, when you close the MDI child form, the menu items associated with the child form are removed from the main menu automatically.

The following code defines an MDI child form that creates its own menu. Create a new Windows application project and add the following class to it:

```
Public Class MDIChildForm
    Inherits System.Windows.Forms.Form

    Public Sub New()
        MyBase.New()
        CreateMenus()
    End Sub
```

```
        Private Sub CreateMenus()
            Dim mnuItem As MenuItem
            Dim mainMenu As MainMenu

            ' create menu for MDI child form
            mainMenu = New MainMenu()

            ' create menu items
            mnuItem = New MenuItem("Child Options")
            mnuItem.MenuItems.Add(New MenuItem("One"))
            mnuItem.MenuItems.Add(New MenuItem("Two"))
            mainMenu.MenuItems.Add(mnuItem)

            ' set form's menu
            Me.Menu = mainMenu

        End Sub

End Class
```

Next, the following code demonstrates an MDI application that allows you to create MDI child forms. Replace the automatically generated form code for Form1 with the following:

```
Imports System.Windows.Forms

Public Class Form1
    Inherits System.Windows.Forms.Form

    Private Sub New()
        MyBase.New()
        CreateMenus()
        ' set this form to be a MDI container
        Me.IsMdiContainer = True
    End Sub

    Private Sub CreateMenus()
        Dim mnuItem As MenuItem
        Dim mnuChild As MenuItem
        Dim mainMenu As MainMenu

        mainMenu = New MainMenu()

        ' create main menu items
        mnuItem = New MenuItem("Main Options")
        mainMenu.MenuItems.Add(mnuItem)
```

```
        ' add submenu items to "Main Options"
        mnuChild = New MenuItem("Create Child Window", _
                             New EventHandler(AddressOf NewMDIChild))
        mnuItem.MenuItems.Add(mnuChild)

        ' add MDI child list to menus
        mnuItem = New MenuItem("Windows")
        mnuItem.MdiList = True
        mainMenu.MenuItems.Add(mnuItem)

        ' set form's menu
        Me.Menu = mainMenu

    End Sub

    Protected Sub NewMDIChild(ByVal sender As Object, ByVal e As System.EventArgs)
        Dim mdiForm As MDIChildForm = New MDIChildForm()
        mdiForm.Text = "MDI Child Form"
        mdiForm.MdiParent = Me
        mdiForm.WindowState = FormWindowState.Normal
        mdiForm.Show()
    End Sub

    Shared Sub main()
        Application.Run(New Form1())
    End Sub

End Class
```

When you run this application, you see the application as shown in Figure 24.20. It has its main menu visible and no child forms. After creating child forms using the Create Child Window menu item, the menu for the new MDI child form is added to the main menu. Figure 24.21 shows the child form and the updated menu.

Figure 24.20: *MDI application.*

Figure 24.21: *MDI child form and its menu.*

One really nice feature that you should take advantage of is the MdiList property on the MenuItem class. If you set this property to True, the MenuItem automatically has child MenuItems added to it for each of the child forms of the MDI application. These newly added menu items can be used to activate the child forms without having to select the forms themselves with the mouse. An example of this is in the previous code example where the MenuItem named Windows has its MdiList property set to True. Figure 24.22 shows the result of doing this.

Figure 24.22: *Automatic menu support for child forms.*

What's Next

In this chapter you learned all about menus. This includes how to quickly add a menu to a form using the Toolbox window and Form Designer window. This also includes basic menus, nested menus, dynamically constructed menus, and owner-drawn menus. In addition, you learned how to define event handlers for menu items for the purpose of responding to the Click event generated by the menu items.

In the next chapter you learn more about the programmatic flow within the UI. In the case of menus, we discussed the simple process of flow between a menu item and its event handler. In the next chapter, UI program flow is covered in more detail so that you can get a better overall picture of the issues involved with developing a user interface in Visual Basic .NET.

NOTE

The answers to "Reviewing It," "Checking It," and "Applying It" are available on our Web site.

REVIEW

Reviewing It

This section presents a review of the key concepts in this chapter. These questions are intended to gauge your absorption of the relevant material.

1. What are the three classes used in creating menus using Visual Basic .NET?

2. What is the simplest way to add a menu to a form?

3. What are event handlers?

4. What is the difference between a mnemonic and a shortcut?

5. What is a context menu?

6. What are owner-drawn menus?

7. What is a menu break?

8. How are shortcut keys supported for menu items?

9. How do you display an ampersand character (&) in a menu?

CHECK

Checking It

Select the correct answer to the following questions.

Multiple Choice

1. What are the two types of menu classes provided with the Microsoft .NET Framework Class Library?

    a. `Menu1` and `Menu2`.

    b. `MainMenu` and `PopupMenu`.

    c. `MainMenu` and `ContextMenu`.

    d. `PopupMenu` and `ContextMenu`.

2. What are menu shortcuts?

    a. A direct route between two menu items.

    b. Quick key access to `MenuItems`.

    c. `MenuItems` with limited text.

    d. All of the above.

3. Dynamic menus require you to respond to what event?

    a. `Click`.

    b. `Select`.

    c. `Build`.

    d. `Generate`.

True or False

Select one of the two possible answers and then verify on our Web site that you picked the correct one.

1. Multiple `MenuItems` can use the same `EventHandler`.

    True/False

2. Menu items that have their `BarBreak` property set to True result in a horizontally displayed menu with vertical bars separating items in the menu.

    True/False

3. `MenuItems` can have sub `MenuItems`.

    True/False

4. `MenuItems` with nested `MenuItems` can generate a `Click` Event.

    True/False

5. All nested `MenuItems` must be specified in code before the application is compiled.

    True/False

6. I can always write my own subclass of `MenuItem` to draw a unique style of menu items.

    True/False

7. Menu separators are created by setting a menu item's Separator property to True.

True/False

APPLY

Applying It

Try to complete the following exercises by yourself.

Independent Exercise 1

Build a context menu on a form that contains three menu items and an event handler for each menu item.

Independent Exercise 2

Build a context menu on a form that contains three menu items and one event handler that handles all three menu items' Click events.

25

Program Flow Control in the User Interface

The past few chapters covered fundamental concepts of user interface programming, Windows forms, menus, and controls. The fundamental concepts presented in Chapter 21, "Programming the User Interface—Fundamental Concepts," which introduces Part IV, is necessary to get you thinking about user interface issues in a broad sense. The next several chapters on forms, menus, and controls are very focused on specific topics in user interface development.

This chapter explains the flow control in your application based on the knowledge you gained from reading the past few chapters. The purpose of this chapter is to give you a bigger picture view of an application so that you can design the overall flow of your applications.

Specifically, this chapter explains the following:

- Application startup and shutdown
- Form initialization and termination
- Form closing
- Event-driven programming

Application Startup and Shutdown

All the user interface examples shown so far in Part IV involve creating a new Form class. When the example is run, the form is magically shown and demonstrates the example it was intended to show. The Form is then closed by clicking on its Close box on the right side of the title bar.

What if your application has more than one Form (which many applications do), which Form is displayed first when the application runs? The easiest way to specify which form is displayed when the application starts is to define the *Startup Object* in your project. The Startup Object is the object which is run when the application starts.

To specify the Startup Object, you need to open the Project Properties window. To do this, you first need to display the Solution Explorer window (if it is not already displayed) by choosing View, Solution Explorer or by pressing the Ctrl+R key combination. You open the Properties window by either of the following two ways:

- Right-click the project in the Solution Explorer window and then click the Properties menu item.

- Select the Project in the Solution Explorer window and then choose Properties from the Project menu in Visual Studio .NET.

Figure 25.1 shows the opened Project Properties window.

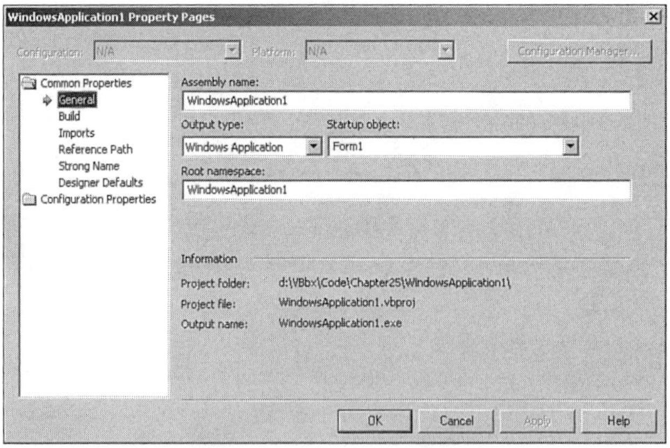

Figure 25.1: *Project Properties window.*

When you create a new Windows application project, the default form is automatically set to be the Startup Object. This means that if you create a new project and then press the F5 key to run it, the default form is automatically displayed. Under the covers, .NET automatically creates a message pump (this may sound familiar to earlier Windows developers) for the application's main thread (as long as the Startup Object is a Form). The message pump deals with automatically dispatching messages from the operating system to your application.

If the Startup Object is not a form, it must then be a public procedure. In this case a message pump is not automatically necessary. If you use a public procedure as the starting point for your application and you show a form in this procedure, you must create a message pump yourself in order for the form to work correctly. This is accomplished by calling the Run method on the shared `Application` object. Sample code that illustrates this is shown later as part of describing the `Sub Main` procedure.

For example, a mouse click message is sent from the operating system to your application through the message pump. After the message is dispatched to a control it is translated into an Event that can be handled using Event Handlers. Handling events is covered in detail in the preceding chapters. Once again, by specifying the Startup Object, this is taken care of for you.

Another way of choosing which Form in your application is displayed when the application starts is by specifying the Startup Object to be `Sub Main`. `Sub Main` should be familiar to Visual Basic 6 developers. It is a shared procedure named Main, which is a well-known procedure to the Visual Basic .NET language. It is commonly used as the initial starting point of an application when it runs.

By default, a `Sub Main` is not created when you create a new Windows application project. In contrast, a Console Application project automatically contains a `Sub Main` procedure. If the project you are working with does not contain a `Sub Main` and you want one, then you can easily add one to your project. To create a `Sub Main` you need to add a module to your project. Modules are used as a container of shared procedures or functions within a project. You can add a module using the Solution Explorer. Right-click the project and then choose Add, Add Module. The Add New Item dialog box is then displayed as shown in Figure 25.2.

The Add New Item dialog box can also be shown using File, Add New Item from the Visual Studio .NET menu or by clicking the Add New Item toolbar button.

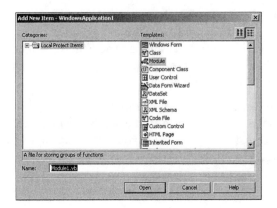

Figure 25.2: *Adding a module to a project.*

After the module is added, you need to create a Sub Main procedure. Here is an example Sub Main procedure:

```
Module Module1

    Public Sub Main()
        Dim form As Form1
        form = New Form1()
        Application.Run(form)
    End Sub

End Module
```

This example defines a form variable whose datatype is Form1. The form variable is set to a newly created instance of the Form1 class. The last line in the Main procedure is the most interesting. The Application class contains several shared methods for getting and setting specific application related data. It also contains a shared Run method, as shown here. The Run method is used to start a message pump for the current thread and then display the form as the controlling form for the thread. These three lines of code inside the body of the Sub Main procedure are identical to defining the Form1 class to be Startup object.

So why bother creating a Sub Main if it is easier just to define the Startup Object to be a specific form? In some cases you may just define the Startup Object to be a form, and this is fine. The benefit of defining a Sub Main to be the Startup Object is that you may have code you want to write when the application is starting. The Sub Main is a good place to put application startup specific code.

The following code shows how you might want to display a splash screen when your application starts:

```
Module Module1

    Private Sub AppStartup()
        ' application startup/initialization code goes here
        System.Threading.Thread.Sleep(5000)
    End Sub

    Public Sub Main()
        Dim splash As SplashScreen
        splash = New SplashScreen()

        splash.Show()
        Application.DoEvents()
        AppStartup()
        splash.Hide()

        Dim form As Form1
        form = New Form1()
        Application.Run(form)

    End Sub

End Module
```

In this example, we created a SplashScreen class that inherits from System.Windows.Forms.Form. The main point of this code is to show how a splash screen could be shown before the application runs. The exact code for the splash screen is not really that important but is shown in the SplashScreen class to give you some ideas on how it is done.

When the Startup Object is set to this Sub Main, you have the opportunity to do stuff before showing your main form. In this case, a splash screen is shown. Other things could be done, such as checking to see whether the application has a correct software license to run.

The first two lines of the Sub Main define and create a SplashScreen object for this application. Next, the splash screen is shown by calling the Show method.

Interestingly enough, the splash screen is not shown at this point. The reason is because there is no working UI message pump to process all of the pending window messages in the message queue. Without this pump, the form cannot handle the necessary events for displaying the form. The next line of code creates a UI message pump to process the messages. This results in the splash screen becoming visible on the screen. Next, there is a call to the AppStartup procedure. You can put any code you like in this procedure, and it will run while the splash screen is visible (if you do any UI tasks you may need to run Application.DoEvents again.)

Upon exiting the AppStartup Procedure, the splash screen is hidden by calling its Hide method. The code continues on to display the application's main form. The end result is that by specifying the Startup Object to be the Sub Main, you can write additional code for specific purposes when the application starts up. These purposes are left up to you as the application developer to define.

The code for the splash screen is shown here to give you an idea of how to write a splash screen for your own applications. The splash screen supports setting a background image on the form so that you can have a nice visual effect representing your application. If you set the background image for the form (using the BackgroundImage property), make sure the image file can be found; otherwise, you may get a runtime exception.

```
Public Class SplashScreen
    Inherits System.Windows.Forms.Form

#Region " Windows Form Designer generated code "

    Public Sub New()
        MyBase.New()

        'This call is required by the Windows Form Designer.
        InitializeComponent()

        'Add any initialization after the InitializeComponent() call

    End Sub

    'Form overrides dispose to clean up the component list.
    Protected Overloads Overrides Sub Dispose(ByVal disposing As Boolean)
        If disposing Then
            If Not (components Is Nothing) Then
                components.Dispose()
            End If
        End If
        MyBase.Dispose(disposing)
    End Sub
    Friend WithEvents Label1 As System.Windows.Forms.Label
    Friend WithEvents Label2 As System.Windows.Forms.Label

    'Required by the Windows Form Designer
```

```
Private components As System.ComponentModel.Container

'NOTE: The following procedure is required by the Windows Form Designer
'It can be modified using the Windows Form Designer.
'Do not modify it using the code editor.
<System.Diagnostics.DebuggerStepThrough()> Private Sub InitializeComponent()
    Dim resources As System.Resources.ResourceManager
    resources = New System.Resources.ResourceManager(GetType(SplashScreen))
    Me.Label1 = New System.Windows.Forms.Label()
    Me.Label2 = New System.Windows.Forms.Label()
    Me.SuspendLayout()
    '
    'Label1
    '
    Me.Label1.BackColor = System.Drawing.Color.Transparent
    Me.Label1.Font = New System.Drawing.Font("Microsoft Sans Serif", _
                                    18!, _
                                    (System.Drawing.FontStyle.Bold Or _
                                    System.Drawing.FontStyle.Italic), _
                                    System.Drawing.GraphicsUnit.Point, _
                                    CType(0, Byte))
    Me.Label1.Location = New System.Drawing.Point(32, 40)
    Me.Label1.Name = "Label1"
    Me.Label1.Size = New System.Drawing.Size(192, 48)
    Me.Label1.TabIndex = 0
    Me.Label1.Text = Application.ProductName
    '
    'Label2
    '
    Me.Label2.BackColor = System.Drawing.Color.Transparent
    Me.Label2.Location = New System.Drawing.Point(216, 184)
    Me.Label2.Name = "Label2"
    Me.Label2.Size = New System.Drawing.Size(64, 16)
    Me.Label2.TabIndex = 1
    Me.Label2.Text = Application.ProductVersion
    '
    'SplashScreen
    '
    Me.AutoScaleBaseSize = New System.Drawing.Size(5, 13)
    Me.BackgroundImage = CType(resources.GetObject("$this.BackgroundImage"), _
                        System.Drawing.Bitmap)
    Me.ClientSize = New System.Drawing.Size(294, 222)
    Me.ControlBox = False
    Me.Controls.AddRange(New System.Windows.Forms.Control() {Me.Label2, _
                                                Me.Label1})
    Me.FormBorderStyle = System.Windows.Forms.FormBorderStyle.FixedSingle
```

```
        Me.MaximizeBox = False
        Me.MinimizeBox = False
        Me.Name = "SplashScreen"
        Me.ShowInTaskbar = False
        Me.StartPosition = System.Windows.Forms.FormStartPosition.CenterScreen
        Me.TopMost = True
        Me.TransparencyKey = System.Drawing.Color.White
        Me.ResumeLayout(False)

    End Sub

#End Region

End Class
```

NOTE

The `System.Windows.Forms.Application` class is useful for other purposes as well. This class has shared methods for getting the executable path and startup path. This is useful if you have application data that exists in the folders where the application is installed and you need to read it within the application code.

Also, the `Application` class provides methods for reading user-specific application Registry data and common application Registry data. This is useful if you store application settings in the Registry and you need to read and write those values from your application code.

So now you know how an application's main form is displayed when the application starts up. This also includes how you would write code that is run before the main form is displayed. In the next section, you'll take a look at how to write code that is run before a form is displayed and after the form is closed. This is more commonly referred to as *form initialization and termination.*

Form Initialization and Termination

A form needs a way of initializing its data before it is displayed on the screen. It also needs a way of cleaning up after itself when the form goes away. In .NET, forms initialize themselves in the New method. Because the New method is called when a new instance of a form is created, you can put your code in the New method (or create another method that is called from the New method) in order to initialize your form.

When you create a new form using Visual Studio .NET, it generates the following code:

```
Public Class Form1
    Inherits System.Windows.Forms.Form
```

```
#Region " Windows Form Designer generated code "

    Public Sub New()
        MyBase.New()

        'This call is required by the Windows Form Designer.
        InitializeComponent()

        'Add any initialization after the InitializeComponent() call

    End Sub

    'Form overrides dispose to clean up the component list.
    Protected Overloads Overrides Sub Dispose(ByVal disposing As Boolean)
        If disposing Then
            If Not (components Is Nothing) Then
                components.Dispose()
            End If
        End If
        MyBase.Dispose(disposing)
    End Sub

    'Required by the Windows Form Designer
    Private components As System.ComponentModel.Container

    'NOTE: The following procedure is required by the Windows Form Designer
    'It can be modified using the Windows Form Designer.
    'Do not modify it using the code editor.
    <System.Diagnostics.DebuggerStepThrough()> Private Sub InitializeComponent()
        components = New System.ComponentModel.Container()
        Me.Text = "Form1"
    End Sub

#End Region

End Class
```

Notice that the New method calls InitializeComponent. The IntializeComponent method does most of the initialization work for the form. If you wanted to add initialization code for the form's class, there is a comment in the New method indicating the spot in which you would add this code.

Alternately, the form can respond to the Load event by providing an OnLoad method. The Load event is sent to the form before it is displayed for the first time:

```
Protected Overrides Sub OnLoad(ByVal e As System.EventArgs)
    MyBase.OnLoad
    'Add any initialization code here
End Sub
```

The Load event just loads the Form object into memory so that it can be used. Once a form is loaded, it is not shown on the screen until its Show method is called. You can also call a form's Hide method to undisplay a form. A hidden form is still around in memory along with its resources. A form is released from memory only after a form is disposed.

The code that cleans up after the form goes away is in the form's Dispose method. The purpose of the Dispose method is to free up any resources used by the form. Just because the automatic garbage collector in .NET will free up the resources automatically, don't assume that you do not need to support the Dispose method. The reason is that the garbage collector may not free up the resources immediately. By supporting the Dispose method, the resources are reclaimed earlier, thereby reducing potential problems. The Dispose method in the previous example code calls the Dispose methods on the components in the form. This also allows each control to perform any specific disposal that each control needs to do.

As you can see, the Visual Studio .NET generated code shows how to support form initialization and termination. If you write your own form class from scratch, make sure you support the New and Dispose methods.

NOTE

Visual Basic 6.0 has the Initialize event that is generated before a form is loaded and the Terminate event that is generated after a form is unloaded. In Visual Basic. NET, the Initialize event is replaced by the New method. The Terminate event is replaced by the Closing and Closed events.

The New method handles when an object is created. The Dispose method is used to free the resources that an object has obtained. What about the case where a form is closed but is still referenced in the application for use later on? The next section covers this case.

Form Closing

It is a common case that you would want to write code that is executed when the form closes. The Closed Event is sent to a form after the form is closed, and the form can handle this event if it has an OnClosed method. The OnClosed method is automatically called on a form if a Closed Event is fired for that form.

Here is a sample `OnClosed` method that shows where you would put your application logic, which is executed when the form is closed:

```
Protected Overrides Sub OnClosed(ByVal e As System.EventArgs)
    MyBase.OnClosed
    'Add code here
End Sub
```

After this method is called, the form is about to be closed, and there is no turning back. What if you wanted to write code to validate the form before it was closed? And, if the form is not validated, then stop the form from being closed? To handle this case, the form needs to handle the `Closing` Event. The `Closing` Event is fired to the form before the `Closed` event and gives you, the developer, an opportunity to intercept the closing of the form.

Just like the `OnClosed` method, there is an `OnClosing` method that can be used. The `OnClosing` method is automatically called when the `Closing` event is fired to the form. The argument to the `OnClosing` method is of type `CancelEventArgs`. The `CancelEventArgs` has a `Cancel` property that can be set to `True`, which forces the close process to stop. This effectively stops the form from being closed, as follows:

```
Protected Overrides Sub OnClosing(ByVal e _
                                As System.ComponentModel.CancelEventArgs)
    MyBase.OnClosing
    'Add code here
End Sub
```

Here is a code example showing the usage of these two methods:

```
Imports System.Windows.Forms

Public Class Form1
    Inherits System.Windows.Forms.Form

    Protected Overrides Sub OnClosed(ByVal e As System.EventArgs)
        MyBase.OnClosed
        MsgBox("The form is now closing.", MsgBoxStyle.OKOnly, "")
    End Sub

    Protected Overrides Sub OnClosing(ByVal e _
                                    As System.ComponentModel.CancelEventArgs)
        MyBase.OnClosing
        If MsgBox("Are you sure you want to close the form?", _
                MsgBoxStyle.YesNo, "") = MsgBoxResult.No Then
            e.Cancel = True
        End If
    End Sub
```

```
Shared Sub Main()
    Dim form As Form1
    form = New Form1()
    Application.Run(form)
End Sub
```

```
End Class
```

When the user clicks on the close box in the form, the `Closing` event is sent to the form first. At this point, the form displays a message asking the user whether he really means to close the form. The code in this example asks a question and tests the response from the user. If the user responds by not wanting to close the form, the `Cancel` property on the argument passed to the `OnClosing` method is set to `True`.

Figure 25.3 shows the message displayed after the user clicks on the close box. If the user clicks on the No button, the form is not closed. If the user clicks on the Yes button, the closing process continues, and a `Closed` event is sent to the form. This causes the `OnClose` method to be called, and the message shown in Figure 25.4 is displayed.

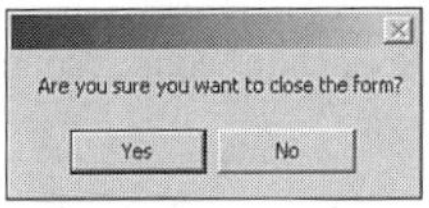

Figure 25.3: *Handling the `Closing` event.*

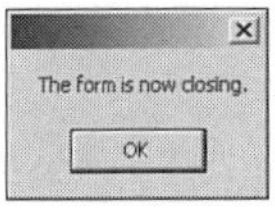

Figure 25.4: *Handling the `Closed` event.*

Now that we've shown how a form is displayed when the application starts along with initializing and terminating the form, the rest of your application's user interface development involves event-driven programming.

Event-Driven Programming

Event-driven programming, as its name implies, involves writing code that responds to events. When developing a user interface, this style of programming is required because you, as the developer, do not know ahead of time the sequence of events that users of your applications will take on a given form. Building a user interface that responds to events enables you to build powerful applications that are easy to use.

When you go about designing your forms, you should be thinking about the goal of the form; whether it is going to display data, edit data, or both. If the form is just going to display data, you just need to populate the form as part of the initialization of the form. Even in this case, however, you probably would put a button on the form to easily support closing the form (even though you may have a close button on the title bar). With a button, you need to handle the `Click` event generated by the button so that the form can be closed by the button.

If the form is used to edit data you need to think about the necessary controls on the form to support editing. For each control placed on the form, you need to decide whether there are any events that the form needs to respond to. If so, define event handlers for the events or override the appropriate method and write the necessary code.

To write an event handler, it is simpler to use the combo boxes on the form code window. Select the Base Class Events option in the combo box at the top left of the code window. This causes the combo box at the top right of the code window to present a list of the available events that can be handled for the form. Selecting an event in this combo box causes an event handler to be injected in the form code to handle the event.

To override a method, select the Overrides option in the combo box at the top left of the code window. This causes the combo box at the top right of the code window to present a list of the available methods that can be overridden for the form. Selecting a method in this combo box causes a method to be injected in the form code to handle the overridden method. Some of these methods are a convenient way to handle events. The naming convention of these methods prepends "On" to the event name. For example, the `OnClick` method handles the `Click` event for the form. This is a simpler and more efficient way to handle an event as opposed to writing an event handler.

Menus are an important user interface feature. They allow your users to view and invoke a set of functionality defined for a form. Consider using menus as appropriate, meaning you choose where and when to use them in context of your own application, and respond to the menu events using event handlers. Refer back to Chapter 24, "Menus," for more information regarding menus.

Drag and drop is also a standard feature of Windows applications. You may choose to spend time thinking about which forms or controls you want to support drag and drop especially because it is easy to implement in .NET.

What's Next

In this chapter you learned about how applications start up. This includes how you would go about adding code during startup and where to put this code. This chapter also covered issues regarding initialization and terminating forms, including how to intercept a form during the close process to validate a form.

In addition, event driven programming was explained in order to get you in the right frame of mind when developing a user interface. It is very important to think in terms of user interface components such as forms, menus, and controls and the events they generate. By responding to these events, you are able to build user interfaces that perform consistently and as the user expects them to perform.

In the next chapter, we continue presenting user interface topics as we cover graphics programming. Graphics programming allows you to draw all kinds of shapes and formatted text using a wide variety of colors, fonts, and brushes directly onto a drawing device. After you understand techniques in graphics programming, you are able to draw sophisticated designs on a form, for example, further enriching your user's experience.

NOTE

The answers to "Reviewing It," "Checking It," and "Applying It" are available on our Web site.

Reviewing It

REVIEW

This section presents a review of the key concepts in this chapter. These questions are intended to gauge your absorption of the relevant material.

1. What is a Startup Object?

2. What is event-driven programming?

Checking It

CHECK

Select the correct answer to the following questions.

Multiple Choice

1. To display a form of type `MyForm` when an application starts, what do you need to do?

   a. Call the `Show` method on a `MyForm` object.

   b. Set the Startup Object to be `Sub Main`.

   c. Set the Startup Object to be `MyForm`.

   d. Handle the `Load` event for `MyForm`.

2. To write code that initializes a form, what do you need to do?

   a. Write code in the `New` method after the `InitializeComponent` method call (if using Visual Studio .NET–generated code).

   b. Write code in the form's `OnLoad` method.

   c. Write code in the form's `Dispose` method.

   d. Both a and b.

3. To write code that is executed when a form closes, what do you need to do?

   a. Write code in the form's `OnClosed` overridden method.

   b. Write code in an event handler for the `Closed` event generated by the form.

   c. Write code in the form's `Dispose` method.

   d. Either a or b.

4. If I want to validate a form, which event should I handle when the form closes?

   a. `Close.`

   b. `Closed.`

   c. `Closing.`

   d. `Open.`

5. Which project type automatically contains a `Sub Main` procedure?

   a. Windows Application.

   b. `Console Application.`

   c. `Class Library.`

   d. `None of the above.`

6. Which project type does not automatically contain a `Sub Main` procedure?

   a. Windows Application.

   b. `Console Application.`

c. Class Library.

d. Both a and b.

True or False

Select one of the two possible answers and then verify on our Web site that you picked the correct one.

1. To write application initialization code when my application starts up, you could set the Startup Object to Sub Main and write the necessary code in Sub Main.

   True/False

2. The Closed event is generated before the Closing event.

   True/False

3. Handling the Closing event allows you to prevent a form from being closed.

   True/False

4. Hiding a form does not imply that the form is released from memory and its resources reclaimed.

   True/False

5. A form's resources are reclaimed after it is disposed and released from memory.

   True/False

6. The termination of a form can be handled in its overridden OnTerminate method.

   True/False

7. The combo boxes in the code window can be used to easily override methods and handle base class events.

   True/False

Applying It

Try to complete the following exercise by yourself.

APPLY

Independent Exercise

Write a simple form with a TextBox and don't allow the form to be closed if the TextBox is empty.

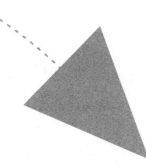

26

Graphics Programming

This chapter explores the graphics capabilities provided by the Microsoft .NET Framework. For most Visual Basic programmers, this chapter may not be of any use. This is because the graphical support that is most needed by programmers is already provided by a broad set of controls that can be used to build interesting applications.

However, for those readers who are interested in understanding and even building more sophisticated user interfaces, this chapter provides a very good introduction to *GDI+*. *GDI+* is Microsoft's successor to *GDI* (Graphics Device Interface) and is provided with the Microsoft .NET Framework.

To give you a better idea of what you will learn in this chapter, here is a list of the topics covered:

- Text
- Fonts
- Page units
- Location and sizing
- String alignment and wrapping
- Pens, lines, and rectangles
- Polygons
- Arcs and ellipses
- Open and closed curves
- Images and icons
- Filling
- Clipping
- Advanced features

Introduction to Graphics in .NET

As already mentioned at the start of this chapter, we will be introducing GDI+ by demonstrating examples that use the classes in the System.Drawing assembly. Most applications don't do any custom drawing on their forms. They just use the common controls provided for displaying data and allowing users to interact with the application. Sometimes though, there is a need to draw rotated text, custom lines, or display icons or bitmaps. GDI+ is used for this purpose. The GDI+ classes can also be combined to create even more complex displays such as a bar graph.

The intent of this chapter is to introduce you to the most common aspects of GDI+. This chapter is not an extensive overview but rather a great first step.

All of the graphics drawing involves using a System.Drawing.Graphics object. This Graphics object is the canvas on which the drawing takes place. It encapsulates the drawing surface of a Form or the printer (as you will see in Chapter 27, "Printing"). In this chapter, all of the examples demonstrate drawing graphics on a form.

When drawing on a form, you would normally override the form's OnPaint method and do the custom drawing there. The OnPaint takes one parameter, which is of type PaintEventArgs. The PaintEventArgs class contains a ClipRectangle and a Graphics object.

The ClipRectangle is the visible area of the form where the drawing takes place. Any drawing outside this ClipRectangle is not sent to the form's display surface.

The Graphics object, again, provides useful methods for doing the drawing (as you'll see).

Let's start by drawing some simple text onto a form.

Text

Here we have a simple example that draws some text onto a form's display area. To demonstrate this, a new form class is created, and the OnPaint method is overridden to provide the custom drawing:

EXAMPLE

```
Imports System.Windows.Forms
Imports System.Drawing

Public Class Form1
    Inherits System.Windows.Forms.Form
```

```
Private Sub New()
    MyBase.New()
End Sub

Protected Overrides Sub OnPaint(ByVal e As PaintEventArgs)
    Dim font As Font
    Dim text As String

    ' define text to be displayed on the form
    text = "Graphics Programming in Visual Basic.NET"

    ' specify the font to use for the text display
    font = New Font("San Serif", 8)

    ' display the text string
    e.Graphics.DrawString(text, font, SystemBrushes.WindowText, 10, 10)

    ' dispose of the font resource
    font.Dispose()

End Sub

Shared Sub main()
    Application.Run(New Form1())
End Sub

End Class
```

RUNIT

You can see the result of the output from this example in Figure 26.1.

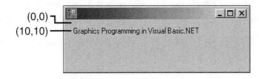

Figure 26.1: *DrawString example.*

This example uses the Graphics object passed in as a property of the parameter passed to the OnPaint method. The DrawString method is invoked on the Graphics object, which causes the string to be drawn on the form. There are several versions of the DrawString method in the Graphics class. The specific version used in this example is defined as

```
Public Sub DrawString(ByVal s As String, _
                      ByVal font As System.Drawing.Font, _
```

```
ByVal brush As System.Drawing.Brush, _
ByVal x As Single, _
ByVal y As Single)
```

The first parameter is the text that is to be displayed. The second parameter is the font that you want the text to be displayed in. The third parameter is the brush that typically defines the color of the text. And, the fourth and fifth parameters are used to specify the starting location of the text.

NOTE

Any point, or location, on a form is described using a pair of x and y values in the form of (x, y). The horizontal direction is indicated by x, and the vertical direction is indicated by y. The origin of a form is the upper left-hand corner of the form. This location is defined as position (0, 0). Therefore, a position of (10, 20) indicates a point 10 units starting from the left side of the form and 20 units from the top of the form. The default unit of measure is a pixel.

Before drawing the text, we had to create a Font object. The Font constructor used in this example takes the name of the installed font and the size of the font as shown here:

```
Public Sub New(ByVal familyName As String, ByVal emSize As Single)
```

Instead of creating a new Brush object like we did with the Font object, the example uses a *system brush*. There are many different system brushes that you can use. Each is defined through the Display Properties in the Control Panel as part of the Microsoft Windows operating system. Using the system brushes, you can develop your application so that the colors are based on the colors you choose as part of your computer setup. This way your users can choose the overall color scheme of an application that should result in a happier user. The last thing you would want to do is specify your own colors and disallow the user any configuration opportunity.

And lastly, a location to start drawing the text is passed to the DrawString method.

After the text is drawn, the Dispose method of the Font is called. This is so that the Font object can free any internal resources before the object goes out of scope. If the object goes out of scope before calling Dispose, there would be no harm based on this example. This is because the Microsoft .NET's garbage collector will reclaim the Font object, forcing the Font's internal resources to be reclaimed. However, it is good practice to call the Dispose method explicitly because the garbage collector may not reclaim the Font object immediately. The longer the delay the higher the potential for contention of resources to occur. So, especially in graphics programming it is good practice to free the resources of fonts, brushes, icons, and images by calling the Dispose method when they are done being used.

Now let's go into more detail regarding fonts.

Fonts

The example in the previous section showed how to create a basic font for use in drawing a string on a form. You can also create fonts with formatting such as bold, italics, underline, and strikethrough. The object-oriented approach of the .NET Framework shows how easy it is to do things like this. You would simply create a new Font object and specify a font style in addition to the font name and size.

Here is an example showing several font styles:

EXAMPLE

```
Imports System.Windows.Forms
Imports System.Drawing

Public Class Form1
    Inherits System.Windows.Forms.Form

    Private Sub New()
        MyBase.New()
    End Sub

    Protected Overrides Sub OnPaint(ByVal e As PaintEventArgs)
        Dim font As Font
        Dim fontName As String
        Dim fontSize As Single
        Dim spacer As Single
        Dim x, y As Single

        ' set starting position
        x = 10
        y = 10

        ' define font to use for example
        fontName = "San Serif"
        fontSize = 12

        ' get height of a string using this font
        font = New Font(fontName, fontSize, FontStyle.Regular)
        spacer = e.Graphics.MeasureString("A String", font).Height + 10
        font.Dispose()

        ' display a string in normal format
        font = New Font(fontName, fontSize, FontStyle.Regular)
```

```vb
    e.Graphics.DrawString("Regular", font, SystemBrushes.WindowText, x, y)
    font.Dispose()

    ' display a string in italic format
    y = y + spacer
    font = New Font(fontName, fontSize, FontStyle.Bold)
    e.Graphics.DrawString("Bold", font, SystemBrushes.WindowText, x, y)
    font.Dispose()

    ' display a string in bold format
    y = y + spacer
    font = New Font(fontName, fontSize, FontStyle.Italic)
    e.Graphics.DrawString("Italic", font, SystemBrushes.WindowText, x, y)
    font.Dispose()

    ' display a string in strikeout format
    y = y + spacer
    font = New Font(fontName, fontSize, FontStyle.Strikeout)
    e.Graphics.DrawString("Strikeout", font, SystemBrushes.WindowText, x, y)
    font.Dispose()

    ' display a string in underline format
    y = y + spacer
    font = New Font(fontName, fontSize, FontStyle.Underline)
    e.Graphics.DrawString("Underline", font, SystemBrushes.WindowText, x, y)
    font.Dispose()

    ' display a string in bold, italic, and underline format
    y = y + spacer
    font = New Font(fontName, fontSize, FontStyle.Bold Or _
                                        FontStyle.Italic Or _
                                        FontStyle.Underline)
    e.Graphics.DrawString("Bold, Italic, and Underline", _
                          font, SystemBrushes.WindowText, x, y)
    font.Dispose()

End Sub

Shared Sub main()
    Application.Run(New Form1())
End Sub

End Class
```

RUNIT

You can see the result of this output in Figure 26.2.

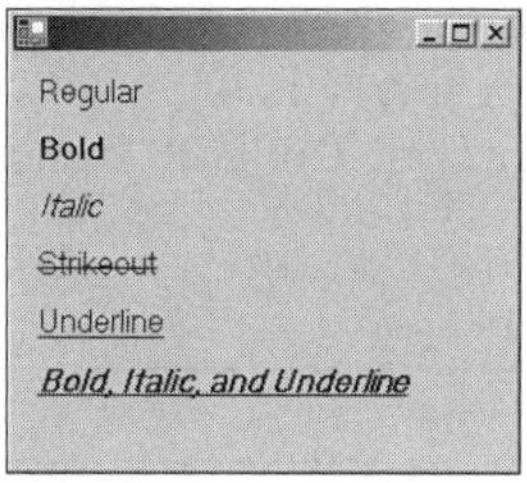

Figure 26.2: *Font example.*

As you can see, the code is based on the first example that illustrated drawing a simple text string. Here, there are six strings being displayed in different font styles. The only difference between the preceding example and the first example is the way in which the Font object is constructed. In the preceding example, the following constructor is used so that the font style could be specified:

```
Public Sub New(ByVal familyName As String, _
               ByVal emSize As Single, _
               ByVal style As System.Drawing.FontStyle)
```

FontStyle is an enumeration used to specify the style for a Font object. Table 26.1 shows the possible values you can use for specifying a font style.

Table 26.1: **FontStyle** *Enumeration Values*

Name	Description
Bold	Displays text in bold
Italic	Displays text in italics
Regular	Displays text in normal style
Strikeout	Displays text with a line through it
Underline	Displays text with an underline

When declaring a Font with a FontStyle, you can specify any combination of styles such as bold and italic. You would combine the styles using the Or operator. This was shown in the previous code example.

Page Units

In Chapter 22, "Forms," and earlier in this chapter, we mentioned units when referring to positioning of elements on a form. Up until now, these units have been in terms of pixels on the screen. This is the default setting, however, and you can change this based on your needs.

The setting that specifies the unit of measurement is the PageUnit property on the Graphics object. The PageUnit property is a System.Drawing.GraphicsUnit enumeration. Table 26.2 shows the GraphicsUnit enumeration.

Table 26.2: **GraphicsUnit** *Enumeration Values*

Name	Description
Display	1/75 of an inch
Document	1/300 of an inch
Inch	Inch
Millimeter	Millimeter
Pixel	1 device pixel (default)
Point	1/72 of an inch
World	Logical world unit

To show the impact of changing the PageUnit, the following example sets the PageUnit to Inch:

EXAMPLE

```
Imports System.Windows.Forms
Imports System.Drawing

Public Class Form1
    Inherits System.Windows.Forms.Form

    Private Sub New()
        MyBase.New()
    End Sub

    Protected Overrides Sub OnPaint(ByVal e As PaintEventArgs)
        Dim font As Font
        font = New Font("San Serif", 12, FontStyle.Regular)

        e.Graphics.PageUnit = GraphicsUnit.Inch

        e.Graphics.DrawString("One inch down, one inch from left.", font, _
                        SystemBrushes.WindowText, 1, 1)

        e.Graphics.DrawString("Two inches down, one inch from left", font, _
                        SystemBrushes.WindowText, 1, 2)

        font.Dispose()

    End Sub
```

```
Shared Sub main()
    Application.Run(New Form1())
End Sub
```

```
End Class
```

The result of this output can be seen in Figure 26.3.

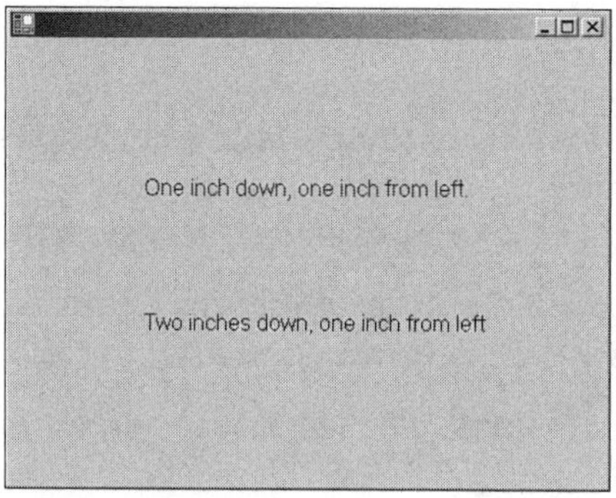

RUNIT

Figure 26.3: PageUnit *example.*

As you can see, the starting location for the displayed strings is now based on inches. Therefore, the example uses numbers like 1 and 2 for specifying the y position. When setting your positions for displaying graphics, make sure you understand the PageUnit the Graphics object is set to and the impact this has on your code.

Location and Sizing

The System.Drawing assembly also provides some handy data types for encapsulating points, rectangles, and sizes. This way you do not need to specify separate parameters for x and y to every DrawString method you call. These data types include Point, Size, Rectangle, PointF, SizeF, and RectangleF.

These three classes store their values as an Integer data type:

- **System.Drawing.Point**. The Point data type defines a location in two-dimensional space. This location is specified by an x coordinate and a y coordinate.

- **System.Drawing.Size**. The Size data type defines a width and a height. Each of these four values is stored as an Integer.

- **System.Drawing.Rectangle**. The Rectangle data type is defined by a Point and a Size.

There are some cases where values of type Integer are not appropriate for defining points, sizes, and rectangles in the System.Drawing assembly. For this reason, these three additional classes were provided to store the values as a Single data type:

- **System.Drawing.PointF**. The PointF data type defines a location in two-dimensional space. This location is specified by an x coordinate and a y coordinate. The x value and y value are stored as Single.

- **System.Drawing.SizeF**. The SizeF data type defines a width and a height. Each of these four values is stored as a Single.

- **System.Drawing.RectangleF**. The RectangleF data type is defined by a PointF and a SizeF.

NOTE

The Point, Size, and Rectangle classes store their location and size information using Integer values.

The PointF, SizeF, and RectangleF classes store their location and size information using Single values.

String Alignment and Wrapping

In addition to drawing single lines of text, you can also wrap a larger amount of text within a defined rectangle. To accomplish this, you need to create a StringFormat object for the purpose of defining how you want the text to be wrapped.

The StringFormat object has two useful properties for controlling the wrapping. These properties are FormatFlags and Alignment. The FormatFlags property is based on the StringFormatFlags enumeration data type. Table 26.3 shows the values defined in this enumeration along with a brief explanation.

Table 26.3: **StringFormatFlags** *Enumeration Values*

Name	Description
DirectionRightToLeft	Specifies text display is right to left.
DirectionVertical	Specifies text display is vertical.

Table 26.3: continued

Name	Description
DisplayFormatControl	Causes control characters to be displayed with a representative glyph in the output if they are present in the text.
FitBlackBox	No text is painted outside of the rectangle.
LineLimit	Only entire lines of text are displayed. If wrapped lines do not fit entirely (based on height of line) in the rectangle then it is not displayed. You must make sure the rectangle is at least as high as one line of text.
MeasureTrailingSpaces	Graphics.MeasureString does not include any spaces at the end of a String unless this option is specified.
NoClip	This option allows overhanging text to be painted outside of the rectangle. The default behavior is to not allow painting of text outside the rectangle.
NoFontFallback	Displaying of text automatically falls back to an alternate font if the specified font is not installed. This option disables this so that there is no fallback to an alternate font.
NoWrap	Specifies that the text does not wrap onto multiple lines.

The Alignment property is based on the StringAlignment enumeration data type. Table 26.4 shows the values defined in this enumeration along with a brief explanation.

Table 26.4: **StringAlignment** *Enumeration Values*

Member Name	Description
Center	Specifies that text is aligned in the center of the layout rectangle.
Far	Specifies that text is aligned far from the origin position of the layout rectangle. In a left-to-right layout, the far position is right. In a right-to-left layout, the far position is left.
Near	Specifies the text be aligned near the layout. In a left-to-right layout, the near position is left. In a right-to-left layout, the near position is right.

The values for the Alignment property are based on the display direction specified by the FormatFlags property. By default, the display direction is from left to right. In this case, if the Alignment property contains the value Near, then the string is aligned to the left. If the Alignment property contains the value Far, then the string is aligned to the right.

In contrast, if the FormatFlags property contains DirectionRightToLeft, then the starting point (or near side) is the right side of the rectangle. So, if FormatFlags is set to DirectionRightToLeft and Alignment is set to Near, then the text is aligned to the right. If the FormatFlags is set to DirectionRightToLeft and Alignment is set to Far, then the text is aligned to the left.

The following example illustrates drawing text on multiple lines and specifying alignment information:

EXAMPLE

```
Imports System.Windows.Forms
Imports System.Drawing

Public Class Form1
    Inherits System.Windows.Forms.Form

    Private Sub New()
        MyBase.New()
    End Sub

    Protected Overrides Sub OnPaint(ByVal e As PaintEventArgs)
        Dim font As Font
        Dim sf As New StringFormat()
        Dim text As String
        Dim rect As New RectangleF(10, 10, 150, 100)

        font = New Font("San Serif", 12, FontStyle.Regular)

        ' specify string formatting
        sf.Alignment = StringAlignment.Near
        sf.FormatFlags = StringFormatFlags.NoClip

        ' draw text
        text = "The quick brown fox jumps over the lazy dog."
        e.Graphics.DrawString(text, font, SystemBrushes.WindowText, rect, sf)

        sf.Dispose()
        font.Dispose()

    End Sub

    Shared Sub main()
        Application.Run(New Form1())
    End Sub

End Class
```

RUNIT

This output results in the image Figure 26.4.

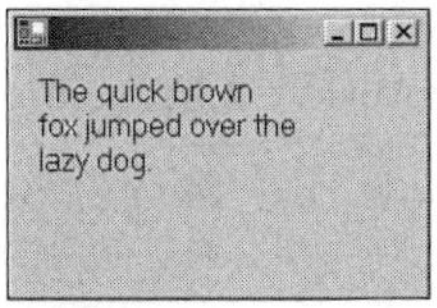

Figure 26.4: *Alignment and wrapping example.*

In this example, a `StringFormat` object is used to specify the formatting information. A `Rectangle` object is used to specify the rectangular area in which the code intends on drawing the text on the form. The alignment is set to `Near`, which translates into align-left because the direction on the form is set to left to right by default. The `NoClip` setting in the formatting allows the text to be painted if by chance the text extends beyond the rectangle area. And lastly, the `Rectangle` and `StringFormat` objects are passed to the `DrawString` method.

This example is quite simple but, as you can see, the alignment and formatting can be combined in many different ways allowing you full control of how to display text using GDI+.

Pens, Lines, and Rectangles

GDI+ allows you to draw more than just text. You can draw lines, rectangles, circles, ellipses, and so on. You can even control the color in which you want to draw these graphical elements.

The `System.Drawing.Pen` class is provided in the .NET Framework to encapsulate colors used during the drawing process. You can create `Pen` objects based on colors you specify and then use these `Pen` objects when drawing text, lines, rectangles, or whatever.

The graphical elements such as lines and rectangles are drawn using methods on the `Graphics` object. The following method is one of several `DrawLine` methods that can be used to draw a line:

```
Public Sub DrawLine(ByVal pen As System.Drawing.Pen, _
                    ByVal pt1 As System.Drawing.PointF, _
                    ByVal pt2 As System.Drawing.PointF)
```

The `DrawLine` method uses a `Pen` object (for the purposes of defining the color in which to draw the line) and two points (representing the starting and ending points of the line).

The following method is one of several `DrawRectangle` methods that can be used to draw a rectangle:

```
Public Sub DrawRectangle(ByVal pen As System.Drawing.Pen, _
                         ByVal rect As System.Drawing.Rectangle)
```

Let's draw a line and a rectangle to see how this works. Here is an example:

EXAMPLE

```
Imports System.Windows.Forms
Imports System.Drawing.Drawing2D
Imports System.Drawing
Public Class Form1
    Inherits System.Windows.Forms.Form

    Private Sub New()
        MyBase.New()
    End Sub

    Protected Overrides Sub OnPaint(ByVal e As PaintEventArgs)
        Dim pointStart, pointEnd As PointF
        Dim rect As Rectangle
        Dim pen As Pen

        pointStart.X = 10
        pointStart.Y = 10

        pointEnd.X = Me.Width - 10
        pointEnd.Y = 10

        pen = New Pen(System.Drawing.Color.Blue)
        pen.Width = 3

        ' draw a blue line
        e.Graphics.DrawLine(pen, pointStart, pointEnd)

        rect.X = 50
        rect.Y = 50
        rect.Height = 100
        rect.Width = 100

        ' draw a blue square
        e.Graphics.DrawRectangle(pen, rect)

        pen.Dispose()

    End Sub
```

```
Shared Sub main()
    Application.Run(New Form1())
End Sub

End Class
```

RUNIT

The preceding output produces what you see in Figure 26.5.

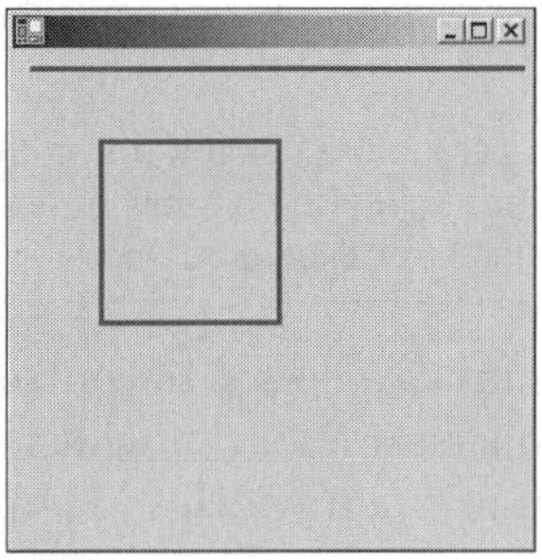

Figure 26.5: *Pen, line, and rectangle example.*

In the OnPaint method, two points are defined that represent the starting and ending points of our example line. Next, create a Pen object and specify its color to be Blue. Notice that the System.Drawing.Color class contains a list of predefined colors that you can use. This list is very extensive, but if you don't find a color you like, you can always create your own if you know the RGB value for the color.

As an example, this code defines a color to use based on an RGB value:

```
pen = New Pen(Color.FromArgb(100, 0, 100))
```

Also, you can use the public properties on the System.Drawing.SystemColors class for obtaining the system colors configured in your operating system. This is very useful if you want to draw graphics and have the colors based on your user's computer setup. For example, to use the Highlight color defined on your computer, you could use this code instead:

```
pen = New Pen(SystemColors.Highlight)
```

In addition to the SystemColors, the .NET Framework provides SystemPens as well. The advantage of using SystemPens over SystemColors is that if a system pen contains more than just a color (such as thickness and a pattern as we'll see later in this chapter) you do not need to redefine a pen object with all of this information to get the same look. You can just use the system pen. For example:

```
pen = SystemPens.Highlight
```

NOTE

If you use a Pen defined in the SystemPens class, be very careful *not* to call the Dispose method of the Pen in your code. This causes the Pen's internal resources to be freed and because the system pens are system-wide resources this may terminate your program prematurely.

To avoid this, you could clone the system pen before using it (using the Clone method). This creates a copy of the pen that you can be free to use in your application. Then you would be free to dispose of the clone (using the Dispose method).

The pen also has a Width property that can be set to control the thickness of the lines drawn using the pen. In this example, the width is set to 3 to make the lines more visible. The default pen width is 1.

The DrawLine method is called on the Graphics object to display the line.

A rectangle of arbitrary position and size is created to illustrate how to draw a rectangle. The DrawRectangle method is called on the Graphics object passing in the Pen object and the defined Rectangle. Notice that the Pen object is being reused again for the rectangle. In your graphics code, you should reuse resources, such as Pens, as often as you can.

The last line of the OnPaint method calls the Pen object's Dispose method to have the Pen free up its internal resources.

Brushes

So far, we have said that Pen objects have a defined color and thickness. They can also have patterns or textures that are defined using Brush objects. Let's start with an example and then we'll discuss this in more detail. Here is an example showing four lines drawn each with different pens:

EXAMPLE

```
Imports System.Windows.Forms
Imports System.Drawing.Drawing2D
Imports System.Drawing
Public Class Form1
    Inherits System.Windows.Forms.Form

    Private Sub New()
        MyBase.New()
    End Sub
```

```vb
Protected Overrides Sub OnPaint(ByVal e As PaintEventArgs)
    Dim pointStart, pointEnd As PointF
    Dim brush As Brush
    Dim rect As Rectangle
    Dim pen As Pen

    pointStart.X = 10
    pointStart.Y = 10

    pointEnd.X = Me.Width - 10
    pointEnd.Y = 10

    pen = New Pen(SystemColors.Highlight)
    pen.Width = 20

    ' show linear gradient brush
    brush = New LinearGradientBrush(pointStart, pointEnd, Color.Blue, Color.Red)
    pen.Brush = brush
    e.Graphics.DrawLine(pen, pointStart, pointEnd)
    brush.Dispose()

    ' show hatch brush
    pointStart.Y += 25
    pointEnd.Y += 25
    brush = New HatchBrush(HatchStyle.SmallCheckerBoard, Color.Green)
    pen.Brush = brush
    e.Graphics.DrawLine(pen, pointStart, pointEnd)
    brush.Dispose()

    ' show texture brush
    pointStart.Y += 25
    pointEnd.Y += 25
    brush = New TextureBrush(New Bitmap("smile.ico"))
    pen.Brush = brush
    e.Graphics.DrawLine(pen, pointStart, pointEnd)
    brush.Dispose()

    ' show solid color
    pointStart.Y += 25
    pointEnd.Y += 25
    brush = New SolidBrush(Color.Coral)
    pen.Brush = brush
    e.Graphics.DrawLine(pen, pointStart, pointEnd)
    brush.Dispose()
```

```
        pen.Dispose()

    End Sub

    Shared Sub main()
        Application.Run(New Form1())
    End Sub

End Class
```

The preceding output results in Figure 26.6.

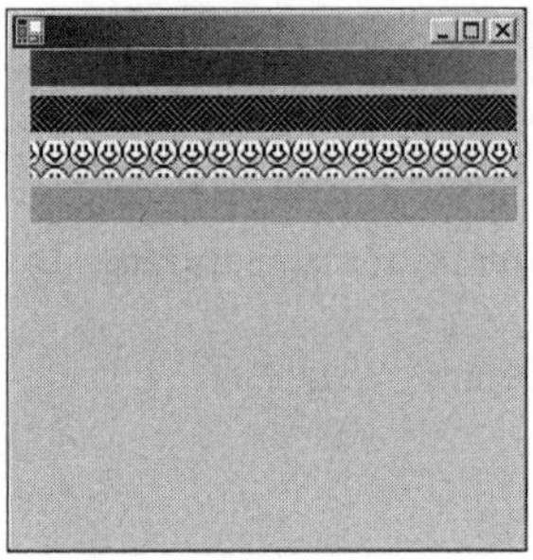

RUNIT

Figure 26.6: Brush example.

In this example, the width of the pen is set to 20 to allow a better view of the brushes used when drawing the lines. There are five types of brushes you can use in GDI+:

- HatchFill
- LinearGradient
- PathGradient
- SolidColor
- TextureFill

In the sample output, the top line uses a LinearGradient brush. As you can see, the LinearGradient brush allows you to specify colors at two specific points on the form, and the LinearGradient brush automatically blends the two colors as they approach each other.

The next line utilizes a HatchFill brush. HatchFill brushes contain a pre-defined pattern and a color. Using these two values, you can draw graphic elements that have color and contain a visibly displayed pattern.

The third line down on the form uses a TextureBrush. A TextureBrush contains an image that is displayed over and over again while the graphic element is being drawn. TextureBrushes can be used to display more interesting graphical drawings without having to draw the image details through code. You just specify the texture, and the brush takes care of the rest for you.

The fourth line down on the form uses a SolidColor brush. In this example, this is the same as setting the Pen color. However, brushes are also used for filling shapes such as rectangles. For filling, you have to use brushes as we will see in the "Filling" section later in this chapter.

PathGradient brushes are similar to LinearGradient except that they support a path, or series of points.

DashStyle

Pens also support dashed lines in addition to solid lines. This is supported through the use of the DashStyle property on the Pen class. The DashStyle property is based on the DashStyle enumeration. This enumeration contains these values:

- Custom

- Dash

- DashDot

- DashDotDot

- Dot

- Solid

To show the effects of setting the DashStyle, this example displays several lines with differing dash styles:

EXAMPLE

```
Imports System.Windows.Forms
Imports System.Drawing.Drawing2D
Imports System.Drawing
Public Class Form1
    Inherits System.Windows.Forms.Form

    Private Sub New()
        MyBase.New()
    End Sub

    Protected Overrides Sub OnPaint(ByVal e As PaintEventArgs)
        Dim pointStart, pointEnd As PointF
        Dim pen As Pen
```

```
                    pointStart.X = 10
                    pointStart.Y = 10

                    pointEnd.X = Me.Width - 10
                    pointEnd.Y = 10

                    pen = New Pen(SystemColors.Highlight)
                    pen.Width = 5
                    pen.DashStyle = System.Drawing.Drawing2D.DashStyle.Dash
                    e.Graphics.DrawLine(pen, pointStart, pointEnd)

                    pointStart.Y += 25
                    pointEnd.Y += 25
                    pen.DashStyle = System.Drawing.Drawing2D.DashStyle.DashDot
                    e.Graphics.DrawLine(pen, pointStart, pointEnd)

                    pointStart.Y += 25
                    pointEnd.Y += 25
                    pen.DashStyle = System.Drawing.Drawing2D.DashStyle.DashDotDot
                    e.Graphics.DrawLine(pen, pointStart, pointEnd)

                    pointStart.Y += 25
                    pointEnd.Y += 25
                    pen.DashStyle = System.Drawing.Drawing2D.DashStyle.Dot
                    e.Graphics.DrawLine(pen, pointStart, pointEnd)

                    pointStart.Y += 25
                    pointEnd.Y += 25
                    pen.DashStyle = System.Drawing.Drawing2D.DashStyle.Solid
                    e.Graphics.DrawLine(pen, pointStart, pointEnd)

                    pen.Dispose()

                End Sub

                Shared Sub main()
                    Application.Run(New Form1())
                End Sub

            End Class
```

RUNIT

The result of this output can be seen in Figure 26.7.

The values for the dash styles are self-explanatory in explaining their visual effects. For example, the DashDotDot value is used to display a line with the repeating pattern of a dash, a dot, and another dot.

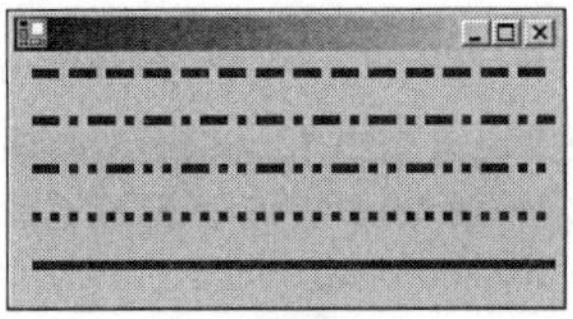

Figure 26.7: DashStyle example.

DashCap

In addition to the dash style, Pen objects also support decorations at either end of each dash in the line. This is supported through the use of the DashCap property in the Pen class. The DashCap property is based on the DashCap enumeration, which contains these values:

- Flat

- Round

- Triangle

The next sample shows examples of each of these three types of dashes you can use in your drawing code:

EXAMPLE

```
Imports System.Windows.Forms
Imports System.Drawing.Drawing2D
Imports System.Drawing

Public Class Form1
    Inherits System.Windows.Forms.Form

    Private Sub New()
        MyBase.New()
    End Sub

    Protected Overrides Sub OnPaint(ByVal e As PaintEventArgs)
        Dim pointStart, pointEnd As PointF
        Dim pen As Pen

        pointStart.X = 10
        pointStart.Y = 10

        pointEnd.X = Me.Width - 10
        pointEnd.Y = 10
```

```
        pen = New Pen(SystemColors.Highlight)
        pen.Width = 10
        pen.DashStyle = System.Drawing.Drawing2D.DashStyle.Dash
        pen.DashCap = System.Drawing.Drawing2D.DashCap.Flat
        e.Graphics.DrawLine(pen, pointStart, pointEnd)

        pointStart.Y += 25
        pointEnd.Y += 25
        pen.DashStyle = System.Drawing.Drawing2D.DashStyle.Dash
        pen.DashCap = System.Drawing.Drawing2D.DashCap.Round
        e.Graphics.DrawLine(pen, pointStart, pointEnd)

        pointStart.Y += 25
        pointEnd.Y += 25
        pen.DashStyle = System.Drawing.Drawing2D.DashStyle.Dash
        pen.DashCap = System.Drawing.Drawing2D.DashCap.Triangle
        e.Graphics.DrawLine(pen, pointStart, pointEnd)

        pen.Dispose()

    End Sub

    Shared Sub main()
        Application.Run(New Form1())
    End Sub

End Class
```

RUNIT

The results of this output can be seen in Figure 26.8.

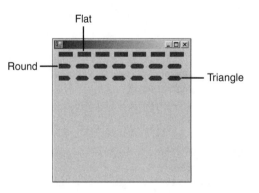

Figure 26.8: *DashCap example.*

LineCap

Just as with the DashCap property, the Pen class also supports decorating the ends of a line with several different decorators. This is supported by setting the LineCap property on a Pen object to one of the following values:

- ArrowAnchor
- DiamondAnchor
- Flat
- Round
- RoundAnchor
- Square
- SquareAnchor
- Triangle

This next example demonstrates a few of the possible LineCap settings:

EXAMPLE

```
Imports System.Windows.Forms
Imports System.Drawing.Drawing2D
Imports System.Drawing

Public Class Form1
    Inherits System.Windows.Forms.Form

    Private Sub New()
        MyBase.New()
    End Sub

    Protected Overrides Sub OnPaint(ByVal e As PaintEventArgs)
        Dim pointStart, pointEnd As PointF
        Dim pen As Pen

        pointStart.X = 20
        pointStart.Y = 20

        pointEnd.X = Me.Width - 30
        pointEnd.Y = 20
```

```
    pen = New Pen(SystemColors.Highlight)
    pen.Width = 10
    pen.StartCap = System.Drawing.Drawing2D.LineCap.ArrowAnchor
    pen.EndCap = System.Drawing.Drawing2D.LineCap.DiamondAnchor
    e.Graphics.DrawLine(pen, pointStart, pointEnd)

    pointStart.Y += 25
    pointEnd.Y += 25
    pen.StartCap = System.Drawing.Drawing2D.LineCap.Flat
    pen.EndCap = System.Drawing.Drawing2D.LineCap.RoundAnchor
    e.Graphics.DrawLine(pen, pointStart, pointEnd)

    pointStart.Y += 25
    pointEnd.Y += 25
    pen.StartCap = System.Drawing.Drawing2D.LineCap.SquareAnchor
    pen.EndCap = System.Drawing.Drawing2D.LineCap.Triangle
    e.Graphics.DrawLine(pen, pointStart, pointEnd)

    pen.Dispose()

End Sub

Shared Sub main()
    Application.Run(New Form1())
End Sub

End Class
```

RUNIT

The preceding output can be seen in Figure 26.9.

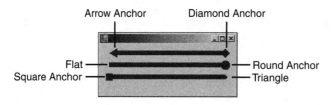

Figure 26.9: *LineCap example.*

Polygons

In addition to drawing text, lines, and rectangles, you can also draw polygons that contain any number of sides. The way you would go about doing this is to first create an array of points that represent the vertices of the polygon. This array of points then is passed to the DrawPolygon method on the Graphics object. The Graphics object takes care of drawing the lines from each point to the next and also from the last point back to the first (to create a closed shape).

Here is a simple example that shows how this is done:

EXAMPLE

```
Imports System.Windows.Forms
Imports System.Drawing.Drawing2D
Imports System.Drawing

Public Class Form1
    Inherits System.Windows.Forms.Form

    Private Sub New()
        MyBase.New()
    End Sub

    Protected Overrides Sub OnPaint(ByVal e As PaintEventArgs)
        Dim points(5) As PointF
        Dim pen As Pen

        points(0) = New PointF(10, 50)
        points(1) = New PointF(30, 25)
        points(2) = New PointF(50, 10)
        points(3) = New PointF(70, 60)
        points(4) = New PointF(40, 80)
        points(5) = New PointF(30, 60)

        pen = New Pen(SystemColors.Highlight)
        pen.Width = 3
        e.Graphics.DrawPolygon(pen, points)

        pen.Dispose()

    End Sub

    Shared Sub main()
        Application.Run(New Form1())
    End Sub

End Class
```

RUNIT

The output of this example can be seen in Figure 26.10.

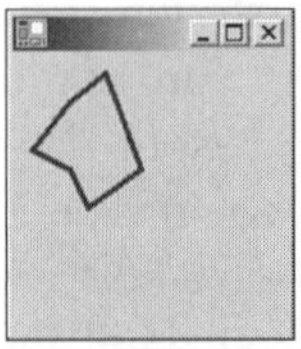

Figure 26.10: *Polygon example.*

Arcs and Ellipses

Arcs and ellipses are additional graphics objects that can be drawn in GDI+ with relative ease. The DrawArc and DrawEllipse methods on the Graphics object provide this capability.

When drawing an arc, you start by defining a rectangle that the arc is bounded by. Next, you specify the starting angle in which to draw the arc. The starting angle is specified in degrees rotating clockwise starting from the x-axis. The last piece of information you need to provide is the ending angle. The ending angle is the number of degrees the arc continues counter clockwise starting from where the arc is first drawn.

Let's discuss a specific example. The following code creates an Arc using an arbitrary rectangle. The starting angle is 0 degrees. This means the arc is going to start from the x-axis. The ending angle is 180 degrees. This means that the arc continues counter clockwise from the x-axis (starting point) until it reaches 180 degrees from the starting point.

Here is the sample code:

EXAMPLE

```
Imports System.Windows.Forms
Imports System.Drawing.Drawing2D
Imports System.Drawing

Public Class Form1
    Inherits System.Windows.Forms.Form

    Private Sub New()
        MyBase.New()
    End Sub
```

```
Protected Overrides Sub OnPaint(ByVal e As PaintEventArgs)
    Dim pen As Pen
    Dim rect As RectangleF
    Dim startAngle As Single
    Dim endAngle As Single

    pen = New Pen(SystemColors.Highlight)
    pen.Width = 3

    rect.X = 30
    rect.Y = 30
    rect.Width = 200
    rect.Height = 100
    startAngle = 0
    endAngle = 180
    e.Graphics.DrawArc(pen, rect, startAngle, endAngle)

    pen.Dispose()

End Sub

Shared Sub main()
    Application.Run(New Form1())
End Sub
```

```
End Class
```

The results of this example can be seen in Figure 26.11.

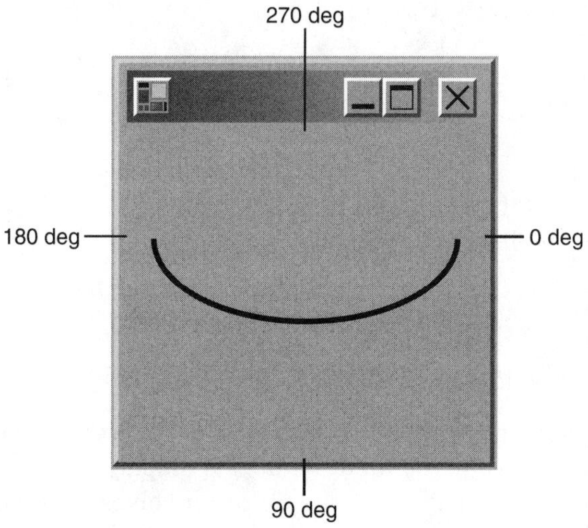

RUNIT

Figure 26.11: Arc example.

Drawing ellipses is much easier because you need to specify only the bounding rectangle. Because the ellipses is a closed arc, the beginning and ending angles are not needed. The following example draws an ellipse. Note that the bounding rectangle is identical to the rectangle using in the arc example. Because of this, the bottom half of the ellipse looks exactly like the Arc in the previous example:

EXAMPLE

```
Imports System.Windows.Forms
Imports System.Drawing.Drawing2D
Imports System.Drawing
Imports System.Drawing
Public Class Form1
    Inherits System.Windows.Forms.Form

    Private Sub New()
        MyBase.New()
    End Sub

    Protected Overrides Sub OnPaint(ByVal e As PaintEventArgs)
        Dim pen As Pen
        Dim rect As RectangleF

        pen = New Pen(SystemColors.Highlight)
        pen.Width = 3

        rect.X = 30
        rect.Y = 30
        rect.Width = 200
        rect.Height = 100
        e.Graphics.DrawEllipse(pen, rect)

        pen.Dispose()

    End Sub

    Shared Sub main()
        Application.Run(New Form1())
    End Sub

End Class
```

RUNIT

Figure 26.12 displays the results of this example.

If in the previous arc example the ending angle were 360 degrees, the resulting display would be identical to the display of the ellipse example. Again, this is because drawing the ellipse involves drawing an arc 360 degrees within the specified bounding rectangle.

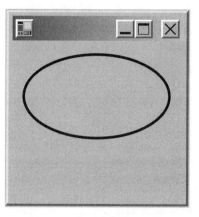

Figure 26.12: Ellipse example.

Open and Closed Curves

Drawing open and closed curves is similar to drawing a series of connected lines. But, instead of having sharp corners where the lines connect, the corners are automatically rounded to give a curving effect. The result is a curve.

Open curves are drawn using the DrawCurve method on the Graphics object. Closed curves are drawn using the DrawClosedCurve method on the Graphics object. Both of these methods take an array of points. The points represent the vertices of the lines that should be drawn (or the points where the line starts to curve in another direction). The only real difference between these two methods is whether the first point and last point are connected by drawing a line that connects them.

This example shows how to draw a curve. To draw a closed curve, the DrawCurve could be replaced with DrawClosedCurve:

EXAMPLE

```
Imports System.Windows.Forms
Imports System.Drawing.Drawing2D
Imports System.Drawing
Public Class Form1
    Inherits System.Windows.Forms.Form

    Private Sub New()
        MyBase.New()
    End Sub
```

```
Protected Overrides Sub OnPaint(ByVal e As PaintEventArgs)
    Dim points(5) As PointF
    Dim pen As Pen

    points(0) = New PointF(10, 50)
    points(1) = New PointF(30, 25)
    points(2) = New PointF(50, 10)
    points(3) = New PointF(70, 60)
    points(4) = New PointF(40, 80)
    points(5) = New PointF(30, 60)

    pen = New Pen(SystemColors.Highlight)
    pen.Width = 3
    e.Graphics.DrawCurve(pen, points)

    pen.Dispose()

End Sub

Shared Sub main()
    Application.Run(New Form1())
End Sub

End Class
```

Figure 26.13 shows the results of this example.

RUNIT

Figure 26.13: *DrawCurve example.*

Replacing the DrawCurve method call in the previous example with DrawClosedCurve results in the display shown in Figure 26.14.

Figure 26.14: *DrawClosedCurve example.*

Images and Icons

Icons are images that have a standard predefined size. Icons are usually 16 pixels high by 16 pixels wide or 32 pixels high by 32 pixels wide (or more commonly referred to as a *small icon* and *large icon*). Icon files usually contain a small version and a large version of the same image to allow applications the option of displaying either size.

Icons are used in user interfaces to aid users in understanding how a particular application works. For example, icons are used in menus that effectively associate a picture with a particular action the user can perform in the application. Then, whenever the user sees this picture, he should expect that action to be available to him.

Images are pictures of any size and are used in applications for any number of reasons. An application could display images as a background to a window to give a more professional look. Also, images are used as data within an application. For example, a product catalog would probably display images of the products so that shoppers could see what is available to purchase.

GDI+ allows you to display images and icons using the Graphics object. Let's take a look at the next example and the resulting display:

EXAMPLE

```
Imports System.Windows.Forms
Imports System.Drawing.Drawing2D
Imports System.Drawing
Public Class Form1
    Inherits System.Windows.Forms.Form

    Private Sub New()
        MyBase.New()
    End Sub

    Protected Overrides Sub OnPaint(ByVal e As PaintEventArgs)
```

```
        ' 1. draws an icon using its original size at a specified location
        e.Graphics.DrawIcon(New Icon("traffic.ico"), 10, 10)

        ' 2. forces icon to fit within the specified rectangle
        e.Graphics.DrawIcon(New Icon("traffic.ico"), New Rectangle(50, 10, 16, 16))

        ' 3. crops icon if does not fit within the bounds of the rectangle
        e.Graphics.DrawIconUnstretched(New Icon("traffic.ico"), _
                                New Rectangle(90, 10, 16, 16))

        ' 4. draws an image using its original size at a specified location
        e.Graphics.DrawImage(New Bitmap("DotNet.bmp"), 10, 90)

        ' 5. forces image to fit within the specified rectangle
        e.Graphics.DrawImage(New Bitmap("DotNet.bmp"), New Rectangle(100, 90, 30, 30))

        ' 6. crops image if does not fit within the bounds of the rectangle
        e.Graphics.DrawImageUnscaled(New Bitmap("DotNet.bmp"), _
                                New Rectangle(160, 90, 30, 30))

        ' 7. example showing usage of system icons
        e.Graphics.DrawIcon(SystemIcons.WinLogo, 10, 170)

    End Sub

    Shared Sub main()
        Application.Run(New Form1())
    End Sub

End Class
```

Figure 26.15 displays the results of the example.

RUNIT

Figure 26.15: *Images and icons example.*

The first image drawn in Figure 26.15 uses the DrawIcon method on the Graphics object. This example constructs a new Icon object by specifying the icon's filename and then passes the Icon object to the DrawIcon method. Also, a starting point to display the icon is specified (10, 10). The result is that the icon is drawn at the desired location. The size of the icon is based on the internal size of the icon, which is 32 by 32 pixels.

The second image drawn uses the DrawIcon method again, but this time a rectangle is specified instead of a starting point. This allows you to force the icon to be displayed in the rectangle. The icon is forced to fit inside the rectangle or is stretched if the rectangle is larger than the icon size.

The third image drawn uses the DrawIconUnstretched method. This allows you to draw an icon within a rectangle. However, using this method does not change the size of the displayed icon. But, if the icon does not fit in the rectangle, then only the part that does is displayed. The rest of the icon that extends outside the rectangle is not drawn.

The fourth image drawn uses the DrawImage method. A new Image object is created using the specified image filename. The starting point for drawing the image is also passed to the DrawImage method. This is virtually identical to the DrawIcon method except that, in this case, an Image object is passed to the method.

The fifth image drawn is forced to be drawn inside the specified rectangle. The DrawImage method is used to do this just as the second image drawn used the DrawIcon method.

The sixth image is drawn without changing the image's size using the DrawImageUnstretched method. Any part of the image that extends beyond the specified rectangle is not displayed.

The seventh and last image drawn in the example shows how to use system icons instead of having to create icon files. There are several system icons available to use. To see which icons are available for you to use, check them out using the Object Browser to view the System.Drawing.SystemIcons class.

Filling

So far in this chapter, we have shown how to create lines, curves, and shapes. But what if you wanted to create solid shapes or shapes that contained a visual pattern? How would you accomplish this? The answer is by filling the shapes using a brush.

We have already covered the types of brushes you can use and the effects they provide earlier in this chapter. Feel free to go back if you need to refresh yourself. This section focuses specifically on filling.

To fill shapes, there are several methods provided on the Graphics object for this purpose. These methods include

- FillClosedCurve

- FillEllipse

- FillPath

- FillPolygon

- FillRectangle

- FillRegion

The next example shows how to fill a rectangle using the FillRectangle. This basic idea can be applied to other shapes using the appropriate Fill method on the Graphics object:

EXAMPLE

```
Imports System.Windows.Forms
Imports System.Drawing.Drawing2D
Imports System.Drawing
Public Class Form1
    Inherits System.Windows.Forms.Form

    Private Sub New()
        MyBase.New()
    End Sub

    Protected Overrides Sub OnPaint(ByVal e As PaintEventArgs)

        Dim textureBrush As Brush
        Dim solidBrush As Brush
        Dim linearBrush As Brush
        Dim hatchBrush As Brush

        Dim rect As RectangleF

        ' create a gradient brush
        rect = New RectangleF(0, 0, 110, 110)
        linearBrush = New LinearGradientBrush(rect, _
                                        Color.Yellow, _
                                        Color.Green, _
                                        LinearGradientMode.Vertical)
```

```
' create a texture brush
textureBrush = New TextureBrush(SystemIcons.Exclamation.ToBitmap())

' create a solid brush
solidBrush = New SolidBrush(Color.CornflowerBlue)

' createa a hatch brush
hatchBrush = New HatchBrush(HatchStyle.DashedDownwardDiagonal, _
                            Color.MediumSlateBlue)

' now fill top left rectangle using textured brush
rect = New RectangleF(10, 10, 100, 100)
e.Graphics.FillRectangle(textureBrush, rect)

' now fill top right rectangle using solid brush
rect.X = rect.X + 110
e.Graphics.FillRectangle(solidBrush, rect)

' now fill bottom left rectangle using gradient brush
rect.X = 10
rect.Y = rect.Y + 110
e.Graphics.FillRectangle(linearBrush, rect)

' now fill bottom right rectangle using hatch brush
rect.X = rect.X + 110
e.Graphics.FillRectangle(hatchBrush, rect)

End Sub

Shared Sub main()
    Application.Run(New Form1())
End Sub

End Class
```

RUNIT

The results of the example are shown in Figure 26.16.

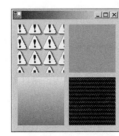

Figure 26.16: *Filling example.*

Clipping

Clipping allows you to ensure your drawing code does not extend outside an area that you define. Basically, you would define an area as the clipping region and then any drawing done to the drawing surface would display its output within the region and not outside the region.

To see how this works exactly, the following code sets a clipping region based on an arbitrary rectangle. Next, a string is drawn to the display surface. Figure 26.17 shows what would be displayed if no clipping region was set. Figure 26.18 shows the result of having the clipping region set. The output is as follows:

EXAMPLE

```
Imports System.Windows.Forms
Imports System.Drawing.Drawing2D
Imports System.Drawing
Public Class Form1
    Inherits System.Windows.Forms.Form

    Private Sub New()
        MyBase.New()
        Me.Width = 225
        Me.Height = 100
    End Sub

    Protected Overrides Sub OnPaint(ByVal e As PaintEventArgs)
        Dim font As Font
        Dim brush As Brush

        e.Graphics().SetClip(New Rectangle(10, 10, 100, 100))

        font = New Font("San Serif", 18)
        brush = New SolidBrush(Color.Black)
        e.Graphics.DrawString("Visual Basic.NET", font, brush, 10, 10)
        brush.Dispose()
        font.Dispose()

    End Sub

    Shared Sub main()
        Application.Run(New Form1())
    End Sub

End Class
```

RUNIT

Figure 26.17: *Example without clipping.*

While Figure 26.17 shows the result of the code if clipping were turned off, Figure 26.18 shows the result of the code with clipping turned on (`SetClip` is called).

Figure 26.18: *Example with clipping.*

As you can see from Figures 26.17 and 26.18, clipping is a good technique to use when you want to ensure your drawing is confined to a particular area on the display surface.

Advanced Features

GDI+ also provides advanced features that are not explicitly covered in this book. These include *scaling*, *rotating*, and *translating*. *Scaling* allows you to support zooming in and out by allowing you to set the scale size on your display surface. It basically allows you to draw all of your elements using the same units (pixels), and the positions are automatically updated using the scale size.

Rotating allows you to draw elements and then rotate them by specifying a rotation degree. *Translating* allows you to draw elements at the desired locations that you can then move, or translate, to new locations.

Another powerful feature is *alpha blending*. Alpha blending allows you to draw semi-transparent graphics elements. This allows elements underneath other elements to blend through, allowing stacked elements to be visually blended together.

What's Next

In this chapter you were introduced to some of the capabilities of graphics programming in .NET. This includes drawing your own text, using fonts, declaring and using different brushes for providing interesting visual effects, pens for adding color to your lines and shapes, and icons and images.

This was basically an introduction into GDI+. There is a lot more to explore in this area if you are really interested in doing your own drawing in your Visual Basic .NET applications.

In the next chapter, you will use some of what you learned here and explore the printing capabilities provided with the .NET Framework. This involves taking a look at the System.Drawing.Printing assembly. The examples show how to deal with printers and the classes involved in providing printing capabilities to your application.

NOTE

The answers to "Reviewing It," "Checking It," and "Applying It" are available on our Web site.

REVIEW

Reviewing It

This section presents a review of the key concepts in this chapter. These questions are intended to gauge your absorption of the relevant material.

1. What is GDI+?

2. How do you draw custom graphics on a form?

CHECK

Checking It

Select the correct answer to the following questions.

Multiple Choice

1. What do you need to use in order to draw text on a form?

    a. Graphics object's DrawText method.

    b. Graphics object's DrawString method.

    c. Graphics object's Draw method.

    d. None of the above.

2. Which is not a valid PageUnit member?

   a. Document.

   b. Pixel.

   c. Centimeter.

   d. Inch.

3. Where is the origin (0,0) on a form?

   a. Top left corner.

   b. Bottom left corner.

   c. Bottom right corner.

   d. Top right corner.

4. Which class stores its information as a Single value instead of an Integer value?

   a. `Point`.

   b. `SizeF`.

   c. `Rectangle`.

   d. None of the above.

5. Lines can be drawn in dashed styles using which class?

   a. `Line` class.

   b. `Pen` class.

   c. `Brush` class.

   d. `Ink` class.

6. Which advanced feature does GDI+ support?

   a. Scaling.

   b. Rotating.

   c. Translating.

   d. All of the above.

7. What is the default PageUnit?

   a. Display.

   b. World.

    c. Pixel.

    d. Point.

8. What is the size of the large version of an icon?

    a. 16 x 16 pixels.

    b. 16 x 32 pixels.

    c. 32 x 32 pixels.

    d. 24 x 24 pixels.

True or False

Select one of the two possible answers and then verify on our Web site that you picked the correct one.

1. Font styles can be combined to create combinations such as italicized and underlined.

   True/False

2. GDI+ has support for string alignment.

   True/False

3. GDI+ does not have support for string wrapping.

   True/False

4. A pen defined in the `SystemPens` class can be used and explicitly disposed in your code without any concerns.

   True/False

5. Different types of decorators can be added to either end of a line.

   True/False

6. To do alpha blending you need to write your own code to support this.

   True/False

7. The `StringFormat` class is used for string alignment and wrapping.

   True/False

APPLY

Applying It

Try to complete the following exercise by yourself.

Independent Exercise

Create a new Windows application project and write code that draws a square on the form. Also display some text in the square. Try to use a colored pen to draw the square.

Printing

This chapter explains how to add printing capabilities to your application. When it comes to developing applications, printing support is more than just writing text to a printer. Applications should give the user the capability to choose a printer, optionally print to a file, a page range for the printout, and ideally the capability to preview the printing on the screen before sending the output to the printer.

The Microsoft .NET Framework provides classes in the System.Drawing. Printing assembly for just this purpose. Using the classes in this assembly you can easily add your own printing support, and you don't need to be an advanced developer to do it.

To give you a better idea of what you will learn in this chapter, here is a list of the topics covered:

- Printing a form
- The `PrintPage` event and `PrintPageEventArgs`
- Printing multiple pages
- `PrintPreview`
- Creating a custom `PrintDocument` class

Introduction to Printing in .NET

Adding printing support to your .NET application is relatively easy, especially after you have read through Chapter 26, "Graphics Programming." Essentially, printing involves writing your custom code. This code then draws on the display surface, which happens to be the printer paper.

The first step involves using an instance of the `System.Drawing.Printing.PrintDocument` class in your application. The `PrintDocument` object is used by the .NET printing process. Events are dispatched to the `PrintDocument` object during the printing process. It becomes your responsibility to respond to these events with your specific printing code.

The code you write that actually draws on the printed page can be as complex as you like. There is a `Graphics` object that represents the surface of the paper on which you are printing. Because it is a Graphics object, you can do some pretty fancy stuff if you choose to (as you have seen in the previous chapter).

In addition, there are two important classes that you should familiarize yourself with. They are `System.Windows.Forms.PrintDialog` and `System.Windows.Forms.PrintPreviewDialog`. These two classes are in the System.Windows.Forms assembly because they are system dialogs. All of the dialogs and user controls used in developing Microsoft Windows applications are found in the Windows.Forms assembly.

The `PrintDialog` class is used to show the standard Print dialog. This dialog is quite simple to incorporate into your application; therefore, we encourage you to use it as it makes your applications more useable. It allows you to select the following:

- The printer
- The page range
- A file as the output device (optional)
- The number of copies you want to print

The `PrintPreviewDialog` is also quite useful and should be used whenever possible. The `PrintPreviewDialog` allows users of the application to see the printed document on your computer screen without having to print it to the printer and wasting printer ink and paper if there are mistakes. If they are printed on the screen (previewed), then the errors in the document could be resolved, by the user, before actually printing to the printer, saving time and money (and trees).

`PrintDocument`, `PrintDialog`, and `PrintPreviewDialog` can be added to a form by dragging each option from the Toolbox window and dropping it onto the form. This is accomplished using Visual Studio .NET while in a form's Design mode. Adding a control to a form creates a data member as part of the form based on the item you dragged from the Toolbox. This drag-and-drop process is exactly the same as dragging an edit control onto a form such as a `TextBox`. You have already seen this with controls in Chapter 23, "Controls."

> **NOTE**
>
> The PrintDocument, PrintDialog, and PrintPreviewDialog controls are in the Windows Forms tab of the Toolbox. Also, these controls are not selectable until a form is visible in Design mode.

Using Visual Studio .NET automatically generates code for you when you add these print-related classes to your form. The following examples do not use the drag and drop. This is done on purpose so that the reader can focus on the Visual Basic .NET language itself and so that the examples can be as concise as possible. After reading this chapter it should be extremely simple to add the appropriate printing classes to your form using Visual Studio .NET (by dragging and dropping); plus you'll have a better understanding of the printing classes themselves.

Let's go over this in more detail using a concrete example in the next section.

Printing a Form

When adding print support to an application or form, the basic idea is to utilize a `System.Drawing.Printing.PrintDocument` object and respond to its events. In responding to those events, you are able to write your specific code to print your form. Table 27.1 lists the specific events generated by instances of the `PrintDocument` class.

Table 27.1: **PrintDocument** *Events*

Event Name	Description
BeginPrint	This event is generated at the start of the printing process.
EndPrint	This event is generated at the end of the printing process.
PrintPage	This event is generated for each page that needs to be printed.
QueryPrinterSettings	This event is generated just before each `PrintPage` event. The reason is because the printer settings could change between each printed page.

To do basic printing, you really only need to associate a `PrintDocument` object with a form and handle the `PrintPage` event by proving your custom code. The following code example shows how to do this. The resulting printed page contains an example string and rectangle. The code is as follows:

EXAMPLE

```
Imports System.Windows.Forms
Imports System.Drawing.Printing
Imports System.Drawing

Public Class Form1
    Inherits System.Windows.Forms.Form

    Private m_menu As MainMenu
    Private WithEvents m_doc As New PrintDocument()

    Private Sub New()
        MyBase.New()
        CreateMenus()
    End Sub

    Protected Sub CreateMenus()
        Dim mnuFile As MenuItem
        Dim mnuItem As MenuItem

        ' create main menu
        m_menu = New MainMenu()

        ' create File menu
        mnuFile = New MenuItem("File")
        m_menu.MenuItems.Add(mnuFile)

        ' add Print menu item to File menu
        mnuItem = New MenuItem("Print...", _
                        New System.EventHandler(AddressOf Print))
        mnuFile.MenuItems.Add(mnuItem)

        ' set the form's main menu
        Me.Menu = m_menu

    End Sub

    Protected Sub Print(ByVal sender As Object, ByVal e As System.EventArgs)
        Dim dlg As New PrintDialog()

        ' set the Print dialog's document
        dlg.Document = m_doc
```

```
            If dlg.ShowDialog() = System.Windows.Forms.DialogResult.OK Then
                ' the OK button was pressed, so let's print the document
                m_doc.Print()
            End If

    End Sub

    Private Sub m_doc_PrintPage(ByVal sender As Object, _
                                ByVal e As PrintPageEventArgs) _
                                Handles m_doc.PrintPage

        ' printing the page
        e.Graphics.DrawString("A Rectangle", _
                              New Font("San Serif", 20), _
                              New SolidBrush(Color.Blue), 200, 200)

        e.Graphics.FillRectangle(Brushes.Red, New Rectangle(200, 500, 400, 500))

    End Sub

    Shared Sub main()
        Application.Run(New Form1())
    End Sub

End Class
```

RUNIT

Let's take a close look at the code. First, notice the imports of System. Drawing.Printing. This allows you to use the printing support classes in the .NET Framework without having to use the fully qualified class name.

Also, notice the following line in the definition of the Form1 class:

```
    Private WithEvents m_doc As New PrintDocument()
```

This line adds a new PrintDocument object as a data member of the Form1 class. Using the WithEvents keyword allows you to define methods that respond to the printing events using the Handles keyword. The m_doc_PrintPage method is declared to handle the PrintPage event sent to the object referenced by the m_doc data member.

You may be wondering why the method is named m_doc_PrintPage. The reason is that this method was generated automatically by Visual Studio .NET. To take advantage of this capability, simply use the two drop-down combo boxes at the top of the edit window. Figure 27.1 shows the left combo box, which displays several interesting items. First, each class that is defined in the current file is listed so that you can quickly navigate to that class in the edit window. Also for each class, the overridable methods are listed as well as the class events. Lastly, all data members that are declared using the WithEvents keyword are also listed.

Left drop-down combo box

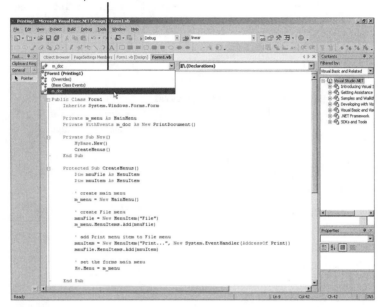

Figure 27.1: *Left combo box.*

Choosing an item in the left combo box affects the contents in the right combo box. If you choose m_doc, the events supported by the m_doc are listed in the right combo box. Figure 27.2 shows the right combo box at the top of the edit window.

Choosing an event in the right combo box generates an event handler in your code for the object selected in the left combo box and for the event selected in the right combo box. Any items in the right combo box in bold indicate that those items already have event handlers defined. The name of the generated method is based on the pattern object_event. In our case this translates into m_doc_PrintPage where m_doc is the name of the object and PrintPage is the name of the event. Later in this chapter, we'll show you how to create your own event handlers in case you want to write them yourself.

In the CreateMenus method, a Print menu item enables the user to initiate the printing of the form. As part of creating the menu item, a delegate is created that references the Print event handler. When the user selects the Print menu item, a Click event is generated that is handled by the Print method.

Right drop-down combo box

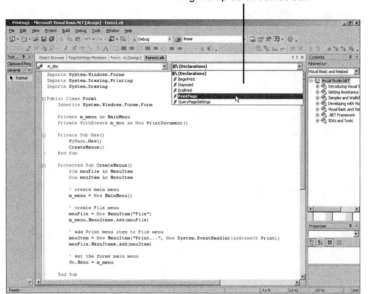

Figure 27.2: *Right combo box.*

Within the `Print` method, a `PrintDialog` object is created. The `PrintDialog` is given a reference to the `m_doc` data member. The `PrintDialog` needs to know which `PrinterDocument` object is going to be printed before the dialog can be displayed. The next line shows the `PrintDialog` and if the user selects the OK button, the `Print` method on the `PrintDocument` object is called. Invoking the `Print` method starts the actual process of printing.

For each page in the printing process, a `PrintPage` event is generated. The sample code handles this event using the `m_doc_PrintPage` method. Essentially, this means that every printed page is performed by the `m_doc_PrintPage`. Our example prints some text and a rectangle just to illustrate that the printing is very similar to the graphics drawing shown in the previous chapter.

After running the previous example, Figure 27.3 shows the form in which the user can select the Print menu for the purposes of printing.

Once the Print menu is selected, the common Print dialog is displayed so that the user can control some of the printing output such as choosing the printer to print to. Figure 27.4 shows the common Print dialog that the application uses.

Figure 27.3: *Print menu.*

Figure 27.4: *Print dialog.*

The PrintDialog is used to give the user more control over what gets printed. After a PrintDialog references a PrinterDocument, it can be shown, thereby allowing the user to choose a printer. In addition, you can selectively give the user more control by allowing the user to print specific pages. Of course, this requires more work on your part, but you have the capability to make that choice. The reason it involves more work is because you have to take into account what pages the user selected and only print those pages. This support is not provided automatically for you because the Microsoft .NET does not know what constitutes a page in regards to your application. Only you, as the developer, know that.

Table 27.2 shows the PrintDialog properties that allow you to control some of the behavior of the Print dialog to discover the print selections created by the user and also the printer settings of the selected printer.

Table 27.2: PrintDialog Properties

Properties	Description
AllowPrintToFile	Boolean property for setting the Print to File check box on the dialog.
AllowSelection	Boolean property that controls whether a user can print only the selected items on the form.
AllowSomePages	Boolean property that controls whether users can select to print using page ranges. If set to True users can print ranges; otherwise they cannot.
PrinterSettings	Contains the printer settings of the selected printer on the dialog. This property is useful during the printing process.
PrintToFile	Contains the value of the Print to File CheckBox on the print dialog.
ShowHelp	Boolean property that controls whether a Help button is displayed on the Print dialog.
ShowNetwork	Boolean property that controls whether the Network button is displayed on the Print dialog. The Network button allows you to access printers installed on the network in addition to the printers connected directly to your computer.

PrintPage Event and PrintPageEventArgs

In the previous example, the PrintPage event handler does not really do anything interesting. It just prints a text string and a rectangle on a single printed page. You need to look at the arguments passed to the PrintPage event handler to do anything useful, specifically, the PrintPageEventArgs argument. This argument contains all the necessary information that is essential for printing a page. For example, you need a Graphics object to draw on. You need page boundaries (including margins) so that you know the area you can draw in. You also need a way to print multiple pages as well as a way to cancel the printing process. This is essentially what the PrintPageEventArgs parameter provides for you, as the developer.

Table 27.3 lists the properties of the PrintPageEventArgs class with a description of each.

Table 27.3: **PrintPageEventArgs** *Properties*

Properties	Description
Cancel	Boolean property that gets or sets whether the printing process should be cancelled.
Graphics	The Graphics object associated with the printer. This represents the drawing surface of the printed page.

Table 27.3: continued

Properties	Description
HasMorePages	Boolean property that gets or sets whether an additional page needs to be printed.
MarginBounds	This property contains the rectangular area of the margins on the page. This is the printable area of the page.
PageBounds	This property contains the rectangular area of the entire printed page.
PageSettings	Contains the page settings for the current page.

The following code shows an example using the `PrintPageEventArgs` parameter when printing a page:

EXAMPLE

```
Imports System.Windows.Forms
Imports System.Drawing.Printing
Imports System.Drawing

Public Class Form1
    Inherits System.Windows.Forms.Form

    Private m_menu As MainMenu
    Private WithEvents m_doc As New PrintDocument()
    Dim m_printFont As Font = New Font("San Serif", 8)
    Dim m_printBrush As Brush = New SolidBrush(Color.Black)

    Private Sub New()
        MyBase.New()
        CreateMenus()
    End Sub

    Protected Sub CreateMenus()
        Dim mnuFile As MenuItem
        Dim mnuItem As MenuItem

        ' create main menu
        m_menu = New MainMenu()

        ' create file menu
        mnuFile = New MenuItem("File")
        m_menu.MenuItems.Add(mnuFile)

        ' add menu items to file menu
        mnuItem = New MenuItem("Print...", _
                            New System.EventHandler(AddressOf Print))
        mnuFile.MenuItems.Add(mnuItem)
```

```vb
    ' set the forms main menu
    Me.Menu = m_menu

End Sub

Protected Sub Print(ByVal sender As Object, ByVal e As System.EventArgs)
    Dim dlg As New PrintDialog()
    dlg.Document = m_doc
    If dlg.ShowDialog() = System.Windows.Forms.DialogResult.OK Then
        m_doc.Print()
    End If
End Sub

Private Sub m_doc_PrintPage(ByVal sender As Object, _
                           ByVal e As PrintPageEventArgs) _
                           Handles m_doc.PrintPage

    Dim xpos, ypos As Single
    Dim lineHeight As Integer
    Dim lineCount As Integer
    Dim msg As String

    msg = "Honey, get me a fork the darn toaster's jammed!"

    ' get the height of a line of text using the print font for this form
    lineHeight = m_printFont.GetHeight(e.Graphics)

    ' set the starting position at the left and top margins
    ypos = e.MarginBounds.Top
    xpos = e.MarginBounds.Left

    ' draw the string the full length of the page
    While (ypos < e.MarginBounds.Bottom)
        e.Graphics.DrawString(msg, _
                             m_printFont, _
                             m_printBrush, _
                             xpos, ypos)
        ypos = ypos + lineHeight
    End While

End Sub

Shared Sub main()
    Application.Run(New Form1())
End Sub

End Class
```

RUNIT

In this example, a Font object and Brush object are created as part of the Form in order to support printing. You could get more elaborate and provide a user interface where the user could select the font and brush used for printing. That would definitely be a better user interface than the one provided by the example. However, the default font and brush created in the example is enough for our purposes here.

In the PrintPage event handler, a text string is printed as many times as possible on the printed page depending on the size of the printed paper and the size of the font to be used. This is accomplished by first getting the height of the font. The height of a font depends on the Graphics object used. This is why the Graphics object is passed to the Font object's GetHeight method. Using the Graphics object associated with the printer, a height is returned that represents the number of units high a printed string will be. Using this number, you can figure out how many strings can be printed on the page.

For this example, the printing starts at the top margin and continues until the bottom margin is reached. After each string is drawn to the page, the position of the next string is updated by the height of the font. The page printing stops after the bottom margin is reached.

Printing Multiple Pages

So far, the examples in this chapter have been focusing on printing a single page. This, however, is not the common case when it comes to printing. More often than not, an application generates printouts that consist of multiple pages. So how is this accomplished? The PrintPageEventArgs parameter that is sent to the PrintPage event handler contains a property called hasMorePages. This property contains a Boolean value indicating whether more pages need to be printed. Because only your code knows this, you need to set this property at the end of the PrintPage event handler. This value defaults to False, which explains why your examples have only printed one page so far.

So how do you know when there are more pages to print? It is up to you to keep track of what you have printed so far and what you have not. Using this information you need to set the hasMorePages property appropriately. To illustrate this with a real example, we updated the previous example to create a simple file viewer application that allows you to open a text file, view it, and print it.

First, we added a RichTextBox control to the main form. This control is used to display the contents of the opened file. The control is named m_view in the example. A `CreateView` method is added to the `Form` class that is responsible for the creation of the `RichTextBox` control and setting its default properties. In our example, we set the control to fill up the form's client area by setting the `Dock` property of the control. Also, the control is set to read-only and to display a vertical scrollbar if necessary. The `CreateView` method is called from the form's constructor.

Next, we added a menu item to allow users to open files. This involved adding another menu item to the File menu and creating another event handler. This new event handler is responsible for displaying a File Open dialog box so that the user can choose a file. After a file is selected, the contents are read into the `RichTextBox` control.

At this point, you have updated your example so that you can open a file and view it. Now let's get to the point of how to print multiple pages. If you remember, you need to keep track of what pages you have printed so that we can correctly set the `hasMorePages` property. Our example uses a `System.IO.StringReader` class to do this for us. A `StringReader` object references a `String` and allows you to read lines from it. Because the `RichTextBox` displays all of the lines of a file, you can pass the value of the `RichTextBox`'s `Text` property to the `StringReader` object and then read each line one at time.

A new data member named `m_reader` is added to the form. This data member's data type is `StringReader`. In the form's `Print` method, the `m_reader` data member is set to the contents of the `RichTextBox` control. Each time the `PrintPage` event handler is called, a new line is retrieved from `m_reader` using the `ReadLine` method. `ReadLine` returns the current line and internally advances to the next line. This allows you to loop through the lines to print a page. At the end of the printing for a specific page, call the `m_reader.Peek()` method. This allows you to see whether there are any remaining lines to print. If the `Peek` method returns -1 this means there are no more lines. Using this technique, you can set the `hasMorePages` property of the `PrintPageEventArgs` parameter to the `PrintPage` event handler.

Here is the example that shows how to print multiple pages:

EXAMPLE

```
Imports System.Windows.Forms
Imports System.Drawing.Printing
Imports System.Drawing

Public Class Form1
    Inherits System.Windows.Forms.Form


    Private m_menu As MainMenu
    Private WithEvents m_doc As New PrintDocument()
```

```vbnet
Dim m_printFont As Font = New Font("San Serif", 8)
Dim m_printBrush As Brush = New SolidBrush(Color.Black)
Dim m_view As RichTextBox
Dim m_reader As System.IO.StringReader

Private Sub New()
    MyBase.New()
    CreateMenus()
    CreateView()
End Sub

Protected Sub CreateMenus()
    Dim mnuFile As MenuItem
    Dim mnuItem As MenuItem

    ' create main menu
    m_menu = New MainMenu()

    ' create file menu
    mnuFile = New MenuItem("File")
    m_menu.MenuItems.Add(mnuFile)

    ' add menu items to file menu
    mnuItem = New MenuItem("Open...", New System.EventHandler(AddressOf Open))
    mnuFile.MenuItems.Add(mnuItem)

    ' add menu items to file menu
    mnuItem = New MenuItem("Print...", _
                          New System.EventHandler(AddressOf Print))
    mnuFile.MenuItems.Add(mnuItem)

    ' set the form's main menu
    Me.Menu = m_menu

End Sub

Protected Sub CreateView()
    ' create the text box to show the opened file contents
    m_view = New RichTextBox()
    m_view.Dock = DockStyle.Fill
    m_view.ScrollBars = RichTextBoxScrollBars.Vertical
    m_view.ReadOnly = True
    m_view.Parent = Me
End Sub
```

```
Protected Sub Open(ByVal sender As Object, ByVal e As System.EventArgs)
    Dim dlg As New OpenFileDialog()
    Dim stream As System.IO.Stream

    ' show the open file dialog box
    dlg.Filter = "txt files (*.txt)|*.txt|All files (*.*)|*.*"
    If dlg.ShowDialog() = System.Windows.Forms.DialogResult.OK Then

        Dim buffer(1024) As Byte
        Dim numToRead As Integer = buffer.Length
        Dim numRead As Integer '
        Dim encoder As New System.Text.ASCIIEncoding()

        ' clear the current view
        m_view.Clear()

        ' open the file
        stream = dlg.OpenFile()

        ' read in each line of the file until there are no more
        Do
            numRead = stream.Read(buffer, 0, numToRead)
            m_view.AppendText(encoder.GetString(buffer))
        Loop Until numRead < numToRead

    End If
End Sub

Protected Sub Print(ByVal sender As Object, ByVal e As System.EventArgs)
    Dim dlg As New PrintDialog()
    m_reader = New System.IO.StringReader(m_view.Text)
    dlg.Document = m_doc
    If dlg.ShowDialog() = System.Windows.Forms.DialogResult.OK Then
        m_doc.Print()
    End If
End Sub

Private Sub m_doc_PrintPage(ByVal sender As Object, _
                           ByVal e As PrintPageEventArgs) _
                           Handles m_doc.PrintPage

    Dim xpos, ypos As Single
    Dim lineHeight As Integer
    Dim lineCount As Integer
```

```
        ' get the height of a line of text using the print font for this form
        lineHeight = m_printFont.GetHeight(e.Graphics)

        ' set the starting position at the left and top margins
        ypos = e.MarginBounds.Top
        xpos = e.MarginBounds.Left

        ' draw the current page
        While (ypos < e.MarginBounds.Bottom)
            e.Graphics.DrawString(m_reader.ReadLine(), _
                                  m_printFont, _
                                  m_printBrush, xpos, ypos)
            ypos = ypos + lineHeight
        End While

        ' check if more pages need to be printed
        If m_reader.Peek() <> -1 Then
            e.HasMorePages = True
        End If

    End Sub

    Shared Sub main()
        Application.Run(New Form1())
    End Sub

End Class
```

RUNIT

So what do you do if it does not make sense to use a StringReader the way this previous example does? This just means that you need to keep track of where you are in your printing process yourself and set the hasMorePages property as you see fit.

Print Preview

If you have already written code to support printing, then supporting Print Preview is quite simple. Supporting Print Preview involves using the System.Windows.Forms.PrintPreviewDialog class. This class has a Document property that needs to reference the PrintDocument object that is used during the printing process. The PrintPreviewDialog class takes care of everything else for you. All you need to do is show the dialog using the ShowDialog method.

To update the previous example to include Print Preview, a menu item must be created. Here is the updated CreateMenus method that adds the Print Preview menu item:

```
Protected Sub CreateMenus()
        Dim mnuFile As MenuItem
        Dim mnuItem As MenuItem

        ' create main menu
        m_menu = New MainMenu()

        ' create file menu
        mnuFile = New MenuItem("File")
        m_menu.MenuItems.Add(mnuFile)

        ' add menu items to file menu
        mnuItem = New MenuItem("Open...", New System.EventHandler(AddressOf Open))
        mnuFile.MenuItems.Add(mnuItem)

        ' add menu items to file menu
        mnuItem = New MenuItem("Print...", New System.EventHandler(AddressOf Print))
        mnuFile.MenuItems.Add(mnuItem)

        ' add menu items to file menu
        mnuItem = New MenuItem("Print Preview...", _
                               New System.EventHandler(AddressOf PrintPreview))
        mnuFile.MenuItems.Add(mnuItem)

        ' set the forms main menu
        Me.Menu = m_menu

    End Sub
```

And here is the code that handles the Click event for the Print Preview menu item:

```
Protected Sub PrintPreview(ByVal sender As Object, ByVal e As System.EventArgs)
    Dim dlg As New PrintPreviewDialog()
    m_reader = New System.IO.StringReader(m_view.Text)
    dlg.Document = m_doc
    dlg.ShowDialog()
End Sub
```

A PrintPreviewDialog object is created that does all of the print preview work. This dialog is shown in Figure 27.5.

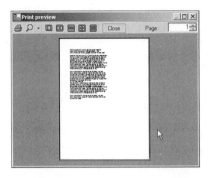

Figure 27.5: *Print Preview dialog.*

The StringReader is set before showing the Print Preview dialog to support the printing of the text in this example. The last two lines in this method hold the key to providing Print Preview. The dialog's Document property is set to the PrintDocument object used during the printing process. The last line actually performs the Print Preview. Calling the ShowDialog method of the PrintPreviewDialog box displays a window on the screen. In this window, you can view each of the printed pages as they would appear if you actually printed them to a printer. This can be a very handy feature for your applications and can also save a lot of paper. Plus, you cam implement this feature at a low cost to you.

Creating a Custom PrintDocument Class

If you dragged and dropped a PrintDocument control from the Toolbox onto a form (in Design mode), you would end up with an additional data member added to the form, and the data member's datatype would be PrintDocument. Then, to handle the events, you would create event handlers for the PrintDocument data member the same way as it was done earlier in this chapter.

Although this works for the purposes of quickly developing a form, there are a couple of problems doing it this way. The resulting code, which performs the actual printing, is part of the Form class itself. This means the code for the form handles the display of the form on the screen and also the printing of the form's data. It seems it would be more natural to somehow separate the code that does the screen display and handling from the code which handles the printing support. This would make the form's code more readable and understandable.

The second problem is related to the reusability of the printing code. Because the printing in the previous examples is tightly coupled with the Form class itself, it is not easy to reuse the printing code for another form or even another application.

Both of these problems could be resolved by creating a custom PrintDocument class and having the form use this custom class for printing.

Let's take a look at how these problems could be resolved. The following code example creates a custom PrintDocument class. The code is based on the printing code shown in previous examples. A new class named TextPrintDocument is created. It inherits from the System.Drawing. Printing.PrintDocument class. The font, brush, and reader data members of the Form class are moved to the TextPrintDocument class because they are used only for printing purposes. You could also expand this class by defining Properties for the font and brush, thereby letting other code tell the TextPrintDocument which font and brush to use.

A public method is also defined for setting the text that is to be printed. Within this method, the text is passed to a StringReader object. The StringReader object is used by the printing process as you have already seen in previous examples.

Finally, the OnPrintPage method is defined, which does the work to print a page. The code in the OnPrintPage is the exact printing code shown in previous examples. However, the benefit here is that this new class handles printing a text document and can be used by any form.

Also, the OnPrintPage method is an overridden method. Instead of having to define an event handler to handle the print events, you can override the OnBeginPrint, OnEndPrint, OnPrintPage, and OnQueryPageSettings methods in your custom PrintDocument class.

```
Imports System.Windows.Forms
Imports System.Drawing.Printing
Imports System.Drawing

Public Class TextPrintDocument
    Inherits System.Drawing.Printing.PrintDocument

    Private m_printFont As Font = New Font("San Serif", 8)
    Private m_printBrush As Brush = New SolidBrush(Color.Black)
    Private m_reader As System.IO.StringReader

    Public Sub SetPrintText(ByVal text As String)
        m_reader = New System.IO.StringReader(text)
    End Sub
```

```
Protected Overrides Sub OnPrintPage(ByVal e AsPrintPageEventArgs)
    Dim xpos, ypos As Single
    Dim lineHeight As Integer
    Dim lineCount As Integer

    ' get the height of a line of text using the print font for this form
    lineHeight = m_printFont.GetHeight(e.Graphics)

    ' set the starting position at the left and top margins
    ypos = e.MarginBounds.Top
    xpos = e.MarginBounds.Left

    ' draw the current page
    While (ypos < e.MarginBounds.Bottom)
        e.Graphics.DrawString(m_reader.ReadLine(), _
                              m_printFont, _
                              m_printBrush, xpos, ypos)
        ypos = ypos + lineHeight
    End While

    ' check if more pages need to be printed
    If m_reader.Peek() <> -1 Then
        e.HasMorePages = True
    End If

End Sub

End Class
```

The Form sample code is updated in the following example so that it uses the TextPrintDocument instead of the PrintDocument. Notice the missing data members because they were moved to the TextPrintDocument class. Also, the m_doc data member is declared as a TextPrintDocument instead of a PrintDocument. Also, the WithEvents is no longer needed because the TextPrintDocument handles the events automatically.

The final changes include calling the document's SetPrintText method so that the document knows what to print. As you can see, there is very little print-related code remaining in the Form class. And, the printing functionality can be reused because it is contained within the TextPrintDocument class.

```
Imports System.Windows.Forms
Imports System.Drawing.Printing
Imports System.Drawing
```

```vb
Public Class Form1
    Inherits System.Windows.Forms.Form

    Private m_menu As MainMenu
    Private m_doc As New TextPrintDocument()
    Dim m_view As RichTextBox

    Private Sub New()
        MyBase.New()
        CreateMenus()
        CreateView()
    End Sub

    Protected Sub CreateMenus()
        Dim mnuFile As MenuItem
        Dim mnuItem As MenuItem

        ' create main menu
        m_menu = New MainMenu()

        ' create file menu
        mnuFile = New MenuItem("File")
        m_menu.MenuItems.Add(mnuFile)

        ' add menu items to file menu
        mnuItem = New MenuItem("Open...", New System.EventHandler(AddressOf Open))
        mnuFile.MenuItems.Add(mnuItem)

        ' add menu items to file menu
        mnuItem = New MenuItem("Print...", New System.EventHandler(AddressOf Print))
        mnuFile.MenuItems.Add(mnuItem)

        ' add menu items to file menu
        mnuItem = New MenuItem("Print Preview...", _
                            New System.EventHandler(AddressOf PrintPreview))
        mnuFile.MenuItems.Add(mnuItem)

        ' set the form's main menu
        Me.Menu = m_menu

    End Sub

    Protected Sub CreateView()
        ' create the text box to show the opened file contents
        m_view = New RichTextBox()
```

```vb
        m_view.Dock = DockStyle.Fill
        m_view.ScrollBars = RichTextBoxScrollBars.Vertical
        m_view.ReadOnly = True
        m_view.Parent = Me
    End Sub

    Protected Sub Open(ByVal sender As Object, ByVal e As System.EventArgs)
        Dim dlg As New OpenFileDialog()
        Dim stream As System.IO.Stream

        ' show the open file dialog box
        dlg.Filter = "txt files (*.txt)|*.txt|All files (*.*)|*.*"
        If dlg.ShowDialog() = System.Windows.Forms.DialogResult.OK Then

            Dim buffer(1024) As Byte
            Dim numToRead As Integer = buffer.Length
            Dim numRead As Integer '
            Dim encoder As New System.Text.ASCIIEncoding()

            ' clear the current view
            m_view.Clear()

            ' open the file
            stream = dlg.OpenFile()

            ' read in each line of the file until there are no more
            Do
                numRead = stream.Read(buffer, 0, numToRead)
                m_view.AppendText(encoder.GetString(buffer))
            Loop Until numRead < numToRead

        End If
    End Sub

    Protected Sub Print(ByVal sender As Object, ByVal e As System.EventArgs)
        Dim dlg As New PrintDialog()
        m_doc.SetPrintText(m_view.Text)
        dlg.Document = m_doc
        If dlg.ShowDialog() = System.Windows.Forms.DialogResult.OK Then
            m_doc.Print()
        End If
    End Sub

    Protected Sub PrintPreview(ByVal sender As Object, ByVal e As System.EventArgs)
        Dim dlg As New PrintPreviewDialog()
        m_doc.SetPrintText(m_view.Text)
```

```
    dlg.Document = m_doc
    dlg.ShowDialog()
End Sub

Shared Sub main()
    Application.Run(New Form1())
End Sub

End Class
```

What's Next

In this chapter, you learned how to add printing capabilities to a form as well as Print Preview support. This entailed using a handful of classes provided by the Microsoft .NET Framework. Overall, adding printing support is fairly straightforward and requires very little additional work on your behalf.

You will learn how to add help to your application in the next chapter. You will learn how to add help to any control, allowing you to provide context-sensitive help in a very simple manner. Of course, showing the table of contents for the application's entire help system is also supported. Examples of each are given so that you will be well on your way to providing help in your own applications.

NOTE

The answers to "Reviewing It," "Checking It," and "Applying It" are available on our Web site.

REVIEW

Reviewing It

This section presents a review of the key concepts in this chapter. These questions are intended to gauge your absorption of the relevant material.

1. Does the process of adding printing support involve lots of tedious code, including code to figure out what printers are available?

2. Given the work involved in adding Print Preview support to an application, is it worth the time to spend adding this support?

3. Do you have the flexibility to print whatever you want, or are you constrained to printing text?

4. Why would you want to create a custom print document?

CHECK

Checking It

Select the correct answer to the following questions.

Multiple Choice

1. A `PrintDocument` object can be added to a form using:

   a. Visual Studio .NET drag and drop from the Toolbox.

   b. Manually adding a `PrintDocument` data member to a form in the code.

   c. Manually creating a custom `PrintDocument` class and adding an instance of this class to a form as a data member.

   d. All of the above.

2. Which dialogs are used for printing?

   a. `OpenFileDialog`.

   b. `PrintDialog`.

   c. `SaveFileDialog`.

   d. None of the above.

3. The `MarginBounds` property on the `PrintPageEventArgs` is:

   a. The size of the margins on the printed page.

   b. The area in which printing can occur on a page (excluding margin area).

   c. Typically set to zero and has little or no meaning.

   d. None of the above.

4. What namespace are the print classes in?

   a. System.Windows.Printing.

   b. System.Windows.Forms.

   c. System.Windows.Forms.Printing.

   d. None of the above.

True or False

Select one of the two possible answers and then verify on our Web site that you picked the correct one.

1. Form printing support requires the use of a `PrintDocument` object.

   True/False

2. The printing process generates four print events that can be handled.

   True/False

3. The `PrintPage` event must always be handled if you want printing to work.

   True/False

4. Supporting Print Preview involves writing your own custom form for displaying the printed output.

   True/False

5. The `PrintPreviewDialog` can be set to allow printing to a file.

   True/False

APPLY

Applying It

Try to complete the following exercises by yourself.

Independent Exercise 1

Create an example project and add printing support using Visual Studio .NET.

Independent Exercise 2

Add Print Preview support to the example in Exercise 1.

Developing a Help System for the User Interface

This chapter explains how to add "Help" support to an application using Visual Basic .NET. Most applications typically do not consider help design issues when first developing an application. This is mostly because developers are focused on finishing the planned features to support the application requirements. More often than not, help support is added at the last minute (if at all).

As part of the Microsoft .NET Framework, the help support for Windows Forms is greatly simplified as compared to developing it for Windows applications in the past. Because the help support is quite easy to integrate into an application, you should consider adding help support from the start of your development. In the event this does not happen, at least you will be able to easily add it later.

Either way, there are a few simple help techniques that you can utilize in your application development. To give you a better idea of what you will learn in this chapter, here is a list of the topics covered:

- `Help` class
- `HelpProvider` component
- Context-sensitive help
- Pop-up help
- ToolTips

Introduction to Help in .NET

Before you start learning how to incorporate help into an application, you first need a help file for this purpose. We used *HTML Help Workshop* to create the help system used for the examples in this chapter. HTML Help Workshop allows you to create a project and incorporate all of the help topics and keywords into a single distributable help file.

HTML stands for hypertext markup language and is commonly used for the purposes of defining Web pages. As applications are becoming more and more Web-centric, creating help content using HTML seems like the natural evolution of help systems. Microsoft HTML Help is now the standard help system for Microsoft platforms.

Visit this Web address for more information on Microsoft HTML Help and to download HTML Help Workshop if needed:

`http://msdn.microsoft.com/library/en-us/htmlhelp/html/vsconhh1start.asp`

HTML Help Workshop uses the project settings and all of the help content to create a compiled html help file (.chm). Because applications built on Microsoft .NET support HTMLHelp 1.x and HTML (in the HTML Help format) the compiled HTML output generated from HTML Help Workshop works just fine for our needs. You can use this tool or a more sophisticated commercial product if you choose. As long as it supports one of these help formats you will be able to use it to provide help with your application.

The focus of this chapter is intended to be on the .NET classes that allow you to provide help in your applications. The background information in this chapter regarding how to create a Help file is just that—background information. If you plan on developing Help content for your applications you need to seek out additional information on authoring Help. The Web link provided previously is a good place to start.

Here is another product that may be of interest to you as well:

`http://www.solutionsoft.com/hlpbrz.htm`

Figure 28.1 shows the sample help file's table of contents when the Contents tab is selected. This table of contents contains two topics labeled "Getting Started" and "New Features." These topics represent sample topics that you may have in your help system. When a topic is selected, the contents of the respective topic is displayed in the window on the right. This sample help file also has two additional tabs. One tab is for viewing the index of keywords that you can search on and the other tab is for displaying a window where you can search on any word in the help file.

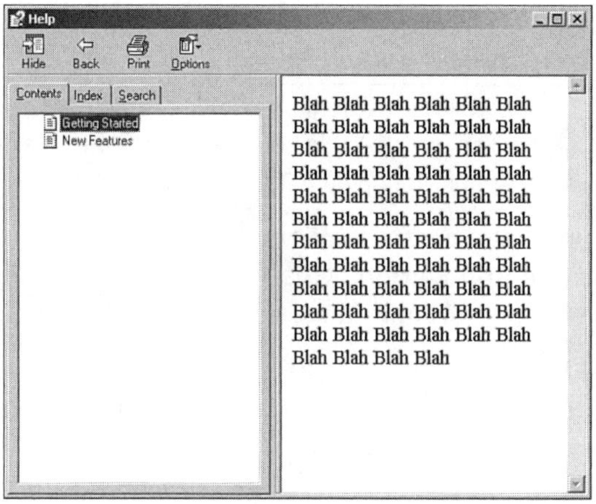

Figure 28.1: *Sample Help file.*

The HTML Help Workshop project along with its supporting files is also provided with the example source code. Check out this project if you want to understand more about creating the actual help file.

Help Class

Our first example of providing application help in this chapter is to display the contents of a help file as a result of selecting a menu item. The goal is to mimic most applications that have a Help menu where the user can display the help contents, help index, or help search for a particular keyword or keywords.

To accomplish this, you are going to use the System.Windows.Forms.Help class. This class contains shared methods that display help in different ways depending on the particular method that is called. You do not need to create an instance of the Help class to use it. In fact, you cannot create a new instance of the Help class. Because the methods are shared methods, you can just call the methods directly as you'll see in just a minute.

First, let's take a look at the three methods defined in the Help class. Table 28.1 shows the three methods of the Help class along with a brief description.

Table 28.1: Help Methods

Method	Description
ShowHelp	Displays the contents of a help file.
ShowHelpIndex	Displays the index or search window of a help file.
ShowPopup	Displays pop-up help at a specific location on the screen.

Using the Help class, the contents of the help file can be displayed to the user directly from an application. This way you can provide application help to allow the user to become more familiar with using the application, which facilitates a faster learning process.

The following example shows how to display the help contents, help index, and help search windows from the application:

```
Imports System.Windows.Forms

Public Class Form1
    Inherits System.Windows.Forms.Form

    Private m_menu As MainMenu
    Private m_help As New HelpProvider()
    Private m_helpFileName As String = "../../htmlhelp/myhelp.chm"

    Private Sub New()
        MyBase.New()
        CreateMenus()
    End Sub

    Protected Sub CreateMenus()
        Dim mnuHelp As MenuItem
        Dim mnuItem As MenuItem

        ' create main menu
        m_menu = New MainMenu()

        ' create menu
        mnuHelp = New MenuItem("Help")
        m_menu.MenuItems.Add(mnuHelp)

        ' add menu items to menu
        mnuItem = New MenuItem("Contents...", _
                            New EventHandler(AddressOf HelpContents))
        mnuHelp.MenuItems.Add(mnuItem)

        ' add menu items to menu
        mnuItem = New MenuItem("Index...", _
```

```
                                  New EventHandler(AddressOf HelpIndex))
        mnuHelp.MenuItems.Add(mnuItem)

        ' add menu items to menu
        mnuItem = New MenuItem("Search...", _
                                  New EventHandler(AddressOf HelpSearch))
        mnuHelp.MenuItems.Add(mnuItem)

        ' set the forms main menu
        Me.Menu = m_menu

    End Sub

    Protected Sub HelpContents(ByVal sender As Object, ByVal e As System.EventArgs)
        Help.ShowHelp(Me, m_helpFileName)
    End Sub

    Protected Sub HelpIndex(ByVal sender As Object, ByVal e As System.EventArgs)
        Help.ShowHelpIndex(Me, m_helpFileName)
    End Sub

    Protected Sub HelpSearch(ByVal sender As Object, ByVal e As System.EventArgs)
        Help.ShowHelp(Me, m_helpFileName, HelpNavigator.Find, "")
    End Sub

    Shared Sub main()
        Application.Run(New Form1())
    End Sub

End Class
```

NOTE

The previous code sample requires myhelp.chm to be in a specific directory in relation to where the application is started from. Keep this in mind when you build your own applications. The easiest approach to take is to just use the help filename (no directory path) and place the help file in the same directory as the installed application.

The example creates a Help menu with three menu items, one menu item for each of the three help tasks: help contents, help index, and help search. A separate event handler is created for each of the menu items. Within each event handler, the Help class is used to display the help file in differing ways. The ShowHelp method is used to display the table of contents for the help. To display the help index, the ShowHelpIndex method is used. And lastly, the ShowHelp method is used to display the help search window.

To display the search window, however, we had to pass more information to the ShowHelp method. There are a few overloaded ShowHelp methods for different purposes. The version of the ShowHelp method used to display the search window takes four parameters. The first parameter is the parent control which, in this case, is the form. The second parameter is the name of the help file. The third parameter is a value from the HelpNavigator enumeration. This is explained in more detail in Table 28.2. The fourth parameter is a string to search on. Because we don't know what the search string is yet, our example uses an empty string. Once the search window is displayed, the user can enter any keyword(s) they choose.

Table 28.2: **HelpNavigator** *Enumeration*

Enumeration Value	Description
AssociateIndex	The index for the specified topic is displayed.
Find	The search page is displayed for the defined help file.
Index	The index page is displayed for the defined help file.
KeywordIndex	The search page is displayed along with the specified keyword to search for.
TableOfContents	The table of contents in the help file is displayed.
Topic	The topic is displayed.

Figure 28.2 shows the previous example running. If you select the Contents menu item, the help is displayed as shown in Figure 28.1.

Figure 28.2: *Help example.*

Although providing application help in this way is useful, this should be considered the minimum level of help support you should provide for your applications. Ideally, help should be more integrated into the application, which this example does not show. For instance, if the user is working on a particular form and presses F1 for help, should he see the help's table of contents or the exact help topic which is relevant for where he is in the application? Probably showing a specific help topic would make more sense.

This capability is commonly referred to as *context-sensitive help*. Context-sensitive help allows the user to get help on a particular control or form immediately without having to search the help system. This allows the users to get the most direct help support provided by your application.

So, how is this done? Once you started down the road of providing more integrated help as part of an application, you need to utilize the HelpProvider component. The next section discusses this control followed by a section on how to provide context-sensitive help.

HelpProvider Component

In addition to the Help class, supporting help in your Windows application is also accomplished by using the System.Windows.Forms.HelpProvider component. The HelpProvider component allows you to associate a particular help file with your application or form. This is necessary in order to support context-sensitive help described in section and the following next section.

A Help Provider component can be added to a form by dragging it from the Toolbox and dropping it onto a form or by adding it to a form manually through code. After it is added, you need to set the HelpNamespace property that defines the help file to use. Once the help file is defined, you add code to call specific methods on the HelpProvider component depending on the type of help support you want.

Let's take a look at the properties and methods of the HelpProvider component so that you can get a better insight to its purpose. Tables 28.3 and 28.4 list the commonly used properties and methods of the HelpProvider component. Feel free to check the Object Browser in Visual Studio .NET for a complete reference. The following set of properties and methods are the key points you need to be aware of and the ones used throughout the examples in this chapter. If you get to know this minimal set of properties and methods, you will be able to add help support with relative ease to your applications.

Table 28.3: HelpProvider Properties (Most Relevant)

Properties	Description
HelpNamespace	This property contains the name of the help file associated with the HelpProvider component.

Table 28.4: HelpProvider Methods (Most Relevant)

Methods	Description
SetHelpKeyword	Sets the help keyword for a specific control. When the user requests help (either by pressing F1 or through a menu), the keyword is used to find the specific help in the help file.
SetHelpNavigator	Defines the help command used when retrieving help from the help file.

Table 28.4: continued

Methods	Description
SetHelpString	Specifies the exact help string for a control.
SetShowHelp	Defines whether help is to be displayed for a specified control.

The SetHelpNavigator method uses an enumeration as one of its parameters. This enumeration contains the help commands used when retrieving help from a help file. Table 28.2 explains the enumeration values earlier in this chapter.

It is also important to note that you can set the HelpKeyword, HelpNavigator, HelpString, and ShowHelp properties using the Form Designer and Properties window in Visual Studio .NET. If you click on a control in the Form Designer window, the Properties window is updated with the properties for the control you just selected. You can then edit the properties as you choose. Once you set the properties, Visual Studio .NET injects the appropriate method call into your code so that you don't have to.

Okay, so now you know that the HelpProvider component is used to display help in an application. Also, you've just seen some relevant properties and methods of the HelpProvider component. So how does this actually work? For the remainder of the chapter, you are going to look at three specific techniques of providing contextual help. You may decide to incorporate any or all of these techniques as you see fit. The techniques are as follows:

- *Context-sensitive help* supports displaying specific help regarding a control or form that has focus at the time the user presses the F1 key. Depending on the control or form that has focus, specific help for the control (or form) is displayed giving the user specific information that is relevant to what they are currently doing.

- *Pop-up help* is similar to context-sensitive help in that you get specific help on a control or form. However, the help information is embedded within the application and not in a separate help file. Also, the manner in which the help is displayed is different as you'll see later.

- *ToolTip help* provides a quick tip when the mouse is hovered over a control or form for a moment. When the mouse moves again, the ToolTip automatically disappears.

Context-Sensitive Help

Context-sensitive help is extremely useful to users of an application. Whenever they want help on a topic, all they need to do is press the F1 key and help appears regarding the area of the application they are currently working on. If done correctly, your users will be able to learn more quickly and as a result be more productive using software that you build.

The most difficult part about developing context-sensitive help is not the coding aspect; it is the writing of the development of the actual help content. If you have the time to write the help that corresponds to the forms and controls in your application, you definitely should invest the coding time to integrate it with your software. It is so easy to do so in Visual Basic .NET.

The basic idea is that you specify the help topic for each control that you want to support context-sensitive help. Then you "turn on" help for the control, and you're done. When the specific control gains focus and the user presses F1, the context-sensitive help defined for the control appears for the user to enjoy.

Here is a code example that illustrates this:

```
Imports System.Windows.Forms

Public Class Form1
    Inherits System.Windows.Forms.Form

    Friend WithEvents m_firstName As System.Windows.Forms.TextBox
    Friend WithEvents m_lastName As System.Windows.Forms.TextBox
    Friend WithEvents m_address As System.Windows.Forms.TextBox
    Friend WithEvents m_city As System.Windows.Forms.TextBox
    Friend WithEvents m_state As System.Windows.Forms.TextBox
    Friend WithEvents m_zip As System.Windows.Forms.TextBox
    Friend WithEvents m_lblFirstName As System.Windows.Forms.Label
    Friend WithEvents m_lblLastName As System.Windows.Forms.Label
    Friend WithEvents m_lblAddress As System.Windows.Forms.Label
    Friend WithEvents m_lblCity As System.Windows.Forms.Label
    Friend WithEvents m_lblState As System.Windows.Forms.Label
    Friend WithEvents m_lblZip As System.Windows.Forms.Label
    Friend WithEvents btnOK As System.Windows.Forms.Button
    Friend WithEvents btnCancel As System.Windows.Forms.Button
    Friend WithEvents m_help As System.Windows.Forms.HelpProvider

    Private Sub New()
        MyBase.New()
        InitializeComponent()
    End Sub

    Shared Sub main()
        Application.Run(New Form1())
    End Sub
```

```vb
Private Sub InitializeComponent()
    Me.m_city = New System.Windows.Forms.TextBox()
    Me.m_lblState = New System.Windows.Forms.Label()
    Me.m_lblZip = New System.Windows.Forms.Label()
    Me.m_zip = New System.Windows.Forms.TextBox()
    Me.btnOK = New System.Windows.Forms.Button()
    Me.m_firstName = New System.Windows.Forms.TextBox()
    Me.m_lblAddress = New System.Windows.Forms.Label()
    Me.m_help = New System.Windows.Forms.HelpProvider()
    Me.btnCancel = New System.Windows.Forms.Button()
    Me.m_address = New System.Windows.Forms.TextBox()
    Me.m_lblFirstName = New System.Windows.Forms.Label()
    Me.m_state = New System.Windows.Forms.TextBox()
    Me.m_lblCity = New System.Windows.Forms.Label()
    Me.m_lastName = New System.Windows.Forms.TextBox()
    Me.m_lblLastName = New System.Windows.Forms.Label()
    Me.SuspendLayout()
    '
    'm_city
    '
    Me.m_help.SetHelpKeyword(Me.m_city, "City")
    Me.m_help.SetHelpNavigator(Me.m_city, HelpNavigator.KeywordIndex)
    Me.m_city.Location = New System.Drawing.Point(80, 104)
    Me.m_city.Name = "m_city"
    Me.m_help.SetShowHelp(Me.m_city, True)
    Me.m_city.Size = New System.Drawing.Size(128, 20)
    Me.m_city.TabIndex = 9
    Me.m_city.Text = ""
    '
    'm_lblState
    '
    Me.m_lblState.Location = New System.Drawing.Point(216, 104)
    Me.m_lblState.Name = "m_lblState"
    Me.m_lblState.Size = New System.Drawing.Size(40, 20)
    Me.m_lblState.TabIndex = 6
    Me.m_lblState.Text = "State:"
    Me.m_lblState.TextAlign = System.Drawing.ContentAlignment.MiddleRight
    '
    'm_lblZip
    '
    Me.m_lblZip.Location = New System.Drawing.Point(40, 136)
    Me.m_lblZip.Name = "m_lblZip"
    Me.m_lblZip.Size = New System.Drawing.Size(32, 20)
    Me.m_lblZip.TabIndex = 7
```

```
Me.m_lblZip.Text = "Zip:"
Me.m_lblZip.TextAlign = System.Drawing.ContentAlignment.MiddleRight
'
'm_zip
'
Me.m_help.SetHelpKeyword(Me.m_zip, "Zip Code")
Me.m_help.SetHelpNavigator(Me.m_zip, HelpNavigator.KeywordIndex)
Me.m_zip.Location = New System.Drawing.Point(80, 136)
Me.m_zip.Name = "m_zip"
Me.m_help.SetShowHelp(Me.m_zip, True)
Me.m_zip.Size = New System.Drawing.Size(72, 20)
Me.m_zip.TabIndex = 11
Me.m_zip.Text = ""
'
'btnOK
'
Me.btnOK.Location = New System.Drawing.Point(256, 8)
Me.btnOK.Name = "btnOK"
Me.btnOK.Size = New System.Drawing.Size(72, 24)
Me.btnOK.TabIndex = 12
Me.btnOK.Text = "Ok"
'
'm_firstName
'
Me.m_help.SetHelpKeyword(Me.m_firstName, "First Name")
Me.m_help.SetHelpNavigator(Me.m_firstName, HelpNavigator.KeywordIndex)
Me.m_firstName.Location = New System.Drawing.Point(80, 16)
Me.m_firstName.Name = "m_firstName"
Me.m_help.SetShowHelp(Me.m_firstName, True)
Me.m_firstName.Size = New System.Drawing.Size(128, 20)
Me.m_firstName.TabIndex = 1
Me.m_firstName.Text = ""
'
'm_lblAddress
'
Me.m_lblAddress.Location = New System.Drawing.Point(16, 72)
Me.m_lblAddress.Name = "m_lblAddress"
Me.m_lblAddress.Size = New System.Drawing.Size(56, 20)
Me.m_lblAddress.TabIndex = 3
Me.m_lblAddress.Text = "Address:"
Me.m_lblAddress.TextAlign = System.Drawing.ContentAlignment.MiddleRight
'
'm_help
'
Me.m_help.HelpNamespace = "../../htmlhelp/myhelp.chm"
'
```

```
'btnCancel
'
Me.btnCancel.Location = New System.Drawing.Point(256, 40)
Me.btnCancel.Name = "btnCancel"
Me.btnCancel.Size = New System.Drawing.Size(72, 24)
Me.btnCancel.TabIndex = 13
Me.btnCancel.Text = "Cancel"
'
'm_address
'
Me.m_help.SetHelpKeyword(Me.m_address, "Address")
Me.m_help.SetHelpNavigator(Me.m_address, HelpNavigator.KeywordIndex)
Me.m_address.Location = New System.Drawing.Point(80, 72)
Me.m_address.Name = "m_address"
Me.m_help.SetShowHelp(Me.m_address, True)
Me.m_address.Size = New System.Drawing.Size(128, 20)
Me.m_address.TabIndex = 8
Me.m_address.Text = ""
'
'm_lblFirstName
'
Me.m_lblFirstName.Location = New System.Drawing.Point(0, 16)
Me.m_lblFirstName.Name = "m_lblFirstName"
Me.m_lblFirstName.Size = New System.Drawing.Size(80, 20)
Me.m_lblFirstName.TabIndex = 0
Me.m_lblFirstName.Text = "First Name:"
Me.m_lblFirstName.TextAlign = System.Drawing.ContentAlignment.MiddleRight
'
'm_state
'
Me.m_help.SetHelpKeyword(Me.m_state, "State")
Me.m_help.SetHelpNavigator(Me.m_state, HelpNavigator.KeywordIndex)
Me.m_state.Location = New System.Drawing.Point(256, 104)
Me.m_state.Name = "m_state"
Me.m_help.SetShowHelp(Me.m_state, True)
Me.m_state.Size = New System.Drawing.Size(40, 20)
Me.m_state.TabIndex = 10
Me.m_state.Text = ""
'
'm_lblCity
'
Me.m_lblCity.Location = New System.Drawing.Point(40, 104)
Me.m_lblCity.Name = "m_lblCity"
Me.m_lblCity.Size = New System.Drawing.Size(32, 20)
Me.m_lblCity.TabIndex = 4
```

```
Me.m_lblCity.Text = "City:"
Me.m_lblCity.TextAlign = System.Drawing.ContentAlignment.MiddleRight
'
'm_lastName
'
Me.m_help.SetHelpKeyword(Me.m_lastName, "Last Name")
Me.m_help.SetHelpNavigator(Me.m_lastName, HelpNavigator.KeywordIndex)
Me.m_lastName.Location = New System.Drawing.Point(80, 40)
Me.m_lastName.Name = "m_lastName"
Me.m_help.SetShowHelp(Me.m_lastName, True)
Me.m_lastName.Size = New System.Drawing.Size(128, 20)
Me.m_lastName.TabIndex = 5
Me.m_lastName.Text = ""
'
'm_lblLastName
'
Me.m_lblLastName.Location = New System.Drawing.Point(16, 40)
Me.m_lblLastName.Name = "m_lblLastName"
Me.m_lblLastName.Size = New System.Drawing.Size(64, 20)
Me.m_lblLastName.TabIndex = 2
Me.m_lblLastName.Text = "Last Name:"
Me.m_lblLastName.TextAlign = System.Drawing.ContentAlignment.MiddleRight
'
'Form1
'
Me.AutoScaleBaseSize = New System.Drawing.Size(5, 13)
Me.ClientSize = New System.Drawing.Size(336, 197)
Me.Controls.AddRange(New System.Windows.Forms.Control() {Me.btnCancel, _
                                                Me.btnOK, _
                                                Me.m_zip, _
                                                Me.m_state, _
                                                Me.m_city, _
                                                Me.m_address, _
                                                Me.m_lblZip, _
                                                Me.m_lblState, _
                                                Me.m_lastName, _
                                                Me.m_lblCity, _
                                                Me.m_lblAddress, _
                                                Me.m_lblLastName, _
                                                Me.m_firstName, _
                                                Me.m_lblFirstName})
Me.Name = "Form1"
Me.m_help.SetShowHelp(Me, True)
Me.ResumeLayout(False)
```

```
      End Sub
End Class
```

The example shows a form for entering a person's name and address as shown in Figure 28.3. For each TextBox on the form, context-sensitive help is defined.

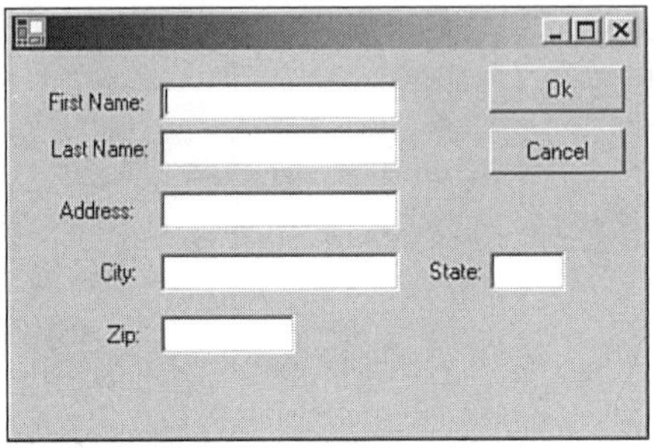

Figure 28.3: Example form.

The HelpProvider's Namespace property is set to the help file used for the form (or application). If you have many forms as part of your application, each form would have its own HelpProvider component. The Namespace property for each of the HelpProvider components could use the same help file. This way you could create one help file for your entire application and have it be used by many HelpProvider components. You also have the option of creating one help file per form. However, this can quickly become a management problem once you start having a large number of forms in your application.

For each control that supports context-sensitive help, there are three methods that need to be called on the HelpProvider component. These methods are SetHelpKeyword, SetHelpNavigator, and SetShowHelp.

The SetHelpKeyword defines the topic ID for the control. For this to work, a topic with the specified topic ID must exist in the help file.

The SetHelpNavigator defines how the help is displayed when the user presses F1. In this example, you specify the name of the control and System.Windows.Forms.HelpNavigator.KeywordIndex.

And lastly, the SetShowHelp method is used to turn on and off the context-sensitive help capability. Our example turns it on for the TextBox controls.

Figure 28.4 shows the help that is displayed if you press F1 when the First Name text box has focus. The help window is displayed with the correct topic content displayed in the window on the right. Also, the index of topics is displayed on the left in the event the user needs to search for help on other topics.

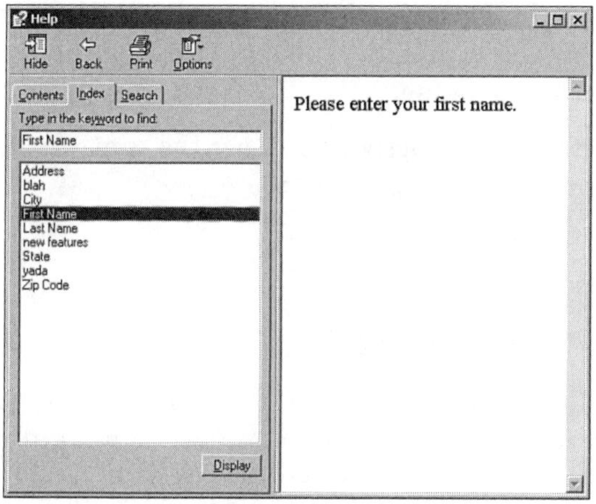

Figure 28.4: Help display.

Pop-up Help

Pop-up help is very similar to context-sensitive help. However, the means by which the help is displayed is different. In addition, the help content is not displayed in an external help file but rather it is embedded in the code.

You need to call two methods on the HelpProvider component to define the Pop-up help. Instead of calling the SetHelpKeyword and SetHelpNavigator, you would just call SetHelpString. This sets the help string for the particular control. The SetShowHelp must also be called for the controls that support help.

When you use the Form Designer in building a form, the HelpString and ShowHelp properties can be set in the Properties window in Visual Studio. NET. If you click on the control in the Form's Designer window, the Properties window shows the properties for the control that is selected. You can then edit the properties for the control directly in the Properties window. As a result, Visual Studio .NET injects the appropriate method calls into your code.

After you set the properties to set the help for the controls (either directly in your code or through the Properties window), you need to tell the form that it is supposed to display Pop-up Help. This is accomplished by turning on the Help button on the form. The minimize and maximize buttons must also be turned off in order for the Help button to be displayed. The Help button is turned on by setting the HelpButton property on the form to True. You would turn off the maximize button by setting the form's MaximizeBox property to False. Finally, the minimize button is turned off by setting the MinimizeBox property to False.

The following code shows exactly how to set the control's help strings and configure the form to show pop-up help:

```
Imports System.Windows.Forms

Public Class Form1
    Inherits System.Windows.Forms.Form

    Friend WithEvents m_firstName As System.Windows.Forms.TextBox
    Friend WithEvents m_lastName As System.Windows.Forms.TextBox
    Friend WithEvents m_address As System.Windows.Forms.TextBox
    Friend WithEvents m_city As System.Windows.Forms.TextBox
    Friend WithEvents m_state As System.Windows.Forms.TextBox
    Friend WithEvents m_zip As System.Windows.Forms.TextBox
    Friend WithEvents m_lblFirstName As System.Windows.Forms.Label
    Friend WithEvents m_lblLastName As System.Windows.Forms.Label
    Friend WithEvents m_lblAddress As System.Windows.Forms.Label
    Friend WithEvents m_lblCity As System.Windows.Forms.Label
    Friend WithEvents m_lblState As System.Windows.Forms.Label
    Friend WithEvents m_lblZip As System.Windows.Forms.Label
    Friend WithEvents btnOK As System.Windows.Forms.Button
    Friend WithEvents btnCancel As System.Windows.Forms.Button
    Friend WithEvents m_help As System.Windows.Forms.HelpProvider

    Private Sub New()
        MyBase.New()
        InitializeComponent()
    End Sub

    Shared Sub main()
        Application.Run(New Form1())
    End Sub

    Private Sub InitializeComponent()
        Me.m_city = New System.Windows.Forms.TextBox()
        Me.m_lblState = New System.Windows.Forms.Label()
        Me.m_lblZip = New System.Windows.Forms.Label()
```

```
Me.m_zip = New System.Windows.Forms.TextBox()
Me.btnOK = New System.Windows.Forms.Button()
Me.m_firstName = New System.Windows.Forms.TextBox()
Me.m_lblAddress = New System.Windows.Forms.Label()
Me.m_help = New System.Windows.Forms.HelpProvider()
Me.m_address = New System.Windows.Forms.TextBox()
Me.m_state = New System.Windows.Forms.TextBox()
Me.m_lastName = New System.Windows.Forms.TextBox()
Me.btnCancel = New System.Windows.Forms.Button()
Me.m_lblFirstName = New System.Windows.Forms.Label()
Me.m_lblCity = New System.Windows.Forms.Label()
Me.m_lblLastName = New System.Windows.Forms.Label()
Me.SuspendLayout()
'
'm_city
'
Me.m_help.SetHelpString(Me.m_city, "Enter City")
Me.m_city.Location = New System.Drawing.Point(80, 104)
Me.m_city.Name = "m_city"
Me.m_help.SetShowHelp(Me.m_city, True)
Me.m_city.Size = New System.Drawing.Size(128, 20)
Me.m_city.TabIndex = 9
Me.m_city.Text = ""
'
'm_lblState
'
Me.m_lblState.Location = New System.Drawing.Point(216, 104)
Me.m_lblState.Name = "m_lblState"
Me.m_lblState.Size = New System.Drawing.Size(40, 20)
Me.m_lblState.TabIndex = 6
Me.m_lblState.Text = "State:"
Me.m_lblState.TextAlign = System.Drawing.ContentAlignment.MiddleRight
'
'm_lblZip
'
Me.m_lblZip.Location = New System.Drawing.Point(40, 136)
Me.m_lblZip.Name = "m_lblZip"
Me.m_lblZip.Size = New System.Drawing.Size(32, 20)
Me.m_lblZip.TabIndex = 7
Me.m_lblZip.Text = "Zip:"
Me.m_lblZip.TextAlign = System.Drawing.ContentAlignment.MiddleRight
'
'm_zip
'
Me.m_help.SetHelpString(Me.m_zip, "Enter Zip Code")
Me.m_zip.Location = New System.Drawing.Point(80, 136)
```

```vbnet
Me.m_zip.Name = "m_zip"
Me.m_help.SetShowHelp(Me.m_zip, True)
Me.m_zip.Size = New System.Drawing.Size(72, 20)
Me.m_zip.TabIndex = 11
Me.m_zip.Text = ""
'
'btnOK
'
Me.btnOK.Location = New System.Drawing.Point(256, 8)
Me.btnOK.Name = "btnOK"
Me.btnOK.Size = New System.Drawing.Size(72, 24)
Me.btnOK.TabIndex = 12
Me.btnOK.Text = "Ok"
'
'm_firstName
'
Me.m_help.SetHelpString(Me.m_firstName, "Enter First Name")
Me.m_firstName.Location = New System.Drawing.Point(80, 16)
Me.m_firstName.Name = "m_firstName"
Me.m_help.SetShowHelp(Me.m_firstName, True)
Me.m_firstName.Size = New System.Drawing.Size(128, 20)
Me.m_firstName.TabIndex = 1
Me.m_firstName.Text = ""
'
'm_lblAddress
'
Me.m_lblAddress.Location = New System.Drawing.Point(16, 72)
Me.m_lblAddress.Name = "m_lblAddress"
Me.m_lblAddress.Size = New System.Drawing.Size(56, 20)
Me.m_lblAddress.TabIndex = 3
Me.m_lblAddress.Text = "Address:"
Me.m_lblAddress.TextAlign = System.Drawing.ContentAlignment.MiddleRight
'
'm_help
'
Me.m_help.HelpNamespace = "../../htmlhelp/myhelp.chm"
'
'm_address
'
Me.m_help.SetHelpString(Me.m_address, "Enter Address")
Me.m_address.Location = New System.Drawing.Point(80, 72)
Me.m_address.Name = "m_address"
Me.m_help.SetShowHelp(Me.m_address, True)
Me.m_address.Size = New System.Drawing.Size(128, 20)
Me.m_address.TabIndex = 8
Me.m_address.Text = ""
'
```

```
'm_state
'

Me.m_help.SetHelpString(Me.m_state, "Enter State")
Me.m_state.Location = New System.Drawing.Point(256, 104)
Me.m_state.Name = "m_state"
Me.m_help.SetShowHelp(Me.m_state, True)
Me.m_state.Size = New System.Drawing.Size(40, 20)
Me.m_state.TabIndex = 10
Me.m_state.Text = ""
'

'm_lastName
'

Me.m_help.SetHelpString(Me.m_lastName, "Enter Last Name")
Me.m_lastName.Location = New System.Drawing.Point(80, 40)
Me.m_lastName.Name = "m_lastName"
Me.m_help.SetShowHelp(Me.m_lastName, True)
Me.m_lastName.Size = New System.Drawing.Size(128, 20)
Me.m_lastName.TabIndex = 5
Me.m_lastName.Text = ""
'

'btnCancel
'

Me.btnCancel.Location = New System.Drawing.Point(256, 40)
Me.btnCancel.Name = "btnCancel"
Me.btnCancel.Size = New System.Drawing.Size(72, 24)
Me.btnCancel.TabIndex = 13
Me.btnCancel.Text = "Cancel"
'

'm_lblFirstName
'

Me.m_lblFirstName.Location = New System.Drawing.Point(0, 16)
Me.m_lblFirstName.Name = "m_lblFirstName"
Me.m_lblFirstName.Size = New System.Drawing.Size(80, 20)
Me.m_lblFirstName.TabIndex = 0
Me.m_lblFirstName.Text = "First Name:"
Me.m_lblFirstName.TextAlign = System.Drawing.ContentAlignment.MiddleRight
'

'm_lblCity
'

Me.m_lblCity.Location = New System.Drawing.Point(40, 104)
Me.m_lblCity.Name = "m_lblCity"
Me.m_lblCity.Size = New System.Drawing.Size(32, 20)
Me.m_lblCity.TabIndex = 4
Me.m_lblCity.Text = "City:"
Me.m_lblCity.TextAlign = System.Drawing.ContentAlignment.MiddleRight
'
```

```
'm_lblLastName
'
Me.m_lblLastName.Location = New System.Drawing.Point(16, 40)
Me.m_lblLastName.Name = "m_lblLastName"
Me.m_lblLastName.Size = New System.Drawing.Size(64, 20)
Me.m_lblLastName.TabIndex = 2
Me.m_lblLastName.Text = "Last Name:"
Me.m_lblLastName.TextAlign = System.Drawing.ContentAlignment.MiddleRight
'
'Form1
'
Me.AutoScaleBaseSize = New System.Drawing.Size(5, 13)
Me.ClientSize = New System.Drawing.Size(336, 197)
Me.Controls.AddRange(New System.Windows.Forms.Control() {Me.btnCancel, _
                                        Me.btnOK, _
                                        Me.m_zip, _
                                        Me.m_state, _
                                        Me.m_city, _
                                        Me.m_address, _
                                        Me.m_lblZip, _
                                        Me.m_lblState, _
                                        Me.m_lastName, _
                                        Me.m_lblCity, _
                                        Me.m_lblAddress, _
                                        Me.m_lblLastName, _
                                        Me.m_firstName, _
                                        Me.m_lblFirstName})
Me.HelpButton = True
Me.MaximizeBox = False
Me.MinimizeBox = False
Me.Name = "Form1"
Me.m_help.SetShowHelp(Me, True)
Me.ResumeLayout(False)

  End Sub
End Class
```

Figure 28.5 shows the running Form. Notice the Help button at the top right of the form.

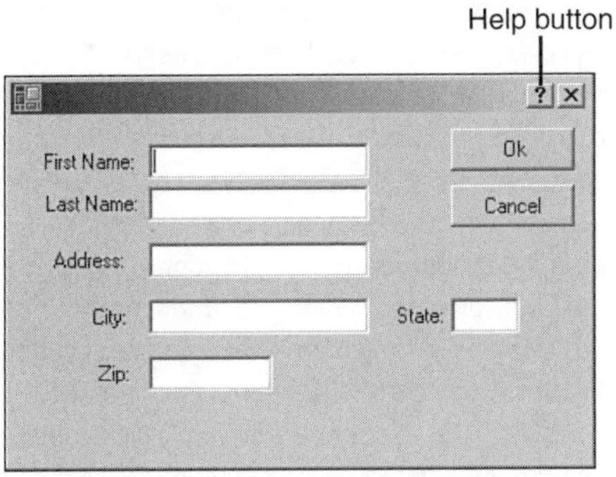

Help button

Figure 28.5: Form with Help button.

So how does one actually show the pop-up help? This works by first clicking the Help button at the top of the form. You should notice the cursor's appearance change to include a question mark. At this point, you can click on any control that has Pop-up help defined, and the help text you defined in your code should appear describing the control you just clicked.

ToolTips

ToolTip Help shows small snippets of help that you define automatically as you hover the cursor over a control. If the control has ToolTip help defined for it, a small window containing the help appears, and when you move the cursor away the help automatically disappears.

ToolTip Help is very simple to provide in your applications. It involves only two steps. First, you need to add a `System.Windows.Forms.ToolTip` component to the form. For each control on the form that you want to provide a ToolTip for, you need to call the `SetToolTip` method on the ToolTip component. This method takes two arguments—a control and the ToolTip help string.

You can call the `SetToolTip` method directly in your code, or you could set it using the Properties window in Visual Studio .NET. That's all you need to do. The following code example illustrates this:

```
Imports System.Windows.Forms

Public Class Form1
    Inherits System.Windows.Forms.Form
```

```
Friend WithEvents m_firstName As System.Windows.Forms.TextBox
Friend WithEvents m_lastName As System.Windows.Forms.TextBox
Friend WithEvents m_address As System.Windows.Forms.TextBox
Friend WithEvents m_city As System.Windows.Forms.TextBox
Friend WithEvents m_state As System.Windows.Forms.TextBox
Friend WithEvents m_zip As System.Windows.Forms.TextBox
Friend WithEvents m_lblFirstName As System.Windows.Forms.Label
Friend WithEvents m_lblLastName As System.Windows.Forms.Label
Friend WithEvents m_lblAddress As System.Windows.Forms.Label
Friend WithEvents m_lblCity As System.Windows.Forms.Label
Friend WithEvents m_lblState As System.Windows.Forms.Label
Friend WithEvents m_lblZip As System.Windows.Forms.Label
Friend WithEvents btnOK As System.Windows.Forms.Button
Friend WithEvents m_toolTip As System.Windows.Forms.ToolTip
Private components As System.ComponentModel.IContainer
Friend WithEvents btnCancel As System.Windows.Forms.Button

Private Sub New()
    MyBase.New()
    InitializeComponent()
End Sub

Shared Sub main()
    Application.Run(New Form1())
End Sub

Private Sub InitializeComponent()
    Me.components = New System.ComponentModel.Container()
    Me.m_city = New System.Windows.Forms.TextBox()
    Me.m_lblState = New System.Windows.Forms.Label()
    Me.m_lblZip = New System.Windows.Forms.Label()
    Me.m_zip = New System.Windows.Forms.TextBox()
    Me.btnOK = New System.Windows.Forms.Button()
    Me.m_firstName = New System.Windows.Forms.TextBox()
    Me.m_lblAddress = New System.Windows.Forms.Label()
    Me.m_address = New System.Windows.Forms.TextBox()
    Me.m_state = New System.Windows.Forms.TextBox()
    Me.m_lastName = New System.Windows.Forms.TextBox()
    Me.btnCancel = New System.Windows.Forms.Button()
    Me.m_lblFirstName = New System.Windows.Forms.Label()
    Me.m_lblCity = New System.Windows.Forms.Label()
    Me.m_lblLastName = New System.Windows.Forms.Label()
    Me.m_toolTip = New System.Windows.Forms.ToolTip(Me.components)
    Me.SuspendLayout()
    '
    'm_city
    '
```

```
Me.m_city.Location = New System.Drawing.Point(80, 104)
Me.m_city.Name = "m_city"
Me.m_city.Size = New System.Drawing.Size(128, 20)
Me.m_city.TabIndex = 9
Me.m_city.Text = ""
Me.m_toolTip.SetToolTip(Me.m_city, "City Field")
'
'm_lblState
'
Me.m_lblState.Location = New System.Drawing.Point(216, 104)
Me.m_lblState.Name = "m_lblState"
Me.m_lblState.Size = New System.Drawing.Size(40, 20)
Me.m_lblState.TabIndex = 6
Me.m_lblState.Text = "State:"
Me.m_lblState.TextAlign = System.Drawing.ContentAlignment.MiddleRight
'
'm_lblZip
'
Me.m_lblZip.Location = New System.Drawing.Point(40, 136)
Me.m_lblZip.Name = "m_lblZip"
Me.m_lblZip.Size = New System.Drawing.Size(32, 20)
Me.m_lblZip.TabIndex = 7
Me.m_lblZip.Text = "Zip:"
Me.m_lblZip.TextAlign = System.Drawing.ContentAlignment.MiddleRight
'
'm_zip
'
Me.m_zip.Location = New System.Drawing.Point(80, 136)
Me.m_zip.Name = "m_zip"
Me.m_zip.Size = New System.Drawing.Size(72, 20)
Me.m_zip.TabIndex = 11
Me.m_zip.Text = ""
Me.m_toolTip.SetToolTip(Me.m_zip, "Zip Code Field")
'
'btnOK
'
Me.btnOK.Location = New System.Drawing.Point(256, 8)
Me.btnOK.Name = "btnOK"
Me.btnOK.Size = New System.Drawing.Size(72, 24)
Me.btnOK.TabIndex = 12
Me.btnOK.Text = "Ok"
'
'm_firstName
'
Me.m_firstName.Location = New System.Drawing.Point(80, 16)
Me.m_firstName.Name = "m_firstName"
```

```
Me.m_firstName.Size = New System.Drawing.Size(128, 20)
Me.m_firstName.TabIndex = 1
Me.m_firstName.Text = ""
Me.m_toolTip.SetToolTip(Me.m_firstName, "First Name Field")
'
'm_lblAddress
'
Me.m_lblAddress.Location = New System.Drawing.Point(16, 72)
Me.m_lblAddress.Name = "m_lblAddress"
Me.m_lblAddress.Size = New System.Drawing.Size(56, 20)
Me.m_lblAddress.TabIndex = 3
Me.m_lblAddress.Text = "Address:"
Me.m_lblAddress.TextAlign = System.Drawing.ContentAlignment.MiddleRight
'
'm_address
'
Me.m_address.Location = New System.Drawing.Point(80, 72)
Me.m_address.Name = "m_address"
Me.m_address.Size = New System.Drawing.Size(128, 20)
Me.m_address.TabIndex = 8
Me.m_address.Text = ""
Me.m_toolTip.SetToolTip(Me.m_address, "Address Field")
'
'm_state
'
Me.m_state.Location = New System.Drawing.Point(256, 104)
Me.m_state.Name = "m_state"
Me.m_state.Size = New System.Drawing.Size(40, 20)
Me.m_state.TabIndex = 10
Me.m_state.Text = ""
Me.m_toolTip.SetToolTip(Me.m_state, "State Field")
'
'm_lastName
'
Me.m_lastName.Location = New System.Drawing.Point(80, 40)
Me.m_lastName.Name = "m_lastName"
Me.m_lastName.Size = New System.Drawing.Size(128, 20)
Me.m_lastName.TabIndex = 5
Me.m_lastName.Text = ""
Me.m_toolTip.SetToolTip(Me.m_lastName, "Last Name Field")
'
'btnCancel
'
Me.btnCancel.Location = New System.Drawing.Point(256, 40)
Me.btnCancel.Name = "btnCancel"
Me.btnCancel.Size = New System.Drawing.Size(72, 24)
```

```
        Me.btnCancel.TabIndex = 13
        Me.btnCancel.Text = "Cancel"
        '
        'm_lblFirstName
        '
        Me.m_lblFirstName.Location = New System.Drawing.Point(0, 16)
        Me.m_lblFirstName.Name = "m_lblFirstName"
        Me.m_lblFirstName.Size = New System.Drawing.Size(80, 20)
        Me.m_lblFirstName.TabIndex = 0
        Me.m_lblFirstName.Text = "First Name:"
        Me.m_lblFirstName.TextAlign = System.Drawing.ContentAlignment.MiddleRight
        '
        'm_lblCity
        '
        Me.m_lblCity.Location = New System.Drawing.Point(40, 104)
        Me.m_lblCity.Name = "m_lblCity"
        Me.m_lblCity.Size = New System.Drawing.Size(32, 20)
        Me.m_lblCity.TabIndex = 4
        Me.m_lblCity.Text = "City:"
        Me.m_lblCity.TextAlign = System.Drawing.ContentAlignment.MiddleRight
        '
        'm_lblLastName
        '
        Me.m_lblLastName.Location = New System.Drawing.Point(16, 40)
        Me.m_lblLastName.Name = "m_lblLastName"
        Me.m_lblLastName.Size = New System.Drawing.Size(64, 20)
        Me.m_lblLastName.TabIndex = 2
        Me.m_lblLastName.Text = "Last Name:"
        Me.m_lblLastName.TextAlign = System.Drawing.ContentAlignment.MiddleRight
        '
        'Form1
        '
        Me.AutoScaleBaseSize = New System.Drawing.Size(5, 13)
        Me.ClientSize = New System.Drawing.Size(336, 197)
        Me.Controls.AddRange(New System.Windows.Forms.Control() {Me.btnCancel, _
                                                      Me.btnOK, _
                                                      Me.m_zip, _
                                                      Me.m_state, _
                                                      Me.m_city, _
                                                      Me.m_address, _
                                                      Me.m_lblZip, _
                                                      Me.m_lblState, _
                                                      Me.m_lastName, _
```

```
                                                        Me.m_lblCity, _
                                                        Me.m_lblAddress, _
                                                        Me.m_lblLastName, _
                                                        Me.m_firstName, _
                                                        Me.m_lblFirstName})

            Me.Name = "Form1"
            Me.ResumeLayout(False)

        End Sub
End Class
```

What's Next

This chapter concludes Part IV of this book. The last several chapters were devoted to working with forms and controls. This basically covered a lot of material (as you already know). You should now be at point where you can design and develop your own user interface using the classes provided in the System.Windows.Forms assembly. This includes forms, controls, menus, customized drawing using the graphics capabilities, printing support, and of course help.

Now you are going to move onto Part V, which involves manipulating data in Visual Basic .NET. You will be using more Microsoft .NET Framework classes and explaining through examples how you can access and manipulate data using a SQL database as well as using XML. After you get through Part V, you should have the knowledge of writing Visual Basic .NET code to work with data. As a result, you should be in a position to take what you have learned in Part IV and Part V and be able to apply it to building a complete Visual Basic .NET application.

NOTE

The answers to "Reviewing It," "Checking It," and "Applying It" are available on our Web site.

REVIEW

Reviewing It

This section presents a review of the key concepts in this chapter. These questions are intended to gauge your absorption of the relevant material.

1. What are the ways an application written in Visual Basic .NET can support help?

2. What's the main difference between pop-up help and context-sensitive help?

3. What are the possible components and/or classes you could use in an application to support help?

4. What is the purpose of the HelpProvider component?

5. How do you turn on and off the context-sensitive help for a control?

6. If you don't want to use an external help file, how would you define a help string for a control?

7. How do you add tooltips for controls on a form?

Checking It

Select the correct answer to the following questions.

CHECK

Multiple Choice

1. To show the table of contents, index page, or search page of an external help file, you need to use the following:

   a. `Help` class.

   b. `HelpProvider` component.

   c. `ToolTip` component.

   d. Pop-up help.

2. To show context-sensitive help you need to use the following:

   a. `Help` class.

   b. `HelpProvider` component.

   c. `ToolTip` component.

   d. Pop-up help.

   e. None of the above.

3. ToolTip help involves:

   a. Using a `ToolTip` component and setting the `HelpNamespace` property.

   b. Using a `HelpProvider` component and calling the `SetToolTip` method.

   c. Using a `ToolTip` component and calling the `SetHelp` method.

d. Using a `ToolTip` component and calling the `SetToolTip` method.

e. None of the above.

True or False

Select one of the two possible answers and then verify on our Web site that you picked the correct one.

1. To display a help file's table of contents you first need to set the `HelpNamespace` property on the `Help` class.

   True/False

2. To use pop-up help, you must set the form's `HelpButton` property to `True`, the `MinimizeBox` property to `False`, and the `MaximizeBox` property to `False`.

   True/False

3. To use pop-up help, you must use a `HelpProvider` component and call the `SetHelpString` and `SetShowHelp` methods.

   True/False

4. To use context-sensitive help you must use a `HelpProvider` component and call the `SetHelpKeyword`, `SetHelpNavigator`, and `SetShowHelp` methods.

   True/False

APPLY

Applying It

Try to complete the following exercises by yourself.

Independent Exercise 1

Use a help authoring tool to create a help file that contains at least two topics. The help file should also have a Table of Contents and an Index.

TIP

Download HTML Help Workshop from this Web site if you don't already have it: http:// www.hyteq.com/help/hh-workshop.html.

Independent Exercise 2

Write a sample Visual Basic .NET form that provides context-sensitive help for each of the controls on the form using the help file created in Exercise 1.

Part V

Manipulating Data with ADO.NET and XML

Introducing Database Access with ADO.NET

DataSets

SQL Commands

XML Data Access

Reading XML

Generating an XML Document

29

Introducing Database Access with ADO.NET

ADO.NET is all about data access. It is the successor to ADO and defines an architecture for reading and writing data. At a high level, ADO.NET consists of two parts: .NET Data Providers and the DataSet.

There are two .NET Data Providers available as part of the .NET Framework Class Library. One is for SQL Server, and the other is for OLEDB. The SQL Server data provider is optimized for data access using SQL Server, while the OLEDB data provider is used to access data using any OLEDB database connection.

The DataSet supports disconnected access to data. A DataSet can be populated with data from a database, XML stream, or directly through your code. Once the data is loaded into a DataSet, it can be used to display and modify the data within an application. The DataSet automatically keeps track of any changes to the DataSet, and the changes can be automatically saved to either a database or an XML file.

Rather than jumping right into DataSets, this chapter starts Part V by presenting the Data Providers in order to explain some of the underlying infrastructure. This allows you to have a better understanding of what is going on behind the scenes once you get to DataSets.

The topics covered in this chapter are

- Database basics
- The .NET Framework Data namespaces
- .NET Data Providers
- The Server Explorer

Database Basics

The purpose of this chapter is to introduce ADO.NET. We assume you have a working knowledge of SQL (Structured Query Language) databases. In the event you do not, a brief database overview is presented here so that you can have a better understanding of the rest of the ADO.NET material. If you are really not that familiar with SQL databases and want to be, you should purchase a book about SQL or relational databases to get more information. Also, for a more in depth SQL tutorial you can visit http:// sqlcourse2.com.

A *database* is used to store information for an indefinite period of time in a structured format. It also provides fast reliable retrieval of the currently stored information. Once the database is defined and available for use, many applications can access the database in order to perform searches and updates.

A database structure is commonly referred to as a *database schema* and includes the following types of objects:

- Tables
- Columns
- Rows
- Primary keys
- Foreign keys
- Indexes

These types of objects are created in a database using *DDL* (Data Definition Language) or an administration tool that comes with the database product you purchased. Each of these types of objects has a specific meaning and has a purpose in the operation of the database.

Tables

Figure 29.1 shows a database table named authors with rows and columns.

Tables contain information about specific elements of your application. Each table has a unique name (within the schema) and contains a set of columns.

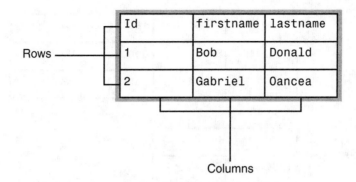

Figure 29.1: Table with rows and columns.

Columns

A *column* is a data element or property within a table. A column is also commonly referred to as a *field*. Columns are defined by having a unique name within the table and a data type. Once a column is defined as part of a table, a row in the table can contain a value for that column.

Rows

A *row* is an entry in a table that contains values for each of the columns of the table. A row is also commonly referred to as a *record*.

Primary Keys

Primary keys are defined as a set of columns within a table that together uniquely identify a row. Primary keys are used internally by the database to enforce referential integrity (discussed as part of foreign keys) as well as by an application in the process of searching for records. Because primary keys are often used, a database typically creates an index on the primary key for faster performance.

In Figure 29.1, the primary key consists of the Id column.

Foreign Keys

Foreign keys are a set of columns in a table that contain values of a primary key of another table (see Figure 29.2). The presence of a foreign key in a table signifies that records in the table are related to records in the table that the foreign key refers to.

Id	firstname	lastname	pid
1	Bob	Donald	1000
2	Gabriel	Oancea	1001

Foreign Key ——

pid	phone
1000	555-1212
1001	555-2121

Figure 29.2: Foreign keys.

Referential integrity exists when all foreign keys reference to an existing rows other tables. If a foreign key contains a value that does not exist in the referenced column in the other table, then referential integrity is broken.

Indexes

An index can be created on a set of one or more columns in a table. They are used internally by the database for faster searching and retrieval of rows from a table.

The .NET Framework Data Namespaces

The .NET Framework provides several namespaces that deal with data access in Microsoft .NET. These namespaces provide an extensive set of classes that support the overall ADO.NET architecture. The following table lists these namespaces along with a brief description. Each of these namespaces and the classes contained within them are covered in the next several chapters.

Table 29.1: .NET Framework Data Namespaces

Namespace	Description
`System.Data`	Provides the base set of classes and interfaces for the ADO.NET architecture. This includes the `DataSet` class, which is at the heart of ADO.NET.
`System.Data.Common`	Provides a set of classes shared by the .NET Data Providers.
`System.Data.OleDb`	Provides the classes that make up the .NET Data Provider for OLEDB.

Table 29.1: continued

Namespace	Description
System.Data.SqlClient	Provides the classes that make up the .NET Data Provider for SQL Server. The classes here are similar to classes in the System.Data.OleDb namespace but are optimized for working with SQL Server.
System.Data.SqlTypes	Provides a set of classes that represent the SQL data types supported by relational databases. These types are used in your code to represent the format of specific information that is stored in the database.
System.XML	Provides a set of classes for working with XML data. This is covered in more detail in Chapters 32, "XML Data Access" and 33, "Reading XML."

.NET Data Providers

A *Data Provider* supports data access through its own specific implementation that supports a common set of interfaces. In .NET, there are two standard Data Providers: SQL Server Data Provider and OLEDB Data Provider.

The OLEDB Data Provider supports data access through any OLEDB driver. If you have an OLEDB driver installed on your computer, your application can use that driver for accessing data stored in the format that OLEDB driver supports. For example, if you have an Oracle OLEDB driver installed you can write an application in .NET to access data in an Oracle database using the OLEDB Data Provider. You cannot use the SQL Server Data Provider to access data in an Oracle database.

If your application supports SQL Server, you could use the OLEDB Data Provider to access data in SQL Server. However, using the SQL Server Data Provider would be better in this case because it is optimized to talk to a SQL Server database.

So what does a Data Provider look like? A *Data Provider* is really just a set of classes that implement a standard set of interfaces. The classes in a Data Provider interact with a database in a standard way from the standpoint of the code using the Data Provider classes (since they are implementing standard interfaces). The database interaction includes connecting to a database, retrieving data, and storing data.

In .NET, the set of classes for a Data Provider are grouped into their own namespaces. Any Data Providers offered in the future would presumably be in their own namespace as well. To get a better idea of the types of classes in a Data Provider, see Table 29.2.

Table 29.2: .NET Data Provider Main Classes

Namespace	Description
Connection	Provides the communication link between application code and a database. Using a connection, an application can issue SQL commands for retrieving and modifying data in a database.
Command	Encapsulates a specific database command with a standard easy-to-use interface.
DataReader	Provides a forward-only read-only cursor.
DataAdapter	Provides a bridge between a database connection and a DataSet. A DataAdapter uses commands for populating a DataSet and for storing changes to a DataSet back to the database.

The basic steps in using a Data Provider are to first obtain a connection to a database and then issue commands to the database for retrieving data or modifying the data in the database. To get a connection, you need to instantiate a database connection object and pass it a connection string. The format of the connection string is based on the particular Data Provider you are using.

The SQL Server Data Provider contains a SqlDbConnection class that supports opening a database connection to a SQL Server Database. The OLEDB Data Provider contains an OleDbConnection class that supports opening a database connection to an OLEDB data source. In each case, a connection string is passed to the database connection object that represents the specific connection information for the particular data source. Connection strings are constructed using named value pairs with each pair being separated by a semicolon.

The simplest way to define a connection string is to create a new file on the desktop or in a folder. This is accomplished by right-clicking on the desktop or in a folder and then clicking New, Text Document. Rename the file so that it has a .udl file extension (answer Yes to the Are You Sure question). Now that the file exists, if you double-click the file to open it, the Data Link Wizard is started. The Data Link Wizard is shown in Figure 29.3. Using the wizard, you can specify the specific connection information to a database to which you want to connection to. When you click the OK Button, the connection information is stored in the file that you double-clicked.

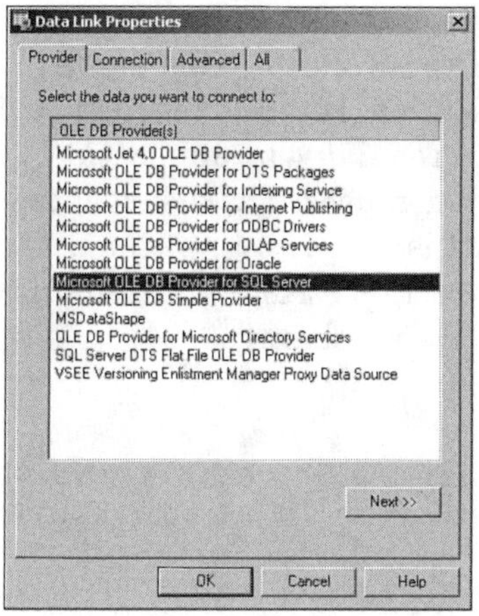

Figure 29.3: *Data Link Wizard.*

The list of OLE DB Data Providers shown in Figure 29.3 varies from computer to computer. This is because some software products install additional OLE DB Data Providers for their products to work. So, this list is actually dependant on what software packages you have installed on your computer.

A UDL file contains textual information that represents a connection string to a database. For example, here are the contents of the UDL file that is created if you use the wizard to define a connection to the pubs database in SQL Server:

```
[oledb]
; Everything after this line is an OLE DB initstring
Provider=SQLOLEDB.1;Persist Security Info=False;User ID=sa;Initial Catalog=pubs;
        Data Source=localhost
```

The previous connection string can be used by explicitly defining it directly in the code. For example, the connection string can be used as follows:

```
Dim connStr As String = "Provider=SQLOLEDB.1;Persist Security Info=False; " & _
                        "User ID=sa;Initial Catalog=pubs;Data Source=localhost"
Dim conn As SqlConnection = New SqlConnection(connStr)
```

Or, it can be used this way:

```
Dim connStr As String = "File Name = myfile.udl"
Dim conn As SqlConnection = New SqlConnection(connStr)
```

The advantage of using the UDL filename in the second approach is that you can change the UDL file if you want to connect to a different database after you have built your application. If the connection string is embedded in your code, you would need to rebuild your application to change the connection string that your application uses. The disadvantage of using a UDL file is that the connection string is parsed every time a connection is opened. Therefore, using a connection string that contains a reference to a UDL file will slow down performance slightly.

NOTE

The *pubs database* is an example database schema that is installed by default with a SQL Server database. The schema also comes populated with sample data. The examples in this chapter uses this database rather than having to construct a new schema. The assumption is that many readers are already familiar with this schema. If you are not familiar with it and you have SQL Server installed, you can browse the schema using the SQL Server Enterprise Manager to open the database server and view the schema.

Once a database connection object is created, you can use it to connect to the database and retrieve information from it by selecting rows from specific tables.

Here are two code examples that connect to a database, read the rows from the authors table in the pubs database, and then print out each author's first and last name.

Following is an example using SQL Server Data Provider:

```
Imports System.Data.SqlClient

Dim query As String = "select au_fname, au_lname from authors"
Dim connStr As String = "Initial Catalog=pubs;Data Source=localhost;" & _
                        "Integrated Security=SSPI;"
Dim conn As SqlConnection = New SqlConnection(connStr)
Dim command As SqlCommand = New SqlCommand(query, conn)
Dim reader As SqlDataReader

Try
    conn.Open()
    reader = command.ExecuteReader()
    While reader.Read()
        Console.WriteLine((reader.GetString(0).ToString & ", " & _
                          reader.GetString(1)))
    End While
Catch ex As SqlException
    Console.WriteLine(ex.Message)
```

```
Finally
    reader.Close()
    conn.Close()
End Try
```

Following is an example using OLEDB Data Provider:

```
Imports System.Data.OleDb

Dim query As String = "select au_fname, au_lname from authors"
Dim connStr As String = "Provider=SQLOLEDB;Data Source=localhost;" & _
                        "Initial Catalog=pubs;User ID=sa;Password="
Dim conn As OleDbConnection = New OleDbConnection(connStr)
Dim command As OleDbCommand = New OleDbCommand(query, conn)
Dim reader As OleDbDataReader

Try
    conn.Open()
    reader = command.ExecuteReader()
    While reader.Read()
        Console.WriteLine((reader.GetString(0).ToString & ", " & _
                        reader.GetString(1)))
    End While
Catch ex As SqlException
    Console.WriteLine(ex.Message)
Finally
    reader.Close()
    conn.Close()
End Try
```

In each example, two strings are declared first. The query string represents the SELECT statement used to read all of the authors' first and last names from the database. The connection string represents the information provided to the connection object to establish a connection to the database. A database connection object is then created using the connection string passed to its constructor. Next, a command is created by passing the query string and the connection object to the command objects constructor.

A Try-Catch block is commonly used around database access calls because frequently a database reports exceptions that you should handle and not just ignore. If, for example, the connection string were not formatted properly, an exception would be thrown. If you did not catch the exception, your program would not exit gracefully, and it would be difficult to track down the problem. You can save yourself some aggravation by using Try-Catch blocks.

The connection is opened by calling the Open method on the connection object. If the connection succeeds, program execution continues to the next line. Otherwise, program execution jumps to the catch section, and the exception message is output to the console. After the connection is opened, the command is executed by calling the ExecuteReader() method. Command objects in ADO.NET are used to define specific SQL commands that can then be executed on the database. In this case, the command object is used to create a reader object for performing a forward only read-only cursor. This allows you to move forward through the list of authors once, and you cannot modify the list. While iterating through the list (by calling the Next method in a While loop), each author's first name and last name is output to the console.

The Finally block is then executed, which closes the reader and the connection objects. Remember to close connections when you are done with them.

Each of these two examples uses a specific Data Provider. This is easy to see because the classes used in the method are either prefixed with SQL (SQL Server Data Provider) or OleDb (OLEDB Data Provider). If you used either data provider, this assumes your application will use only that data provider for the life of your application. This is fine if this is your intent. There is an alternative approach, which is described next.

Each of the classes in the Data Providers implements a standard interface in the System.Data namespace. If you used the interfaces in the System.Data namespace instead, you would be able to write code that did not distinguish between which Data Provider was being used by your application. To show this more clearly, take a look at the following code:

```
Imports System.Data.OleDb

Dim query As String = "select au_fname, au_lname from authors"
Dim connStr As String = "File Name = myfile.udl"
Dim conn As IDbConnection = New OleDbConnection(connStr)
Dim command As IDbCommand = New OleDbCommand(query, conn)
Dim reader As IDataReader

Try
    conn.Open()
    reader = command.ExecuteReader()
    While reader.Read()
        Console.WriteLine((reader.GetString(0).ToString & ", " & _
                          reader.GetString(1)))
    End While
Catch ex As SqlException
    Console.WriteLine(ex.Message)
Finally
    reader.Close()
    conn.Close()
End Try
```

The only difference between this code example and the example using the OLEDB Data Provider is the lines in bold. Each of the variables is defined using a standard interface from the System.Data namespace. It is true that this example instantiates a connection and command object from the OLEDB Data Provider, but you could also factor out this code so that your application instantiated Data Provider objects in a centralized place and the rest of your code used interfaces defined in the System.Data namespace, thereby making the rest of your code Data Provider–independent.

A .NET Data Provider also includes a specific data adapter class that implements the System.Data.IDataAdapter interface. Data adapters are used to populate DataSet objects and to store the DataSet object changes back to the database. A data adapter accomplishes this by using command objects that can communicate with the database through the opened connection.

Because a DataAdapter is used in conjunction with a DataSet, it is difficult to explain one without the other. Therefore, the DataAdapter is explained in more detail in Chapter 30, "DataSets." However, the next section includes an example of an easier way to retrieve author information from the pubs database. This example incidentally involves a DataAdapter.

Server Explorer

Up to this point in this chapter, the coding examples relied on the programmer to type in code. Visual Studio .NET provides a much easier way to get the same results. This easier way was not presented first because we felt it would be better for you to understand some of the classes and objects first. This way the following examples will have more meaning and hopefully be better understood.

The Server Explorer window, which is shown in the same frame as the Toolbox, can be displayed using the Ctrl+Alt+S keys. It contains information about defined Data Connections, known Servers such as the computer you are working on and other Servers you have added to this list by using the Add Server option, Crystal Report services, Event logs, Message Queues, Performance Counters, Services, and known SQL Server databases. Figure 29.4 shows the Server Explorer window in your Visual Studio .NET workspace.

You can expand the tree in the Server Explorer window to browse its contents. Figure 29.5 shows the Server Explorer window expanded to show the tables in the pubs database on my computer.

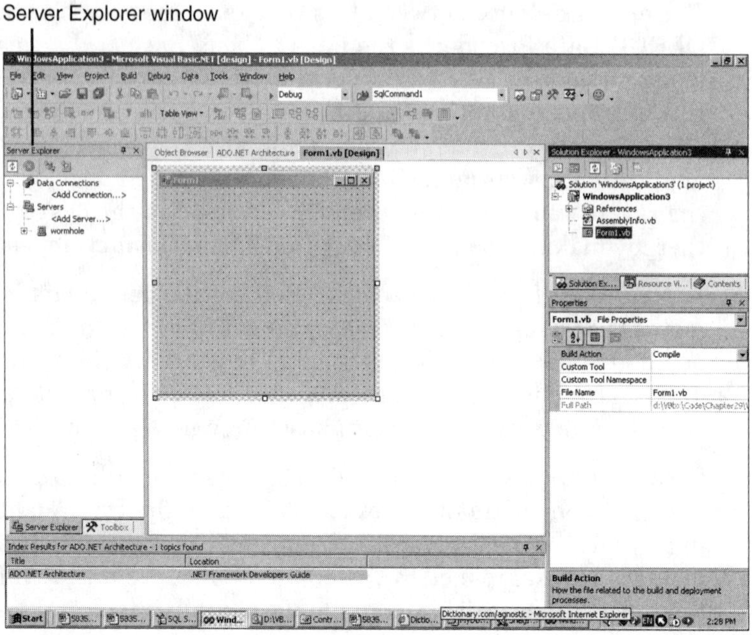

Server Explorer window

Figure 29.4: *Server Explorer window.*

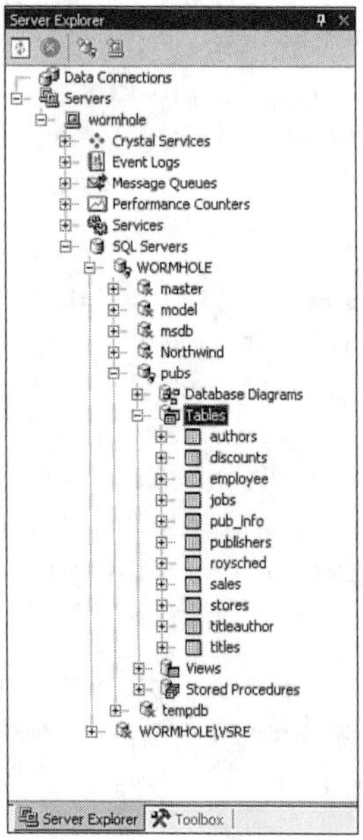

Figure 29.5: *Server Explorer window expanded.*

If you want to get information from the authors table as part of a form that you are developing, you can click on the table and drag it onto your form. By selecting the authors table and dragging it onto the form, a Connection object and a DataAdapter object are automatically created for the form. Also, all of the specifics regarding the connection string and the SQL statements are defined for you rather than having to do it yourself. Figure 29.6 shows the SqlConnection and SqlDataAdapter objects at the bottom of the form.

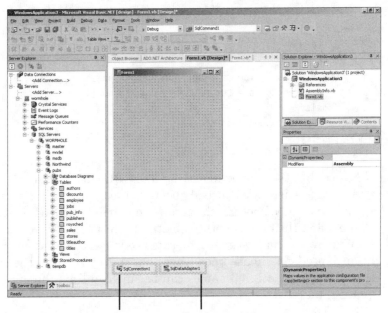

SqlConnection object   SqlDataAdapter object

Figure 29.6: *SqlConnection and SqlDataAdapter on form.*

If you click on the Connection object at the bottom of the Form Designer window, you are then able to see the properties for the Connection object. The properties include the ConnectionString, which is modifiable. If you need to modify the connection string you could do it by entering a new value for the ConnectionString property.

If you click on the DataAdapter object at the bottom of the Form Designer window, you are able to see its properties as well. Notice that the DataAdapter has four command properties: SelectCommand, InsertCommand, UpdateCommand, and DeleteCommand. These commands represent the SQL statements for automatically reading and writing data to the authors table. You do not need to write these commands by hand.

At this point, I can start accessing the data. To show this, I added a button on the form and wrote the following code that responds to the button's Click event:

```
Imports System.Data.SqlClient

Private Sub Button1_Click(ByVal sender As System.Object, _
                          ByVal e As System.EventArgs) Handles Button1.Click
    Try
        Dim reader As System.Data.SqlClient.SqlDataReader
        Me.SqlConnection1.Open()
        reader = Me.SqlSelectCommand1.ExecuteReader()
        While reader.Read()
            System.Console.Out.WriteLine(reader.Item("au_fname").ToString & " " & _
                                        reader.Item("au_lname").ToString)
        End While

    Catch ex As system.Data.SqlClient.SqlException
        System.Console.Out.WriteLine(ex.Message)
    Finally
        Me.SqlConnection1.Close()
    End Try
End Sub
```

Notice that the connection string and SQL statements are not defined in this code. These have already been defined when the table was dropped on the form. To be specific, the connection string and SQL statements are defined in the code generated by the Form Designer. You can see this in the "Windows Form Designer generated code" section of the form's code. The only specific database knowledge that this code has is the column names. And, even the column names can be shielded from the application code by using `TableMappings`.

If you click on the DataAdapter in the Form Designer window and then click on the value for the `TableMappings` property, you can specify the mappings between the columns in the table and the columns in the DataSet. Figure 29.7 shows the Form for specifying the mappings.

The columns in the DataSet are the columns to which your application refers. When commands are sent to the database, the values for the columns defined in the DataSet are translated to the specific columns in the database using the defined TableMappings. This way you can write application code that does not depending specifically on knowing the column names. You still need to update and rebuild your code if column names change in the database; however, your code changes are isolated to the TableMappings and can be done relatively easily.

The great part about this approach of dragging and dropping from the Server Explorer is that you don't need to concern yourself about the specifics to start writing database code. This allows you to develop code using database access in a much faster timeframe.

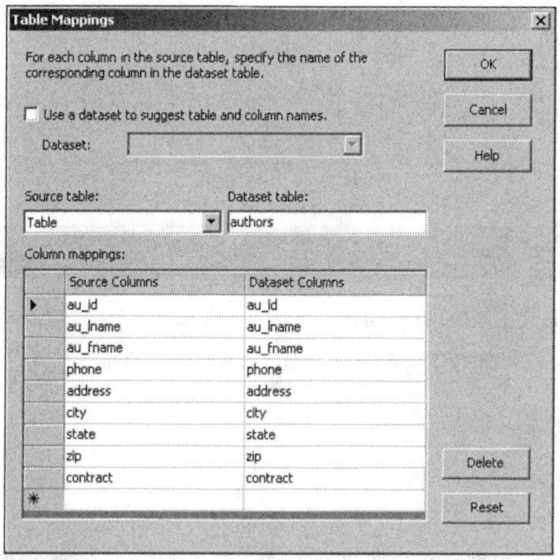

Figure 29.7: *Table Mappings form.*

What's Next

This chapter introduces ADO.NET by explaining what a database is. It then goes on to explain what Data Providers are and how they are used in .NET. The chapter ended by showing how the Server Explorer can be used to simplify database development by dragging and dropping the desired tables onto a form. At that point, the coding effort to use the desired tables is very manageable.

The intent of this chapter was to get you started in learning ADO.NET by focusing on Data Providers. This includes Connections, Commands, and briefly. DataAdapters.

The next chapter focuses on the heart of ADO.NET, which is DataSets. A *DataSet* represents a data structure that contains disconnected data. The benefit of supporting disconnected data is that an application can retrieve information from a database and display it in different ways without having to go back to the database again. For example, if you retrieve a set of information and wish to filter it or sort it differently, this can be done within the DataSet itself and does not require you to go back to the database. DataSets also allow you to move data across the wire (network) because it supports serializing its data to XML, and it keeps track of the changes made to it so that it can intelligently save data back to the database when the application desires.

NOTE

The answers to "Reviewing It," "Checking It," and "Applying It" are available on our Web site.

REVIEW

Reviewing It

This section presents a review of the key concepts in this chapter. These questions are intended to gauge your absorption of the relevant material.

1. What are Data Providers?

2. What is the Server Explorer?

CHECK

Checking It

Select the correct answer to the following questions.

Multiple Choice

1. A row in a database represents:

    a. A record.

    b. A set of values for each column in a table.

    c. a and b.

    d. None of the above.

2. Primary keys are used to:

    a. Connect to a database.

    b. Uniquely identify rows in a database table.

    c. Unlock the secrets of the database.

    d. None of the above.

3. Which namespace defines the interfaces implemented by a .NET Data Provider?

    a. System.Data.

    b. System.Data.OleDb and System.Data.SqlClient.

    c. System.Data.SqlTypes.

    d. System.Data.Provider.

4. What are the two Data Providers provided with the .NET Framework?

    a. OLEDB Data Provider and XML Data Provider.

    b. SQL Server Data Provider and XML Data Provider.

    c. OLEDB Data Provider and SQL Server Data Provider.

    d. SQL Server Data Provider and Oracle Data Provider.

True or False

Select one of the two possible answers and then verify on our Web site that you picked the correct one.

1. ConnectionStrings are named value pairs used to specify a connection to a database.

    True/False

2. The Data Link Wizard can be used to define a ConnectionString.

    True/False

3. You can browse a database using the Server Explorer.

    True/False

4. A table can contain columns, primary keys, and foreign keys.

    True/False

5. The SQL Server Data Provider consists of classes with their names prepended with SqlServer.

    True/False

6. The OLEDB Data Provider consists of classes with their names prepended with OleDb.

    True/False

APPLY

Applying It

Try to complete the following exercise by yourself.

Independent Exercise

Create a new Windows Application project and use the Server Explorer to select any table from any database and drop it onto a form. Then write some code that iterates through the table and outputs some values from each of the rows.

30

DataSets

The heart of ADO.NET, as we mentioned in the previous chapter, is the DataSet. A *DataSet* represents a data structure that contains disconnected data. The benefit of supporting disconnected data is that an application can retrieve information from a database and display it in different ways without having to go back to the database again. For example, if you retrieve a set of information and wish to filter it or sort it differently, this can be done within the DataSet itself and does not require you to go back to the database. DataSets also allow you to move data across the wire (network) since it supports serializing its data to XML, and it keeps track of the changes made to it so that it can intelligently save data back to the database when the application desires.

DataSets are used in conjunction with DataAdapters. DataAdapters populate DataSets with data from a specific data store such as a database or an XML file. DataAdapters are also used to store changes made to a DataSet into a data store as well.

Examples in this chapter will show how to use DataSets in several different ways, and by the end of the chapter you will understand the essence of ADO.NET.

The topics covered in this chapter include

- Using a DataSet to read and modify data
- Sorting and filtering a DataSet
- Binding a DataSet to a control
- Multi-table DataSets and relations
- Typed and untyped DataSets

Using a DataSet to Read and Modify Data

In the previous chapter, we showed how to read data from a database using a `DataReader` object. Here we show how to read data using a `DataSet` object. The difference here is that the `DataSet` object is populated with data from the database and then used for managing the data. The `DataSet` object keeps track of any changes made to the data in the DataSet. The DataSet modifications can be saved back to the database at any point.

When reading data into a DataSet, the idea is to use a `DataAdapter` object to fill the DataSet. The `DataAdapter` uses a `Connection` object and a query string (SQL statement) for retrieving the desired rows from the database. After the DataSet is populated with data, the database connection can be closed because it is no longer necessary until the changes are saved back.

In order to illustrate this, create a Windows application project and drag the authors table (in the pubs database) onto the form. This automatically creates a SqlConnection object and a SqlDataAdapter object that knows how to read data from and write data to the authors table in the pubs database. Then add a Button to the form and double-click it to open the code window at the point of the generated event handler for the Button's Click event. At the top of the form include the following line so that the project has a reference to the correct namespace:

```
Imports System.Data.SqlClient
```

Here is a code example within the button's event handler that retrieves each author's first and last name:

```
Imports System.Data.SqlClient

Dim query As String = "select au_fname, au_lname from authors"
Dim ds As DataSet = New DataSet()
Dim rowIndex As Integer
Dim table As DataTable
Dim row As DataRow

Try

    SqlConnection1.Open()
    SqlDataAdapter1.Fill(ds)
    SqlConnection1.Close()

    ' output data from DataSet
    table = ds.Tables.Item(0)
    For rowIndex = 0 To table.Rows.Count - 1
```

```
        row = table.Rows.Item(rowIndex)
        Console.WriteLine("{0} {1}", row("au_fname"), row("au_lname"))
    Next

Catch ex As SqlException
    Console.WriteLine(ex.Message)
End Try
```

The code that populates the DataSet is rather minimal. The `SqlConnection1` and `SqlDataAdapter1` objects were constructed as a result of dropping the authors table onto the form.

A `DataSet` variable is defined and set to a new `DataSet` instance. Within the Try-Catch block, the connection is opened, the adapter fills the DataSet, and then the connection is closed. Technically, this example does not need to explicitly open or close the connection because the data adapter will do this automatically. The example opens and closes the connection on purpose to show that the DataSet's data can be used even when the database connection is closed. This demonstrates the disconnected aspect of DataSets.

The example code iterates through the DataSet and writes out the data to the Output window. The DataSet contains a set of tables represented by the `Tables` property. This property contains a list of `DataTable` objects. A `DataTable` contains a set of rows for that table. This set is represented by the `Rows` property, which contains a list of `DataRow` objects. The `Rows` property is a `DataRowCollection` object that contains a list of `DataRow` objects.

A `DataRow` object contains values for each of the columns in the row. The values are stored in the DataRow's `Item` collection. The column values can be accessed by an index number starting at zero or by a string that represents the name of the column. Alternatively, a value for a column in a row can be accessed directly from the row object by passing in the column name as shown in the previous example. This is a shorthand way of accessing column values and is more readable.

Okay, now what's the advantage of using a DataSet? Well, the DataSet is now disconnected from the database. This allows an application to use the DataSet as a memory storage of data. The data can be filtered, sorted, added to, modified, removed, and so on. There is no need to go back to the database again until you want to commit the changes back to the database. In a Windows application or a Web application, this can improve performance and scalability because the database does not need to be requeried each time the data needs to be filtered or sorted, for example. The DataSet can also improve performance if the data needs to be cached in memory for quick access.

The next few examples start to get more interesting as we show how to add, modify, and remove data from a DataSet and then save the changes back to the database.

Adding Data Using a DataSet

Adding data to a database using a DataSet is accomplished by adding rows to a table in the DataSet. The following example uses a `SqlDataAdapter` to populate a `DataSet` object. After the data is loaded, a row is added to the table, and the columns in the row are given some values.

Using the same project created in the previous example, add another Button to the form and double-click it to generate and event handler. The following code is placed in the event handler to show how to add data to the DataSet:

```
Dim ds As DataSet = New DataSet()
Dim table As DataTable
Dim row As DataRow

Try

    SqlDataAdapter1.Fill(ds)

    table = ds.Tables.Item(0)
    row = table.NewRow()
    row("au_id") = "123-45-5678"
    row("au_fname") = "Bob"
    row("au_lname") = "Donald"
    row("contract") = True
    row("phone") = "555-555-5555"
    table.Rows.Add(row)

    SqlDataAdapter1.Update(ds)

Catch ex As SqlException
    Console.WriteLine(ex.Message)
End Try
```

After the connection is opened and the DataSet is filled with data, the code in bold adds data to the DataSet. This is done by getting the table object from the DataSet that contains the loaded data. This example assumes there is only one table and, therefore, uses the index 0 to get the table. In the "Multi-Table DataSets and Relations" section later in this chapter, you will see how DataSets can store multiple tables.

After you have the table, a new row is created by calling the NewRow method. This method returns a new row to which you can add data. For each column in the row, the example sets some sample values. The row object is then added to the table object. This is because the NewRow method creates a new row object and does not automatically add it to the table. You have to add it using the Add method on the Rows collection property.

When you are done with the DataSet and want to save the DataSet changes back to the database, you need to call the Update method only on the adapter passing in the DataSet object.

Updating Data Using a DataSet

Updating data in a database using a DataSet is done by changing values in a row within the DataSet. After the row has been updated, you would store the changes back to the database by calling the Update method on the adapter object just like in the previous example.

Using the same project again, add another Button to the form and double-click it to generate and event handler. The following code is placed in the event handler to show how to update data in the DataSet:

```
Dim ds As DataSet = New DataSet()
Dim rowIndex As Integer
Dim table As DataTable
Dim row As DataRow

Try

    SqlDataAdapter1.Fill(ds)

    table = ds.Tables.Item(0)
    For rowIndex = 0 To table.Rows.Count - 1
        row = table.Rows.Item(rowIndex)
        If row("au_fname") = "Bob" And row("au_lname") = "Donald" Then
            row("contract") = False
        End If
    Next

    SqlDataAdapter1.Update(ds)

Catch ex As SqlException
    Console.WriteLine(ex.Message)
End Try
```

After the DataSet has been populated, this code searches for a particular row and modifies the contract column. After that, the DataSet changes are persisted back to the database using the data adapter.

The search approach taken in this example is one example way of doing a search. Later in this chapter, you'll see how you can use filtering to find a set of one or many records in a DataSet.

Deleting Data Using a DataSet

Deleting data from a database using a DataSet is done by removing specific rows from the DataSet. This is accomplished by calling the Delete method on any row object that you want deleted. Internally, the DataSet keeps track of the rows that were deleted so that when you call the Update method on the adapter, the data can be removed from the database.

Once again in the same project, add another Button to the form and double-click it to generate an event handler. The following code is placed in the event handler to show how to delete rows in the DataSet:

```
Dim ds As DataSet = New DataSet()
Dim tableIndex, rowIndex As Integer
Dim table As DataTable
Dim row As DataRow


Try

    SqlDataAdapter1.Fill(ds)

    table = ds.Tables.Item(0)
    For rowIndex = 0 To table.Rows.Count - 1
        row = table.Rows.Item(rowIndex)
        If row("au_fname") = "Bob" And row("au_lname") = "Donald" Then
            row.Delete()
        End If
    Next

    SqlDataAdapter1.Update(ds)

Catch ex As SqlException
    Console.WriteLine(ex.Message)
End Try
```

A row is deleted from a DataSet by calling the a row object's Delete method. This example searches for a known author record and calls Delete on the row if it is found. The DataSet changes are then persisted to the database by calling the Update method on the adapter.

In each of the examples that showed how to add rows, update rows, and delete rows, the changes to the DataSet were persisted back to the database using the Update method on the DataAdapter object. The Update method we used accepted a DataSet object. This is acceptable and very straightforward. However, there is a finer grained option if you choose to use it. You can extract all of the changes from a DataSet by calling the DataSet's GetChanges method. This method creates a new DataSet object and populates it with the changes that were made to the DataSet. So, instead of calling Update and passing a potentially large DataSet that has only a few changes, you could write code like this:

```
If ds.HasChanges() Then
    adapter.Update(ds.GetChanges())
End If
```

This code checks to see whether the loaded DataSet has any changes. If it does, the changes are returned from the GetChanges method. The result is a new DataSet that only contains the rows that were changed. The adapter now presumably has a smaller DataSet to persist, and this conceptually makes more sense.

There is also another variation of the GetChanges method that allows you to get specific types of changes such as just the added rows or just the modified rows. The following code shows how to save only the added and modified rows:

```
If ds.HasChanges() Then
    adapter.Update(ds.GetChanges(DataRowState.Added or DataRowState.Modified))
End If
```

The parameter to the GetChanges method is a DataRowState enumeration. Table 30.1 shows the possible values in the DataRowState enumeration along with a description of each.

Table 30.1: **System.Data.DataRowState** *Enumeration*

Value	Description
Added	Means the row has been added to a DataRowCollection (Rows property) using the Add method. After the data has been saved to the database, the state reverts back to Unchanged.
Deleted	Means the row has been removed from a DataRowCollection (Rows property) using the Delete method. After the DataSet is saved to the database, the row is removed from the DataSet.
Detached	Means the DataRow object has been created but not added to a DataRowCollection yet.
Modified	Means the row has been updated but not saved to the database yet. After the DataSet changes have been saved to the database, the state reverts back to Unchanged.
Unchanged	The DataRow object has not been changed.

Filtering and Sorting of data within a DataSet is an extremely useful capability of a DataSet. So let's discuss this next.

Sorting and Filtering DataSets

Rows in a DataSet can be filtered and sorted as needed. There are two ways of doing this. The simple way is to use the Select method on the DataSet object. The Select method allows you to pass in SQL like strings for selecting a set of rows and optionally sorting those rows. When you call the Select method, the database is not queried again. Only the rows that exist in the loaded DataSet are used for satisfying the filtering request. This can improve application performance if the application needs to load some data and then display it in several different ways. In this case, the data is loaded once and then filtered and sorted as needed in memory.

The second way of performing filtering and sorting of DataSets is by using System.Data.DataView objects. DataView objects are a layer or a facade on top of a DataTable (which exists in a DataSet). The DataView uses the DataTable as the data source and the view presents the data depending on the filtering and sorting defined in the DataView. Also, there can be many DataView objects using the same DataTable. This allows you to set up several different views of the same data in your application. If you change the data in the DataTable, all of the views have the benefit of presenting the same change.

Let's start with an example showing how to use the DataSet's Select method. In the following example, the desired table is referenced from the DataSet. The Select method is then called on the DataTable object passing in a SQL-like filter string. In this case, the filtering is defined to find the same author that the For-Next loop found in the earlier examples. This approach is simple and presumably more efficient. The result of the Select method is an array of DataRow objects. As an array, you can iterate through the DataRow objects and do what you want with them. This example just displays the first and last name to the console.

Add another Button to the form and double-click it to generate an event handler. The following code is placed in the event handler to show how to filter rows in the DataSet::

```
Dim ds As DataSet = New DataSet()
Dim rowIndex As Integer
Dim table As DataTable
Dim row As DataRow
Dim rows() As DataRow

Try
```

```
    SqlDataAdapter1.Fill(ds)

    table = ds.Tables.Item(0)
    rows = table.Select("au_fname = 'Johnson' AND au_lname = 'White'")

    For rowIndex = 0 To rows.Length - 1
        row = rows.GetValue(rowIndex)
        Console.WriteLine("{0} {1}", row("au_fname"), row("au_lname"))
    Next

Catch ex As SqlException
    Console.WriteLine(ex.Message)
End Try
```

The next example shows how to perform sorting using the Select method. The second parameter is optional and if provided defines a SQL sort string. The result of using the sort string means that the returned rows are sorted by the defined sort string.

Add another Button to the form and double-click it to generate an event handler. The following code is placed in the event handler to show how to sort rows in the DataSet:

```
Dim ds As DataSet = New DataSet()
Dim rowIndex As Integer
Dim table As DataTable
Dim row As DataRow
Dim rows() As DataRow

Try

    SqlDataAdapter1.Fill(ds)

    ' output data from DataSet
    table = ds.Tables.Item(0)
    rows = table.Select("au_lname > 'M'", "au_lname ASC")

    For rowIndex = 0 To rows.Length - 1
        row = rows.GetValue(rowIndex)
        Console.WriteLine("{0} {1}", row("au_fname"), row("au_lname"))
    Next

Catch ex As SqlException
    Console.WriteLine(ex.Message)
End Try
```

As stated earlier, the other approach is to use a `DataView` object. A `DataView` object can be filtered and sorted as well. The following example shows the instantiation of a `DataView` object by passing in a DataTable to its constructor. After the DataView is created, it is bound to the DataTable given to it in its constructor. The DataTable can be set (or get) using the DataView's `Table` property as well.

Add another Button to the form and double-click it to generate an event handler. The following code is placed in the event handler to show how to filter rows in a `DataView`:

```
Dim ds As DataSet = New DataSet()
Dim rowIndex As Integer
Dim table As DataTable
Dim row As DataRowView
Dim dv As DataView

Try

    SqlDataAdapter1.Fill(ds)

    dv = New DataView(ds.Tables.Item(0))
    dv.RowFilter = "au_fname = 'Johnson' AND au_lname = 'White'"

    For rowIndex = 0 To dv.Count - 1
        row = dv.Item(rowIndex)
        Console.WriteLine("{0} {1}", row("au_fname"), row("au_lname"))
    Next

Catch ex As SqlException
    Console.WriteLine(ex.Message)
End Try
```

After the DataView object is created, the filter is set using the DataView's `RowFilter` property. This property contains a string that represents the SQL-like filter expression. After the filter is set, the DataView shows only the DataRows that match the filter expression from the DataTable.

The next example shows how to sort a DataView using the DataView's `Sort` property. The `Sort` property is a SQL sort expression that defines which columns to sort on and the direction of the sort. This example shows how to sort by last name in ascending order.

Also notice in this example that two `DataView` objects are using the same DataTable. This is an example of how two different views of the same DataTable can be created and used at the same time in an application. The advantage of this is that you don't have to create two different queries against the database to get two different results back. You can just get the data you need for both views once and then decide how to filter and sort the data as needed.

Add another Button to the form and double-click it to generate an event handler. The following code is placed in the event handler to show how to filter and sort rows in the DataView:

```
Dim ds As DataSet = New DataSet()
Dim rowIndex As Integer
Dim table As DataTable
Dim row As DataRowView
Dim dvAtoM As DataView
Dim dvMtoZ As DataView

Try

    SqlDataAdapter1.Fill(ds)

    ' create data view of authors' last
    ' names from A to L
    dvAtoM = New DataView(ds.Tables.Item(0))
    dvAtoM.RowFilter = "au_lname < 'M'"
    dvAtoM.Sort = "au_lname ASC"

    ' display DataView
    For rowIndex = 0 To dvAtoM.Count - 1
        row = dvAtoM.Item(rowIndex)
        Console.WriteLine("{0} {1}", row("au_fname"), row("au_lname"))
    Next

    ' create data view of authors' last
    ' names from M to Z
    dvMtoZ = New DataView(ds.Tables.Item(0))
    dvMtoZ.RowFilter = "au_lname >= 'M'"
    dvMtoZ.Sort = "au_lname ASC"

    ' display DataView
    For rowIndex = 0 To dvMtoZ.Count - 1
        row = dvMtoZ.Item(rowIndex)
        Console.WriteLine("{0} {1}", row("au_fname"), row("au_lname"))
    Next

Catch ex As SqlException
    Console.WriteLine(ex.Message)
End Try
```

Binding a DataSet to a Control

One of the most exciting aspects of DataSets is that they can be bound to a control. This allows controls to automatically display the data within a DataSet without you having to write any specific code. Let's walk through an example of how to do this using a simple application.

First, create a new Windows application project. On the main form in the Form Designer window, drag the authors table from the Server Explorer window onto the main form exactly as described in the previous chapter. (This involves navigating the Server Explorer tree into the installed SQL Server database installed on your machine—assuming you have SQL Server.) This adds a SqlDataConnection and a SqlDataAdapter to the Form class. Update the names of the SqlConnection and SqlDataAdapter to more meaningful names such as m_connection and m_adapter, respectively.

Next, add a DataSet control from the Toolbox onto the form and name it m_dataset. When you add a DataSet to a form, a dialog box appears and asks you whether you want to create a Typed DataSet or an Untyped DataSet. These two types are explained later in this chapter. For this example, create an Untyped DataSet. This results in a DataSet added to the form with the name DataSet1.

Add a button on the form that, once clicked, will populate the DataSet. Set the display text on the button to be Read and name the button btnRead. Double-click the button on the form to automatically generate an event handler. Here is the code for populating the DataSet:

```
Private Sub btnRead_Click(ByVal sender As System.Object, _
                          ByVal e As System.EventArgs) Handles btnRead.Click
    Try
        ' fill the data set with authors
        m_adapter.Fill(m_dataset)
    Catch ex As System.Data.SqlClient.SqlException
        Console.WriteLine(ex.Message)
    End Try
End Sub
```

Add a button to the form so that you can save the DataSet as well. Name the button btnSave and change its display text to "Save." Add code to the Save button's Click event to save the DataSet data back to the database. Here is the code to do this:

```
Private Sub btnSave_Click(ByVal sender As System.Object, _
                          ByVal e As System.EventArgs) _
                          Handles btnSave.Click
```

```
If m_dataset.HasChanges Then
    m_adapter.Update(m_dataset.GetChanges())
End If
```

```
End Sub
```

The last step is to add a control to the form and bind the DataSet to the control. The DataGrid control is perfect for this exact case so let's use it. Add the DataGrid to the form from the Toolbox and change its name to m_datagrid.

At this point, the form looks something like the form shown in Figure 30.1.

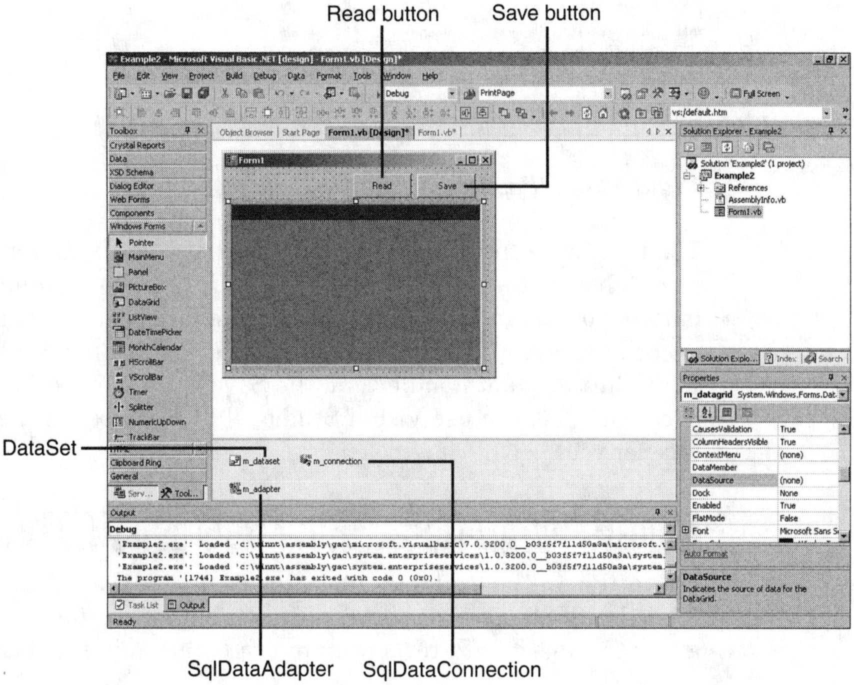

Figure 30.1: Example DataSet binding.

To set up the binding, you need to set the DataSource property on the DataGrid control to the DataSet. In this example, this means the following code needs to be defined:

```
m_datagrid.DataSource = m_dataset
```

The best way to do this is to use the Properties window in Visual Studio. NET. Select the DataGrid control by clicking it once. Then set the DataSource property by selecting a DataSet from the list. When you run this application and click the Read Button, the data grid is populated with the data that resides in the loaded DataSet. You need to click on the DataGrid to expand it. Once you do this, you will see a form similar to the one shown in Figure 30.2.

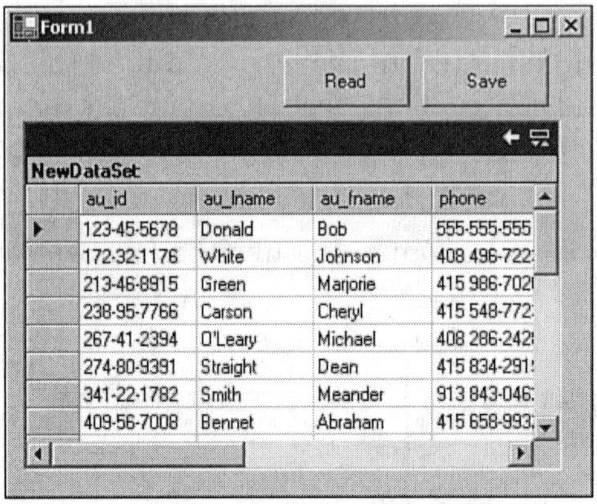

Figure 30.2: Populated DataGrid control.

The DataGrid control allows you to see what is in the DataSet. And, it allows you to change it as well. If you change any of the data and click the Save button, your changes will be saved to the database. The amount of code needed to accomplish this functionality is limited to the code shown in the Read Button event handler and the Save Button event handler (assuming, of course, that you use Visual Studio .NET because it generates a lot of the code for you).

Multi-Table DataSets and Relations

Up until now, the examples have demonstrated DataSets using a single table. DataSets also support multiple tables. Therefore, you are able to fill a `DataSet` object with rows from multiple tables in the database.

Essentially, a DataAdapter is responsible for populating a DataSet from a specific table in the database. If you create a DataSet for each table that you want to populate a DataSet with, you can then use each DataAdapter object to populate the `DataSet` object. This results in populating a DataSet with many types of records. The number of different types of records depends on the number of adapters you use to populate a DataSet.

Remember in our earlier examples where we used the Tables property on a DataSet? In those examples, the number of tables was only one because you were dealing only with single tables. When a DataSet is filled with data from multiple DataAdapters, a DataTable object is added to the Tables property of the DataSet. To access data using a particular table in the DataSet, you first need to find the appropriate DataTable object and then filter the rows to get the specific rows you want to deal with in a particular table. You can either iterate through the Tables property (which is a DataTableCollection containing DataTable objects), or you can reference the specific table by name using the following notation where ds is a variable of type DataSet:

```
Dim table As DataTable
table = ds.Tables("authors")
```

At this point let's walk through an example that fills a DataSet with data from the pubs database again. This time, let's load data from the titles table and the publishers table. First create a new Windows application project and then drag and drop the titles table and publishers table onto a form in a project. Rename the DataConnection object to m_connection. Rename the DataAdapter for the titles table to m_titles. And, rename the DataAdapter for the publishers table to m_publishers. And finally, add an untyped DataSet to the form and name it m_ds.

Add a button to the form, name it btnRead, and create an event handler for it by double-clicking it. Now, reading the data from these two tables into a DataSet is accomplished by the following code (make sure that you import the System.Data.SqlClient namespace at the top of the form's code):

```
Private Sub btnRead_Click(ByVal sender As System.Object, _
                          ByVal e As System.EventArgs) _
                          Handles Button1.Click
    Try

        m_connection.Open()
        m_titles.Fill(m_ds)
        m_publishers.Fill(m_ds)
        m_connection.Close()

    Catch ex As SqlException
        Console.WriteLine(ex.Message)
    End Try
End Sub
```

This can be useful if you need to have a single cache of data within your application where you want to store several different types of data. Another, more appropriate, reason for doing this is so that you can relate rows within the DataSet and easily navigate them. For example, the code example loads book information and publisher information into a DataSet. Wouldn't it be nice if you could easily find the books that a publisher published? As it turns out, this is very simple to do.

Here's an example that shows this. This example expands on the same project created in the previous example that populated the DataSet. First, take a look at Figure 30.3.

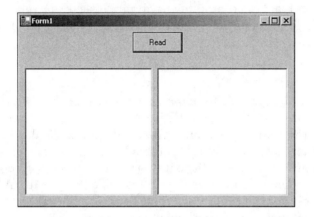

Figure 30.3: *Form with button and two list boxes.*

You are going to create a form with a single button and two list boxes. When the user clicks on the button, the DataSet is loaded with book information and publisher information. In addition, the list box on the left side of the form is going to be populated with publishers. Then, when the user clicks on a publisher the list box on the right side of the form displays a list of books associated with the selected publisher.

The ability to get books associated with a given publisher is based on the idea of relations. In a DataSet, you can define how tables are related to one another. This is done by creating a `DataRelation` object that defines which column in the parent table is associated to which column in the child table.

Add two ListBox controls to the form and name the one on the left `lbPublishers` and name the one on the right `lbTitles`.

At this point, you need to change the code that responds to the `Click` event of the button. When the button is clicked the code needs to load the DataSet and define the relation between the tables. Here's the code to do this:

```
Private Sub btnRead_Click(ByVal sender As System.Object, _
                ByVal e As System.EventArgs) _
                Handles btnRead.Click
```

```
    Dim parentCol As DataColumn
    Dim childCol As DataColumn
    Dim relCustOrder As DataRelation
    Dim table As DataTable
    Dim rowIndex As Integer

    Try

        'load DataSet
        m_connection.Open()
        m_titles.Fill(m_ds)
        m_publishers.Fill(m_ds)
        m_connection.Close()

        'define relationship in DataSet
        parentCol = m_ds.Tables("publishers").Columns("pub_id")
        childCol = m_ds.Tables("titles").Columns("pub_id")
        relCustOrder = New DataRelation("Titles", parentCol, childCol)
        m_ds.Relations.Add(relCustOrder)

        ' update listbox
        table = m_ds.Tables("publishers")
        For rowIndex = 0 To table.Rows.Count - 1
            lbPublishers.Items.Add(table.Rows.Item(rowIndex)("pub_name"))
        Next

    Catch ex As SqlException
        Console.WriteLine(ex.Message)
    End Try

End Sub
```

After the DataSet is populated with data, the code moves on to define a DataRelation between the two loaded tables. A DataRelation involves three pieces of information—the name of the relation, the parent column, and the child column. This code gets the pub_id column from the publishers table (which is the primary key) and gets the pub_id column from the titles table (which is the foreign key). These two columns are added to a DataRelation object along with a name for the relation. We'll see the impact of this as you read on.

After the relation is defined, the rest of the code iterates through the publishers table and fills the ListBox control with publisher names.

The next thing you want to do in this example is display the appropriate list of books in the list box to the right of the form depending on which publisher was selected in the list box at the left of the form. This is accomplished by handling the SelectedIndexChanged event for the list box. Double-click the publishers listbox on the right and enter the following code in the SelectedIndexChanged event handler:

```
Private Sub lbPublishers_SelectedIndexChanged(ByVal sender As System.Object, _
                                    ByVal e As System.EventArgs) _
                                    Handles
lbPublishers.SelectedIndexChanged
    Dim pubName As String
    Dim table As DataTable
    Dim rows() As DataRow
    Dim childRows() As DataRow
    Dim i As Integer

    ' clear titles list box and get selected publisher
    lbTitles.Items.Clear()
    pubName = lbPublishers.SelectedItem

    ' get list of books for the selected publisher
    table = m_ds.Tables("publishers")
    rows = table.Select("pub_name = '" & pubName & "'")

    ' display books
    If rows.Length = 1 Then
        childRows = rows(0).GetChildRows("Titles")
        For i = 0 To childRows.Length - 1
            lbTitles.Items.Add(childRows(i)("title"))
        Next
    End If

End Sub
```

This code does three basic steps:

1. The ListBox control at the right of the form is cleared so that no residual information remains in the user interface. In addition, the name of the selected publisher is discovered by checking the selected item in the publishers ListBox.

2. The row that represents the publisher information is found by getting the publishers table and then calling its Select method to retrieve the specific publisher row.

3. Using the publisher row, a call to the GetChildRows method allows us to get the books associated with the known publisher. The GetChildRows method uses the name of a previously defined DataRelation object. Using the information defined in the

DataRelation object, the DataSet can navigate to the child rows and return only those child rows that exist in the database. Once again, this data querying and navigation does not involve communicating with the database again. It is all done within memory.

Figure 30.4 shows the form running. In the figure, the user selected the second publisher from the top, and the list box on the right is displaying the books for the selected publishers. The user can click through the entire list of publishers to display the appropriate book information. The only database communication cost is the initial loading of the DataSet. Without this capability, most applications typically dealt with this scenario by querying the database each time the selected publisher changes.

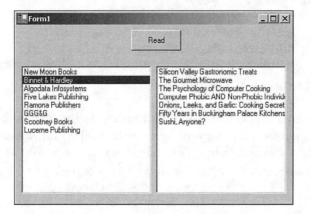

Figure 30.4: Displaying book information for a specific publisher.

Typed and Untyped DataSets

Untyped DataSets is a term that refers to instances of the DataSet class itself. A DataSet class all by itself does not represent a specific type of a DataSet. It's just a regular DataSet. *Typed DataSets* on the other hand is a term used to describe subclasses of a DataSet. Typed DataSets, in addition to being a subclass of DataSet, have properties and methods specific to the type of DataSet it is.

Let's create a typed DataSet and see what this all really means.

Create a new Windows application project and drag the authors table onto the form. Now, right-click the SqlDataAdapter control and click the Generate DataSet menu item. You should see the dialog shown in Figure 30.5. In this dialog, enter a name for the generated DataSet. In our example, we left the name as MyDataSet. When the OK Button is clicked, a typed DataSet is generated for the form.

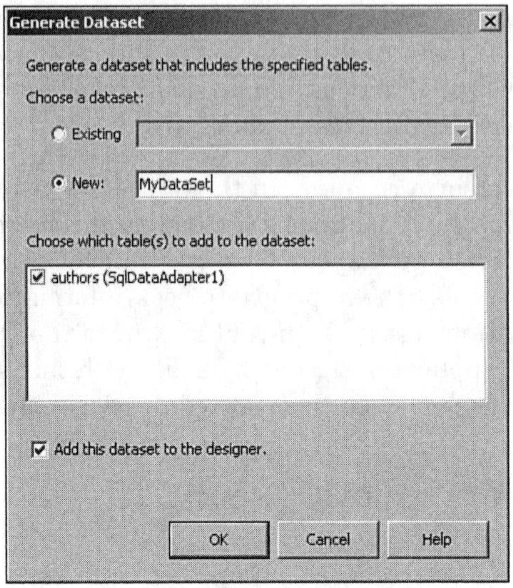

Figure 30.5: Generate DataSet form.

To see how to use this DataSet, add a button to the form and write some
code in the button's `Click` event handler to read an author and printout the
author's first and last name. The code to do this is as follows:

```
Private Sub Button1_Click(ByVal sender As System.Object, _
                    ByVal e As System.EventArgs) _
                    Handles Button1.Click

    Try

        SqlConnection1.Open()
        SqlDataAdapter1.Fill(MyDataSet1)
        SqlConnection1.Close()

        Console.WriteLine(MyDataSet1.authors(0).au_fname)
        Console.WriteLine(MyDataSet1.authors(0).au_lname)

    Catch ex As SqlException
        Console.WriteLine(ex.Message)
    End Try
End Sub
```

When writing out the author's first name and last name, notice that the
DataSet has a property named `authors`. This property represents a list of
rows in the `authors` table that is part of the DataSet. In a typed DataSet,
you can refer to a table using a property name, and you don't have to do the
following:

```
table = m_ds.Tables("authors")
```

Also, each row in the authors table contains properties for the specific column values. Notice that the author's first and last name values can be accessed directly by using the au_fname and au_lname properties on the row.

Typed DataSets can also be used like an untyped DataSet because a Typed DataSet inherits from a DataSet. Given that, you don't lose anything by using typed DataSets. In fact, you gain an advantage because the compiler can check typed DataSets against using invalid table or column names.

What's Next

In this chapter, we presented how to populate DataSets from a database, modify the data, and save the changes back to the database. Examples also showed how to deal with multiple tables and relationships within a DataSet.

After a DataSet has been loaded you can filter and sort the data as needed to present different views of the data without issuing a command back to the database again.

Data binding also showed you how to load data in a standard format, easily display the data, modify the data, and finally save the changes back to the database with relative ease using Visual Studio .NET and Visual Basic .NET.

In the next chapter, we explain the Commands used by DataAdapters for the purposes of reading rows, adding rows, modifying rows, and deleting rows in the database. Because you now have an understanding of Data Providers and DataSets, it makes sense to explain how the data is actually saved to the database. Depending on your programming experience you may never need to know anything about Commands. However, if you take the time to understand how Commands work, you will have a better understanding of the data access layer of your application.

NOTE

The answers to "Reviewing It," "Checking It," and "Applying It" are available on our Web site.

REVIEW

Reviewing It

This section presents a review of the key concepts in this chapter. These questions are intended to gauge your absorption of the relevant material.

1. What is an untyped DataSet?

2. What is a typed DataSet?

3. What is a DataRelation?

4. How do you filter a DataSet?

5. How do you sort a DataSet?

6. How do you populate a DataSet?

7. What is data binding?

8. How do you save changes in a DataSet back to a database?

CHECK

Checking It

Select the correct answer to the following questions.

Multiple Choice

1. DataSet changes are saved to the database using the:

   a. Save method.

   b. Update method.

   c. Fill method.

   d. None of the above.

2. DataSets are loaded from the database using the:

   a. Load method.

   b. Read method.

   c. Fill method.

   d. None of the above.

3. Multiple views of a DataSet are handled by using:

   a. Multiple View objects.

   b. Multiple DataView objects.

   c. Multiple DataSetView objects.

   d. None of the above.

4. Sorting supports:

   a. Ascending order.

   b. Descending order.

   c. Ascending and descending order.

   d. None of the above.

True or False

Select one of the two possible answers and then verify on our Web site that you picked the correct one.

1. DataSets can be filtered.

   True/False

2. DataSets can be sorted.

   True/False

3. DataSets keep track of the changed rows.

   True/False

4. DataSets support multiple tables.

   True/False

5. Typed DataSets are generated from a DataAdapter.

   True/False

6. DataView objects can be used to filter rows in a DataTable.

   True/False

7. DataView objects can be used to filter rows in a DataTable.

   True/False

APPLY

Applying It

Try to complete the following exercises by yourself.

Independent Exercise 1

Create a new Windows application and use the Server Explorer. Select any table from any database and drop it onto a form. Then write some code that populates a DataSet and then iterates through the DataSet and outputs some values from each of the rows.

Independent Exercise 2

Create a new Windows application and show how Data Binding works with DataSets and controls.

31

SQL Commands

This chapter focuses on SQL commands used to communicate directly with a database. In the previous two chapters, we presented an overview of ADO.NET, Data Providers, and the DataSet. In presenting these topics, SQL commands were briefly discussed and intentionally not explained in detail. Now that you have a good understanding of ADO.NET, this chapter explains SQL commands so that it is clear how direct access to a database works in .NET.

There are two goals to this chapter. The first goal is to briefly explain the syntax of the four most common commands in the SQL language. These commands are SELECT, INSERT, UPDATE, and DELETE. The second goal is to show how you would invoke these databases commands using the .NET Framework Class Library.

The topics covered in this chapter include

- SQL primer
- SqlCommands and SqlParameters

SQL Primer

SQL is the language used to read and write records to many brands of relational databases including SQL Server, Oracle, Informix, etc. This chapter does not attempt to present an overview of the entire SQL language. However, you should be familiar with the basic commands if you want to understand how DataAdapters in ADO.NET actually work with a database. So to get a better understanding, the four most common SQL commands (SELECT, INSERT, UPDATE, and DELETE) are presented here.

If you plan on writing your own SQL commands directly in your code, then we assume you already have some familiarity with SQL. If you don't have this familiarity and require more information regarding SQL than what is provided in this chapter, you should purchase a book devoted to the SQL language. This could be helpful if you plan on writing your own SQL commands in your application instead of relying on the automatic capabilities provided by Visual Studio .NET and the .NET Framework.

Table 31.1 lists the four common commands used when accessing and modifying data in a relational database.

Table 31.1: Most Common SQL Commands

SQL Command	Description
SELECT	Selects records from one or more tables
INSERT	Inserts a record into a table
UPDATE	Updates a record (or records) in a table
DELETE	Deletes a record (or records) from a table

Each of these commands is explained in more detail in the following sections. The *pubs* database that comes with SQL Server is again used to present real examples.

You should also read the help in Visual Studio .NET—"SQL commands, overview."

SELECT

The syntax of the SQL SELECT command is as follows:

```
SELECT    [DISTINCT] item(s)
FROM      table(s)
[ WHERE     condition ]
[ GROUP BY fields
[ HAVING    condition ]
[ ORDER BY fields]
[ UNION SQL_SELECT]
```

This command selects records from one or more tables. You must specify a list of fields to return or use the * character to signify the retrieval of all fields in the specified tables.

Using the DISTINCT keyword removes any duplicate rows from the list of returned records.

The FROM keyword is used to specify from which tables records are to be retrieved.

The WHERE keyword is optional and is used to specify a condition. Only records that satisfy the condition are retrieved.

The GROUP BY keywords are optional and are used to group the rows together that contain the same value for the specified fields.

The HAVING keyword is optional and is used in conjunction with the GROUP BY clause. The "condition" in the HAVING clause is used to place a condition on each group as specified by the GROUP BY clause. For example, specifying COUNT(*) > 4 as the condition in the HAVING clause means that only groups that contain more than four records are retrieved. You cannot use the HAVING clause without the GROUP BY clause.

The ORDER BY keywords are optional and are used to order resulting rows on the specified field values.

The UNION keyword is used to specify a subquery (SELECT statement). The results of the subquery return the records that exist in the results of main query and the results of the subquery.

Here is an example that selects all books from the database where their respective price is less than $10:

```
SELECT * FROM titles WHERE price < 10.00
```

This query selects all of the columns from the titles table and returns all of the rows specified by the WHERE clause. This WHERE clause specifies only the rows that contain a value for the price column and the value is greater than 10.

Here is an example that retrieves the year-to-date sales figures for each book in the database:

```
SELECT title, ytd_sales FROM titles, sales
WHERE titles.title_id = sales.title_id
```

This query selects two columns from the titles table and the sales table. The WHERE clause specifies how each row in the titles table is matched to a row in the sales table.

INSERT

The syntax of the SQL INSERT command is as follows:

```
INSERT
INTO    table [ ( field [, field ] ... ) ]
VALUES  ( literal [, literal ] ... )
```

or

```
INSERT
INTO    table [ ( field [, field ] ... ) ]
subquery
```

The first format inserts a new row into a specified table and sets the specified fields to the specified values. The second format evaluates the subquery, and the resulting rows of the subquery are inserted into the specified table. The specified fields are set to the values in the resulting subquery. The first value in the resulting subquery is set to the first specified field, the second value to the second specified field, and so on. Also, the number of columns in the results of the subquery must match the number of columns specified in the SQL INSERT statement. Also, the commands themselves do not need to be uppercase. You can choose to use lowercase, uppercase, or mixed case depending on your preference.

Following is an example that inserts a new record into the authors table:

```
INSERT INTO authors (au_id, au_fname, au_lname, contract)
VALUES ('123-45-6789', 'Bob', 'Donald', 1)
```

This statement inserts a row into the authors table. It lists the columns that are going to be affected in the row. The actual value for each corresponding column is listed after the VALUES keyword.

UPDATE

The syntax of the SQL UPDATE command is as follows:

```
UPDATE  table
SET     field = scalar-expression
    [, field = scalar-expression ] ...
[ WHERE  condition ]
```

This command updates records in the specified table, setting each field to its new specified value. All records in the table that satisfy the "condition" in the WHERE clause are modified.

Following is an example that updates a record in the authors table and sets the contract to the equivalent of a "true" value.

```
UPDATE authors SET contract = 1 WHERE au_id = '123-45-6789'
```

DELETE

The syntax of the SQL DELETE command is as follows:

```
DELETE
FROM    table
[ WHERE   condition ]
```

This command deletes all records in a table that satisfy the "condition" in the WHERE clause.

Here is an example that deletes all authors from the pubs database that don't have a contract.

```
DELETE FROM authors WHERE contract = 0
```

Using SqlCommands and SqlParameters

After you create the SQL statements in your code, how do you actually send the statements or commands to the database? The answer depends on the Data Provider your application is using. You have the option of using the OLEDB Data Provider or the SQL Server Data Provider. There will probably be other Data Providers made available in the future as well.

If you want to use the SQL Server Data Provider, you should use the classes defined in the System.Data.SqlClient namespace. If you want to use the OLEDB Data Provider, you should use the classes defined in theSystem.Data.OleDb namespace. And, if you want to write code that does not assume any particular Data Provider you would use the interfaces defined in System.Data. This latter approach is advanced and assumes that you use interfaces to define your variables and instantiate specific DataProvider objects.

The following statement defines a connection using the SQL Server Data Provider:

```
Dim conn As SqlConnection = New SqlConnection("File Name = myfile.udl")
```

The following statement defines a connection using the OLEDB Data Provider:

```
Dim conn As OleDbConnection = New OleDbConnection("File Name = myfile.udl")
```

This next example defines a connection variable that is unaware of any particular Data Provider connection. The variable is set to a specific OLE DB connection object that is part of the OLE DB Data Provider:

```
Dim conn As IDbConnection = New OleDbConnection("File Name = myfile.udl")
```

The most common approach is to pick a Data Provider and standardize on using that Data Provider throughout your code. For the remainder of this chapter, we will be using the SQL Server Data Provider for all of the examples. Using the OLE DB Data Provider is done by using the OleDb prefixed classes such as OleDbConnection instead of SqlConnection.

When you want to issue SQL commands directly against the database, you first need to create a connection object and then a command object that uses the connection object. We'll start with an example that sends a SQL SELECT statement to the database for the purposes of retrieving author information.

```
Dim query As String = "select au_fname, au_lname from authors"
Dim connStr As String = "Initial Catalog=pubs;Data Source=localhost;" & _
                        "Integrated Security=SSPI;"
Dim conn As SqlConnection = New SqlConnection(connStr)
Dim command As SqlCommand = New SqlCommand(query, conn)
Dim reader As SqlDataReader

conn.Open()
reader = command.ExecuteReader()
Try
    While reader.Read()
        Console.WriteLine((reader.GetString(0).ToString & ", " & _
                           reader.Item("au_lname")))
    End While
Finally
    reader.Close()
    conn.Close()
End Try
```

The connection string is for my local server and should work for you as well if you are connecting to SQL Server on your local computer. If it does not, update the connection string for your particular setup.

In this example, a SqlConnection object is created using the connection string defined. The fifth line creates a SqlCommand object that uses the command string and connection object. The command string in this example is a SQL SELECT statement. SqlCommand objects are used to handle SQL statements including SELECT, INSERT, UPDATE, and DELETE.

The eighth line calls the Open method on the connection object. This opens a connection to the database defined in the connection object's connection string property. After a connection is opened, you can send as many SQL commands to the database as you like. In the nineth line, the SQL SELECT statement is sent to the database by calling the ExecuteReader method on the command object. The ExecuteReader sends the command to the database and returns a SqlDataReader object for the purposes of reading the retrieved information.

A $SqlDataReader$ represents a read-only forward-only stream of rows that are retrieved from the database. At the risk of being redundant, this means you can only go forward through the $SqlDataReader$ object once, and you cannot modify the data in the database using the $SqlDataReader$ object. You need to create $SqlCommand$ objects for this purpose as you'll see later in this chapter.

Using the $SqlDataReader$ object, you can iterate through the returned rows by calling the $Read$ method. This method returns $True$ if another row is read. Once a row is read, you can access the row's values (or columns) using any one of several Get methods or by accessing the $Item$ property. The example retrieves the first value in the row by passing the value 0 to the $GetString$ method. The value you pass to this method corresponds to the index of the column in the query ($SELECT$ statement) you passed to the $SqlCommand$ object. The example also shows how to access values by column name using the $Item$ property on the $SqlDataReader$ object.

The example ends by closing the reader and connection objects by calling their respective $Close$ methods.

When you send commands to the database, you have the option of using any of four execute methods on the command object. Here we showed an example that used the $ExecuteReader$ method. Table 31.2 lists the execute methods and a description for each. The first three in the table will be shown in this chapter. The fourth will be shown in the next chapter when you learn about XML.

Table 31.2: Execute Methods on **SqlConnection, OleDbConnection** *Classes and* **IDbConnection** *Interface*

Value	Description
ExecuteReader	Executes a SQL SELECT statement against a database and returns a SqlDataReader object that can by used to read the retrieved rows.
ExecuteScalar	Retrieves a single value from the database. The single value returned is based on the first column in the resultset.
ExecuteNonQuery	Used to send INSERT, UPDATE, and DELETE statements to the database and returns the number of rows affected.
ExecuteXmlReader	Executes a SQL SELECT statement that contains a "FOR XML" clause and returns an XmlReader object that provides forward-only read-only data in XML format. Please note that this is specific to SQL Server 2000.

In addition to retrieving multiple rows, you can also retrieve a single value. For example, you may want to find out how many rows there are in a table or query. To do this, you would use the ExecuteScalar method on the SqlCommand object. This method returns the value defined in the SQL statement defined in the command object. The following example shows how to retrieve the number of authors in the pubs database on my local server:

```
Dim query As String = "select count(*) from authors"
Dim connStr As String = "Initial Catalog=pubs;Data Source=localhost;" & _
                        "Integrated Security=SSPI;"
Dim conn As SqlConnection = New SqlConnection(connStr)
Dim command As SqlCommand = New SqlCommand(query, conn)

conn.Open()
Try
    Console.WriteLine("Number of authors is: " & command.ExecuteScalar())
Finally
    conn.Close()
End Try
```

The SQL statement uses the SQL count() function to count the number of rows defined by the query. The query involves all of the rows in the authors table. The command object is created using this SQL statement. The ExecuteScalar method executes the query and returns the single value returned from the query that is the count of author rows. This number is then written out to the console. This is an easier way of retrieving a single value instead of having to retrieve a SqlDataReader object, retrieving a row, and then getting a column value from it.

The next example involves inserting rows into a database. Inserting rows is done by sending SQL INSERT statements to the database. You can define SQL INSERT statements in your code and use SqlCommand objects to execute the statements. Because an insert does not return rows, you would use the ExecuteNonQuery method on the SqlCommand object to do this. This method returns the number of rows affected, which should be 1 if you are inserting a record.

This example shows adding an author to the database:

```
Dim commandStr As String = "insert into authors" & _
                           "(au_id, au_fname, au_lname, contract) " & _
                           "values (@ssn, @firstName, @lastName, @contract)"
Dim connStr As String = "Initial Catalog=pubs;Data Source=localhost;" & _
                        "Integrated Security=SSPI;"
Dim param As SqlParameter
Dim rowsAffected As Integer
Dim conn As SqlConnection = New SqlConnection(connStr)
```

```
Dim command As SqlCommand = New SqlCommand(commandStr, conn)

param = New SqlParameter("@ssn", SqlDbType.VarChar)
param.Value = "123-12-1234"
command.Parameters.Add(param)

param = New SqlParameter("@firstName", SqlDbType.VarChar)
param.Value = "Bob"
command.Parameters.Add(param)

param = New SqlParameter("@lastName", SqlDbType.VarChar)
param.Value = "Donald"
command.Parameters.Add(param)

param = New SqlParameter("@contract", SqlDbType.Bit)
param.Value = True
command.Parameters.Add(param)

Try
    conn.Open()
    rowsAffected = command.ExecuteNonQuery()
    Console.WriteLine("Rows affected = " & rowsAffected)
Catch ex As SqlException
    Console.WriteLine(ex.Message)
Finally
    conn.Close()
End Try
```

Notice that the SQL INSERT statement defined in the example contains values that are prefixed with the @ sign. Most SQL Statements are not fully known when you write your code. This is because an application does not know every author that is going to be added to a database before the application runs. Therefore, application code needs a way to construct the SQL statements when the application runs. Typically, this example would have an author form where a user can enter the relevant information. This information would then be used to construct the INSERT statement to add the author to the database. Rather than constructing the exact SQL string in your code, you can use placeholders that are later used to automatically place values. These placeholders are also commonly referred to as *parameters*. There are four parameters defined in the SQL INSERT statement in this example.

After a command object is created using the defined SQL statement, you can substitute values for the parameters by using SqlParameter objects. A *SqlParameter object* is created by passing in the placeholder name (*@ssn*) and the database type for the value represented by the placeholder. The database type is defined in the database. After a parameter object is created, its value can be set using the Value property. The SqlParameter object is then added to the command's collection of parameters by calling the Add method on the Parameters property of the SqlCommand object. This process is repeated for each parameter defined in the SQL statement.

The ExecuteNonQuery method is used to execute the SQL INSERT statement. At this point, each of the values in the parameter objects is bound to the statement, and the INSERT statement results in creating a new author record that contains the values defined in the parameter objects. Using parameters in this way allows you to reuse the same SQL INSERT statement for any author that is added to the database. You only need to update the parameter objects with the correct values for each author added.

The ExecuteNonQuery method returns the number of rows affected in the database. Because this example inserts a single row, the value of 1 is returned from this method call.

The following example shows how to update a row in the database. To update a row, you need to create a SQL UPDATE statement and use a SqlCommand object to issue the command to the database. Using the same authors table, this example defines a SQL statement that updates the row that matches a specific value for the au_id column and sets the value for the phone column to a new value.

The SQL UPDATE statement is defined and passed to a SqlCommand object along with a connection object. Just like the INSERT example, parameters are used to replace the placeholders with specific values. And, the ExecuteNonQuery method is used to send the command to the database that updates the row defined by the UPDATE statement. The returned value of the ExecuteNonQuery method is the number of rows affected. In this example, this value is 1 if there is a matching row and 0 if there is no matching row in the database. The reason the returned value is not greater than one in this example is because the au_id column is unique in this table. Therefore, there cannot be more than one row with the same values in the au_id column.

```
Dim commandStr As String = "update authors set phone = @phone " & _
                           "where au_id = @ssn"
Dim connStr As String = "Initial Catalog=pubs;Data Source=localhost;" & _
                        "Integrated Security=SSPI;"
Dim param As SqlParameter
Dim rowsAffected As Integer
Dim conn As SqlConnection = New SqlConnection(connStr)
Dim command As SqlCommand = New SqlCommand(commandStr, conn)
```

```
param = New SqlParameter("@phone", SqlDbType.VarChar)
param.Value = "123-555-1234"
command.Parameters.Add(param)

param = New SqlParameter("@ssn", SqlDbType.VarChar)
param.Value = "123-12-1234"
command.Parameters.Add(param)

Try
    conn.Open()
    rowsAffected = command.ExecuteNonQuery()
    Console.WriteLine("Rows affected = " & rowsAffected)
Catch ex As SqlException
    Console.WriteLine(ex.Message)
Finally
    conn.Close()
End Try
```

If the WHERE clause was not included in the SQL statement, all rows in the authors table would be updated and their phone numbers set to the specified value. In this case, the return value of the ExecuteNonQuery method results in the number of the rows affected by the update, which would be the number of rows in the authors table.

The next example shows how to delete records from the database. In this example, a SQL DELETE statement is defined and includes a placeholder for the author ID. A command object is created by passing in the SQL statement along with a connection object. A parameter object is created and added to the command. The parameter's value is set to the author ID that is going to be deleted. The ExecuteNonQuery method executes this SQL DELETE statement and returns the number of row affected. If there exists a row in the database with the defined author id the value returned by ExecuteNonQuery is 1; otherwise 0 is returned.

```
Dim commandStr As String = "delete from authors where au_id = @ssn"
Dim connStr As String = "Initial Catalog=pubs;Data Source=localhost;" & _
                        "Integrated Security=SSPI;"
Dim param As SqlParameter
Dim rowsAffected As Integer

Dim conn As SqlConnection = New SqlConnection(connStr)
Dim command As SqlCommand = New SqlCommand(commandStr, conn)

param = New SqlParameter("@ssn", SqlDbType.VarChar)
param.Value = "123-12-1234"
command.Parameters.Add(param)
```

```
Try
    conn.Open()
    rowsAffected = command.ExecuteNonQuery()
    Console.WriteLine("Rows affected = " & rowsAffected)
Catch ex As SqlException
    Console.WriteLine(ex.Message)
Finally
    conn.Close()
End Try
```

If the WHERE clause was not including in the SQL statement, all rows in the authors table would be deleted. In this case, the return value of the ExecuteNonQuery method results in the number of the rows deleted.

Stored procedures are also very important aspects of a relational database. They are basically custom functions that you can be defined in a database and can be called directly from your application code. In the pubs database, there exists a stored procedure named byroyalty that takes as input a percentage royalty. This percentage is then used to find all books whose royalty matches the input value. Each book that matches is returned as part of the result.

The advantages of Stored Procedures is that you can execute database specific code within the database, thereby reducing the database specific logic in your application code. In addition, multiple applications can then benefit from Stored Procedures without needing to rewrite the application code each time.

The next example shows how to invoke the stored procedure and how to read the returned values.

```
Dim commandStr As String = "byroyalty"
Dim connStr As String = "Initial Catalog=pubs;Data Source=localhost;" & _
                        "Integrated Security=SSPI;"
Dim param As SqlParameter
Dim rowsAffected As Integer
Dim reader As SqlDataReader
Dim conn As SqlConnection = New SqlConnection(connStr)
Dim command As SqlCommand = New SqlCommand(commandStr, conn)

command.CommandType = CommandType.StoredProcedure

param = New SqlParameter("@RETURN_VALUE", SqlDbType.VarChar)
param.Direction = ParameterDirection.ReturnValue
command.Parameters.Add(param)
```

```
param = New SqlParameter("@percentage", SqlDbType.Int)
param.Value = CType(30, Integer)
command.Parameters.Add(param)

Try
    conn.Open()
    reader = command.ExecuteReader()
    Dim val As String
    Console.WriteLine("{0}", reader.GetName(0))
    While reader.Read()
        Console.WriteLine("{0}", reader.GetString(0))
    End While
Catch ex As SqlException
    Console.WriteLine(ex.Message)
Finally
    conn.Close()
End Try
```

The command string contains only the name of the stored procedure. This string is passed to the constructor of the command object. Once the command object is constructed, the command type is set to StoredProcedure by setting the CommandType property. Next, a parameter is created for the return value of the stored procedure and a parameter for the input value (the percentage royalty). If you want to read the return value from a stored procedure, you must add the return value parameter to the command before any other parameters.

The stored procedure is invoked by calling the ExecuteReader method on the command object. This method also returns a DataReader object that is used to read multiple returned rows if they exist. Each call to the Read method on the DataReader object retrieves another row from the return value of the stored procedure.

Now that we have gone through examples showing how to directly invoke SQL commands including SELECT, INSERT, UPDATE, and DELETE as well as stored procedures, you may find that using a DataSet object is easier and more useful. Either way, Microsoft .NET provides the DataSet for a richer data structure and database command objects for performing low-level data access directly with the database.

What's Next

This chapter presented SQL commands and the necessary classes in .NET to invoke those commands on a relational database. This includes an overview of SQL syntax followed by examples using the SQL Server Data

Provider to send SQL commands directly to the database. Hopefully this chapter explained how to send your own commands directly to the database and, equally important, how the DataSet uses commands to persist its data.

In the next three chapters, we continue exploring how to deal with data in Microsoft .NET. The next chapter explains data access using XML followed by a chapter explaining reading XML and another chapter explaining writing XML. These chapters will be focusing primarily on the set of classes used to read and write XML. It is assumed the reader has some cursory knowledge of XML already. If not, you may want to read "XML, DTD, and SML Schema Fundamentals," on our Web site to get more background information regarding XML first.

NOTE

The answers to "Reviewing It," "Checking It," and "Applying It" are available on our Web site.

REVIEW

Reviewing It

This section presents a review of the key concepts in this chapter. These questions are intended to gauge your absorption of the relevant material.

1. What are the three types of objects (classes) needed to send SQL commands to a database using the SQL Server Data Provider?

2. What are parameters in SQL statements?

3. What are the four common SQL commands used to retrieve and modify data in a SQL database?

4. Why would you want to use the ExecuteScalar method on a connection object?

5. When would you want to use the ExecuteNonQuery method on a connection object?

CHECK

Checking It

Select the correct answer to the following questions.

Multiple Choice

1. SQL SELECT statements are sent to a database using:

   a. SqlConnection and its ExecuteReader method.

   b. SqlCommand object and its ExecuteNonQuery method.

c. `SqlCommand` object and its `ExecuteReader` method.

d. `SqlParameter` object and its `Execute` method.

2. SQL `INSERT` statements are sent to a database using:

a. `SqlConnection` and its `ExecuteReader` method.

b. `SqlCommand` object and its `ExecuteNonQuery` method.

c. `SqlCommand` object and its `ExecuteReader` method.

d. `SqlParameter` object and its `Execute` method.

3. SQL `UPDATE` statements are sent to a database using:

a. `SqlConnection` and its `ExecuteReader` method.

b. `SqlCommand` object and its `ExecuteNonQuery` method.

c. `SqlCommand` object and its `ExecuteReader` method.

d. `SqlParameter` object and its `Execute` method.

4. SQL `DELETE` statements are sent to a database using:

a. `SqlConnection` and its `ExecuteReader` method.

b. `SqlCommand` object and its `ExecuteNonQuery` method.

c. `SqlCommand` object and its `ExecuteReader` method.

d. `SqlParameter` object and its `Execute` method.

5. Stored procedures are invoked using:

a. `SqlConnection` and its `ExecuteReader` method.

b. `SqlCommand` object and its `ExecuteNonQuery` method.

c. `SqlCommand` object and its `ExecuteReader` method.

d. `SqlParameter` object and its `Execute` method.

6. Retrieving a single value from a returned row involves using:

a. `SqlConnection` and its `ExecuteReader` method.

b. `SqlCommand` object and its `ExecuteNonQuery` method.

c. `SqlCommand` object and its `ExecuteScalar` method.

d. `SqlParameter` object and its `Execute` method.

True or False

Select one of the two possible answers and then verify on our Web site that you picked the correct one.

1. When inserting, updating, or deleting records, you can obtain the number of affected rows from the operation.

   True/False

2. The return value from a stored procedure must be the first parameter defined in the command.

   True/False

3. Values retrieved from a database using a command object and a SELECT statement can be accessed in the command object using a numeric index value only.

   True/False

4. When calling a stored procedure, the CommandType property of a command object needs to be set to StoredProcedure.

   True/False

APPLY

Applying It

Try to complete the following exercise by yourself.

Independent Exercise

Write your own example to read the number of books available in the pubs database.

XML Data Access

ADO.NET has taken a major step forward with the advent of the DataSet and Data Providers. Now, data can be loaded from a relational database and managed in a disconnected cache, modified, and persisted back into the database in a very manageable fashion.

XML has become the standard for sharing data amongst different tiers of a multitiered application. A major reason for this is that XML is self-describing data that is independent of any platform or programming language. In addition, XML is supported by the software industry as more and more products are supporting XML, thereby solidifying a strong foothold.

Because XML is used for communicating data across the wire (the network), it makes sense that ADO.NET and XML are integrated to provide the best of both worlds (managing data and shipping data). This chapter explains how ADO.NET and XML are integrated to support a broader level of services. The topics covered in this chapter include

- Exposing XML and XML Schema from a DataSet
- Writing XML and XML Schema from a DataSet
- Reading XML and XML Schema into a DataSet
- Synchronizing XML and DataSets

NOTE

This chapter assumes you have a working knowledge of XML. If you do not, you should read "XML, DTD, and XML Schema Fundamentals," on our Web site before reading this chapter.

Exposing XML and XML Schema from a DataSet

As you have already learned, DataSets contain tables, and each table contains columns. A set of values for the columns in the tables can be added to a DataSet (also known as a row). This can be described more simply this way: A DataSet contains structure and data. The structure is defined by the tables and columns defined in the DataSet. The data is defined by the rows (or values) in the DataSet.

XML also adheres to this concept of structure and data. The integration between DataSets and XML revolve around seamlessly converting the structure and data between these two formats. Previously, we showed an example of using a DataSet and iterating through the DataSet to print out the rows in the DataSet to the console window. Here is a simple example Console Application project that shows how to output data from a DataSet as XML to the console window.

```
Imports System.Data.SqlClient
Imports System.Data.Common

Module Module1

    Sub Main()

        Dim query As String = "select * from authors"
        Dim connStr As String = "Initial Catalog=pubs;Data Source=localhost;" & _
                                "Integrated Security=SSPI;"
        Dim conn As SqlConnection = New SqlConnection(connStr)
        Dim adapter As SqlDataAdapter = New SqlDataAdapter(query, conn)
        Dim ds As DataSet = New DataSet()

        adapter.TableMappings.Add(New DataTableMapping("Table", "authors"))

        Try

            adapter.Fill(ds)
            Console.WriteLine(ds.GetXml())

        Catch ex As SqlException
            Console.WriteLine(ex.Message)
        End Try

    End Sub

End Module
```

The bulk of the code contains nothing new. First, a new `DataTableMapping` is defined for the adapter. This mapping is used when the DataSet gets loaded from the adapter. The resulting table in the DataSet has the name `authors` instead of the default name of `Table`. This is useful, as you'll see in the XML output.

A DataSet is created by opening a connection and filling it with data from the authors table in the pubs database. After the DataSet is loaded, the data can be output to the console window as XML using the `GetXml` method on the DataSet. This method uses the defined structure in the DataSet to create the XML structure (or schema) and populate it with the data from the DataSet. Here is output of this example:

```
<NewDataSet>
  <authors>
    <au_id>172-32-1176</au_id>
    <au_lname>White</au_lname>
    <au_fname>Johnson</au_fname>
    <phone>408 496-7223</phone>
    <address>10932 Bigge Rd.</address>
    <city>Menlo Park</city>
    <state>CA</state>
    <zip>94025</zip>
    <contract>true</contract>
  </authors>
  <authors>
    <au_id>213-46-8915</au_id>
    <au_lname>Green</au_lname>
    <au_fname>Marjorie</au_fname>
    <phone>415 986-7020</phone>
    <address>309 63rd St. #411</address>
    <city>Oakland</city>
    <state>CA</state>
    <zip>94618</zip>
    <contract>true</contract>
  </authors>
  <authors>
    <au_id>238-95-7766</au_id>
    <au_lname>Carson</au_lname>
    <au_fname>Cheryl</au_fname>
    <phone>415 548-7723</phone>
    <address>589 Darwin Ln.</address>
    <city>Berkeley</city>
    <state>CA</state>
    <zip>94705</zip>
    <contract>true</contract>
  </authors>
```

```xml
<authors>
  <au_id>267-41-2394</au_id>
  <au_lname>O'Leary</au_lname>
  <au_fname>Michael</au_fname>
  <phone>408 286-2428</phone>
  <address>22 Cleveland Av. #14</address>
  <city>San Jose</city>
  <state>CA</state>
  <zip>95128</zip>
  <contract>true</contract>
</authors>
<authors>
  <au_id>274-80-9391</au_id>
  <au_lname>Straight</au_lname>
  <au_fname>Dean</au_fname>
  <phone>415 834-2919</phone>
  <address>5420 College Av.</address>
  <city>Oakland</city>
  <state>CA</state>
  <zip>94609</zip>
  <contract>true</contract>
</authors>
<authors>
  <au_id>341-22-1782</au_id>
  <au_lname>Smith</au_lname>
  <au_fname>Meander</au_fname>
  <phone>913 843-0462</phone>
  <address>10 Mississippi Dr.</address>
  <city>Lawrence</city>
  <state>KS</state>
  <zip>66044</zip>
  <contract>false</contract>
</authors>
<authors>
  <au_id>409-56-7008</au_id>
  <au_lname>Bennet</au_lname>
  <au_fname>Abraham</au_fname>
  <phone>415 658-9932</phone>
  <address>6223 Bateman St.</address>
  <city>Berkeley</city>
  <state>CA</state>
  <zip>94705</zip>
  <contract>true</contract>
</authors>
<authors>
  <au_id>427-17-2319</au_id>
```

```
    <au_lname>Dull</au_lname>
    <au_fname>Ann</au_fname>
    <phone>415 836-7128</phone>
    <address>3410 Blonde St.</address>
    <city>Palo Alto</city>
    <state>CA</state>
    <zip>94301</zip>
    <contract>true</contract>
  </authors>
  <authors>
    <au_id>472-27-2349</au_id>
    <au_lname>Gringlesby</au_lname>
    <au_fname>Burt</au_fname>
    <phone>707 938-6445</phone>
    <address>PO Box 792</address>
    <city>Covelo</city>
    <state>CA</state>
    <zip>95428</zip>
    <contract>true</contract>
  </authors>
  <authors>
    <au_id>486-29-1786</au_id>
    <au_lname>Locksley</au_lname>
    <au_fname>Charlene</au_fname>
    <phone>415 585-4620</phone>
    <address>18 Broadway Av.</address>
    <city>San Francisco</city>
    <state>CA</state>
    <zip>94130</zip>
    <contract>true</contract>
  </authors>
  <authors>
    <au_id>527-72-3246</au_id>
    <au_lname>Greene</au_lname>
    <au_fname>Morningstar</au_fname>
    <phone>615 297-2723</phone>
    <address>22 Graybar House Rd.</address>
    <city>Nashville</city>
    <state>TN</state>
    <zip>37215</zip>
    <contract>false</contract>
  </authors>
  <authors>
    <au_id>648-92-1872</au_id>
    <au_lname>Blotchet-Halls</au_lname>
    <au_fname>Reginald</au_fname>
```

```
      <phone>503 745-6402</phone>
      <address>55 Hillsdale Bl.</address>
      <city>Corvallis</city>
      <state>OR</state>
      <zip>97330</zip>
      <contract>true</contract>
  </authors>
  <authors>
    <au_id>672-71-3249</au_id>
    <au_lname>Yokomoto</au_lname>
    <au_fname>Akiko</au_fname>
    <phone>415 935-4228</phone>
    <address>3 Silver Ct.</address>
    <city>Walnut Creek</city>
    <state>CA</state>
    <zip>94595</zip>
    <contract>true</contract>
  </authors>
  <authors>
    <au_id>712-45-1867</au_id>
    <au_lname>del Castillo</au_lname>
    <au_fname>Innes</au_fname>
    <phone>615 996-8275</phone>
    <address>2286 Cram Pl. #86</address>
    <city>Ann Arbor</city>
    <state>MI</state>
    <zip>48105</zip>
    <contract>true</contract>
  </authors>
  <authors>
    <au_id>722-51-5454</au_id>
    <au_lname>DeFrance</au_lname>
    <au_fname>Michel</au_fname>
    <phone>219 547-9982</phone>
    <address>3 Balding Pl.</address>
    <city>Gary</city>
    <state>IN</state>
    <zip>46403</zip>
    <contract>true</contract>
  </authors>
  <authors>
    <au_id>724-08-9931</au_id>
    <au_lname>Stringer</au_lname>
    <au_fname>Dirk</au_fname>
    <phone>415 843-2991</phone>
    <address>5420 Telegraph Av.</address>
```

```
    <city>Oakland</city>
    <state>CA</state>
    <zip>94609</zip>
    <contract>false</contract>
  </authors>
  <authors>
    <au_id>724-80-9391</au_id>
    <au_lname>MacFeather</au_lname>
    <au_fname>Stearns</au_fname>
    <phone>415 354-7128</phone>
    <address>44 Upland Hts.</address>
    <city>Oakland</city>
    <state>CA</state>
    <zip>94612</zip>
    <contract>true</contract>
  </authors>
  <authors>
    <au_id>756-30-7391</au_id>
    <au_lname>Karsen</au_lname>
    <au_fname>Livia</au_fname>
    <phone>415 534-9219</phone>
    <address>5720 McAuley St.</address>
    <city>Oakland</city>
    <state>CA</state>
    <zip>94609</zip>
    <contract>true</contract>
  </authors>
  <authors>
    <au_id>807-91-6654</au_id>
    <au_lname>Panteley</au_lname>
    <au_fname>Sylvia</au_fname>
    <phone>301 946-8853</phone>
    <address>1956 Arlington Pl.</address>
    <city>Rockville</city>
    <state>MD</state>
    <zip>20853</zip>
    <contract>true</contract>
  </authors>
  <authors>
    <au_id>846-92-7186</au_id>
    <au_lname>Hunter</au_lname>
    <au_fname>Sheryl</au_fname>
    <phone>415 836-7128</phone>
    <address>3410 Blonde St.</address>
    <city>Palo Alto</city>
    <state>CA</state>
```

```
      <zip>94301</zip>
      <contract>true</contract>
    </authors>
    <authors>
      <au_id>893-72-1158</au_id>
      <au_lname>McBadden</au_lname>
      <au_fname>Heather</au_fname>
      <phone>707 448-4982</phone>
      <address>301 Putnam</address>
      <city>Vacaville</city>
      <state>CA</state>
      <zip>95688</zip>
      <contract>false</contract>
    </authors>
    <authors>
      <au_id>899-46-2035</au_id>
      <au_lname>Ringer</au_lname>
      <au_fname>Anne</au_fname>
      <phone>801 826-0752</phone>
      <address>67 Seventh Av.</address>
      <city>Salt Lake City</city>
      <state>UT</state>
      <zip>84152</zip>
      <contract>true</contract>
    </authors>
    <authors>
      <au_id>998-72-3567</au_id>
      <au_lname>Ringer</au_lname>
      <au_fname>Albert</au_fname>
      <phone>801 826-0752</phone>
      <address>67 Seventh Av.</address>
      <city>Salt Lake City</city>
      <state>UT</state>
      <zip>84152</zip>
      <contract>true</contract>
    </authors>
</NewDataSet>
```

The root XML element is named NewDataSet and contains the remaining elements that represent the data in the DataSet. For each row in the DataSet, an element is created that has its name based on the name of the table. In this case, the element is named authors. Each authors element contains child elements, one for each column in the table. Each of these child elements has the name of the column and contains the column value as the value of the XML element. As you can see, you can create an XML string that represents the data within a DataSet very easily by invoking the GetXml method. This allows you to load a DataSet and then package up the data in XML to do as you please. One common use case would be to send the data to another component in your application for processing or across the network to a client browser for display purposes. In either case, there is very little work on your part to create the XML content.

In addition to constructing the XML content, you also have the option of getting the XML Schema definition from a DataSet. Internally, this involves inspecting the DataSet structure in terms of tables, columns, and data types and then generating an XML Schema from it. The previous example is modified to also generate the XML Schema as follows:

```
Imports System.Data.SqlClient
Imports System.Data.Common

Module Module1

    Sub Main()

        Dim query As String = "select * from authors"
        Dim connStr As String = "Initial Catalog=pubs;Data Source=localhost;" & _
                                "Integrated Security=SSPI;"
        Dim conn As SqlConnection = New SqlConnection(connStr)
        Dim adapter As SqlDataAdapter = New SqlDataAdapter(query, conn)
        Dim ds As DataSet = New DataSet()

        adapter.TableMappings.Add(New DataTableMapping("Table", "authors"))

        Try

            adapter.Fill(ds)

            Console.WriteLine(ds.GetXmlSchema())
            Console.WriteLine(ds.GetXml())

        Catch ex As SqlException
            Console.WriteLine(ex.Message)
        End Try

    End Sub

End Module
```

For obvious reasons, we are not going to list the output of the GetXml method here again because the data has not changed. However, the XML Schema is shown here to give you an idea of the schema generated for this DataSet containing author data from the pubs database:

```
<xsd:schema id="NewDataSet" targetNamespace="" xmlns=""
xmlns:xsd="http://www.w3.org/2001/XMLSchema" xmlns:msdata="urn:schemas-microsoft-
com:xml-msdata">
  <xsd:element name="NewDataSet" msdata:IsDataSet="true">
    <xsd:complexType>
      <xsd:choice maxOccurs="unbounded">
        <xsd:element name="authors">
          <xsd:complexType>
            <xsd:sequence>
              <xsd:element name="au_id" type="xsd:string" minOccurs="0" />
              <xsd:element name="au_lname" type="xsd:string" minOccurs="0" />
              <xsd:element name="au_fname" type="xsd:string" minOccurs="0" />
              <xsd:element name="phone" type="xsd:string" minOccurs="0" />
              <xsd:element name="address" type="xsd:string" minOccurs="0" />
              <xsd:element name="city" type="xsd:string" minOccurs="0" />
              <xsd:element name="state" type="xsd:string" minOccurs="0" />
              <xsd:element name="zip" type="xsd:string" minOccurs="0" />
              <xsd:element name="contract" type="xsd:boolean" minOccurs="0" />
            </xsd:sequence>
          </xsd:complexType>
        </xsd:element>
      </xsd:choice>
    </xsd:complexType>
  </xsd:element>
</xsd:schema>
```

Once again, if you are not familiar with XML or XML Schema, you should check our Web site to familiarize yourself with this technology before continuing with this chapter.

The XML Schema defines an XML element based on a row in the authors table. This element can exist any number of times in the XML stream because it is an unbounded list of author records.

Writing XML and XML Schema from a DataSet

The XML content and XML Schema generated from a DataSet can also be saved to files. There are convenient methods on the DataSet for providing this capability. These methods are WriteXmlSchema and WriteXml.

The following example again shows loading a DataSet from the authors table:

```
Imports System.Data.SqlClient
Imports System.Data.Common

Module Module1
```

```
Sub Main()
    Dim query As String = "select * from authors"
    Dim connStr As String = "Initial Catalog=pubs;Data Source=localhost;" & _
                            "Integrated Security=SSPI;"
    Dim conn As SqlConnection = New SqlConnection(connStr)
    Dim adapter As SqlDataAdapter = New SqlDataAdapter(query, conn)
    Dim ds As DataSet = New DataSet()

    adapter.TableMappings.Add(New DataTableMapping("Table", "authors"))

    Try

        adapter.Fill(ds)

        ds.WriteXmlSchema("Authors.xsd")
        ds.WriteXml("Authors.xml")

    Catch ex As SqlException
        Console.WriteLine(ex.Message)
    End Try

    End Sub

End Module
```

After the DataSet is loaded, the schema can be saved using the
WriteXmlSchema method. This generates the schema displayed earlier
except the schema information is stored in a file that can be used later.
The XML content is generated and saved to a file using the WriteXml
method. This content is identical to the XML output displayed earlier
except it is now saved to a file.

Unless a path is specified, the files are saved to the folder from which
the application was started. If you are running this project from Visual
Studio .NET, then the place where the files are saved is in the "bin"
subfolder of the current project.

Reading XML and XML Schema into a DataSet

In addition to loading a DataSet from records in a database, you can also
construct a DataSet and populate it using a defined XML Schema and content defined in an XML file. This allows you to load XML data and work
with it as a DataSet. Here is an example Console application project that
loads a DataSet from XML:

```
Imports System.Data.SqlClient
Imports System.Data.Common
```

```
Module Module1

    Sub Main()

        Dim ds As DataSet = New DataSet()

        Try

            ds.ReadXmlSchema("Authors.xsd")
            ds.ReadXml("Authors.xml")

            Console.WriteLine(ds.GetXmlSchema())
            Console.WriteLine(ds.GetXml())

        Catch ex As SqlException
            Console.WriteLine(ex.Message)
        End Try

    End Sub

End Module
```

NOTE

In order to read these files, they must be in the "bin" folder of the current project.

The structure of the DataSet is defined by reading in XML Schema from the Authors.xsd file by invoking the ReadXmlSchema method on the DataSet object. This creates all of the necessary tables and columns based on the structure defined in the XML Schema. After the structure is defined, you can load the XML data using the ReadXml method. If the structure of the XML data is different than the structure defined in the XML Schema an exception is thrown informing you of the problem.

What if you have an XML document but don't have an XML Schema defined for it? You can still load it, but you need to infer a schema for the XML document. This is accomplished by calling the InferXmlSchema method. This method takes an XML document you wish to generate a schema for and infers the schema as it is loaded.

This example infers a schema from the XML document:

```
Imports System.Data.SqlClient
Imports System.Data.Common

Module Module1

    Sub Main()
```

```
    Dim ds As DataSet = New DataSet()

    Try
        ds.InferXmlSchema("Authors.xml", Nothing)
        Console.WriteLine(ds.GetXmlSchema())
    Catch ex As SqlException
        Console.WriteLine(ex.Message)
    End Try

End Sub

End Module
```

The result of this example is that a schema is inferred from the XML document and the corresponding structure defined in the DataSet. However, the data in the XML document is not loaded. You still need to call `ReadXml` if you need to load the XML document after inferring its schema.

Synchronizing XML and DataSets

So far in this chapter, we focused on converting XML to a DataSet or a DataSet to XML. It is also possible to make changes to a DataSet or the XML and have the changes reflected back in the other format. For example, if I load a DataSet I can get an updateable XML view of the DataSet. If I make changes to the XML, the changes are immediately reflected in the DataSet. If I make changes to the DataSet, the changes are immediately reflected in the XML.

Let's walk through an example showing this. Here is an XML Schema defining an XML document that contains company information. The file is named Company.xsd and includes department and employee information:

```
<?xml version="1.0" standalone="yes"?>
<xsd:schema id="Company" xmlns:xsd="http://www.w3.org/2001/XMLSchema"
xmlns:msdata="urn:schemas-microsoft-com:xml-msdata">
  <xsd:element name="Company" msdata:IsDataSet="true">
    <xsd:complexType>
      <xsd:choice maxOccurs="unbounded">
        <xsd:element name="Department">
          <xsd:complexType>
            <xsd:sequence>
              <xsd:element name="Name" type="xsd:string" minOccurs="0"
msdata:Ordinal="0" />
              <xsd:element name="Employee" minOccurs="0" maxOccurs="unbounded">
                <xsd:complexType>
                  <xsd:sequence>
                    <xsd:element name="EmployeeId" type="xsd:string"
```

```
minOccurs="0" msdata:Ordinal="0" />
                    <xsd:element name="FirstName" type="xsd:string" minOccurs="0"
msdata:Ordinal="1" />
                    <xsd:element name="LastName" type="xsd:string" minOccurs="0"
msdata:Ordinal="2" />
                    <xsd:element name="DateOfHire" type="xsd:string"
minOccurs="0" msdata:Ordinal="3" />
                    <xsd:element name="Salary" type="xsd:string" minOccurs="0"
msdata:Ordinal="4" />
                </xsd:sequence>
                <xsd:attribute name="Department_Id" type="xsd:int"
use="prohibited" />
            </xsd:complexType>
          </xsd:element>
        </xsd:sequence>
        <xsd:attribute name="Department_Id" msdata:AutoIncrement="true"
type="xsd:int"
                    msdata:AllowDBNull="false" use="prohibited" />
      </xsd:complexType>
    </xsd:element>
  </xsd:choice>
</xsd:complexType>
<xsd:unique name="Constraint1" msdata:PrimaryKey="true">
  <xsd:selector xpath=".//Department" />
  <xsd:field xpath="@Department_Id" />
</xsd:unique>
<xsd:keyref name="Department_Employee" refer="Constraint1"
msdata:IsNested="true">
  <xsd:selector xpath=".//Employee" />
  <xsd:field xpath="@Department_Id" />
</xsd:keyref>
  </xsd:element>
</xsd:schema>
```

Here is the sample XML file, named Company.xml, that is validated by the previous XML Schema:

```
<?xml version="1.0" standalone="yes"?>
<Company>
  <Department>
    <Name>Sales</Name>
    <Employee>
      <EmployeeId>1001</EmployeeId>
      <FirstName>John</FirstName>
      <LastName>Smithfield</LastName>
      <DateOfHire>03-12-2001</DateOfHire>
      <Salary>100,000</Salary>
    </Employee>
    <Employee>
```

```
      <EmployeeId>1002</EmployeeId>
      <FirstName>John</FirstName>
      <LastName>Smithfield</LastName>
      <DateOfHire>03-12-2001</DateOfHire>
      <Salary>100,000</Salary>
    </Employee>
  </Department>
  <Department>
    <Name>Marketing</Name>
    <Employee>
      <EmployeeId>1003</EmployeeId>
      <FirstName>Sally</FirstName>
      <LastName>Rores</LastName>
      <DateOfHire>01-11-1987</DateOfHire>
      <Salary>100,000</Salary>
    </Employee>
    <Employee>
      <EmployeeId>1004</EmployeeId>
      <FirstName>Jacob</FirstName>
      <LastName>Gallagher</LastName>
      <DateOfHire>09-24-1995</DateOfHire>
      <Salary>80,000</Salary>
    </Employee>
  </Department>
  <Department>
    <Name>Engineering</Name>
    <Employee>
      <EmployeeId>1005</EmployeeId>
      <FirstName>Al</FirstName>
      <LastName>Hacker</LastName>
      <DateOfHire>05-24-2001</DateOfHire>
      <Salary>150,000</Salary>
    </Employee>
    <Employee>
      <EmployeeId>1006</EmployeeId>
      <FirstName>Jason</FirstName>
      <LastName>Knowitall</LastName>
      <DateOfHire>02-01-1999</DateOfHire>
      <Salary>90,000</Salary>
    </Employee>
  </Department>
</Company>
```

Figure 32.1 shows an example application that can be used to edit an XML document. This example is currently hard wired to use the Company.xsd and

Company.xml files just shown. However this could be modified very easily to support browsing for any XML Schema file and XML document for generic use.

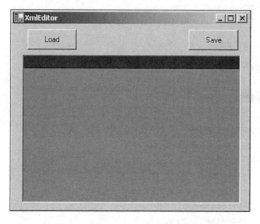

Figure 32.1: Example XML Editor.

The application has two buttons and one data grid. The Load button loads the XML document and binds the data grid to a DataSet. Using the data grid control, users can browse the contents of the XML and modify the data. They can even add data if they want to. At any point, the Save button can be clicked to save the XML document back to the same file. As a result, this application uses an XML file as a mini-database for retrieval of information and storage of modifications.

So how does saving the data grid contents to XML work? Keep in mind that the data grid control can data bind to a DataSet and not to an XML document. Our goal is to load the XML document but data bind to a DataSet. The trick is to use an XmlDataDocument object to support the synchronization between the loaded XML data and the DataSet. Here is the complete set of code for the application shown in Figure 32.1:

```
Imports System.Xml

Public Class Form1
    Inherits System.Windows.Forms.Form

    Private m_doc As XmlDataDocument

#Region " Windows Form Designer generated code "

    Public Sub New()
        MyBase.New()
```

```vbnet
    'This call is required by the Windows Form Designer.
    InitializeComponent()

    'Add any initialization after the InitializeComponent() call

End Sub

'Form overrides dispose to clean up the component list.
Protected Overloads Overrides Sub Dispose(ByVal disposing As Boolean)
    If disposing Then
        If Not (components Is Nothing) Then
            components.Dispose()
        End If
    End If
    MyBase.Dispose(disposing)
End Sub
Friend WithEvents DataGrid1 As System.Windows.Forms.DataGrid
Friend WithEvents btnLoad As System.Windows.Forms.Button
Friend WithEvents btnSave As System.Windows.Forms.Button

'Required by the Windows Form Designer
Private components As System.ComponentModel.IContainer

'NOTE: The following procedure is required by the Windows Form Designer
'It can be modified using the Windows Form Designer.
'Do not modify it using the code editor.
<System.Diagnostics.DebuggerStepThrough()> Private Sub InitializeComponent()
    Me.DataGrid1 = New System.Windows.Forms.DataGrid()
    Me.btnLoad = New System.Windows.Forms.Button()
    Me.btnSave = New System.Windows.Forms.Button()
    CType(Me.DataGrid1, System.ComponentModel.ISupportInitialize).BeginInit()
    Me.SuspendLayout()
    '
    'DataGrid1
    '
    Me.DataGrid1.Anchor = (((System.Windows.Forms.AnchorStyles.Top Or _
                    System.Windows.Forms.AnchorStyles.Bottom) _
                    Or System.Windows.Forms.AnchorStyles.Left) _
                    Or System.Windows.Forms.AnchorStyles.Right)
    Me.DataGrid1.DataMember = ""
    Me.DataGrid1.HeaderForeColor = System.Drawing.SystemColors.ControlText
    Me.DataGrid1.Location = New System.Drawing.Point(16, 48)
    Me.DataGrid1.Name = "DataGrid1"
    Me.DataGrid1.Size = New System.Drawing.Size(264, 216)
    Me.DataGrid1.TabIndex = 0
    '
    'btnLoad
    '
```

```
        Me.btnLoad.Location = New System.Drawing.Point(16, 8)
        Me.btnLoad.Name = "btnLoad"
        Me.btnLoad.Size = New System.Drawing.Size(80, 32)
        Me.btnLoad.TabIndex = 1
        Me.btnLoad.Text = "Load"
        '
        'btnSave
        '
        Me.btnSave.Anchor = (System.Windows.Forms.AnchorStyles.Top Or _
                            System.Windows.Forms.AnchorStyles.Right)
        Me.btnSave.Location = New System.Drawing.Point(200, 8)
        Me.btnSave.Name = "btnSave"
        Me.btnSave.Size = New System.Drawing.Size(80, 32)
        Me.btnSave.TabIndex = 2
        Me.btnSave.Text = "Save"
        '
        'Form1
        '
        Me.AutoScaleBaseSize = New System.Drawing.Size(5, 13)
        Me.ClientSize = New System.Drawing.Size(292, 273)
        Me.Controls.AddRange(New Control() {Me.btnSave, _
                                            Me.btnLoad, _
                                            Me.DataGrid1})
        Me.Name = "Form1"
        Me.Text = "XmlEditor"
        CType(Me.DataGrid1, System.ComponentModel.ISupportInitialize).EndInit()
        Me.ResumeLayout(False)

    End Sub

#End Region

    Private Sub btnLoad_Click(ByVal sender As System.Object, _
                            ByVal e As System.EventArgs) _
                            Handles btnLoad.Click
        Dim ds As DataSet = New DataSet()

        Try

            ds.ReadXmlSchema("Company.xsd")
            m_doc = New XmlDataDocument(ds)
            m_doc.Load("Company.xml")

            DataGrid1.SetDataBinding(ds, "Department")

        Catch ex As Exception
            MsgBox(ex.Message)
```

```
        End Try
    End Sub

    Private Sub btnSave_Click(ByVal sender As System.Object, _
                        ByVal e As System.EventArgs) _
                        Handles btnSave.Click
        Try
            m_doc.Save("Company.xml")
        Catch ex As Exception
            MsgBox(ex.Message)
        End Try
    End Sub

End Class
```

The Form class contains a private data member for the XmlDataDocument. This way the XmlDataDocument object is around for the life of the form.

The btnLoad_Click method creates a DataSet object and reads in the schema defined in the Company.xsd file. Next, a new XmlDataDocument is created by passing the DataSet into the constructor. This associates the XmlDataDocument with the DataSet. The XML data is then loaded by calling the Load method on the XmlDataDocument object. At this point because both the XmlDataDocument object and the DataSet are synchronized, the DataSet object contains the loaded data in addition to the XmlDataDocument.

Given that the DataSet contains data, the call to SetDataBinding binds the DataSet with the data grid and specifies the viewing start point to be Departments.

After clicking the Load button, the application appears as shown in Figure 32.2.

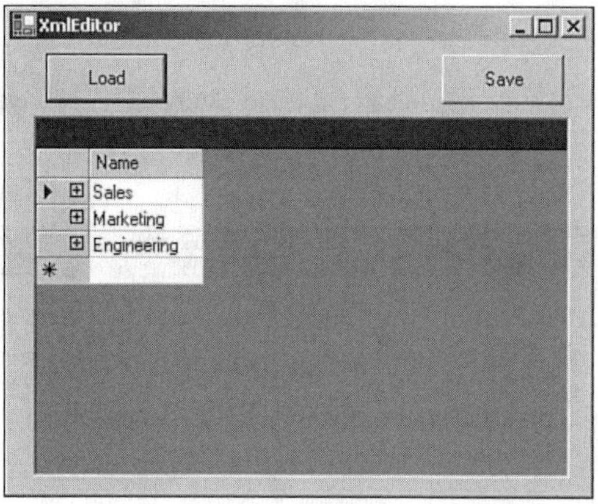

Figure 32.2: Example XML Editor loaded with data.

You can add data to the DataSet using the `DataGrid` control. Any changes to the datagrid are saved in the DataSet and consequently in the `XmlDataDocument` as well. By clicking the Save button, the changes are saved back to the XML file that was originally loaded. This is accomplished in the `btnSave_Click` method by calling the `Save` method on the `XmlDataDocument`. Again, remember that the `XmlDataDocument` contains the changes as well.

That's really all there is to it. This technique of data binding a DataSet to a control where the DataSet was loaded from XML can be quite useful. It's especially useful in cases where you need to utilize a DataSet or XML services but don't want to consider up front the details involved with using XML before developing some code.

What's Next

The intent of this chapter was to expose the integration points of ADO.NET and XML as well as introduce the synchronization capability between DataSets and XML.

In this chapter we explained how DataSets can read and write XML data. In addition, we showed how DataSets and XML data can be synchronized so that you can have differing views of the same data. We did not actually show how to programmatically walk through and read the XML data (other than using the DataSet directly) or how to manually construct an arbitrary XML document.

Both of these topics (reading and writing XML) are covered in the next two chapters. The next chapter explains the classes involved in reading the XML data once it is loaded. Chapter 34 explains how to manually construct an XML document.

NOTE

The answers to "Reviewing It," "Checking It," and "Applying It" are available on our Web site.

REVIEW

Reviewing It

This section presents a review of the key concepts in this chapter. These questions are intended to gauge your absorption of the relevant material.

1. What are the advantages of having XML integrated with the DataSet in ADO.NET?

2. How is XML data loaded into a `DataSet` object?

3. How is DataSet data saved to an XML document?

4. How is XML data retrieved from a `DataSet` object?

5. What do you do if you need an XML schema that represents data in a `DataSet` object?

CHECK

Checking It

Select the correct answer to the following questions.

Multiple Choice

1. How do you get an XML representation of a DataSet?

   a. Call the `GetXml` method on the DataSet.

   b. Call the `GetXmlData` method on the DataSet.

   c. Write custom code.

   d. None of the above.

2. How do you get an XML Schema from a DataSet?

   a. Call the `GetSchema` method on the DataSet.

   b. Call the `GetXmlSchema` method on the DataSet.

   c. Call the `GetDataSchema` method on the DataSet.

   d. None of the above.

3. How do you control the structure of the XML Schema using the DataSet?

   a. Define the Tables in the DataSet.

   b. Define the Columns in the DataSet.

   c. Define the TableMappings in the DataSet.

   d. All of the above.

4. How do you write the XML from a DataSet to a file?

   a. Call the `Save` method on the DataSet.

   b. Call the `Write` method on the DataSet.

   c. Call the `WriteXml` method on the DataSet.

   d. None of the above.

5. How do you write the XML Schema from a DataSet to a file?

   a. Call the `SaveSchema` method on the DataSet.

   b. Call the `WriteSchema` method on the DataSet.

   c. Call the `WriteXmlSchema` method on the DataSet.

   d. None of the above.

6 What class is used to synchronize XML with a DataSet?

   a. `XmlSynchronizer`.

   b. `XmlReader`.

   c. `XmlDataDocument`.

   d. None of the above.

True or False

Select one of the two possible answers and then verify on our Web site that you picked the correct one.

1. You can retrieve data in a DataSet as XML.

   True/False

2. You can retrieve the structure of a DataSet as XML Schema.

   True/False

3. You can infer the structure of a DataSet using an XML document.

   True/False

4. You can save the data in a DataSet as an XML document.

   True/False

5. You read an XML document data into a DataSet.

   True/False

APPLY

Applying It

Try to complete the following exercises by yourself.

Independent Exercise 1

Create an XML file containing the data in the `titles` table in the pubs database in SQL Server. Hint: Use a DataSet.

Independent Exercise 2

Create an XML Schema for the XML document created in Exercise 1.

Reading XML

This chapter covers how to read the contents of an XML document using the classes provided in the Microsoft .NET Framework Class Library. In the last chapter we explained the integration of XML and DataSets but didn't really explain how to read the XML contents or how to programmatically construct an XML document. Here, we actually get into the specifics of reading the XML content itself.

This involves explaining the process of loading an XML document into an in-memory structure, traversing the XML structure, and reading the XML data (content).

This chapter includes

- Loading XML
- Traversing XML
- Finding specific nodes and elements
- Reading the content

Overview

The Microsoft .NET Framework provides extensive support for dealing with XML. In fact, the amount of information related to XML in Microsoft .NET is too vast to be completely explained by just a few chapters; especially because this book is about Visual Basic .NET. Therefore, this chapter focuses on the basics of using the XML classes to read XML data using Visual Basic .NET. We also assume that you have a basic understanding of XML before reading this chapter. If you are not comfortable with your understanding of XML, you should first read "XML, DTD, and XML Schema Fundamentals," on our Web site as it provides an introduction to XML, DTDs, and XML Schemas.

Reading this chapter is a great first step for understanding how to deal with XML in Visual Basic .NET. After you have finished this book, if you want to expand your knowledge in this area you should consider purchasing a book (or books) on XML, XSL, and detailing the classes in the `System.Xml` assembly, which contains the `System.Xml`, `System.Xml.Schema`, `System.Xml.Serialization`, `System.Xml.Xpath`, and `System.Xml.Xsl` namespaces.

You can also visit `http://msdn.microsoft.com/library/default.asp` for more information regarding XML.

This chapter explains how to read in an XML document and validate it against an XML Schema if you choose. After the XML is loaded, we explain how to navigate the structure for reading the content. In addition, we explain how to query the XML structure for specific XML nodes or elements instead of having to manually search for the desired content yourself. After you complete this chapter you will be able to write code to load any XML document, validate it against an XML Schema, and read the content appropriately.

Loading the XML Document

Dealing with XML starts with the `System.Xml.XmlDocument` class. This class supports loading, manipulating, and saving XML data.

NOTE

In the last chapter you learned about the `System.Xml.XmlDataDocument` in regards to synchronizing data between XML and a DataSet. The `XmlDataDocument` class is a subclass of `XmlDocument`. Therefore, everything discussed in this chapter and the next chapter also applies to `XmlDataDocument`.

Loading XML in your code is performed by calling the `Load` or `LoadXml` methods on an `XmlDocument` object. The `Load` method reads data using a filename or an `XmlReader` object. The `LoadXml` method is used to load an XmlDocument by directly passing in a string that contains XML.

Here is an example XML document, named contacts.xml, which is used for several examples in this chapter. It contains a list of Person elements. Each Person element contains a first name, last name, email address, and phone number. Also, this XML document defines the namespace `http://www.myexample.org/Contacts`. This namespace is here for example purposes only.

```
<Contacts xmlns="http://www.myexample.org/Contacts">
  <Person gender="male">
    <FirstName>Bob</FirstName>
    <LastName>Donald</LastName>
    <Email>bdonald@xyz.com</Email>
    <Phone>555-5555</Phone>
  </Person>
  <Person gender="male">
    <FirstName>Gabriel</FirstName>
    <LastName>Oancea</LastName>
    <Email>goancea@xyz.com</Email>
    <Phone>555-4444</Phone>
  </Person>
</Contacts>
```

NOTE

In order to use this XML document in the following examples, the file must exist in the current project's "bin" subfolder.

To load this XML document into memory, you need to create a `System.Xml.XmlDocument` object and call its `Load` method. Here is a Console application project that shows this:

```
Imports System.Xml

Module Module1

    Sub Main()

        Dim doc As XmlDocument

        Try
            doc = New XmlDocument()
            doc.Load("contacts.xml")
```

```
        Catch ex As Exception
            MsgBox(ex.Message)
        End Try

    End Sub

End Module
```

In this example, a new `XmlDocument` object is created, and its `Load` method is called by passing in a filename. If there is an error in the document or the file does not exist, an exception is thrown and displayed on the screen. The `Load` method checks to make sure the document is well formed (for example, all elements have a corresponding end element), but it does not validate the document against a DTD or XML Schema.

This next example shows loading XML from an XML string in memory. A new `XmlDocument` object is created, and its `LoadXml` method is called passing in a string that contains XML.

```
Imports System.Xml

Module Module1

    Sub Main()

        Dim doc As XmlDocument

        Try
            doc = New XmlDocument()
            doc.LoadXml("<Person><Name>Harry</Name></Person>")
            Console.WriteLine(doc.DocumentElement.OuterXml)
            Console.WriteLine(doc.DocumentElement.InnerXml)
        Catch ex As Exception
            MsgBox(ex.Message)
        End Try

    End Sub

End Module
```

The `LoadXml` method checks to make sure the XML is well formed but does not validate it. After the XML is loaded into the `XmlDocument` object, the XmlDocument contains a value for the `DocumentElement` read-only property. The `DocumentElement` is an instance of `System.Xml.XmlElement` and represents the root element in the loaded XML. In our previous example, the root element in the XML is `Person`, and the `DocumentElement` property contains an `XmlElement` object containing the data for the Person element.

The content `DocumentElement` property is displayed in the console window using its read-only `OuterXml` and `InnerXml` properties. The `OuterXml` property contains XML that includes itself and all child XML elements. The `InnerXml` contains XML for child elements only. Here is the output from the previous example:

```
<Person><Name>Harry</Name></Person>
<Name>Harry</Name>
```

The first line represents the outer XML, and the second line represents the inner XML for the root element.

An XML document can be formatted as one single long line of text, or it can be spread out on multiple lines. Typically, XML is formatted on multiple lines to make it easier to read by humans. When you load an XML document into memory you may want to preserve the formatting, or you may choose not to. This all depends on your requirements. For example, if you are sending an XML document across the wire to be consumed by code on the other end you probably don't care about preserving the formatting because the program at the other end is not affected either way.

The `XmlDocument` class contains a `PreserveWhitespace` property to allow you to control how the formatting is preserved. A `True` value preserves the whitespace (spaces, tabs, and so on), and a `False` value removes the whitespace.

Here is a Console application project example that loads the XML document shown earlier and outputs the XML content to the console window.

```
Imports System.Xml

Module Module1

    Sub Main()

        Dim doc As XmlDocument

        Try
            doc = New XmlDocument()
            doc.PreserveWhitespace = True
            doc.Load("contacts.xml")
            Console.WriteLine(doc.DocumentElement.OuterXml())
        Catch ex As Exception
            MsgBox(ex.Message)
        End Try

    End Sub

End Module
```

The output generated from this example is

```
<Contacts xmlns="http://www.myexample.org/Contacts">
  <Person gender="male">
    <FirstName>Bob</FirstName>
    <LastName>Donald</LastName>
    <Email>bdonald@xyz.com</Email>
    <Phone>555-5555</Phone>
  </Person>
  <Person gender="male">
    <FirstName>Gabriel</FirstName>
    <LastName>Oancea</LastName>
    <Email>goancea@xyz.com</Email>
    <Phone>555-4444</Phone>
  </Person>
</Contacts>
```

As you can see, when the `PreserveWhitespace` property is set to `True` before loading the formatting is preserved.

This next example sets the `PreserveWhitespace` property to `False`, and you can see the difference. The unnecessary whitespace between elements is removed.

```
Imports System.Xml

Module Module1

    Sub Main()

        Dim doc As XmlDocument

        Try
            doc = New XmlDocument()
            doc.PreserveWhitespace = False
            doc.Load("contacts.xml")
            Console.WriteLine(doc.DocumentElement.OuterXml())
        Catch ex As Exception
            MsgBox(ex.Message)
        End Try

    End Sub

End Module
```

The output displayed in the console window is shown here:

```
<Contacts xmlns="http://www.myexample.org/Contacts"><Person gender="male">
<FirstName>Bob</FirstName><LastName>Donald</LastName><Email>bdonald@xyz.com
```

```
</Email><Phone>555-5555</Phone></Person><Person gender="male"><FirstName>Gabriel
</FirstName><LastName>Oancea</LastName><Email>goancea@xyz.com</Email><Phone>
555-4444</Phone></Person></Contacts>
```

The Load method on the XmlDocument class also supports passing in an XmlReader object. The XmlReader class is abstract so you can't use an instance of this class directly. There are three implementations of the XmlReader class that are useful in loading an XML document. These are XmlTextReader, XmlNodeReader, and XmlValidatingReader.

The XmlTextReader class inherits from XmlReader class and provides fast non-cached forward-only access to XML data. The XmlTextReader checks the XML to make sure it is well formed. It does not do any XML validation.

This Console application project example loads an XML document using an XmlTextReader object:

```
Imports System.Xml

Module Module1

    Sub Main()

        Dim doc As XmlDocument
        Dim reader As XmlTextReader

        Try
            doc = New XmlDocument()
            reader = New XmlTextReader("contacts.xml")
            doc.Load(reader)
        Catch ex As Exception
            MsgBox(ex.Message)
        End Try

    End Sub

End Module
```

The XmlNodeReader class inherits from XmlReader class and provides fast non-cached forward-only access to XML data using an XmlNode. Because the data is already loaded into an XmlNode, the XML is already guaranteed to be well formed. Also, this class does not perform an XML validation. XmlNode refers to any type of data that exists in an XML document. Examples of nodes include elements, attributes, entities, etc. Since everything in an XML document is basically a node, you are able to traverse an entire XML document using nodes.

The following example loads a source document and then loads the target document from the source document using an XmlNodeReader object. The XmlNodeReader object is constructed using the root node (or DocumentElement) of the source document. The XmlNodeReader starts with the root node and is used to read the entire contents of the source document.

```
Imports System.Xml

Module Module1

    Sub Main()

        Dim docSource As XmlDocument
        Dim docTarget As XmlDocument
        Dim reader As XmlNodeReader

        Try

            docSource = New XmlDocument()
            docSource.Load("contacts.xml")

            docTarget = New XmlDocument()
            docTarget.Load(New XmlNodeReader(docSource.DocumentElement))
            Console.WriteLine(docTarget.DocumentElement.OuterXml())

        Catch ex As Exception
            MsgBox(ex.Message)
        End Try

    End Sub

End Module
```

The XmlValidatingReader class is used to validate an XML document as it is being read. The XmlValidatingReader actually uses another XmlReader object to read the XML. However, the XmlValidatingReader adds the functionality of validating the read XML against a DTD, XML Schema, and so on.

The XmlValidatingReader generates a ValidationEventHandler event when an error is detected. It is you, as the programmer, who is responsible for handling this event if you want validation to actually occur. In handling this event, you can choose to throw an exception to stop the XML processing. You can also perform additional custom validation in code and throw an exception appropriately or just ignore the validation error entirely. You have the control to perform the level of validation that you prefer. But just remember that you must handle the ValidationEventHandler event if you want to perform any kind of XML validation.

To show how this works, an XmlValidator class is shown here that contains an instance of an XmlDocument as a private data member. This class also has an event handler defined to handle the ValidationEventHandler event generated from the XmlValidatingReader object.

This event handler just writes the error to the console window for the purposes of tracking down programming bugs. In a real-world situation you would probably throw an exception in this event handler to stop the processing.

Create a new Console application project and add this class to the project:

```
Imports System.Xml
Imports System.Xml.Schema

Public Class XmlValidator

    Private WithEvents m_reader As XmlValidatingReader
    Private m_doc As XmlDocument
    Private m_valid As Boolean = True

    ' Loads the specified XML document using the specified schemas. While loading,
    ' this class keeps track of any errors generated by the XmlValidatingReader.
    ' If there are any errors, the valid flag is set to false.
    Public Sub Load(ByVal fileName As String, ByVal schemas As XmlSchemaCollection)
        Try
            m_doc = New XmlDocument()
            m_reader = New XmlValidatingReader(New XmlTextReader(fileName))
            m_reader.ValidationType = ValidationType.Schema
            m_reader.Schemas.Add(schemas)
            m_doc.Load(m_reader)
        Catch ex As Exception
            Console.WriteLine(ex.Message)
        End Try
    End Sub

    ' Write any validation errors to the console window
    Private Sub ValidationError(ByVal sender As Object, _
                            ByVal e As ValidationEventArgs) _
                            Handles m_reader.ValidationEventHandler
        Console.WriteLine(e.Message)
        m_valid = False
        ' throw exception here if you wish to stop the loading process
```

```
        ' otherwise loading continues
    End Sub

    ' Get the loaded document
    Public ReadOnly Property Document()
        Get
            Return m_doc
        End Get
    End Property

    ' Get the valid state of the loaded document
    Public ReadOnly Property Valid()
        Get
            Return m_valid
        End Get
    End Property
End Class
```

NOTE

Visual Studio .NET supports creating XML files, XML Schema files, and XSLT files. Use Ctrl+Shift+N while in Visual Studio .NET to bring up the New File dialog and choose the appropriate type of file you want to create. When creating an XML file, the editor is XML aware in that it automatically creates the corresponding end tags for you as you edit the file.

To show how this works, let's first take a look at the XML Schema for the example XML file. This file is saved as contacts.xsd using Visual Studio .NET:

```
<?xml version="1.0" encoding="utf-8"?>
<xsd:schema targetNamespace="http://www.myexample.org/Contacts"
            elementFormDefault="qualified"
            xmlns:tns="http://www.myexample.org/Contacts"
            xmlns:xsd="http://www.w3.org/2001/XMLSchema">
    <xsd:complexType name="person">
        <xsd:sequence>
            <xsd:element name="FirstName" type="xsd:string" />
            <xsd:element name="LastName" type="xsd:string" />
            <xsd:element name="Email" type="xsd:string" />
            <xsd:element name="Phone" type="xsd:string" />
        </xsd:sequence>
        <xsd:attribute name="gender" type="xsd:string" />
    </xsd:complexType>
    <xsd:complexType name="contacts">
        <xsd:sequence>
            <xsd:element name="Person" type="tns:person" maxOccurs="unbounded" />
        </xsd:sequence>
```

```
    </xsd:complexType>
    <xsd:element name="Contacts" type="tns:contacts" />
</xsd:schema>
```

Now we are going to modify the example XML file so that it is no longer valid. There are two changes to the example XML file that cause it to be invalid. The first is that the LastName element is before the FirstName element as part of the second Person element. The second change is that we added a Baboon element to the XML document, which is not defined in the XML Schema. This file is saved as contacts invalid.xml using Visual Studio .NET.

```
<?xml version="1.0" encoding="utf-8"?>
<Contacts xmlns="http://www.myexample.org/Contacts">
  <Person gender="male">
    <FirstName>Bob</FirstName>
    <LastName>Donald</LastName>
    <Email>bdonald@xyz.com</Email>
    <Phone>555-5555</Phone>
  </Person>
  <Person gender="male">
    <LastName>Oancea</LastName>
    <FirstName>Gabriel</FirstName>
    <Email>goancea@xyz.com</Email>
    <Phone>555-4444</Phone>
  </Person>
  <Baboon>
  </Baboon>
</Contacts>
```

Now we will validate the XML document. In the same project, this code demonstrates the usage of the XmlValidator class:

```
Imports System.Xml.Schema

Module Module1

    Sub Main()

        Dim validator As XmlValidator = New XmlValidator()
        Dim schemas As XmlSchemaCollection = New XmlSchemaCollection()

        schemas.Add("http://www.myexample.org/Contacts", "contacts.xsd")
        validator.Load("contacts_invalid.xml", schemas)
        Console.WriteLine("XML Document is valid: {0}", validator.Valid)

    End Sub

End Module
```

When validating an XML document using an XML Schema you need to specify the XSD file that contains the schema. Also, if your XML file contains a particular namespace for the elements you are validating, you need to specify those namespaces. Both of these are accomplished by adding the XSD filename and namespace to an XmlSchemaCollection for each XSD file and namespace used. This XmlSchemaCollection is passed to the XmlValidator's load method along with a filename to validate.

Here is the output of running this previous example. The appropriate errors are reported to the console window for each validation error. This is because we did not quit processing while reading the XML data. Each error is reported and a flag is set by the XmlValidator class indicating the document is invalid.

```
Element 'http://www.myexample.org/Contacts:Person' has invalid content. Expected
'http://www.myexample.org/Contacts:FirstName'. An error occurred at
file:///d:/VBbx/Code/Chapter33/WindowsApplication1/bin/contacts_invalid.xml(10, 6).
Element 'http://www.myexample.org/Contacts:Contacts' has invalid content. Expected
'http://www.myexample.org/Contacts:Person'. An error occurred at
file:///d:/VBbx/Code/Chapter33/WindowsApplication1/bin/contacts_invalid.xml(15, 4).
The 'http://www.myexample.org/Contacts:Baboon' element is not declared. An error
occurred at
file:///d:/VBbx/Code/Chapter33/WindowsApplication1/bin/contacts_invalid.xml(15, 4).
XML Document is valid: False
```

Traversing XML

After an XmlDocument is loaded, it is represented by an in-memory hierarchical structure of XmlNode objects. An *XmlNode* is an abstract class in the .NET Framework that is the base class for many different node types. The XmlNode class contains a read-only property named NodeType that contains a value in the enumeration XmlNodeType that represents the node's actual type. Table 33.1 lists the values in the XmlNodeType enumeration.

Table 33.1: **XmlNodeType** *Enumeration*

Value	Description
Attribute	An attribute.
CDATA	A CDATA section.
Comment	A comment.
Document	A root document node.
DocumentFragment	A node or subtree associated with this document that is part of another document.

Table 33.1: continued

Value	Description
DocumentType	The document type declaration represented by the DOCTYPE tag.
Element	An element start tag. For example, <Person>.
EndElement	An element end tag. For example, </Person>.
EndEntity	The entity that is resolved by an EntityReference.
Entity	An entity declaration.
EntityReference	A reference to an entity.
None	Current value is not a node. When an XMLReader has not had its Read method called, the XMLReader's NodeType property is None because the current node has not been read.
Notation	A notation in a DTD. For example, <!NOTATION ...>
ProcessingInstruction	A processing instruction.
SignificantWhitespace	Whitespace between markup in a mixed content model.
Text	Text content of an element.
Whitespace	Whitespace between markup (spaces, tabs, and so on).
XmlDeclaration	The XML declaration node at the top of the file. For example, <?xml version="1.0" encoding="utf-8"?>

Each of these node types has a corresponding class defined in the .NET Framework Class Library for handling that particular node type. Here is the list of XmlNode subclasses that are used to represent these node types:

XmlAttribute

XmlCDataSection

XmlComment

XmlDocument

XmlDeclaraction

XmlDocumentFragment

XmlDocumentType

XmlElement

XmlEntity

XmlEntityReference

XmlNotation

XmlProcessingInstruction

XmlSignificantWhitespace

XmlText

XmlWhitespace

We show examples of these, most notably XmlElement and XmlAttribute, later in this chapter.

Because each of these classes inherits from the XmlNode class, they can all be treated as an instance of an XmlNode. This easily supports implementing code that traverses the XML structure in a uniform fashion because the XmlNode class provides several properties that can be used for traversing XmlNodes.

Table 33.2 shows the subset of properties on the XmlNode class that aid in writing code that traverses and inspects the structure of a loaded XML document.

Table 33.2: **XmlNode** *Properties*

Property	Description
ChildNodes	Property containing a list of child nodes.
FirstChild	Property containing the first child in the list of child nodes.
HasChildNodes	Property indicating whether the node has child nodes or not.
Item	Property that represents the first child that matches the specified node name.
LastChild	Property containing the last child in the list of child nodes.
Name	The name of the node.
NamespaceURI	The namespace for the node.
NextSibling	The next sibling in relation to the current node's parent.
NodeType	The type of the node.
OwnerDocument	The document containing the node.
ParentNode	The parent node of the node.
PreviousSibling	The previous sibling in relation to this node's parent.
Value	The value for the node.

Using these properties, it is quite simple to iterate through the nodes and child nodes for the purposes of reading the XML content. Shown next is an example Console application project that contains a PrintNodes function to demonstrate traversing the XML document.

```vb
Imports System.Xml

Module Module1

    Public Sub PrintNodes(ByVal node As XmlNode)
        Dim i As Integer
        Dim attr As XmlAttribute

        ' print node information
        Console.WriteLine("Node: {0}", node.Name)
        Console.WriteLine("   type: {0}", node.NodeType)
        Console.WriteLine("   value: {0}", node.Value)
        Console.WriteLine("   namespace: {0}", node.NamespaceURI)

        ' print node's attribute information
        If Not node.Attributes Is Nothing Then
            If node.Attributes.Count > 0 Then
                For i = 0 To node.Attributes.Count - 1
                    attr = node.Attributes.Item(i)
                    Console.WriteLine("   attribute: {0}", attr.Name)
                    Console.WriteLine("        type: {0}", attr.Value)
                    Console.WriteLine("       value: {0}", attr.Specified)
                Next
            End If
        End If

        Console.WriteLine("")

        ' now print child nodes
        If node.HasChildNodes Then
            For i = 0 To node.ChildNodes.Count - 1
                PrintNodes(node.ChildNodes.Item(i))
            Next
        End If

    End Sub

    Sub Main()

        Dim doc As XmlDocument
        Dim reader As XmlTextReader
        Dim node As XmlNode
        Dim element As XmlElement

        Try
            doc = New XmlDocument()
```

```
        reader = New XmlTextReader("contacts.xml")
        doc.Load(reader)
        PrintNodes(doc)
    Catch ex As Exception
        MsgBox(ex.Message)
    End Try

End Sub
```

```
End Module
```

The PrintNodes function, given an XmlNode, prints out the node's name, type, value, and namespace as well as information on each of the node's attributes. Then, each of the node's child nodes is passed to the PrintNodes function in a recursive manner. The result is that all of the nodes (starting with the first node passed to the PrintNodes function) are outputted to the console window.

The Main procedure loads the XML document and calls the PrintNodes function.

Let's use this example document (contacts.xml) again:

```
<?xml version="1.0" encoding="utf-8"?>
<Contacts xmlns="http://www.myexample.org/Contacts">
  <Person gender="male">
    <FirstName>Bob</FirstName>
    <LastName>Donald</LastName>
    <Email>bdonald@xyz.com</Email>
    <Phone>555-5555</Phone>
  </Person>
  <Person gender="male">
    <FirstName>Gabriel</FirstName>
    <LastName>Oancea</LastName>
    <Email>goancea@xyz.com</Email>
    <Phone>555-4444</Phone>
  </Person>
</Contacts>
```

And here is the result of running the sample code. Take a moment and review the output and try to match up the output with each node in the example XML document.

```
Node: #document
    type:  Document
    value:
    namespace:
```

```
Node: xml
   type:  XmlDeclaration
   value: version="1.0" encoding="utf-8"
   namespace:

Node: Contacts
   type:  Element
   value:
   namespace: http://www.myexample.org/Contacts
   attribute: xmlns
        type: http://www.myexample.org/Contacts
        value: True

Node: Person
   type:  Element
   value:
   namespace: http://www.myexample.org/Contacts
   attribute: gender
        type: male
        value: True

Node: FirstName
   type:  Element
   value:
   namespace: http://www.myexample.org/Contacts

Node: #text
   type:  Text
   value: Bob
   namespace:

Node: LastName
   type:  Element
   value:
   namespace: http://www.myexample.org/Contacts

Node: #text
   type:  Text
   value: Donald
   namespace:

Node: Email
   type:  Element
   value:
   namespace: http://www.myexample.org/Contacts
```

```
Node: #text
    type:  Text
    value: bdonald@xyz.com
    namespace:

Node: Phone
    type:  Element
    value:
    namespace: http://www.myexample.org/Contacts

Node: #text
    type:  Text
    value: 555-5555
    namespace:

Node: Person
    type:  Element
    value:
    namespace: http://www.myexample.org/Contacts
    attribute: gender
        type: male
        value: True

Node: FirstName
    type:  Element
    value:
    namespace: http://www.myexample.org/Contacts

Node: #text
    type:  Text
    value: Gabriel
    namespace:

Node: LastName
    type:  Element
    value:
    namespace: http://www.myexample.org/Contacts

Node: #text
    type:  Text
    value: Oancea
    namespace:

Node: Email
    type:  Element
    value:
    namespace: http://www.myexample.org/Contacts
```

```
Node: #text
   type:  Text
   value: goancea@xyz.com
   namespace:

Node: Phone
   type:  Element
   value:
   namespace: http://www.myexample.org/Contacts

Node: #text
   type:  Text
   value: 555-4444
   namespace:
```

Finding Specific Nodes and Elements

In addition to being able to walk the entire XML document as shown in the previous section, you can also automatically select nodes using expressions defined in *XPath* (XML Path Language). The XPath standard can be found at http://www.w3.org/TR/xpath.

Basically, XPath allows you to define an expression that can be used to retrieve one or many nodes from the XML document, which you can then process. This allows you to write code that deals only with the nodes you care about. You don't have to write lots of code just to find the nodes your application uses.

The XmlNode class defines two methods that you can use to evaluate an expression and retrieve the resulting nodes. These methods are SelectNodes and SelectSingleNode. *SelectNodes* evaluates the expression and returns all child nodes that match the expression. The result is returned as an XmlNodeList object that contains a list of nodes. The *SelectSingleNode* evaluates the expression and returns the first node that matches the expression. This node could be several levels deep depending on the how complicated the expression is.

This example code fragment loads the contacts.xml document again and demonstrates the use of the SelectNodes and SelectSingleNode methods using an XPath expression.

```
Dim doc As XmlDocument
Dim reader As XmlTextReader
Dim nodes As XmlNodeList
Dim node As XmlNode
```

```
Try

    doc = New XmlDocument()
    reader = New XmlTextReader("contacts.xml")
    doc.PreserveWhitespace = True
    doc.Load(reader)

    Dim nsmgr As XmlNamespaceManager = New XmlNamespaceManager(doc.NameTable)
    nsmgr.AddNamespace("ns", "http://www.myexample.org/Contacts")

    ' select all person nodes that have a first name containing 'Gabriel'
    nodes = doc.SelectNodes("/ns:Contacts/ns:Person[ns:FirstName='Gabriel']", _
                            nsmgr)
    Console.WriteLine("Nodes found: {0}", nodes.Count)

    ' select the first person node that has a first name containing 'Gabriel'
    node = doc.SelectSingleNode("/ns:Contacts/ns:Person[ns:FirstName='Gabriel']", _
                                nsmgr)
    Console.WriteLine(node.OuterXml)

Catch ex As Exception
    MsgBox(ex.Message)
End Try
```

In this example, an XmlNamespaceManager object is created so that we can define the namespace that exists in the contacts.xml document. This is because the nodes in the document need to be referenced by their fully qualified names within the expression. The XmlNamespaceManger object is used in the selection process to expand the node names defined in the expression to their fully qualified names.

The call to SelectNodes uses an expression that should return all Person elements that also have a FirstName child element that contains the value Gabriel. In our example, this results in finding a single node all in one line of code.

The call to SelectSingleNode uses the same expression. The difference here is that processing stops as soon as any node matches the expression and the result is a single XmlNode object.

The output of this previous example is:

```
Nodes found: 1

<Person gender="male" xmlns="http://www.myexample.org/Contacts">
    <FirstName>Gabriel</FirstName>
    <LastName>Oancea</LastName>
```

```
    <Email>goancea@xyz.com</Email>
    <Phone>555-4444</Phone>
</Person>
```

The Item property in the XmlNode class is also useful for finding immediate children using a node name. By passing a node name to the Item property, the first child node that matches the node name is returned and null if there are no matches. The following code shows how to get the FirstName element of the first Person element in the document.

```
Imports System.Xml

Module Module1

    Sub Main()

        Dim doc As XmlDocument
        Dim reader As XmlTextReader
        Dim node As XmlNode

        Try

            doc = New XmlDocument()
            reader = New XmlTextReader("contacts.xml")
            doc.PreserveWhitespace = True
            doc.Load(reader)

            node = doc.Item("Contacts").Item("Person").Item("FirstName")
            Console.WriteLine(node.OuterXml)

        Catch ex As Exception
            MsgBox(ex.Message)
        End Try

    End Sub

End Module
```

Using the same sample XML file again, the output of this code is

```
<FirstName xmlns="http://www.myexample.org/Contacts">Bob</FirstName>
```

If you deal with XML documents that utilize attributes of type ID and IDREF, you can also retrieve these elements directly by calling the GetElementById method on the XmlDocument class. As long as the document is loaded and has the appropriate DTD or XML Schema defined for the attributes of type ID, the GetElementById method accepts a String containing the ID for which to search. If found, the XmlElement is returned.

The `XmlDocument` and `XmlElement` classes also have a method named `GetElementsByTagName` that accepts a tag name and returns all descendant elements that have the same tag name.

Reading the Content

The actual content of an XmlDocument is represented by the `Value` property of each `XmlNode` object. Well, not exactly each XmlNode. Remember earlier in this chapter we basically said that everything in an XmlDocument is an XmlNode? This includes XmlElements and XmlAttributes among others. Depending on the actual type of each XmlNode, the `Value` property might contain a value, or it might not at all. It depends on the type of the node. Table 33.3 describes the value stored in the `Value` property of an XmlNode depending on the actual NodeType of the node.

Table 33.3: `XmlNode.Value` *Depending on NodeType*

Class	**Content of `Value` Property**
`XmlAttribute`	The value of the attribute.
`XmlCDataSection`	The content of the CDATA section.
`XmlComment`	A content of the comment.
`XmlDeclaraction`	The content of the declaration.
`XmlDocument`	Nothing.
`XmlDocumentFragment`	Nothing.
`XmlDocumentType`	Nothing.
`XmlElement`	Nothing.
`XmlEntity`	Nothing.
`XmlEntityReference`	Nothing.
`XmlNotation`	Nothing.
`XmlProcessingInstruction`	The entire content of the processing instruction.
`XmlText`	The content of the text node.
`XmlSignificantWhitespace`	The whitespace characters.
`XmlWhitespace`	The whitespace characters.

To get the value of an `XmlElement` object, you should use the `InnerText` property that represents the content for an XML element. Take this XML fragment for example:

```
<abc>xyz</abc>
```

This fragment represents one `XmlElement` object containing some content—the `XmlElement` being abc and the content being xyz. This fragment also represents two `XmlNode` objects. The first `XmlNode` object is abc. This node has a `NodeType` of Element, and the `Value` property does not contain a value. The second `XmlNode` object is the xyz. This node has a `NodeType` of `Text`, and its

Value property contains the string xyz. So, to get the content for an element, you could call the InnerText method on the XmlElement object, or you could get the FirstChild and retrieve the value for that node.

The following code illustrates this point:

```
Imports System.Xml

Module Module1

    Sub Main()

        Dim doc As XmlDocument
        Dim reader As XmlTextReader
        Dim node As XmlNode

        Try

            doc = New XmlDocument()
            reader = New XmlTextReader("contacts.xml")
            doc.PreserveWhitespace = True
            doc.Load(reader)

            node = doc.Item("Contacts").Item("Person").Item("FirstName")
            Console.WriteLine(node.InnerText)
            Console.WriteLine(node.FirstChild.Value)

        Catch ex As Exception
            MsgBox(ex.Message)
        End Try

    End Sub

End Module
```

Here is the output generated by this code:

```
Bob
Bob
```

The Value property type is a String. Because it is a String, the actual value could be any number of different formats however the value is stored in a String representation. So whenever you read data from an XML file and the data is a number, for example, you must read the Value property and convert it to the appropriate number type.

To simplify your work, the .NET Framework provides an XmlConvert class that handles converting CLR (Common Language Runtime) data types to XSD (XML Schema) data types and vice versa. So, after you load an XML document into memory, you should convert the values in the XmlNode `Value` properties to an appropriate value before using it. The `XmlConvert` class is very useful in providing this conversion support.

Table 33.4 lists the conversion methods available.

Table 33.4: XmlConvert Methods

Method	Description
ToBoolean	Converts a String to a `Boolean`.
ToByte	Converts a String to a `Byte`.
ToChar	Converts a String to a `Char`.
ToDateTime	Converts a String to a `DateTime`.
ToDecimal	Converts a String to a `Decimal`.
ToDouble	Converts a String to a `Double`.
ToGuid	Converts a String to a `Guid`.
ToInt16	Converts a String to an `Int16`.
ToInt32	Converts a String to an `Int32`.
ToInt64	Converts a String to an `Int64`.
ToSByte	Converts a String to an `SByte`.
ToSingle	Converts a String to a `Single`.
ToString	Converts strongly typed data to a `String`.
ToTimeSpan	Converts a String to a `TimeSpan`.
ToUInt16	Converts a String to a `Uint16`.
ToUInt32	Converts a String to a `Uint32`.
ToUInt64	Converts a String to a `Uint64`.

What's Next

This chapter explained how to load an XML document into memory, traverse the entire XML structure, find selected XML nodes, and read the actual content.

Generating XML documents is explained in the next chapter. At that point you will see how to generate your own XML documents in Visual Basic .NET.

NOTE

The answers to "Reviewing It," "Checking It," and "Applying It" are available on our Web site.

REVIEW

Reviewing It

This section presents a review of the key concepts in this chapter. These questions are intended to gauge your absorption of the relevant material.

1. What is the minimal set of classes required to load and traverse an XML document?

2. How do you validate an XML document against a specific XML Schema?

3. How do you find specific nodes in an XML document?

CHECK

Checking It

Select the correct answer to the following questions.

Multiple Choice

1. How can you load an XML document into an XmlDocument object?

   a. Use the XmlDocument Load method along with a filename.

   b. Use the XmlDocument Load method and an XmlTextReader object.

   c. Use the XmlDocument Load method and an XmlValidatingReader object.

   d. All of the above.

2. How do you validate an XML document?

   a. Use the XmlDocument Load method.

   b. Use the XmlDocument Validate method.

   c. Use an XmlValidatingReader and handle the ValidationEventHandler event.

   d. None of the above.

3. How would you find specific nodes in a loaded XML document?

   a. Call the Find method on the XmlDocument object.

   b. Call the SelectNodes method on the XmlDocument object.

   c. Call the Search method on the XmlDocument object.

   d. None of the above.

4. Given an `XmlNode` object, how can you figure out what type of node it is?

   a. Call the `GetType` method.

   b. Read the `NodeType` property.

   c. Read the `Type` property.

   d. Call the `GetNodeType` method.

5. How would you find an XmlElement and XmlDocument if you had the element's ID?

   a. Call the XmlDocument's `Find` method.

   b. Call the XmlDocument's `GetElementById` method.

   c. Call the XmlDocument's `GetElement` method.

   d. None of the above.

6. How should you convert a `DateTime` object so that it can be safely stored in an XML document?

   a. Use the `XmlConvert.ToString` method.

   b. Use the `DateTime.ToString` method.

   c. Use the `XmlDocument.Store` method.

   d. None of the above.

True or False

Select one of the two possible answers and then verify on our Web site that you picked the correct one.

1. The `XmlTextReader` class provides fast read-only forward-only access to XML data.

   True/False

2. XML documents are validated by default when loading.

   True/False

3. Whitespace in an XML document can be preserved by setting the `XmlDocument` object's `PreserveWhitespace` property value to `True` before loading the document.

   True/False

4. The `SelectNodes` and `SelectSingleNode` methods accept XPath expressions for finding the specific nodes.

   True/False

5. The `Value` property contains the actual value for an `XmlNode` object.

   True/False

Applying It

Try to complete the following exercises by yourself.

Independent Exercise 1

Create the following XML document using Visual Studio .NET.

```
<?xml version="1.0" encoding="utf-8" ?>
<Book>
    <Chapter title = "Introduction">
    </Chapter>
    <Chapter title = "More Information">
    </Chapter>
    <Chapter title = "Advanced Information">
    </Chapter>
</Book>
```

Independent Exercise 2

Create a new Console application project. Using the XML document created in Exercise 1, write code to load the document, and find the "More Information" chapter node.

34

Generating an XML Document

This chapter explains how to write code that generates XML documents using Visual Basic .NET and the classes provided in the Microsoft .NET Framework Class Library. This chapter assumes that you have a basic working knowledge of XML. If you need more detailed knowledge of XML, feel free to read "XML, DTD, and XML Schema Fundamentals," on our Web site.

The last chapter covered the aspects of reading XML. In that chapter, you learned the different structural parts of XML, such as elements and attributes. And you learned how to navigate this structure after the XML data is loaded. This chapter goes further to explain how you can create your own XML documents programmatically.

Because the Microsoft .NET platform (and distributed Web applications in general) leverage XML, you will undoubtedly need to create an XML document at some point. The goal of this chapter is not to be a complete XML generation reference but rather to provide a solid foundation for learning how to generate XML documents in Visual Basic .NET.

This chapter includes information about

- Creating elements and attributes
- Creating comments
- Creating text
- Writing nodes
- Saving XML documents
- XSL transformations

Creating Elements and Attributes

The most common items found in an XML document include elements and attributes. When creating a new XML document, the basic idea is that you instantiate a new System.Xml.XmlDocument object in memory and add instances of System.Xml.XmlElement to the document object. For each element, you can also define attributes that are represented as System.Xml.XmlAttribute object.

XmlElement objects can be added as children to other XmlElement objects, resulting in a nested structure. The final XML document contains data based on the code that generated the XML. This is typically dependant on the type of XML content your application is creating.

To show how this works exactly, create a new Console application project and add the following code to create an in-memory XML document and then save the document to a file.

```
Imports System.Xml

Module Module1

    Sub Main()

        Dim doc As XmlDocument = New XmlDocument()
        Dim games As XmlElement
        Dim game As XmlElement
        Dim attr As XmlAttribute

        ' create the XML declaration header for the document
        doc.AppendChild(doc.CreateXmlDeclaration("1.0", "", ""))

        ' create a new element and add it to the document
        ' (making it the root element)
        games = doc.CreateElement("ComputerGames")
        doc.AppendChild(games)

        ' create a new element, set its attributes, and
        ' append it as a child of another element.
        game = doc.CreateElement("Game")
        game.SetAttribute("name", "Diablo II")
        game.SetAttribute("type", "RPG")
        games.AppendChild(game)

        game = doc.CreateElement("Game")
        game.SetAttribute("name", "Quake III")
```

```
        game.SetAttribute("type", "First Person Shooter")
        games.AppendChild(game)

        game = doc.CreateElement("Game")
        game.SetAttribute("name", "Unreal Tournament")
        game.SetAttribute("type", "First Person Shooter")
        games.AppendChild(game)

        ' save the document to a file
        doc.Save("games.xml")

    End Sub

End Module
```

To start with, a new instance of XmlDocument is created that is used to contain the XML content. The content is created in the remaining lines of code in the example. Next, an XML declaration is created and added to the document. This identifies the content of the document to contain XML (version 1.0) data along with the encoding format. The default encoding format (if none specified) is UTF-8.

The root element, ComputerGames, is then created and added to the document. Just before adding it to the document, two attributes on the element are updated with values. The pattern shown here is to call a method on the document to create the desired node in the XML document. Each create method on the document returns an object as denoted by the return value of the method. The object returned from the method call can be modified appropriately and then added to the document typically by appending it as a child of another node. The objects are not added to the document during any of the Create methods. You must specifically add them to the document in the desired order by appending them as children of the document or children of a node within the document.

The CreateElement method takes a name that represents the element tag name. If you plan on using namespaces in your XML documents, the CreateElement method can also take a namespace string as the second parameter. The example here does not use a namespace.

The SetAttribute method supports setting an attribute value using an attribute name and a value. This method also supports using namespaces by specifying three parameters instead of two. These parameters represent the name, namespace, and value of the attribute.

The ComputerGames element is added to the document by appending it as a child of the document. This effectively makes it the root element. If, for some reason, you appended multiple elements to the document itself you would get an error on the second appending. This is because only one element can be added to a document as the root.

The last line in the example saves the XML document to the file named games.xml. This file is saved in the same folder that the application is started from. When running projects from Visual Studio .NET this is the "bin" folder under the folder for the current project. The content of the generated XML file is shown here:

```
<?xml version="1.0"?>
<ComputerGames>
  <Game name="Diablo II" type="RPG" />
  <Game name="Quake III" type="First Person Shooter" />
  <Game name="Unreal Tournament" type="First Person Shooter" />
</ComputerGames>
```

This previous example did not include XML namespaces in order to simplify the example. Namespaces allow you to define elements in an XML file that don't interfere with someone else's definition of an XML element using the same name. In our example, this allows us to define an XML element named Games that does not conflict with someone else's element named Games. XML element names are unique based on the element tag name and the namespace it belongs in. This allows developers to freely define XML elements within their own namespace (assuming their namespace name is unique). Programming errors and confusion occurs when you are using XML elements (with the same tag name) defined by two different XML Schemas (meaning the elements have different structures to them); the namespaces are the same (or not used); and the XML elements are used in the same XML document.

Methods are provided in the Framework Class Library that support defining namespaces for elements, attributes, and so on. The following example is a Console application project that demonstrates the previous example again with the addition of namespaces. A String defining the namespace is defined. This String is then passed as a parameter when creating elements and setting attributes. The output is shown immediately following the example code.

```
Imports System.Xml

Module Module1

    Sub Main()

        Dim doc As XmlDocument = New XmlDocument()
        Dim games As XmlElement
```

```
        Dim game As XmlElement
        Dim attr As XmlAttribute
        Dim ns As String

        ns = "MyNamespace"

        ' create the XML declaration header for the document
        doc.AppendChild(doc.CreateXmlDeclaration("1.0", "", ""))

        ' create a new element and add it to the document
        ' (making it the root element)
        games = doc.CreateElement("ComputerGames", ns)
        doc.AppendChild(games)

        ' create a new element, set its attributes, and
        ' append it as a child of another element.
        game = doc.CreateElement("Game", ns)
        game.SetAttribute("name", ns, "Diablo II")
        game.SetAttribute("type", ns, "RPG")
        games.AppendChild(game)

        game = doc.CreateElement("Game", ns)
        game.SetAttribute("name", ns, "Quake III")
        game.SetAttribute("type", ns, "First Person Shooter")
        games.AppendChild(game)

        game = doc.CreateElement("Game", ns)
        game.SetAttribute("name", ns, "Unreal Tournament")
        game.SetAttribute("type", ns, "First Person Shooter")
        games.AppendChild(game)

        ' save the document to a file
        doc.Save("games.xml")

    End Sub

End Module
```

The generated output from this example is

```
<?xml version="1.0"?>
<ComputerGames xmlns="MyNamespace">
  <Game n1:name="Diablo II" n1:type="RPG" xmlns:n1="MyNamespace" />
  <Game n1:name="Quake III" n1:type="First Person Shooter" xmlns:n1="MyNamespace" />
  <Game n1:name="Unreal Tournament" n1:type="First Person Shooter"
xmlns:n1="MyNamespace" />
</ComputerGames>
```

Namespaces are not defined as part of the remainder of the code examples for the purposes of simplifying the code. However, adding namespaces is just a matter of simply adding a parameter when creating elements, attributes, and so on.

Creating Comments

XML supports comments for the purposes of injecting additional documentation into an XML document. Comments are solely intended to help the human reader of an XML document. If you think a person is going to be frequently reading an XML document that you generated (rather than a computer program), you should consider adding comments as necessary to your XML documents. When generating larger documents, this greatly simplifies the process of developing a program that generates the XML document and reviewing the results of the code. This allows you to see the comments and get a better idea of where you are in the XML document if you are reading the XML document using a text editor.

> **NOTE**
>
> If you are developing code in Visual Studio .NET that generates an XML file, a useful technique is to open the generated XML file in Visual Studio .NET after the first time the XML file is generated. As you make changes to your code and run it, Visual Studio .NET detects when the generated XML file has changed and asks you whether you want to reload it. This allows you to quickly see the changes as they happen instead of continuously opening and closing the file to see the reflected changes.

Here is another Console application project that generates an XML document with comments :

```
Imports System.Xml

Module Module1

    Sub Main()

        Dim doc As XmlDocument = New XmlDocument()
        Dim games As XmlElement
        Dim comment As XmlComment
        Dim game As XmlElement
        Dim attr As XmlAttribute

        doc.AppendChild(doc.CreateXmlDeclaration("1.0", "", ""))

        games = doc.CreateElement("ComputerGames")
        doc.AppendChild(games)
```

```
        comment = doc.CreateComment("This is an awesome game that " & _
                                    "requires teamwork.")
        games.AppendChild(comment)

        game = doc.CreateElement("Game")
        game.SetAttribute("name", "Diablo II")
        game.SetAttribute("type", "RPG")
        games.AppendChild(game)

        comment = doc.CreateComment("id Software revolutionized " & _
                                    "the gaming industry.")
        games.AppendChild(comment)

        game = doc.CreateElement("Game")
        game.SetAttribute("name", "Quake III")
        game.SetAttribute("type", "First Person Shooter")
        games.AppendChild(game)

        comment = doc.CreateComment("Very cool game.")
        games.AppendChild(comment)

        game = doc.CreateElement("Game")
        game.SetAttribute("name", "Unreal Tournament")
        game.SetAttribute("type", "First Person Shooter")
        games.AppendChild(game)

        doc.Save("games.xml")

    End Sub

End Module
```

Comments are added to an XML document by creating an instance of an XmlComment. This instance is created by calling the CreateComment method on the document itself. The CreateComment method takes a parameter that represents the actual comment and returns an instance of an XmlComment. This object is then added as a child to a node of your choosing. This example adds the comments to the root node (ComputerGames). Here is the output of the previous example:

```
<?xml version="1.0"?>
<ComputerGames>
  <!--This is an awesome game that requires teamwork.-->
  <Game name="Diablo II" type="RPG" />
  <!--id Software revolutionized the gaming industry.-->
  <Game name="Quake III" type="First Person Shooter" />
  <!--Very cool game.-->
```

```
    <Game name="Unreal Tournament" type="First Person Shooter" />
</ComputerGames>
```

Creating Text

In XML, the value of an element is the text contained between the start and end tags. Text can be stored in either of two ways in an XML document. The first is to store the text in a Text Node. This requires the actual text to obey the rules of XML and not have inappropriate characters in the text. For example, the text cannot contain less than (<) or greater than (>) characters. Otherwise, the XML document would not be well-formed and, therefore, would not load. The second way to store text is to place the text in a CDATA section in the XML document. CDATA sections safely support storing any free-formed text in an XML document.

The following Console application project example demonstrates each of these ways of storing text:

```
Imports System.Xml

Module Module1

    Sub Main()

        Dim doc As XmlDocument = New XmlDocument()
        Dim games As XmlElement
        Dim comment As XmlComment
        Dim game As XmlElement
        Dim description As XmlText
        Dim cdata As XmlCDataSection
        Dim attr As XmlAttribute

        doc.AppendChild(doc.CreateXmlDeclaration("1.0", "", ""))

        games = doc.CreateElement("ComputerGames")
        doc.AppendChild(games)

        comment = doc.CreateComment("This is an awesome game that " & _
                                    "requires teamwork")
        games.AppendChild(comment)

        game = doc.CreateElement("Game")
        game.SetAttribute("name", "Diablo II")
        game.SetAttribute("type", "RPG")
        description = doc.CreateTextNode("Awesome Game!")
        game.AppendChild(description)
        games.AppendChild(game)
```

```
        comment = doc.CreateComment("id Software revolutionized " & _
                                    "the gaming industry.")
        games.AppendChild(comment)

        game = doc.CreateElement("Game")
        game.SetAttribute("name", "Quake III Arena")
        game.SetAttribute("type", "First Person Shooter")
        cdata = doc.CreateCDataSection("Awesome Game <really cool>!")
        game.AppendChild(cdata)
        games.AppendChild(game)

        comment = doc.CreateComment("Very cool game.")
        games.AppendChild(comment)

        game = doc.CreateElement("Game")
        game.SetAttribute("name", "Unreal Tournament")
        game.SetAttribute("type", "First Person Shooter")
        games.AppendChild(game)

        doc.Save("games.xml")

    End Sub

End Module
```

The `CreateTextNode` method is used to create a node that contains text. This text must follow the appropriate XML rules concerning text. This method passes back an `XmlText` object that contains the text passed into the method as an argument.

The `CreateCDataSection` method is used to create a CDATA section containing the specified text. This method creates an `XmlCDataSection` object and assigns it the text passed in as a parameter.

The output of the code example is as follows:

```
<?xml version="1.0"?>
<ComputerGames>
  <!--This is an awesome game that requires teamwork-->
  <Game name="Diablo II" type="RPG">Awesome Game!</Game>
  <!--id Software revolutionized the gaming industry.-->
  <Game name="Quake III Arena" type="First Person Shooter"><![CDATA[Awesome Game
<really cool>!]]></Game>
  <!--Very cool game.-->
  <Game name="Unreal Tournament" type="First Person Shooter" />
</ComputerGames>
```

NOTE

When writing out data to an XML document, you are required to store the data in a text format. How do you store non-text data? Use the XmlConvert.ToString method to convert different data types to String. This method safely converts data types specifically for the purpose of storing the result in an XML document.

The following example creates an XML document with a single element that contains a value. The value is generated by calling the XmlConvert. ToString and passing in the Boolean value. The ToString converts the Boolean value into a text string that can be stored in the document.

```
Imports System.Xml

Module Module1

    Sub Main()

        Dim doc As XmlDocument = New XmlDocument()
        Dim elem As XmlElement
        Dim text As XmlText

        doc.AppendChild(doc.CreateXmlDeclaration("1.0", "", ""))

        elem = doc.CreateElement("abc")
        doc.AppendChild(elem)

        text = doc.CreateTextNode(XmlConvert.ToString(True))
        elem.AppendChild(text)
        doc.Save("abc.xml")

    End Sub

End Module
```

Here is the generated XML document from this example:

```
<?xml version="1.0"?>
<abc>true</abc>
```

The XmlConvert class can be used to convert the text back into a Boolean value when the document is read back in.

Writing Nodes

You have the option of creating an XML document by writing code that creates specific objects as you construct the XML. For example, you can call the CreateElement method to create an XmlElement object that you can deal with. However, similar to what we did when showing how to read an XML document, you can choose to write code that writes an XML document using $XmlNodes$ only.

The $XmlDocument$ class provides the method $CreateNode$ that can be used for this purpose. Actually, this method has several versions depending on your needs. The version used in the following code example takes three arguments. The first is a NodeType (defined in Chapter 33, "Reading XML," in Table 33.1) that represents the type of node to create. The second parameter is the name of the node. The third parameter is the namespace for the node.

The following code demonstrates generating the same XML document again—this time using nodes.

```
Imports System.Xml

Module Module1

    Sub Main()

        Dim doc As XmlDocument = New XmlDocument()
        Dim games As XmlNode
        Dim comment As XmlNode
        Dim game As XmlNode
        Dim description As XmlNode
        Dim attr As XmlNode
        Dim cdata As XmlNode

        doc.AppendChild(doc.CreateXmlDeclaration("1.0", "", ""))

        games = doc.CreateNode(XmlNodeType.Element, "ComputerGames", "")
        doc.AppendChild(games)

        comment = doc.CreateNode(XmlNodeType.Comment, "", "")
        comment.Value = "This is an awesome game that requires team work"
        games.AppendChild(comment)

        game = doc.CreateNode(XmlNodeType.Element, "Game", "")

        attr = doc.CreateNode(XmlNodeType.Attribute, "", "name", "")
        attr.Value = "Diablo II"
        game.Attributes.Append(attr)

        attr = doc.CreateNode(XmlNodeType.Attribute, "", "type", "")
        attr.Value = "RPG"
        game.Attributes.Append(attr)
```

```
        description = doc.CreateNode(XmlNodeType.Text, "", "")
        description.Value = "Awesome Game!"
        game.AppendChild(description)
        games.AppendChild(game)

        comment = doc.CreateNode(XmlNodeType.Comment, "", "")
        comment.Value = "id Software revolutionalized the gaming industry."
        games.AppendChild(comment)

        game = doc.CreateNode(XmlNodeType.Element, "Game", "")

        attr = doc.CreateNode(XmlNodeType.Attribute, "", "name", "")
        attr.Value = "Quake III Arena"
        game.Attributes.Append(attr)

        attr = doc.CreateNode(XmlNodeType.Attribute, "", "type", "")
        attr.Value = "First Person Shooter"
        game.Attributes.Append(attr)

        cdata = doc.CreateNode(XmlNodeType.CDATA, "", "")
        cdata.Value = "Awesome Game <really cool>!"
        game.AppendChild(cdata)
        games.AppendChild(game)

        comment = doc.CreateNode(XmlNodeType.Comment, "", "")
        comment.Value = "Very cool game."
        games.AppendChild(comment)

        game = doc.CreateNode(XmlNodeType.Element, "Game", "")

        attr = doc.CreateNode(XmlNodeType.Attribute, "", "name", "")
        attr.Value = "Unreal Tournament"
        game.Attributes.Append(attr)

        attr = doc.CreateNode(XmlNodeType.Attribute, "", "type", "")
        attr.Value = "First Person Shooter"
        game.Attributes.Append(attr)

        games.AppendChild(game)

        doc.Save("games.xml")

    End Sub

End Module
```

As you can see, this code produces the same result using more code. However, it allows you to write code that treats all of the objects as nodes. The decision of which approach to use is based on your stylistic fancy.

Saving XML Documents

The examples shown so far in this chapter have saved the generated XML documents to a file using the `Save` method on the `XmlDocument` class. The `Save` method uses the filename passed as a String to the method for saving the XML content to a file.

In fact, there are several versions of the `Save` method that collectively use a `String`, `System.IO.Stream`, `System.IO.TextWriter`, or a `System.Xml.XmlWriter` to save the content of the XML document.

The `Console.Out` property is an instance of `System.IO.TextWriter` that can be used to output text to the console window. Therefore, you can display the content of an XML document by calling the object's save method and passing in the `Console.Out` object. For example:

```
doc.Save(Console.Out)
```

The `System.Xml.XmlWriter` class supports writing out an XML document to a file. The `XmlWriter` class also provides more support for indentation in the generated XML file. This is accomplished through the use of the `Formatting`, `Indentation`, and `IndentChar` properties of the `XmlWriter` class.

The `Formatting` property is an enumeration that can contain one of two possible values—`Indented` or `None`. If this property is set to `Indented`, the `Indentation` property contains the number of characters to be indented for each level in the XML structure. The `IdentChar` property contains the character used for indenting. This is a space character by default.

If the `Formatting` property is set to `None`, no indenting is performed in the saved XML file.

Using the document object created in the preceding examples, here is an example that saves the document without formatting:

```
Dim writer As XmlTextWriter
writer = New XmlTextWriter("games1.xml", System.Text.Encoding.UTF8)
doc.WriteTo(writer)
writer.Flush()
writer.Close()
```

The generated output is this:

```
<?xml version="1.0"?><ComputerGames><Game name="Diablo II" type="RPG"
/><Game name="Quake III" type="First Person Shooter" /><Game name="Unreal
Tournament" type="First Person Shooter" /></ComputerGames>
```

Now, let's turn on the formatting so that the saved file contains some visible indentation.

```
Dim writer As XmlTextWriter
writer = New XmlTextWriter("games2.xml", System.Text.Encoding.UTF8)
writer.Formatting = Formatting.Indented
writer.Indentation = 4
doc.WriteTo(writer)
writer.Flush()
writer.Close()
```

The `Formatting` property is set to `Indented`, causing the outputted XML to be indented. The indentation is set to four characters wide. Here is the generated XML file based on the previous code:

```
<?xml version="1.0"?>
<ComputerGames>
    <Game name="Diablo II" type="RPG" />
    <Game name="Quake III Arena" type="First Person Shooter" />
    <Game name="Unreal Tournament" type="First Person Shooter" />
</ComputerGames>
```

XSL Transformations

XSL (eXtensible Stylesheet Language) is very useful for generating custom displays based on XML. If you don't know XSL already, we encourage you to learn more about this powerful technology as it is being leveraged more and more by maturing applications.

XSL is used to transform XML documents into another XML document or another format such as HTML. The XML document is used as a data source for the stylesheet. The stylesheet uses the XSL language to select content from the XML document and to output the content in another format. The format is totally defined by the stylesheet.

XSL is used today in applications for the purpose of generating HTML pages using XML documents that contain the data for the particular page. This allows a clean separation between the data and how the data is displayed on a Web page. XSL is also used for generating other XML documents or combining XML documents.

The Microsoft .NET Framework Class Library provides support for XSL primarily through the use of the `System.Xml.Xsl.XslTransform` class. This section, once again, assumes you have working knowledge of XML and XSL. If you require more information regarding XML, you may want to read "XML, DTD, and XML Schema Fundamentals," on our Web site before continuing. For more information on XSL, you can visit `http://www.w3.org/TR/xslt`.

To show how you can transform an XML document using XSL, we are going to walk through an example that generates an XML document and then transforms the document to HTML using XSL. Create a Console application project for the purpose of this example. To create the XML document, the example code needs to use reflection to get a list of all the interfaces and classes in the System.XML assembly.

NOTE

Reflection allows you to write code that can read and interpret running code. For example, using reflection you can write code that figures out classes that exist in an assembly, or the methods that are defined as part of a class, or even the number and types of parameters to a method.

Here is the code to generate the XML document:

```
Imports System.Xml

Module Module1

    Sub Main()

        Dim doc As XmlDocument = New XmlDocument()
        Dim classLib As XmlElement
        Dim ns As XmlElement
        Dim member As XmlElement
        Dim attr As XmlAttribute
        Dim assemblyName As String = "System.Xml"
        Dim objAssembly As System.Reflection.Assembly
        Dim types() As System.Type
        Dim t As System.Type

        ' use reflection to obtain the assembly
        objAssembly = System.Reflection.Assembly.LoadWithPartialName(assemblyName)
        types = objAssembly.GetTypes()

        ' create the xml declaration header for the document
        doc.AppendChild(doc.CreateXmlDeclaration("1.0", "", ""))

        ' create a new element and add it to the document
        ' (making it the root element)
        classLib = doc.CreateElement("ClassLibrary")
        doc.AppendChild(classLib)

        ' create an element for the namespace
        ns = doc.CreateElement("Namespace")
```

```
            ns.SetAttribute("name", assemblyName)
            classLib.AppendChild(ns)

            ' create elements for all of the public interfaces
            ' and public classes in this namespace
            For Each t In types
                If t.IsInterface And t.IsPublic Then
                    member = doc.CreateElement("Interface")
                    member.SetAttribute("name", t.Name)
                    ns.AppendChild(member)
                ElseIf t.IsAnsiClass And t.IsPublic And Not t.IsInterface Then
                    member = doc.CreateElement("Class")
                    member.SetAttribute("name", t.Name)
                    ns.AppendChild(member)
                End If
            Next

            ' save the document to a file
            Dim writer As XmlTextWriter
            writer = New XmlTextWriter("example.xml", System.Text.Encoding.UTF8)
            writer.Formatting = Formatting.Indented
            writer.Indentation = 4
            doc.WriteTo(writer)
            writer.Flush()
            writer.Close()

    End Sub

End Module
```

The result of this code generates a file named `example.xml` that contains the XML content regarding the interfaces and classes defined in the `System.Xml` assembly. Note that the classes and interface elements are intermingled under the Namespace element. Here is the resulting XML file:

```
<?xml version="1.0"?>
<ClassLibrary>
    <Namespace name="System.Xml">
        <Class name="XPathNavigator" />
        <Interface name="IHasXmlNode" />
        <Class name="XPathNodeIterator" />
        <Class name="EntityHandling" />
        <Interface name="IXmlLineInfo" />
        <Class name="XmlNameTable" />
        <Class name="NameTable" />
        <Class name="ReadState" />
        <Class name="ValidationType" />
```

```
<Class name="WhitespaceHandling" />
<Interface name="IXPathNavigable" />
<Class name="XmlNode" />
<Class name="XmlAttribute" />
<Class name="XmlNamedNodeMap" />
<Class name="XmlAttributeCollection" />
<Class name="XmlLinkedNode" />
<Class name="XmlCharacterData" />
<Class name="XmlCDataSection" />
<Class name="XmlNodeList" />
<Class name="XmlComment" />
<Class name="XmlConvert" />
<Class name="XmlDeclaration" />
<Class name="XmlDocument" />
<Class name="XmlDocumentFragment" />
<Class name="XmlDocumentType" />
<Class name="XmlWriter" />
<Class name="XmlTextWriter" />
<Class name="XmlElement" />
<Class name="XmlEntity" />
<Class name="XmlReader" />
<Class name="XmlTextReader" />
<Class name="XmlEntityReference" />
<Class name="XmlNodeChangedAction" />
<Class name="XmlException" />
<Class name="XmlImplementation" />
<Class name="XmlNamespaceManager" />
<Class name="XmlNodeChangedEventArgs" />
<Class name="XmlNodeChangedEventHandler" />
<Class name="XmlNodeOrder" />
<Class name="XmlNodeReader" />
<Class name="XmlNodeType" />
<Class name="XmlNotation" />
<Class name="XmlParserContext" />
<Class name="XmlProcessingInstruction" />
<Class name="XmlQualifiedName" />
<Class name="XmlResolver" />
<Class name="XmlSignificantWhitespace" />
<Class name="XmlSpace" />
<Class name="XmlText" />
<Class name="XmlTokenizedType" />
<Class name="XmlUrlResolver" />
<Class name="XmlValidatingReader" />
<Class name="XmlWhitespace" />
<Class name="Formatting" />
<Class name="WriteState" />
```

```
<Class name="XPathExpression" />
<Class name="XsltContext" />
<Class name="XPathDocument" />
<Class name="XPathException" />
<Class name="XmlSortOrder" />
<Class name="XmlCaseOrder" />
<Class name="XmlDataType" />
<Class name="XPathResultType" />
<Class name="XPathNamespaceScope" />
<Class name="XPathNodeType" />
<Interface name="IXsltContextVariable" />
<Class name="XsltArgumentList" />
<Interface name="IXsltContextFunction" />
<Class name="XsltException" />
<Class name="XsltCompileException" />
<Class name="XslTransform" />
<Class name="XmlSchemaDatatype" />
<Class name="ValidationEventArgs" />
<Class name="ValidationEventHandler" />
<Class name="XmlSchemaObject" />
<Class name="XmlSchema" />
<Class name="XmlSchemaAnnotated" />
<Class name="XmlSchemaParticle" />
<Class name="XmlSchemaGroupBase" />
<Class name="XmlSchemaAll" />
<Class name="XmlSchemaAnnotation" />
<Class name="XmlSchemaAny" />
<Class name="XmlSchemaAnyAttribute" />
<Class name="XmlSchemaAppInfo" />
<Class name="XmlSchemaAttribute" />
<Class name="XmlSchemaAttributeGroup" />
<Class name="XmlSchemaAttributeGroupRef" />
<Class name="XmlSchemaChoice" />
<Class name="XmlSchemaCollection" />
<Class name="XmlSchemaCollectionEnumerator" />
<Class name="XmlSchemaContentModel" />
<Class name="XmlSchemaComplexContent" />
<Class name="XmlSchemaContent" />
<Class name="XmlSchemaComplexContentExtension" />
<Class name="XmlSchemaComplexContentRestriction" />
<Class name="XmlSchemaType" />
<Class name="XmlSchemaComplexType" />
<Class name="XmlSchemaContentProcessing" />
```

```
<Class name="XmlSchemaContentType" />
<Class name="XmlSchemaDerivationMethod" />
<Class name="XmlSchemaDocumentation" />
<Class name="XmlSchemaElement" />
<Class name="XmlSchemaException" />
<Class name="XmlSchemaExternal" />
<Class name="XmlSchemaFacet" />
<Class name="XmlSchemaNumericFacet" />
<Class name="XmlSchemaLengthFacet" />
<Class name="XmlSchemaMinLengthFacet" />
<Class name="XmlSchemaMaxLengthFacet" />
<Class name="XmlSchemaPatternFacet" />
<Class name="XmlSchemaEnumerationFacet" />
<Class name="XmlSchemaMinExclusiveFacet" />
<Class name="XmlSchemaMinInclusiveFacet" />
<Class name="XmlSchemaMaxExclusiveFacet" />
<Class name="XmlSchemaMaxInclusiveFacet" />
<Class name="XmlSchemaTotalDigitsFacet" />
<Class name="XmlSchemaFractionDigitsFacet" />
<Class name="XmlSchemaWhiteSpaceFacet" />
<Class name="XmlSchemaForm" />
<Class name="XmlSchemaGroup" />
<Class name="XmlSchemaGroupRef" />
<Class name="XmlSchemaIdentityConstraint" />
<Class name="XmlSchemaXPath" />
<Class name="XmlSchemaUnique" />
<Class name="XmlSchemaKey" />
<Class name="XmlSchemaKeyref" />
<Class name="XmlSchemaImport" />
<Class name="XmlSchemaInclude" />
<Class name="XmlSchemaNotation" />
<Class name="XmlSchemaObjectCollection" />
<Class name="XmlSchemaObjectEnumerator" />
<Class name="XmlSchemaObjectTable" />
<Class name="XmlSchemaRedefine" />
<Class name="XmlSchemaSequence" />
<Class name="XmlSchemaSimpleContent" />
<Class name="XmlSchemaSimpleContentExtension" />
<Class name="XmlSchemaSimpleContentRestriction" />
<Class name="XmlSchemaSimpleType" />
<Class name="XmlSchemaSimpleTypeContent" />
<Class name="XmlSchemaSimpleTypeList" />
<Class name="XmlSchemaSimpleTypeRestriction" />
```

```
<Class name="XmlSchemaSimpleTypeUnion" />
<Class name="XmlSchemaUse" />
<Class name="XmlSeverityType" />
<Class name="XmlAttributeEventHandler" />
<Class name="XmlAttributeEventArgs" />
<Class name="XmlElementEventHandler" />
<Class name="XmlElementEventArgs" />
<Class name="XmlNodeEventHandler" />
<Class name="XmlNodeEventArgs" />
<Class name="UnreferencedObjectEventHandler" />
<Class name="UnreferencedObjectEventArgs" />
<Class name="CodeIdentifier" />
<Class name="CodeIdentifiers" />
<Interface name="IXmlSerializable" />
<Class name="SoapAttributeAttribute" />
<Class name="SoapAttributeOverrides" />
<Class name="SoapAttributes" />
<Class name="SoapCodeExporter" />
<Class name="SoapElementAttribute" />
<Class name="SoapEnumAttribute" />
<Class name="SoapIgnoreAttribute" />
<Class name="SoapIncludeAttribute" />
<Class name="SoapReflectionImporter" />
<Class name="SoapSchemaExporter" />
<Class name="SoapSchemaImporter" />
<Class name="SoapSchemaMember" />
<Class name="SoapTypeAttribute" />
<Class name="XmlAnyAttributeAttribute" />
<Class name="XmlAnyElementAttribute" />
<Class name="XmlAnyElementAttributes" />
<Class name="XmlArrayAttribute" />
<Class name="XmlArrayItemAttribute" />
<Class name="XmlArrayItemAttributes" />
<Class name="XmlAttributeAttribute" />
<Class name="XmlAttributeOverrides" />
<Class name="XmlAttributes" />
<Class name="XmlChoiceIdentifierAttribute" />
<Class name="XmlElementAttribute" />
<Class name="XmlElementAttributes" />
<Class name="XmlEnumAttribute" />
<Class name="XmlIgnoreAttribute" />
<Class name="XmlIncludeAttribute" />
```

```
        <Class name="XmlMapping" />
        <Class name="XmlMemberMapping" />
        <Class name="XmlMembersMapping" />
        <Class name="XmlReflectionImporter" />
        <Class name="XmlReflectionMember" />
        <Class name="XmlRootAttribute" />
        <Class name="XmlSchemaExporter" />
        <Class name="XmlSchemas" />
        <Class name="XmlSerializationReader" />
        <Class name="XmlSerializationFixupCallback" />
        <Class name="XmlSerializationCollectionFixupCallback" />
        <Class name="XmlSerializationReadCallback" />
        <Class name="XmlSerializationWriter" />
        <Class name="XmlSerializationWriteCallback" />
        <Class name="XmlSerializer" />
        <Class name="XmlSerializerNamespaces" />
        <Class name="XmlTextAttribute" />
        <Class name="XmlTypeAttribute" />
        <Class name="XmlTypeMapping" />
        <Class name="XmlCodeExporter" />
        <Class name="XmlSchemaImporter" />
    </Namespace>
</ClassLibrary>
```

Now, to transform this document into HTML using XSL we need to have an XSL document defined that describes the transformation. Here is a simple XSL document, named example.xsl, that creates an HTML document containing a list of interfaces and a list of classes. Note that the result contains two lists, one of interfaces and one of classes. This does not require the XML data to be in any particular order.

```
<?xml version="1.0"?>

<xsl:stylesheet xmlns:xsl="http://www.w3.org/1999/XSL/Transform" version="1.0">

<xsl:template match="/">
  <html>
    <head>
      <title>Microsoft.NET Class Library</title>
    </head>
    <body>
      <xsl:apply-templates select="*"/>
    </body>
  </html>
</xsl:template>
```

```
<xsl:template match="Namespace">
  <h1><xsl:value-of select="@name"/></h1>
  <h2>Interfaces:</h2>
  <xsl:apply-templates select="./Interface"/>
  <h2>Classes:</h2>
  <xsl:apply-templates select="./Class"/>
</xsl:template>

<xsl:template match="Interface">
  <p><xsl:value-of select="@name"/></p>
</xsl:template>

<xsl:template match="Class">
  <p><xsl:value-of select="@name"/></p>
</xsl:template>

</xsl:stylesheet>
```

By applying this XSL template onto the generated XML document, we can generate an HTML file with the display we want. To actually perform the transformation, you need to use the XslTransform class. The following code loads the XSL document into an instance of the XslTransform class and then calls the Transform method to evaluate the stylesheet.

Add the following code to the code shown in the previous example. The code should be added at the end of the Sub Main procedure. Keep in mind the resulting HTML file is created in the bin folder under the current project's folder.

```
' now transform the xml file to html
Dim transformer As System.Xml.Xsl.XslTransform
transformer = New System.Xml.Xsl.XslTransform()
transformer.Load("example.xsl")
transformer.Transform("example.xml", "example.html")
```

The Transform method takes two arguments. The first argument is the source XML file, and the second argument is the resulting file that contains the output of the transformation process.

Figure 34.1 shows the resulting HTML file visible in a browser.

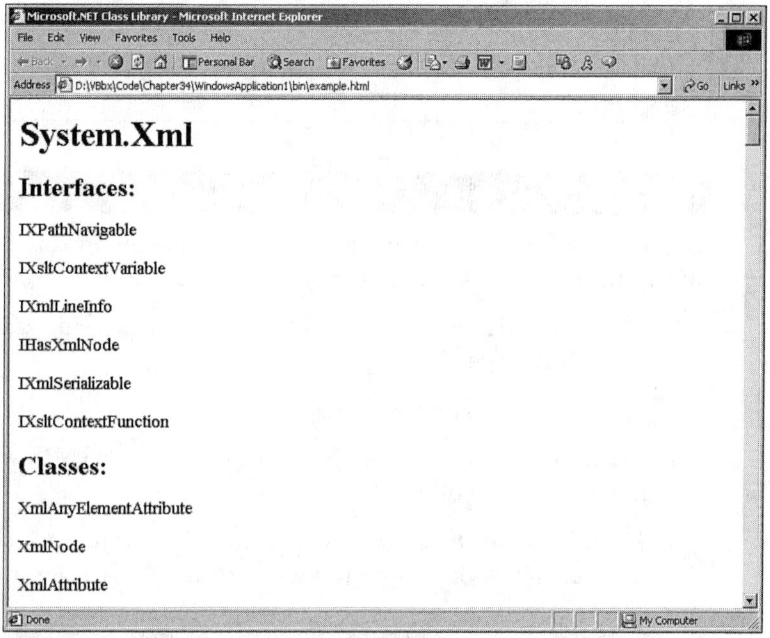

Figure 34.1: Example HTML.

What's Next

This chapter explained how to generate XML documents using the classes provided in the Microsoft .NET Framework Class Library. In addition to generating the XML documents directly through code, an example was shown on how to generate another file containing XML or HTML from a source XML document. You should now be able to generate your own XML documents using Microsoft .NET.

The next chapter starts to introduce Visual Basic .NET and Web development. This involves explaining Web Forms and examples showing how to build Web Forms using Visual Basic .NET. The next few chapters are useful if you are interested in Web development using Microsoft .NET, but they are not extensive coverage of the topic. If you plan on developing Web applications using Microsoft.NET, you should read a book that specifically targets Web development after you finish reading the next few chapters.

NOTE

The answers to "Reviewing It," "Checking It," and "Applying It" are available on our Web site.

REVIEW

Reviewing It

This section presents a review of the key concepts in this chapter. These questions are intended to gauge your absorption of the relevant material.

1. How are XML documents created and saved using the Visual Basic .NET language?

2. What are XML namespaces used for?

3. If I wanted to convert an XML document to HTML, what is a good approach to doing this?

4. In addition to the classes shown in this chapter, are there more classes in Microsoft .NET that support additional XML features?

CHECK

Checking It

Select the correct answer to the following questions.

Multiple Choice

1. How do you define the `<?xml version="1.0"?>` markup in an XML document?

   a. Use the `CreateXmlElement` method on the `XmlDocument` class.

   b. Use the `CreateXmlDeclaration` method on the `XmlDocument` class.

   c. Use the `CreateXmlHeader` method on the `XmlDocument` class.

   d. All of the above.

2. How do you create elements in an XML document?

   a. Use the `CreateXmlElement` method on the `XmlDocument` class.

   b. Use the `CreateElement` method on the `XmlDocument` class.

   c. Use `new XmlElement()` to instantiate a new element object.

   d. All of the above.

3. How do you set an attribute value on an element?

   a. Call the SetAttribute method on an XmlElement object.

   b. Use the CreateNode method to create an attribute, set the attribute's Value property, and then append it to the element.

   c. Set the Value property of the XmlAttribute object.

   d. All of the above.

4. How to you create comments in an XML document?

   a. Call the CreateComment method on the XmlDocument class.

   b. There is no easy way to do this.

   c. Comments are useless and should be avoided.

   d. None of the above.

5. How do you save text data in an XML document?

   a. Call the CreateTextNode method on the XmlDocument class and then append the node to an existing node in the document.

   b. Call the CreateCDataSection method on the XmlDocument class and then append the node to an existing node in the document.

   c. Call the CreateNode method on the XmlDocument class and then append the node to an existing node in the document.

   d. All of the above.

6. How do you save an XML document including indentation?

   a. This is by default when saving.

   b. Use an XmlTextWriter object and specify the Formatting and Indentation properties.

   c. Use XSL.

   d. None of the above.

True or False

Select one of the two possible answers and then verify on our Web site that you picked the correct one.

1. The classes used to generate XML documents do not support defining namespaces.

   True/False

2. XSL is used to transform XML documents into another file format defined by the rules in the XSL stylesheet.

   True/False

3. Indentation in XML is turned off by default.

   True/False

4. The CreateNode method on the XmlDocument class supports creating any type of node within an XML document.

   True/False

5. The XmlConvert class is used to convert several data types to string values for the purpose of saving into an XML document.

   True/False

Applying It

Try to complete the following exercise by yourself.

APPLY

Independent Exercise

Start with the example code used to generate the interfaces and classes in the System.XML namespace and expand it to include the methods defined in the interfaces and classes. Also, update the XSL stylesheet so that the methods are outputting to the generated HTML file.

Part VI

Developing for the Web

Introduction to Web Forms

Developing Applications for the Web

Web Services

35

Introduction to Web Forms

The chapters in this part of the book are dedicated to teaching the basis of developing distributed applications that run on the World Wide Web (or, in short, Web applications). We'll discuss the following topics:

- Fundamental concepts
- The first Web application
- The Web Forms properties and methods
- Controls used on Web Forms
- The event model of a Web Form

We will start by looking at the fundamental concepts required to understand how a Web application works. We will compare a Web application with a normal Visual Basic .NET application and point out the common characteristics and the major differences.

Next you will create a simple Web application, consisting of one Web Form (one page), and you will compile and run the application.

Next you will learn the most important properties and methods of a Web Form and how to use them.

You will then look at some of the most common controls used on a Web Form and their properties.

Lastly you will look at the event model for a Web Form, compared to the event model for a regular WinForm. You will use a more complete example, including retrieving and modifying data from a database.

Fundamental Concepts

The Internet is a large network of computers, which are exchanging information in various formats, using a number of *protocols*. You can think of a *protocol* as a convention (or a set of conventions) that describes the formatting of data exchanged between the computers of this network. You have to keep in mind that the Internet is made of a very large number of interconnected computers of various types (from large mainframes to small wireless devices), running an even larger variety of operating systems (all flavors of Windows, Unix, and so on). To ensure that the applications running on all these computers can exchange data in a useful fashion, a number of protocols have been adopted over time. One of the most commonly used is the HTTP protocol, which is the basis for the World Wide Web (WWW). This is the protocol that is used when you browse the Internet.

NOTE

The description of the Internet, the WWW, and the protocols that govern the data exchange are presented only as a superficial overview. There are books and specifications dedicated to the detailed presentation of the architecture of the Internet and the protocols used. One good resource is *A Guide to the TCP/IP Protocol Suite, Second Edition*, by Floyd Wilder (Artech House, 1998, 089006976X). Another is *TCP/IP Illustrated, Vol. 1: The Protocols*, by W. Richard Stevens (Addison-Wesley, 1994, 0201633469). We will just introduce the fundamental concepts required to learn how to develop a Web application using the .NET Framework and Visual Studio .NET.

The HTTP protocol is a *stateless* protocol. A client application (normally a Web browser) connects to a Web server and submits a request to the server. The server sends back a response to the client's request and closes the connection to the client. Hence the stateless: The server does not maintain state (information about the clients connecting to it).

NOTE

You will see later on that this fact can become an issue in some applications that require the server to maintain state. You will learn about state and how to maintain it in Chapter 36, "Developing Applications for the Web."

The request is normally in the format of a Universal Resource Locator (URL). This normally means a request for an HTML page, like the one that follows. You can enter the following example in a browser's address line and see what happens.

```
http://www.yahoo.com/index.html
```

The first part of the URL (http:) is the protocol used (HTTP in this case). The protocol is followed by a server name, in this case it is //www.yahoo. com. The rest of the URL consists of the name of a file and eventually some other data. In our example this is `/index.html`. Translated into English the request means: Give me the file `/index.html` from the server `//www.yahoo.com` using the HTTP protocol.

Keep in mind that the actual requests can be more complicated than this example shows; the file can be missing completely, or it may not be a file, or it may be an offset into a file. The filename can be followed by some parameters (known as a query string). We will explain some of these cases as we encounter them in the rest of the chapters in Part VI.

The browser takes the request you enter, parses it, and tries to connect the server you specified. It then uses the HTTP protocol to get the page you requested. If the server cannot be found, or the page that you requested is not available on the server, you will get an error. One of the most common errors is the HTTP 404 error `Page not found`, which means that the server does not have the HTML page you requested.

The pages requested are normally in a format known as HTML (Hyper-Text Markup Language). The HTML format is widely used by servers and recognized by all browsers. It consists of text formatted in a certain way, using markup tags. These tags and the general syntax of HTML are similar to the XML syntax you have studied in the previous chapters. It is beyond the scope of this book to discuss the HTML syntax. And as you will see, using Visual Studio .NET makes direct editing of the HTML pages rather unnecessary. If you wish to look closer into the HTML specification, you can go to the site `http://www.w3.org/MarkUp`.

As you probably know, HTML pages can contain links to other pages; they can be used to gather user input, display query results, and in general act in a similar fashion to an application. The development of a *Web application* consists of developing a group of related pages and deploying them on a Web server.

Web applications developed using Visual Studio .NET use ASP.NET, part of the .NET Framework, to develop the pages and the Internet Information Server (IIS) as a Web server. The pages developed with Visual Studio .NET are also known as *Web Forms*. These forms are similar to regular Visual Basic .NET forms: They have properties and events and may contain other controls. Therefore, a Web application developed in Visual Studio .NET consists of a number of Web Forms and a few auxiliary files.

When the application is built, the Web Forms are compiled and deployed under the IIS server. When a client requests a page represented by a Web Form, the server translates the output of the page to an HTML page and sends it to the client requesting the page.

We will continue with an example of how to develop a simple Web application with one Web Form.

The First Web Application

You will now look at the steps involved in creating and deploying a Web application. Your tasks as developer of a Web application consist of the following:

1. Create the project for the Web application.

2. Create the Web Forms, which are part of the project.

3. Add controls to the Web Forms.

4. Add code to handle events for the form(s).

5. Build and run the application.

The first step is relatively simple. In the Visual Studio .NET create a new project and select the ASP.NET Web application, give it a name, and select a location on the IIS server where the project will be deployed.

> **NOTE**
>
> You need IIS version 5 or later and .NET Framework installed, with the latest service packs installed on the machine that will be the Web server. During development time, this will normally be your machine.

The wizard will create the project and a number of files for you. These files are as follows:

- `Web.config`—An XML configuration file that holds information for all forms used in the project.

- `Global.asax`—An optional file that handles application-level events. It is named `Global.asax.vb` in its uncompiled form.

- `Styles.css`—This is a supporting style-sheet file used in the project.

- `AssemblyInfo.vb`—This is a file that contains information about the assemblies used in the project.

- `<ProjectName>.vsdisco`—This is an XML discovery file, and it contains links to resources providing discovery information for Web Services used.

- `WebForm1.aspx`—This is a Web Form generated by the project wizard for you. It also has a related `WebForm1.aspx.vb` file, which contains the code behind the page, your code, which handles the miscellaneous events fired by the page.

We will spend most of our development efforts in modifying the design of the Web Form and adding event handler code to the .vb file that underlies the Web Form. When the project wizard is finished, you will notice that this is the only window open. A Web Form inherits from the class Page in the System.Web.UI assembly.

Next add a label to the form. From the Toolbox select the WebForms tab. Click on the Label control and then draw a label on the form.

The label is now selected, and its properties are displayed. Change the Text property to "Hello Web World" or any text you wish. At this point you should see something similar to Figure 35.1.

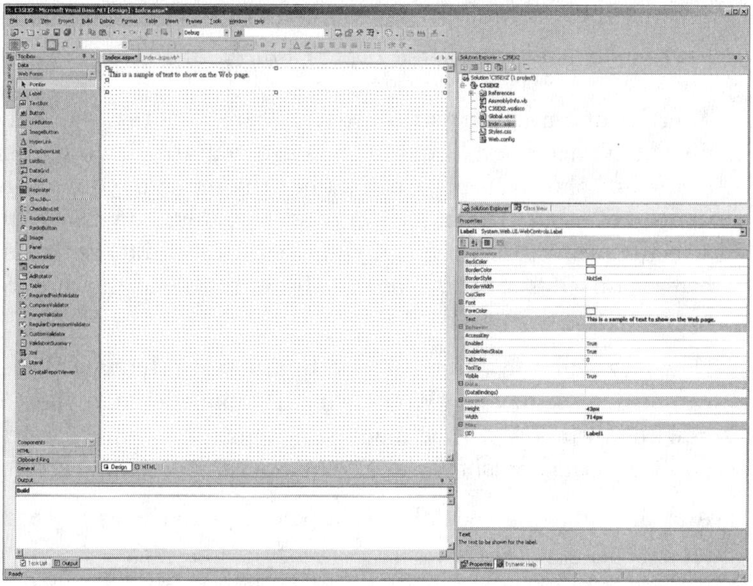

Figure 35.1: *The first Web Form.*

You probably have noticed that the Web Forms Label has a different set of properties compared to the Label used in WinForms. We will look at these properties more closely a bit later.

You can now build and run the Web application. You will notice that the Internet Explorer (or your selected browser) is activated, and the page displayed should look like the one shown in Figure 35.2.

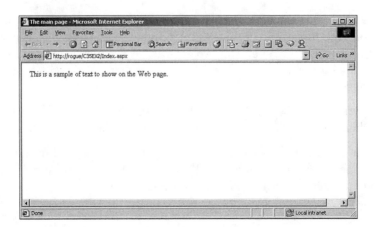

Figure 35.2: *The first Web Form running in IE.*

There is not much to your first Web form: The text you entered is displayed. Notice the address of the page you are viewing, it should be similar to the one shown in Figure 35.2, but the name of your server is shown instead of rogue (the name of my server). Also the project name you have selected (WebApplication1, if you used the default) replaces the name of the project I used (C35EX2). Close the browser to end the application and return to the IDE.

Now let's add a few lines of code to illustrate the way Visual Basic .NET can be used to develop Web Forms. Double-click anywhere on the form. A new code window will be displayed (Index.aspx.vb). You will see some code similar to the one shown in Figure 35.3.

Add the following code shown in bold type to the Page_Load event handler:

```
Private Sub Page_Load(ByVal sender As System.Object, _
                    ByVal e As System.EventArgs) _
    Handles MyBase.Load
    Label1.Text = "You are using " + Request.Browser.Type + _
                " version " + Request.Browser.Version
End Sub
```

When the Web Form loads (which is somewhat similar to a regular WinForm Load event) the Page_Load event handler is called. We use this opportunity to detect the type and version of the browser the client calling us is using. We achieve this by using the Request object, a property of our base class Page. The Request property returns an object of type HttpRequest, which wraps a lot of information about the client that called us. We will make use of this object and its counterpart, the Response object, in a few places in our code.

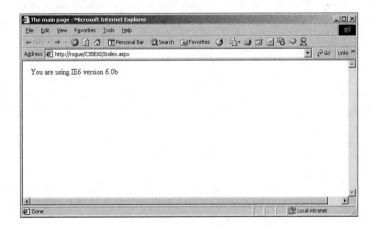

Figure 35.3: *Adding code to the Web Form.*

If you run the application again, you will notice that the text shown now in the browser indicates the type and version of the browser you are using. You should get something like Figure 35.4.

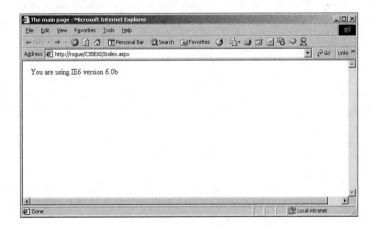

Figure 35.4: *Running the Web Form again.*

Web Form Properties and Methods

You have seen briefly that a Web Form consists of two elements: the actual page (the .aspx file) and the code behind it (the .aspx.vb file, also known as the code-behind-the-page class).

The actual page properties can be seen in the visual property editor, after clicking anywhere on the page. Some of the most used ones are summarized here:

- $aLink$—The color of all active links (to other URLs) in the document
- $vLink$—The color of visited links on the page
- $link$—The color of unvisited links on the page
- $background$—A picture tiled as a background for the page (if provided)
- $bgProperties$—The properties of the picture (if any)
- $bgColor$—Page background color
- $text$—Page foreground (text) color
- $pageLayout$—The model of the page layout (can be $Grid$ or $Flow$)
- $title$—Title of the page

There are also other properties like margins, language, and culture settings, keywords associated with the page, debug and trace settings, and others, which are self-explanatory. Another subset of properties includes the more advanced properties. We will explain some of these properties when we encounter them.

At this point you will look at some of the most important properties and methods of the $Page$ class, which is the base class for your Web page. The $Page$ class inherits from the $TemplateControl$ class, which in turn inherits from the $Control$ class.

The $Control$ is the base class for all ASP.NET controls. It defines the properties, methods, and events that are the base for all controls in ASP.NET and for any custom controls created by you. It can contain other controls, and it has a $Controls$ collection that contains references to these controls. Among the most notable properties of the $Control$ class are

- ID—The name (programmatic identifier) of the control.
- $Visible$—Is $True$ if the control is visible (not hidden).
- $Controls$—A collection of the controls that are contained within this control (applies to container controls only).

- **EnableViewState**—Indicates whether the control preserves its view state between calls. More on this property when we learn of state management in the next chapter.

- **Parent**—The container of this control. It is Nothing if the control is a Page.

The TemplateControl is the base for the Page and UserControl classes and provides them with a basic implementation of the properties and methods in the Control base class. It does not add any properties, but it has a few extra methods.

We will now enumerate some of the most important and/or often used properties of the Page class:

- **IsPostBack**—If true, the page is loaded as a response to a post-back from the client; otherwise, it is loaded for the first time.

- **Session**—Gets the session object (an instance of HttpSessionState class) as provided by the ASP.NET infrastructure. This object has session state information properties about one user connection.

- **Server**—An object representing the server (HttpServerUtility). It has a few general HTTP and URL utility methods.

- **Request**—The HTTP request object (HttpRequest). It provides access to the request object from the client. Useful in getting properties about the client browser, language, and so on.

- **Response**—The HTTP response object (HttpResponse). It provides access to the response that goes out to the client and can be used to write directly to the output as text or binary.

- **User**—Information about the user making the request (an instance of an implementation of the IPrincipal interface).

- **ErrorPage**—A string indicating the error page to which the user is redirected if an unhandled error occurs while processing this page.

Before we explain and exemplify the use of some of these properties you need to understand how the Web page is constructed at runtime, when a client makes a request.

Figure 35.5 shows the sequence of events that takes place when a client makes a request for a new Web page. When the page is first requested, the server (using ASP.NET runtime services) loads the page, fires the appropriate events, (for example, Load), and then renders the page to an HTML document. This rendering is based on the form design you have done in Visual Studio .NET. Then the rendered form is shipped back to the client browser, which displays its contents. The Web Form is unloaded after rendering it. The server may cache the class, the HTML output, or both.

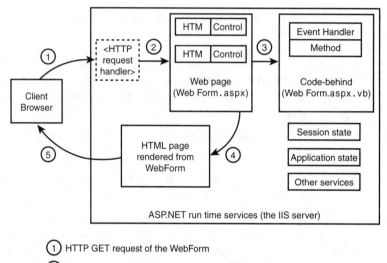

1. HTTP GET request of the WebForm
2. The WebForm aspx is actuated
3. Load event is fired (in the code-behind)
4. The WebForm page is rendered to HTML
5. The HTML output is returned to the client

Figure 35.5: *Runtime handling of the Web page.*

When the user takes some action that requires the form to fire an event, the form sends a message to the server, requesting the server to execute the appropriate event handler on the code-behind class, and then re-render the form. This is known as a *post-back* request, and it is used to update data on the form as a result of the user typing in a query of some sort. A similar set of steps occurs in the case of a *post-back*: The form is loaded (but the IsPostBack property is true this time), and the appropriate event is fired (for example a button click event). Then the form is rendered again and re-sent to the client browser, eventually with modified data.

Because HTTP is a stateless protocol, the server has no standard means to determine that it is the same client that is reconnecting to do a post-back, versus a new client requesting the same page. This is a problem that can be solved in a few different ways, using the server or the client, each one with advantages and disadvantages. One of these mechanisms (server-side) is keeping a state of the client session on the server (hence the Session property of the Page). Other state-keeping mechanisms include use of cookies, hidden fields, and using query-strings, which are all client-side mechanisms. These mechanisms are discussed in detail in the next chapter.

The Request and Response objects can be used to get and set data about the HTTP request/response. The Response can be used to construct the HTML page on-the-fly, by outputting HTML tags directly to the output stream. The following example uses some of these properties to construct a dynamic HTML page. In a new ASP.NET Web application project, add this code to the .vb file (and no controls on the page).

```
Private Sub Page_Load(ByVal sender As System.Object, _
                      ByVal e As System.EventArgs) _
    Handles MyBase.Load
    Response.Write("<p><b>Browser Capabilities:</b></p>")
    Response.Write("Type = " & Request.Browser.Type & "<br>")
    Response.Write("Name = " & Request.Browser.Browser & "<br>")
    Response.Write("Version = " & Request.Browser.Version & "<br>")
    Response.Write("Platform = " & Request.Browser.Platform & "<br>")
    Response.Write("<br>")
    Response.Write("Machine name = " & Server.MachineName & "<br>")
    Response.Write("<br>")
    Response.Write("User name = " & User.Identity.Name & "<br>")
    Response.Write("<br>")
    Response.Write("Session ID = " & Session.SessionID & "<br>")
End Sub
```

You will probably notice that the User.Identity.Name is empty; this is because the user was not authenticated (using some sort of login dialog); therefore the user is unknown.

Controls Used on Web Forms

There are two categories of visual controls that can be used to construct Web forms: HTML controls and Web controls. We used the Web control Label in the first example in this chapter.

The HTML controls are grouped in the System.Web.UI.HtmlControls namespace. These controls are a collection of classes that map directly to the standard HTML tags supported by Internet browsers. Using this type of controls allows you to use a scripting language (like JavaScript) to control programmatically the elements of the HTML page. If you are familiar with HTML and ASP development, you may want to use these types of controls. These controls are not discussed in this book because they have almost no connection with the Visual Basic .NET language.

NOTE

The HTML controls can be used as server-side controls, in which case you can write VB code to handle some events. However, the same or better functionality is achieved using the Web controls.

The Web controls are more involved in terms of properties and events, and they have a close resemblance to the regular WinForm controls that you have seen so far in the book. For example there are controls like `Label`, `TextBox`, `Button`, `DropDownList`, `Image`, and so on. We will look in more detail at these controls next.

The next example illustrates a few of the most common controls placed on a page. In Figure 35.6 you can see the Web page design.

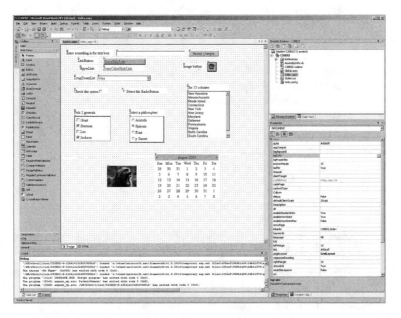

Figure 35.6: *A Web page with common controls.*

And in Figure 35.7 you can see the page in the browser.

All the controls in the namespace `System.Web.UI.WebControls` are derived from the base class `WebControl`, which itself is derived from `Control`. The `WebControl` class implements a set of common properties, methods, and events common to all the Web controls. It has the usual set of UI properties (`AccessKey`, `BackColor`, `ForeColor`, `BorderColor`, `BorderStyle`, `BorderWidth`, `Font`, `Height`, `Width`, `Enabled`, `TabIndex`, and `ToolTip`). The `ID` property (inherited from `Control`) represents the name of the control. The `Page` property (also inherited from `Control`) represents the page this control is on.

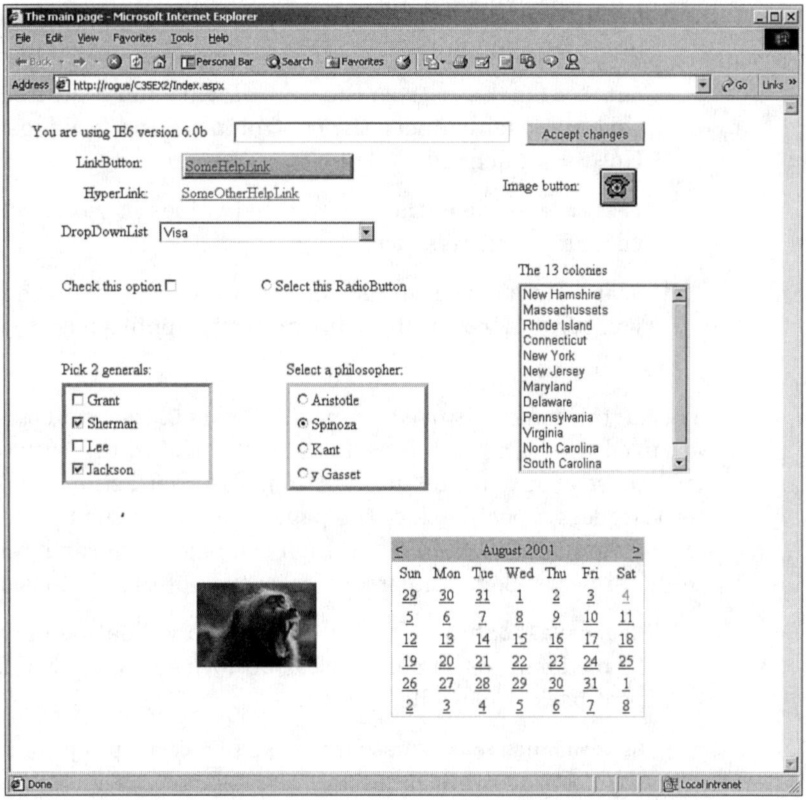

Figure 35.7: *The Web page from Figure 35.6, running in the browser.*

The Label control serves the same purpose as the Label control in WinForms. It has a Text property that is the text displayed when the page is rendered.

The TextBox control is very similar to the System.Windows.Forms.TextBox control, and it is used primarily as a data-gathering control. The following properties are commonly used:

- Text—Get and set the text of the control; can be changed by the end user (in the browser).

- MaxLength—Sets the maximum number of characters allowed in the control.

- Columns—Sets the width of the control in number of characters (depending upon the font used).

- ReadOnly—Disables user input into the control.

- **Rows**—Sets the height (number of lines of text) of a multi-line control, based on the font size used.

- **AutoPostBack**—If True, the control will send a post-back request every time the user changes the control (after the focus leaves the control). Not recommended.

- **TextMode**—One of the enumerated values in TextBoxMode: SingleLine, Multiline, or Password.

- **Wrap**—If true, the text in the control will wrap on the next line, else it will scroll horizontally. This property applies only to multi-line controls.

The Button control is used primarily for its Click and Command events, which are fired when the end user clicks the control in the browser. We will discuss these events in the next section. The user action (clicking on the button) triggers a post-back of the page, when both the Click and the Command event handlers are called, and then the page is re-rendered and sent back to the browser. Some important properties of the Button control are

- **CausesValidation**—If True (default), a validation of the page is performed before the post-back is performed. If the validation fails, the post-back is cancelled.

- **CommandArgument**—A string passed back as an optional parameter to the Command event handler.

- **CommandName**—A string passed back as an optional parameter to the Command event handler.

- **Text**—The text displayed in the browser (button caption).

The Image control is used primarily to display an image on the page. Some of its specific properties are

- **ImageUrl**—An URL pointing to the image file (usually an image file which is part of the application). It is recommended that you use a standard (therefore, widely supported) image format like JPEG, PNG, or GIF.

- **AlternateText**—If the image cannot be displayed (the image file is not found, the browser does not support it, or any other reason), this string is displayed instead.

- **ImageAlign**—Indicates how the image should be displayed on the page. This property is usually used when the page layout is a FlowLayout. It can have any value from the ImageAlign enumeration and defaults to NotSet.

The `ImageButton` control is a combination of the `Image` control (which is the base class of this control) and the `Button` control behavior. It does have the same properties and behavior as both controls; therefore, it can fire a `Command` event, and it can cause validation.

The `HyperLink` control is specific to Web pages, and it is used to navigate to another URL (page). It directs the browser to open the specified URL. Depending upon the `Target` property, it can be displayed in the same browser window or frame, or in a new one. Some of its most important properties are

- `NavigateUrl`—The URL to navigate to. For example: `http://www.yahoo.com`.

- `Target`—The name of the target window or frame to open the new URL in. It is a string and can have the following special values:

Value	Description
_blank	Opens a new browser window
_parent	Opens in the parent of the current frame
_self	Opens in this frame
_top	Opens in the same window as this frame

- **Text**—The text to display as a link on the page (normally a user-friendly name of the URL).

- **ImageUrl**—An URL to an image that will be used instead of the `Text`, if it is set and the image is available.

The `LinkButton` control looks like a `HyperLink` control but behaves as a `Button`. It has the same properties and events of the `Button` class. It is used normally when the URL to which it links is to be determined programmatically—that is, when you want to control in code what URL is open by this `LinkButton`. Therefore, the control does not have the `NavigateUrl` or any of the other properties of the `HyperLink` control.

The `CheckBox` and `RadioButton` controls are very similar to their WinForms counterparts. The `RadioButton` inherits from `CheckBox`. The most important shared properties of the controls are

- **AutoPostBack**—If `True` the control will send a post-back request every time the user clicks the control. Not recommended.

- **Checked**—Can be used to get/set the checked state of the control.

- **Text**—The text displayed in the control.

- **TextAlign**—Enumerated value with two members: `Right` (default) and `Left`.

The only difference between the two controls is the way they are rendered: One displays a check box; the other one a radio button.

The abstract `ListControl` class is the base for four other controls with similar behavior: `ListBox`, `DropDownList`, `CheckBoxList`, and `RadioButtonList`. It abstracts the behavior of a list of items, each item being of `ListItem` type. The properties of the `ListItem` class are shown here:

- **Text**—A string property used to display the item in the list.

- **Value**—A string property that holds a value associated with this item.

- **Selected**—A Boolean indicating whether the item was selected (checked). It is used normally to determine which items in the collection were selected by the user.

The main properties of the `ListControl` class are shown in the following list:

- **Items**—The collection of all items in the list. Can be used to add and remove items to/from the list.

- **SelectedItem**—The selected item in the list. If more than one item is selected, it is the item with the lowest index.

- **SelectedIndex**—The index of the selected item in the list. If more than one item is selected, it is the lowest index of the selected items.

- **AutoPostBack**—If true, a post-back is executed every time the selection of the list changes. Not recommended.

- **DataSource**—A `DataSource` object used to automatically populate the items in the list. If it is used, it is normally a `DataSet`.

- **DataMember**—A table in the DataSource.

- **DataField**—A field in the DataSource (or DataMember) used to populate the list items (the `Text` property).

- **DataValueField**—A field in the DataSource (or DataMember) used to populate the `Value` property of the list items. Normally used to uniquely identify the table row that was the source of the `Text` property, or alternatively to store a code value associated with the `Text` displayed.

- **DataTextFormatString**—A formatting string that determines how the `Text` is rendered in the list. Can be used to format numbers, currency, and so on.

The items in a list can be set in a few different ways: at design time using the Items collection property of the list, or at runtime, when the page is loaded or posted back, either from a data source or from another source. For this example, we set the items at design time; we will show a more involved example using a data source in the next chapter.

The ListBox and DropDownList controls are very similar, with the only difference that the DropDownList does not allow multiple selections. They are also similar to their WinForms counterparts. The ListBox has a Rows property, which is similar to the multi-line TextBox.Rows property; namely it indicates the number of visible rows in the list.

The CheckBoxList and RadioButtonList are lists of items represented with a check box or a radio button associated to each item, allowing in this fashion for multi-selection. These types of lists can be displayed as a regular list (using one column) or using multiple columns (in a table format). Their most distinctive properties are listed here:

- **CellPadding**—Used to get/set the distance (in pixels) between the border and the cells (rendered list items).

- **CellSpacing**—Used to get the spacing between adjacent cells (items).

- **RepeatColumns**—The number of columns to use for display when the list is a multi-column one.

- **RepeatDirection**—The repeat direction of multi-column lists. Can be Horizontal or Vertical (both members of the RepeatDirection enumeration).

- **RepeatLayout**—An enumerated value indicating whether this list should be rendered as a table or as a flow of items. The RepeatLayout enumeration has two members: Table and Flow.

- **TextAlign**—Indicates whether the check box or radio button is to the right or to the left of the item text. Default is Right.

Another control that can be useful in some applications is the Calendar control. It displays a calendar month, and it has many UI features (the capability to customize almost all settings of the control). You can set the colors and styles for the days of this month, the current day (today), the days of other months, the headers, and so on.

There are other important controls, such as validation controls, data grid, and data list controls, that we will discuss in the next chapter as we get into more advanced concepts.

In order to understand how a Web form works, we need to understand the Web controls' properties, methods, and events. We looked briefly at the Web controls' properties and methods. Next we will look at the Web controls' events.

The Event Model of a Web Form

The event model of an application using Web controls is different from the event model in a regular WinForms application. You have seen (in Figure 35.5) that in response to a client (usually browser) request, the .aspx page is rendered to an HTML document, which is then sent back in the HTTP response. The HTML page contains code (developed usually in a scripting language, such as JavaScript) that runs on the client, inside the browser. This code is generated when the page is rendered, and it is responsible to call back the server every time an event that requires a post-back is triggered.

Although this mechanism may seem innocuous (because it happens behind the scenes from what you have learned so far), it may have serious side effects on performance of the application in general, if misused.

For example, assume you have a page that contains a number of TextBox controls with the AutoPostBack property set to True. Every time the user changes the content of one of the controls and switches focus to another control, the scripts in the HTML page will do a post-back to the server. This results in a new instance of the page being loaded and rendered on the server and then sent to the client, which must now refresh its display. This type of behavior is unacceptable from both the server's and the client's point of view, hence the use of the AutoPostBack property is not recommended.

Therefore, the most important paradigm in developing a well-behaved Web application is to create pages that do not post-back until the user has finished entering the whole set of data. That is, reduce the number of event handlers to an absolute minimum. This normally means for a data entry page that you have one Submit button (or its equivalent).

From the point of view of the programmer, the events are handled in a very similar fashion to the events on regular WinForms: For each event that you wish to handle, write a handler procedure with the appropriate parameters and associate it with the control. On a Web page, this task is easily achieved by double-clicking on the control for which you wish to handle the event.

Let's look at an example of page that will update data in the Shippers table of the Northwind database that comes by default with SQL Server. The table has three columns: shipperId (Integer), companyName (String), and phone (String). The project consists of one Web page and a data access class, in a separate Visual Basic .NET library, which performs all database operations.

NOTE

It is a bad idea to have SQL statements (data access code) spread into the Web pages themselves. The Web pages are presentation layer code and as such should contain as little business logic and data access code as possible. It is considered a much better approach to isolate the business logic and data access code in separate layers (assemblies); in this way one reduces complexity of all layers and makes changes to each layer easier (because it is self-contained).

The code in the DataAccess assembly contains only one class, named Shipper, which has methods to retrieve and store data into the database. You have sent this type of code in the previous chapters; therefore, no further details are given in regards to the code in this class. Note that you will need to provide the name of your SQL Server machine (instead of ROGUE).

```
Imports System.Data.OleDb

Public Class Shipper
    Protected m_shipperId As Integer
    Protected m_companyName As String
    Protected m_phone As String

    Private Shared s_connStr = "Provider=SQLOLEDB.1;" + _
                               "Data Source=ROGUE;" + _
                               "Initial Catalog=NORTHWIND;" + _
                               "User ID=sa;" + _
                               "Password="

    Public Property shipperId() As Integer
        Get
            Return m_shipperId
        End Get
        Set(ByVal Value As Integer)
            m_shipperId = Value
        End Set
    End Property

    Public Property companyName() As String
        Get
            Return m_companyName
        End Get
```

```
        Set(ByVal Value As String)
            m_companyName = Value
        End Set
    End Property

    Public Property phone() As String
        Get
            Return m_phone
        End Get
        Set(ByVal Value As String)
            m_phone = Value
        End Set
    End Property

    Public Sub New()
        m_shipperId = 0
        m_companyName = "New Shipper"
        m_phone = ""
    End Sub
    Public Sub New(ByVal shipperId As Integer, _
                   ByVal companyName As String, _
                   ByVal phone As String)
        m_shipperId = shipperId
        m_companyName = companyName
        m_phone = phone
    End Sub

    Public Function Find(ByVal shipperId As Integer) As Boolean
        Dim conn As OleDbConnection
        Dim comm As OleDbCommand
        Dim dr As OleDbDataReader
        Dim bFound As Boolean
        Dim sSQL As String
        sSQL = "SELECT Shippers.CompanyName, Shippers.Phone " + _
               "FROM Shippers " + _
               "WHERE shipperId = " + Str(shipperId)
        Try
            conn = New OleDbConnection(s_connStr)
            conn.Open()
            comm = New OleDbCommand(sSQL, conn)
            dr = comm.ExecuteReader(CommandBehavior.SingleRow)
            If dr.Read() Then
                m_shipperId = shipperId
                m_companyName = dr.GetString(0)
                m_phone = dr.GetString(1)
                bFound = True
```

```
        End If
    Catch e As OleDbException
        Console.Out.WriteLine(e.Message)
    Finally
        If Not dr Is Nothing Then dr.Close()
        If Not conn Is Nothing Then conn.Close()
    End Try
    Return bFound
End Function

Public Sub Insert()
    Dim conn As OleDbConnection
    Dim comm As OleDbCommand
    Dim sSQL As String
    sSQL = "INSERT INTO Shippers (companyName, phone) " + _
            "VALUES('" + m_companyName + "', '" + m_phone + "')"
    Try
        conn = New OleDbConnection(s_connStr)
        conn.Open()
        comm = New OleDbCommand(sSQL, conn)
        comm.ExecuteNonQuery()
    Catch e As OleDbException
        Console.Out.WriteLine(e.Message)
    Finally
        If Not conn Is Nothing Then conn.Close()
    End Try
End Sub

Public Sub Update()
    Dim conn As OleDbConnection
    Dim comm As OleDbCommand
    Dim sSQL As String
    sSQL = "UPDATE Shippers SET " + _
            "CompanyName = '" + m_companyName + "', " + _
            "Phone = '" + m_phone + "' " + _
            "WHERE shipperId = " + Str(m_shipperId)
    Try
        conn = New OleDbConnection(s_connStr)
        conn.Open()
        comm = New OleDbCommand(sSQL, conn)
        comm.ExecuteNonQuery()
    Catch e As OleDbException
        Console.Out.WriteLine(e.Message)
    Finally
        If Not conn Is Nothing Then conn.Close()
    End Try
```

```
End Sub

Public Sub Remove()
    Dim conn As OleDbConnection
    Dim comm As OleDbCommand
    Dim sSQL As String
    sSQL = "DELETE FROM Shippers " + _
            "WHERE shipperId = " + Str(m_shipperId)
    Try
        conn = New OleDbConnection(s_connStr)
        conn.Open()
        comm = New OleDbCommand(sSQL, conn)
        comm.ExecuteNonQuery()
    Catch e As OleDbException
        Console.Out.WriteLine(e.Message)
    Finally
        If Not conn Is Nothing Then conn.Close()
    End Try
End Sub
End Class
```

The actual page in design mode is illustrated in Figure 35.8.

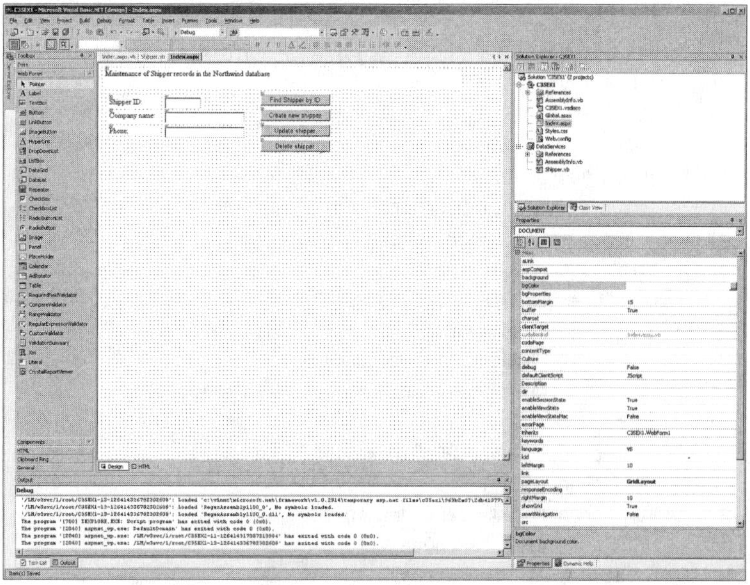

Figure 35.8: *The layout of the* Shipper *maintenance page.*

The TextBox controls are named txtShipperId, txtCompanyName, and txtPhone, respectively. The buttons are used to retrieve a shipper from the database, create a new shipper, update a shipper's data, and delete a shipper from the database, respectively.

Each button handles the Click event, and the handler code is shown here:

```
Public Class Index
    Inherits System.Web.UI.Page
    Protected WithEvents Label2 As System.Web.UI.WebControls.Label
    Protected WithEvents txtShipperId As System.Web.UI.WebControls.TextBox
    Protected WithEvents Label3 As System.Web.UI.WebControls.Label
    Protected WithEvents txtCompanyName As System.Web.UI.WebControls.TextBox
    Protected WithEvents Label4 As System.Web.UI.WebControls.Label
    Protected WithEvents txtPhone As System.Web.UI.WebControls.TextBox
    Protected WithEvents cmdFindShipper As System.Web.UI.WebControls.Button
    Protected WithEvents cmdInsert As System.Web.UI.WebControls.Button
    Protected WithEvents cmdUpdate As System.Web.UI.WebControls.Button
    Protected WithEvents cmdDelete As System.Web.UI.WebControls.Button
    Protected WithEvents Label1 As System.Web.UI.WebControls.Label


    ' Web Form Designer Generated Code omitted

    Private Sub Page_Load(ByVal sender As System.Object, _
                    ByVal e As System.EventArgs) _
    Handles MyBase.Load
        '
    End Sub


    Private Sub cmdFindShipper_Click(ByVal sender As System.Object, _
                        ByVal e As System.EventArgs) _
    Handles cmdFindShipper.Click
        Dim m_shipper As DataServices.Shipper

        m_shipper = New DataServices.Shipper()
        If m_shipper.Find(Val(txtShipperId.Text)) Then
            txtCompanyName.Text = m_shipper.companyName
            txtPhone.Text = m_shipper.phone
        Else
            txtCompanyName.Text = ""
            txtPhone.Text = ""
            txtShipperId.Text = "Not found!"
        End If
    End Sub


    Private Sub cmdInsert_Click(ByVal sender As System.Object, _
                        ByVal e As System.EventArgs) _
    Handles cmdInsert.Click
        Dim m_shipper As DataServices.Shipper
```

```
        m_shipper = New DataServices.Shipper(txtShipperId.Text, _
                                             txtCompanyName.Text, _
                                             txtPhone.Text)

        m_shipper.Insert()
    End Sub

    Private Sub cmdUpdate_Click(ByVal sender As System.Object, _
                        ByVal e As System.EventArgs) _
    Handles cmdUpdate.Click
        Dim m_shipper As DataServices.Shipper

        m_shipper = New DataServices.Shipper(txtShipperId.Text, _
                                             txtCompanyName.Text, _
                                             txtPhone.Text)

        m_shipper.Update()
    End Sub

    Private Sub cmdDelete_Click(ByVal sender As System.Object, _
                        ByVal e As System.EventArgs) _
    Handles cmdDelete.Click
        Dim m_shipper As DataServices.Shipper

        m_shipper = New DataServices.Shipper(txtShipperId.Text, _
                                             txtCompanyName.Text, _
                                             txtPhone.Text)

        m_shipper.Remove()
    End Sub
End Class
```

Each of the handler procedures uses a DataServices.Shipper object to retrieve or store data from/into the database. They also use the values entered by the user in the browser to either find, insert, update, or remove a shipper row into the Shippers table. These values are the Text properties of the txtXXX controls.

The Find methods will set the values to the values retrieved from the database if the row is found. Otherwise, the text fields txtCompanyName and txtPhone are blanked, and the txtShipperId is set to be Not found!, to indicate to the user that the row does not exist. In Figure 35.9 you can see the application running in the browser, after a successful find.

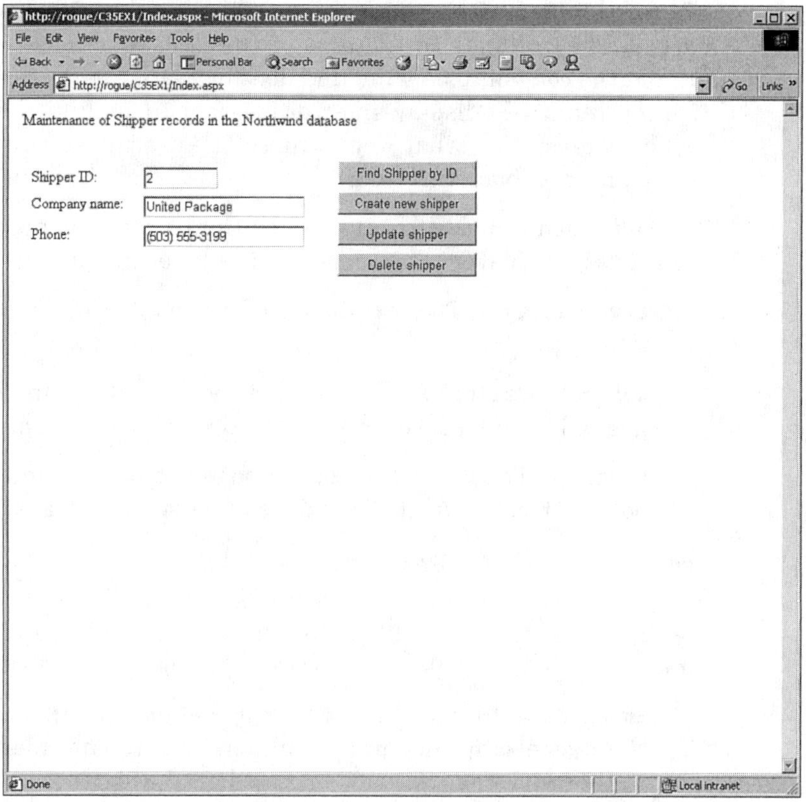

Figure 35.9: The Shipper maintenance page running in browser.

Client-side Validation and Validator Controls

What would happen if the user enters the wrong information in one of the TextBox fields, when making a post-back request to the server? An error would occur in the server code and you, as a programmer, would need to take corrective action. This means that the page needs to be redisplayed with some sort of error message telling the user what was the error. It would be nice if we could detect this error condition in the HTML page, before posting the page back to the server. This would save us an unnecessary round trip to the server and back.

It turns out that you can achieve this result by adding some validation controls to the form. The validation controls work on the client (in the browser, if the browser supports it) and ensure that the page is not posted back unless all validation controls are satisfied. If the browser does not support client script validation (older browsers do not), the validation takes place on the server.

The validation controls act as an invisible text box attached to one `TextBox` control. They validate the data when the focus leaves the text control. If the data in the control to be validated does not satisfy the criteria of the validation control, it will display an error message (usually near the offending text control) stating what went wrong. The user must correct the input before any post-back can occur.

The validation controls are all derived from a common abstract base class named `BaseValidator`. This class has the following notable properties:

- `ErrorMessage`—The text displayed as an error message when validation fails.

- `ControlToValidate`—The name of the control to validate (on the same page). In the IDE, select from the drop-down list a name.

- `Display`—The way the error message is allocated and displayed. It can be one of the enumerated values (`ValidatorDisplay`):

Value	Description
None	The message is never displayed.
Static (default)	The text is statically allocated on the page.
Dynamic–	The text is allocated dynamically if the validation fails.

- `EnableClientScript`—If set to true (default) it will attempt to use client-side script to perform validation. If the browser does not support it, the validation will be performed on the server.

- `Enabled`—If true (default) the validator is enabled; otherwise it is disabled.

- `IsValid`—If true, the control is valid; otherwise, it is not.

There are four classes derived from the `BaseValidator`: `BaseCompareValidator`, `CustomValidator`, `RegularExpressionValidator`, and `RequiredFieldValidator`. The `BaseCompareValidator` is further specialized in `CompareValidator` and `RangeValidator`.

Each one of the concrete (non-abstract) validator classes have their own special properties, briefly presented here.

The **RequiredFieldValidator** simply requires that the validate control is not empty (that it contains some data). It has no other properties, besides those inherited from its base.

The **BaseCompareValidator** has a property called `Type`, which is the data type for the values being compared. It is an enumerated value and can be any one of `Currency`, `Integer`, `Date`, `String`, and `Double`.

The `CompareValidator` is derived from `BaseCompareValidator`, and it is used to ensure that the value of a control satisfies a comparison to a fixed value or to the value of another control. The following properties are usually used:

- `ValueToCompare`—The value to compare to the `ControlToValidate` value.

- `Operator`—Relational operator to use for comparison. It is an enumerated value and can be any of the standard relational operators (=, >, >=, <, <=, <>) and the special `DataTypeCheck` enumerated value. The latter is used to ensure that the value entered by the user can be converted to the data type specified in the `Type` property.

- `ControlToCompare`—An alternative to the `ValueToCompare`, it is used when the comparison is made between two values, both entered by the user in two controls.

The `RangeValidator` is used to ensure a value is within a range (between the `MinimumValue` and the `MaximumValue` properties). It uses the inherited `Type` property to determine the data type of the values.

The `CustomValidator` is used to create a custom validation for a control. It involves handling a `ServerValidate` event and creating a script function to handle the validation on the client. We will not use this control because it requires knowledge beyond the scope of this book.

The `RegularExpressionValidator` is used to ensure that the value of a control matches a specified pattern (a sequence of characters in a specified order, such as a telephone number, social security number, and so on). The control uses the class `System.Text.RegularExpressions.Regex` to validate the expression. The `ValidationExpression` property is used to enter the pattern that the control value must match.

NOTE

See the `System.Text.RegularExpressions.Regex` class for a complete reference to the syntax of regular expressions.

For example, the pattern for a U.S. telephone number is

`((\(\d{3}\) ?)|(\d{3}-))?\d{3}-\d{4}`

This pattern would match a phone number like `(123) 456-7890`, but it would not match a value like `2S-3456`.

We will continue our example by adding three validators to our page. A `CompareValidator` will ensure that the `txtShipperId` value is positive. The `ControlToValidate` is set to be `txtShipperId`, the `ValueToCompare` is `0`, and the `Operator` is `GreaterThan`.

A `RequiredFieldValidator` will ensure that the `txtCompanyName` field is not empty, and a `RegularExpressionValidator` will ensure that the telephone number is formatted correctly as a U.S. number. Figure 35.10 shows the `.aspx` page in Design mode.

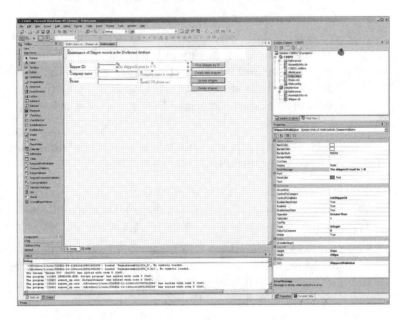

Figure 35.10: *The Shipper page with validators.*

If you run the modified page and intentionally enter invalid values you would get the error messages displayed in Figure 35.11. The page will not be posted back until you fix the errors.

Form and Control Events and Their Order

Both the page and controls on it have a number of events that are fired when the form is requested. You will now look at the most important of these events, as well as the order in which they are fired.

Both the Page class and the Web control classes have as parent the Control class, which has the following important events:

- **Init**—The page or control is initialized (the first step in the control life). Seldom used, it is automatically generated by the wizard.

- **Load**—The page or control is loaded. This is frequently used to initialize the controls on the page.

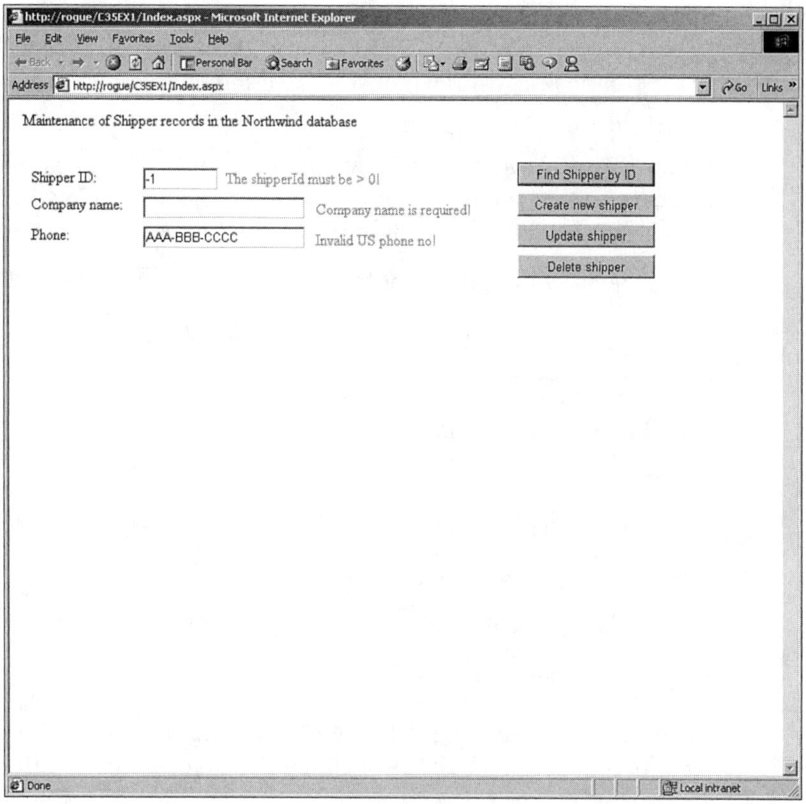

Figure 35.11: *The modified Shipper page running in browser with validation errors.*

- **PreRender**—Called when the page or control is about to be rendered. It is sometimes used to make final changes to the state of the controls before rendering.

- **Unload**—The page or control is unloaded from memory. It is in general used to clean up resources used by the page.

Some controls have control-specific events, besides those inherited from the Control class. Notably, the Button class and its descendants and related classes (LinkButton, ImageButton) have an event named Click and one named Command. Both events are fired when the user clicks on the button. The Click event is a regular EventHandler. The Command receives a special argument of type CommandEventArgs, which contains the values of the two strings properties defined at design time: CommandName and CommandArgument.

The classes derived from $ListControl$ (all list classes) have an event named $SelectedIndexChanged$, which is a standard $EventHandler$. This event occurs (as its name suggests) when the selection changes in the list, as a result of user input.

Other controls have specific events; most of them have a similar event that indicates when the user changed the control data. We will look in some detail to a few of these events in the next chapter.

The order in which the events occur when a form is loaded is

1. Controls receive $Init$.

2. Page receives $Init$.

3. Page receives $Load$.

4. Controls receive $Load$.

5. Page receives $PreRender$.

6. Controls receive $PreRender$.

7. Controls receive $Unload$.

8. Page receives $Unload$.

In the $Load$ you can check for the $IsPostBack$ status to find out whether a page is requested for the first time or is loaded as a result of a post-back.

The following sample code can be used to test this event order:

```
Public Class WebForm1
    Inherits System.Web.UI.Page
    Protected WithEvents Label1 As System.Web.UI.WebControls.Label
    Protected WithEvents Button1 As System.Web.UI.WebControls.Button


#Region " Web Form Designer Generated Code "

    'This call is required by the Web Form Designer.
    <System.Diagnostics.DebuggerStepThrough()> Private Sub InitializeComponent()

    End Sub

    Private Sub Page_Init(ByVal sender As System.Object, _
                        ByVal e As System.EventArgs) _
    Handles MyBase.Init
        'CODEGEN: This method call is required by the Web Form Designer
        'Do not modify it using the code editor.
```

```
        InitializeComponent()
        System.Diagnostics.Debug.WriteLine("*** PAGE_INIT ***")
    End Sub

#End Region

    Private Sub Page_Load(ByVal sender As System.Object, _
                        ByVal e As System.EventArgs) _
    Handles MyBase.Load
        System.Diagnostics.Debug.WriteLine("*** PAGE_LOAD ***")
    End Sub

    Private Sub Page_PreRender(ByVal sender As Object, _
                            ByVal e As System.EventArgs) _
    Handles MyBase.PreRender
        System.Diagnostics.Debug.WriteLine("*** PAGE_PRERENDER ***")
    End Sub

    Private Sub Page_Unload(ByVal sender As Object, _
                        ByVal e As System.EventArgs) _
    Handles MyBase.Unload
        System.Diagnostics.Debug.WriteLine("*** PAGE_UNLOAD ***")
    End Sub

    Private Sub Page_Disposed(ByVal sender As Object, _
                            ByVal e As System.EventArgs) _
    Handles MyBase.Disposed
        System.Diagnostics.Debug.WriteLine("*** PAGE_DISPOSED ***")
    End Sub

    Private Sub Button1_Click(ByVal sender As System.Object, _
                            ByVal e As System.EventArgs) _
    Handles Button1.Click
        System.Diagnostics.Debug.WriteLine("*** B_CLICK ***")
    End Sub

    Private Sub Button1_Init(ByVal sender As Object, _
                            ByVal e As System.EventArgs) _
    Handles Button1.Init
        System.Diagnostics.Debug.WriteLine("*** B_INIT ***")
    End Sub

    Private Sub Button1_Load(ByVal sender As Object, _
                            ByVal e As System.EventArgs) _
```

```
     Handles Button1.Load
        System.Diagnostics.Debug.WriteLine("*** B_LOAD ***")
     End Sub

     Private Sub Button1_PreRender(ByVal sender As Object, _
                                   ByVal e As System.EventArgs) _
     Handles Button1.PreRender
        System.Diagnostics.Debug.WriteLine("*** B_PRE_RENDER ***")
     End Sub

     Private Sub Button1_Unload(ByVal sender As Object, _
                                ByVal e As System.EventArgs) _
     Handles Button1.Unload
        System.Diagnostics.Debug.WriteLine("*** B_UNLOAD ***")
     End Sub

     Private Sub Button1_Command(ByVal sender As Object, _
        ByVal e As System.Web.UI.WebControls.CommandEventArgs) _
     Handles Button1.Command
        System.Diagnostics.Debug.WriteLine("*** B_COMMAND ***")
     End Sub
End Class
```

The System.Diagnostics.Debug object is used to output the text to the output window of the IDE, so that you can see the order in which the server fired the events. The Output pane is one of the tabs of the Debug window, normally situated in the lower-left corner of your IDE.

What's Next

This concludes your introduction to developing Web applications using Visual Basic .NET. You have learned the fundamental concepts behind Web development, the basis of using the Web pages derived from the Page class, and you have seen the most common controls in action.

You also learned how to handle events and how to do some elementary data validation, all in the context of a simple database application.

Next you will learn some more advanced concepts, how to use bound data and state management options, as well as how to develop a user control for a Web application.

NOTE

The answers to "Reviewing It," "Checking It," and "Applying It" are available on our Web site.

REVIEW

Reviewing It

This section presents a review of the key concepts in this chapter. These questions are intended to gauge your absorption of the relevant material.

1. Describe the steps involved in getting a Web page developed in Visual Studio .NET from the server into a client browser.

2. What does a Web Form consist of?

3. What is the base class for both the Page and Web control classes? Enumerate some of its most important properties.

4. How can you add items to a list-type of control on a page?

5. What is the most important rule to keep in mind when developing the event handlers for a page?

6. What is the order in which the page events are fired?

CHECK

Checking It

Select the correct answer or answers to the following questions.

Multiple Choice

1. Is validation using Validator classes taking place on the client or on the server?

   a. On the client.

   b. On the server.

   c. On the client if possible; if not, on the server.

   d. Both on the client and the server.

2. Can you output text and HTML tags to the Web page directly?

   a. Yes, using the `Response` object.

   b. No, it must be done through Web controls.

   c. Yes, using `HtmlControls`.

   d. Both a. and c.

3. What would be the equivalent of opening another form when using Web pages?

   a. Doing a post-back.

   b. Navigating to another URL.

    c. Navigating to another URL within the same application.

    d. There is no equivalent.

4. To open another page into a different window of the browser you must use:

    a. A `HyperLink` control.

    b. A `LinkButton` control.

    c. A `HyperLink` control with the `Target` property set to `_top`.

    d. A `HyperLink` control with the `Target` property set to `_blank`.

True or False

Select one of the two possible answers and then verify on our Web site that you picked the correct one.

1. The HTTP protocol is a stateless protocol.

    True/False

2. Firing of an event from a control of a Web page requires a post-back of the page to the server.

    True/False

3. For better performance it is recommended that you place all data access code (SQL statements and so on) directly into the page code.

    True/False

4. All list control classes are derived from the `ListBox` class.

    True/False

5. A validator uses either client or server code, depending upon the browser capabilities.

    True/False

6. The `Load` event is the event to use to initialize controls on the page.

    True/False

APPLY

Applying It

Try to complete the following exercises by yourself.

Independent Exercise 1

Try to reproduce (without looking) the diagram describing the steps involved in a client requesting a page, up to the point when the page is returned to the client browser.

Independent Exercise 2

Write a small Web application that is composed of two pages, with some controls. Each page should be able to call (`activate`) the other page.

36

Developing Applications for the Web

In this chapter you will find out more about developing Web applications. You will learn new techniques related to data access, state management, and user controls. The topics covered in this chapter include the following:

- Data access using data bound controls

- State management

- Web user control development

You will start with a step-by-step example on how to build a Web page that displays a list of rows from a database table, as well as a detailed view of each row once the user selects the row.

Next we will discuss state management options and how to use them in real-life applications. We will present an example using different state management techniques.

Lastly, you will learn how to develop a user Web control. We will walk you through all the steps required to create a simple user control and then use the control in one of your Web pages.

Data Access Using Data Bound Controls

The example in this section requires knowledge of data access, which you learned in Part V, "Manipulating Data with ADO.NET and XML." We will only briefly present the steps required to create data adapters and data sets, assuming that you are already familiar with these techniques.

Most Web controls have a set of data binding properties and methods. These properties are meant to allow a particular control to automatically get its data from a data source (for example a DataSet or a DataView). These properties are grouped under the category Data in the Properties window, in the same way the data properties for the regular controls are grouped. For example, a Label control has a DataBindings property visible in the Properties window. If you open the property dialog associated with it, you will get a dialog like the one shown in Figure 36.1.

You can open the Data Bindings dialog by clicking Data Bindings in the Properties pane and then clicking on the ellipsis button to the right of the property.

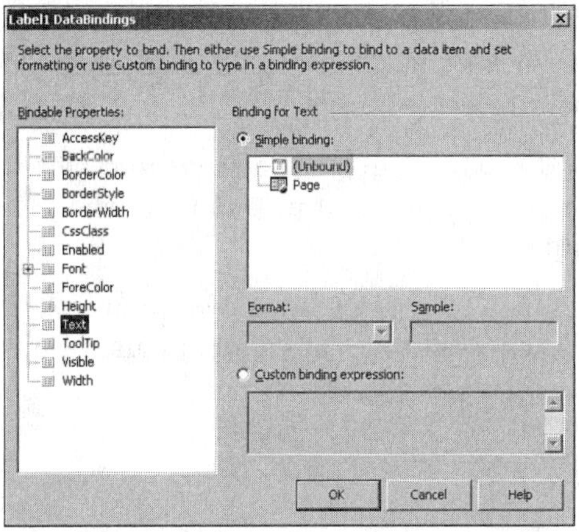

Figure 36.1: *Data binding properties of the Label control.*

The right-hand side of the tree contains all the bindable properties of the control—Text, Font, color settings, and so on. A *bindable property* is a property that can draw its value from the value of a data source, to which is linked (bound).

On the right-hand side we have the sources to which the property selected on the left-hand side is bound to. In Figure 36.1 we see the Text selected on the left and that it is bound to nothing (unbound). The binding can be simple (a table column from a data set) or custom (an expression). We will return with more details on both the simple and the custom binding later in this section and in the section "Developing Web User Controls."

The next example shows how to create a Web page that will display a list of all the orders from the Orders table in the Northwind database. When a user selects a row by clicking on the order ID, a detailed view of the order will be shown. The following steps are required to implement the example:

1. Create the project and add a data access component class.

2. Add and configure the data source.

3. Create a method to populate the DataSet.

4. Create the DataSet and DataGrid controls on the Web page.

5. Configure the DataGrid control.

6. Add configure detail bound Label controls.

7. Implement the SelectedIndexChanged event.

Step 1. Create the Project and Add a Data Access Component Class

The first step is to create an empty ASP.NET Web application project. Follow the same steps we used in the previous examples. The data source could be added directly to the Web Form, but in order to simulate a real life situation, we will create a component that deals with all data access.

Add a new component to the project by right-clicking on the project name in the Solution Explorer and selecting the Add Component menu. Select the default option—Component Class. A component is a custom class derived from System.ComponentModel.Component. A new component class will be created and added to the project. The Design view of the class will be shown (see Figure 36.2). Give the component a meaningful name.

We can now add the data source to the component.

Step 2. Add and Configure the Data Source

We will use the Northwind database that comes with SQL Server. In the ToolBox, select the Data tab. Drag the SqlDataAdapter to the Component Design window. If you use another database (such as Oracle), you must use the OleDbDataAdapter instead. When you drop the SqlDataAdapter on the component, the Data Adapter Configuration Wizard dialog will be displayed. Select the New Connection button. This action will open the Data Link Properties dialog. Enter the information required to connect to your database. Figure 36.3 illustrates the dialog after the settings are entered.

You will need to provide your server name and also the user ID and password. Select the Northwind database and make sure to test the connection.

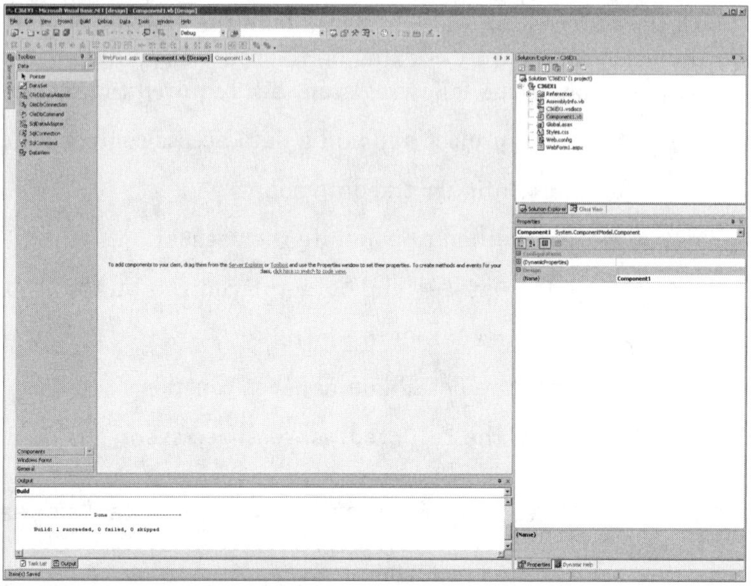

Figure 36.2: *The Design view of the component class.*

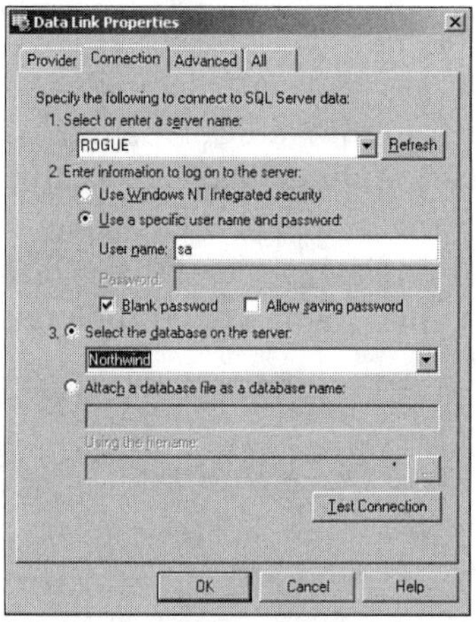

Figure 36.3: *The Data Link Properties dialog.*

Back in the Data Adapter Configuration Wizard, select the Next button. Leave the default selection (Use SQL Statements) and click Next again. Now we need to select the data tables that will be used by the data adapter to create the DataSet. Click on the Query Builder button, and the Query Builder dialog will be shown.

Select the Orders and Customers tables, click Add, and then close. This will bring the two tables into the Query Builder, and we can now select the columns that we want in the DataSet. Note that the relationship between the two tables is correctly shown in the builder. Select the columns from the two tables so that they match the ones shown in Figure 36.4 and then click OK.

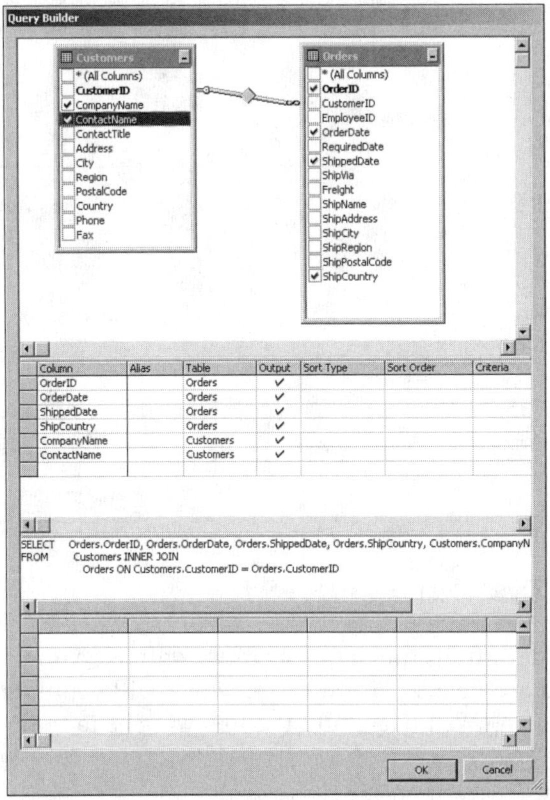

Figure 36.4: *The Query Builder dialog.*

We are now back in the wizard; select Next. You will get warnings stating that the INSERT, UPDATE, and DELETE operations cannot be created due to having selected multiple tables in the adapter. This is correct, but we can safely ignore the warnings because we do not intend to do any updates to the database. Select the Finish button on the wizard, and the wizard will create the SqlConnection object for you and exit.

Step 3. Create a Method to Populate the `DataSet`

Now we need to create a `DataSet`. Right-click on the `SqlAdapter1` object in the component designer and select Generate Dataset. Check the New radio button and enter a name for the DataSet, for example `DsCustomers`, and then click OK. The new DataSet is created and added to the project as `DsCustomers.xsd`. You can view the schema of the data set by double-clicking on it. If should look similar to the one shown in Figure 36.5.

Figure 36.5: The `DsCustomers` DataSet.

To access the data from the data source we defined, you need to create a public method on the component class, which will populate a `DataSet` object passed in from the Web page. Add the following code to the component class:

```
Public Class Component1
    Inherits System.ComponentModel.Component

    ' Component Designer generated code

    Public Sub PopulateDS(ByRef ds As DsCustomers)
        SqlDataAdapter1.Fill(ds)
    End Sub

End Class
```

The PopulateDS method takes a reference to the DsCustomers data set you created and will fill it with the data from the database, using the sqlDataAdapter1 object (created for you by the wizard).

Step 4. Create the DataSet and DataGrid Controls on the Web Page

In the Designer view of the .aspx page, create a new DataSet control by dragging the DataSet control from the Data tab of the ToolBox to the page. The Add Dataset dialog is shown, and the DsCustomers class you created should be the default selection. Click OK to accept the selection. A new data set control is now displayed in the lower (non-visual) part of the designer.

Now drag a DataGrid control on the page from the Web Forms tag of the ToolBox. The page should now look similar to the one shown in Figure 36.6.

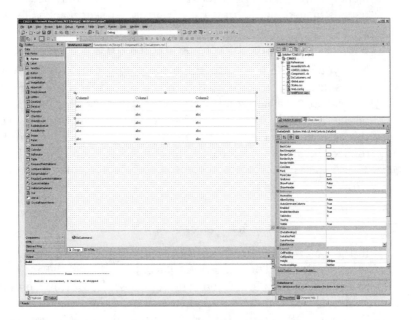

Figure 36.6: *The Web Page Design window after adding the DataSet and grid.*

Now you need to add code to create a new component in the Web page, initialize it, and populate the data set we created on the page. Open the code editor for the Web page and enter the code as shown in bold type:

```
Public Class WebForm1
    Inherits System.Web.UI.Page
    Protected WithEvents DsCustomers1 As C36EX1.DsCustomers
```

```
Protected WithEvents DataGrid1 As System.Web.UI.WebControls.DataGrid
Protected theComponent As New Component1()

' Web Form Designer Generated Code

Private Sub Page_Load(ByVal sender As System.Object, _
                      ByVal e As System.EventArgs) _
Handles MyBase.Load
   If Not IsPostBack Then
      theComponent.PopulateDS(DsCustomers1)
   End If
End Sub
End Class
```

This code adds theComponent object to the Web page and when the page loads, will populate the DsCustomers1 data set from theComponent, if the page is loaded for the first time (that is, if IsPostBack is false).

Step 5. Configure the DataGrid Control

Now you need to bind the grid to the data set and configure the columns to be displayed in the grid. Select the grid control on the page (in design view) and set its DataSource property to the DsCustomers1 DataSet. You will notice that the grid was refreshed to show all the columns we selected in the data set. This may be enough is some cases, but we will further customize the grid control. Right-click on the grid and select Property Builder. The Property Builder dialog will be shown. This dialog has a few tabs; we will walk through the steps required to set up the grid.

In the first tab (General) select the DataMember (the Customers table) and then in the DataKey field select OrderID.

In the Columns tab uncheck the Create Columns Automatically at Run Time check box. Then add the OrderDate and CompanyName columns to the Selected Columns list. Then scroll down to the Button Column node in the Available Columns tree and expand it. Add the Select button to the Selected Columns and then use the arrow buttons on the left to move it up to the first position. Set the HeaderText to be Order ID and then from the Text field drop-down list select OrderID. Figure 36.7 illustrates the property builder dialog at this stage.

These actions have defined the column OrderID to be a select button, instead of simple text. This means that when the user clicks on the OrderID (shown as a LinkButton in the list) a SelectedIndexChange event will occur. We will use this event shortly to show some details of the order.

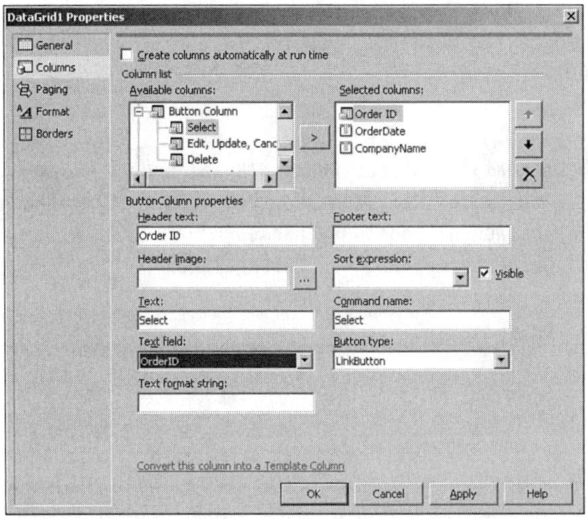

Figure 36.7: *The Property Builder dialog for the* `DataGrid1` *control.*

In the Paging tab check the Allow Paging check box, which will allow the browser to display a limited number of rows (a page) at a time. This is especially useful when dealing with large sets of data.

In the Format tab select the Header in the tree on the right and set its style to Bold (check the Bold check box). This will ensure the header text is displayed in bold type to distinguish it from regular text.

Click OK to accept and apply the changes. Note how the display is now changed to reflect all the modifications we made to the grid. Note at the bottom of the grid the navigation buttons for getting the next and previous pages.

We now need to add some code to bind the control to the data set returned from the component and to handle the paging. In the code view of the page, enter the code in bold type as shown:

```
Public Class WebForm1
    Inherits System.Web.UI.Page
    Protected WithEvents DsCustomers1 As C36EX1.DsCustomers
    Protected WithEvents DataGrid1 As System.Web.UI.WebControls.DataGrid
    Protected theComponent As New Component1()

    ' Web Form Designer Generated Code

    Private Sub Page_Load(ByVal sender As System.Object, _
                          ByVal e As System.EventArgs) _
    Handles MyBase.Load
```

```
    If Not IsPostBack Then
        theComponent.PopulateDS(DsCustomers1)
        DataGrid1.DataBind()
    End If
End Sub
Private Sub DataGrid1_PageIndexChanged(ByVal source As Object, _
    ByVal e As System.Web.UI.WebControls.DataGridPageChangedEventArgs) _
    Handles DataGrid1.PageIndexChanged
    DataGrid1.CurrentPageIndex = e.NewPageIndex
    theComponent.PopulateDS(DsCustomers1)
    DataGrid1.DataBind()
End Sub
End Class
```

The DataBind method executes the binding to the DataSet, as defined by us previously. The PageIndexChanged event must be handled to refresh the data displayed in the grid. We need to update the CurrentPageIndex property of the DataGrid control to the value passed in the property NewPageIndex of the argument e (of type DataGridPageChangedEventArgs). Then we need to refresh the data source and rebind the grid (basically repeat the code in the Load event handler).

At this point we are ready to run a first test and see the result of the data binding at work. Run the project; the browser will load, and you can see the rows from the table join that is our DataSet. You can navigate up and down the list using the previous and next page buttons at the bottom of the grid. Figure 36.8 is an illustration of how the page looks like in Internet Explorer.

Step 6. Add and Configure Detail Bound Label Controls

The first step is to create a new DataView control, which will provide bindings for the detail view labels. From the Data tab of the ToolBox select the DataView, drag it, and drop it on the non-visual part of the page designer; then select it by clicking on it. In the Properties window select the Table property and expand it. Select the DsCustomers1 data set and expand it; then select the Customers table.

Now we can add a detailed view of each row (represented by a few Label controls), which will be updated when the user selects a row by clicking on the OrderID LinkButton. This allows us to see more information about the selected row. Modify the design of the page to look similar to the one shown in Figure 36.9; that is, add the eight Label controls and set the names for the ones to the left as shown.

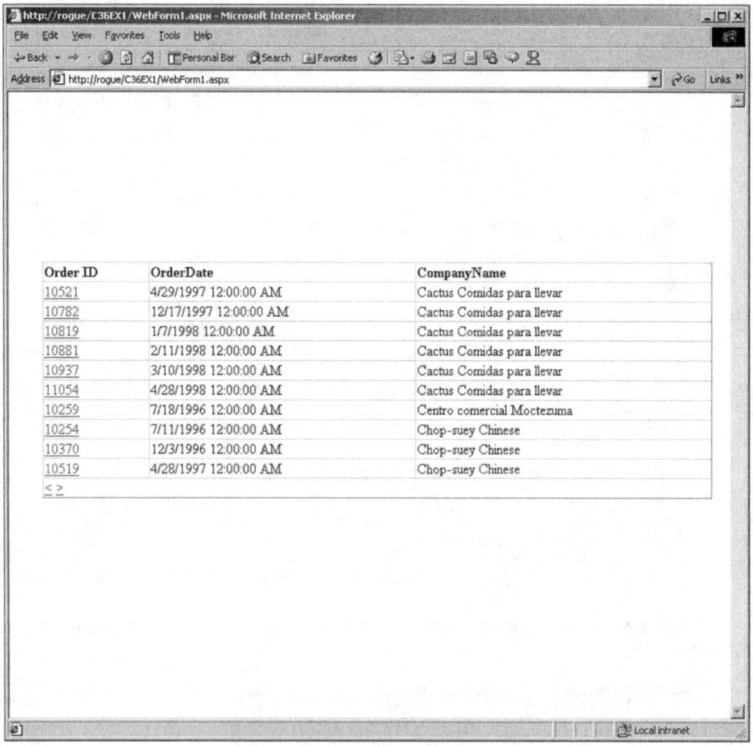

Figure 36.8: The Web page running (1).

Now we need to bind the labels on the right to the columns in the DataView controls so that the label contents are automatically populated by the DataView. Select the label to the right of the one labeled OrderID. In the Properties window click on the DataBindings property to open the Bindings dialog. Select the binding to the OrderID column of the DataView1 data source, from the DataView1[0] node, as illustrated in Figure 36.10. Click OK when done. Repeat the procedure for the other three labels on the right, binding them to ShippedDate, ShipCountry, and ContactName, respectively.

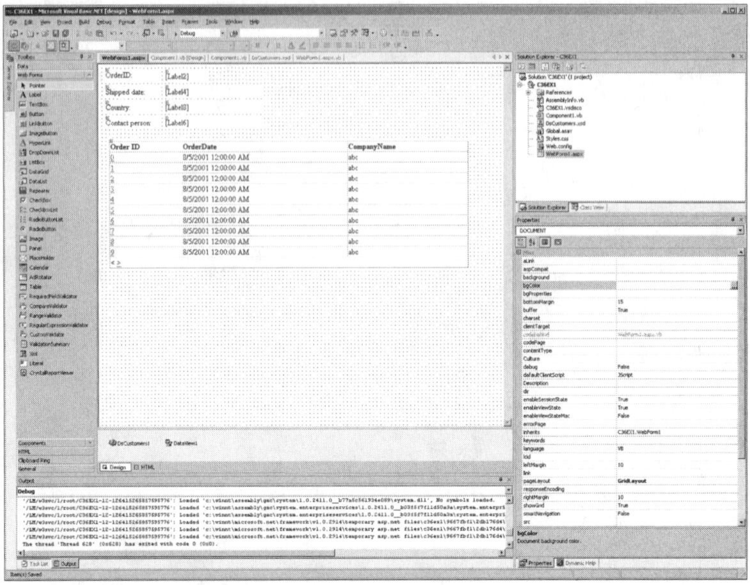

Figure 36.9: *The page with the detail labels in Design mode.*

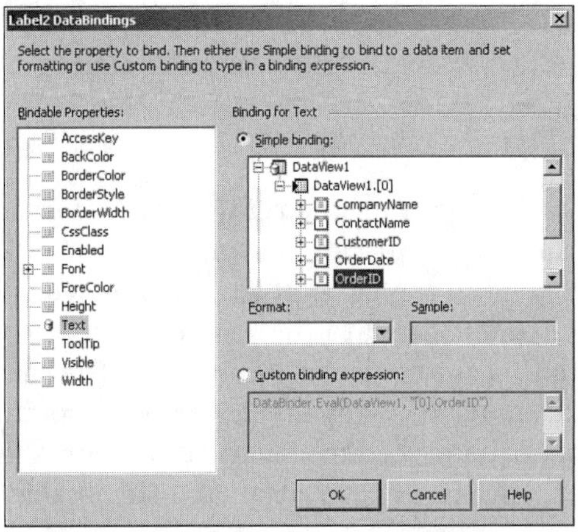

Figure 36.10: *Creating the label bindings.*

Step 7. Implement the `SelectedIndexChanged` Event

The last thing to add to our application is a handler for the
`SelectedIndexChanged` event of the `DataGrid`, which is required to update
the detail view (the bound labels) defined previously. Add the code as
shown:

```
Public Class WebForm1
    Inherits System.Web.UI.Page
    Protected WithEvents DsCustomers1 As C36EX1.DsCustomers
    Protected WithEvents DataGrid1 As System.Web.UI.WebControls.DataGrid
    Protected WithEvents DataView1 As System.Data.DataView
    Protected WithEvents Label1 As System.Web.UI.WebControls.Label
    Protected WithEvents Label2 As System.Web.UI.WebControls.Label
    Protected WithEvents Label3 As System.Web.UI.WebControls.Label
    Protected WithEvents Label4 As System.Web.UI.WebControls.Label
    Protected WithEvents Label5 As System.Web.UI.WebControls.Label
    Protected WithEvents Label6 As System.Web.UI.WebControls.Label
    Protected WithEvents Label7 As System.Web.UI.WebControls.Label
    Protected WithEvents Label8 As System.Web.UI.WebControls.Label
    Protected theComponent As New Component1()


    ' Web Form Designer Generated Code


    Private Sub Page_Load(ByVal sender As System.Object, _
                          ByVal e As System.EventArgs) _
    Handles MyBase.Load
        If Not IsPostBack Then
            theComponent.PopulateDS(DsCustomers1)
            DataGrid1.DataBind()
        End If
    End Sub


    Private Sub DataGrid1_PageIndexChanged(ByVal source As Object, _
        ByVal e As System.Web.UI.WebControls.DataGridPageChangedEventArgs) _
    Handles DataGrid1.PageIndexChanged
        DataGrid1.CurrentPageIndex = e.NewPageIndex
        theComponent.PopulateDS(DsCustomers1)
        DataGrid1.DataBind()
    End Sub


    Private Sub DataGrid1_SelectedIndexChanged(ByVal sender As System.Object, _
        ByVal e As System.EventArgs) Handles DataGrid1.SelectedIndexChanged
        theComponent.PopulateDS(DsCustomers1)
        Dim index As Integer = DataGrid1.SelectedIndex
        'System.Diagnostics.Debug.WriteLine("** index = " + index.ToString)
        Dim key As String = DataGrid1.DataKeys(index).ToString()
        'System.Diagnostics.Debug.WriteLine("** key = " + key)
        DataView1.RowFilter = DataGrid1.DataKeyField & "=" & key
        Label2.DataBind()
        Label4.DataBind()
```

```
        Label6.DataBind()
        Label8.DataBind()
    End Sub
End Class
```

The algorithm is very simple: first we retrieve DsCustomers1 (using the PopulateDS method of theComponent). Then we get the SelectedIndex of the DataGrid1 (which is the row on which the user clicked in the browser). Then we get the unique key of the data set for the row, using the DataKeys property of the DataGrid. We then set the RowFilter property of the DataView1 object to be the key value we found, as an expression of type key = value. And finally we update the binding for all labels bound to this DataView. If you have problems running the code, uncomment the debugging statements shown in code to get some information on what went wrong.

We are now ready to run the final version of the application. Figure 35.11 shows the page running in the browser, with the details for an order shown above the grid.

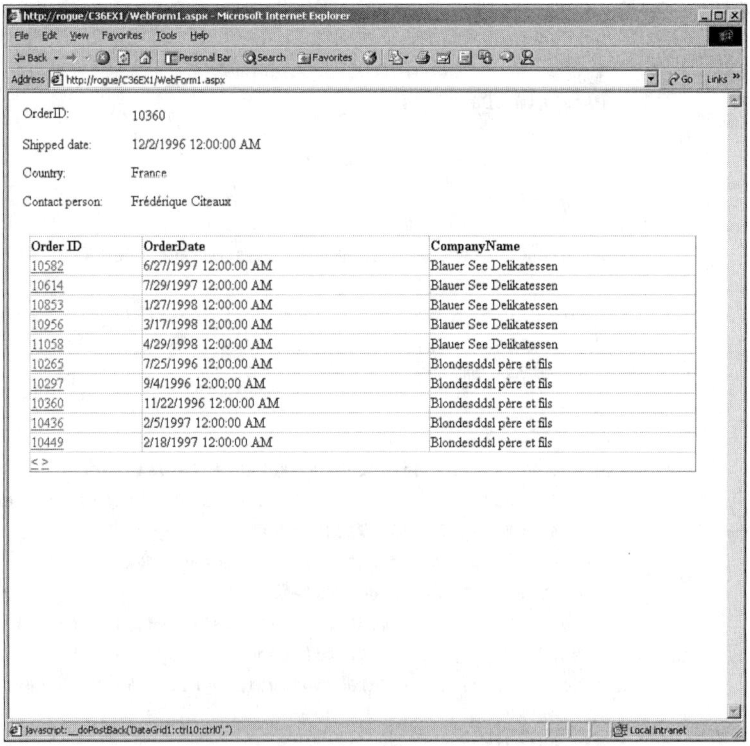

Figure 36.11: *The final application running.*

State Management

You have learned so far that Web pages are loaded during each HTTP GET and POST. The data associated with the page and its controls will be lost every time the page is posted back. For instance, if the end user enters some data into a text box, that data is lost in the round trip from the browser to the server. In a normal HTML page in order to preserve this data, you have to reload manually the control with the value entered by the user. However, the .NET framework (namely the ASP.NET part) can automatically save the state of the page and its controls. Optionally, it can also save application or session-specific information. The process of managing this data is known as *state management*.

The .NET framework provides a number of ways to manage state information. These ways can be classified in *client-side* and *server-side* state management techniques. Among the client-side methods are cookies, hidden fields, query strings, and view state. The server-side methods are application state, session state, and database state support. Each one of these techniques has its distinct advantages and disadvantages. We will look next at the most important state management techniques.

Cookies (Client-Side)

A cookie is a small amount (usually less than 4KB) of data stored on the client machine. It is normally stored as a text file known as a *persistent cookie*. If the browser does not support persistent cookies, it can be stored in-memory, and is known as a *temporary cookie*. Cookies can be used to store information about a particular client, which you can use later. They are meant mainly for tracking settings, for example a unique session ID. They are stored on the client machine and when the browser requests a page, it will also send the data in the cookie. The Web server will use the data to identify the client and take appropriate action.

The advantages of using cookies are that it requires no server resources; it is simple to use; and it is relatively secure (the browser can send only the cookie back to the server that created it). The disadvantages are that it may be refused by the browser (if the user has disabled cookie support); it has a limited size; and it may pose potential security risks (for example, if the user tampers with the cookie contents).

The next example shows how to create and read a cookie, using the Response and Request properties of the Page class. Each one of the two contain a property called Cookies, which is a collection of the known cookies for this page. You can add your own cookies to the Response.Cookies collection, and they will be saved on the client:

```
Public Class WebForm1
    Inherits System.Web.UI.Page
    Protected WithEvents Button1 As System.Web.UI.WebControls.Button

    ' Web Form Designer Generated Code

    Private Sub Page_Load(ByVal sender As System.Object, _
                          ByVal e As System.EventArgs) _
        Handles MyBase.Load
        Dim cookie As HttpCookie
        cookie = Request.Cookies.Get("MyCookie")
        If cookie Is Nothing Then
            ' we need to create a new cookie
            cookie = New HttpCookie("MyCookie", "The cookie value!")
            cookie.Expires = Now.AddDays(5)
            cookie.Secure = False
            Response.Cookies.Add(cookie)
        Else
            ' we got the cookie we created earlier
            Response.Write("Cookie: " & cookie.Name & "<br>")
            Response.Write("Expires: " & cookie.Expires & "<br>")
            Response.Write("Secure:" & cookie.Secure & "<br>")
            Response.Write("Value:" & cookie.Value & "<br>")
        End If
    End Sub

    Private Sub Button1_Click(ByVal sender As System.Object, _
                              ByVal e As System.EventArgs) _
        Handles Button1.Click
        ' this is for postback
    End Sub
End Class
```

Add a button to the form, which does a simple post-back, as shown in the sample code (Sub Button1_Click). When you first run this application, the cookie will be created. If you press the button (which does nothing except a post-back) the cookie will be found, and its properties displayed on the post-back page. The classes used are HttpCookieCollection and HttpCookie.

Hidden Fields (Client-Side)

The hidden fields are standard HTML controls (implemented in ASP.NET as the HttpInputHidden class). They are controls that are invisible to the end user, but whose content is sent back to the server when the page is posted back. A hidden field stores a single variable, containing any page-specific information you deem necessary. The control will appear as a regular control in the Controls collection of the page, when it is posted back.

The hidden fields are normally used to store small amounts of information that changes frequently. The advantages of using hidden fields are being an HTML standard they are almost universally supported, they are simple to use, and use no server resources. Disadvantages are that they are not secure (they can be viewed in the browser if the user looks at the HTML source for the page), and they have limited storage characteristics (both volume and structure).

Query Strings (Client-Side)

Query strings can be thought of more as a mechanism of passing parameter information to a page through the HTTP request, rather than a state management method. A query string is a collection of parameters and their values in the form of a string, which is appended to the HTTP request for a page. For example:

```
http://www.myserver.com/index.aspx?type=MAP&x=20&y=31
```

This query string contains three parameters (type, x, and y) and their values (MAP, 20, and 31, respectively). The syntax is simple: the query string starts with the question mark ? and is followed by a number of parameter-value pairs, delimited by the ampersand &. The parameter name and value are delimited by the equal (=) sign.

The .NET Framework provides good support to retrieve the parameters and their values, through the Request.QueryString property, as illustrated by the next example:

```
Imports System.Collections.Specialized
Public Class WebForm1
    Inherits System.Web.UI.Page

    ' Web Form Designer Generated Code

    Private Sub Page_Load(ByVal sender As System.Object, _
                        ByVal e As System.EventArgs) _
    Handles MyBase.Load
        Dim c As NameValueCollection = Request.QueryString
        Dim a As String() = c.AllKeys
        Dim i As Integer
        For i = 0 To a.Length - 1
            Response.Write("Parameter name: " & a(i) & _
                        ", value: " & c.Get(a(i)) & "<br>")
        Next
    End Sub
End Class
```

Figure 36.12: Parsing a query string.

In Figure 36.12, you can see the output of this code. Note the query string (?type=MAP&x=20&y=31) entered manually in the browser's address window.

The query strings have the same advantages as the hidden fields: simple to use, broad support on most browsers, and (as any client-state management method) no server resources are required to support them. The disadvantages include the fact that query strings are not secure and that their size is limited to 256 bytes on most browsers.

View State (Client-Side)

This method is similar to the hidden fields method. It uses the Control. ViewState property to store name-value pairs used between multiple invocations of the same page. Unlike the hidden fields, though, the data is both encrypted and compressed. When the page is posted back, the server automatically decrypts and populates the ViewState property of the controls. It has the advantage of being secure, simple to implement and not requiring any server resources. It can have a negative impact on page loading performance, if large amounts of data are stored in the ViewState.

The following example is a simple illustration of the usage of the ViewState property.

```
Public Class WebForm1
    Inherits System.Web.UI.Page
    Protected WithEvents Button1 As System.Web.UI.WebControls.Button

    ' Web Form Designer Generated Code

    Private Sub Page_Load(ByVal sender As System.Object, _
                        ByVal e As System.EventArgs) _
    Handles MyBase.Load
        If Not IsPostBack Then
            ' set the value
            ViewState("mySetting") = "myValue"
        Else
            ' get and display all values
            Dim n As IEnumerator = ViewState.Keys.GetEnumerator()
            Do While n.MoveNext()
                Dim s As String = CType(n.Current, String)
                Response.Write("Parameter name : " & s & "<br>")
                Response.Write("Parameter value: " & ViewState.Item(s) & "<br>")
            Loop
        End If
    End Sub

    Private Sub Button1_Click(ByVal sender As System.Object, _
                            ByVal e As System.EventArgs) _
    Handles Button1.Click
        ' used for post-back
    End Sub
End Class
```

Add a button to the form, which does a simple post-back, as shown in the sample code (Sub Button1_Click). Figure 36.13 illustrates the browser after the button was pressed (to trigger a post-back).

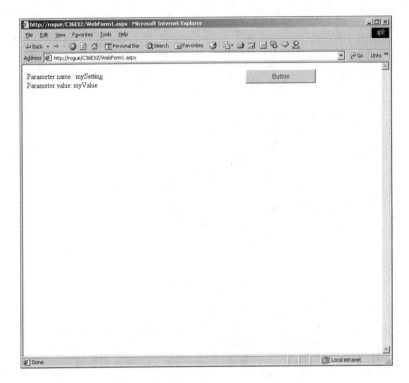

Figure 36.13: *Using the ViewState property.*

Application State Object (Server-Side)

The .NET Framework allows you to maintain global application state using an instance of the HttpApplicationState class per application. This instance is known as the Application State object. It is used as a global storage mechanism accessible from all pages in the current application. It should be used as a mechanism to store data shared among pages in the same Web application. It consists of a set of ordered name-value pairs (a dictionary). You can add to the application state object application-specific data that you need to store between page requests; the server will manage it. You can think of the named values you add to the application object as global variables of the application. Because of this fact, it is a good idea to limit the number of such variables to the minimum required. Use other mechanisms to store session or page specific data. The next example illustrates how to set and get a named value into the Application object.

```
Public Class WebForm1
    Inherits System.Web.UI.Page
    Protected WithEvents Button1 As System.Web.UI.WebControls.Button
```

```
' Web Form Designer Generated Code

Private Sub Page_Load(ByVal sender As System.Object, _
                      ByVal e As System.EventArgs) _
Handles MyBase.Load
   Dim connectionString As String = Application.Get("connectionString")
   If connectionString Is Nothing Then
      Application.Add("connectionString", "DSN=pubs")
   Else
      Response.Write("Application connection string is: <b>'" _
                     & connectionString & "'</b><br>")
   End If
End Sub

Private Sub Button1_Click(ByVal sender As System.Object, _
                          ByVal e As System.EventArgs) _
Handles Button1.Click
   ' used for postback
End Sub
End Class
```

Figure 36.14 illustrates the browser window after the button was pressed (to trigger a post-back). The application value named connectionString is displayed.

Session State Object (Server-Side)

A similar mechanism to the application state, the session state allows you to maintain the state for one session, i.e., for one instance of the Web application created for one user. It involves the use of the session state object (an instance of the HttpSessionState class). The Web server will create one object of this type when a user connects for the first time and requests a page. The Web server will keep the session object around for a (configurable) period of time, so that if the same user connects again, the server will have the session data available.

This object is a dictionary—a sorted set of named values (similar to the application object). Apart from storing session data, this object can be also used to raise session management events and allows you to write code to manage these events (Session_OnStart and Session_OnEnd).

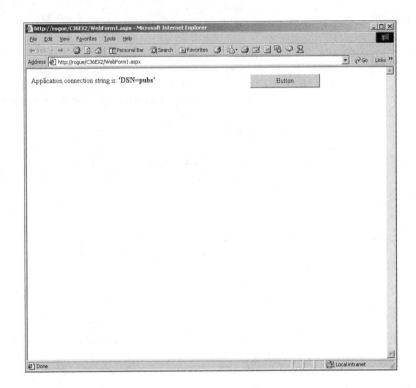

Figure 36.14: *Using the Application object.*

The session state is the most convenient and easy way to store client-specific data. The session object itself can be stored in one of a few different modes, all members of the SessionStateMode enumeration in the System.Web.SessionState namespace:

- **Off**—Session state is disabled.
- **InProc**—Session state is kept in process.
- **SQLServer**—Session state is saved in a SQL Server database.
- **StateServer**—Session state is saved on a special (dedicated) serve.

The last two modes allow the session data to survive a crash of the server process or thread that is processing a request. They also support *server farms*, that is, multiple machines clustered together to form a bigger Web server.

The usage of the session is similar to that of the application object (use the public Session object to set and get data as named value pairs). It is normally used to store client data common to all pages in the application, such as username, profile data, shopping cart info, and so on.

NOTE

It is strongly recommended that you limit the amount of data stored in the session object to the minimum required. The data is kept for the whole duration of a session, which can be around 10–30 minutes. For a server serving 10 hits per second 30 minutes means 18,000 session objects. Multiply this value with the average size of each session, and you will arrive to some pretty big numbers in terms of memory requirements. If you expect a heavy-loaded server, consider using the SQLServer or StateServer modes of operation, described previously.

Database State Support (Server-Side)

This mechanism is actually used in two distinct cases: in conjunction with cookies to save custom data for a client for longer periods of time and also in conjunction with the session object (as we mentioned previously, when using the SQLServer mode of the Session object).

In the first case the cookie stores a unique user identifier on the client machine, an identifier that is supplied every time the user requests a page. In the database, a custom set of data is added for each client, uniquely identified by the ID value in the cookie. When the client connects, the application gets the cookie value and retrieves the information from the database. The data stored can be anything from user preferences to stock and portfolio data.

Most Web applications today use database state support in one form or another because user data needs to be stored someplace, and relational databases are the most common and affordable way to store it.

State Management Summary

The state management options usage can be summarized in Table 36.1.

Table 36.1: State Management Usage Summary

Method	Best Used When
Cookies	Amount of data to be stored is small and security is not an issue.
Hidden fields	Amount of data to be stored is small and the page will post-back itself. Security is not an issue.
Query string	Transferring small amount of data from one page to another and security is not an issue.
View state	Amount of data to be stored is small and a medium level of security is required.
Application state	Application (global) data is stored and infrequently changed. Size of data is small or medium.

Table 36.1: continued

Method	Best Used When
Session state	Session data stored in a secure way for short periods of time. Data size should be small.
Database support	Same as session state, but the data size can be large. Data will be preserved if the server fails. Allows for transactions and distributed Web farms.

The most common methods are cookies and query strings, as well as session state. In .NET we expect the Database support method to be quite popular.

Developing Web User Controls

Web user controls are similar to normal Windows controls: They consist of a number of other controls grouped together under one class. They expose properties, methods, and events like any other Web controls.

The base class for all Web user controls is `UserControl`. The user controls are treated as contained Web pages, which can be displayed only within the context of another page. Their main use is to provide a reusable group of controls, when the intention is to frequently use them in an application.

We will show an example of creating a simple menu-like selection list control that will post-back to the page when an item in the menu is selected, using a query string. This example also illustrates one of the more advanced Web controls: the `DataList`.

The first step in creating a user control is to add it to the project. Create a new Web application and in the Solution Explorer window right-click on the solution name and select the Add/Add Web user control menu. This action will open the Add New Item dialog. Make sure the Web User Control item is selected and then give the control a name, such as `Menu.ascx`.

The wizard creates and opens the Design view of the control. Our control will consist of one `DataList` control in which every item is a `HyperLink` control. We will bind the `Text` and `NavigateURL` properties of each `HyperLink` control in the list using a custom binding function.

The `DataLink` control is used to present a list of items to the user. Each item can be any combination of controls. It can be a list of images and labels, a list of buttons, and so on. The way the list is displayed is controlled at design time through the templates associated with the `DataList` control.

Add a `DataList` control to the `Menu.ascx` control. In the Properties window set its `RepeatDirection` property to `Horizontal`. This setting will direct the list to display the items horizontally rather than vertically. In the Style section of the Properties pane, select the `SelectedItemStyle` property, open the `Font`, and set its `Bold` property to `True`.

TIP

You can double-click on the property name to toggle between `True` and `False` for any property of type `Boolean`.

Now we will set the templates for displaying the list. Right-click on the `DataList` control and select the menu item Edit Templates/Separator template. In the box under the SeparatorTemplate label enter a vertical bar character (|). You can add a space on each side of the vertical bar character, if you wish. This string is going to be used to delimit the items in our list, which will look like this:

```
Item1 | Item2 | …
```

Now we need to set up the `DataList` items. Right-click again on the control and select Edit Templates/Item Templates. Drag a `HyperLink` control and drop it in the space under the ItemTemplate label. Now we need to bind its properties to the container (`DataList`) properties. In the Properties window select `DataBindings` and click on the ellipsis button. This will open the Data Bindings dialog, as shown in Figure 36.15.

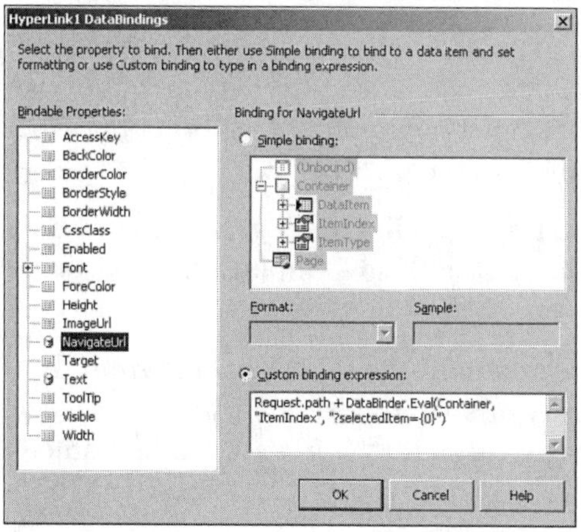

Figure 36.15: *Binding the properties of the `HyperLink` control.*

First we need to expand the `Container` node in the tree on the right (under the Binding for Text label). Select the `DataItem` node. Now, in the tree on the left select the `NavigateUrl` property. In the bindings tree on the right now select the `ItemIndex` property. In the `Format` text box enter the following string:

```
?selectedItem={0}
```

Now if you check the Custom binding expression radio button, the custom expression will become:

```
DataBinder.Eval(Container, "ItemIndex", "?selectedItem={0}")
```

Add the following string in front of the expression:

```
Request.path +
```

It will then become:

```
Request.path + DataBinder.Eval(Container, "ItemIndex", "?selectedItem={0}")
```

What we have done is to bind the `Text` property of each `HyperLink` control in the list to the `DataItem` member of the container (the `DataList`). We also bound the `NavigateUrl` property of the `HyperLink` control to a custom string that will be constructed at runtime, based on the expression. The `Request.Path` is the actual name of the page the control is on. The `DataBinder.Eval` is a method that will evaluate the expression ItemIndex of the container (`DataList`) and replace it in the format string `?selectedItem={0}`. It will replace the `{0}` with the actual value of the `ItemIndex` of the `DataList` (0, 1, and so on). So in effect our string expression when evaluated will look something like:

```
http://rogue/C36EX4/WebForm1.aspx?selectedItem=1
```

The first part of the expression (non-bold type) is the actual URL of the page the control will run on. The second part is a query string we constructed using the `DataList` custom binding function, where the `{0}` placeholder was replace by `ItemIndex` value 1.

Select OK to exit the Data Binding dialog. Right-click on the `DataList` control and select the menu item End Template Editing to return to the normal view of the control.

Now we need to specify where the binding come from. In this example we will use a simple array of strings. Press F7 to open the code-behind editor, and add the following code to it (the file should be named `Menu.ascx.vb`):

```
Public MustInherit Class Menu
    Inherits System.Web.UI.UserControl
    Protected WithEvents DataList1 As System.Web.UI.WebControls.DataList
    Public values() As String
    Public selection As Integer = -1
```

```
' Web Form Designer Generated Code

Private Sub Page_Load(ByVal sender As System.Object, _
                      ByVal e As System.EventArgs) _
   Handles MyBase.Load
      DataList1.DataSource = values
      DataList1.SelectedIndex = selection
      DataList1.DataBind()
   End Sub
End Class
```

The values and selection properties are added so that the clients of this
control (other pages in the project) can set the content of the menu list. We
will see how this is done shortly.

In the Load event handler we add the binding code: we set the DataSource
and SelectedIndex properties of the DataList1 control. We then call the
DataBind() method, to enable the bindings.

This is all we need to do to implement the control. We can now use it on
any form in the project. Switch back to the main form of the project
(WebForm1.aspx) and drag the control (Menu.ascx) from the Solution
Explorer window to the page. Create a Label underneath the control, which
will be used to display the selected menu item. Now switch to the code
behind the form.

The first thing to do is to add a class member for the user control. The wizard does this step for you for all standard controls, but not for user controls.
Therefore, it generates the declaration for Menu1 in the code below.

```
Public Class WebForm1
   Inherits System.Web.UI.Page
   Protected WithEvents Label1 As System.Web.UI.WebControls.Label
   Protected Menu1 As Menu

   ' Web Form Designer Generated Code

   Private Sub Page_Load(ByVal sender As System.Object, _
                         ByVal e As System.EventArgs) _
      Handles MyBase.Load
         Dim values() As String = New String() _
            {"Weekly", "Monthly", "Quarterly", "Yearly"}
         Menu1.values = values
         Dim si As String = Request.Params("selectedItem")
         If si <> "" Then
            Dim i As Integer = CInt(si)
            Menu1.selection = i
            Label1.Text = "Display report: " & values(i)
```

```
        End If
    End Sub
End Class
```

To populate the menu control we also declare an array of strings (values). When the Page_Load event occurs, we initialize the control's values property and then we get the query string parameter selectedItem (the one we set in the custom binding for the HyperLink control above). If it is present, we set the selection property of the Menu1 control and the value of the Label1.

We are now ready to build and run the application. When you run and click on any of the links, the value of the label will change, as illustrated in Figure 36.16.

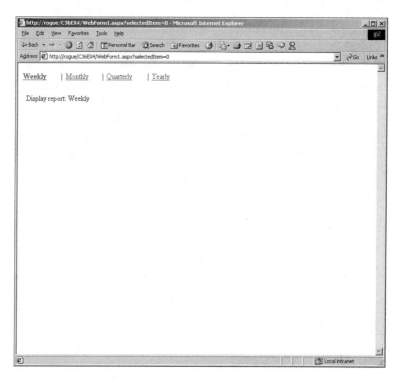

Figure 36.16: *The page with Menu user control running.*

In a real-life situation you will do more than display the selection in a label. You would likely refresh the display contents of a grid control, or of another data list, and so on.

What's Next

In this chapter we have looked at a few more advanced issues related to developing Web applications. We have looked at examples on how to bind data controls and how to configure some of the more advanced controls.

You also have learned about state management and what are the available options to implement it. You have seen the advantages and disadvantages of each method of managing state.

And finally we constructed a Web user control and learned the steps required to implement it, as well as to use it.

In the next chapter we will look briefly at Web Services: what they are and what you need to know to implement one. We will use a few simple examples to illustrate how to develop and use Web Services.

NOTE

The answers to "Reviewing It," "Checking It," and "Applying It" are available on our Web site.

REVIEW

Reviewing It

This section presents a review of the key concepts in this chapter. These questions are intended to gauge your absorption of the relevant material.

1. What is a bindable property?

2. What is a good approach when dealing with potentially large rowsets that need to be displayed?

3. Enumerate the state management mechanisms available using the client side.

4. What are the differences between the `Application` and `Session` objects?

5. What is a Web user control?

6. What is the base class of the Web user controls?

CHECK

Checking It

Select the correct answer(s) to the following questions.

Multiple Choice

1. Which of the following properties of a Label cannot be bound?

   a. BorderColor.

   b. Font name.

   c. EnableViewState.

   d. Height.

2. What must be done at design time to get a SelectedIndexChange event from a DataGrid control?

   a. Must add a key column to the grid.

   b. Must add a Select Button column.

   c. Must add a HyperLink column.

   d. Either b or c.

3. What is the best state management option, assuming that we have a small amount of data, we must not use server resources, and we need it to be moderately secure. Select all options in order from best to worse.

   a. Cookie.

   b. Hidden field.

   c. Query string.

   d. ViewState.

4. What type of items can be displayed in a DataList control?

   a. Anything.

   b. Any one Web control.

   c. Any combination of Web controls and text.

   d. Any combination of Web and HTML controls and text.

True or False

Select one of the two possible answers and then verify on our Web site that you picked the correct one.

1. `DataSet` and `DataView` can be both used as data sources.

   True/False

2. In a paged `DataGrid` you need to do `DataBind()` only once (in `Page_Load`).

   True/False

3. A state management mechanism is required because HTTP is a stateless protocol.

   True/False

4. The disadvantage of using cookies is the limited size and potential that the end user has the cookies option disabled.

   True/False

5. The advantage of using a database or state server to store state on the Web server versus using in-process session state is increased performance.

   True/False

6. The advantage of creating a user control from groups of frequently used controls is that it promotes reusability and saves time.

   True/False

APPLY

Applying It

Try to complete the following exercises by yourself.

Independent Exercise 1

Modify the user control example and add an icon (image control) to each menu item (in the `DataList`).

Independent Exercise 2

Based on the example in the section "Data Access Using Data Bound Controls" earlier in this chapter, write a Web application with two pages. The first page allows the user to select a product category (from the Categories table in the Northwind database). When the selection is made, the second page should be displayed, showing a list of all products in that category. HINT: The CategoryID column in the Products table should be used as a filter.

37

Web Services

In the previous two chapters you learned the fundamentals required to develop a Web application using Web pages and controls. In this chapter you will continue to learn about Web development, but from a different angle. You will learn about Web Services, or how to develop distributed applications using the Visual Studio .NET and the Web Services infrastructure. The chapter is structured in the following topics:

- Introduction to Web Services

- Example of developing a Web Service

- Attributes as a language extension mechanism

- Using the Web Services in a client application

In the first part of this chapter you will learn the basics about Web Services: what they are and an overview of the components involved in a Web Service.

Next, you will learn the steps required to implement a Web Service, using a simple example. The example will walk you through the process of developing a Web Service from initial project setup to building and deployment.

The next section is dedicated to *attributes* as a mechanism of extending the .NET languages. We will use the same example developed in the "Example of Developing a Web Service" section.

In the last part of the chapter you will learn how to use the Web services from a client application. You will develop both a Web application and a regular Windows Forms client application, and access the service from both. In the final part of this section you will read a brief discussion on when and how to best make use of the Web Services.

Introduction to Web Services

Web Services are one of the new and exciting features introduced in the .NET Framework. They are a mechanism that allows any client application to call a method on a remote component, residing on a server machine. For example a Web application (page) can invoke a method `getStockInfo()` on a `StockQuote` component residing on a different machine to get information about a specific stock. The application would pass in the name of the stock as a parameter to the method and would get back the current value of the stock.

This mechanism is known as *Remote Procedure Call* (RPC), and it may be familiar to you if you used DCOM or the Remote services in Visual Basic 6. The same principle is used in many other platforms and languages (Java, CORBA, and so on). The implementation of the mechanism is totally different in the .NET Framework compared to any other implementations.

The server is said to provide Web Services to any client that connects to it. The server can be configured to be secure and provide access only to some clients, based on some form of authentication. The protocol used to communicate between the server and the clients, as well as the protocol used to discover (describe) the functionality offered by the server are transparent to you, if you use the Visual Studio .NET to develop your application (server and client). If your client application is developed in another language or on a different platform, it is your responsibility to implement the client RPC handling.

The protocol used for communication between the server and the client is known as *Simple Object Access Protocol* (SOAP), and it is based on XML. It uses XML messages, validated using the XML Schema specification. The detailed specification for this W3C protocol is at `http://www.w3.org/TR/SOAP/`.

The protocol used for the description of the services provided by a server (the metadata protocol) is named *Web Services Description Language* (WSDL), and it is also an XML based W3C protocol. Its specification is at `http://www.w3.org/TR/WSDL.html`.

The *Universal Description, Discovery and Integration* (UDDI) protocol is used by clients to identify the specific server and by servers to list their services in a directory fashion. It is based on XML and SOAP. This protocol is not currently a W3C recommendation, rather it was developed in collaboration by Microsoft, IBM, and Ariba. You can find out more about it at `http://www.uddi.org`.

A simplified overview of the Web Services architecture is presented in Figure 37.1.

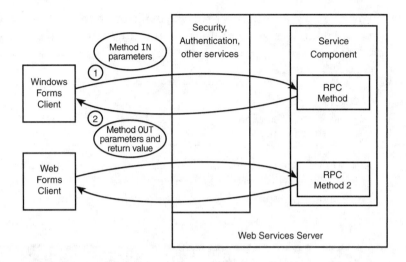

Figure 37.1: *Web Services overview.*

A client application can call a method of a server component, passing in a number of parameters known as IN parameters (1 in Figure 37.1). For example, it could pass in the stock name (symbol). The server will invoke the component method, passing in the parameter values from the client. The component will then return the outbound parameters and eventually the return value to the client (2 in Figure 37.1). For example, it would return the current value of the requested stock, either as a return value or as an OUT parameter. This process can be initiated by any application that can use SOAP, although it is greatly simplified if you use the Visual Studio .NET IDE and wizards.

NOTE

Things are a bit more complicated if you look under the surface (which you do not have to!). The .NET Framework on the client side actually will translate the method call made by the client into a SOAP message and will place the inbound parameter data, as well as the correct server, component, and method identifiers in the message. Then it will send the message and wait for the response.

The server will receive the SOAP request message and will decode it. It will then verify and authenticate the client. If the security check is passed, the requested component methods will be invoked with the data (IN parameters) passed in from the client. Upon the return of the method, the outbound data (OUT parameters and return value) is encoded into a SOAP response message and sent back to the client.

The client code will then decode the SOAP response and return the data to the client method which called the remote method. From the client's point of view, this process is almost transparent, but if you plan to develop industrial strength applications, it is better if you understand what goes on underneath the hood.

Web Services are similar to a Web application in that both use a disconnected (stateless) protocol to communicate between clients and servers: The client makes a request; the server replies with an answer; and then the connection is closed.

> **NOTE**
>
> Similarity to a Web application is extended by the fact that most SOAP implementations are based on HTTP.

Although the details behind the Web Services implementation seem to be quite complex (and some of them are), you will see next that the actual process of developing a Web Service is relatively simple and straightforward.

Example of Developing a Web Service

The steps involved in creating a Web Service are as follows:

1. Create the Web Service project.

2. Create the component class.

3. Implement the desired methods.

4. Build, deploy, and test the server.

You will create a simple service example that will return a description for a catalog item requested by the client. You will add two methods to the component, one to get the description, based on the item identifier, and a second one to get a list of all known identifiers for this server. You will then implement a client application as a Web page, which will use the services you developed.

Step 1. Create the Web Service project

The first step is to create a new project and select the Web Service from the New Project Wizard dialog. The wizard will create a new Web Service project and a default component called `Service1`.

> **NOTE**
>
> You need the IIS installed and operational to create a Web Service project, as you do for any other Web-based application.

The next step is to rename the `Service1.asmx` component to `ResourceServer.asmx`. You can do this in the Properties window, under the `FileName` property. By double-clicking anywhere on the design page of the component, you will open the code window. In code, change the class name to `ResourceServer` to match the `.asmx` filename.

Step 2. Create the Component Class

The component class generated by the wizard inherits from the `WebService` class in the `System.Web.Services` namespace and contains (as usual) some designer-generated code. Let's look first at the base class.

The `WebService` class is used to derive all Web Services components. It is itself derived from the `Component` class in the `System.ComponentModel` namespace, which in turn is derived from the abstract `MarshalByRefObject` class from the `System` namespace.

The `MarshalByRefObject` class is used as a base for all objects that need to be *marshaled* by reference. Marshaling is the action of passing parameters to a method call in a different process. Marshaling can be done *by value* or *by reference*.

Marshaling by value means that the object data is copied from the calling process into the called process memory space, and the object is reconstructed there. That is, a copy of the object is passed to the called process.

Marshaling by reference means that the object reference is passed from the calling process into the called process, but the object state (data) is not copied. The object is used by means of the reference passed. The semantic meaning of the marshaling is similar to the `ByVal` and `ByRef` passing of parameters that you learned earlier in the book.

The most significant methods of the `MarshalByRefObject` class are `CreateObjRef` (used to create a new object reference) and `InitializeLifetimeService`. These are low-level advanced methods, and you will not deal with them directly.

The `Component` is a base class for the remotable components and provides a default implementation for the `IComponent` interface. It is, as you have learned, the base class for all Windows `Forms` classes.

The `WebService` class has a few important properties and methods, presented in the following list:

- `Application` is a property that returns an instance of the `HttpApplicationState` class. This is a singleton (single object) per application, same as for the regular ASP.NET Web applications.

- `Session` returns a `HttpSessionState` instance, which represents a user session. It is the same object you have seen in the previous chapter, in the section on maintaining state.

- **User** returns a User object, the same as for any other Web application.

- **Context** the HttpContext instance for the current request. This is the same class as the one used in any Web application in .NET.

As you can see, all of the preceding properties are equivalent to the properties with the same name of the Page class. They have similar semantics and usage as in the case of the Web pages. For example, the Application property can be used to access application-wide data, while the Session is used to hold information about one client session.

Step 3. Implement the Desired Methods

You create Web Services by extending the WebService class and adding public methods to it. The following code shows the implementation of the two methods to get a resource description and get a list of all known resources for this server:

```
Imports System.Web.Services
Imports System.Collections

Public Class ResourceServer
    Inherits System.Web.Services.WebService

    Private m_resources As Hashtable

#Region " Web Services Designer Generated Code "

    Public Sub New()
        MyBase.New()

        'This call is required by the Web Services Designer.
        InitializeComponent()

        'Add your own initialization code after the InitializeComponent() call
        m_resources = New Hashtable(5)
        m_resources.Add("Scimitar", _
            "Short sword having a curved blade with the edge on the convex side")
        m_resources.Add("Saber", _
            "Cavalry sword with a medium length curved blade and guard")
        m_resources.Add("Broadsword", _
            "Large heavy sword with a broad blade used for cutting")
        m_resources.Add("Katana", _
            "Long single-edged sword slightly curved used mostly in Japan")
        m_resources.Add("Rapier", _
            "Straight double-edged sword with a narrow pointed blade")
```

```
End Sub

'Required by the Web Services Designer
Private components As System.ComponentModel.Container

'NOTE: The following procedure is required by the Web Services Designer
'It can be modified using the Web Services Designer.
'Do not modify it using the code editor.
<System.Diagnostics.DebuggerStepThrough()> Private Sub InitializeComponent()
    components = New System.ComponentModel.Container()
End Sub

Protected Overloads Overrides Sub Dispose(ByVal disposing As Boolean)
    'CODEGEN: This procedure is required by the Web Services Designer
    'Do not modify it using the code editor.
End Sub

#End Region

    <WebMethod()> _
    Public Function GetResource(ByVal resourceName As String) As String
        Dim o As Object = m_resources.Item(resourceName)
        If o Is Nothing Then Return Nothing
        Return CType(o, String)
    End Function

    <WebMethod()> Public Function GetKnownResources() As String()
        Dim keys As ICollection = m_resources.Keys
        Dim e As IEnumerator = keys.GetEnumerator()
        Dim knownResources As String() = New String(keys.Count) {}
        Dim i As Integer = 0
        Do While e.MoveNext()
            knownResources(i) = e.Current
            i += 1
        Loop
        Return knownResources
    End Function
End Class
```

To implement the resource holder you use a Hashtable field, m_resources. The field is initialized in the Sub New, which is located inside the code generated by the designer (the code in bold type). You add five named resource strings to the Hashtable. These are going to be used to return a description and a list of resource names to the clients.

NOTE

In a real-life application you would use a database to store the resources and the descriptions. The GetResource method could then be implemented as a search into the database. However, the example is intended to teach you how to create Web Services, so we decided to keep unnecessary and already learned features out of the example. This is the reason we use a memory Hashtable of hard-coded strings.

The two public functions GetResource and GetKnownResources are the methods we want to expose from this component. The GetResource is simply looking for a resource with the specified name in the m_resources Hashtable. The GetKnownResources constructs an array of all resource names from the Keys collection of the Hashtable and returns it to the client.

We will explain the meaning of the <WebMethod()> tag prefixing the two functions in the next section, when we talk about attributes.

Step 4. Build, Deploy, and Test the Server

You can now run the project. Because this is a service that has no visible parts to it, you would need a client application to test it. However, the Visual Studio .NET IDE provides a quick and easy way to test a Web Service without a client. The IDE will generate a default client Web page for you, so that you can call the methods of your component. To test a Web Service, mark the .asmx file as a start-up page (right-click on the file in the Solution Explorer and select the Set As Startup Page menu item). When you run the project, you should get a Web page in the browser, as illustrated in Figure 37.2.

The Web page will list all the known methods for your component. You can click on the links with the method names to test them. Following are some generated recommendations, code samples, and links. If you click on the GetResource link, you will get another browser page, similar to the one illustrated in Figure 37.3.

For each parameter of the method the IDE will generate a TextBox control, in which you can type the values you want to use to test the method. Below the table of parameters and values there is a sample of the SOAP messages that will get generated, as well as the HTTP request and response. The placeholders in bold letters would be replaced by real values (either entered by you or calculated). If you enter one of the resource names (the sword types defined previously) in the text box (say Katana) and click the Invoke button, you will get a response back, similar to the one shown in Figure 37.4.

You can close this new page to test with other values. You can also go back to the previous page and test the GetKnownResources method.

Figure 37.2: Web Service test page.

Attributes as a Language Extension Mechanism

Both the `GetResource` and `GetKnownResources` functions are prefixed by a special tag enclosed in angle brackets, `<WebMethod()>`. This tag is known as an *attribute*, and it is used as a language extension mechanism. In the example in the previous section, it tells the compiler that the two methods marked by the `<WebMethod()>` attribute are the ones the component will expose to the outside world, through the Web Services server. It is important to understand that *attribute* in this context is different from the UML concept of an attribute. It is a .NET-specific way to extend a language by adding special notations to some of its elements. This is the meaning that is attached to the *attribute* concept within this chapter, unless otherwise noted.

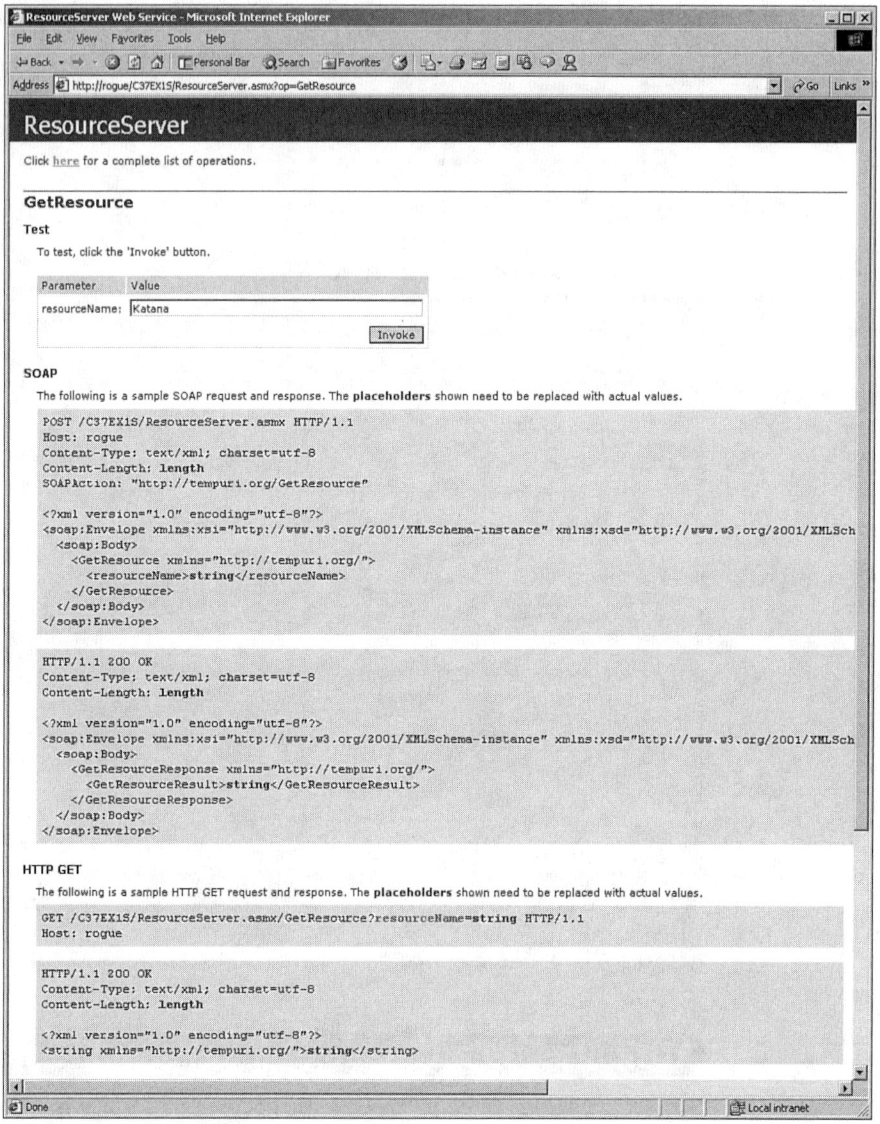

Figure 37.3: Web Service test method page.

In Visual Basic .NET these notations are represented as tags delimited by the angle brackets < and > placed before an language element.

Assemblies, namespaces, classes, properties, and methods are examples of language elements that can have attributes attached to them. The .NET Framework includes a number of predefined attributes, and you can define custom attributes if you need to.

Figure 37.4: *Web Service test results page.*

Attributes can have parameters and values. For example, you can modify the code to add a description for the two methods:

```
Imports System.Web.Services
Imports System.Collections

Public Class ResourceServer
   ' the rest of the code is unchanged

   <WebMethod(Description:="Get a resource string by name")> _
   Public Function GetResource(ByVal resourceName As String) As String
      Dim o As Object = m_resources.Item(resourceName)
      If o Is Nothing Then Return Nothing
      Return CType(o, String)
   End Function

   <WebMethod(Description:="Get an array of all known resources")> _
   Public Function GetKnownResources() As String()
      Dim keys As ICollection = m_resources.Keys
      Dim e As IEnumerator = keys.GetEnumerator()
      Dim knownResources As String() = New String(keys.Count) {}
      Dim i As Integer = 0
      Do While e.MoveNext()
         knownResources(i) = e.Current
         i += 1
      Loop
      Return knownResources
   End Function
End Class
```

If you run the program now, you will notice that the generated test Web page now includes the two descriptions for the two methods. You can also add attributes to the Web Service class:

```
Imports System.Web.Services
Imports System.Collections
```

```
<WebService(Namespace:="http://ROGUE/WebServices/", _
            Description:="This is a resource server Web Service.")> _
Public Class ResourceServer
   ' the rest of the code is unchanged
End Class
```

You can set the Namespace and Description properties of the WebService attribute. The Namespace is important, and it is the actual server path used to identify the *Web Services Description Language* (WSDL) service descriptor. This is a file that contains the full description of what this service looks like, and it is used by client applications to gather information about a specific service. The WSDL file is automatically generated using the class definition you create.

If you run the application now (see Figure 37.5), you will notice that the recommendations at the bottom of the browser window have disappeared because you added a real namespace, and the descriptions for both the service and the methods are there.

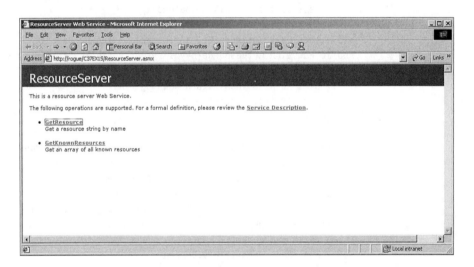

Figure 37.5: *Web Service test running.*

The attributes are implemented using .NET classes. For example the WebMethod attribute is implemented using the WebMethodAttribute class, in the System.Web.Services namespace. All attributes are derived from the base class Attribute, and by convention the class names end in the word Attribute (WebMethodAttribute, WebServiceAttribute, and so on).

They are regular classes, and indeed, you can define your own attributes to extend the language. However, this is an advanced subject, and we will not present it in this book. See the online documentation "Extending Metadata Using Attributes" for details, should you want to pursue this matter further.

Next you will look at the most significant properties of the
WebMethodAttribute and the WebServiceAttribute classes. All these public
properties can be specified using the syntax shown in the previous examples and are summarized next:

`AttributeClass(Property:=Value, Property2:=Value2, …`

The AttributeClass is a placeholder for an attribute name (like WebMethod);
Property is a placeholder for the property name (for instance Description);
and Value is a placeholder for an appropriate value for that property (for
example "This is the description property").

WebMethodAttribute

The most significant WebMethodAttribute class properties are summarized
as follows:

- **EnableSession**—This is a Boolean property indicating whether the session state is enabled for this service method. By default this is False;
  the session is disabled. Warning: the session data is per user/
  connection (as it is for the Web applications), so setting this to
  true means server overhead.

- **Description**—The Web service method description. This is used to
  communicate to client application developers (or any other consumers
  of the method) what the method does.

- **BufferResponse**—Also a Boolean property. If it is True (the default), it
  indicates that the response should be buffered in memory until the
  method exits, and then it should be sent back to the client. If it is
  False, no buffering is done, and data is sent back to the client as it is
  written to the buffer. This is less efficient and should not be used,
  unless large amounts of data are transferred.

- **TransactionOption**—Indicates whether a transaction should be associated with the method. The default is no transaction is associated. If
  you wish to enable a transaction option, you must set one of the
  Supported, Required, or RequiredNew settings. See the .NET reference
  TransactionOption enumeration for details.

- **CacheDuration**—Used to indicate how long a response should be kept
  in cache after sending it back to the client. This property is useful if it
  is expected that the same client request will be repeated often. By
  default the value is 0—that is, no caching is done. This property
  should be used with care because caching large amounts of data can
  damage the overall server performance.

WebServiceAttribute

The WebServiceAttribute class properties are listed here:

- **Description**—The Web service description. This is used to communicate to client application developers (or any other consumers of the method) what the service does.

- **Namespace**—It is the XML namespace to use for the description of this service. Each Web Service has a descriptor, which is in WSDL format. This property specifies the URI (normally a URL) for this description.

- **Name**—Indicates the name of the service to use publicly. Normally it is the same as the class name, therefore is not frequently used.

Assembly-Level Attributes

Another set of attributes that are frequently used in most applications (Web and regular) is attached to the assembly in which the project is created. If you look at the file named AssemblyInfo.vb in the project (double-click on it in the Solution Explorer), you will see code like this:

```
Imports System.Reflection
Imports System.Runtime.InteropServices


' General Information about an assembly is controlled through the following
' set of attributes. Change these attribute values to modify the information
' associated with an assembly.

' Review the values of the assembly attributes

<Assembly: AssemblyTitle("")>
<Assembly: AssemblyDescription("")>
<Assembly: AssemblyCompany("")>
<Assembly: AssemblyProduct("")>
<Assembly: AssemblyCopyright("")>
<Assembly: AssemblyTrademark("")>
<Assembly: CLSCompliant(True)>

'The following GUID is for the ID of the typelib if this project is exposed to COM
<Assembly: Guid("46373112-DA98-4F78-99D6-C9A0500104D7")>

' Version information for an assembly consists of the following four values:
'
'       Major Version
'       Minor Version
'       Build Number
'       Revision
'
```

```
' You can specify all the values or you can default the Build and Revision
Numbers
' by using the '*' as shown below:
```

```
<Assembly: AssemblyVersion("1.0.*")>
```

This file is used to set some of the attributes of the assembly that you created. Some of the attributes have self-explanatory names, for example `AssemblyTitle`, `AssemblyDescription`, and so on. Others are less explicit. The version of the assembly (`AssemblyVersion`) is probably the one that you would use most often. The `CLSCompliant` attribute indicates whether the assembly is compliant with the Common Language Specification (CLS) specifications. All the projects in Visual Basic .NET are CLS-compliant, so you should leave the value of `CLSCompliant` to `True`.

NOTE

If you want detailed information about any attribute or attribute class, you can look it up in the .NET reference help. Use the Index and type in the name of the attribute.

The next step is to create a client application that will use the service you developed.

Using the Web Services in a Client Application

Now that you're familiar with Web Services, you can write a simple Web application that uses Web Services. The rest of this section is dedicated to the steps required to build this example.

Developing a Web Application client

You will use a Web application with one page to create a client for your service. Create a new ASP.NET Web application using the wizard and adding it to the solution (rather than creating it as a separate solution). You can do this by checking the Add to Solution radio button on the New Project dialog.

On the Web page design add two labels, a text box and a button, as shown in Figure 37.9. You will use the text box to allow the user to enter the resource name and the second label to display the result of calling the Web service `GetResource` method.

Now you need to add to the project a reference to the Web Service that you wish to use. You can do this in the Solution explorer window by right-clicking on the project name and selecting the Add Web Reference menu item. The Add Web Reference dialog is shown, as illustrated in Figure 37.6.

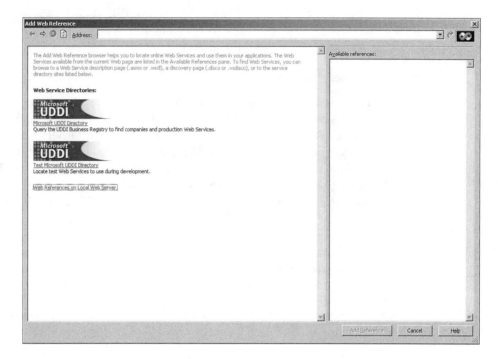

Figure 37.6: *The Add Web Reference dialog.*

From here you have a few options: You can use one of the UDDI services provided by the links in the dialog; you can use the local server references link; or you can enter the address of a known server in the address text box. Regardless of the method you use, a list of available Web Service and Web application servers will be shown in the right pane of the dialog. For this example, click on the Web References on Local Web Server hyperlink. You will get a result similar to the one shown in Figure 37.7.

From the right pane select the service you created in the previous example; this service is named C37EX1S. In the left pane you should get a description of the service, similar to the one shown in Figure 37.8. This is a UDDI (discovery) XML document.

In the right pane of Figure 37.8 there are two links, View Contract and View Documentation. Select the View Contract link to see the WSDL description of the service in the left pane. Note the two methods you implemented previously are now showing in the WSDL document. You can now select the Add Reference button to add a reference of this service to your project.

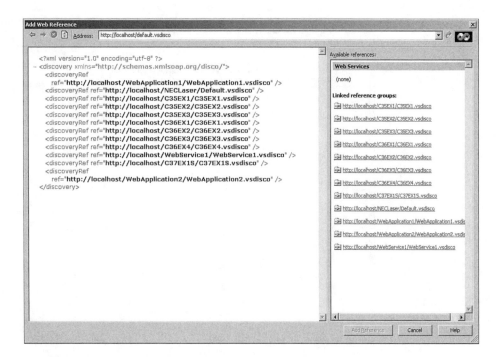

Figure 37.7: *The Add Web Reference dialog—selecting a server.*

In the Solution Explorer you will now see a Web Reference entry, with a single node named `localhost`. This is your local machine, functioning as a server for the Web Service you developed. You can now add code to use the service. Double-click on the button control on the page to add an event handler for the `Click` event. Enter the code as shown:

Imports WebApplication2.localhost

```
Public Class WebForm1
    Inherits System.Web.UI.Page
    Protected WithEvents Label1 As System.Web.UI.WebControls.Label
    Protected WithEvents TextBox1 As System.Web.UI.WebControls.TextBox
    Protected WithEvents Button1 As System.Web.UI.WebControls.Button
    Protected WithEvents Label2 As System.Web.UI.WebControls.Label

    ' Web Form Designer-Generated Code

    Private Sub Page_Load(ByVal sender As System.Object, _
                    ByVal e As System.EventArgs) _
    Handles MyBase.Load
        'Put user code to initialize the page here
    End Sub
```

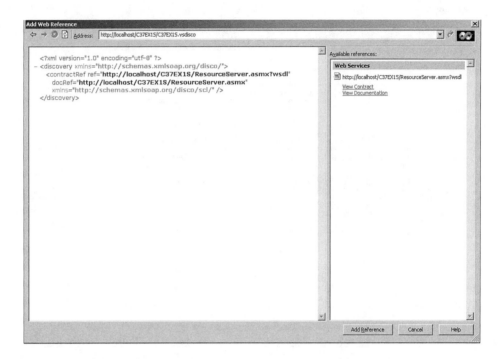

Figure 37.8: The Add Web Reference dialog—selecting a service.

```
    Private Sub Button1_Click(ByVal sender As System.Object, _
                              ByVal e As System.EventArgs) _
    Handles Button1.Click
        Dim svc As ResourceServer = New ResourceServer()
        Label2.Text = svc.GetResource(TextBox1.Text)
    End Sub
End Class
```

Normally, you would change the WebApplication2 to a more meaningful name. The Imports statement at the top is not mandatory, it just saves some typing: With it you can use the ResourceServer class without its namespace, not localhost.ResourceServer.

In the Click event handler of the button you have the call to the remote object. As you see this call is quite transparent. You create a new instance of the ResourceServer class and call its GetResource method as you would call any regular Visual Basic .NET method. You place the returned value (a String) into the Label2 so that the user of the browser can see it.

You are now ready to run the client example. Make sure you select the client Web application to be the start-up project (in the Solution Explorer window). The browser will display the page; you can enter a resource name;

and (if it is valid) you will get a description back in the Label2. Figure 37.9 illustrates the application running.

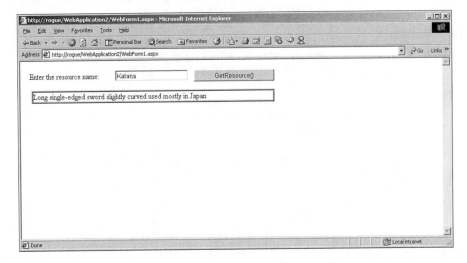

Figure 37.9: *The client Web application running.*

This concludes our simple Web application example of using a Web Service. Next you will develop a Windows Forms application client, using the same services.

Developing a Windows Forms Application client

You also can use as a client a regular Windows application. Create a new Windows application using the wizard. Add the application to the same solution (the one you are currently working on). Add a Label control, a ComboBox control, and a read-only text box control to display the results of the Web Service method call. Use Figure 37.10 as a guide for placing the controls.

Now you need to add a Web Reference to the project, using the same path as you did for the Web application. Follow the exact same procedure and select the ResourceServer service from localhost or from your service deployment machine.

This time we would like to get all the known resource names and place them in the combo box, for the user to pick one. Add the code as shown:

```
Imports WSClientExample.rogue

Public Class FMain
    Inherits System.Windows.Forms.Form
```

```
' Windows Form Designer-generated code

Private Sub FMain_Load(ByVal sender As System.Object, ByVal e As
System.EventArgs) Handles MyBase.Load
    Dim svc As ResourceServer = New ResourceServer()
    Dim rNames As String() = svc.GetKnownResources()
    Dim i As Integer, s As String
    For i = 0 To rNames.Length - 1
        s = rNames(i)
        If Not s Is Nothing Then
            ComboBox1.Items.Add(s)
        End If
    Next
    If i > 0 Then ComboBox1.SelectedIndex = 0
End Sub

Private Sub Button1_Click(ByVal sender As System.Object, ByVal e As
System.EventArgs) Handles Button1.Click
    Dim svc As ResourceServer = New ResourceServer()
    Dim rName As String = ComboBox1.Text
    TextBox1.Text = svc.GetResource(rName)
End Sub
End Class
```

The Imports statement in this case uses the machine name (rogue) as a namespace. It will be different in your case. The form-level Load event handler is used to call the GetKnownResources() method of the ResourceServer service, which returns an array of strings (the names of the known resources). You use this array to populate the combo box control.

The Click event handler of the button is used (as you did before) to call the GetResource method of the service. You pass in the currently selected resource name from the combo box, and you place the returned description in the text box.

You are now ready to run the application (make sure you set this project as a startup project first). When you run it, select a resource name and click the button to get a description. Figure 37.10 illustrates the application running.

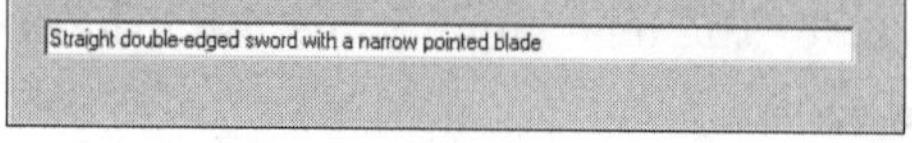

Figure 37.10: The client Windows application running.

As you see from this code, the usage of the Web Service classes is also transparent and very similar to the usage in a Web application. You create a remote object and use it as you would use any regular object.

Web Services Recommendations and Discussion

You have learned how to build Web Services and how to use them from a client application. Now you may have questions about when you would want to use a Web Service and what pitfalls you should try to avoid when developing and using a Web Service.

The first important concept that you must understand is that the service objects are *remote*. This is very important, and easy to forget, especially with the ease of use provided by the IDE. The fact that they are remote has a number of implications, which are outlined as follows:

- The referenced object is accessed over the wire; that is, you can get disconnected, the server may be busy, or any number of network exceptions can happen.

- The fact that it is over the network means that the performance will be worse than when calling a local assembly. Normally it is accepted that the connection speed would be an order of magnitude less (10 times slower).

- The performance takes another hit because data transmitted over the wire must be transformed into XML format and encoded into SOAP, then at the other end decoded and parsed back into values. The response data then will follow the exact same path in reverse.

These implications must be considered when developing and using a Web server. You should try to follow the following recommendations:

- Try to keep the amount of data transmitted to a minimum. This will reduce both network and parsing time.

- Try to use standard (.NET framework) classes as parameters and return values when developing the service. In this way the clients do not need to download your classes (and, therefore, do not depend on the changes you make to your code).

- Try to use by-value classes (structures), with no references to other classes. This will limit the number and size of data sent over the wire.

- Try to group multiple calls to an object's properties (for example) into one call (return a structure containing all the object state). This is a known distributed development pattern, and it is usually called using *value objects*, or data structures.

- Do not keep session state if possible, because this will decrease server performance.

It is in general a good idea to develop a Web Service if you plan to offer the service as a commercial service or allow unknown clients (at development time) to connect to it. It is not recommended to use Web Services for large-scale applications that require high-performance data access.

What's Next

We have reached the end of our journey together in learning the Visual Basic .NET language and the .NET Framework Class Library in general. We hope that the knowledge you gained from the book is going to help you become a better software developer.

If you want to further your knowledge, there are a few directions that we can suggest, depending upon your general preferences and/or job requirements.

If you want to learn more about design and object-oriented methodologies, search for a few books on UML, analysis, and design. Some examples include *The Unified Modeling Language Reference Manual* by James Rumbaugh et al (ISBN: 020130998X); *Design Patterns* by Erich Gamma et al (ISBN: 0201633612); and *Object-Oriented Analysis and Design with Applications* by Grady Booch (ISBN: 020189551X).

If you will develop a lot of applications for the Web, a good book on ASP.NET and HTML would help.

If you are developing Windows applications and IT applications and frameworks in general, an advanced book to the .NET Framework and programming in general will be of use.

If you plan on developing large-scale enterprise applications, you will need a better understanding of relational databases, ADO.NET, and XML.NET, as well as notions of distributed computing.

NOTE

The answers to "Reviewing It," "Checking It," and "Applying It" are available on our Web site.

REVIEW

Reviewing It

This section presents a review of the key concepts in this chapter. These questions are intended to gauge your absorption of the relevant material.

1. What are Web Services?

2. What are the protocols used by Web Services infrastructure?

3. Describe what happens when a client application calls a method of a remote object.

4. What does it mean to marshal data?

5. What are attributes (when we speak of .NET-specific features)?

6. What type of clients could use a Web Service?

CHECK

Checking It

Select the correct answer(s) to the following questions.

Multiple Choice

1. The SOAP protocol is:

   a. A stateful protocol.

   b. A stateless protocol.

   c. A stateless protocol based on XML.

   d. A stateless protocol based on HTML.

2. A .NET Web Service is implemented as a class derived from:

   a. `System.Web.UI.Page`.

   b. `System.Web.HttpRequest`.

   c. `System.componentModel.Component`.

   d. `System.Web.Services.WebService`.

3. What is required for a method of a component to become a Web method? Select all that apply.

   a. Must have Public access.

   b. Must be a Function, not a Sub or Property.

   c. Must have a `WebMethod` attribute.

   d. Must have a `WebService` attribute.

4. What special care must be taken when invoking a Web method from a client application? Select all that apply.

   a. Convert all parameters to `Strings`.

   b. Prefix the call with a `WebMethod` attribute.

   c. Use a try-catch block to catch any network/server errors.

   d. Nothing special must be done.

True or False

Select one of the two possible answers and then verify on our Web site that you picked the correct one.

1. SOAP is an HTTP-based protocol.

   True/False

2. Setting the `EnableSession` property of the `WebMethodAttribute` class to `True` will degrade server performance.

   True/False

3. `Namespace` is a property of the `WebServiceAttribute` used as a URI for the WSDL metadata for the service.

   True/False

4. Visual Basic .NET uses the angle brackets < and > to delimit attributes (of the language elements).

   True/False

5. UDDI is used to identify the server within the TCP/IP network.

   True/False

6. Performance of a Web Service–based distributed application is improved if the amount of data and number of server call is reduced.

   True/False

APPLY

Applying It

Try to complete the following exercises by yourself.

Independent Exercise 1

Modify the sample Web client project in this chapter to use the `GetKnownResources` method, in a similar fashion to what the Windows application does.

Independent Exercise 2

Modify the example Web Service code to use a database to store the data currently hard-coded in the Hashtable. Use a DataSet to get the data in the table.

Part VII

Appendix

UML Crash Course

UML Crash Course

This appendix presents a quick overview of the notation and the most important features of the Unified Modeling Language (UML), as they relate to the material presented in this book.

This is not a complete UML course, and there are UML topics that are not presented at all in this appendix, either because of the level of complexity of the notions involved, or because of the degree of relevance to the subject of the book. If you need to further your knowledge in UML or modeling and design in general, please consult a specialized UML book. Some examples include *The Unified Modeling Language Reference Manual* by James Rumbaugh et al (ISBN: 020130998X); *Design Patterns* by Erich Gamma et al (ISBN: 0201633612); and *Object-Oriented Analysis and Design with Applications* by Grady Booch (ISBN: 020189551X).

This appendix is structured in three parts:

- Brief introduction to modeling and design

- Classes, attributes, and operations

- Relationships

We will start with a short introduction to the field of design and modeling. Then you will learn about the notation used to represent classes and their attributes and operations.

The third section is dedicated to relations between classes—that is, association, aggregation, inheritance, and realization.

To understand the code examples and some concepts of this appendix, it is assumed that you have learned the fundamental concepts presented in Parts II, "Language Basics," and III, "Working with Objects."

Brief Introduction to Modeling and Design

Software complexity has increased dramatically over the past few decades, due to both advances in hardware and customer demand. Indeed, very few of us would be satisfied today with a green or amber text-only terminal style application of the 70s and early 80s. The increase in software complexity has created the ever-increasing demand for some sort of development process, to ensure both an increase in reliability and maintainability of the software produced. Starting to code in the first day of a project and adding the final changes at 3 a.m. the night before the delivery date is hardly a recipe for a successful system.

In the 80s, roughly at the same time as the emergence of the first commercial Object Oriented (OO) programming languages, a few design and modeling methodologies appeared. The three methodologies that were most widely adopted were Booch (developed by G. Booch), OMT (developed by J. Rumbaugh and others) and Jacobson (developed by I. Jacobson). Between the three of them, they held more than 90 percent of the market of OO analysis, modeling, and design. Each one of the three methodologies had its own strengths and weaknesses.

About seven years ago, the three methodologies were united (first Booch and Rumbaugh, then Jacobson joined them), taking the best parts from each, and resulting in what we know today as UML.

The UML standard is currently owned by the Object Management Group (OMG). The version 2.0 of the UML specification is in work at the time this book was written. You can find the UML specification at the `http://www.omg.com`.

Any software system or subsystem can be modeled in UML. A software system can be represented as a *UML model*. A UML model consists of many UML *entities* and of the relations between these entities. Examples of entities are classes, attributes, operations, associations, categories, packages, and so on. Each one of these entities has attributes. For example, a UML class entity has a name, a collection of attributes, and so on. A set of these entities forms an instance of an UML model. For example, all classes in the .NET Framework can be grouped and represented as one instance of a UML model. For each class, structure, and enumeration in the .NET Framework we will have a UML class representing it. For each field and/or property in a class, we will have a corresponding UML attribute.

The entities in a UML model are usually viewed in *diagrams*. A diagram is a graphics representation of the model. Usually the models are too large to be viewed in a single diagram. Therefore, the statement should be rephrased to reflect that diagrams are usually *views* of parts of the model.

An analogy can be made to a word processor window (the diagram), which shows just a part of the whole document (the whole model).

There are many kinds of diagrams in UML, differentiated by purpose. There are *class diagrams*, which are used to represent classes and relations between them. There are *sequence diagrams* and *collaboration diagrams*, which are used to represent interactions between objects (instances) of the classes in the model. There are use-case diagrams, state diagrams, activity diagrams, and so on. This appendix will focus on the class diagrams.

Each type of diagram has its own rules on how to represent certain entities in the model. For example, a class in a class diagram is represented as a rectangle with one, two, or three compartments. The same entity can be represented differently in different diagrams. For example, an object (class instance) is represented as a rounded rectangle in a collaboration diagram, but it is represented as a vertical narrow rectangle in a sequence diagram.

The UML standard specifies how each entity should be represented, but it allows some flexibility at the detail level. This flexibility allows different tools to use slightly different icons to represent some model entity properties. Figures A.1 and A.2 illustrate the same UML class in two different tools (Rational Rose and Microsoft Visio).

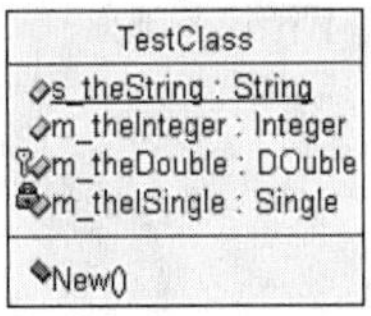

```
TestClass
◇s_theString : String
◇m_theInteger : Integer
◇m_theDouble : DOuble
◇m_theISingle : Single
◆New()
```

Figure A.1: *UML class in Rational Rose.*

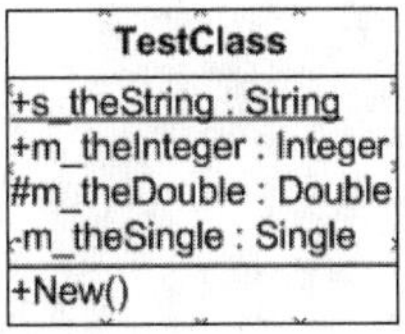

```
TestClass
+s_theString : String
+m_theInteger : Integer
#m_theDouble : Double
-m_theSingle : Single
+New()
```

Figure A.2: *UML class in Microsoft Visio.*

There are many UML tools available, each with its own features and capabilities. They go from free (open-source) tools to tools that sell for a few tens of thousands of dollars. Many of them are listed here:

`http://www.objectsbydesign.com/tools/umltools_byCompany.html`. You can sort them by company, product, platform, or price.

Classes, Attributes, and Operations

A UML class is represented as a rectangle with one, two, or three compartments. Figures A.1 and A.2 illustrate a class with three compartments: The top one is used to show the class name and eventually a *stereotype*. We will explain shortly what a stereotype is. The second (middle) compartment is used to display the class attributes. The third (lower) one is used to display the class operations (including constructors). Either the middle or the lower compartment or both can be omitted. Most UML tools provide a way to hide either one. This is sometimes helpful, especially when dealing with classes that have many operations, for example.

The class name compartment can also contain a *stereotype*. In UML a stereotype is a mechanism to further refine the model, by adding categories to some of the UML entities. For example, to make a distinction between classes and structures (a distinction that UML does not make), you can add the stereotype `<<structure>>` to the class entity that represents the structure. Stereotypes extend the basic modeling entities to add new meanings or create new entities that are specific to a project or system. An example of a structure using the stereotype is shown in Figure A.3.

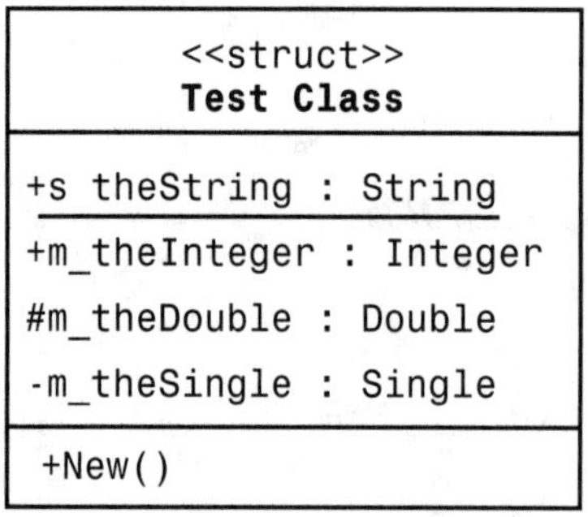

```
          <<struct>>
          Test Class

+s theString : String
+m_theInteger : Integer
#m_theDouble : Double
-m_theSingle : Single

 +New()
```

Figure A.3: *Class diagram of the* `TestClass` *with a stereotype.*

The class attributes are represented in the second (middle) compartment, using the notation

`attributeName : TypeName`

Where the `attributeName` is the name of the attribute, followed by the `TypeName` data type of the attribute (and separated by a literal colon—`:`).

The type name is that of a Visual Basic data type, a .NET Framework class, or one of your classes. For example:

```
m_name : String
```

Represents an attribute named m_name of the predefined type String.

The name of the attributes (and also of operations) is proceeded by a symbol which indicates its visibility:

- + Plus sign is used to denote Public attributes.
- # Pound sign is used to denote Protected attributes.
- − Minus sign is used to denote Private attributes.

If no sign is used, the visibility is Friend (which in UML is generally known as *implementation visibility*).

Shared attributes (which are known in UML as *static*) are either underlined (as s_theString shown in Figure A.3) or are prefixed with a $ (dollar sign).

If the attribute has a default value, the value is represented by placing it after the attribute type, as shown:

```
attributeName : TypeName = value
```

For example:

```
m_name : String = "The default value"
```

or

```
s_pi : Double = 3.141592
```

Default values are typically used for constant attributes.

A UML attribute represents usually a class property and its underlying field (data member). A UML tool may allow you to specify how the attribute will be implemented when the class code is generated. The following code illustrates a possible implementation for the class TestClass, used in the preceding examples.

```
Public Class TestClass
    Private Shared s_theString As String

    Private m_theInteger As Integer
    Private m_theDouble As Double
    Private m_theSingle As Single

    Public Shared Property theString() As String
        Get
            Return s_theString
        End Get
```

```
    Set(ByVal Value As String)
        s_theString = Value
    End Set
End Property

Public Property theInteger() As Integer
    Get
        Return m_theInteger
    End Get
    Set(ByVal Value As Integer)
        m_theInteger = Value
    End Set
End Property

Protected Property theDouble() As Double
    Get
        Return m_theDouble
    End Get
    Set(ByVal Value As Double)
        m_theDouble = Value
    End Set
End Property

Public Sub New()
    '
End Sub
End Class
```

In this case, all fields are implemented as private, and the visibility defined in the UML model is interpreted as the visibility of the properties associated with the respective field. Properties were generated for all public and protected fields, but not for the private field m_theSingle. This is a common way to implement the TestClass model.

NOTE

Private fields are visible only in the class that declares them, making implementation of a Private Property superfluous. For this reason private properties are seldom used.

UML attributes have also a property indicating whether the attribute is read-only, and a property called *multiplicity*, indicating the size of the array (if the attribute is an array). Note that we are speaking of properties of an UML attribute here, not properties in the .NET sense.

Operations are represented in the third (lower) compartment of the class rectangle. They can be represented only by the name of the operation, followed by a pair of parenthesis, as illustrated by the New() operation in

Figure A.3. The operations use the same conventions to represent their visibility and static properties as the attributes.

Operations can be also be represented using the full operation signature: parameter list and return type, as illustrated by the SetValues method in Figure A.4.

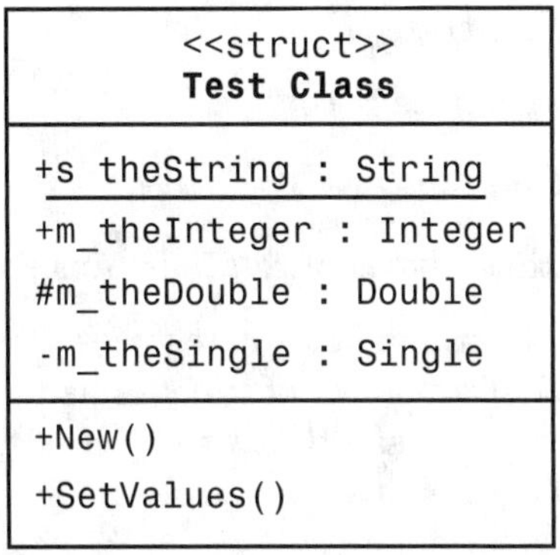

```
          <<struct>>
          Test Class

+s theString : String
+m_theInteger : Integer
#m_theDouble : Double
-m_theSingle : Single

+New()
+SetValues()
```

Figure A.4: *A full operation signature in UML.*

The name of the method (SetValues) is followed by the parameters list (if any) enclosed in parenthesis and then followed by the operation return type (if any). Each parameter follows the same notation as an attribute—that is, it has a name and a data type, and eventually a default value (for the optional parameters). In addition, each parameter may have a prefix indicating whether the parameter is IN or OUT or IN-OUT. In Visual Basic IN parameters are represented by using the ByVal prefix, when implementing the operation. The OUT and IN-OUT parameters are implemented as ByVal parameters. The SetValues operation could be implemented as shown:

```
Public Function SetValues(ByVal x As Short, Optional ByVal y As Short = 0) As
Double
    ' function body omitted
End Function
```

In addition to the features specified here, UML operations can specify what exceptions are thrown from the operation, how the operation is synchronized, and others.

The class, attribute, and operation (as well as many other model entity) properties can be accessed and edited in a tool-specific fashion (i.e., depends on the tool—if it is a dialog box, a property page, or some other way to access these entities). Most tools offer a "properties" or "specification" style dialog, or window for each model entity type.

Relationships

A relationship between two classes is a UML entity that represents the fact that the classes are somehow related to each other. Examples of relationships are:

association—class A is associated with class B.

aggregation—class A aggregates class B.

inheritance—class A inherits from class B.

realization—class A implements interface IB.

We will give examples of all these types of relationships shortly.

We can classify relationships in two general categories: *has-a* type of relationships (when we can say that an object of type A has an object of type B), and *is-a* relationships (when we can say that an object of type A is also of type B). Association and aggregation are *has-a* relationships. Inheritance and realization are *is-a* type relationships.

All relationships are represented as lines that connect two classes. Depending upon the relation type and properties, different adornments (symbols) are used at line ends. For example, a regular association is usually represented by a line terminated by a v-shaped arrow, as illustrated in Figure A.5.

Association

Two classes are said to be *associated* when instances of one or both classes hold a reference to instances of the other class. This type of relationship is represented as shown in Figure C.5.

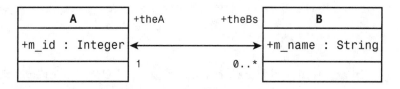

Figure A.5: *Association between classes A and B.*

The association consists of the double-arrow line connecting classes A and B and the text fragments (theA, 1, theBs, and 0..*), above and below the line ends. The line ends, and the text near them are known as *UML* *roles*. Therefore, each relationship consists of two roles, one towards each end of the line representing the relationship. The roles are UML entities that show what role the other class plays towards this (current) class, in the context of this relationship. In simpler terms, each role corresponds to the attribute that implements the relationship, in each class. Each role has a name (theA and theBs) and a *multiplicity*. The multiplicity indicates the number of instances of each kind associated with one instance at the other end. It is normally represented as a whole number like 1, 2, and so on, or a range represented like 0..5 (meaning between 0 and 5 objects), or 1..* (meaning at least one object). In our example, instances of class A will have a collection of instances of the class B (named theBs), which will hold any number of B objects (0 or more). Instances of class B will have a reference to exactly one object of type A. The following code illustrates a possible implementation of the association represented in Figure A.5.

```
Public Class A
    Public m_id As IntegerGo
    Public m_theBs As B()
End Class


Public Class B
    Public m_name As String
    Public m_theA As A
End Class
```

The role names are shown in bold type. You will also notice that the multiplicity of theBs role is implemented as an array of B instances.

It is legal (and common) for an association to have only one role. In this case, it is said that the association is *navigable* only in one direction, or it is a one-way relationship. Figure A.6 illustrates the UML representation.

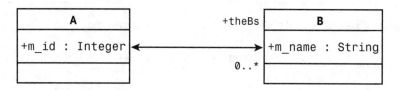

Figure A.6: *One-way association between classes* A *and* B.

Note that the arrow is now pointing in one direction only (towards B). The following code shows a possible implementation:

```
Public Class A
    Public m_id As Integer
```

```
    Public m_theBs As B()
End Class

Public Class B
    Public m_name As String
End Class
```

Note that class B no longer has the reference to A (theA), which corresponds to the missing UML role.

When the multiplicity is greater than 1, the role is implemented usually as a collection of instances. This collection can be a simple bounded or unbounded array, an ArrayList, a Hashtable, and so on. Normally the UML design tool would allow you to specify the class to use when generating the code for the relationship.

Aggregation

Aggregation is a particular case of association, which indicates a container-part type of association. That means that one of the objects is the container, while the other is a part. There are many examples in real life of aggregation: a PurchaseOrder class aggregates the OrderItems, an Engine class aggregates the Parts, and so on. Aggregation is represented with a diamond shaped adornment on the line, toward the class that is the container. The UML diagram shown in Figure A.7 modifies the previous example to add aggregation.

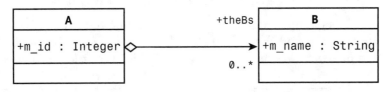

Figure A.7: *Aggregation between classes* A *and* B.

The code for the aggregation is shown here:

```
Public Class A
    Public m_id As Integer
    Private m_theBs As B()

    Public ReadOnly Property theBs(ByVal i As Integer) As B
        Get
            Return m_theBs(i)
```

```
        End Get
    End Property
End Class

Public Class B
    Public m_name As String
End Class
```

As you have probably noticed, there is only one small difference between the examples modeled in Figures A.6 and A.7 (the array is now private, and the class implements an accessor method to it). The difference between the association and aggregation is mostly semantic. Aggregation imposes as a restriction in the fact that a part (aggregated) object cannot be owned by two different containers at the same time. An order line item cannot be owned by two orders, an engine part cannot exist in more than one engine (not at the same moment, anyway). That means that the class behavior must be implemented such that it enforces the fact that the B instances are contained within A. For example, it may implement a copy constructor, which does a deep copy of the collection of Bs (that is, clones all objects in the collection, not only the collection itself).

You have now seen that a part (aggregated) object cannot be owned by more than one container at any time, but that it can be transferred from one container to the other.

A special case of aggregation is known as *composition*. In the case of composition, the aggregated objects (parts) cannot exist outside their containers, and they cannot be transferred or moved to a different container. In this case, the life span of the composed (part) object overlaps that of its container (in this case normally called a *composite*). For example, it is created when the container is created and destroyed when the container is destroyed. In this case, the relationship is represented as shown in Figure A.8.

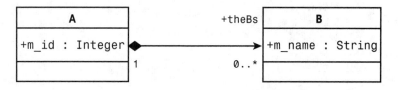

Figure A.8: Composition between classes A and B.

The code is similar with the one shown above for aggregation:

```
Public Class A
    Public m_id As Integer
    Private m_theBs As B()

    Public ReadOnly Property theBs(ByVal i As Integer) As B
      Get
          Return m_theBs(i).Clone()
      End Get
    End Property
End Class

Public Class B
    Public m_name As String
End Class
```

In this case class A should provide a method that creates the B objects and adds them to the array, and never return a reference to a B contained in the class, but rather a clone of the object in the array.

Being a special case of aggregation, the composition should be treated the same as aggregation, with the one caveat that the part objects cannot be moved outside the container.

Inheritance

The inheritance relationship represents the typical case of an *is-a* relationship. A base class is extended or specialized by its derived classes. A derived class extends, specializes, or inherits from a base class.

The inheritance is illustrated by a line connecting the two classes, which ends with a hollow triangle towards the base class. This is illustrated in Figure A.9.

The code in this case is quite simple:

```
Public Class B
    Public m_name As String
End Class

Public Class D
    Inherits B
    Public m_age As Single
End Class
```

Although this type of relationship also has properties (like name and stereotype), they are very seldom used.

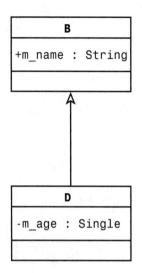

Figure A.9: *Inheritance example.*

The .NET Framework supports only single inheritance. There are languages (like C++) that support multiple inheritance; that is, a class can extend more than one class. The .NET Framework achieves the same result using *interface realization.*

Realization

A class can inherit only from one base class, but it can implement any number of interfaces. In UML this type of relationship is known as *realization.* It is said that class D *realizes* interface IE if it implements all methods declared by that interface. This could be represented in UML form as shown in Figure A.10.

The code is also straightforward, as shown here:

```
Public Class B
    Public m_name As String
    Public m_theA As A
End Class

Public Interface IE
    Sub DoSomething(ByVal i As Integer)
End Interface
```

```
Public Class D
    Inherits B
    Implements IE

    Public m_age As Single

    Sub DoSomething(ByVal i As Integer) Implements IE.DoSomething
        ' do something
    End Sub
End Class
```

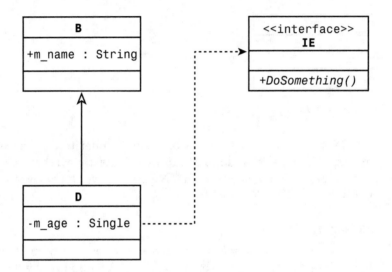

Figure A.10: *Interface implementation (realization) example.*

Class D can now be used anywhere a reference to a B object is expected, or to an instance of a class that implements interface IE. Similar to inheritance, this type of relationship also has properties (like name and stereotype), but they are very seldom used.

This concludes our brief presentation of the basic UML concepts required in the course of the book.

Index

J–L

M

Learning Java™

Related titles from O'Reilly

Creating Effective JavaHelp™

Database Programming with JDBC and Java™

Developing Java Beans™

Enterprise JavaBeans™

Java™ 2D Graphics

Java™ & XML

Java™ and XSLT

Java™ Cookbook

Java™ Cryptography

Java™ Distributed Computing

Java™ Enterprise in a Nutshell

Java™ Examples in a Nutshell

Java™ Foundation Classes in a Nutshell

Java™ I/O

Java™ in a Nutshell

Java™ Internationalization

Java™ Message Service

Java™ Network Programming

Java™ Performance Tuning

Java™ Programming with Oracle JDBC

Java™ Programming with Oracle SQLJ

Java™ Security

JavaServer™ Pages

JavaServer™ Pages Pocket Reference

Java™ Servlet Programming

Java™ Swing

Java™ Threads

Jini™ in a Nutshell

Learning Java™

Also available

The Java™ Enterprise CD Bookshelf

Java™ Professional Library